20 Years of Alternative Music:

Original
writing
on rock,
hip-hop,
techno
and beyond

dean martin

June 20, 1990

Mr. Robert Lloyd, you are one helluva guy in my book!

My son, Ricci, brought your article (April 1, 1990) in SPIN to me and I can tell you it made me one <u>very</u> happy man.

It is by far the finest piece ever written about this old crooner.   And I mean that.

It amazed me that you and SPIN would think so highly of my body of work.

Again, Thanks.   I needed that.

Most sincerely your friend,

Dean Martin

DM:ew

Goth, emo, grunge, indie rock, alt-rock, rap rock, gangsta rap, alt-rap, synth-pop, Brit-pop, post-punk, punk funk, electronica, deep house, acid house, industrial, trip hop, alt-country, riot grrrl, hair metal, speed metal, garage rock, jam band rock, heroin rock, and OutKast.

SPIN

20 Years of Alternative Music:

Original
writing
on rock,
hip-hop,
techno
and beyond *

edited by Will **Hermes** with Sia **Michel**

THREE RIVERS PRESS
NEW YORK

Published in the United States by Three Rivers Press, an
imprint of the Crown Publishing Group, a division of Random
House, Inc., New York.
www.crownpublishing.com

Three Rivers Press and the Tugboat design are registered
trademarks of Random House, Inc.

Portions of this work appeared previously in SPIN magazine.

Library of Congress Cataloging-in-Publication Data
SPIN: 20 years of alternative music / edited by William
Hermes with Sia Michel.—1st ed.
1. Alternative rock music—history and criticism. 2. Popular
culture—history—20th century. I. Hermes, Will. II. Michel, Sia.
III. SPIN (New York, N.Y.)
ML3534.S648 2005
781.66—dc22
2005012418

ISBN 0-307-23662-5

Printed in the United States of America

Design by A. Galperin

10 9 8 7 6 5 4 3 2 1

First Edition

Acknowledgments

This book was a massive project undertaken with a hilariously tight deadline (which we blew—repeatedly), so any appearance of effortlessness is a front. It's hard to know who to thank first, so I'll begin by giving it up for Lindsay Barnes, Henry Bowles, Lane Brown, Ashley Bryan, Arielle Castillo, Jennifer Clay, Morgan Clendaniel, Andrea Grimes, Peter Hamby, Jessica Pasko, Jenna Payne, Scott Rosen and Lisa Tauber, the crunk-tastic interns who combed our "library" of back issues—some rescued from beneath Charles Aaron's collection of DC hard-core 45s—photocopying stacks of crumbling yellow pages, inputting them for digital posterity, and fact-checking dubious material. Is this what you'll find when you head out into the world of "real" magazines? Let us know.

Laura Sinagra did the first round of archival excerpting, a huge task, and the shape and tone of this collection has a lot to do with her sharp ear for critical bon-mots and telling soundbites. Lisa Corson found the hot photos, usually on first try 'cause she's such a pro, and never balked when we wanted her to keep digging. (For the Q-Bert shot alone, she deserves mad props.) Additional thanks go to Melissa Maerz, Jennifer Edmondson, Michelle Ha, John Espinosa at Retna, Edwin Garcia at LFI, Andrew Conti at Corbis, Rachel Crowe at Outline, Richard Kolnsberg at Star File, Genevieve Harley at Getty, and Chuck Musse at Rex for their help with getting our images sorted.

The fabulous Anne Galperin designed and art directed this thing under highly unusual and often stressful circumstances—ie: living with the editor—and really made it dance. To our daughter Gia, thanks for napping in the afternoon (most of the time) and for providing comic relief when we were freaking out.

To Carrie Thornton (our editor) and Brandi Bowles at Crown, and Jim Fitzgerald (our agent), thanks for making it happen and for keeping things on track without resorting to violence.

Immeasurable thanks go out to the SPIN massive. Charles Aaron and Doug Brod helped immensely—with top editing, contributions, archival tips, and encouragement even when we were at our most harried. Ditto Jon Dolan and Chuck Klosterman, who along with Greg "Microfiche" Milner, provided historical perspective and necessary sarcasm over high-carb lunches. Caryn Ganz, Kyle Anderson, and Phoebe Reilly fielded endless, pitiable cries for info and general assistance with grace and good cheer; Kyle and Phoebe, along with the exacting Rebecca Milzoff and others, also pulled some crucial 11th hour fact-checking. Thanks for making us all look smarter than we are. Further thanks to Dave Iztkoff and Chuck for joke doctoring, Jeanann Pannasch for handling legal matters, and publisher Jake Hill for taking care of business.

To Sia Michel, this book's editorial super-ego: thanks for the enthusiasm, for carrying the torch, keeping it real, bringing the steak, and knowing where to find the coolest handbags in the East Village.

Lastly, to all the SPIN writers and photographers, past and present, whose work constitutes this book, as well as those who space constraints kept us from including—in the end, it's all about y'all.

To paraphrase Robert Wyatt from his excellent 1982 Rough Trade LP *Nothing Can Stop Us*, any errors you find in here—and I'm sure you'll find some—are entirely deliberate and should be read as evidence of our humanity. —WH

Contents

When I'm interviewed about editing SPIN, I usually mention that I've been reading the magazine since the very first issue.

That's a lie.

Sort of.

/ Sia **Michel**

Growing up in a small city in the early 1980s, it was tough to be a fan of what was then called "college rock." The only major rock magazine in the country was putting actors like Dudley Moore on the cover. The only place to buy a magazine was the grocery store; there were no mega-bookstores stocking zines or British new-wave weeklies. There was no cool record shop, and if I wanted, say, the Dead Kennedys album that a friend's suddenly punk older brother had taped at college, there was no way to get it unless I convinced someone to drive me two hours to Pittsburgh, or I sent a money order to the label and waited months for it to (probably not) arrive. There was no Internet, no downloading, no MySpace, no official band sites, no message boards—virtually no easy way to listen to, or get info on, an even marginally underground band. MTV took awhile to come to our town, so I watched videos on BET, and then got pissed that I couldn't find Grand-master Flash singles, either.

I attended an all-girls high school where there was one other person who shared my obsession. We always griped that we felt isolated and uninformed. I'd sit on the floor and stare at the cover of R.E.M.'s *Murmur* with no sense of what the band was all about, where they were from, whether they were part of an interesting scene, or what other people thought of them. It drove me fucking crazy.

When SPIN started publishing in 1985, I naturally had no idea it existed. A couple of summers later, while I was in college, I sublet a decrepit, sweltering attic in West Philadelphia, which I shared with identical twin sisters who despised each other and kept throwing each other's clothes out the only unstuck window. (This was a very big deal, as it overlooked the backyard, which was so filthy with trash, rats, and empty crack vials that no one dared enter it.) The previous tenant had left all of his junk, including a huge stash of magazines. It was mostly porn and National Lampoon, but stacked on a milk crate were the first two years of SPIN. The premier issue alone featured the Replacements, Run-D.M.C., Hüsker Dü, Roxy Music. The second one even had a write-up on Grandmaster Flash. By then I'd been reading zines and knew plenty of underground music devotees, but they could be perplexingly narrow-minded (Jesus and Mary Chain fans mocked Smiths fans, who in turn dissed Eric B. & Rakim fans—at the time, many indie rockers didn't consider hip-hop "real music"). But SPIN enthusiastically covered every innovative sound, regardless of genre. I was immediately, permanently hooked.

So, back to my lie: I have read every issue of SPIN—I just started two years late. And a decade afterward, when I went on to work for, and then eventually run, the magazine, I always kept the frustrations of kids like me in mind. For most of our readers, dedicating yourself to what was eventually dubbed "alternative music" involves so much more than the appreciation of cool new bands. It's about refusal, transformation, possibility. This will sound corny, but that's okay, because trying to describe musical epiphanies always does: Discovering alternative music completely redefined my life. Growing up female and working class during the Reagan era, I had miserably low expectations (as do many young people in the Dubya era). I didn't know

anything about activism, but all it took was hearing a few outraged rappers and punks to realize that I didn't have to sit back and passively consume whatever the administration or entertainment industry fed us. All it took was a few cryptically literate indie rockers to make me want to read better books, get a real education, travel the world, or at the very least, move to the East Village and lean menacingly against a brick wall, just like the Ramones. (Ironic how music associated with slackerdom and negation can often inspire ambition.) Even when SPIN is at its most irreverent, our writers and editors never forget how meaningful music can be.

That respect is in every page of this book. In the same way that SPIN saw a void in music magazines 20 years ago, we wanted to fill a major gap in the world of music books. While there are many excellent histories of specific genres or moments in alternative music—techno, post-punk, hip-hop, etc.—we longed to read a larger, more comprehensive look at this fascinating, confusing, still-beating movement.

I signed on to this project under one condition: It had to be helmed by Will Hermes, a former SPIN editor, a good friend, a formidable music encyclopedia, and the kind of guy you'd trot out to talk to the cops when they tried to bust your house party. I thank him for practically killing himself to get this done so quickly, and for handling my panic attacks, blown deadlines, and existentialist e-mails of darkness with Jedi-like calm.

We hope you enjoy the book, even if you end up reading it in a hot, dirty attic, two years late, while hateful twins beat each other with broken mop handles.

So what's this "alternative" music, you ask?

That question hasn't gotten any less pesky since Eric Weisbard smacked it around in the Introduction to the tasty *SPIN Alternative Record Guide*, published in 1995 on the occasion of the magazine's 10th anniversary. Now, staring down SPIN's 20th anniversary with a medium-grade hangover, I frankly don't feel like unpacking it. Let's just say that, being young and impulsive, the mag got "alternative" tattooed on its ass after a long, debauched night and has had to learn to live with it.

What? Sorry…I'm now being told that I need to "expand on that."

OK, how's this?:

"Alternative" designates certain things that come along when certain other things, mainstream things, begin sucking.

These "alternative" things are usually distinguished by innovation (ie: they do stuff no things before them have done in quite the same way) and/or by extreme passion (the do familiar stuff with unfamiliar intensity). The pop marketplace being what it is, alternatives become mainstream in short order. But there is often a weird, magically precarious period when things are simultaneously alternative and mainstream. Think about Prince in the mid-'80s, or Nirvana post-*Nevermind*.

The initial premise of SPIN, launched in the mid-'80s, was that mainstream music writing, like mainstream music—Prince notwithstanding—had been sucking for quite a while. SPIN was cooked up by a guy with some dough (Bob Guccione Jr.) and a bunch of young writers who together pushed a vision holding punk and rap and indie-rock to represent the vital future of popular music. In this, needless to say, they were right.

But SPIN has been a lot of things over the years. An earnest crusader for aesthetic goodness. A jaded curmudgeon. A smart-ass (pseudo-)intellectual. A committed activist. A slack motherfucker. A shameless marketplace 'ho. It is what it has always championed—an indie that naively wanted to go big-time without compromising or "selling out" its vision to The Man, simultaneously alternative and mainstream. That created a conflict that's never been resolved and never will be. But it also created a magazine that's published some pretty hot writing over the years, to which this book hopefully testifies.

Let's be clear: this isn't an encyclopedia of "alternative music"—which, however you want to define it, began before 1985, the year SPIN began publishing and the year this book takes as its effective starting point. It isn't even a comprehensive history of SPIN, which ran some remarkable political and other non-music writing in addition to the stuff surveyed here. Instead, *20 Years of Alternative Music* is a kind of DJ mix—a mash-up, if you will—of some of the magazine's best music riffs, spliced into chapters with brand-new essays that address an artist, or a trend, or some other phenomena that impacted the scene over the past two decades.

Our take is admittedly subjective; the choice of excerpts often has as much to do with how smart or deep or funny or startling or stupid (in a good way) the piece sounds than with how well it tells the "whole" story. After all, if the past twenty years have taught us anything, it's that history, like journalism, is a subjective game. And if SPIN has done anything consistently, it has captured history—and the fleeting, bone-deep pleasures of music—in some highly personal, highly subjective voices. That it counts top-shelf storytellers like Elizabeth Gilbert, Dennis Cooper, Barry Hannah, Darcy Steinke, William T. Vollman, Sarah Vowell, Thomas Beller, Joy Williams, Chuck Klosterman, Dave Eggers and J.T. Leroy among its past contributors testifies to that.

SPIN writing also tends to be opinionated, frequently lurching into the obnoxious. Sometimes it's heartfelt, sometimes erudite, sometimes ridiculous, pretentious, over-the-top. Sometimes it strives for greatness; sometimes it talks shit in the back of the club into the wee hours until the bouncer finally pushes it out towards the street and the shaky walk home. Sometimes it has been patently false, as John Leland mentions in his Introduction—yet hopefully, like all worthy fiction, striving for greater truth than facts would allow. Sometimes, frankly, it's just been lame. But we left that stuff out here (like I said, history is a subjective game).

SPIN's mission has shifted in the current era. The kid in Utah who once relied on it as his main source of data on "alternative" music now has hundreds of free options on the internet, and as far as being first to expose a new band or MC, bloggers with zero lead time are generally gonna beat SPIN to the punch. But maybe that's for the best. It leaves the magazine free to be obnoxious, heartfelt, erudite, and ridiculous with a little more perspective, spitting opinions and telling stories which will no doubt bear re-reading when someone remixes them into *SPIN: 30 Years of Alternative Music*, due in bookstores in 2015.

: Back in the Day

The horrible truth about Myanmar

/ John **Leland**

During my senior year in college,

I went to see Mission of Burma at Max's Kansas City. The gig drew so few people that Clint Conley, the bass player, stepped down from the stage in mid-set to shake people's hands. "Hi, I'm Clint," he said. This was in the year 5 B.S., or five years before the start of SPIN, and the indie world that we take for granted now, linked by national alt-rock magazines, college radio promoters, and a fully paved tour circuit, was still a work in progress. There was no reason to believe it would go the way it did. Burma were heroes in Boston, playing to a dozen strangers in New York.

The band was an event that did not exist, except in retrospect, and this was fine, because in the post-punk world of the early '80s—an unformed stretch between the relatively well-defined punk outburst of the 1970s and the alt-rock takeover of the '90s—for the most part *events* did not exist either, at least as we know them today. There were just gigs and records, sometimes great ones. You took for granted that in a week or a month you could catch the band again at a similar club, and that in a few months the musicians would break up because of "creative differences."

Looking at Mission of Burma then vs. now, when their name inspires a kind of awe, offers one way to consider the 20 years of SPIN that passed in between. When we started, sharing an office with *Penthouse Letters* and a short-lived dirty mag called *New Look*, it was in a much different time. I don't mean just that more people attach themselves to Mission of Burma now, but that the nature of this attachment is different—and that this change both reflects and made possible the two decades of culture described in this book. In things like the rise of Interpol and the Killers, who look and sound like a lot of the stuff in those early SPIN issues, or the return of Burma and Big Audio Dynamite, that era appears to be with us again. But the music and the values it represents have changed in the process, in ways that say less about the early '80s than about the time that has passed in between.

What strikes me over this period is the extent to which the punk of those B.S. years, which was proudly marginal and ephemeral, has solidified into a value system for large swaths of young America, in ways that extend far beyond music or fashion. Punk is less a music than a code. You can live in it, shop in it, start your own indie business under its aegis. It has its own menu and décor, and a program that is more moral than aesthetic: in a world of hucksters and hypesters, backstabbers and backsliders, punk is now the responsible thing to do. This is why some punks can be deemed fake, even if they look or sound pretty much like the real thing. Even as punks got younger, punk as an ethic is now mature—hell, it is *maturity*. No one is as punk as a punk vegan who recycles.

SPIN arrived in the early part of this transition: after those delightfully fun years when punk was just you and your friends, but before the greater vegan/Seven Sisters nation got on board. Most of us from the early days (I started a column in the second issue and went to work at the magazine a few years down the line) were to some degree shaped by punk, but in ways that were more refractory than literal, and more evident collectively than individually. We had seen punk and hip hop make music fun again not by improving what was musical about it, but by pulling this apart. Rock'n'roll had acquired too many strengths, and these were weighing it down; punk and hip hop simply cast these aside. To the extent that SPIN had a mission, it was to do something comparable to the music magazine: to dismantle what was responsible and sober about it. That and to get into clubs for free.

Or maybe this is overstating things. Most of us privately harbored our own grand schemes for the magazine, which were promptly dashed whenever founder Bob Guccione Jr. met someone at a party who happened to have his or her own vision for SPIN. There were grand clashes. When Richard Gehr in a review called the Red Hot Chili Peppers a minstrel act, Glenn O'Brien wrote a rebuttal accusing Richard of playing Depeche Mode in the office. They did this on typewriters because we were not on computers yet, and maybe this had an effect on the magazine—it was easier to flaunt our mistakes than to correct them. In one issue the middle-of-the-road singer John Waite reviewed a Frank Sinatra album. This confused me until I learned that the editor had meant to ask Tom Waits, but got confused. Often there seemed to be no grown-up minding the store. Scott Cohen and I, puzzled that Chris Lowe of the Pet Shop Boys never seemed to do anything, invented a biography for him as a Delta bluesman—a seventh son, a manchild, a son of a gun—and published it as if it were true. I often wonder what Lowe thought of this.

Over the last 20 years, the magazine has built on the strengths of those early issues, as the music has built on the strengths of the bands of the time. But what has been lost, I think, as the financial stakes for both have gotten higher, is the space for the mistakes we made back then. This is what I mean by the difference between Burma (or, say, the Minutemen or Hüsker Dü), then and now, and what this difference has to do with the 20 years of SPIN. Certain things that were fun about these bands then—the gleeful sense of destruction, the essentially antisocial squawk—do not apply now, while things that are rewarding about them now—the formal purity, the sense of permanence—could not be heard in the empty spaces at Max's then. What were once pleasures of excess are now pleasures of discipline. And what was once a unifying experience for bands of the early '80s—being ballers at home, facing an empty room two towns over—now seems an anomaly, something to tell the kids about.

Or else it no longer exists, even in memory. Even the name Mission of Burma has changed its meaning, referring to a nation that now calls itself Myanmar. SPIN came about to make nonexistent events like that night at Max's Kansas City exist: to present a band like Burma, which blustered through scrappy fanzines, in the glossy format suited to Madonna or U2. In the pages of the magazine, we treated both as material to reshape. Some people in the early years called SPIN a fanzine with a big budget; little did we know how well these words, with just a little tweaking, anticipated the major label alt-rock world of a half-decade later, when multinational corporations invested fortunes in stylized street cred. In both cases, I mean this for better and for worse.

Oh, and the Burma show at Max's? It rocked.

: The R.E.M. method

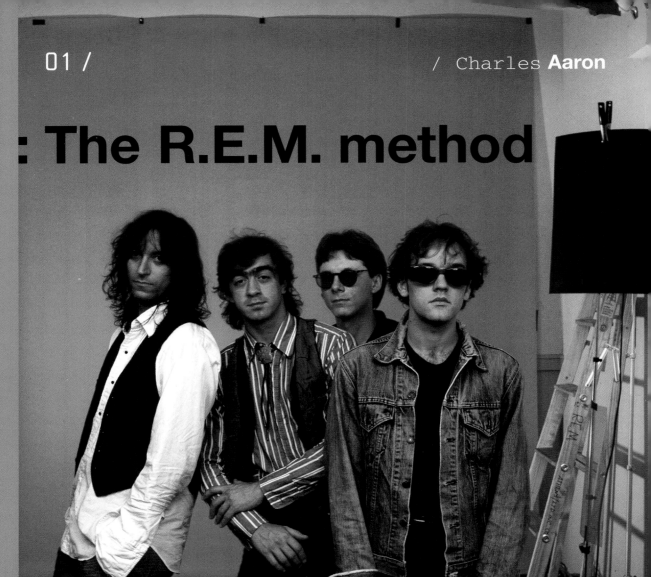

and other rites of passage

How indie rock learned to stop worrying
and love itself in the morning

ATHENS, GEORGIA, 1985. The acid had lost its come-hither bouquet and the speed had snapped everyone's nerves like twigs. The run-down Victorians weren't such a steal anymore and the days of buying an armful of thrift-store dresses for a quarter were long gone. Two years before, *People* magazine had run a photo of a group of obscure local musicians gathered around a Confederate memorial downtown to illustrate an article about America's so-called rock renaissance. Considering that the South was where punk and new wave had been met, at best, with piss-off slurs, this was a little hard to fathom. But now, Athens bands were multiplying at a dizzying rate, and wannabe rockers were even making pilgrimages to this bucolic college town.

One sunny afternoon, I was driving near Barber Street (where penniless bands once flopped in "Munsters" houses, as Pylon drummer Curtis Crowe put it) and a friend in the passenger seat pointed out the window and casually commented: "You know, Pete Buck just bought a house over there."

"What?!" I exclaimed.

"No, it's true," he answered with a slight smirk. Like many, he'd grown weary of the scene's self-image as a bohemian arcadia, full of demure aesthetes, untainted by ambition.

But I was flashing back a few years, to when Buck was just another unwashed face in the crowd: a babbling record-store clerk who gave me the hard sell on Pere Ubu, the New York Dolls, the Velvet Underground, and racks of other older bands that he touted as more "punk" than the hardcores I worshipped like Black Flag, Circle Jerks, and Dead Kennedys. To my surprise, he was also in a local band called R.E.M. (lower-case, blurry letters on a yellow flyer I pulled off a telephone pole) who played a cool black-and-white Rickenbacker guitar with an impressive panache for someone who clearly couldn't even fake a solo. R.E.M. weren't incensed punks or stylish, wound-up new-wavers, and even though they played familiar covers ("Gloria," "Toys in the Attic"), they never really *rocked*. Instead, they sketched out shadowy moods in a swirl of twitchy melodies and rhythmic turnarounds. Rag-doll singer Michael Stipe would convulse, withdraw, and collapse into an introverted, sway-ing trance that, in retrospect, was a more languid version of Joy Division's Ian Curtis. But at the time, I thought he was the antithesis of every rock singer I'd ever seen. His phonetic lyrics, sung in a reedy near-drawl, made no apparent sense, but his voice felt totally original—intimate yet enigmatic. And he gave off a sexuality that had nothing to do with rock's usual your-girlfriend-wants-to-fuck-me bombast.

R.E.M. soon began to tour—visiting towns largely unmarked by punk (from New Orleans to Memphis to Albuquerque), in addition to New York, Boston, Los Angeles, and San Francisco. Their shows were famously intense, whether playing for a bar of hostile drunks in Detroit or four curious hardcore brats in Birmingham. Buck became a true-believing advocate for scores of new underground acts— Minutemen, Jason and the Nashville Scorchers, Let's Active, the Dream Syndicate, etc. And gradually, as more bands toured widely, an outsider circuit emerged based around independent labels and record stores, college radio stations, and fanzines. As a result, throughout the '80s, strong scenes formed in places almost as unlikely as Athens—Minneapolis, Austin, Seattle, Chapel Hill.

This may not seem like a righteous cause today, but at the beginning of the ominously moralizing Reagan era, you took what you could get. For just about any kid who wasn't an aspiring Christian careerist in khaki duck pants, the country could seem heartless and remote (there was no Internet-driven sense of community), and the music business, with its craving for baroquely produced, drum-machine Euro-pop, seemed just as inaccessible. Hardcore punks raged against the U.S.'s cultural and political depravity, but this new group of underground bands (like R.E.M.) had an oddly traditional, even patriotic, chip on its shoulder. It was as if they were say-ing, "There's so much great music here that's being ignored, why can't people just wake up and appreciate it?" The Los Angeles punk poets X stated it plainly: "Will the last American band to get played on the radio, please bring the flag?"

R.E.M., in its way, made the country feel less foreboding and more inclusive, replacing hardcore's iconoclasm with a warm invitation to less-hip kids who didn't live in California or the northeast. "When I was 15 years old in Richmond, Virginia, they were a very important part of my life, as they were for all members of our band," said Bob Nastanovich of '90s indie-rock doyens Pavement. "They were this uniting force. People who liked Black Flag liked 'em and people who liked the Dead liked 'em. They were the first [underground] band that the frat guys looked at and didn't say, 'Oh, let's beat up some fags.'"

R.E.M. weren't selfless ambassadors, though; they were also role models because they succeeded. From early on, the band made sure business was taken care of so that it didn't interfere with their music. In fact, ever since, people have talked about, and envied, the so-called "R.E.M. Model," a series of basic, easier-said-than-done career moves—hire a manager and lawyer as soon as you make any money; tour like a circuit preacher; sign to an "independent" label that has major-label backing; move to a major only when you've built a substantial following; insist on "creative control" (you make decisions on the producer, the single, and the video); split the money fairly among the band members; don't fear the power ballad.

By 1985, R.E.M. were about two-thirds of the way through this process, but it was already obvious that their music was paying off, and that their future was secure. They'd shown how far an underground, punk-inspired rock band could go within the industry without whoring out its artistic integrity in any obvious way. They'd figured out how to buy in, not sell out—in other words, they'd achieved the American Bohemian Dream.

A couple of years later, the anarchic Texas hardcore band the Butthole Surfers performed an incendiary version of "The One I Love," R.E.M.'s 1987 attempt at a prosaic pop single, while singer Gibby Haynes devilishly burned dollar bills onstage. Haynes was obsessed with R.E.M.—in fact, he'd briefly moved his band to Athens in the mid-'80s, partly due to his curiosity about their mythos. It amazed him that they'd maintained such an aura of purity, despite consistently burnishing their music and hardballing their business operation (R.E.M. Inc. is now one of the most powerful companies in Athens). As a Trinity College accounting grad turned lawless, shit-slinging prankster, Haynes was careening in another direction—his band's name couldn't even be mentioned in a newspaper—and he didn't trust how efficiently the Model was humming. Didn't there have to be some deal with the devil that we didn't know about?

Or maybe it was just envy (the Buttholes eventually signed their own major-label deal years later). But as I was driving on that sunny Athens afternoon, pondering *Pete Buck: Homeowner*, I could relate. How did R.E.M. pull it off? And was there something wrong with the rest of us if we couldn't develop our own plan for making a living off the scene?

As I gazed dumbly ahead, thoughts racing, my friend turned to me, his smirk now suspiciously deadpan. Then he delivered the kicker.

"You know, he's got a pool, too."

+ +

WE ARE THE UNDERBELLY OF ROCK'N'ROLL... WE ARE HUMAN IDIOTS; WE ACT LIKE BUFFOONS. WE DON'T HAVE TO SMOKE DOPE OR DRINK ALCOHOL TO DO THAT. WE GET MESSED UP JUST WITH OUR OWN THOUGHTS. WE USE OUR PROFICIENCY WITH THE INSTRUMENTS TO RAKE PEOPLE'S BRAINS OVER THE COALS.
— Curt Kirkwood, Meat Puppets

By the mid-'80s, the raw sprawl of post-hardcore "underground rock" was coalescing, and after R.E.M.'s success, a number of bands started to think that they could also buy in. Major-label reps were showing more interest, and it seemed like a new generation might be ready to have its day. (It's no coincidence that SPIN published its first issue in May of 1985, though by putting Madonna on the cover, we were still hedging our bets.) But like the brilliantly

SPIN | **20 Years of Alternative Music**

unhinged Arizona burnouts in the Meat Puppets, many of the underground's "stars" did live lives that could seem idiotic and buffoonish, and performed brain-raking music that genuinely freaked people out. Business was not their métier. Still, in 1985, the most incorrigibly ill-behaved rock band in America, Minneapolis' Replacements, signed to Sire and released their major-label debut *Tim*, a perfectly ragged collection of anthemic pleas written by singer-guitarist Paul Westerberg. If the rock masses embraced the 'Mats, maybe a change was coming. But *Tim* was a commercial stiff, as was X's *Ain't Love Grand!*, a last-gasp by the exquisitely corrosive underground elders to domesticate their sound. Former hardcore punks Hüsker Dü (Minneapolis natives like the Replacements), recorded their major-label debut, *Candy Apple Grey*, for Warner Bros., a 10-song stunner of feverish punk-pop headtrips, but it never earned a nod from commercial radio. The moment's hopeful ambition faded. And in a tragic coda, D. Boon, singer-guitarist for agit-blurt virtuosos Minutemen, and possibly the underground's most impassioned figure, died in an auto accident in December of '85.

But this period of disenchantment would have just as permanent an impact on rock's next ten years as R.E.M.'s crafty breakthrough. As major labels moved on to hump the L.A. hair-metal ass-party, underground rockers began to lose their craving for mainstream validation. The new role models became uncompromising label owners like Greg Ginn of Southern California's SST, and Ian MacKaye of Washington, D.C.'s Dischord. SST, which had started in the late '70s with Ginn's pioneering Black Flag, was a relentless force, signing up the most significant underground bands of the early-mid-'80s—Minutemen, Hüsker Dü, Meat Puppets, Sonic Youth, Dinosaur Jr., etc; MacKaye stayed local, assiduously documenting the D.C. punk scene of groups like Government Issue, Dag Nasty, and Rites of Spring. Both were consumed by the idea that a self-sustaining independent framework was necessary for compelling music to thrive. (MacKaye went so far as to break up his powerhouse hardcore band Minor Threat after the other members wanted to consider signing to a major label).

As this shift took place in the underground scene, a new tag for the music began to crop up: "Indie rock." A nod to the importance of independent labels, it was the rare genre name rooted in economics rather the sound of the bands involved. It could be traced to the early '80s, Marxist-inspired British indie scene, where labels viewed their business arrangements—no contracts, 50/50 split of costs and receipts, the band's ownership of their recordings—as a political statement. The American version was more individualistic than militant, and the music itself was much less self-consciously disaffected.

A classic case was Amherst, MA, trio Dinosaur Jr., who released their self-titled debut in 1985. Singer-guitarist J Mascis, though hidden behind a curtain of scraggly hair, unleashed a shitstorm of distorted riffs that could practically cave in a club's ceiling. His songs, which sounded like Neil Young as a pissed D&D geek, were a roaring, revelatory purge. "Dino were part of this thing I saw with the later punks and hardcores—these guys who were too young to react against rock'n'roll," wrote the Minutemen's Mike Watt for a reissue of the band's first three albums. "A lot of the '70s punks were trying to be ironic and satirical about the whole paradigm of rock'n'roll...I was into a kind of ideological war, but for these guys, it wasn't that much of an issue."

A multitude of underground bands flourished during the latter half of the '80s, and their music gave indie rock a creative rush that mirrored the late-'80s "golden age" of hip-hop—just substitute Run-D.M.C. for R.E.M. A band like Rites of Spring was obviously trapped in a post-hardcore malaise, but Guy Picciotto sang like he was setting himself free by ripping up diary entries in the middle of Dupont Circle, while guitarist Ed Janney looted a fakebook of melodies behind him (Rites' sound was dubbed "emo-core" for its emotional bent, later shortened to "emo"). Picciotto then moved on to play guitar and sing with Ian MacKaye's new band Fugazi, a hurtling blur of scratchy rhythms and open-hearted, anti-sexist manifestos. The band's ascetic idealism—playing all-ages shows for five dollars—was almost as bracing as their timebomb-ticking songs.

In the D.C. suburb of Arlington, Virginia, Mark Robinson's Teenbeat label was a cheekier proposition. His band Unrest mixed winsome, strummy love songs with a brash, pop-culture irony that would later become indie-rock's defining identity (Camper Van Beethoven were the hippie-ish Northern California corollary). Unrest's peak, the 1991 7-inch "Yes, She Is My Skinhead Girl," a sugary ode to a punk crush, was co-released with like-minded Olympia, Washington-based K Records (K and Teenbeat were both partial to 7-inch singles with hand-made artwork, which carried a tinge of nostalgic innocence, especially as CDs became more prevalent). Known for its minimalist, almost childlike aesthetic, K was founded in the early '80s by Calvin Johnson, whose band Beat Happening was the embodiment of the label, playing rudimentary, defiantly gawky songs about sexual coming-of-age from both male and female perspectives (Heather Lewis sang and played drums).

K also ambitiously mapped out the International Pop Underground, a network of heady indie acts—most notably Olympia singer-songwriter Lois Maffeo, Canadian folk-punk duo Mecca Normal, and scruffy Scottish romantics the Vaselines (led by singer-guitarists Eugene Kelly and Frances McKee); the culmination was 1991's IPU Festival in Olympia, featuring Fugazi, and all-female bands Scrawl, L7, and Bikini Kill. The international indie-pop scene reached as far as New Zealand, where the label Flying Nun released records by a remarkable group of bands (the Clean, the Chills, Verlaines, the Bats) who matched fanciful lyricism with tremulous guitars.

But the most exceptional aspect of all the above bands was their distinct lack of macho posturing and objectifying lyrics, and as a result, they would inspire great numbers of women to start their own bands and labels. The prominence of so many male-female duos also gave the music a different level of complexity and a more revealing, if at times awkward, intimacy. The jangly, droning Velvet Underground-influenced sound of Hoboken's Yo La Tengo, for instance, took on a more affecting edge when drummer Georgia Hubley tempered the feverishly boyish excursions of singer-guitarist Ira Kaplan.

Bookending this period were two bands: Sonic Youth, who spent the pre-indie era as a cooler-than-you, downtown New York art-noise clique before developing into a R.E.M.-like presence through the mid-late-'80s; and Boston's Pixies, who bypassed the U.S. indie circuit, first finding success for their abstract pop squall in the U.K. Both were led by male-female duos—Sonic Youth's Thurston Moore and Kim Gordon, the Pixies' Black Francis and Kim Deal—and their music could feel like an ongoing 3 A.M. heart-to-heart, flipping from eerie whispers to alien croons to gnomic shouts. So when they signed to major labels—Pixies to Elektra in 1988 and Sonic Youth to Geffen in 1990—it was an acknowledgement that indie's reinvigorated version of rock might finally be market-ready.

But when the crossover came, it was from a scene that had little to do with the aforementioned aesthetic and social shifts (which might explain its commercial potential). Seattle had been an isolated and gloomy zone for underground and indie rock through much of the '80s, a place where metalheads and '70s-style rockers were still grinding it out in rainy anonymity. And the city's important post-hardcore indie bands—Green River (which which split into Mudhoney and Pearl Jam), Melvins, and Soundgarden—started by putting a punk spin on '70s titans like Black Sabbath, Led Zeppelin, and Aerosmith. Though they might not have been the most progressive, Seattle's best were ferocious live—their shirtless swagger and stomping, sludgy riffs headbanged with a shot of irony and humor.

Local indie label Sub Pop latched onto this so-called "grunge" sound, aggressively promoting and branding it like a mini-major label (even hosting British journalists, who went home crowing about Seattle as the center of America's new rock revolution). The band who benefited the most was, of course, Nirvana, whose singer, Kurt Cobain, was a flannel-metal kid, but also loved underground punk bands (Black Flag, Butthole Surfers, Big Black) and indie rock (he said that K was his favorite record label). With the release of their second album, *Nevermind* (now on major-label Geffen instead of Sub Pop), Nirvana took all these disparate elements to the top of the pop charts, seemingly confirming that punk and indie music was capable of appealing to a mainstream audience (if given the right production and promotion). And in their wake, a series of bands were solicited and signed by majors.

But none would have the cultural impact of Nirvana, and few would see any financial windfall. While Cobain became deeply conflicted about the media notoriety that came with *Nevermind*'s popularity (he was constantly referred to as the voice of generation), indie artists also grew ambivalent. Was Nirvana's success, and even Sonic Youth's safe major-label passage, a case of "we won," or just a pathetic grab for validation from the type of people who used to stuff "us" into gym lockers? Did former indie kids—now referred to as "alternative rockers"—really believe that major labels would bestow them with expense accounts and not ask for serious concessions? Nirvana had cited the R.E.M. Model as a way to maintain artistic integrity while doing business on a larger stage. But like Hüsker Dü and the Replacements in the mid-'80s, most other indie bands couldn't meet the Model's demands. And ultimately, neither could Cobain—who became disillusioned and committed suicide in 1994.

This ambivalence, and Cobain's drugged-out breakdown, pushed indie-rock in two self-conscious directions: the "lo-fi" scene and the "riot grrrl" movement. Lo-fi devotees curled up and hid from the mainstream, favoring hissy four-track recordings and confessional, self-mocking lyrics (best represented by Sebadoh, Guided By Voices, and Pavement); an Olympia, Washington, and Washington, D.C., nexus, "riot grrrl," was overtly political, led by the bands Bikini Kill and Bratmobile and the label Kill Rock Stars. It matched a passionate, spray-the-room critique of rock and media sexism with a playfully artless attitude toward musicianship. Their best songs were like nursery-rhyme fatwas.

While riot grrrl was a radical indictment that helped lead to an actual "women in rock" surge at major labels in the mid-'90s, lo-fi was a strategic withdrawal—sincere and coy, meant to zero in on the music's emotional core and deflate rock-star pretensions. There was a willfully ingenuous quality at the heart of lo-fi, a longing for a time before the temptations and pressures to cash in. Dinosaur Jr. had moved on to a major, but bassist Lou Barlow left to form the contentious trio Sebadoh, where he flayed himself as a needy, selfish jerk, in stripped-bare, often acoustic songs. Then there were the "slowcore" bands—Low, Codeine, Bedhead—who replayed moments of despair and isolation at ever more torpid tempos, as if to stop-focus every troubling detail. Punkish scrappers Superchunk tore out of North Carolina with the 7-inch anthem, "Slack Motherfucker," a stirring refusal to work for anyone but themselves. And perhaps the genre's most celebrated artist, Liz Phair, straddled lo-fi and riot grrrl, singing affectless post-feminist kiss-offs to an indie world she saw as increasingly dominated by indulgent guys.

But the bands that came to exemplify indie rock in this period, and still define the term in many people's minds, were Pavement and Guided By Voices. A furtive collective from Northern California, led by singer-guitarists "SM" (Stephen Malkmus) and "Spiral Stairs" (Scott Kannberg), Pavement created lo-fi bedroom dramas that romanticized the misty bewilderment of college kids on the cusp of entering the adult straight world. Their free-associating lyrics over melodies that seemed embedded in the staticky fuzz of a transistor radio were a cryptic denial of alt rock's ambition. Malkmus had a gift (like Kurt Cobain) for inside-joke aphorisms that felt like generational broadsides. On the 1992 album *Slanted and Enchanted*, he mused with a stricken hauteur: "I've got a lotta things I want to sell/ But not here, babe" and "All the things we had before/ You sold us out and took it all." Guided By Voices, led by thirtysomething Dayton, Ohio, schoolteacher Robert Pollard, had been churning out cruddy-sounding recordings for years, but their literate, elliptical bursts of British Invasion-tinged rock never caught much attention. But with the release of 1994's breathtakingly composed

Bee Thousand, they were suddenly a mini-cause celebre, a symbol of the uncompromising, self-reliant indie artist who eventually gets the recognition he deserves.

As the '90s progressed, indie rock became less of an oppositional cause—alternative had become a mainstream proposition, in an albeit attenuated form (Nirvana gave way to Pearl Jam which gave way to Stone Temple Pilots and Silverchair), and many of the music's fans had grown up to work in mainstream industry jobs. "Indie" was now more of a pejorative for a sound (disaffected guitars and lyrics) and a stance (nerdy white college boys who prized their record collections). Many influential indie labels—like Sub Pop and Matador—cut deals with majors for financial support, and the indie/mainstream dichotomy became harder to parse. At this point, underground hip hop more closely resembled indie rock's '80s ideal.

When alt rock finally collapsed into the sexually assaultive arena schlock of Korn and Limp Bizkit in the late '90s, there was a quiet backlash in favor of more modest indie bands. These groups, unlike, say, Beat Happening, Bikini Kill, or even Pavement, had no real agenda or sense of a larger context—they just wanted to put on a good rock show that wasn't a moronic embarrassment (a rarity at the time). The White Stripes (a male-female duo who got their first breaks opening for Pavement and riot-grrrl progeny Sleater-Kinney) and the Strokes (worshippers of Guided By Voices) wrote great songs that sounded like direct tributes to other great songs. And they looked cool while doing it. In this version, "indie rock" was simply a smart aesthetic choice. Unsurprisingly, both bands enjoyed commercial success, signing lucrative record deals and giving the industry a fresh burst of energy.

Meanwhile, boosted by an economic trickle-down from alternative's payday and the growth of the Internet, the indie/underground scene continued to professionalize. It was far easier for small labels to distribute records, and the touring circuit was lively and profitable. Artists were able to sell their songs to movie soundtracks and commercials to supplement their income and gain exposure. In effect, the indie scene was a viable career option and a major-label farm team, grooming bands for the next level. The R.E.M. Model had become the norm.

In October of 2003, singer-songwriter Elliott Smith committed suicide in Los Angeles at age 34 after a long, tortured battle with addiction and depression. Smith, who emerged from the Pacific Northwest indie-rock scene, was, like Cobain, one of the most talented songwriters of the '90s. His hushed, wounded, folk-punk songs movingly reflected the fallout from alternative rock's early-'90s circumstance. After releasing three indie albums (two on Kill Rock Stars) that built a moderate cult audience, he signed to the major label DreamWorks. But his inability to endure the demanding industry routine, especially after somewhat disappointing record sales, took its toll. He gradually found more comfort in drugs than music.

For fans of today's commercially successful, blithely shambling indie-rockers—the Shins, Death Cab for Cutie, Interpol—Smith's dilemma may be difficult to grasp, like an artifact from another generation. Sure, these bands express troubled emotions, but they never seem to be in any real danger. Listening to Death Cab's Ben Gibbard, there's a sense that no matter how badly things go for him, he'll always find a soft place to fall. Is that maturity, or just the security that comes from the groundbreaking accomplishments of others? And does it have anything to do with the quality of today's music? How you answer that question probably depends on how much you've invested in the indie saga, and how much you've been able to make its lessons pay off.

3:20 P.M. MONDAY AFTERNOON: BROOKE JOHNSON, R.E.M.'S LOVELY, TALENTED, AND RUTHLESSLY ORGANIZED ASSISTANT, RETURNS FROM LUNCH TO FIND TWO WRITERS BUSY AT WORK IN HER OFFICE. Jim Greer is beginning this story on the official R.E.M. typewriter, while Mark Blackwell thumbs through a Rolodex, copying down the addresses of as many rock stars as he can. "You guys reek," Brooke says by way of greeting. "What have you been doing?"

The writers had arrived promptly at 11:00 A.M. and had met Brooke along with band manager Jefferson Holt (immortalized by the line "Jefferson, I think we're lost" on *Reckoning*) and Bertis Downs, R.E.M.'s lawyer. Upon discovering that the band was tied up in a photo shoot, Mark and Jim set about interviewing local bartenders. But finally things seemed to be getting underway.

Soon Michael Stipe arrives. He needs to run some errands, so Jim and Mark offer to drive him around.

Michael: We need to go by my house, but you have to swear to God never to tell anybody where it is.

Mark: Don't worry. You can trust us.

Michael: I've been burned by journalists too many times.

Jim: Don't worry.

Michael: You guys want a raw carrot?

Mark and Jim: Sure.

Michael pulls a bunch of carrots out of his leather bag. Later, as Mark slams on the brakes to avoid killing a cat, the singer's bag falls to the floorboard and out spills a pile of little brown cubes.

Mark: Sorry about that.

Michael; It's okay. You guys want some baked tofu?

Mark and Jim: Sure.

Michael gives directions to his friend's place, where a huge oak tree covered in strings of lights stands in the backyard, harboring an elaborate house in its higher branches. The three climb up the tree and get down to business.

— "Going for Baroque" / Mark Blackwell and Jim Greer / March '91

JOE LEVY: DID YOU SEE THE MICHAEL STIPE INTERVIEW ON MTV? He wouldn't look at the camera. They'd ask him questions and he'd stare over to the side as though he was in high school and he thought, "If they look me in the eyes they'll steal my soul."

Christian Logan Wright: R.E.M. songs are like recorded versions of little things you'd scribble on the back of your notebook during Survey of Art.

Levy: It's all so private—Stipe won't address the audience. I don't understand why he won't be a rock star. I wish more of these guys would be rock stars. The saddest thing about the Replacements record—and it's a sad record—is that half of it is an aping of Paul Westerberg's favorite rock star, Alex Chilton, and the guy wasn't even ever a real star. I mean, I own Alex Chilton records, and I haven't let it ruin my life.

— review of R.E.M.'s *Green*, The Replacement's *Don't Tell a Soul*, and Matthew Sweet's *Earth* / Joe Levy and Christian Logan Wright / March '89

"YOU COULD OPEN UP *CMJ* [*COLLEGE MEDIA JOURNAL*] AND THERE WAS THIS LITTLE PICTURE OF THE COUNTRY, AND YOU COULD LOOK AT THE COLLEGE STATIONS, 'CAUSE COLLEGE STATIONS, THAT'S ALL THERE WAS TO LISTEN TO. Well, there were modern-rock stations that played the Cure, the Fixx, Siouxsie and the Banshees. But if you wanted to hear Hüsker Dü or the Replacements or anything like that, you had to listen to college radio. Once [The Pixies' *Come on Pilgrim*] came out, we could see our name listed, like, in the Top Ten. We could say, "Wow, lookit, a college in North Carolina is playing us." And we could go there and play a show. I don't think I realized that it was probably a wattage that didn't even penetrate the campus—that probably two people were listening."

— Kim Deal (The Pixies), 2004

"TO ME, THE SOUL OF ROCK'N'ROLL IS MISTAKES. IN GENERAL, MUSIC THAT'S FLAWLESS IS USUALLY UNINSPIRED. The people who go with the flow and make the mistakes and turn that into something special are the ones with guts—that's what we've always tried to do. People who play it safe have no business playing rock'n'roll."

— Paul Westerberg, 1991

ACCORDING TO VETERAN PRODUCER JIM DICKINSON (RY COODER, BIG STAR, AS WELL AS THE REPLACEMENTS' *PLEASED TO MEET ME*), "[PAUL] WESTERBERG IS THE BRAINS OF THE REPLACEMENTS, BUT TOMMY [STINSON] IS THE BALLS. The fire, the energy I keyed in on was Tommy. He and Chris [Mars] are a great rhythm section, just fabulous. Tommy's this great existential hero, which is a rare breed nowadays. Every morning, or after-noon, Tommy wakes up and decides whether or not he wants to be Tommy. His brother Bob [an original Replacement] used to force him to play the bass when he was a little kid. If he didn't he'd get backhanded, so Tommy hates the bass, but he loves it, too. It's that fight between the positive and the negative that creates the tension that makes great music. The Stones had it, and so do the Replacements." (When I ask Westerberg if he agrees that Tommy is the balls of the group, he remarks, "Tommy's the balls and the dick.")

"Those guys don't just have a few beers," Dickinson continues. "They wake up and start drinking vodka. If they're trying to be good they drink wine. Westerberg wouldn't know how to be sober. I recorded him in the dungeon, which is not actually a studio, but it's got four concrete walls that give it a nice natural echo, and he got so drunk that we had to duct-tape mattresses to the walls to keep him from hurting himself. Westerberg is a real good guitar player, though, if you catch him just drunk enough. He can't play sober and he can't play completely shitfaced, but if you catch him in between he's real good."

— "They Might Be Giants" / Michael Corcoran / April '89

SITTING ON A FALLEN TREE ON A SMALL ISLAND IN THE MIDDLE OF A FROZEN MINNEAPOLIS LAKE, BOB STINSON IS A SHAKY DEFENSE FOR THE ROCK LIFE-STYLE. Heineken propped up in the snow, thrift-store suit jacket pulled tight against the 10-degree cold, he blows his nose into the wind, belches, and shivers. An unrepentant alcoholic for more than ten years, Stinson insisted we buy a six-pack and do the interview out here, near where the speedboats race in the summer. "It's completely untouched by screw-ups," he marvels, blood-shot blue eyes squinting into a bright blue midday sky.

Still best known as an ex-Replacements guitarist more than six years after being fired from the band he started in his mom's house, Stinson is harshly defined by the past. Every other Replacement, including *his* replacement, guitarist Bob "Slim" Dunlap, will release an album this year. Meanwhile, Stinson, 33 and holding on, is an unemployed cook, divorced, killing time in a youthfully Stones-y bar band and living in a dorm-style apartment wallpapered with rock posters (Jimmy Page, Ace Frehley) and

Madonna pin-ups. A pink dress, a relic of Replacements past, hangs on a broken mic stand.

Long before Kurt Cobain's bank card became an indie-rock talisman, the Replacements were self-destructively struggling with the post-punk myth of "selling out" (they refused to even show their faces for their first video, 1986's "Bastards of Young"). The band flaunted its volatile dynamic. Stinson, a burly, gentle Yes fan who favored thrift-store frocks, played Shakes the Clown to Westerberg's half-assed Pagliacci. Grinning like a vagrant crashing an office party, he would petulantly refuse to play a solo, then spew out some grossly beautiful racket that was equal parts Kiss baby-food-metal, Robert Quine art-mangle and pure-pop trash. Westerberg—a moody fuck-up much like Stinson—would inevitably smirk and cigarette-rasp a heart-wrenching, no-future-in-frontin' chorus. His best songs ("Shiftless When Idle," "Color Me Impressed," "Unsatisfied") scripted the self-deprecating middle-class vulnerability of the '80s just as sharply as Dylan sketched the pretentious middle-class dreams of the '60s. Stinson's half-brother Tommy, 11 when he joined as bassist, struck airborne rock poses and flashed his I'm-too-young-to-know-better glance at college girls. Chris Mars, a dead ringer for an ABC After School Special "loner," hunched over his drums, slight frame pounding away like somebody was chasing him. There was never much tawdry glamour with the Replacements, just raw nerves.

But as boredom and fear of semi-fame crept up on the band, they more often sputtered through a schlock-block of stunted covers ("Detroit Rock City," "Smokin' in the Boys' Room") like janitors throwing a smoke bomb down the toilet. Night after night, they heckled themselves: It's a filthy job but somebody's gotta screw it up. And Bob, the band's most recklessly troubled member, became a symbol of how rock dangles redemption, and then laughs in your face when it's snatched away.

He is offhandedly brutal about his risks and disappointments:

"You know, I'd really like to meet myself sometime. I'd probably beat the shit out of myself for letting opportunities go by."

The Stinson family definitely was "no Leave It to Beaver," as Bob puts it. Mom, now seven years sober, was an alcoholic throughout his childhood. His father, an alcoholic who left when Bob was two, has no contact with the family. Tommy's dad, his mother's longtime boyfriend, is dead. Bob was pulled out of ninth grade for being "incorrigible and self-destructive" and traveled through the entire juvenile system. "The last group home I was at was where I learned to drink, get good drugs, and play guitar, all at the same time," he says.

When Bob returned to the family, Tommy became his personal project. "He was throwing stones through gas station windows and shit like that, and my mom said, 'Something's got to be done.'" So Bob bought his brother an amp and appointed him bass player of Dogbreath, Bob and Chris Mars's first band. Eventually, Tommy left school, also in the ninth grade, to play with them full-time. The Stinson brothers co-existed uneasily —sometimes not communicating with each other for a year at a time since Bob was dumped from the Replacements in 1986, reportedly for excessive drug use and his unwillingness to (or inability to) learn the more "mature" material being written by Westerberg.

Expectations for the Replacements raged after 1984's *Let It Be*—a perfectly torn flannel shirt of '60s garage-pop, '70s blues-metal, and '80s hardcore. As did doubts about Bob. In 1989, Westerberg told *Musician*, "[Bob] believed the image we played onstage. He didn't understand, 'Oh we gotta play some music too.'" Here was the readily embraced mythology: Bob was a balls-to-the-walls slob holding back the band's aesthetic development. But what Bob embodied and what Westerberg would not admit (except in his songs,) was a specifically post-punk burden of truth. Like it or not, the Replacements' brilliance became tangled up with their pathos. They rocked because they felt pathetic. But then they still felt pathetic, so Westerberg's aching ballads about stunted hopes were even more poignant. After Bob was gone, that dynamic was lost.

"It was never the same after he left," says Mars. "Once somebody got together, like, a thousand cardboard cutouts of Bob's face for the show and passed them around for everybody to put on, including Slim. They were protesting, they wanted Bob back."

— "Hold My Life" / Charles Aaron / June '93

BOB STINSON WAS FOUND DEAD OF "NATURAL CAUSES" IN FEBRUARY 1995 IN HIS MINNEAPOLIS APARTMENT. Though there was a syringe next to his couch, the death was not technically the result of a drug overdose. Instead, doctors characterized it as complicated by "chemical dependency with acute and chronic alcoholism, hepatic cirrhosis, intravenous narcotism with recent opiate use, and bipolar affective disorder." A medical examiner put it more concisely: "Even though he was 35 years old, he wore his body out."

— "Top Spin" / Charles Aaron / May '95

HÜSKER DÜ DIDN'T QUITE SOUND LIKE A PUNK BAND, BUT IT DIDN'T SOUND LIKE ANYTHING ELSE, EITHER.

From the beginning, the prettiness and emotional heft of Bob Mould's and Grant Hart's songs didn't jibe with the one-dimensional scream-fest that constituted so much early '80s punk rock.

It wasn't an obviously innovative sound—in fact, next to R.E.M.'s poetic textures and the Replacements' crazy looseness, Hüsker Dü sounded almost reactionary—but its narrowness was a very complicated thing that wound up influencing a huge array of subsequent bands. Green Day borrowed Hüsker Dü's harsh tunefulness. Nirvana discovered a palatable format for depressive fury. My Bloody Valentine studied their feedback. The list of admirers and protégés is as long and various as that of any band's in rock.

— "The Ten That Matter Most '85-'95 (#6: Hüsker Dü)" / Dennis Cooper / April, '95

LIKE THE GOLD COINS CALIGULA USED TO DUMP FROM HIS ROOFTOP ONTO THE CROWDED STREETS, SONIC YOUTH'S LATEST RECORD—DESPITE ITS COLD BLUE MASK—WILL BURN YOUR FINGERS. Sure, it's no substitute for the live thing, but you already knew that, and have learned to cope with it. *Sister* has other virtues. Stripped of its coat-of-many-overtones, SY's intricately structured noise gleams like polished bones: Turns out this band can write *songs*. Their sense of dynamics continues to develop, and the "weird tunings" now seem to add to, more than they distract from, the music—not just because some of the novelty's worn off, but because the tunings are now built around songs.

The two best tracks here ("Catholic Block" and "Tuff Gnarl"), show why some long-time fans are screaming bloody sell-out over this record (usually a good sign

[SONIC YOUTH]

in a band's musical development). Both songs splice melody and mayhem together as if the combination were as natural as meat and cookies, and the result works almost as well. There's no band who uses noise as musical weapon quite so well, and no other rock group whose textures are as deep, as colorful, or as affecting.

Buy this record. Play it over and over. In ten years everyone will be trying to sound like this.
— Review of Sonic Youth's *Sister* / James Greer / April '88

"THE WORD *INDEPENDENT* IS QUICKLY LOSING ITS MEANING," SAYS FUGAZI'S IAN MACKAYE. "In the early '80s, when people started putting out their own independent records, the impact they had on the underground music scene and the independent music scene was massive. So massive that of course sooner or later the majors were going to come down to it."

But MacKaye isn't interested.

"The only thing major labels can really offer is distribution," he says. "They can get your records all over the place. But I think we can get our records almost all over the place, and the fact that we can't get our records in every 7-Eleven across the country is just not important. It's not our ambition. The goal of Fugazi is to be a band. And we've succeeded in that."

Fugazi is in a unique situation. They are a "popular band" (their latest release, *Repeater*, has sold more than 100,000 copies), but don't subscribe to any promotional pressure. They're known for their five-dollar shows; they won't play if it will cost people more.

Some major labels also offer complete creative control, but that doesn't surprise MacKaye.

"I think that labels are so completely out of touch with music that they are willing to turn creative control over to the band," he asserts. "Because they're buying out of the independent thing. And of course they can't tell independent bands how to play their music—they already know. These are bands that have played dozens to hundreds of shows. And you can't tell a band like D.O.A. how to play music. It's just crazy. The same thing with Sonic Youth. How the

fuck can Geffen tell Sonic Youth how to sound? There's no way, no way."
— "Underground: Dischord" / Daniel Fidler / February '91

"MAYBE YOU SHOULD COME OVER AND FELLATE MY GUITAR, STEVE." Sonic Youth guitarist Thurston Moore is lying on his back on the foil-covered floor of a downtown Manhattan production studio. He wants drummer Steve Shelley to give his guitar a blowjob because the band are shooting a video. These guys know what plays well on MTV.

Actually, they were going to call the new album *Blowjob*, but settled instead on *Goo*. Which probably made their new record company, Geffen, happy until its executives saw the cover art: a drawing by renowned underground artist Raymond Pettibon. The drawing itself of a guy and girl in a car presented no problems. But the accompanying text—which read in part, "Within a week we killed my parents and hit the road"—gave some Geffenites fits.

"They were still talking at sales meetings about an alternative cover, even though our A&R person knew quite well that there was no way we were going to do that," says bassist Kim Gordon.

After nine years of pretty much doing anything they want, Sonic Youth are finding the adjustment to corporate-label status somewhat difficult.

— "Kool Things" / Jim Greer / September '90

FOR SOME OF US, THE THROWING MUSES' 1986 DEBUT WAS ONE OF THOSE RECORDS, THE KIND THAT LEAVES YOU FEELING YOUR LIFE HAS BEEN CHANGED IN WAYS YOU CAN'T DEFINE. Women friends have testified that it was the first time they encountered a purely female music of rage and bewilderment that spoke directly to them. Where male angst is directed outward at the world, female violence is implosive, turned inward to take shape in obsessive symptoms like anorexia or "delicate self-cutting."

Kristin Hersh's fractured lyrics and hemorrhaging voice seemed to be a musical equivalent, or possibly an alternative, to these self-destructive practices. But the ravaged grace of her "falling apart" never seemed like mere wallowing in misery, but rather, it was the first step toward rebuilding herself. Boys could identify too, since Hersh's songs were as much about adolescence as specifically female trauma.

— review of Throwing Muses' *The Real Ramona* / Simon Reynolds / May '91

THAT NIGHT AT YALE, DINOSAUR JR. TAKE TO THE POORLY LIT STAGE LOOK-ING LIKE A HARDCORE BAND OUT OF *LORD OF THE RINGS*. Except for his goofy orange ski cap with a rainbow band and a big furry pompom, J Mascis is an example of the lanky, elfin strain of Deadheads: straight sub-nipple hair, droopy brown sweater, orange knit neck-lace. Murph (just Murph) bashes his drums like a bearded hobbit. Beneath his Wilderness Division sweatshirt decorated with Eskimos, he wears a Squirrel Bait T. Lou Barlow, in torn jeans, half turns towards his amp, confronting the audience only when he takes to the mic for his occasional screams. Even then he hides behind his shaggy dog mop.

They jam electric drool, grunge from the heart of the broken forest, feedback and sludgy riff doodles leaking out between the cracks in the set like glue.

Unlike the Jesus and Mary Chain, who layer feedback and screech on top of catchy songs, Dinosaur Jr.'s tunes emerge from the noise itself. They lunge into "Sludgefeast," a midtempo melting pot of minor-chord metal, '70s leftovers, and misty mountain pop. Mascis, gazing vacantly over the audience, spatters electricity everywhere, surrounding himself in noise before pleading, "I'm waiting/ Please come back/ Got the guts now/ To meet yer eye." Murky matter bubbles up from beneath the surface of the song: solitude, yearning, love that falls short of friendship. The wood-folk melody and Mascis' plaintive warble thread through the massive hooks and monstrous guitar sludge like small flowers growing on hills of black sulfurous muck. And once you step in it, yer stuck.

And why does Mascis enjoy playing at such high volume? "It's basically because I don't like to play. The guitar's such a wimpy instrument, and it's the only way to make it halfway bearable. I mean, I like *listening* to guitar, but to me it's never loud enough because it's so weird and undynamic as an instrument."

[DINOSAUR JR.]

"You really don't like to play guitar?"

"No."

"Why do you do it?"

"Dunno."

— "Just Like Heaven" / Erik Davis / August '89

"IT WAS A COMPLETELY CONFUSED TIME, A POST-GULF WAR TIME," says Lou Barlow of the recording of *Sebadoh III.* "We were all broke, and I was being supported by my girlfriend. I was angry. And we were alone." But mostly, Barlow was still pissed at J Mascis for kicking him out of Dinosaur Jr. two years earlier. He began writing songs that pitilessly dissected his psyche, gushed about true love, analyzed his need to masturbate, and railed against Mascis. Among this last category is the opener, "The Freed Pig," one of the finest songs ever written about hating someone as much as you hate yourself.

— "The 90 Greatest Albums of the '90s / Greg Milner / September '99

THE BREEDERS' SECOND ALBUM SPINS OUT AS A LITANY OF SUMMER—OR RATHER, A SUMMER OF ROCK'N'ROLL. Its bright cymbal sound flashes off submerged lyrics about sunshine and water and steaming metal; the broiling guitars reek occasionally of surf. There's a stubbornly harmonious pop song ("Do You Love Me Now," from last year's *Safari* EP), a bunch of effervescent pop rocks ("Cannonball," "Divine Hammer," "Saints"), and the now–obligatory acoustic country shuffle ("Driving on 9"). Singer-guitarist Kim Deal and guitarist Kelly Deal jumpstart the whole shebang with two minutes of the blistering "New Year"—as in "I am the sun/ I am the new year"—and 12 songs later, Kim's lazily sassing "summer is ready when you are," as if the season's some archetypal willing babe.

Or not. That line's ambiguity (when will you be ready?) pulls us down into the tangle of gender politics under *Last Splash's* sun-fun surface noise. For in the mainstream, where rock music meets summer, girls haven't had a lot to do besides don halter tops and dance on their boyfriends' shoulders. And wear tight dresses to meet someone on a rooftop. And look really sleek in Daddy's convertible. But what happens when the woman is the "I," the man the "you," and the summer is seen from a girl's-eye-view?

— review of The Breeders' *Last Splash* / Terri Sutton / September '93

ROBERT POLLARD WRITES INSANELY AMAZING SONGS THAT STICK IN YOUR HEAD LIKE AN UNPLEASANT RELATION-SHIP, AND CALLS THEM THINGS LIKE "KICKER OF ELVES" AND "I AM A SCIENTIST." He does an awkward shaman dance like a nerdy Jim Morrison, sings like my dream boyfriend, and adores the Beatles. He's been making music for years, as well as teaching elementary school and hanging with his kids. He has no interest in being a rock star, which is why he'll probably be one. This is his band's ninth LP and I worship it.

— review of Guided by Voices' *Bee Thousand* / Gail O'Hara / August '94

KURT COBAIN'S GOT A TATTOO ON HIS ARM. It's the K Records symbol, representing the Olympia, Washington, indie label run by Beat Happening's Calvin Johnson. This summer Johnson helped stage the International Pop Underground Convention, where, unlike other so-called new music conventions, they really did showcase only new talent, along with holding barbecues, parades, and disco dances. It was very pure.

Cobain says, "It's the event of the year. I vowed months ago that nothing was going to get in the way of me attending it—but unfortunately this year we missed it because we played the Reading Festival in England. But I've had the tattoo since last summer. It was a home job. Dave taught me."

"You can do it with just a regular sewing needle, string, and some India ink," instructs Nirvana drummer Dave Grohl. "Wrap the thread around the needle, dip it in the ink, and jab it in."

"But when I did it, the thread unraveled," says Cobain. "So I ended up jabbing in the needle and pouring ink all over my arm."

— "Heaven Can't Wait" / Lauren Spencer / January '92

SO I'M SITTING IN MY HOTEL ROOM WATCHING MTV, AND THAT DAMN DUSTDEVILS VIDEO COMES ON AGAIN. What is this, like the fifteenth time today? I wonder how much Matador had to pay to get that thing in heavy rotation. I mean the girl is cute, but….

Okay, maybe not. Maybe there isn't a Dustdevils video in heavy rotation on MTV. Maybe there isn't a Dustdevils video at all—Matador can scarcely afford to keep its back catalogue in print, much

less dole out the bucks for a video. But that's not the point, is it?

At Matador, New York City's coolest new independent rock label in years, the point is music, not exposure. Label founders Chris Lombardi and Gerard Cosloy (you may remember him from Homestead Records, the label he ran in the mid-to-late '80s that served as erstwhile home of such indie luminaries as Sonic Youth and Dinosaur Jr.) aren't looking for any particular *sound*—this isn't a Sub Pop thing waiting to happen. In fact, it pleases the boys if you say you really hate one or more of the bands almost as much as if you say you love them. It pleases them because they are looking to provoke a reaction.

"We signed the Shams and the Unsane at the same time," says Lombardi. "Their music is almost exactly opposite—the Shams are sort of folk-pop and the Unsane are kind of noisy."

The label's roster, while unquestionably diverse, does tend to be weighted more heavily towards the "noise" end of the indie-rock spectrum. Labelmates Railroad Jerk, Dustdevils, the Unsane, and H.P. Zinker (Matador's first release, in January 1990) all bear superficial resemblance to each other in terms of the powerful dissonance each trades in. The thing about noise bands, though—good ones, anyway, and the ones on Matador are mostly good ones—is that the noise is beside the point. It's a means to an end, and the ends are as diverse as the personalities that comprise the bands.

Probably the most successful band currently on the Matador roster is the Scottish noise-pop combo Teenage Fanclub, whose debut, *A Catholic Education*, was easily one of the best records of 1990. They are planning to start work soon on a follow-up LP that Matador hopes to release sometime this summer. It'll probably be the band's last album for the label, however, as wolf packs of major record labels have been heard baying at Teenage Fanclub's door.

But even if the majors snap them up, Matador is sure to come up with enough innovative, exciting new bands to keep your interest over the next few years. Maybe they'll even sell enough records to make a Dustdevils video one of these days.

— "Cool Record Labels: Matador" / Jim Greer / May '91

[THE BREEDERS]

THE BIG-BUDGET BOMBAST OF THE BUTCH VIG-*NEVERMIND* SOUND IS AS OPPRESSIVELY OMNIPRESENT AS DANIEL LANOIS-*JOSHUA TREE* STRATOSPHERICS WERE IN THE MID-'80S. But, thank the Lord, there's an alternative to CD-friendly alternative in the form of the lo-fi underground: avant-garage bands such as Royal Trux, Trumans Water, Thinking Fellers Union Local 282, Wall Drug, Fantastic Palace, God Is My Co-Pilot, and droves of more miniature miscreants every month. Too motley to be a movement, these bands do share common roots in the more warped tributaries of the pre-punk and post-punk underground (Captain Beefheart, Can/Faust/Neu, Pere Ubu, the Fall). They're fond of thrift-store, ultracheesy guitar effects and antiquated technology pushed to the breaking point. And their ramshackle songs have cryptic titles, absurdist wit, Dada doggerel lyrics, and loose ends galore. The absolute ruler of this particular mess-thetic is, of course, Pavement.
— review of Pavement's *Westing (By Musket and Sextant)* / Simon Reynolds / June '93

WITH A $1,500 ADVANCE FROM MATADOR (THE LABEL THAT WAS TO INDIE ROCK WHAT SUB POP WAS TO GRUNGE), THE TRIO TOOK THE MUSIC STEPHEN MALKMUS HAD DAYDREAMED AS A SECURITY GUARD AT NEW YORK'S WHITNEY MUSEUM AND HAPHAZARDLY FASHIONED A LEGEND. On *Slanted and Enchanted*, the reluctant anthem "Summer Babe" and the sing-songy "Trigger Cut" (in which Malkmus somehow turns "Lies and betrayals/ Fruit-covered nails/ Electricity and lust" into a call to arms) slapped five with song snippets that treated slackness as a birthright. Earlier indie had rooted its greatness in revitalizing rock; this stuff exploded like genius let out of a bottle.

"For a certain generation of people, *Slanted* was, like, a big thing," Malkmus says. "That's never going to happen with another Pavement record for them because we grew up. But it's nice to be known for something, I guess. Even if it is a lo-fi Fall rip-off album."
— "The 90 Greatest Albums of the '90s / Eric Weisbard / September '99

"[PAVEMENT'S] STEPHEN MALKMUS IS GREAT. It's the Stockton [CA] part of him, you know? If it was just the East Coast thing he'd be gross. And he's so well-bred. He's like the Grace Kelly of indie rock."
— Courtney Love, 1994

PAVEMENT'S OBLIQUENESS WAS ORIGINALLY ROOTED IN A SHARED SENSE OF RIGHTEOUS OBSCURITY. By *Wowee Zowee*, they had bailed on the idea of Indie Nation, and recast themselves as a blur, as chooglin' culture-jammers on the periphery of pop. But by that time, Blur were recasting themselves as Pavement, and Pavement were naming albums after John Ashbery poems. This was indeterminacy as art. Though it seemed gracefully off-the-cuff at the time, it was nonetheless a strategy. What makes *Terror Twilight* feel fresh is that it tried to break the spell, with something like a commitment to clarity. "It's all right to shake to fight to feel," Malkmus sings on the record's most fetching tune, "…and Carrot Rope," and throughout you feel him trying to shake in new ways. "…and Carrot Rope" is full of positively good vibes and wah wah wah—you almost expect a brass section to materialize and knock you back to a '70s Top 40 countdown. "Major Leagues" once would have suggested their tangled feelings regarding major-label life, but all that's meaningless now. Now the "major leagues" means emotional commitment, means "relationships hey-hey-hey," and Malkmus says he's ready.

But he's not quite there yet. Alongside the directness there's an overripe worldweariness or, more accurately, decadence. At various points Malkmus role-plays a lech coming on to a boy; confesses his girlfriend makes him feel so good he wants to "spit on a stranger"; and indelibly shrieks, "I've got a right to sit on that face." There's a breathy, jaded tone to his singing, too; ever since *Wowee Zowee*'s opener, "We Dance," a gust of pomp has been blowing through it, and here it's like the Santa Ana winds. At times he conveys the grandiosity of Liberace delivering his famous funeral oration for Victor Herbert, lamenting the death of refinement.
— review of Pavement's *Terror Twilight* / RJ Smith / June '99

FUGAZI LEADER IAN MACKAYE LOOKS PRETTY MUCH LIKE HE DID WHEN HE WAS TEARING UP STAGES WITH MINOR THREAT 20 YEARS AGO: The stubble on his head is graying and starts a bit farther back on his scalp than it did in the early '80s, but he's trimmer than most guys his age, decked out in an old T-shirt and baggy shorts. Dischord Records co-founder Jeff Nelson is likewise still rail thin, but he's assumed a professorial air, wearing a neat plaid shirt and glasses, free of the shock of brown hair that he sports on the back of the box set (in a photo that shows him getting pummeled by a fellow mosher). Today, he's eating a leftover slice of Domino's pizza, which he seems to have brought over for the sole purpose of irritating his vegan business partner. "Would you like to keep the dipping sauce?" Nelson asks MacKaye with a shit-eating grin. MacKaye tosses the offending condiment before sitting down to pour himself a cup of tea, which he drinks from a Christmas mug with a broken handle.

This domestic tableau is far from the combat-boot cliché of D.C. punk, perhaps the most stridently ideological music scene in rock history: no drugs, no sexism, no "rock'n'roll bullshit," as Government Issue put it in a 1981 single. But myths are more convenient than reality, and the true story of this loud music has often been drowned out by the even louder conversation about its creators' lifestyles. "We always get asked about Ian," says John Davis of Q and Not U, a young band that joined Dischord in 2000. "'Does he smoke pot?' 'Does he drink? I hear he drinks.'"

"He's almost a cultlike figure," says Kim Coletta, co-owner of the record label DeSoto and bassist for the now-defunct Dischord band Jawbox. Even cultlike figures consider him a cultlike figure. "I don't really want to meet him—I'd be scared out of my mind," says Dashboard Confessional's Chris Carrabba, who, like thousands of kids, pinpoints a Fugazi show as the site of his greatest live-music epiphany. "I respect them for sticking to their ideals so ardently," he says. "But it's gotta be hard. I bet in the '90s Fugazi got a different major-label offer every day. They've been at this 20 years—touring around in a van is really hard, and it must take strength to say, 'This is where we started; this is where we're gonna stay.'"

The great irony of Ian MacKaye's career is that despite his band's aversion to the mass-culture shell game—famously singing "You are not what you

[FUGAZI]

own," refusing to make videos or sell T-shirts, and avoiding the mainstream press—he has engendered more mythological speculation than willing media darlings like Sum 41 ever will.

"There's a lot of conversations," says MacKaye. "Take the straight-edge thing. I understand there's, like, a phenomenon that has occurred—now the word *straight edge* is in the dictionary. That's insane. It's cool!"
— "Out of Step with the World" / Andrew Beaujon / May '03

"WHAT HAPPENS TO PEOPLE? They turn new wave, they move away, they mate, they take drugs, they watch TV, they get in car crashes, they get lucky, they get stabbed, they get rich, they go crazy, they go to Philadelphia and never return…."
— Henry Rollins, 1985

: MTV

Giving the people what they want
[Jesus—is this really what they want?]

[DURAN DURAN
Rio, 1983]

■

> **MTV is the worst thing to happen to music since *Saturday Night Fever*. It's bringing back every stupid cliché, sexism, racism. Part of [our song] "MTV Get Off the Air" is when the DJ says, "Don't create, be sedate." That's what they're pushing: don't think, consume! Don't go outside and see what our country's like. Sit inside and watch television. They've finally figured out a way to get people to watch television commercials 24 hours a day.**
> – JELLO BIAFRA (Dead Kennedys), 1986

Whenever people use MTV as a metaphor

(either as the surrogate for an entire generation, or as the driving aesthetic for all modernity), it always serves the same purpose: The reason you compare something to MTV is to show how something is *sad*. Or vapid. Or disposable. Or—at the very least—"extreme." And very often, the analogy has merit; at various points throughout its existence, MTV has been all of those things. However, what nobody will admit about MTV (or maybe never considered) is how it consistently demonstrates how the music industry does not know what it's doing, and how it effortlessly proves that Americans never really know what they want until they see it.

MTV emerged in 1981, an exceptionally weird time for rock'n'roll; this was a period when obscuring what a band looked like was pretty much the whole idea. Five years earlier, Boston had put a cartoon spaceship on the cover of their album and sold 17 million records. Styx records featured surreal zebras and demonic robots; Foreigner was content to market themselves with the number "4." The concept, it seemed, was to turn bands like REO Speedwagon and Journey and Toto into faceless, interchangeable entities that could then be formatted into the same FM radio category; this way, every FM station would sound like one long song. This would stop people from twisting the dial, and that was ideal for companies who wanted to buy FM advertising. Moreover, it was assumed that *this was what people wanted*. If people liked the way Boston sounded, what the guys in Boston looked like probably didn't matter.

This, of course, is where record labels were confused. As David Foster Wallace pointed out in *Infinite Jest*, the battle between radio and television was not a technological gap between audio and video; television is audio *plus* video. It was never a fair fight, which is why TV so easily won. It was not that video killed the radio star; it was that TV became a more compelling type of radio. MTV allowed teenagers to engage with music in a new way, especially kids who happened to live in places where bands never played and rock stars didn't exist. Almost immediately after MTV began beaming itself to rural America, original MTV marketing chief Tom Freston met a barber in Wichita who suddenly had teenage boys asking him for Rod Stewart haircuts. Clearly, this was something new.

The number of acts whose success can be directly linked to MTV is (of course) staggering. Duran Duran, Bon Jovi, and Madonna are among the most obvious early examples, but a connection can be made between MTV and almost any artist who sold a lot of albums during the 1980s (this even includes the bands who *weren't* on the station—a big part of Metallica's early credibility was their refusal to make videos). On the Stray Cats first U.S. tour in 1982, the group only played in cities where MTV was available, since those were the only communities where anyone knew who they were. The dominance of Mötley Crüe's "Home Sweet Home" on MTV's all-request program, *Dial MTV*, completely altered who their audience was and subsequently transformed the arc of their career. When *Yo! MTV Raps* debuted in August of 1988, it was the first time most white people heard (and certainly the first time most white people saw) hip-hop. MTV became—almost irrefutably—the most accurate reflection of what consumer culture was. It was (and is) populism in practice.

MTV changed the way its audience thinks about *everything*, including the channel itself. In the summer of 1992, MTV was still operating like a Top 40 station; if you watched an hour of programming on any Friday night, you would inevitably see Pearl Jam's "Jeremy" and the Black Crowes' "Remedy" and Sir Mix-A-Lot's "Baby Got Back" and three or four other clips that happened to fall into heavy rotation. But that same summer, MTV debuted *The Real World*; around the same time, they became obsessed with the "Choose or Lose" get-out-the-vote campaign and the notion that it was suddenly a news channel. In every year that followed, MTV seemed to show fewer and fewer videos, replacing music with the kind of programming they had originally been the alternative to. And everyone complained about this, insisting they preferred music videos to *Beavis and Butt-head* marathons or endless episodes of *Singled Out*.

But evidently they did not, because MTV's ratings immediately improved when they introduced conventional block programming. Young audiences had begun consuming videos as autonomous four-minute shows: Anytime they grew bored with any individual video, they switched to something else. Showing 12 videos in the span of an hour provided 12 opportunities to change the channel, and music video jump-cuts only made trigger-fingers itchier. This was bad news for advertising; it created the same problem FM radio had tried to fix with self-conscious facelessness in the 1970s. Economically, it became more efficient to show four straight episodes of *Newlyweds* for 120 consecutive minutes.

This is why MTV barely plays videos anymore. They accelerated culture so successfully that they forced themselves to suck.

1980

Devo, "Whip It" Jerking around the barnyard in UPS/S+M uniforms and black-plastic, Kmart frames, these Ohio spuds lasso Nerd Chic.

1983

Michael Jackson, "Billie Jean" The fluid moves of soul and Hollywood jazz, oh sure, but mixed with the song's stalker vibe, Michael creates a world of heavy-metal intensity.
+ Duran Duran, "Rio" Exteriors, darling, are everything for playboy synth-pop bands specializing in exotic escapism. Monaco? We did that last season. And the light sucked.
+ Eurythmics, "Sweet Dreams (Are Made of This)" The culture of deal-making reigned so completely in the '80s that art-popsters couldn't resist visualizing sex in similar terms.

1984

Van Halen, "Jump" Who needs a story line when you're a guitar band, by God? Swathed in spandex, on-fucking-stage, lights blaring, cigarettes burning between frets, sticking it in your ear.
+ John Cafferty & the Beaver Brown Band, "On the Dark Side" When rockers are on the run, it's always through back-streets and alleys, dodging trash cans, rats, and piles of garbage.
+ Michael Jackson, "Thriller" MGM, Cinerama, horrorcore amusement park, Spielberg, Lucas: everything you can jam into one of these things.
+ Madonna, "Like a Virgin" High-filtered, gauzy shots of lions, Italy, overstuffed hotel sofas, black lingerie, ropy pearls, and Madonna herself. Yuppie opulence equals shameless sex.

1985

a-ha, "Take on Me" After A Flock of Seagulls, cartoons were no leap, and the animation got slicker and cooler: Flintstones, out; Jetsons, in.
+ 'Til Tuesday, "Voices Carry" Pop songs have their melodrama, relationships have awful domestic stress. The symbol of both? Shattering glass—in white-knuckle-slo-mo.
+ Prince, "Raspberry Beret" Trees turn pink, perhaps chartreuse, guys throw Day-Glo jackets over ruffled shirts. It's *Sgt. Pepper*'s with more intricate hairstyles.

1986

Janet Jackson, "What Have You Done For Me Lately?" Choreography that's as jagged, elegant, designed and up-close-and-personal as the revamped black pop it accompanies.

1988

R.E.M., "Stand" The video as equal-opportunity employer—ordinary people, crooked smiles, T-shirts, high school reunions. The result: populism that charms.

1989 **Garth Brooks**, "The Dance" According to the canniest country artist/marketeer in pop history, the last 50 years of mainstream American myth belong to Nashville.
+ 2 Live Crew, "Me So Horny" Starring the derriere.
—"'80s Images We've Come to Love and Hate" / James Hunter / August '97

An assistant turned on a tape cassette of ZZ Top.

"Dance!" the man said.

We rehearsed the dancing. I tried to look enthusiastic, even though under no circumstance could I ever imagine myself dancing enthusiastically to ZZ Top on the roof of a boat with five typecast strangers.

"Put some streamers around their necks," the woman told the assistant. So he threw red and pink streamers over us.

"OK," the man said. "This time, when you dance, go really crazy. You—" he pointed at a girl with a blond frou-frou hairdo—"you shake up the bottle of beer while you dance and spray it on everyone."

This time the camera was on. The boat began to rock from side to side. The sky grew overcast. We danced wildly to the tape, a boy picked up a handful of greenish potato salad and stuffed it into his mouth, the other boy pretended to play the barbeque tongs as if it was a guitar, the girl shook up the bottle and sprayed it over all of us. The crepe-paper streamers, wet with beer, began to bleed streaks of bloody red down everyone's clothes. The girls jiggled back and forth, laughing furiously, clapping their hands. The boat was rocking harder now. Near the Statue of Liberty, I began to think I might possibly throw up. Yet I noticed the camera focusing on my face. I smiled wanly as I danced, shaking my head from side to side to demonstrate joy and good will.

"OK," the man said, "Now, in the next scene, pick up this vat of chicken and toss it overboard, vat and all."

"I feel sick," the boy who had eaten the potato salad said. "That potato salad—there was something wrong."
— "I Was an Elderly Teenage Bimbo for MTV" / Tama Janowitz / September '86

[DEVO *"Whip It,"* 1980]

Which is more violent: A man burning alive or a nuclear explosion?

MTV feels safer with an atomic bomb than a man in flames. Programmers at the network refuse to put "666," by Christian rock group DeGarmo & Key, on the air because it showed a character being burned alive. But when the band replaced the human torch with a nuclear blast, the video went into light rotation.

"We won't run videos with senseless violence," says David Horowitz, president and chief executive officer of MTV.

— "Thou Shalt Obey MTV" / Andrew Roblin / July '85

It's a fiercely hot March day in the middle of spring break in Lake Havasu City, Arizona.

MTV is here to celebrate the season by taping several shows. They've invited all the spring breakers to be in the audience, but not everyone cares to. Being in the *MTV Spring Break* audience means parting with your keg for a few hours, and there are a bunch of kids at the beach who simply don't consider that an option. Besides, down here at the beach, a group of about 300 young men just found an old-fashioned way to relax together. They're having fun the way people used to have fun, back before television was invented. They're crowding by the water's edge, pounding their fists up and down in the air. They're chanting, "Show us your tits! Show us your tits!"

The subjects of this zany prank are a couple of bikini-clad coeds on a boat just offshore. One of the more clever girls decides to leave the safety of her boat and wade into the midst of this throng. She's passed around by dozens of groping hands, in a scene that resembles an open casting call for *The Accused*. Finally, she shows those coveted tits. She earns herself a savage roar of approval and is swallowed by the chanting crowd.

Soon, another boat drifts by. A young man on it grabs his girlfriend and leads the beach crowd in the "Show us your tits" chant. She won't do it. He shrugs apologetically to his 300 college buddies onshore, who take the disappointment as bravely as they can. (They switch their cry to "Fuck you! Fuck you!" and throw beer cans at the girl.) Now a third boat drifts by. No ladies on board, but the skipper is blasting "Smells Like Teen Spirit." The crowd changes their chant again, this time to "Nir-van-a! Nir-van-a!"

From where I'm standing, it sounds like as good an explanation for Kurt Cobain's suicide as anything I've ever heard.

The press is welcome to visit MTV's spring break coverage, but journalists are strongly discouraged from canvassing any part of the massive compound without publicity's supervision. I manage to build up points for good behavior, and on a few occasions, I'm actually allowed to walk over to the port-a-potties by myself. Aside from this subversive act, almost nothing is left to chance this week. Every moment has been planned, every word meticulously scripted.

I spend a morning watching two MTV employees write cue cards for their talent show *Fame or Shame*.

One panicked cue-card writer asks another, "Where's the card for Dr. Dre to welcome everyone back after the commercial break?"

She searches the pile frantically. To her great relief, she finds the cue card. WELCOME BACK! it reads.

On a few occasions, I'm allowed to talk to the kids in the audience. Publicity hangs a few paces back, making sure no network secrets are inadvertently divulged.

This is the kind of dangerous stuff I overhear:

"Um ... Lisa?" one girl asks another. "Um ... like, what'd you put in your hair today?"

"Um ... everything?" Lisa says.

I manage to find a small group of dissident audience kids who are actually bitter toward MTV. They're angry. They feel they've been betrayed. We lower our voices and share. Turns out the students are upset that they weren't selected by MTV recruiters to perform their particular talents on *Fame or Shame*.

"I snorted three quarters up my nose, and they didn't even pick me," one guy complains.

"But they picked the girl who drank ketchup," his girlfriend snaps.

"Drinking ketchup is not a talent," the quarter-snorter sniffs archly.

"MTV came out to our motel because they heard my buddy could bark like a dog and they wanted him on the show," another guy adds.

This revelation brings group outrage. "Bark like a dog?" the students say in disgust. "And he gets to be on MTV? Who can't bark like a dog?"

Much competitive barking follows to prove this point.

During the taping, a college kid seeks fame by drinking a milk shake concocted in his buddies' mouths. Ed Lover invents a quick little tune. "You are famous!" Ed sings to the milk-shake man. "You are no longer an anus! You were on MTV for a short period of time!" He trails off. "Now get the hell out of here.... "

— "Dumb and Dumber" / Elizabeth Gilbert / July '95

Since handily trouncing the 4,000 hopefuls who entered MTV's "I Wanna Be a VJ" contest in April 1998, Jesse Camp, the 18-year-old "homeless" kid with the loopy stoner vibe, has blown up, as he puts it, "like a-a-a-a-a thing that blows up!"

The only thing stranger than the on-air essence of a self-proclaimed semi-literate who wears makeshift thighwarmers, speaks of "spreading the love," and proudly cops to an '80s glam jones is the clamor for a piece of him: Versace and Kenneth Cole are considering him for national print campaigns. Record labels are vying to sign him. Movie studios want him under contract. Visiting celebrities take to him instantly—one day it's Green Day woofing pizza and blunts with Jesse in their dressing room; the next it's Warren Beatty soliciting conversation over Cuban cigars. Teenage girls cluster outside the MTV studios in Manhattan, and when Camp emerges, they trail his gaunt, 6' 5" frame through Times Square, giddily seeking shade under the outside brim of his floppy blue hat. "It's bizarre," says his perplexed colleague Kurt Loder. "When you meet him, you expect him to ask you for a quarter. But he just has sparkle. He doesn't have that TV patina."

— "The Accidental VJ" / Maureen Callahan / August '98

/ Eric **Weisbard**

: **Madonna**

Icon of
mall rats,
Ph.D.
candidates,
and the
rest of us.

At this point you could shred everything that's been written about Madonna and have enough paper to treat her to an old fashioned New York City ticker tape parade.

So I won't even pretend to have done my homework. Anyway, a true chronicle of Her Blonde Ambition would be multi-media, not written—an as yet unbuildable three-dimensional memory theater of her forays into sound, spectacle, and society.

That sci-fi installation would permit a glimpse of the rarest Madonna of all. Not unreleased compositions. Not her naked body in one last unfashioned pose, or an anecdote that never made it onto Page Six. I mean her personal sublime, the moments that made her shiver, giggle, compete. The DJs, photographers, parties, painters, films and books, icons, and gurus who would take us beyond clubland's Jellybean Benitez or Vogue's Herb Ritts and into some sense of her full spectrum.

In place of this kind of aesthetic summation, which I believe would reveal a vision of pop as unprecedented and usable as the vision of Americana that Dylan revealed in *Chronicles: Volume One* (where "Down in Florida on a Hog" by Darby & Tarlton unexpectedly looms as large as "Tutti Frutti"), let me suggest a few notes toward a unified theory of Madonna.

George W.S. Trow once wrote a *New Yorker* article called "Within the Context of No Context," a phrase now used for pseudopop epiphenomena like the O.J. trial, or many other things which Madonna actually isn't. Another Trow piece was called "Within that Context, One Style: Eclectic, Reminiscent, Amused, Fickle, Perverse (Ahmet Ertegun)." Ertegun had built Atlantic Records on R&B but by then was partying at Studio 54 with Mick Jagger. We'll start from there.

Context: This was the party that Madonna took over. The saga of white men propping their own myth on a sentimental vision of black music. The saga of Andy Warhol connecting art students and pop commerce. The saga of new wave as the latest pop music to cross over from England to America. The saga of punk, disco, and other unmentionables.

Context: Madonna made her 1980s records for Sire Records, which had tried to break the Ramones, who still best exemplify the SPIN magazine version of "alternative": rock bands with obvious intelligence playing in a manner populist enough to reach kids hungry for something new. Sire failed with the Ramones. With Madonna, they broke the bank. Where that reality left the "alternative" dream has never been clear. Or postmodernism and cultural studies, two versions of the same impulse to sanctify a sliver of pop. Madonna, instead, went ahead and seized pop.

Context: In 1965, as an outgrowth of Civil Rights, the Johnson administration lifted barriers on immigration that had kept the U.S. isolated from non-Northern European influxes since the 1924 Immigration Restriction Act (or before if you were Chinese). It took a good while to register, but WASP-Americans began moving from majority to plurality. Cultural studies became post-colonial studies. Globalism slew post-modernism. No term replaced alternative, but Coachella or The Killers felt staid next to crunk, poly-pop *Now!* compilations, or L.A. rappers with accordians. Arjun Appadurai writes in *Modernity at Large*: "neither popular nor academic thought in this country has come to terms with the difference between being a land of immigrants and being one node in a postnational network of diasporas." *TRL* Nation. Hip-hop Nation. Queer Nation. Republican Nation. Voguing—instead of rocking.

Madonna did come to terms with Appadurai's diasporas. Or seemed to, in as much as she won't or can't talk about her work in any way that adds new layers to our appreciation of it (her inarticulate appearance on Nightline to discuss the censoring of "Justify My Love" being but one example).

Here's the funny part, though. Madonna justified our love by seeming to represent a more ecumenical future: The "Into the Groove" dream that even Sonic Youth were a little envious of. You saw it in those shopping mall wannabes of all racial varieties; in the songs that proved themselves by how intercontinentally they could stretch without cracking; in her synthesizing Danceteria, NYC, 1982 (from Latin hip-hop and Jean-Michel Basquiat to Blondie) into a cyber anti-punk as blandly all powerful as ABBA.

That was then. Now, Madonna is married to a cool boy British film director and lives in the U.K. She makes albums when she feels like it that are as deep as any singer-songwriter's. She grooves to French techno. She's more old school Anglo-America alternative by the minute. Which suggests two conclusions. First, that unlike virtually every diva, boy band, or Roc-A-Fella who succeeded her, she made her proto-21st-century pop landmarks with a foot still planted in the tradition she was burying. She may have killed new wave, but she still was part of new wave: its sense of cultural critique, futurism, and sugary aesthetics.

And second, that like much of the Western world she found true globalization, as it emerged out of the end of the cold war, to be much less groovy than she might have imagined. Less willing to exchange fundamentalism for pop utopia—abroad, and here too. And so she retreated, praying in her own fashion.

I've barely mentioned a song. They were all burned in her fire, trademarked by history, taken from the midnight hour. Try and hear something new in any of the big hits from *The Immaculate Collection*. It's tough. So leave it as a question: Can she be experienced again with a sense of wonder and revelation? Will Madonna ever re-enter our personal sublime? We've lived so long, after all, in the ever-stretching boundaries of hers.

"I HAVE THE MOST PERFECT BELLY BUTTON: AN INNY, AND THERE'S NO LINT IN IT. I NEVER WORE A JEWEL IN MY BELLY, BUT IF I DID IT WOULD BE A RUBY OR AN EMERALD. WHEN I STICK MY FINGER IN MY BELLY BUTTON, I FEEL A NERVE IN THE CENTER OF MY BODY SHOOT UP MY SPINE. IF 100 BELLY BUTTONS WERE LINED UP AGAINST A WALL, I COULD DEFINITELY PICK OUT WHICH IS MINE."

— Madonna, 1985

In the beginning was the sound: electrobeats booming from passing cars, the chatter of party people on the sidewalk, city radio stations bleeding in and out of each other. Madonna tried to cram all this sound onto one record. Madonna was a stranger in New York, an Italian-American from Iggy Stooge's Detroit. But having worked as a drummer in a punk band as well as having been a dance student and Paradise Garage clubgoer, she'd sampled enough of the city's sounds to know how she wanted her own version to sound. She took the vaguely disco-y edge of post-punk DOR and amped it up into a new kind of robotic sleaze, listening to the tastes of the gay, black, and Latin club audiences. Listening to how, say, "Material Girl" fused Lene Lovich's 1981 Teutonic DOR smash "New Toy" with Vivien Vee's 1982 hi-NRG club hit "Heartbeat" is a lesson in how adventurous Madonna's sound really was.

As the sound turned Madonna into a star, she became a true rebel-rock icon. She was about sex, insisting on physical appetites for fast beats as rock'n'roll's bottom line. She was about gender, foregrounding femininity as construction and even masquerade. She was about Catholicism, delivering the rock-'n'roll answer to *Mean Streets* that Bruce Springsteen and Billy Joel had only promised. But she had her own sound, and all those iconographic twists and turns of personality feel mighty real as long as you can hear her physical attraction to that sound. And a physical attraction, as she sang, is "nothing to be ashamed of."

After two self-penned club smashes, "Everybody" and "Burning Up," Madonna recorded her debut album as a quickie, with

the dance-floor savvy of mixer Jellybean Benitez spicing up producer Reggie Lucas's more straightforward R&B sound. Although the hits were the attention grabbers, Madonna fleshed out their abrasively uptempo sound with "Borderline," where she chased a glock-enspiel up and down the scale, and "Physical Attraction," her definitive electrothrob statement. *Like A Virgin* is even better, with

Nile Rodgers putting more bounce into the beats. Her best hits are here—"Like a Virgin," "Material Girl," "Dress You Up"—alongside the peerless "Angel," which flutters with a helium-fueled urgency. On a roll, Madonna contributed two of her greatest songs to the *Vision Quest* soundtrack, the swoony "Crazy for

You" and the fierce aggro-disco "Gambler," where she sneers,"you're just jealous 'cause you can't be me."

True Blue is Madonna's least eventful '80's album. "White Heat" and "Open Your Heart" are strong but not comparable to past glo-

ries, and the weak songs get even slushier than the dreary TV movie "Papa Don't Preach." The only stunner is "Live To Tell," which simmers

with enough vocal and melodic intensity to support every "secret" that fans have projected onto it. *You Can Dance* shows off how far Madonna's sound had come over the previous four years, remixing her old songs with splashes of Miami disco and Latin hip-hop into a noisy transcultural groove. Shep Pettibone's seven-minute rewiring of "Where's The Party," using screeching tires as a percussion device, is the most powerful Madonna music on record.

Like A Prayer expands Madonna's signature sound by building on the melodic invention of "Live To Tell" rather than on the

rhythmic invention of "Into The Groove." Her gritty vocals make ballads such as "Oh Father" and "Promise To Try" exhilarating musically

as well as verbally. The dance tracks filter a grab bag of styles through the keyboards until they sound like, well, Madonna. *Like A Prayer* is Madonna's most conventionally songful album, but because she's still a loud-mouth weirdo expressing herself with enough Catholic angst to fill a basilica, it's also her most intensely emotional. "Like A Prayer" is a confession on speaker-phone, channeling her obsessions into a soliloquy that explodes into a parking-lot block party. The gospel choir obviously got off at the wrong bus stop, but they hang around long enough to outchant the Benedictine Monks. The album ends with a true punk rock moment, adding some guitar feedback to centuries-old Catholic chart-topper "Act of Contrition." Twelve Our Fathers and twelve Hail Marys for you, Maddie.

With comic show tunes and Bette Midler homages "inspired" by the movie Dick Tracy, *I'm Breathless* is not quite as campy as

it thinks it is, and the piano-ballad format forces Madonna to abandon her own sophisticated sense of rhythm, rhythm she never had

trouble exploiting for comic effect in "Dress You Up" or "White Heat."

Immaculate Collection is an eccentric selection of her radio hits, skipping an actual Number One ("Who's That Girl") along with such other Top Fivers as "True Blue" and

"Angel." These compact hits get sped up and faded out early—"Into the Groove" doesn't even have a chance to build to the climactic

"Now I know you're mine/ Now I know you're mine" verse before the plug gets pulled. Conceptually, it's brilliant, not too far from the Ramones, and yet Madonna fans are likely to get bored hearing such incandescent songs briefly evoked rather than acted out in all their blood and glory. The radio does a livelier job of winnowing Madonna's music down to its money shots than *Immaculate*, and *You*

Can Dance does a livelier job of flaunting the rhythmic breaks and techno-utopian bravado that make the money shots worth hearing.

Her 1991 documentary film *Truth or Dare* was a must-see at the time, but as the steam has gone out of Madonna's musical boiler-room, *Truth or Dare* has become a disheartening souvenir of a moment when so little was happening in pop music that Madonna was asked to shoulder cultural burdens far beyond any star's—or audience's—capability. She felt compelled to try anyway, and the result was *Erotica*, which ignored the swaggering dance hooks of her past in favor of tepid eclecti-

cism, classy ballads, and abstract studio experimentation. It was as if Elvis had answered his '50's critics by cutting a cool-jazz record with

Dave Brubeck to prove he wasn't just a dumb hick. *Bedtime Stories* sounded even less like a Madonna album, filled with not-terrible renditions of perfectly good soft-soul ballads in an exemplary case study of the Daryl Hall Fallacy.

Both these albums debuted high on the charts before dropping abruptly once word got around that they sucked, giving the lie to the media impression that Madonna had lost her audience. What Madonna has lost is her sound, and while she still has a huge audience, what this audience wants is music that sounds like Madonna, not product that alludes to the Madonna phenomenon. She'll be back as soon as she remembers how to write catchy songs.

— "Madonna" / Rob Sheffield / from *The Spin Alternative Record Guide* (1995)

Madonna:

"At one point, I was living in New York and eating out of garbage cans. Actually, it was not a garbage can on the street; it was a garbage can in the Music Building on Eighth Avenue where I lived with Steve Bray, the guy I write songs with. [Ed. note: He's Useful Male #2 or #3, depending upon which article you read.]

I had been squatting in a loft, living there illegally, but it was burned down. There was no heat or hot water, so I had all these electric space heaters around this little piece of carpeting I slept on. I woke up in the middle of the night surrounded by a ring of fire. One of the heaters had set fire to the rug and it was spreading. I jumped up and dumped water on the fire, which made it spread more. Then my nightgown caught on fire. So I took it off, got dressed, grabbed a few things, like underpants and stuff—all my important things like tapes and instruments were already over at the Music Building three blocks away—and I went over to the Music Building and started sleeping there."
— 1985

SPIN: Who are your heroes?
Madonna: Most of them are women, and a lot of them were painters; Georgia O'Keefe, Frieda Kahlo, Tamara DeLempicka. All those women were married to successful, ambitious men, yet they managed to retain a strong sense of themselves, and do their own work, while maintaining relationships with brilliant men. They suffered a lot in order to do it too, because it's not easy for people like O'Keefe and Stieglitz—people with so much ego—to be together. To be that kind of person and be with that kind of person is the ultimate challenge.
— 1988

SPIN: What's your favorite Madonna song?
Madonna: That I've written? "Live to Tell."
Why?
Because it sums up all of my yearning and a lot of my pain, really.
What's your least favorite?
"Material Girl." *Blecch.* It makes me want to throw up. Barf.
— 1996

Madonna:
I look at pictures of myself 15 years ago or watch myself on television and think, "Who is that?" It's like looking at your high school graduation picture and you sit there and go, "What a geek! Why did I have my hair like that?"
— 1998

SPIN: What's your spiritual life like?
Madonna: I feel that talking about it trivializes it. [Deep breath] I've been studying the Cabala, which is the mystical interpretation of the Torah. I've studied Buddhism and Hinduism and I've been practicing yoga and obviously I know a lot about Catholicism. There are indisputable truths that connect all of them, and I find that very comforting and kind. My spiritual journey is to be open about everything. Pay attention to what makes sense, be absorbed. For me, yoga is the closest thing to our real nature.

I used to call the balancing positions 'the humiliation positions.' I just kept falling and falling. Then little by little I got there, but as soon as you figure something out, there's something a lot harder you've got to go to next. It's actually a good metaphor for life.
— 1998

During the extended New York swing of her 1985 Virgin tour, the newly ubiquitous Madonna reportedly indulged her taste for Hispanic studs by cruising Manhattan's sketchy Alphabet City in a limo, looking for boys to toy with. Few refused her salacious solicitations to come for a "ride." As told by cruising buddy Erica Bell in Christopher Andersen's *Madonna Unauthorized*, the beautiful stranger usually just kissed her catches: "But if she really liked the kid, she'd just rip off his clothes and do whatever she liked with him. We'd end up driving around with two or three guys at a time, [then] we'd drop them off right where we found them." And dozens of lives were changed forever.
— "The 100 Sleaziest Moments in Rock" / Jessica Letkemann / October '00

Madonna's book, *Sex*, is a rip-off. Because it's not about sex, it's about hatred of it or, more exactly, I think, a hatred and a disdain for average people, communicated in a ritualistic dismantling of sex, a draining of its lifeblood, which is emotion.

The book is not erotic, although the poses are. Or should be. Heaven knows, strangers performing oral sex on Madonna in an S&M club should at least titillate. But it doesn't. The threesomes, the lesbians, sex on the dinner table, the toe sucking—even the toe sucking!—is all somehow, astonishingly, dead. As sexy as a body chart at the doctor's office. Because it's just as precise and soulless.
— "TopSpin" / Bob Guccione, Jr. / January '93

Madonna:
"You can't be a pop star and have an opinion. Some unknown entity can put out a magazine with erotic photographs, but a famous person young girls identify with can't do that and make money off of it. I think men can deal with those fantasies when a man is in control of them and in charge.... It's a man's point of view, a man's fantasy. *Sex* was my fantasy, and I made money off of it. That is a no-no."
— 1995

By titling her new album *American Life,* Madonna promises to examine the country's mood, as anyone running a good campaign should. Glaring defiantly from the album cover like Patti Smith in a Patti Hearst beret, she seems poised to stir up controversy as never before—i.e., without taking off her clothes. The record inside, though, is less radical, a suite of faux-folkie electro that fuses the introspection of *Ray of Light* with *Music*'s fast-food dance licks—autocratic words on top of democratic beats. If it feels unsettled and transitional, perhaps it reflects the state of the union all too well.
— review of *American Life* / James Hannaham / June '03

Most Desperate Grab for Relevance (or Weirdest Children's Book Promo) of the Year: The Madonna-and-Britney Kiss

It was only a matter of time before today's saucy pop princesses shared the spotlight with the queen mother. So there was an air of inevitability when Madonna strode onto the MTV Video Music Awards stage, eyed Britney and Christina decked out in virginal white, and slipped Britty some tongue. (Once again, Christina Aguilera was relegated to never-a-bride status: Her kiss was decidedly less French.) With Madonna's latest stab at social commentary landing as flat as her abs, and Britney desperately celebrating that, yes, she is finally a woman, this foray into frat-boy titillation left a bittersweet taste (at least in our mouths). The two seemed to cement a sort of career-survival pact during their special moment—Madge appears on Britney's single "Me Against the Music." But considering the S&M tinge in the song's video, only time will tell who's truly dominant in this relationship.
— "The Rest of the Best" / Caryn Ganz / January '04

/ Alan **Light**

Funky sex god

PRINCE

Prince strode over to the side of the stage,

and without interrupting the ferocious guitar solo he was unleashing, leaned over to me and whispered, "You see how hard it is when you can play anything you hear?"

He's certainly not a man known for concision, but this remark during a soundcheck at San Francisco's Civic Auditorium does a pretty fine job of encapsulating the peaks and valleys of one of pop music's most remarkable careers. Songwriter, producer, one-man band, balladeer, ass-shaker, svengali, guitar hero, sex god, preacher—in terms of raw talent, Prince may have no competition; Stevie Wonder is probably the only living figure worthy of comparison. And much like Wonder, Prince had about a decade-long run of one jaw-dropping, genre-bending smash after another before seeming to get bored with just writing hits and moving on to other, less crowd-pleasing concerns.

He was just 20 years old (though claimed to be 18) in 1978 when his first album, *For You*, came out as the first release under a contract with Warner Bros. that gave him complete creative control, unprecedented for a new artist. But it wasn't until his third album, 1980's new-wave-inflected *Dirty Mind*, that he hit his stride sonically (the flawless "When You Were Mine"), satyrically ("Head"), and sartorially (garter belts and trench coats). After that, the floodgates opened—the double-disc pop breakthrough *1999* (in 1982), the global takeover of the 15-times platinum *Purple Rain* (1984), and his unqualified masterpiece *Sign 'O' the Times* (1987). And that's not to mention the hits from "I Wanna Be Your Lover" to "Do Me Baby" to the breathtaking "Kiss," or the versions of his songs by Sinead O'Connor, Chaka Khan, and the Bangles,

all while he maintained an aura of mystery and silence. Throughout the '80s, Prince was omnipresent, and the signature synth-and-drum slam that came to be known as "The Minneapolis Sound" made him unquestionably the most influential artist of the decade.

In song after song, he didn't so much break the rules as ignore them and come up with new paradigms. The droning angularity of "When Doves Cry"—which didn't even have a bass line—sounded impossible coming out of the radio in 1984, and yet became the year's biggest single. Metal, psychedelia, funk, and folk all melded together in records full of fearless arrangements and unshakable melodies. (Plus he could even recreate them onstage, backwards, in platform heels!) But then, perhaps inevitably, his focus began to wane.

After the success of the film *Purple Rain* (in which the riveting performance footage narrowly defeated a cartoonish script), Prince turned his sights to movie stardom. But the thunderous flops *Under the Cherry Moon* (1986) and *Graffiti Bridge* (1990) put the brakes on that notion. The dawn of the '90s saw Prince struggling with the impact of hip-hop, and with the burdens of maintaining both his commercial presence and his musical experimentation. Neither he nor his fans could quite decide if he was really a superstar celebrity, or simply the world's biggest cult artist.

After several middling albums, Prince began his fateful stand-off with his label, Warner Bros. Arguing that the suits were inhibiting his output and his creativity, and that "if you don't own your masters, your master owns you," he changed his name to an unpronounceable symbol in 1994 and appeared on television with the word "SLAVE"

scrawled on his face. His preferred appellation was The Artist Formerly Known as Prince, which, as the fight dragged on to widespread indifference, Howard Stern memorably rendered as The Artist People Formerly Cared About.

But there were consistent signs that the fire hadn't gone out. As ♀, he released the gloopy 1994 ballad "The Most Beautiful Girl in the World" on the independent Bellmark label and it went to No. 1. The triple-disc *Emancipation* (1996), while obviously way too long, included some of his best music of the decade. And always, any time he got on a stage, he was simply capable of performances that no one else alive could pull off. You got the feeling that he was always one song away—that he just needed to decide he wanted to get back in the game.

That's what happened in 2004, exactly 20 years after *Purple Rain* made him a household word. Freed from the last of his contracts, he reclaimed his name, opened the Grammy Awards ceremony, was inducted into the Rock and Roll Hall of Fame, and released *Musicology*—if not his finest album, definitely a solid and satisfying display of songwriting flair and irresistible grooves. The tour that followed was the biggest box-office of the year, and suddenly he was back on magazine covers and video channels, insisting that it couldn't be a comeback if he never went away (and from Gwen Stefani to Basement Jaxx, there's no question that his influence never really waned). In the meantime, the collapse of the major-label system and the rise of digital distribution made it seem as if Prince wasn't such a kook after all, but something of a visionary—and still the baddest motherfucker in the atmosphere.

9 examples of practical sex advice from Prince songs:

1. **If you have sex with someone once, but you utilize no more than 23 different positions during the encounter, you should call this person the next day—not because it's nice, but because you need to remind him or her that this did, in fact, happen.** ("Gett Off") 2. **Women masturbating in hotel lobbies will likely be open to myriad sexual suggestions.** ("Darling Nikki") 3. **The fact that a woman has a pocket full of used condoms is no reason not to have sex with her.** ("Little Red Corvette") 4. **If your sister is exactly twice your age, feel free to make love to her.** ("Sister") 5. **You can tell a lot about a woman by the degree to which her breasts bounce.** ("Peach") 6. **When attempting to remove clothing from a woman of larger proportions, it is somehow sexy to request that she "move [that] big ass 'round this way so I can work on that zipper, baby."** (Gett Off") 7. **Women who are about to get married will still perform oral sex, as this is not really infidelity.** ("Head") 8. **Threesomes are emotionally difficult, but we must overcome this if we are truly in love.** ("When You Were Mine") 9. **Dude, it's the body, not the mind.** ("Sexy M.F.")

— The Ultimate List Issue / April '03

꧁ꑄ꧁ꑄ꧁ꑄ꧁ꑄ꧁ꑄ꧁ꑄ꧁ꑄ꧁ꑄ꧁ꑄ꧁

MY MOTHER PHONES LONG-DISTANCE AND ASKS ME TO EXPLAIN PRINCE'S NEW ALBUM TO HER BECAUSE IT SURE AIN'T LIKE *PURPLE RAIN.* From out Berkeley way, my cantankerous walkboy Craig keys me up to say he likes the mug because it ain't like *Purple Rain* and besides which it represents the first time since Hendrix a black rock artist has gotten away with indulging his muse at the expense of commercial potential, the way white artists do all the time. Melvin tells me the LP reminds him of Sly's "There's A Riot Goin' On" inasmuch as it sees Prince doing what Sly did then, which was dare to move to the left of musical trends he'd set in motion. Barry in Baltimore relates to me that down his way the brothers and sisters are going for the psychedelic hornswaggle in a big way, while Sharon, a Newark homegirl, says everybody she's talked to says the record ain't shit. Nothing like stirring up a little controversy, is there, Mr. Nelson?

— review of *Around the World in a Day* / Greg Tate / July '85

IN THE YEARS FOLLOWING *PURPLE RAIN*, A NUMBER OF BLACK BANDS MOVED TO MINNEAPOLIS TO LAUNCH CAREERS. Why not? The movie made it look like a Black Rock Coalition rendering of Mecca. Almost without exception, these bands moved out.

The thriving, racially-mixed scene Prince portrayed in *Purple Rain* was something he made up. It had nothing to do with Minneapolis, which has a relatively small black population, but it had everything to do with the emotional reality of growing up black, talented, and ambitious in Minneapolis.

Starting as a stranger in his hometown, Prince invented a polyglot, multiracial community in his mind; "Uptown" (from *Dirty Mind*) was its anthem. He then reinvented himself as the high priest of Uptown, freak flag flown high. It involved calculated fictions, as his detractors always claimed.

The self-mythologizing reached its apotheosis with *Purple Rain* the movie, which Prince called his "emotional autobiography." It was a staggering feat, both as music and as rock careerism. The radio never sounded better in the '80s than in the summer bracketed by "When Doves Cry" and "Let's Go Crazy." But *Purple Rain* also proved how perilously alone Prince was. On his subsequent tour, Prince seemed petrified onstage and off.

At any rate, *Purple Rain* certainly had the effect of isolating him even further. In the next two years he made some fine music, but he also acted out a basic confusion about *which* took precedence, the music or the cult of personality. The self-obsession reached an embarrassing crescendo in 1986 with "Under the Cherry Moon," a bad movie made worse by being so heartfelt on some level.

If the self-mythologizing became even more circumspect after that, the pace at which Prince reinvented himself musically redoubled. Each record was radically different from the last.

Of them all, *Parade* was the only post-*Purple Rain* album to elaborate on musical ideas from its predecessor. Otherwise, the cardinal rule was change. It made Prince the most intriguing figure in rock, not to mention the most maddening. Prince's approach favored revolution over evolution, and solitary composition over collaboration. All through the latter half of the '80s, he hit big or he missed big.

Prince's most exciting strides in the second half of the '80s came as a live performer and band leader, not in the studio. The *Sign O' the Times* and *Lovesexy* tours were amazing spectacles, both musically and visually. Lacking contemporaries who could challenge him creatively, he put together a band that kept him honest, and he shared some of his finest moments with them.

Sex may be Prince's best known obsession, but it's always gone hand in hand with a longing for larger connections. Images like Uptown, Paisley Park, and the New Power Generation are all attempts to imagine communities where he's at once a member, prophet, and benevolent dictator. What he crafted onstage with the *Lovesexy* band is as close as he'd ever come to realizing it, and confronting its contradictions. That tour gave a breadth and depth to his music that it never suggested so clearly before.

For someone who used to seem determined to usher in the Apocalypse or wear out his dancing shoes trying, that's a mark of growth. So what now? Well, if part of his problem in the '80s was a lack of creative stimulation from his peers, that should change in the '90s as pop struggles to integrate the profound innovations of hip-hop.

All that may not matter if he holes up in Paisley Park, but if he's willing to walk through the door he opened on the *Lovesexy* tour, his best work is still ahead of him.

— "The 10 Most Interesting Musicians of the Last 5 Years: Prince" / Steve Perry / April '90

꧁ꑄ꧁ꑄ꧁ꑄ꧁ꑄ꧁ꑄ꧁ꑄ꧁ꑄ꧁ꑄ꧁ꑄ꧁

OPEN "10-2-7" TUESDAY THROUGH SATURDAY AND "12-2-5" SUNDAYS, THE NEW POWER GENERATION BOUTIQUE IN UPTOWN MINNEAPOLIS IS CRAMMED TO THE GILLS WITH RICK JAMES MERCHANDISE. Just kidding. Like Spike Lee before him, Prince, er, Mr. Name Change, has opened a promotional outlet to keep his street cred de la street as he masterminds his next career coup. In the New Power Generation, if Prince didn't play it or produce it, he at least approved it.

Cedric Ellis, the maitre d' bodyguard, greets you as you step through the silk-curtained entrance. "How y'all doin'?" Dark, sparkling, almost Tibetan, it feels like Prince's bedroom in *Purple Rain*. CDs, posters, and jewelry make up most of the inventory, though there are vanity items—Prince-brand pheromones, for instance ($7.95 per bottle), or Prince-brand pheromone atomizers ($150, but extremely ornate). Theoretically, you can put a bid on anything: the motorcycle, "the last ring worn before the name change," the (unpronounceable symbol) signs that foliate the shop like duckweed.

But then why have they roped off that staircase? Is he up there doing payroll? Oiling his wahwah? Maitre d'Ellis kindly shows you to the second floor. It's home to a People's Choice Award (Favorite Male Performer 1985) and a TV room with floor pillows. There, "for a small fee," you can watch all the dirty videos they never showed on MTV.

Another kid has snuck under the rope. Fingering a platinum album, he asks Ellis, "Does he come here at all?"

"Perhaps, I can't say yes or no."

"So it's kinda like a museum?"

"No," Ellis laughs, "everything's for sale."

"Everything?" asks the kid.

Ellis stops laughing. "*Every*thing."

— "News Flashes" / Mike Mattison / February '94

꧁ꑄ꧁ꑄ꧁ꑄ꧁ꑄ꧁ꑄ꧁ꑄ꧁ꑄ꧁ꑄ꧁ꑄ꧁

FROM 1982–1995, WHILE RECORDING MUCH GENUINELY AMAZING MUSIC, PRINCE ALSO WROTE AND PRODUCED ALBUM AFTER ASTOUNDINGLY INTERCHANGEABLE ALBUM OF MACHINE-TOOLED BUBBLE-FUNK FOR WOMEN EVERYONE ASSUMED HE MUST BE NAILING. At least Sheila E. was a great percussionist; there was never any evidence Vanity 6 (originally dubbed Vagina Sex) , Apollonia 6, or Carmen Elektra could do anything but look amazing in fetishwear. And does anyone even remember Ingrid Chavez or Jill Jones? Prince's shagadelic vibe wasn't confined to his pet projects. He offered hit musical come-ons to the Bangles ("Manic Monday") and Sinead O'Connor ("Nothing Compares 2U"). Any exculpatory evidence that he wasn't using his musical skills as a dating service was erased when he married Mayte, his last notable Svengali project (see the dreaded *Child of the Sun*). Meanwhile, Vanity did what any sane woman would do after her purple per diem: She dated Nikki Sixx, did some acting, then became a born-again Christian. And Carmen Elektra became, uh, Carmen Elektra.

— "Dirty Mind"/ Joe Gross / October '00

/ Ann **Powers**

: **U2** Revelation & **Lust**

U2'S FABLES, PART I:

*A small boy lived
in a small house in Dublin,*
*with a flower garden in the back. He played among the flowers every day and sometimes
he would sing. One day, he noticed a tiny bee sitting on a leaf. He reached toward it. His
mother, standing in the doorway, started to shout, "Don't do that, Paul, you'll get stung!"
But something made her bite her tongue. The little boy did not know to fear the bee, and so
the bee did not know to behave ferociously. The boy sang a song to the bee, stroked its
wings, and set it down. From then on, the boy, who grew up to be a very famous singer,
refused to fear what others thought would sting him, like artistic ambition, sweeping statements, and leaps of faith. And he never got stung.*

MORAL: *Move forward with confidence and the path will be clear.*

The Greatest. What does that title get you? If you're a boxer, brain damage; if
you're a sexpot, an overdose of sleeping pills; if you're a rock band, a nasty
breakup and a legacy that will haunt you the rest of your lives. Unless you're U2,
that is. After a quarter-century of testing rock's vertical limit and evolving past
each plateau unrelentingly—as golden youths and then world conquerors in the
1980s, models of maturity in the '90s, and reanimated 21st-century superstars—
Ireland's champions have seemingly defied every curse of fame and fortune.

U2'S FABLES, PART II:

*On a rainy Dublin day, a young drummer tacked a piece of paper on a bulletin board at
his high-school:* LOOKING FOR BANDMATES. *Soon enough, he found himself with
three new friends: an introverted guitarist, a bassist with a droll smile, and a singer who
made everyone else alternately nervous and eager to play. They all began talking at once,
but then somehow caught each others' eyes long enough to stop and just start playing. The
next thing they knew, they were part of a scene. The other groups were much more fashionable, dressing in interesting costumes and naming themselves after fruit. But the three fel-
lows in the drummer's band, which sometimes seemed like the singer's band or the guitarist's
or even the bemused bass player's band, just kept their eyes locked on each other and played.
Eventually, all the cooler bands started arguing about their outfits and publicity campaigns. The drummer's band was the only one left in the end, and ruled the world.*

MORAL: *Know your friends as you know yourself.*

Envy U2, everyone. None have beaten the odds so beautifully. The original quartet
of high-school New Wavers has stayed intact and aged with grace. The group's
identity, which drifted into bloat in the late '80s and got a bit wheezy again a
decade later, has coalesced around the dignified pursuit of rigorous musical form
and meaningful emotional function. Members' extracurricular pursuits, most
famously the global activism of singer/holy fool Bono, don't impede the accomplishments of the whole. And those musical accomplishments still hit with the

45

ESSAY CONTINUES ON NEXT PAGE >

impact of the band's first feverish outbursts. The band's last two releases, 2000's *All That You Can't Leave Behind* and 2004's *How to Dismantle an Atomic Bomb*, show less concern for demographic trends than ever—no crunk, neo-punk, alt-country shuffle, or duets with Gwen Stefani here, yet millions of fans still adore the music's mountainous majesty, and critics have praised its increasing subtlety and grace.

It's almost boring, all this success. It doesn't seem like a rock'n'roll story—aren't the masters of this fiery form supposed to explode and fade and fall, or else become good-natured, self-directed jokes, taking the piss out of their own youthful dreams? U2 has refused to do either, and thus become a sort of anomaly, the role models no one seems to be able to emulate.

U2'S FABLES, PART III:

The drummer's band made an album, and gained friends throughout the land. The time came for the foursome to go into the recording studio again, and everyone did his part to prepare: The guitarist sharpened his fingernails, the bassist popped some popcorn, the drummer tuned his snare. But the singer, who was always busy chasing new thoughts, ran so fast one evening that he dropped all of the ones he'd already come up with into a deep, dark hole. "I've lost my notebook!" he told his mates. The new recording seemed doomed. But the singer screwed up his courage and opened his heart before the studio microphone, and something moved through him, and songs formed. The band held him up like a crowd-surfer as he spoke in tongues.

MORAL: *Never fear the sound of a forming thought.*

U2's singularity is rooted in the relationship between the band's music and the life of the band as an artistic unit. Three of U2's members embraced evangelical Christianity as youths, only to abandon their organized beliefs for the secular spirituality of rock'n'roll; that moment of switched alliances added a huge sense of mission to their musical pursuits. It's a misinterpretation of Gen-X attitude to think that most rock artists of the '80s and '90s didn't care about having an impact on the larger culture, but many in the rock world believed that self-fulfilling inaccuracy, and so artistic striving, spiritual or otherwise, often was concealed by obscurantism or irony. Not so for U2. They crave revelation, for themselves and everyone.

From the group's very first single, "Out of Control," released in 1979, all the way through the band's 2004 downloadable hit "Vertigo," Bono's lyrics and the band's bursting-at-the-seams music have embodied the desire to hyper-articulate: to say more than was acceptable or even possible within the available circumstances. Each player in U2 has developed his approach upon this principle. The Edge's trademarked atmospheric playing pioneered the use of effects and sustain in pushing the lexicon of rock guitar closer to the boundaries of synthesizer, sampling, and even percussion. Larry Mullen Jr. and Adam Clayton brought a melodicism into their rhythm work that connected to jazz and world music, without losing rock's hard edge. And Bono—well, he's a preacher, and like another great pop testifier, Al Green, he tends to run at the mouth. But he's also a self-made intellectual, and each new lyric he writes is a kind of analysis of his previous chatter—a Talmudic commentary on his artist's journey into the language of the soul.

U2'S FABLES, PART IV:

The guitarist's band decided that music sounded better at high altitudes, and so they scaled the world's tallest peaks, one after the other. The documents they made of these journeys inspired many would-be travelers, but the bandmates themselves started to notice that their ropes had frayed. They took them in to a man with a mysterious name—Eno—for repair, and he patched them with dirt and Latex. For a while after that, the bandmates misplaced the ropes altogether, they were having so much fun on the ground. One day, though, the nervous singer realized he had become strangely nearsighted—the close air of the lowlands seemed to have glued his sunglasses to his face. He went through his closets to find some grease to remove them, and there were the ropes. He pulled them out, and a few months later, after much discussion, his mates agreed to accompany him on a climb. This time, though, they went more slowly. And the ropes, with their Latex and dirt, stayed intact.

MORAL: *A lesson lived is a lesson remembered.*

The writer C.S. Lewis, like Bono and his mates, was an artist who sought to bring divinity to the dining room table. He once wrote, "Aim at heaven and you will get earth thrown in; aim at earth and you get neither." His pronouncement's somewhat gloomy conclusion is contradicted by all the rockers who've made contact with God (or whatever they choose to call her) through expressions of sex or mere bodily joy. But the first half definitely applies to U2. The ardent idealism of the band's first decade created a field of inquiry large enough to suit most artists, but this band's desire to wrap its arms around the world required eventual deep contact with matters of the flesh. On 1991's *Achtung Baby*, U2 finally got earth—not just sex, but all the vices of the modern world: self-centered freneticism, dissolute materialism, confusion between reality and the media dream. The following decade has been a gradual return to a more innocent place. Not innocent as in naive, or even pure. Innocent as in forgiven. Only from that perspective, in which human limitation is accepted as the basis for all striving, can a person, or a rock band, become whatever The Greatest means to them.

U2'S FABLES, PART V:

Four old friends set out to see the world, each on his own terms. One, the guitarist, crawls deep inside his instrument to try to find the perfect chord. The bassist gets stuck on the dangerous side of town, but pulls himself back and becomes a master of self-discipline. The drummer, a practical sort, soon decides to stay mostly at home, quiet except for his motorcycle rides. And the one known as "Good Voice" actually tries to touch the hearts of everyone he meets, his pockets filling up with all the dreams he pulls out of those beating chests. Eventually, though, the four friends grow suspicious that they'll never find what they're looking for, no matter how far they roam. One by one, each realizes the obvious: The world is round! Their paths lead back to each other. There they are today, standing together in the room where they started, and the whole world is now in there with them, too.

MORAL: *Life's possibilities are infinite, but satisfaction is possible (even for a rock'n'roll band).*

FIN.

"SOME PEOPLE EXPECT U2 TO COME ON LIKE A POLITICAL BAND, using the stage as a soapbox—that we're going to ram Northern Ireland down their throats. Other people see us as prophets. Some see us as pop stars and think we're going to come on in tight leather pants and makeup. And we're not any of those things. We're probably all of them. I don't know what we are."
— Bono, 1985

"I ALWAYS RESENTED BEING ON A STAGE. I always resented that barrier between us and the audience, and this led to that infamous gig in Los Angeles where I ended up falling off the balcony and a riot ensued and people could have got hurt. The band took me aside backstage and said, 'Look, you're a singer in a band. People in the audience understand the situation…you don't have to remind them all the time of the fact that U2 aren't stars to be worshipped. They already *know* that.'"
– Bono, 1987

SPIN: I was talking to The Edge about music and spirituality, and I would like to know if you see any relation between the old concept of religion and modern music?

BONO: I do. I think all singers, when they're dragging things out of themselves that they didn't know were there, become very aware of their spirit—the third part of their being. For me it's been a release, while my belief in God is so personal that I just shut my mouth all the time lest I trash it into the ground because I feel so awkward trying to express it. That's what the song "Gloria" is about—the failure to express that belief. It says, "I try to stand up, but I can't find my feet, I try to speak up, but only in you am I complete." It resorts to Latin even, because I cannot explain.

I think that failure to express our emotions drive the effort to make great music. That's why John Lennon made great music all the time. He was trying to cut through hypocrisy and find out who he was. For me it's also important if people will give of themselves to the music, because I think the truth is like a sword—it really cuts through. You can tell if that singer onstage is adopting a stance or if it is he himself that is on the line.

— 1985

AT BEST, U2 IS A BAND THAT LIVES UP TO ITS PRETENSIONS. Committed, naive, and original, they've matured by learning in the studio to modify and moderate their heavy-handed techniques with variety and subtlety. *The Joshua Tree* is their first wholly successful album because it finally breaks free from the seductive but limiting chant-and-drone approach of earlier material. There's nothing as powerful as "Sunday Bloody Sunday" or "Pride (In the Name of Love)" on this LP. But there's nothing as facile as "Surrender" or plainly awful as "Elvis Presley and America," either. There isn't a bad song on the record, and songs are what *The Joshua Tree* is made of.

— review of *The Joshua Tree* / John Piccarella / June '87

"I don't think I'm a good singer, but I think I'm getting to be a good singer.

On *Unforgettable Fire* I think something broke in my voice, and it's continuing to break on *The Joshua Tree*, but there's much, much more in there. See, I'm loosening up as a person about my position in a rock'n'roll band, but for years I really wasn't sure who I was, or who U2 were, or really if there was a place for us. People say U2 are self-righteous, but if ever I pointed a finger, I pointed it at myself. I was defensive about U2, therefore I was on the attack. When I hear U2 records, I hear my voice, and I hear an uptightness. I don't hear my real voice." – Bono, 1987

"Wim Wenders says it best when he says, 'America has colonized our subconscious.'

It's for this reason that we did *The Joshua Tree*, for this reason we confined the album to the desert, for this reason I said: 'I live in Ireland but my imagination is on the loose in America.' Amerika, spelled with a K, is the universal America. It is not the geography of America but the idea of Amerika. We would be foolish to deprive ourselves of their good ideas." — Bono, 1993

BONO HAS GLADLY GIVEN UP WANDERING ACROSS THE PLAIN FOR LURKING IN THE CORNER OF THE HOTEL BAR. In the end, he didn't have to get wise, or even smart, because he got jaded. His new role model seems to be the angels in buddy Wim Wenders' *Wings Of Desire*, who, having finally managed to transcend, wish for nothing more than the messy, painful joy of earthliness.

Zooropa, an album of even riskier material recorded around the same time as *Achtung Baby*, bubbles and scrapes with Brian Eno and Flood's effects and Edge's now truly edgy guitar. And despite the inclusion of proto-plainsman Johnny Cash as guest vocalist on one track, *Zooropa* firmly places U2 within a European cosmopolitanism that Wenders also inhabits, in which both America and heaven are faraway future dreams overshadowed by the burdens of history, border-dissolving technology, and personal regret.

— "U2"/ Ann Powers / *SPIN Alternative Record Guide* (1995)

Here's the real *zoo:* laminate-bearing henchmen and women, walkie-talkies strapped to their sides, power-walking with tight, urgent faces down endless corridors; phones constantly gurgling; tattooed strongmen barking incomprehensible Irish orders; wheeled crates full of unidentifiable but doubtless phenomenally costly equipment hurtling down corridors; strange wispy men in capes. I have no idea what any of these people do. (Is this Kafka-esque or Fellini-esque? I can't remember.) Compared to this maelstrom, the show itself is almost anticlimactic.

Resulting perhaps partly from the behind-the-scenes anarchy, certain weird hierarchical inconsistencies crop up backstage on the Zoo TV tour. Little things, mainly, most of which aren't probably even under the purview of the band members themselves, but they look to me like clues. For instance: Even though the Pixies have been hand-picked as opening band for the first leg of the North American tour (the Edge and Bono are reportedly big fans), U2, which has gone to the trouble of printing up signs for just about every conceivable subset of its own organization, can't manage better than to slap "Support Act" signage on the Pixies' dressing room.

Last night in Montreal, Dave Grohl from Nirvana came to say hello to Support Act, of which he's a major fan, and Larry from U2 made his (and the band's) only appearance of the tour in the Support Act's dressing room. Apparently Dave was a big enough star to warrant his slumming. Later, Dave was also treated to a grandfatherly talk by Bono, who spent an hour lecturing him on the evils of success ("Don't let it go to your head") and didn't take his wrap-around fly-shades off the whole time.

— "Animal Farm" / Jim Greer / July '92

"People find it hard to accept artists working above their station," says the Edge.

"But the most interesting stuff comes from people doing things they shouldn't really be doing, acting outside of the boundaries of convention. I'm not in the least bit apologetic if people think we're pretentious."

More than his bandmates, Bono has taken that risk by playing ambassador to the stars, showing up at Cannes or behind the bar at the hottest new Soho nightspot. But he claims he'd never want to get stuck in the in crowd. "I hang out with every set," he says. "Anyone will tell you that. From the penthouse to not just the pavement but under the pavement. I'll go anywhere there's an idea hatching or a great party being thrown."

"There are seven women who work in that pub, and they're all named Angela," he informs me one afternoon when we've stopped for a pint. One of the seven Angelas has just walked by and enjoyed a brief conversation with him. It's a sunny day, so we've taken our Guinness across the street to the river's edge, and Bono waves and yells whenever a passing car gives him a honk. He never seems to tire of the attention. "I'm not very inhibited," he says, stating the obvious. "My strongest trait is curiosity. I'm just lifting stones, you know, opening doors. Looking out windows, around corners, up skirts."

This mischievous Bono is a recent incarnation. For years his fans thought Bono a saint, and critics accused him of playing that role falsely even when he was just trying to be himself. "I used to think that my image was something to live up to, " he says. "Now I feel it's almost a duty to let people down." The only way Bono could dodge his own shadow was by assuming its cartoonish opposite—becoming MacPhisto, or the Fly, modern devils as degraded as his previous public self was holy. "One thing I might regret from the early times was just showing that one side of me," he says. "The egomaniac was always there, too."

— "The Future Sound of U2" / Ann Powers / March '97

"We're gonna give these kids a ride,"

says Bono. I look over my right shoulder at the girl from Austria, and I witness someone's mind being blown out of her skull; I can almost see her brains and blood splattered across the rear window. The car takes off. Bono drives recklessly, accelerating and braking at random. "Do you want to hear the new album?" he asks the glassy-eyed teenagers. This is more than a month before *How to Dismantle an Atomic Bomb* will be released. They say, "Yes." Bono punches up track four, "Love and Peace or Else." He hits PLAY, and it's loud; it sounds like someone dropping the throttle on a Harrier Jump Jet. Bono starts singing along, harmonizing with himself. He's playing air drums while he drives. The music changes, and he exclaims, "This is the Gary Glitter part!" The music changes again. "This is the Brian Wilson moment." The teenagers aren't even talking. They're just kind of looking at each other, almost like they're afraid this is some Celtic version of *Punk'd*.

One of the kids asks to hear "Miracle Drug," which makes Bono nervous. An early version of the album was stolen in July, and he is worried that it may have been leaked to the Internet. But he plays the track anyway, still singing along and he turns the volume even higher when we get to the lyrics, "Freedom has a scent/ Like the top of a newborn baby's head." He calls these two lines the best on the album. This behavior is incredibly charming, a little embarrassing, and amazingly weird. We eventually get to the hotel, and Bono drives up on the sidewalk. He unloads the kids' bags, and they walk away like zombies. The two of us amble into the Clarence and shake hands in the lobby, and then Bono disappears into the restaurant to meet the elderly painter I've never heard of. And I find myself thinking, "Did this really just happen? Am I supposed to believe he does this kind of thing all the time, even when he doesn't have a reporter in the front seat of his car? And does that even matter? Was that car ride the greatest moment in those four kids' lives? Was this whole thing a specific performance, or is Bono's *entire life* a performance? And if your entire life is a performance, does that make everything you do inherently authentic? Is this guy for real, or is this guy full of shit?"

— "Mysterious Days" / Chuck Klosterman / December '04

> > >

: Run-D.M.C.
The Kings of Queens

/ Nelson **George**

One member has been murdered. Another has given his life to the Lord. The third soldiers on, trying to build a solo career. Two decades after three black men from Queens jump-started the biggest musical movement since rock'n'roll, everything's changed and yet, fundamentally, nothing's changed. In the mid-1980s, Run-D.M.C. emerged as hip-hop's most important pioneers, and despite the rigors of time, their centrality to the culture has not diminished. In fact, the trio's stature has actually grown, due to the outpouring of love generated by Jason "Jam Master Jay" Mizell's unsolved shooting death in 2002, and the ongoing '80s revival.

Let's be frank: If Run-D.M.C. hadn't existed, it's possible that rap on record would have remained a novelty that generated an occasional hit. It might not have become a mass, global culture or a commercial cash cow. Judged against every important criterion of musical stardom—records, image, innovation, attitude—Run-D.M.C. remain the platinum standard for rhyming over a beat.

The music, or more accurately, the *sounds* made for Run-D.M.C. records were as minimalist as John Cage's, but much tougher, with bass lines, pretty chords, and melodies eschewed for drum machines, turntable scratches, and phat, distorted heavy-metal guitar riffs. Though Rick Rubin gets well-deserved credit for "reducing" the group's biggest hit, 1986's "Walk This Way" (a rap cover of a 1975 Aerosmith song), Run-D.M.C.'s sonic aesthetic was conceived by original producers Larry Smith and Def Jam co-founder Russell Simmons on early tracks such as "It's Like That," "Sucker MCs," and "Rock Box" (from their self-titled 1984 debut album). These were "beat" as opposed to "groove" records, meaning they weren't just R&B records with rhymes on them (like hits by the Sugar Hill Gang or Kurtis Blow); they emphasized the same raw breakbeats that a street DJ would. In this way, Run-D.M.C. drew a dividing line between themselves and the black pop mainstream.

Early rappers moved right from the stage to the studio, so they tended toward a bombastic delivery. No one epitomized this aggressive style like Run (Joseph Simmons) and D.M.C. (Darryl McDaniels), who often simply shouted at the top of their lungs. To casual listeners, they sounded angry, even dangerous, despite rhymes that advocated staying in school and learning a trade. Run-D.M.C. weren't the lyrical assassins later MCs like Rakim would strive to be ("Peter Piper picked peppers but Run rocked rhymes" was a typical line). Yet there was a sense of violence and threat in Run's and D.M.C.'s voices that scared cultural gate keepers of all colors. When the guitars kicked in on "Rock Box" and "King of Rock" with the two MCs bellowing over them, the combination felt organic, clearing the way for the legion of rap-rockers to come.

None of the above would have mattered as much if the threesome weren't so damn fly. Jay was already sporting a black fedora when manager Russell Simmons (Run's brother) got the group to ditch their checkered jackets of early gigs for black leather, Lee jeans, and those laceless, shell-toe Adidas sneakers. D.M.C.'s lensless Cazal frames were an essential hip-hop accessory circa 1984. To this day, the image of the band in their leather stagewear, arms folded across their chests in the classic b-boy stance, represents the '80s as fully as a Ronald Reagan or Jesse Jackson speech. Add the band's block-letter logo and the tour T-shirts with lyrics immortalized on the back, and Run-D.M.C.'s iconography was as stylized, memorable, and vibrant as anything conceived by peers like Madonna or Michael Jackson.

Thanks to their marriage of rap and rock, of street style and self-conscious design, Run-D.M.C. became the Jackie Robinsons of hip hop. They opened doors in almost every medium, including television (the first rap group in regular rotation on MTV and the first on *American Bandstand*) and movies (appearing in 1985's *Krush Groove* and 1988's *Tougher Than Leather*). They were the only rap group to play the historic Live Aid charity concert in 1985, and became the genre's first multi-platinum act when 1986's *Raising Hell* sold three million copies. With all due respect to KRS-One and Jay-Z, there is only one blueprint for mass-appeal hip hop and its architects are the kings from Queens.

"BEFORE US, RAP RECORDS WERE CORNY. EVERYTHING WAS SOFT. NOBODY MADE NO HARD BEAT RECORDS. EVERYBODY JUST WANTED TO SING, BUT THEY DIDN'T KNOW *HOW* TO SING, SO THEY'D JUST RAP ON A RECORD.... BEFORE RUN-D.M.C. CAME ALONG, RAP COULD HAVE BEEN A FAD." — Jam Master Jay, 1986

Run: "You know I had that line on 'King of Rock,' 'There's three of us but we're not the Beatles.' I thought there were three Beatles. Didn't you, D?"
D.M.C.: [shrugs] "Naw."
Run: "You knew I was fucking up?"
D.M.C.: "Yeah."
Run: "I can't believe you didn't say anything if there was four."
D.M.C.: "Well, one of them died."
— "The Years of Living Dangerously" / Scott Mehno + John Leland / May '88

BABY BACK RIBS
(The way Bannah McDaniels, D.M.C.'s mom, makes 'em):
Steam one slab baby back ribs for 20 minutes. Towel dry. Sprinkle with garlic salt and pepper, cover in soy sauce, and soak overnight in refrigerator. The next day, grill slowly, brushing with remaining marinade until brown on both sides (roughly 30 minutes). Then brush with any commercial BBQ sauce, thinned with mustard and a little vinegar, and grill until blackened. — July '88

At the brightly lit Pop and Kim grocery, there seems to be a hundred people inside, and they all know D.M.C. "You look fat. Do some sit-ups," says one of them with a laugh. We're here to catch up with some "40 dogs"—40-ounce bottles of Olde English 800 malt liquor, which D considers liquid gold. "We never leave home without it," he says. "It's like American Express/ And it tastes the best/ Gotta be cold/ when you're drinking Olde Gold." Pop and Kim keep it frozen—the coldest beer in New York.

They have no rap for Wong's Chow Mein, a Chinese fast-food place in Laurelton, Queens—they're too busy devouring to come up with rhymes. They order large, salty portions of shrimp toast and shrimp egg foo young. It's probably the largest group this mostly take-out restaurant has ever served (there are only three or four tables). Stock in the shrimp industry is skyrocketing as we eat.

One of the D posse says he'd love to be "one of those critics that eat food and review it and shit." Someone passes gas and it's commented that it "sounds like you stepped on a duck." "I gotta get my stomach pumped," someone says. "Word up," says D. They all pee in the street.

The last food stop is Discount Bar B Q, which has home-baked pies, chicken, catfish, seafood, pork chops, beef, fried okra, stuffing, biscuits, and cornbread, and on the same premises, a repair service for gas boilers, stoves, and water heaters. Very little is consumed—only one slice of sweet potato pie, actually—though they all consider the repair service. At the 7-11, I get a coffee to restimulate, and D buys *Black Beat*, *People,* and *National Lampoon* magazines and heads home. "I was gonna see a girl," he says, "but I think I'll lie down."
— "D.M.C.'s Culinary Guide to Queens" / Michael Musto / October '88

"The best musical moment was in '86 at Madison Square Garden. That night it was sold out. We were sold out all over the world, the time of *Raising Hell*. I told people to hold up their Adidas and the whole place took their Adidas off their feet and put them in the air. When I got offstage, the Adidas representative was there and he told me that night that we would have our own line of Adidas."
— Run, 1993

INSIDE THE BOOTH OF THE STUDIO WHERE AEROSMITH AND RUN-D.M.C. ARE RECORDING "WALK THIS WAY," PRODUCER RICK RUBIN IS FIDDLING WITH THE DRUM MACHINE, turning up first the cymbal, then the kick drum, trying out faster and slower tempos. Joe Perry stands by the board and plays the "Walk This Way" riff through the monitors.

"Yo, call Budgie," Darryl "D.M.C." McDaniels shouts to Run. He leans against the water fountain, flicking it on and off, on and off. "It's already three o'clock."

"They said if we don't have the car back today, we're going to jail," says Run. He dials 411. "Hello, can I have the number for Budget Rent-A-Car?"

Steven Tyler and Perry are introduced to Rubin, manager Russell Simmons, Darryl, Run, and Jam-Master Jay, and all huddle together on risers to fit into one shot for the MTV camera. Tyler is wired, jabbing his finger at the lens, mugging for a close-up, rapping. He bear hugs people while Perry looks embarrassed. Run and Russell quietly argue under their breath.

"C'mon, do we have to do any more?" asks Tyler. "We've got a lot of work and only a little time." (Rush Productions reportedly paid Aerosmith $8,000 to have Tyler and Perry in the studio for one day.) Tyler's girlfriend, Teresa, walks up to him with a jeweled cigarette case, and they disappear into a bathroom and emerge noticeably refreshed. The last photos taken, Rubin returns to the booth and decides to lay down the guitar part first. Perry does the first take in deep concentration, oblivious to the clinking of Lite beer bottles. His back to the growing crowd of spectators, he plays a blond Schecter with "Protest and Survive" burned into the front of the head. Simmons tells Run and Darryl to go outside and get the lyrics down with Tyler. > > >

"I want it to be b-boy language," says Run.

"I keep telling you, it already is," says Simmons.

"Hey diddle diddle with the titty in the middle," says Run.

"Hey diddle diddle with the *kitty* in the middle," corrects Tyler. "Get me some paper and I'll write it down for you."

Someone hands him a sheet and he kneels on the floor, Magic Marker in hand.

"No, that's OK, we know it," says Run. "We're just gonna do one take, then we gotta leave. We gotta return the car."

By 9 PM the session's over and everyone has left, except Rubin and Simmons, who are waiting for an engineer to dupe cassettes of the rough mix.

"The original is a classic, but some of the things Steven and Joe did today—this could also be very interesting," says Rubin.

— "Burning the Kingdom" / Sue Cummings / July '86

Much as any fan prayed for it, the success of Run-D.M.C.'s "Walk This Way" leaves a bad taste in my mouth.

It's one thing to take a cynical approach to a racist problem, another to watch it succeed, thereby validating all your original cynicism. So a track that's far from the band's best suddenly warms the ears of AOR and CHR programmers who wrote off "Rock Box" and "King of Rock" as black music and therefore not fit for their airwaves. This is a breakthrough? Run-D.M.C. deserve the success, but on their own terms. And what's up for them now? Are those new friends going to play the next single the way they did "Walk This Way?" Or is the group gonna have to team up with the Allman Brothers to have another hit? This question is the measure of their success.

— "Singles" / John Leland / December '86

Five nights earlier, Run-D.M.C.'s Jam Master Jay, 37, was in his recording studio, 24/7, on nearby Merrick Boulevard.

He was rocking a brown leather hat and Adidas sneakers, playing Xbox football with a buddy, and chatting with an aspiring singer named Lydia. Then a man wearing a ski mask entered the studio lounge, walked up to Jay, put a .40-caliber pistol behind his left ear, and shot him, leaving powder burns on his shirt. The shooting also left a widow, three kids, and a legacy of uplifting music.

Run-D.M.C. ruled an era when you could rock parties and star on MTV while boasting that you went to St. John's University. In fact, this was their point—the

no-frills clothes and workaday rhymes were supposed to declare a less show-biz, more "real" hip-hop age. By all accounts, Jay never left that era. He stayed in his community, cofounded the Scratch DJ Academy for young DJs, produced local acts at his studio, and became the unofficial mayor of Hollis. "Tinted windows don't mean nothin'/ They know who's inside," goes a Run D.M.C. lyric. Jay's solution was not to hide.

Various motives for the murder have been suggested, including feuds within the rap game. But Jay's only link to industry beef was an association with Queens rapper 50 Cent, a.k.a. Curtis Jackson, whom Jay discovered and whose songs ("How to Rob," "Wanksta") taunted so-called studio gangstas. While these songs may have led to the rapper's shooting two years ago, police have not connected them to Jay's death. The subsequent murder of 50 Cent's promoter, Kenneth Walker, in the Bronx also remains unlinked.

— "In the City, It's a Pity" / Chris Norris / February '03

On November 4, outside the J. Foster Phillips Funeral Home in Jamaica, Queens, hundreds of cameramen, reporters, and fans braved the rain to gaze at a long line of mourners. Shoutouts erupted whenever a hip-hop celebrity like Grandmaster Flash arrived, and a few ill-mannered folks even handed out business cards. Metal police barricades separated the spectators from the official guests, and a tall, tight-faced officer ordered people around as if they were waiting to get into a rap concert. The scene seemed like a parody of a celebrity wake.

Even inside the funeral home, there was a cartoonish aspect to the proceedings. Jason Mizell, 37, who was murdered on October 30, was laid in an open coffin, garbed as "Jam Master Jay"—black leather pants and jacket, shell-toe Adidas sneakers, a big black Stetson hat, and a thick gold chain with a miniature sneaker pendant. The tears in the viewing room, though, were for Jason, father of three, husband of 11 years, and longtime Queens resident. Yes, there were flowers from Jazzy Jeff and L.L. Cool J. Yes, Ad-Rock and MCA of the Beastie Boys stood against a wall looking dazed. But this was no photo-op grief. For the artists who were there when Run-D.M.C. lifted hip-hop out of the underground in the early 1980s, Mizell was a symbol of stability, maturity, and support. L.L. Cool J's floral arrangement featured STUDENT written in red roses, a reflection of the fact that Mizell was a mentor to so many—not exactly a father figure, more like a very cool big brother.

Two days after the wake, Run-D.M.C. announced that they were retiring, which was both incredibly disheartening and quite appropriate.

— "Jam Master Jammin'" / Nelson George / February '03

: The Smiths +
Morrissey

Beautiful misery

In the late 1800s, a writer named Oscar Wilde
stunned the English-speaking world
with his brilliance and unwavering devotion to,
and defense of, art for art's sake.
He carried around sunflowers and peacock feathers,
and cherished his collection of blue china.
His writing was effete and lily-delicate, but at the same time
full of aphorisms so viciously witty
that he was alternately feared, lionized, and loathed
by the society-types of London.
Speculation about Wilde's sexuality—

he was married with children, but maintained a long-time relationship with a younger man—brought him first societal opprobrium, then imprisonment, and soon after, financial and familial ruin. He died in Paris at age 46, but his works—*The Importance of Being Earnest*, *De Profundis*, and *The Picture of Dorian Gray* among them—endure, because he was utterly unafraid of existing in a perpetual state of aesthetic flamboyance. Like many who grow elaborate gardens in the soil of their pain and isolation, he was first lauded for his candor and artistic sensitivity, then more or less killed for same.

About a century later, the first that many young people, particularly those living in certain suburbs of Chicago, heard of Oscar Wilde was when a British band called the Smiths mentioned him in a song called "Cemetery Gates" on 1986's *The Queen Is Dead*. The relevant lyrics: "Dreaded sunny day/ So let's go where we're wanted/ And I meet you at the cemetery gates/ Keats and Yates are on your side/ but you lose/ because weird lover Wilde is on mine." The writer of these words was named Stephen Patrick Morrissey, but he went by his last name only. He wore his hair in a kind of pompadour, and was blandly handsome in a way that suggested film actors of the 1950s. He seemed, at first at least, to be, like Wilde, doomed by his own vulnerability.

Morrissey's reference to Wilde helped his devotees place the singer in the proper context. Like Wilde's, his writing was full of seemingly innocuous wordplay and bon mots, but was, at its core, passionate, often furious. He was, to employ a dubious metaphor that will be regretted by its author, a vengeful sort of butcher, wielding a knife with a gorgeously carved handle. "I decree today that life is simply taking and not giving/ England is mine and it owes me a living/ But ask me why and I'll spit in your eye," he sings on "Still Ill." Like Wilde's, Morrissey's sexuality was

a source of much speculation, at least initially. The cover of the band's self-titled debut album from 1984 features a shirtless man with his head bowed in shyness or shame. The lyrics were often interpreted to be expressing the alienation of a young gay man struggling to find love or acceptance—or a moment of lust.

There was a happy sort of song called "This Charming Man," but for the most part the album was dour and frustrated, even morbid, at one point mulling a recent tragedy—the abduction and murder of several children—from the Smith's gloomy hometown of Manchester. The music was jangly and lush, but still raw, never overproduced. While many of the Smiths' contemporaries, including the Cure—with whom they were often and erroneously compared—employed elaborate studio arrangements, it was clear that everything on the Smiths' debut had been played with guitar, drums, and bass. There was nothing frilly about it, which underscored both how tortured Morrissey sounded, and how ridiculously pretty—even stripped down to almost nothing—guitarist Johnny Marr's music could be.

By the second album, 1985's *Meat Is Murder*, a cult of devotees read Morrissey's lyrics as they would pictograms on a newly found tomb of a long-dead prophet. He seemed to be the only lyricist at the time willing to be lyrical; he seemed alone in being at once terribly witty and deeply soulful, at once self-lacerating and self-aggrandizing. This dichotomy is best exemplified in "Frankly Mr. Shankly" and "I Know It's Over," which run in succession on *The Queen Is Dead*. "I'd rather be famous/ than righteous or holy" he sings in the first song, while the second features the couplet, "Oh mother, I can feel/ the soil falling over my head." In fact, Morrissey's self-abuse—the very extent and quality of it—was in a strange way the source of his pride. He was, perhaps, the best self-loather/self-parodist the world had ever known.

ESSAY CONTINUES ON NEXT PAGE >

"MORRISSEY," REMEMBERS [JOURNALIST
AND NEIGHBOR] PAUL MORLEY,
"WAS ALWAYS LAUGHED AT IN MANCHESTER
WHEN WE WERE KIDS.

He was the village idiot. That's the ironic thing—now he's the poet of a generation. But in those days, he was 'that-one-in-the-corner, Steve the Nutter.'"

— "Spirit in the Dark" / Jessica Berens / September '86

"NOW, I'M NOT SAYING HE'S
JOHN LENNON, AND I'M NOT SAYING
HE'S THE MONKEES.

But you gotta admire a guy who can rhyme 'rusty spanner' with 'play pianner' and who can espouse the beauty of a doubledecker bus collision."

— review of The Smiths' *The Queen Is Dead* / Rich Stim / August '86

JOHNNY ROGAN IS THE AUTHOR OF THE
INFLAMMATORY 1992 BOOK *Morrissey & Marr:
The Severed Alliance*, ABOUT WHICH
MORRISSEY IS ON RECORD AS SAYING
"I WOULD SOONER LOSE THE USE
OF BOTH LEGS THAN READ."

But there the Miserable One was, parked outside of Book Soup in L.A. one September evening as Rogan read from and then signed copies of his book. Store manager Guy Adams noted that at least half of the hundred or so people who had congregated in the store poured out into the parking lot to get something, anything, signed. After about ten minutes of frenzied autographing, Morrissey leapt into a chauffeur-driven black Mercedes-Benz and sped off, closely followed by several carloads of fans. Rogan was amused that Morrissey never entered the store. "The idea of Morrissey actually confronting me—I don't think he'd do that in a million years."

— "L.A. Spawned a Monster"/ December '93

"I CAN'T IMAGINE ANYONE LOVING MADONNA AND WANTING TO GET
ONSTAGE, AND HOLD HER, AND SQUEEZE HER, AND NOT LET GO.
She doesn't inspire that. She may sell millions upon millions of records~similarly with George Michael or Michael Jackson~but I don't know that people really, really love them in the way that I feel that I am loved by the people who come and see me."

— Morrissey, 1992

> ESSAY CONTINUES FROM PREVIOUS PAGE

Morrissey spoke to and for bookish types, or for less-bookish types when they were feeling bookish. He spoke to and for those who loved a well-turned phrase, and who especially loved it when such a phrase was sung with a flip of the chin and a roll of the *r*. He spoke to and for those who felt that life was so intensely, wretchedly gorgeous that it was too much to bear. Morrissey spoke to and for those adolescents who would ride their bikes around their neighborhoods, alone in the dark, listening to the Smiths on a six-pound Walkman, looking into the windows of homes, seeing everyone as doomed and full of perfection and destined to die miserably. He spoke to and for those teenagers who would listen to his music while sitting on the grass outside the Art Institute of Chicago, where they were taking summer classes, while thinking of a girl who smoked and was older, one who seemed unimprovable in every way—starting with the fact that she was older and, impossibly, lived on a street named Goethe.

Morrissey, though, was not always good to those who cared for him. In 1986, one of these teenaged devotees traveled to Milwaukee for a chance to see the Smiths play in a perfectly decrepit burgundy-curtained venue, but the Smiths were not good. And they did not appear to care. They played for precisely 43 minutes and left without an encore. At one point, during "The Queen Is Dead," Morrissey walk-danced listlessly around the stage holding a sign that said—what? what did it say?—"The Queen Is Dead."

It was the beginning of a complicated period for Morrissey. By 1987, as the Smiths released both *Louder Than Bombs* (a collection of singles and B-sides) and a final studio album, *Strangeways Here We Come*, the devoted were not sure what to think of him anymore. He spoke the gospel, and was always the prettiest writer in the music world, but he seemed eternally distant, and had increasing trouble writing from his core—or what his listeners imagined was his core. Much of his work after *The Queen Is Dead* seemed to reach for subject matter, every so often drifting into camp, à la the musically divine but lyrically silly "Girlfriend in a Coma" ("Girlfriend in a coma / I know I know, it's serious/ Bye bye bye bye bye baby goodbye").

The band broke up acrimoniously after *Strangeways*, and Marr went on to play for many different bands, guest-appearing on over a dozen or so albums. Morrissey's solo career has been, for the most part, every bit as fascinating and full of brilliance as the Smith's, though he only intermittently gets the respect his writing warrants. His first solo foray, 1988's *Viva Hate*, contains easily six songs that would have fit happily on any Smiths album. *Your Arsenal* (1992) is even better. No longer stretching for subject matter, he's become more politically engaged, exploring British identity amid globalization and a tidal wave of immigration and American influence. As he approaches Wilde's age of demise, we can at least be thankful that Morrissey, after eight years in reclusion, could return with an album, 2004's *You Are the Quarry*, of great honesty and artful fury. Though it appeared for some time that Morrissey would be, as Wilde was, swept under the tide that is always ready to kill the eccentric and exquisitely sensitive, it appears now that Morrissey will be with us as long as he wants.

SPIN:
Are you lonely?
MORRISSEY:
Yes, I am extremely lonely.

SPIN: How would you think about solving that?

Morrissey: I don't think about that now, because when you've struck the grand old age of 33, you have to come to some basic conclusions about your life-style and practically every night of my life has been the same, so it's not as if I've had ups and downs. The day always ends the same way, with exactly the same scenario. I'm closing the door and putting the lights out and fumbling for a book. And that's it. I find that very unfortunate, but then, I could have a wooden leg.

SPIN: But isn't the point that everyone is, just by the nature of human existence, so incredibly lonely, that the only thing you can do is to try to mitigate that somehow?

Morrissey: Yes, but most people try to do that by pretending that the word "lonely" doesn't exist in the dictionary. The strain for me is that most people don't talk in a personal way. I don't want to sit down with head bent and shoulders arched, with a crack in the voice, 24 hours a day, talking about every human ill imaginable. But I would like people to talk to me directly. And I would like people to say, well, "Why do you live this way?"

SPIN: But I just have!

Morrissey: But nobody else ever does.

SPIN: Maybe they're just frightened?

Morrissey: But what of? I know what you're going to say (laughs), but I just want to hear you say it.

SPIN: Because, for example, people are constantly telling me all the things that Morrissey doesn't do. You know: "He doesn't want to talk about the Smiths. He won't discuss the Rogan book (*Morrissey & Marr: The Severed Alliance*). He doesn't

have drinks. He won't come out to dinner." And one thinks, what the hell am I supposed to talk about? And all the time there's this self-fulfilling prophecy going on: "I'm incredibly lonely, but could you please fuck off."

Morrissey: Very elegantly put (laughs).

SPIN: But if I were your therapist, I might say that, at some point, it might be advisable for you to break that cycle for your own peace of mind.

Morrissey: Well, yes, I do actually realize that. I realized that in 1970. However, well, it's only life.

SPIN: Yes, but it's the only one you've got.

Morrissey: Yes, but it will end. And all this will seem so frivolous.

SPIN: Do you like yourself?

Morrissey: No, I don't. That is the actual truth, but I know that there is no way that that sentence can be printed and not seem like anything other than extreme nonsense.

—"The Sorrow and the Pity" / David Thomas / November, '92

Boasting the most fervid fans in the pop universe, Morrissey drew 2,500 starry-eyed acolytes to his April 27 in-store appearance in New York City's Tower Records. Among them:

Vicky, 19
(first in line, waited 37 hours)
"I've waited nine years for this. He was signing my album and he was like, 'Well, you haven't said anything yet.' And I just couldn't get a word out. He just stood there with this sorry look on his face and patted me on the head with my album and said, 'It's just life.' And then he gave me a hug."

James, 21
"I gave him a card with the Little Prince on it because he likes the Little Prince, and he opened it and he laughed, and then I made him feed me a strawberry. And then (crying) I hugged him."

Iva, 20
"I wear black on the outside because black is how I feel on the inside. That's my model. I took it from Morrissey's own lyrics. Black is happiness. White is depressing to me. I think Morrissey has one of the blackest hearts ever."

Joe, 20
"I'm here to get an autograph for my friend Abigail from California because her mom is a Jehovah's Witness. She never gets anything for her birthday because they don't believe in celebrating birthdays. I'm gonna get him to sign: 'Abigail, have an *unhappy birthday.*' You know, from that Smiths song. She'll get it. "

— "Hopelessly Devoted" / August '94

I FINALLY GOT TO INHALE MORRISSEY'S SWEAT IN 1992. The man played my local high-school auditorium with his flashy new glam-rockabilly band and, aside from being the most excellent night of my entire life, it was a really good show, eliciting squeals from the gladiola-clutching kids swarming around me. Onstage the guitarists circled Morrissey with wreaths of feedback as he gave voice unto the undulations within his very soul while ripping off his gold lamé shirt. A friend managed to snag a shred of Morrissey's frock and let me sniff it, so I can tell you authoritatively that even the Mozzer's sweat bears the aroma of genius. And just a few months ago I spent a weekend's food money on an import CD called *Beethoven Was Deaf*, which only contained near identical live versions of songs I already knew by heart. It sounds sub-fuckin'-lime.

Ten years of mindless devotion to a compulsively ironic rock star with flabby pectorals and an Oscar Wilde fetish makes no sense, I know. But then, Morrissey makes no sense. He's rock 'n' roll's untamed shrew, frivolous and coy, heterosexually unintelligible, our prodigal prince of frippery and froppery. Long before pop culture fixated on cyberspace and virtual reality, Morrissey took you through the looking glass with a shamelessly excessive vocal style, a fey parody of all the contradictions and illusions built into the human voice. These days, of course, there are Morrissey news groups in cyberspace on the Internet—just what his fans need, another reason never to leave the apartment—but it's still more vertiginous to listen in on his musical tea party. He serves fiber-optic cables coiled around cucumber sandwiches and hashish fudge.

The new *Vauxhill and I* takes a big step away from the frantic guitar havoc of 1992's *Your Arsenal*, which guitarists Boz Boorer and Alain Whyte made the most exuberantly gorgeous album of Moz's career. Although Boorer and Whyte are still on hand, producer Steve Lillywhite has muted their roar until *Vauxhall* sounds soft and dreamy, more like the early Smiths than a Morrissey solo album. Although I wish there were a single track as stunning as "Certain People I Know" or "We Hate it When Our Friends Become Successful," the overall flow is powerful. Delicate acoustic textures weave through haunting drones and synthesized strings. The sweetest tune here, "Why Don't You Find Out For Yourself," warns about "The glass/ Hidden in the grass," gloating over all the traps you'll fall into following in Morrissey's footsteps. "Speedway" could be Oscar Wilde singing on the witness stand and flirting with the judge: "All of the rumors/ Keeping me grounded/ I never said that they were/ Completely unfounded." Although the draggy tempos and lush settings make *Vauxhall* sound unbecomingly mellow on the surface, Morrissey does his best to get on your nerves.

American critics will probably never forgive the Mozzer for his vocal overreacting. Minimalist he's not, and his modifier-to-noun ratio is still over the legal limit in many states. He doesn't fit in with the terse, tight-lipped diction of more sensible songwriters, what Lester Bangs called "the Lou Reed 'I walked to the chair/ Then I sat in it' school of lyrics." British critics slam Morrissey for hanging around too long, associating him with their other adolescent miseries: scurvy, rickets, mutton, getting caned, not being chosen head prefect because they played cricket with socialists, etc. But the Morrissey audience is now big enough to support a music business of its own, as insular and self-sufficient as the Christian Contemporary or Spanish-speaking industries. Suede is our own hard rock, the Auteurs are our own roots music. Stereolab is our own New Age, and so on. Even noise-rock kings Pavement quoted a stray Morrissey lyric in the *Slanted and Enchanted* CD booklet: "I'm the end of the family line." The irony is that Morrissey's line isn't ending at all, merely recombining and mutating into new strains of personality. If by chance you get your own fatal taste of it, don't blame me if you're still tuning in ten years after *you're* old enough to know better.

— review of Morrissey's *Vauxhall and I* / Rob Sheffield / April '94

SOME PEOPLE FEEL NERVOUS AROUND CRUZ RUBIO. That's unfair, but it's true. He's a badass: The dude is 20 years old, he's from East Los Angeles, the sleeves are ripped off his flannel shirt, and he looks like an extra from the movie *Colors*. I have no doubt whatsoever that he could kick the shit out of me. But I am not nervous around Cruz Rubio, because he is telling me how Morrissey makes him weep.

"Some nights I lay in my bedroom and I listen to 'There is a Light That Never Goes Out,' and I cry," he tells me. "I cry and cry and cry. I cry like a little bitch, man."

Perhaps you are wondering what a cut-like-marble Latino could possibly see in a quintessentially British, marvelously effeminate white guy best known for reading Oscar Wilde and wearing his espoused asexuality on his sweater sleeve. Frankly, there's no concrete answer to that question. But Cruz Rubio is definitely seeing *something*, because he is not the exception; within the walls of the sixth annual Smiths/Morrissey convention in Hollywood's Palace Theater, he is the rule.

For two days in April, fans of a disbanded Mancunian pop group and its forgotten frontman smoked clove cigarettes, picked over U.K. bootlegs, and danced to "Hairdresser on Fire" like dehydrated Helen Kellers, which is how people at Smiths conventions are supposed to behave. Yet these fans are not the glowering white semi-goths you'd expect to encounter; this scene looks like a 1958 sock hop in Mexico City. To argue that Morrissey's contemporary audience skews Hispanic would be inaccurate; Morrissey's contemporary audience *is* Hispanic, at least in L.A. Of the 1,400 people at this year's convention, at least 75 percent of the ticket buyers—and virtually all under 20—were Latino. For reasons that may never be completely understood, teenage Hispanics tend to be the only people who still care about Manchester's saddest sack. And they care a lot.

"He speaks to us, man. As Latinos. He addresses us personally," Rubio explains. "His music fits our lifestyle. I mean, where was the one place Morrissey always said he was dying to tour? It was Mexico, man. That's where his heart is."

Moments later, 23-year-old construction worker Albert Velazquez expresses a nearly identical sentiment. "The last time I saw him live, he looked into the audience and said, 'I wish I had been born Mexican, but it's too late now.' Those were his exact words. And the crowd just exploded. He loves the Mexican culture, and he understands what we go through."

Velazquez is 235 pounds and 6'5" (6'8" if you count the pompadour). He plans to celebrate Morrissey's birthday on May 22; everybody at this convention knows that date. Velazquez also tells me he's going to drink a few Coronas that afternoon, because that's Morrissey's favorite beer. Everyone seems to know that, too. Morrissey once sang that we must look to Los Angeles for the language we use, because London is dead. And so it is: The question is no longer "How soon is now?"; the question is "¿Es realmente tan extraño?"

— "Viva Morrissey!" / Chuck Klosterman / August '02

"ARE YOU AWARE OF THE EMO MOVEMENT?" I ASK MORRISSEY.

He arches an eyebrow. "No. I was born yesterday."

"What do you make of nü-metal bands like the Deftones citing the Smiths as an influence as well?"

"I think it certainly is a modern trend to expose the emotions, more so than ever before. And whether it's as far-reaching as groups like the Deftones or System of a Down, everybody is 'coming out,' and I don't mean sexually. I mean throwing their emotions out there. Everybody seems to know what they need. They don't necessarily attain it, but they know what they want to say [about it]."

"What do you make of the fact that many of your new fans are so young?" I ask.

"It's fascinating," he says. "Year after year, it seems to absolutely catch the 14-year-olds and capture their imaginations somehow. I think [being a teenager] is a time in your life when you gravitate toward a somewhat dark realism, and you want people to stop talking to you as if you were a child. You want people to give it to you straight. And I think my singing voice has always sounded like a real voice. It's never sounded like it's been heavily treated, and I don't sound like a person who's terribly happy. God knows how that started, given my natural exuberance."

"But as a 44-year-old, it must be awkward to have fans who are 14."

"Not really," he says. "It's not as if I take them home and bake them pies. I can put it in perspective. And I'm thankful that anybody should listen—when I've often been told nobody should."

—"These Things Take Time" / Marc Spitz / May '04

: Goth

SUBURBAN HIGH SCHOOLS, THE CURE, AND THE SECRET OF HAPPINESS

Goth, short for Gothic, is a post-punk subculture whose aesthetics are rooted in both the romantic and grotesque mid-19th-century fiction of Shelley, Stoker, and Poe (the capes, sweeping hair, and lace-up boots) and the flashy, trashy late-20th century glitter rock movement (the makeup, the drugs, and the stacked boot heels). "Telegram Sam" by T. Rex is as Goth as Tod Browning's *Dracula* (starring Bela Lugosi, who is dead). Most people don't credit Goth with rockin' but then Goth is the most misunderstood of all enduring subcultures. Sometimes these prejudices are harmless (see the recurring late '90s Saturday Night Live skit *Goth Talk*, which should have been adapted to replace *A Night At The Roxbury* as Chris Kattan's big screen spinoff bid). Sometimes they're serious (Death row inmate and Goth Damien Echols, one of the West Memphis Three depicted in the *Paradise Lost* documentaries, is probably not a child murderer, but definitely a Cure fan).

Goth garb is the most visually theatrical of all the subcultural dress codes, with nods to both witchcraft and the occult (punk Johnny Rotten claimed "I am an anti-Christ" but didn't really look like one). This has not helped the easily spooked public understand or explore why a good kid, raised on Journey or Britney, would one day decide to dress like Winona Ryder in *Beetlejuice*. Still, every high school in America has a Goth faction (every high school in the suburbs anyway). So, as a public service, I will now reveal precisely why Goth culture has attracted kids for 25 years and will never abate.

Getting up two hours before the bus comes to spike your hair, ringing your eyes with black Kohl liner, wearing black wool in the summertime...it's all very practical. In an existential sense anyway. If you see a Goth walking your streets, you will probably assume that he or she is on the way to the graveyard to weep. More often than not, however, the Goth is thinking, "Did I shut down my computer?" Or "A grilled cheese sandwich would taste good right now."

Goths have dispensed with morbid preoccupations that haunt rave kids, hippies, and fans of Shania Twain and are uniquely able to enjoy graveyards for what they are: cool places to get high. Maybe you'll flee in fear or notify the police that some pedestrians of doom are on their way to shoot up the high school. The lesser but just as valid truth about Goths is that they want to drink blood or sacrifice your firstborn about as much as the hip-hop head on his way home from a long shift at Coconuts wants to whip out a 9 and bust a cap or even a rhyme. A true Goth would rather dance (popular moves include the "Oh, no, it's started to rain I must cover my head with my bat wings" or the "Pick up the penny! Pick up the penny!") In its purest form, Goth is nothing if not a tool designed to liberate oneself from the constant fear of Death by embracing and appreciating and

fetishizing all reminders that life is fleeting and, yeah, scary. If every day is Halloween, like Ministry once sang (before abandoning the genre for it's abrasive offshoot, Industrial, although I always preferred the *With Sympathy* era), then superstition and a heightened, often troubling awareness of the unknown becomes routine shit.

By 1985, when SPIN began publishing, Goth's first and most significant wave had long since peaked. With the exception of some brilliant singles by Siouxsie and the Banshees ("Cities in Dust," "Peek-A-Boo") or Sisters of Mercy ("This Corrosion"), most of the classic Goth icons were past it. Joy Division became New Order (after singer Ian Curtis hung himself) and started making disco music for imaginary John Hughes movies. The Birthday Party became Nick Cave and the Bad Seeds and started wearing tailored suits. Bauhaus became Love and Rockets and stopped covering Bowie and Bolan. Southern Death Cult became The Cult and started covering Steppenwolf.

The Cure were the only band from first wave to remain essentially Goth, and by that I don't mean they kept their hair the same (they did). Rather, they understood that Goths are fundamentally free. What else but a true Goth act could follow up the bleakest heroin record since Lou Reed's *Berlin* (1982's *Pornography*) with boppy jazz for 4th graders (the 1983 single "The Lovecats"). Some fans accused them of going pop with 1985's *The Head on the Door* and 1987's *Kiss Me, Kiss Me, Kiss Me*, but they missed the point. If you're an unrepentant Goth, you can go pop. You can even go disco (as they did on their *All Mixed Up* remix album in 1990). You can release singles about being eaten alive by giant, nocturnal spiders (1989's "Lullaby") and sell out Giants Stadium. To this day, The Cure succeed by confounding, and confound by succeeding. They will always seem vital and fresh and surprising because a great contingent of cynics will always expect them to merely whine about dying lonely and misunderstood. People are actually starting to respect them for this, and in the case of Interpol and entire sub-genres of punk and heavy metal, emulate it. The Cure used to be as much a punch line as they were a cult. Now they're a paradigm.

"I actually think I'm the most grown-up person I've ever met," Robert Smith told me when I interviewed him in 2004, "in that I run a huge business and have been married to the same person for years. I'm more emotionally mature than anyone I know." He was 45 years old then, wearing smeared red lipstick and raccoon eye makeup. But I believed him completely—and not just because "Catch" was playing while I lost my virginity. One underestimates a true Goth like Smith (who by the way, doesn't consider himself a Goth, which only makes him more quintessentially Goth) at one's own peril. The Cure, allegedly obsessed with Death, have enjoyed more life as an unassailable rock

That's Goth!

Steak is Goth. Salad is not.

Meth is Goth. Cocaine is not.

Cats are Goth. Dogs are not.

Murder ballads are Goth (especially when sung by Johnny Cash). Power ballads are not.

Nina Simone was Goth. So is Diamanda Galas. Tori Amos is not.

Bowie is Goth. Lou Reed is not (although the first Velvet Underground album with Nico certainly is).

Easter is Goth. Christmas is not (although *The Nightmare Before Christmas* absolutely is).

Jesus was way Goth. Buddha is not. Jews are not really Goth although we have great empathy for Goths.

Kurt was Goth. Eddie Vedder was not.

Wes Borland from Limp Bizkit is extremely Goth. Fred Durst is not.

Edward Gorey was Goth. Emily The Strange is not Goth despite the fact that she's marketed to Goths who couldn't buy her products anyway cause they're broke from buying all that crystal.

Winona Ryder in *Beetlejuice* should not be Goth but actually is.

> ESSAY CONTINUED FROM PREVIOUS PAGE

institution as any rock band. And Robert Smith is probably happier than you and me. There are rumors that he's a big soccer fan.

It actually is Halloween as I write this. Today, I watched a bunch of little kids running up Bleecker Street in Greenwich Village dressed up as skeletons and vampires and the Dresden Dolls. Some of them will grow up to look like Nick Lachey. They'll fear the Reaper and take solace in smooth R&B. Others will remain in vampire drag. They'll look miserable and sickly and hungry for blood but, secretly, they'll awake elated over each new sunrise, hungry for eggs.

SPIN: You don't want to be another Ian Curtis?
Robert Smith (The Cure): I think one for each generation is enough. (1988)

The Cure and its supporters are one of America's more obvious secrets, a youth culture as substantial and central to people's lives as heavy metal or hip hop. They are an obsession. The last time the Cure played San Francisco, on July 27, 1986, a member of the audience climbed onstage and stabbed himself repeatedly in the chest. The crowd of 18,000, thinking this had to be part of the entertainment, cheered wildly.
     "We find Americans a little obsessive and sinister," says Robert Smith.
— "The Cure Melts Down" / Ted Mico / July '89

"To do something like 'Friday I'm in Love' and to have that video and still have people say 'the doom and gloom merchants,' it's just irritating. But we'll always be stuck with it. When we did *Disintegration*, people said we were going back to our roots, whereas in fact our roots are 'Boys Don't Cry' and that sort of idiot pop."
— Robert Smith / '93

"Without the Cure, there would probably have been no Deftones. They were one of the main reasons I started singing."
— Chino Moreno (Deftones) / '98

"My oldest brother, Matt, gave me a cassette [of the Cure's *Staring at the Sea: The Singles*] when I was in the third grade. It was the first thing I owned myself. I would go into my room with my boom box and just play it forever."
— Conor Oberst (Bright Eyes) / '04

To this day, Siouxsie remains a vastly influential fashion icon: Her wild hair, stark black makeup, and black costume may be seen on any number of young women in any city. Although she disclaims a certain amount of responsibility, the "goths," almost hippie punks, are very much Siouxsie's children; they share her dream of something else.
     Despite almost defining the female goth, she's nevertheless capable of self-mockery; she bursts out laughing when she reveals that the engineer chosen to complete *Tinderbox* was selected because of his name—Steve Churchyard.
— "High Priestess" / Jon Savage / June '86

> **The Cure have made dreamy synth-pop out of art-rock's hoariest clichés because Robert Smith has managed to fuse the brain of Jim Morrison with the soul of the Pillsbury Dough Boy.**
> — "The Cure"/ Rob Sheffield / SPIN Alternative Record Guide (1995)

If you had to describe the decorating scheme of Jim Brennan's basement bedroom, you might call it modern headbanger.

The lighting has two settings: dim and dark. Pictures of Skrape, Slipknot, and Mudvayne cover the wood-paneled walls, and the TV flickers with a video called *Necrophagia: Through Eyes of the Dead*, which shows a burly redneck hacking apart a woman to the thud of a double bass drum.

Brennan lives with his mother in Gracemore, a neighborhood in Kansas City, Missouri, in a small house behind an amusement park called Worlds of Fun. This is ironic, since Brennan, who is 19, with black, spiked hair and faraway eyes, spends most of his time searching for—and complaining about the absolute lack of—anything fun.

This June night is no different.

Brennan and his best friend, Jason McCarthy, along with McCarthy's girlfriend, Jaime Beaman, are sitting, stoned, on a couch in his room. It's Thursday night and no one has heard of a party. The last good concert (downthesun) was months ago; the next one (Cradle of Filth) is weeks away. There was some talk of walking out to the driveway, drinking kerosene, lighting a match, and breathing fire. Too bad it's raining.

Brennan wants to broaden his social circle. Until recently, he had spent many evenings in the parking lot outside the Barnes & Noble at Independence Commons, a nearby mall. Lured by the store's café and relatively late hours, Goths began to gather out front—as many as 50 swarmed the entrance on some nights. "Everybody had similar interests," Brennan says. "We were all drawn to the darker side. I thought maybe I'd meet a girl there."

Among the regulars were Traci Russell, who wore fishnet stockings and resembled a large black-widow spider; a pale fellow named Jared Hughes, who called himself Xerxes; and David, a tall kid who wore a black trench coat and talked about casting spells. Brennan, who owns a big wooden box filled with spiked chokers and chunky boots, fit right in; McCarthy would wear a set of vampire fangs.

Then something unexpected happened. A few officers from the Youth Outreach Unit in neighboring Blue Springs began to take notice of the Barnes & Noble kids. Y.O.U. is a division of the Blue Springs Police Department that deals with what it calls "at-risk" youth; to the cops, the kids at the bookstore—with their unnaturally dark hair, all-black clothes, and multiple piercings—looked like tinder sticks, ready to ignite.

Then something truly unexpected happened. The U.S. Department of Education awarded the city of Blue Springs $273,000 to study Goths, with the intent of preventing kids involved in the subculture from inflicting harm on themselves or the community. The so-called Goth Grant kicked in last April and ends on March 31. (In response to a flood of negative publicity and ridicule and because its mandate has broadened, it has since been renamed the Counter Culture Grant.)

There was initial concern that Blue Springs would go "goth hunting," harassing and possibly arresting kids based solely on appearance. While that hasn't happened, the grant has affected the Goths in subtler ways: Kids who already feel keenly different from others have had the notion reinforced by no less an authority than the federal government.

When I ask Brennan about the grant and the negative attention it has placed on him and his friends, he is blunt. "Some dumb fucks at Columbine shot somebody, and now we all have to pay the price," he says.

Because the media (mistakenly) referred to the Columbine shooters as Goths, kids who can be categorized as belonging to the subculture, however loosely, have drawn particular suspicion. The movement, which largely grew out of '70s British punk, originally combined spook-show fashion with atmospheric or macabre music, but now any kid who shops at Hot Topic, watches horror movies, and listens to metal could be construed as Goth.

— "Village of the Darned" / Steve Kurutz / March '04

12 Essential Goth Records

1.

The Cure
Pornography
(1982)

2.
Siouxie and the Banshees
The Scream
(1978)

3.

Bauhaus
The Sky's Gone Out
(1982)

4.
Joy Division
Unknown Pleasures
(1979)

5.
Joy Division
Closer
(1980)

6.

The Birthday Party
Junkyard
(1982)

7.
This Mortal Coil
It'll End in Tears
(1984)

8.
Sisters of Mercy
Floodland
(1987)

9.

Dead Can Dance
Dead Can Dance
(1984)

10.
Cocteau Twins
Treasure
(1984)

11.

The Cramps
Songs the Lord Taught Us
(1980)

12.
The Cure
Disintergration
(1989)

[MARILYN MANSON]

Whether he's embodying the Antichrist, morphing into an asexual alien drug advocate, or merely dressing like a dandyish Goth vampire, Marilyn Manson never stops keeping it unreal. Ever since his music was blamed for the 1999 Columbine school shootings, he has struggled with commercial failure (2000's *Holy Wood* album sold poorly) and personal complexity (he endured a breakup with actress Rose McGowan and the departure of longtime musical collaborator, Twiggy Ramirez). But one thing about Manson has not changed—he's still really, really funny.

Spin: Is *The Golden Age of Grotesque* still moving your aesthetic toward nihilism, or are you moving away from that concept?
Marilyn Manson: This record spits in the face of nihilism. I feel like I've already directed and confronted my ideas against the outside world, and I think closing that chapter and trying to look at things in a different way is what I'm doing now. This album is meant to be about relationships, some of which are personal and some of which deal with the relationship between chaos and order. I took a lot of influences from Berlin and decadence and censorship and fascism and Dada. It's antiauthoritarian in a simpler sense.

You mention absinthe—is it safe to say that *The Golden Age of Grotesque* is the first "absinthe-fueled" album of the modern era?
Well, it's not the first album I've made while drinking absinthe, but this album does embrace the release of imagination that absinthe taps into. Listen to the title track: That song was completely written and recorded in 12 hours, on one bottle of absinthe. That song sounds like absinthe.

Would you say your life is less sleazy than it was five years ago?
Well, I just finished watching a film I made of myself having a threesome with conjoined twins, so I would say no.

Was it real sex, or was it staged?
I don't know what "staged" means. When you have sex with anybody, it's staged, isn't it? You're worried what they're thinking; they're worried what you're thinking. But I had to worry what two people were thinking. And I had to film it.

Who's the sleaziest rock star you've ever partied with?
If Courtney Love was still a rock star, I'd say her. She had razor bumps on her bikini line, and that almost made me vomit. She was always bruised and dirty, and at least in the beginning, there was a lot of charm to it. To her credit, she probably wears that crown really proudly. I don't dislike her.

What would be harder for you: to never be able to have sex again or to never be able to consume drugs, alcohol, and red meat for the rest of your life?
I'd shoot myself.

That's not an acceptable answer. There's no death option. You have to pick.
[Long pause] I suppose I'd cut off my dick and smoke it. That's the only thing I could do. Get the ultimate high and then bleed to death.

You have a song on this album titled "Slutgarden." What's in a slutgarden?
Well, what do *you* think is in a slutgarden?

Well, besides the sluts.
Let me put it this way—what would you find in a normal garden?

Oh, I don't know—carrots, potatoes, maybe flowers....
Flowers. Yes. Flowers. And dirt. And a gardener. So there you go.

— "Who: Marilyn Manson" / Chuck Klosterman / June '03

"Goth is basically glam without its sense of humor, replacing glam's bubblegum self-mockery with prog-rock delusions of grandeur."
— review of *The Pink and the Black: A Goth & Glam Collection* / Chuck Eddy / August '98

Don't let anyone tell you the Age of Irony is over. It's alive and well in California, and here's proof: Goth kids love Disneyland. On the final Sunday of every August, droves of goth-tacular witches and warlocks drive to Anaheim and enter the foreboding inner sanctum of Mickey's Toontown. Welcome to Bats Day in the Fun Park, the annual SoCal collision of goth culture and family fun.

"L.A. Goth is very different from Goth everywhere else in America," explains Bats Day coordinator and Disney superfan Noah Korda, the diminutive 31-year-old who spearheads the pilgrimage. "I mean, it's cold everywhere else. In places like Chicago, it's gloomy. But Goths in California are mostly happy people. I was just the kind of person who was always interested in creepy crap. For me, this has never been about being sad or alienated."

Bats Day began in 1998. At the time, it was just an excuse to be weird: A few regulars from Hollywood Goth clubs like Helter Skelter and Perversion decided to drop acid and walk around Disneyland on a summer afternoon. The following year it was officially dubbed "Bats Day," and it has grown ever since. When the sun was at its zenith on August 25 of this year, more than 500 black-cloaked iconoclasts were tromping around Mickey's playland.

It is not, however, a Disney-sanctioned event.

"We don't contact the park," says Korda. "And they probably wouldn't care, but just in case, I don't want to give them a chance to come up with a reason to shut it down. But it's got to be pretty obvious that this is going on."

At times during Bats Day, it was impossible to swing a dead cat in Disneyland without hitting a Goth (of course, if you *had* swung a dead cat around at Disneyland, a few of these kids probably would have found that pretty awesome). Here's a Dionysian diary from the day of the Disney Dead:

11:07 am: My first error: I see a goateed guy wearing a skull T-shirt, accompanied by a black-haired girlfriend with more tattoos than Tupac and a complexion the color of cocaine. I ask him how many years he has participated in Bats Day in the Fun Park, but it turns out he has no idea what I'm talking about. "We just came here for the hell of it," says the 27-year-old Brandon Stratton. "I had no idea any of this was going on." Stratton and I then have a brief conversation about Tim Burton movies while his girlfriend stares at me silently, probably fantasizing about how I would look swinging from a gallows.

Noon: The highlight of our mass photograph in front of The Sleeping Beauty Castle is the appearance of Snow White's nemesis, the Evil Queen, an uber-wicked woman roundly cheered by hundreds of Goth minions who evidently see her as some kind of role model. These guys certainly dig the black-hearted bitches. Moments later, an actress portraying the virginal Snow White tries to get into the picture, and everyone boos her into submission.

5:32 pm: I find myself inside a log on an underground river. Everything smells like chlorine and Hot Topic. The girls in front of me are giggling at the animatronic rabbits surrounding us, and I find myself thinking, "How did America become terrified of these people?" Two trench-coat-clad kids in Colorado may have become twisted killing machines and ruined it for everybody else, but most of these Goths are the kind of folk who laugh at fur-covered robots.

The ride concludes when the log plummets 50 feet into a mini tsunami. I bid my soaked newfound acquaintances good-bye as they reapply their makeup.

— "Something Wicked This Way Comes" / Chuck Klosterman / December '02

/ Simon **Reynolds**

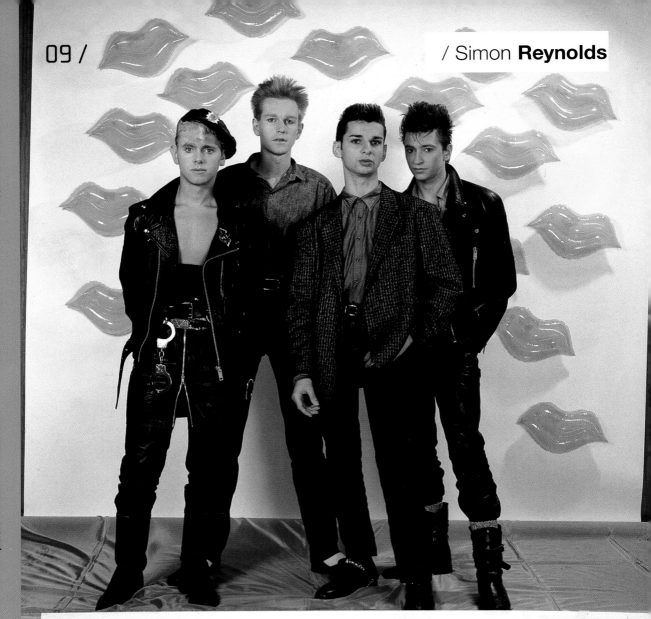

[DEPECHE MODE]

: Synth-Pop
Depeche Mode,
The Human League,
and the soul of the machine

Synthesizers in pop go back further than you might think.

Prog rockers loved 'em: ELP's Keith Emerson let rip many a Moog solo, Rick Wakeman from Yes performed behind a vast bank of keyboards, and German bands such as Tangerine Dream sketched the face of the cosmos with Mellotrons and ARPs. At the other end of the spectrum, Stevie Wonder pioneered the use of electronics in R&B (with tech guidance from two white geeks who went by the name Tonto's Expanding Head Band). And the blurts of abstract noise from Brian Eno's EMS VCS3 on those first two Roxy Music albums turned a generation on to the avant-pop potential of synths.

Still, the synth-pop era as commonly understood—the early '80s Britwave of Human League, Gary Numan, Soft Cell, Depeche Mode—really started in 1977, with two epochal singles: Kraftwerk's "Trans Europe Express" and Donna Summer's "I Feel Love." The missing link between Beethoven and Paul Van Dyk, "Trans Europe Express" conjured the spiritual dimension of technological progress—"all the dynamism of modern life" as K-werk commandant Ralf Hutter put it—with its arching Doppler synths and tireless machine beats. Produced by Giorgio Moroder, "I Feel Love" was the first disco record to be made entirely from synthetic sounds; its clockwork-precise bassline and coldly glittering electronics helped make it a massive worldwide hit.

For many young musicians who'd been mobilized by punk's do-it-yourself rallying cry, the impact of these two tracks was revolutionary: Suddenly the format of guitars, bass, and drums seemed archaic, exhausted. By happy coincidence, just at this moment, synths—hitherto the preserve of wealthy prog-rockers—became affordable, portable, and user-friendly. New items like the Wasp were like orchestras in a box, which is one reason why synth-pop was full of duos that split roles neatly between a singer/lyricist and a composer/machine-operator: Soft Cell, Eurythmics, DAF, Pet Shop Boys, Erasure.

You simply didn't need a whole band of instrumentalists, and that became even more the case when programmable drum machines like the Linn emerged at the end of the '70s. That said, two notable exceptions to the duo norm also happen to be probably the most famous synth-pop outfits of all time: The Human League and Depeche Mode.

From the North-of-England industrial city of Sheffield, The Human League began as two synth nerds (Ian Craig Marsh, Martyn Ware), a singer with a presciently lopsided hair style covering half his face (Phil Oakey), and a fellow who projected Pop Art-influenced slides behind the band (Adrian Wright). In 1979, David Bowie proclaimed The Human League to be the sound of the future. But after two modest-selling albums of almost-pop, the group split acrimoniously.

Everyone assumed the synth boffins, who'd formed a new group called Heaven 17, would make it, and that the vocalist and Director of Visuals were the talent-free rump doomed to obscurity. But Oakey recruited two teenagers, Joanne Catherall and Susanne Sulley, as backing singers after spotting them at a Sheffield nightclub. With the "ordinary girl" charm of their fallible voices and amateurish dance moves, Catherall and Sulley humanized the League for the first time. Brunette and blonde respectively, the girls' presence created an Abba-like visual chemistry while also banishing the group's geeky science-student image, something further enhanced when Oakey stopped writing songs inspired by Philip K. Dick and black holes and started singing about L.O.V.E.

The second masterstroke came when they found their own Giorgio Moroder in producer Martin Rushent, a bearded music-biz veteran who combined arrangement skills acquired by working for the likes of James Bond soundtrack diva Shirley Bassey with a gear-head's passion for the latest music technology. The result was a perfect sequence of U.K. hits—"The Sound of the Crowd," "Love Action," "Open Your Heart," "Don't You Want Me"—that demolished the synthesizer's image as cold and soul-less. "Don't You Want Me" reached Number 1 on both sides of the Atlantic, boosted by its classic promo clip, which, Jean-Luc Godard style, depicted the band making its own video.

Compared to Human League's postmodern wit or the kinky noir imagery of Soft Cell, Depeche Mode initially

seemed like lightweights, with disposable ditties such as "New Life" and "Just Can't Get Enough." When their main songwriter Vince Clarke quit to form Yaz, people assumed Depeche would be forgotten within a year. But the group, originally signed to the adventurous independent label Mute, had their own edgy aspirations. Stepping in as chief writer, Martin Gore started to explore life's deviant precincts. He split up with his prim Christian girlfriend and spent time in Berlin, checking out everything from sleazy bondage clubs to performances by metal-bashing avant-primitivists Einsturzende Neubauten.

Depeche Mode also admired Neubauten's U.K. counterparts, Test Dept, a gang of left-wing skinheads whose clangorous steel symphonies celebrated the might of the working class, even as they were being rendered obsolete by the decline of heavy industry. Borrowing Test Dept's Constructivist imagery, Depeche titled their 1983 album *Construction Time Again* and put a hammer on the front cover, echoing the Soviet hammer-and-sickle. The single "Everything Counts" featured a desolate refrain that sounded like a socialist wringing his hands in the wake of Thatcher's reelection, while the lyrics critiqued '80s enterprise culture: "the grabbing hands grab all they can… it's a competitive world." Full of metal-on-metal percussion and sampled noises, Depeche's next hits, "People Are People" and "Master and Servant," took Neubauten and Test Dept's ideas into the pop

ESSAY CONTINUES ON NEXT PAGE >

"Rock'n'roll all goes back to R&B, but to me it's not very relevant. **Kraftwerk is much more relevant.** I didn't really even listen to the Beatles. What they got away with was absolute murder; people wouldn't get away with that now. What they did was almost nursery rhymes. If we came out with something on that level, like 'she loves you, yeah, yeah, yeah,' for our first single, forget it."

— Duran Duran's Nick Rhodes / '87

[DURAN DURAN]

As groups like Duran Duran and Human League blasted through MTV and Top 40 radio, Depeche Mode remained a faceless enigma. They were reluctant to have their picture on albums or magazines. They preferred to let their songs speak for themselves. Fronted by Vince Clarke (who left early on to form Yaz, then Erasure), Depeche Mode were four suburban teens devoted to a then-experimental instrument—the synthesizer.

"To us, it was a punk instrument," explains the group's songwriter Martin Gore. "It was an instant, do-it-yourself kind of tool. And because it was still new, its potential seemed limitless." The music was a reaction to the '70s mega-rock legacy—big names, big jam sessions, big egos. "We found it all a bit impersonal," says keyboardist Andy Fletcher. "We don't think you have to be a great musician to be allowed to play and get a message out. I guess that's what punk was all about, getting rid of the ego and getting right down to it without having to be a session guitarist. We certainly didn't know anything about playing music when we first started."

"There's a great tenderness and sadness to our music sometimes," he continues, "and I know this is going to sound like a stereotype, but gays in general seem to be more open and receptive to these types of lyrics."
— "Pop à la Mode" / Marisa Fox / July '90

Thank You is the most ill-conceived, worst-timed move since Sinead O'Connor's *Am I Not Your Girl?*, something that should have been released as a rarities package in 2003, or might have found ironic vitality if circulated as a bootleg. Witness, for example, the version of Grandmaster Flash's "White Lines." Simon LeBon had to hire Grandmaster Flash and Melle Mel to do most of the rap; the few lines he whines stand out like Newt Gingrich in Compton. The band rhythmically alters the familiar two-chord riff and transforms it mainly into a guitar line. An audacious move, one that could work for someone (can't think who), but the final result sounds more like a soft-drink commercial than an anti-drug rant. The version of Public Enemy's "911 Is A Joke" is a joke, and not one in particularly good taste. They say they covered it because they knew it would piss people off, but coming from a band devoid of rebellion, it sounds as convincing as Amy Grant covering GG Allin. And not as funny.

Duran disgraces itself, Love and Rockets, and the Temptations simultaneously with "Ball of Confusion." "Watching the Detectives" distorts that passable Brit-reggae rave-up into Holiday Inn lounge fare. It takes two mixes of "I Wanna Take You Higher" [sic] to come up with a watered-down version of U2's "Mysterious Ways" that's halfway listenable. LeBon does an excellent impression of Robert Plant being catheterized with a shrimp de-veiner on their version of "Thank You."
— review of *Thank You* by Duran Duran / James Hannaham / May '95

> ESSAY CONTINUES FROM PREVIOUS PAGE

mainstream. Lyrically informed by Gore's forays through Berlin's S&M underworld, "Master and Servant" connected bedroom and boardroom to make a witty personal-is-political allegory about power games: "It's a lot like life," he sings, so "forget all about equality." Proceeding through a check-list of Weighty Subjects with methodical determination, Depeche tackled religion on 1984's "Blasphemous Rumours," which impudently suggested that "God's got a sick sense of humor."

In the late '80s, Depeche Mode's music got more sophisticated and melodically haunting with albums like *Black Celebration* and *Music For the Masses*. They scored their first genuine U.S. hits with "Personal Jesus" and "Enjoy the Silence" and built a reputation as a fierce live act. Depeche's tours of America took in ever-larger audiences, peaking with a 1988 show at the Pasadena Rose Bowl witnessed by 70,000 ecstatic fans. By this point, Depeche Mode were second only to U2 as a big-in-America band from the British Isles. Depeche's music got rockier too. As with other synth-pioneers such as Human League, Soft Cell, and Eurythmics (all of whom they'd outlasted commercially), at a certain point the only way forward for Depeche was to incorporate non-synthetic instrumental textures.

All this culminated in the bluesy grind of 1993's "I Feel You."

Around this time, singer Dave Gahan underwent a bizarre transformation. Dumping his wife and kids, he moved to Los Angeles and got deeply into tattoos, facial hair, and drugs. Suicide attempts and drug overdoses followed. For Depeche's original following, all this rockist nonsense must have been deeply puzzling. After all, for sensitive and maladjusted types, a huge part of the appeal of being into all that "faggy" music by eyeliner-wearing Anglo fops was that it served as a potent form of dissidence: a way of defining yourself against the standard high-school fare of Mötley Crüe and Ozzy. But here was formerly fresh-faced Gahan mutating into …well, Dave Navarro, basically. The horror….

Grunge returned guitars to dominance for most of the '90s. Eighties synth-pop was either completely forgotten or recalled only as a joke—all those preposterous New Romantic haircuts and fey eyeliner boys playing one-finger synth melodies. Then, gradually, the contempt turned to amused affection, and by the eve of the new millenium, a full-blown early-'80s revival got rolling. It began as a retro-ironic fad within the techno world, with groups like Adult and Les Rhythmes Digitales, whose "Hey You What's That

Sound" came with a video that skewered the charmingly clumsy graphic effects that seemed so futuristic in 1983. Soon scenes blossomed in the hipsterlands of Brooklyn, Berlin, and elsewhere, with clubbers rocking a mash-up of new-wave-style signifiers— asymmetrical haircuts, skinny ties worn over collar-less T-shirts, studded belts and wristbands. The soundtrack mixed classics with new tracks by artists like Miss Kittin and Vitalic, who studiously deployed vintage synth sounds, vocoderized cyborg-vocals, 16th-note basslines, and archly inflexible drum machine beats. Known as "electroclash" or "nu-wave", the revival was the big hype of 2002, but it never penetrated the mainstream, and soon the hipsters moved on to pillaging another seam of retro (late '70s postpunk).

What few noticed was that '80s synth-pop had already resurfaced on the charts in the most unlikely guise: nü-metal. Multi-platinum selling Linkin Park roar at the choruses, sure, but their verses drip with the wan and slightly wussy melancholy of prime-era Depeche Mode, suggesting that the band was born at precisely that moment in the early '90s when MTV would play "Enjoy the Silence" back to back with ballads by Queensryche and Metallica.

We have a confession to make: We screamed like teenage girls while reporting this item. Sure, we scream like teenage girls all the time, but this meant so much to us. Like a birthday or a pretty view. It was, after all, the first U.S. Duran Duran concert featuring the original lineup since Live Aid back in 1985! The reunited New Romantic icons—Simon Le Bon, Nick Rhodes, and the still-quite-handsome-in-middle-age John, Andy, and Roger Taylor—packed Sunset Strip nightclub the Roxy in July and treated die-hard fans and celeb Durannies Beck, Gwen Stefani, Tony Kanal, and Mark McGrath to a set full of classics ("Hungry Like The Wolf," "Girls On Film," "Notorious") and potential new material from their forthcoming comeback album (the upbeat "What Happens Tomorrow"). Nobody seemed to mind the Sri-Lankan rain forest-style swelter inside the relatively tiny venue. "I love that face-to-face thing you get in little clubs where you can smell each other," Le Bon told us after the show.
— "Noise: Boys Gone Wild" / Marc Spitz / October '03

SPIN: People have always seemed to either love Depeche Mode and possess your every remix, or hate you and think synth-pop is the devil incarnate.

Dave Gahan: Those are good reactions.... If nothing else, Depeche Mode has changed the idea of what a rock band is. To be this band of doom and yet to go on stage and have 20,000 people screaming at the top of their lungs—what more can you want?
— May 1997

Essential Synth-Pop

Dismissed by rock chauvinists as a trendy haven for fops, wimps, geeks, and cyborgs and beloved by fops, wimps, geeks, and cyborgs as a computer-world improvement on punk, disco, and soul, synth-pop has endured and mutated for more than two decades. Though largely a singles format in its '80s heyday, it's also produced some pretty brilliant albums.

Gary Numan
The Pleasure Principle
(Atco, 1979)

Numan gave us "Cars," a Beach Boys song idling on Kraftwerk's Autobahn, and the rest of his debut is a study in droll futurism. "Metal," "Airlane," "Engineers," and "Complex" all deadpan the same routine—a bored machine hums rudely over a parodic, sterile groove until you just give up and admit it's kinda funky. Basement Jaxx thought so—they sampled "M.E." on "Where's Your Head At?"

The Human League
Dare
(A&M, 1981)

On the surface, these ice-planet pretties sounded like they'd learned about love from J.G. Ballard's "Crash." Beneath the surface—well, there was no beneath the surface. *Dare*'s creeping, bleeping anthems about consumption and desire cut like a knife because they're only skin deep. When the band finally warm up—on "Don't You Want Me"—it feels like the rebirth of soul music.
also try: Heaven 17's *The Luxury Gap* (Virgin, 1983), a Eurotrashed glimpse into the tyranny of fun.

Prince
Dirty Mind
(Warner Bros., 1980)

The synth was practically the only instrument Prince didn't play on *Dirty Mind* (he only left that in the capable hands of Dr. Fink), but his most concise statement of polymorphous freakery was the ideal middle-ground between the Gap Band's drop-the-bomb bass bounce and the Cars' feathered-and-leathered new-wave whoosh.

New Order
Power, Corruption, and Lies
(Qwest, 1983)

The holy grail of post-punk dance pop. The guitars are jealous of the electronics, singer Bernard Sumner wishes he had the drum machine's nerve, and the songs sway from indie funeral dirges to dawn-of-rave epistles. "Sound formed in a vacuum may seem a waste of time," wonders Sumner, sweeping out the ashes of Joy Division. Then it's "Blue Monday" and his future comes calling.

Scritti Politti
Cupid & Psyche 85
(Warner Bros., 1985)

Green Gartside's posh-boy melodies were as effortless as his use of the word *hermeneutic*. He had a voice like a pixie stick, but Gartside was a pop maverick, rewriting the book of love from the inside. Best feminist anthem ever by a lovelorn dandy: "The Word Girl," about the word *girl*.

Depeche Mode
Catching Up With Depeche Mode
(Sire, 1985)

The sound of Chic-y gloom monkeys in love with technology ("New Life"), kinky repetition ("Just Can't Get Enough"), and their own transcendently elegant narcissism ("Dreaming Of Me"). Things went downhill after genius songwriter Vince Clarke left to form Yaz, but at the bottom of that hill sits "Somebody," synth-pop's purest power ballad.
also try: OMD's *Architecture & Morality* (Virgin, 1981), the thinking man's Mode.

Pet Shop Boys
Introspective
(EMI, 1988)

From its AIDS allegory to its prayer for "revolution in South Africa," the Boys' Chicago-house missive is also one of the best political records of the '80s. They read rebellion into buying a new Chihuahua, they give Willie Nelson a defiant mirror-ball makeover, and the whole thing can transport anyone to their own private Ibiza.

The Magnetic Fields
The Charm of the Highway Strip
(Merge, 1994)

Synth-pop was all about alienation. And what could be more alienating than camped-up Casio country songs by an Ecstasy-era Oscar Wilde from New York's East Village? Stephin Merritt imagines hand-me-down American archetypes—Daniel Webster, Calamity Jane—as extras in an Erasure video.

Book of Love
I Touch Roses—The Best Of The Book Of Love
(Reprise, 2001)

For all the attacks on synth-pop as "pussy music," women were usually treated as decoration in some dude's knob-twisting fantasy. Not so with Philadelphia's Book of Love, three warm *Heathers*-ettes (and one guy) proclaiming, "I'm not a boy," and filling clubs with a single about masturbation called "I Touch Roses."

Black Box Recorder
The Facts of Life
(Jetset, 2001)

Songs about Depeche Mode fans at middle age crying over old mix tapes. Luke Haines, John Moore, and Sarah Nixey write lush micro-ballads that nail the moment when tingle becomes chill. "The English Motorway System" hotwires "Cars" to go in circles; "The Art of Driving" takes "Don't You Want Me" from marriage to mortgage.

— Jon Dolan / March '04

10 /

/ Dave **Itzkoff**

: ’80s teen movies

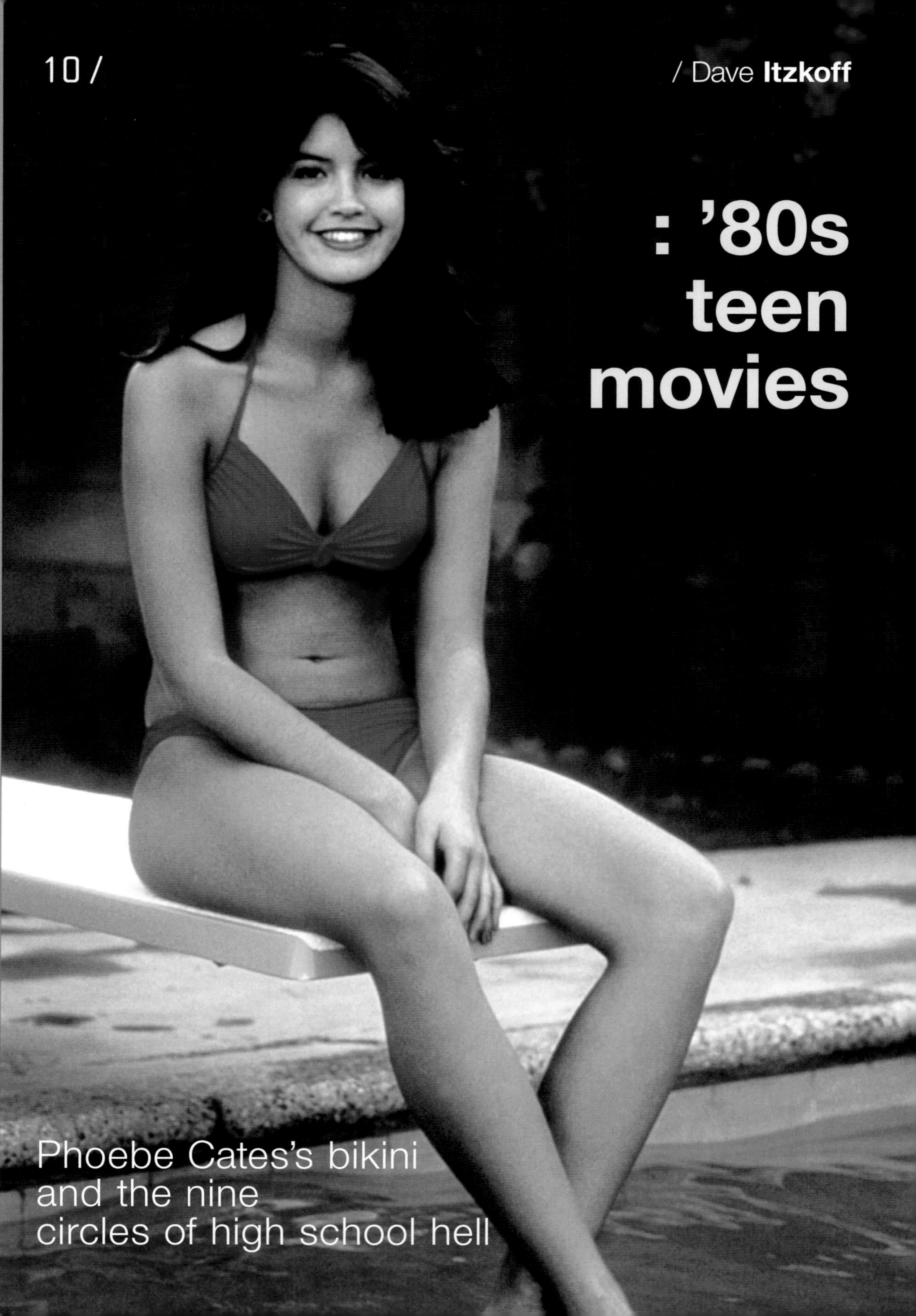

Phoebe Cates’s bikini and the nine circles of high school hell

Having spent the 1980s focused exclusively on films about heroes who wielded lightsabers, leather whips, and Batarangs,

I must confess that I missed the original theatrical run of nearly every teen movie released that decade. This in and of itself was not so detrimental to my upbringing —the problem was that my introduction to almost every single one of these titles came via censored versions on network television. Not only did I grow up thoroughly perplexed by much of Judd Nelson's dialogue in *The Breakfast Club* ("No, Dad, what about you? Flip you!"), I also had no clue there was a sequence in which the Breakfast Clubbers got high together. And when my father told me that there was a scene in *Fast Times At Ridgemont High* where Phoebe Cates took off her bikini top, I insisted he was lying.

Never mind why my dad and I were watching *Fast Times* together—my point is that I never even suspected these moments had been excised, because I had no reason to believe such scenes ever existed. Up until the '80s, Hollywood had a proud tradition of depicting young people behaving in ways they'd never really behave, doing things they'd never really do. James Dean's Jim Stark was a rebel without a cause who didn't smoke dope or use dirty words; Frankie Avalon spent the '60s chasing Annette Funicello through a series of beach-party movies, and

never once tried to cop a feel underneath her blanket.

Chalk it up to whichever factor you want—the groundbreaking screenplay by Cameron Crowe (who had just barely emerged from his teenage years), a generation of filmgoers whose senses had been overstimulated by tits-and-slash exploitation films like *Friday the 13th*, or the fact that Phoebe Cates and Jennifer Jason Leigh just needed the exposure, but everything changed with *Fast Times*. Sure, it showed the kids of Ridgemont High doing the sort of things normal American teenagers did (i.e., whatever the hell they felt like doing), but it also showed how they were affected by the consequences of their actions. They cut class and got stoned, they stole one another's cars and girlfriends, they jerked off and they fucked, they quit their McJobs at the drop of a paper hat. They also felt guilty and angry and humiliated, and they got pregnant and had abortions. Tell me this movie was made solely to swindle mallrats out of their hard-earned allowance dollars, and I'll toss a pot of hot coffee in your face, Judge Reinhold-style.

What's surprising is that so many of the teen movies that followed (aside from the unimpeachable oeuvre of John Hughes) didn't aspire to a similar sense of realism. The first two films of the John Cusack Trilogy, *Better Off Dead* and *One Crazy Summer* (from director "Savage" Steve Holland), were absurdist comedies, and its concluding chapter, *Say Anything...* (also written and directed by Cameron Crowe), abandons any sense of verisimilitude the moment Cusack shows up in Ione Skye's driveway with a boombox atop his head. The basic premise of *Heathers*, one of the finest movies of the '80s in any genre, is totally preposterous, but behind Winona Ryder and Christian Slater's plan to kill their

way through the graduating class of Westerburg High is a more fundamental pact between its filmmakers and its viewers: If we trust them enough to follow their morbidly pitch-black comedy from start to finish, they'll show us just how deeply they understand the attendant angst of the teenage experience, and how much trust they place in the intelligence of their audience. When Winona challenges her cliquish tormentors to lick up her vomit—a line that no oppressed high schooler would ever really utter—she's speaking for every adolescent who's always known how real life can suck losers dry.

Even in a world where Columbine never happened, it's impossible to imagine that a film like *Heathers* could get made now, because that basic trust no longer exists. Today's teens are so media-savvy that only self-aware silliness like the *American Pie* and *Scary Movie* franchises can draw them to the theaters, and the current studio system is so risk-averse that it will only greenlight inspirational pablum starring former Disney Channel princesses. Shamelessly swiping pages from the *Fast Times* playbook probably won't be enough to resurrect the genre at this point: Had Lindsay Lohan taken her top off in the hopelessly cynical *Mean Girls*, it might have made the high-school boys happy, but it wouldn't have made for a better film. Are Mandy Moore's *How to Deal* and Hilary Duff's *A Cinderella Story* the best that 21st-century high-schoolers are entitled to? Hard to believe, but that era bookended by Jeff Spicoli and Lloyd Dobler was a minor cultural renaissance, one that isn't likely to be repeated any time soon, but one that lives on in perpetuity in basic-cable reruns and expanded director's cut DVDs at your local Wal-Mart. Lick it up, baby. Lick it up.

John Hughes

/ Elvis **Mitchell**

There's a reason that '80s teen movies run on TNT under the rubric "the new classics." Yes, it's mostly because the movies are terrible and someone is trying to give them a new marketing lease on life. But in their day—way before the WB used the formula on "Smallville" to turn the Superman mythos into melodrama after abandoning the black…um, urban sitcom audience—these films did something unusual. For one thing, it was the first time teenagers onscreen were portrayed by actors actually still in their teens, or who at least could pass for teenagers. (There wouldn't be a WB without the stack of color-Xeroxes of John Hughes' sensibility—from "Popular" to "Gilmore Girls" to "Smallville" to "One Tree Hill" and beyond, a yellow-brick road of the sincerest form of flattery.) For an example of what I mean, dig under that moldering stack of your dad's Nintendo cartridges in the basement and pull out his VHS copy of the teen raunch-out *Porky's*, in which the high school students seem the same age as the teachers. Keep in mind that there was once a time in which African-Americans were portrayed by whites in make-up (or Michael Jackson).

And it was the first time that the young audiences weren't being patronized by the filmmakers, an attitude which often manifested itself as middle-aged producers apparently leering at the girls onscreen. In the case of the man who single-handedly made the '80s teen movie a viable commodity whose influence still dictates the way movies for younger filmgoers are made—John Hughes—the movies had a deeply felt sense of yearning, a streak of oil on the glass left by noses pressed against the window that wouldn't be out of place in F. Scott Fitzgerald's tale of misplaced longing, "The Great Gatsby," or "Bernice Bobs Her Hair." As simply and compellingly articulated by the extraordinarily empathetic Molly Ringwald, who grew up in Hughes' movies, there was an emotional intelligence in the director's characterizations that spoke to a demographic—Holler!—which had never been the recipient of such sincerely communicated teenage feelings onscreen.

Ringwald's emotions dwelled just beneath the surface of her skin, and were always unashamedly visible; she possessed a capacity for unadorned directness that shamed trained actresses twice her age, who generally displayed emotion with trembling chins and eyelash batting that contained all of the subtlety of spam mail on combating erectile dysfunction. In addition to finding the right performer to radiate his sensibility, a filmic surrogate for the director (in absolute terms, Molly Ringwald was the Robert De Niro to his Martin Scorsese, the Arnold Schwarzenegger to his James Cameron, the Zach Braff to his Zach Braff), Hughes' essential gift as a filmmaker and storyteller was an instinctive understanding of the sheer, harrowing import of minute-to-minute life in the secondary education years, where choosing the wrong T-shirt was a tragedy of epic and sweeping proportions. His films were a reaction to years of miscalculated, second-rate teen movies tackier—and more artificial—than Mango Melon Starbursts.

It helped, too, that Hughes chose songs for his films—a thoughtful selection of don't-let-me-be-misunderstood, hothouse post-punk—that came directly out of his temperament. They functioned as an aural camera obscura, and the self-absorbed angst of those songs added to the willful dramatic ambience: a cinema of stubborn, superficial outsiders. He went so far as to name one of his movies after a Psychedelic Furs song about playful sexual obsession, "Pretty in Pink." By cleaning up the subtext, since the title refers to nudity, it became the equivalent of using the La's wrenching ode to heroin addiction, "There She Goes," for a birth control commercial (but thank God something like that could never really happen).

Unfortunately, "Pretty in Pink," with its connotations of rosy flesh, could have been the title of any Hughes' movies. Despite his capability for rendering pre-college heartbreak ("The Breakfast Club," "Sixteen Candles") or the occasional triumph over high school anxiety ("Ferris Bueller's Day Off"), the paleface panorama in his films is off-putting; his movies are whiter than an episode of "Friends," or the Hollywood issue of *Vanity Fair*. Lisa Bonet reportedly turned down the role that Lea Thompson eventually took in "Some Kind of Wonderful" because she didn't want to shoulder the burden of being the only chocolate chip in the acres of vanilla-frosted Angel Food cake seen in Hughes' movies. It'd be nice to note things have changed in teen movies since the '80s and I suppose they have. But not quite, to quote Brad Pitt in "Ocean's Eleven," more than somewhat.

It's probably worth noting that TV has assumed the mantle of suburban, written-in-the-sand suffering and made a whole new industry of it. "Freaks and Geeks" used the misery scrawled in the margins of high school yearbooks for satire, and Claire Danes and Jared Leto emerged with careers from "My So-Called Life," a fusing of Hughes and the anguish of "thirtysomething" from the latter's creators. Imagine that: an intergenerational intersection of heartbreak. Suddenly, Hughes seems like the Roy Lichtenstein of film.

"What's scarier than high school? What's scarier than adolescence?"

— Sarah Michelle Gellar, 1997

A Blizzard of White Panties:
Celebrating Nearly 50 Years of Awesomely Shameless Teen Entertainment

[**note**: The teensploitation rating (TX RATING) is an assessment of how much an entry flaunts teen stereotypes, not of the quality of the entry.]

J.D. flicks
Film genre, 1955-60
TX rating: 8.0
J.D. stands for "juvenile delinquent": your bad seed; your moody, brooding type; your loner who runs in packs. Like the inner-city hoods of *Blackboard Jungle* or their anti-authoritarian middle-class suburban counterparts in *Rebel Without a Cause*. The enterprising thugs of *The Cool and the Crazy* take special care to stay in school; it's good for their pot dealership. The rich-kid racketeer of *High School Caesar* cares so much about school spirit that he rigs a student election in his favor. **LEGACY**: The Sweathogs.

Mamie van Doren
Icon, 1957-60
TX rating: 9.7
This buxom, bottle-blond bomb-shell (the original 28-year-old teenager) finds herself playing either the bad girl or the very bad girl in a string of B-pitchers. In succession, she does hard time on a girls' prison farm (*Untamed Youth*); gets all bollixed up with reefer-mad beatnik teens (*High School Confidential, The Beat Generation*); lands in the stir a second time, in a juvy jail run by nuns (*Girls Town*); and, foreshadowing today's coeds, is a high-IQ stripper/academic (*Sex Kittens go to College*)—all in time for her 30th birthday in 1961. **LEGACY**: In 1990, a 42-year-old Luke Perry wins a starring role on *90210*.

The Many Loves of Dobie Gillis
TV show, 1959-63
TX rating: 7.5
Dobie Gillis, a none-too-ambitious-or-attractive high-schooler, lives for three things: girls; his best buddy, the dirty, lazy, jazz-digging beatnik Maynard (a pre-*Gilligan* Bob Denver); and girls. **LEGACY**: Gillis does that talking-directly-to-the-viewers thing *Ferris Bueller's Day Off* later swipes; first TV appearance of the goatee.

AIP's Frankie and Annette Beach Movies
Film genre, 1959-65
TX rating: 6.9
In American International Pictures' *Beach Party* (and its countless sequels), Frankie Avalon and Annette Funicello soak up the rays, fend off 50-year-old bikers, and shimmy in the sand to the latest musical acts both cool (Dick Dale, James Brown, Stevie Wonder) and corny (future *Dynasty* star Linda Evans, Mickey Rooney). **LEGACY**: *Baywatch*.

Bye Bye Birdie
Film, 1963
TX rating: 7.2
Singing sensation Conrad Birdie (Jesse Pearson) joins the Army, to the consternation of every female under the age of 18. The first musical explicitly about teens and rock'n'roll has plenty of the former and precious little of the latter. Based on the real-life Elvis-gets-drafted panic felt in all teen quarters. **LEGACY**: Future rock musicals all have some actual rock content.

Wild in the Streets
Film, 1968
TX rating: 9.8
Inexplicably, the voting age is lowered to 14, and civic-minded young Americans naturally cast their ballots for their fave teen rocker, Max Frost. As a result of his election, the nation's capital, unlike real-life Washington, becomes rife with sex, drugs, and rock'n'roll. President Frost locks away everyone over the age of 30 and force-feeds them LSD. **LEGACY**: Voting age lowered to 18 in 1971.

Badlands
Film, 1973
TX rating: 7.6
One of the most artful and poetic articulations of teen angst yet, *Badlands* stars Sissy Spacek as a virginal 15-year-old who falls for local rebel Martin Sheen. Thwarted in his affections by Spacek's over-protective father, Sheen blows him away before setting fire to the house, and the two embark on a cross-country killing spree. **LEGACY**: *True Romance* (down to the score), *Natural Born Killers*.

American Graffiti
Film, 1973
TX rating: 8.0
The greatest coming-of-age-in-the-'50s saga—ostensibly about a night in the life of two California 18-year-olds (Richard Dreyfuss and Ron Howard) facing graduation and an uncertain adult future—actually takes place in 1962. The cast is a future *Who's Who* of Hollywood; the soundtrack is a greaser's dream; and the result is nothing less than a practice run in epic mythmaking for its director, George Lucas. **LEGACY**: *Happy Days, The Lords of Flatbush, The Hollywood Knights.*

Sarah T: Portrait of a Teenage Alcoholic
TV movie, 1975
TX rating: 8.5
When she has a tough time adjusting to her new school, Linda Blair turns to booze and develops a Texas-size drinking problem. **LEGACY:** The maxim that intensive substance abuse invariably leads to turning tricks.

Carrie
Film, 1976
TX rating: 8.1
The girl-power progenitor who gets back at the bitches who pelt her with tampons and the Jesus-freak mother who locks her in the closet with the Day-Glo crucifix and the kids who vote her prom queen just to see her slathered in pig's blood by using her telekinetic powers to kill them all. **LEGACY:** Carrie II; 1,001 prom jokes.

Dawn: Portrait of a Teenage Runaway
TV movie, 1976
TX rating: 7.0
Twenty-two-year-old Eve Plumb, four years removed from her role as the only Brady more boring than Alice, tries to prove she can handle edgier roles by playing a runaway teen prostitute. **LEGACY:** The "I can so play a tramp" career strategy employed by a long line of wholesome sitcom teens (Dana Plato, Alyssa Milano, et. al.).

James at 15
TV show, 1977-79
TX rating: 7.5
O.G. teen-angst TV drama with the dewy-eyed Lance Kerwin breaks the fourth wall during its second season when it acknowledges that James is actually getting older. *James at 15* becomes *James at 16*. **LEGACY:** *My So-Called Life*; that show with James Van Der Beek.

Corvette Summer
Film, 1978
TX rating: 6.0
Just after *Star Wars* and his disfiguring car wreck, Mark Hamill plays a teen who buys a trashed Corvette and tricks it out (righthand drive to better check out babes on the street!). After it's stolen, he's off to Vegas to get it back. On the way he meets a young Annie Potts, also heading to Vegas. To become a hooker. **LEGACY:** Movie poster quote: "The eternal triangle...a boy, a girl, and a car."

Halloween
Film series, 1978-present
TX rating: 9.5
Slashings of post-coital topless girls and sleepy boys; running up the staircase instead of out the front door (or, better yet, hiding from the knife-wielder in a closet); foolishly thinking the killer who fell two stories after getting shot five times might really be dead. Rad. **LEGACY:** Too many to list.

Brooke Shields
Teen poster girl, 1978-81
TX rating: 8.0
In the early '80s, Shields creates a teen dream that's adorable, shagable, and marketable. After a scandalous role as a preteen hooker in *Pretty Baby*, she hits stride in *Endless Love*, featuring fire-lit orgasms that piss off Dad and get Mom all hot. Public declaration of arrested virginity cools career, despite more faux nudity amid monkey-strewn tropicalia of *The Blue Lagoon*. **LEGACY:** The Lionel Richie/Diana Ross theme song is a perennial roller disco couples-only fave.

Meatballs
Film, 1979
TX rating: 6.0
Hot Canadian camp counselors have adult-style parties on canoes while awkward newbies wrassle with self-esteem. Even more pressing: Who's gonna win the Camp Olympics? See also *Meatballs IV* (Corey Feldman on water skis). **LEGACY:** Spaz.

Over the Edge
Film, 1979
TX rating: 9.0
Knife-wielding juvenile delinquents vandalize and terrorize planned suburban community New Granada. Too young to do time, they shoot BBs at cop cars, smoke pot, snort speed, joyride, ignore curfew, and listen to lots of Cheap Trick. Good clean fun till they get hold of a real gun. Next thing you know, the PTA is on fire. **LEGACY:** Matt Dillon.

Rock'n'Roll High School
Film, 1979
TX rating: 7.0
Like the Davy Jones episode of the Brady Bunch, except P.J. Soles is Marcia and Joey Ramone is Davy. **LEGACY:** The Donnas.

Foxes
Film, 1980
TX rating: 9.5
Four best girlfriends spend a lot of time sleeping late, cutting school, and having an extremely active nightlife. Jodie Foster is the moral center, Scott Baio rides a skateboard, and the Runaways' Cherie Currie is the heart-of-gold friend who's got everyone chasing her around town as she boozes it up and cuddles down with just about anyone. **LEGACY:** Girl Power.

Times Square
Film, 1980
TX rating: 6.5
Bad girl rocker Robin Johnson, a Joan Jett clone, busts good girl misfit Trini Alvarado out of the psych ward in a stolen ambulance. A knife makes them blood sisters; rock-'n'roll sets them free. Alvarado's politico pop cries, "Kidnapper!" Late-night DJ Tim Curry cries, "Folk heroine!" "I'm not kidnapped," yells Alvarado, "I'm me-napped!" **LEGACY:** Johnson's "Damn Dog," a campy, glam club fave.

Tom Cruise
Actor, 1981-83
TX rating: 9.0
Losin' It may be *Risky Business* if you don't have *All the Right Moves*. But if you have a minor role in *The Outsiders*, you may have already found *Endless Love*. **LEGACY:** Wayfarers.

Hot for Teacher Flicks
Film mini-genre, 1981-84
TX rating: 10.0
Dropping grades? How about dropping drawers? Cinematic school-reform proposals such as *Homework*, *My Tutor*, and *The Substitute* argue that if the teachers are hot and put-out, Johnny-underachiever is Harvard-bound. Ultimate schoolboy wet dream lends new meaning to term "study hard." **LEGACY:** "Don't Stand So Close to Me"; Mary Kay Letourneau.

Ladies and Gentlemen, the Fabulous Stains
Film, 1981
TX rating: 9.6
Corinne (a curiously-coiffed Diane Lane) leads a brash, untalented girl-teen punk trio down the slippery slope of looming stardom amid a cutthroat music scene. The two Sex Pistols guys nobody cares about play a rival punk group in this early-'80s straight-to-HBO rock satire. Rare. Unparalleled. **LEGACY:** Riot grrrls; "Suckers! I'm perfect. And I don't put out."

Porky's
Film, 1981
TX rating: 10.0
Peeping cheerleaders through a hole in the women's locker room showers inspires Pee-Wee, Meat, and the phallocentrically named gang at Angel Beach High to lose their virginities at the local whorehouse, run by porcine titular character. Racial tolerance subtext (Jews are people too) tossed in as an attempt to give homophobic breast-fest social value. **LEGACY:** "Meat" as nickname.

Class of 1984
Film, 1982
TX rating: 9.5
Hitching rides on the backs of school buses, marijuana smokin', graffiti, vandalism, violence, teachers with guns, new wave girls, cartoon punks in shreds, P.D.A.s, knives, and metal detectors—then the opening credits stop rolling. This under-the-top, *Warriors*-like movie puts so much fear in your heart, you might end up rooting for the adults. **LEGACY:** Strangely, Michael J. Fox's career.

Phoebe Cates
Icon, 1982-83
TX rating: 9.5
The Catesploitation Trilogy. Part One: Taking the *Blue Lagoon* paradigm to another level, she checks Brooke's prissy body double at the door and frolics with Willie Aames and a dodgy English accent in *Paradise*. Part Two: *Fast Times at Ridgemont High*, an international landmark, contains legendary cumming-to-Cates-coming-out-of-the-pool scene. Part Three: On a beach in *Private School*, a naked Cates says goodbye to virginity and hello to Matthew Modine's modine. **LEGACY:** Schooling a generation of girls in giving proper head.

Fast Times at Ridgemont High
Film, 1982
TX rating: 10.0
Scripter/culture-narc Cameron Crowe goes deep cover at actual So-Cal high school, files classic report exposing jocks, surfers, sluts, stoners, scalpers, and Mr. Hand. Bitchin' like a Camaro, director Amy Heckerling makes household names out of entire cast and forever links the Cars' "Moving in Stereo" to visions of Phoebe Cates' dripping-wet breasts, bouncing, bouncing, bouncing in eternal slo-mo. **LEGACY:** Side One, *Led Zeppelin 4*.

Square Pegs
TV show, 1982-83
TX rating: 5.0
Prime-time effort to capitalize on the new wave craze features skinny ties, Elvis Costello-esque nerds, and a theme song by the Waitresses—not to mention Sarah Jessica Parker and '80s babe-role mainstay Jami Gertz as non-slut, uppity Muffy Tupperman. **LEGACY:** The shades/Walkman combo.

Zapped!
Film, 1982
TX rating: 7.0
Give a teenage girl telekinetic powers and half the school ends up getting impaled by sharp objects. Bestow the same gift upon a teenage boy, and the results are far less lethal. Durable sitcom plug-in Scott Baio stars as a horny science geek who discovers a new way to see Hooters-style breasts without paying a cover. **LEGACY:** Nicholson Baker's *The Fermata*.

John Cusack
Actor, 1983-95
TX rating: 9.5
All the films he did previous to 1989—movies in which he plays not necessarily the most glamorous guy, but the one with the most heart (*Better Off Dead*, *The Sure Thing*, *Sixteen Candles*)—are really just preparation for Cusack's role in *Say Anything...* as Lloyd Dobler, the echt boyfriend of all time. **LEGACY:** "I don't want to sell anything, buy anything, or process anything..." and so on.

[SEAN PENN / *Fast Times at Ridgemont High*]

Screwballs
Film, 1983
TX rating: 9.0
Tensions run high as Taft and Adams High School ("T & A") prepares for the big homecoming game. But what a drag: Purity Busch, the homecoming queen, is a virgin. As the boys in uniform try to loosen her up, the unexpected ensues: a strip bowling contest, detention, and somebody spikes the P.T.A. punch bowl with an aphrodisiac! LEGACY: *Loose Screws: the Sequel.*

Suburbia
(a.k.a. The Wild Side)
Film, 1983
TX rating: 7.0
In this fictional follow-up to her landmark documentary, *Decline of Western Civilization*, Penelope Spheeris adds a plot where none is needed. Featuring museum-quality us-against-the-world dialogue ("If we didn't have each other, we wouldn't have anything") and the film debut of Flea. LEGACY: 924 Gilman Street.

Rumble Fish
Film, 1983
TX rating: 6.5
Gang legend Motorcycle Boy (Mickey Rourke, in his prime) is back in town, being ambiguously cool and bumming slightly 'tarded younger bro Rusty (Matt Dillon, also in his prime) by not being as nostalgic about the good ol' days of gang warware. Filmed in stunning black-and-white, which doesn't for a minute hinder the sight of Diane Lane (in *her* nymphy prime). LEGACY: *The Outsiders*; a like-named Sunset Strip glam band.

Valley Girl
Film, 1983
TX rating: 8.5
Can Randy (Nic Cage) and Julie (Deborah Foreman) fall in love, despite the fact she's from the San Fernando Valley and he walks the mean streets of Hollywood? Does Modern English stop the world and melt with you? Dumb and shiny as a Christmas tree, Julie represents everything punk-rock Randy stands against, and yet... LEGACY: *Clueless.*

Angel
Film, 1984
TX rating: 6.0
This year Angel turns 30. She's no longer honor student by day/hooker by night looking for the killer John, nor the law student who returns to hooking to avenge her cop-pal killer. One wonders what Angel is doing now: Did she keep her executive job after she found her long-lost sister who also fell to hooking? LEGACY: Teen hookers with hearts of gold.

Footloose
Film, 1984
TX rating: 9.0
Ren MacCormack (Kevin Bacon) reads *Slaughterhouse Five* and cuts a mean rug back in the big city where he comes from. After about one day in the Bible Belt, he learns that fancy learnin' and slow-dancing with skinny ties and such are branded the work of the Devil. But even the Devil ends up giving the boy a hand when he sees Ren playing chicken in a tractor. LEGACY: Pat Benatar's "Invincible."

The Wild Life
Film, 1984
TX rating: 8.0
Topless bars. Head-butting. Chris Penn as a charm-free Jeff Spicoli. Did the same Cameron Crowe who wrote *Fast Times at Ridgemont High* and *Say Anything...* actually write this movie? We can't be sure, but we're guessing lots of cocaine may have been involved. Soundtrack features an uncredited track by Edward Van Halen. Dude! LEGACY: Sundry beer commercials.

The Breakfast Club
Film, 1985
TX rating: 7.0
A pan-high-school collection of teen stereotypes—the jock, the snob, the delinquent, the geek, the freak—are assigned to Saturday detention and learn that deep inside, we're all the same. As if. LEGACY: "Chicks can't hold de smoke, dat's what it is."

Girls Just Want to Have Fun
Film, 1985
TX rating: 5.0
Sarah Jessica Parker disobeys her militant father to enter the Richard Blade-hosted TV dance show contest. Bad clothes, bad music, bad dancing, and then the baddest prank: getting back at the snobettes by inviting—gasp!—all the punkers in town to her debutante ball! Where they line dance. LEGACY: Helen Hunt as a comedian.

Tuff Turf
Film, 1985
TX rating: 9.1
Bad-ass loner James Spader can peg a cockroach from across the room with his BB gun but can he survive the first day of high school? A gang of J.D.s in "Beat It" drag aren't gonna make it easy. After beatdowns, showdowns, and chicken games, poet rocker Jim Carroll performs "It's Too Late" at the big dance (with bare-chested Robert Downey Jr. on drums), inspires Spader to serenade his misty-eyed gal with Journey-informed ballad "I Walk the Night." LEGACY: The word "tuff."

Weird Science
Film, 1985
TX rating: 9.8
With Mom and Dad out of town, horny geeks Anthony Michael Hall and Ian Mitchell Smith hack into the government's computer and create über-babe Kelly LeBrock ("like Frankenstein but cuter"). The nurturing LeBrock helps them get paid, laid, and wasted at climactic par-tay fulla "sex, drugs, rock'n'roll, chips, dips, chains, whips, your basic high school orgy type of thing." LEGACY: "Lisa, give me the keeeze!"; Bill Paxton's acting career; TV spinoff.

Nicole Eggert
Film, 1986-93
TX rating: 9.0
Long before she appears on *Baywatch* and is immortalized on Sugar Ray's *Lemonade and Brownies*, Aames, Baio, Feldman, and Haim try to soak up Eggert's sundrenched allure and Orange County cheerleader realness in *The Double O Kid*, *Anything for Love*, and *Charles in Charge*. Power Eggert: getting naked with Haim in *Blown Away* as they enjoy wanton sex after a car bomb kills her mom. LEGACY: Most notable for not appearing in the Feldman-centric *License to Drive*. That's Heather Graham.

River's Edge
Film, 1986
TX rating: 8.8
Crispin Glover's finest moment. "I happen to know my friends, fucking know them. We're a fucking team, we're like Starsky and Hutch." Glover as a black-eyeliner-wearing, leader-of-the-pack freak is better than Glover as nerd-boy freak or kung fu freak. Featuring a naked corpse, a blowup doll, and vintage Ione Skye and Keanu. Genius. LEGACY: *Blue Velvet*, *Twin Peaks*, *Gummo*.

Degrassi Jr. High/
Degrassi High
TV show, 1986-92
TX rating: 10.0
Imagine *90210*, but cast with age/acne-appropriate Canadian adolescents. It's a revelation. LEGACY: The slang "broomhead" as a catchall insult.

Less Than Zero
Film, 1987
TX rating: 7.0
The colorful world of your average rich Beverly Hills post-high school teen in the superficial '80s. Unruly decadence of all sorts abounds, though it never looks all that fun. But that's the gist: Cocaine ain't all that fun. LEGACY: The curse on Robert Downey Jr.

21 Jump Street
TV show, 1987-92
TX rating: 5.1
Are you Johnny Depp? Are you Johnny Depp? Who wants to know! Who wants to know! LEGACY: Richard Grieco, Skeet Ulrich.

Bill and Ted's Excellent Adventure
Film, 1989
TX rating: 5.0
Who says Keanu can't act? Director Stephen Herek creates mind-boggling, unforgettable combinations of the words "excellent" and "dude." And that air-guitar sound. LEGACY: Dogstar.

Gleaming the Cube
Film, 1989
TX rating: 9.0
Frosted skaterat Christian Slater and his buds clean up their act and skate around town in order to solve the murder of his adopted Vietnamese brother, Vinh. "Gleaming the cube" is alleged skater slang for achieving the ultimate rush. LEGACY: "Gleaming the cube."

Heathers
Film, 1989
TX rating: 7.1
The original ending is even blacker than the rest of the movie—Veronica supposedly joins forces with J.D. instead of stopping the violence. But a movie that compromises with a frustrated homicidal teenage maniac strapping himself with TNT is still pretty punk. LEGACY: *Jawbreaker.*

Saved by the Bell
TV show, 1989-93
TX rating: 4.0
Aggressively dimpled actors doing stupid-teen tricks in Dolby™ Surround Laugh-Track Sound. LEGACY: The classically trained Elizabeth Berkley.

Beverly Hills, 90210
TV show, 1990-present
TX rating: 7.2
Fans loyal since Minnesota twins Brandon and Brenda first arrived are determined to illuminate to the masses the genius subtext, which will probably only be recognized years from now. Someday, some smarty-pants semiotics major's thesis will be titled "The Homoeroticism of Steve Sanders." LEGACY: White boys calling each other brother on TV.

House Party
Film, 1990
TX rating: 5.0
Kid is sneaking out of the house, hiding from gangs, and running from the law—all to get to Play's house party. Kudos are given by critics for the positive portrayal of middle-class black youth. Kudos are given by audiences for lots of big booty. LEGACY: Tisha & Mar-tiiin!

[WINONA RYDER & CHRISTIAN SLATER / *Heathers*]

Pump up the Volume
Film, 1990
TX rating: 7.6
Enigmatic pirate-radio DJ Hard Harry's nocturnal transmissions inspire fellow repressed Arizonan teens to "Kick Out the Jams," write bad sex poetry, and piss off their sell-out Boomer parents, fascist principal, and the FCC. Shit gets off the hook when they start exploding microwave ovens and blowing off their heads. **LEGACY:** Samantha Mathis's breasts.

Neve Campbell
Actor, 1992-present
TX rating: 8.1
Remember, on 90210, how Shannen Doherty used to spit out every single word with unnecessary bile and sarcasm, and how her line readings always had this stilted, staccato rhythm, and how she loved to punctuate trenchant points with a scowl, and how she left the show to pursue a movie career but eventually wound up back on TV? **LEGACY:** JLH.

Dazed and Confused
Film, 1993
TX rating: 8.0
Richard Linklater feathers the hair of more indie icons than we can count and dresses shopworn "last day of school, where are we headed, gang?" spiel in polyester, pot-fogged drag. **LEGACY:** Matthew McConaughey; That '70s Show.

Jennifer Love Hewitt
Budding mini-industry, 1994-1998
TX rating: 9.3
Building a career using the Alyssa Milano template: release some CDs in Japan; do a dance workout video; become a series regular; do some films; make a TV movie about the life of a complicated woman with a really difficult accent (Hewitt tried her hand at Audrey Hepburn). Next up: her own series. **LEGACY:** Lacey Chabert?

My So-Called Life
TV Show, 1994–1995
TX rating: 7.5
In just one season, Claire Danes' Angela Chase manages to drop her childhood friend, dye her hair red, and emerge as the voice-over of a generation with intrepid commentary such as, "My parents keep asking how school was. It's like saying, 'How was that drive-by shooting?' You don't care how it was; you're lucky to get out alive." **LEGACY:** Every teen show on TV today.

Sweet Valley High
TV Show, 1994-1997
TX rating: 5.0
Blond-haired, blue-eyed twins Elizabeth (the nice one) and Jessica (the naughty one) Wakefield get into much mischief, usually involving boys, parties, and/or gossip. Inspired by the hugely successful pre-teen book of the same title. **LEGACY:** Their Doublemint Commercials.

The Basketball Diaries
Film, 1995
TX rating: 9.4
Halfway through Jim Carroll's autobiographical tale about his life as a teen junkie, Leo DiCaprio enters a confessional. Priest: "Have you engaged in impure deeds?" Leo: "Oh Father, you have no idea. I've done all kinds of crazy shit." Including, but not limited to: huffing, snorting, shooting, dealing, hustling, carjacking, screwing, and overacting. **LEGACY:** "Time sure does fly when you're young and jerking off."

Clueless
Film, 1995
TX rating: 8.0
Sweet 'n' clever Beverly Hills relocation of Jane Austen's Emma invents credible teen vernacular eventually adopted by actual teens. **LEGACY:** The dizzying rise and fall of Alicia Silverstone; TV spinoff series.

The Doom Generation
Film, 1995
TX rating: 9.7
Rose McGowan stars as a frisky teen squeeze-toy with Tourette syndrome-like demeanor—no wonder Marilyn Manson asked her out after watching this movie. Featuring bad dialogue masquerading as intentionally bad dialogue, The Doom Generation (which follows All F****d Up and precedes Nowhere) firmly establishes Gregg Araki as the Ed Wood of the punk underground. **LEGACY:** Steamy three-way photo spread in Barely Heterosexual.

Empire Records
Film, 1995
TX rating: 8.0
Indie record store staff of alternababes and post-grunge fellas wrestle with their hearts, their fears, the Man, and pin-up Maxwell Caulfield's libido during one wacky day-shift that reinforces the existential gospel: Let's go crazy 'cause a spontaneous pot-luck kegger will save us all. **LEGACY:** Edwyn Collins' one hit, "A Girl Like You."

Kids
Film, 1995
TX rating: 11.0
Kids was billed as a "wake-up call to America," but it plays like softcore teen porn with an indie-rock soundtrack. Oh sure, there's that AIDS subplot, but Kids is really a day on the prowl with Telly, "the virgin surgeon," who spends his downtime smoking blunts, drinking 40s, committing misdemeanors, and dispensing mealy-mouthed sex tips to his peeps. **LEGACY:** Gummo; Chloe Sevigny's unexpected acting career.

The Craft
Film, 1996
TX rating: 6.0
A foursome of highly attractive social misfits go Wiccan, but childish pranks give way to white-hot evil. Easy on those incantations, girls, or you'll go mad, mad, mad! **LEGACY:** "We are the weirdos, mister."

Fear
Film, 1996
TX rating:8.0
Reese Witherspoon's suave-at-first stalker boyfriend "Marky" Mark Wahlberg scratches a NICOLE 4 EVA tattoo on his chest and decapitates the family dog after he "pops her cherry" to a Bush song. One of the best Marky-Mark stalking-teen movies ever. **LEGACY:** Finger-fun on roller-coasters.

Foxfire
Film, 1996
TX rating: 8.5
Roguish, avenging, feminist Zen orphan "Legs" (Angelina Jolie) directs her anger toward teachers who molest students, jocks who bitch-slap girlfriends, and fathers who beat daughters. **LEGACY:** Celebrating that natural non-lesbian lesbian thing.

Freeway
Film, 1996
TX rating: 11.0
Reese Witherspoon in an over-the-top turn as the world's sweetest pistol-whipping, trash-talking, shoplifting sociopath. An update of Little Red Riding Hood by way of Jerry Springer, Freeway features crack-smoking, incest lite, maternal prostitution, and teen illiteracy. All in the first five minutes. **LEGACY:** Luckily, none.

Romeo & Juliet
Film, 1996
TX rating: 6.0
Claire Danes makes a movie star bid as Juliet in Baz Luhrmann's glam, neon-lit, MTV-ready version of Shakespeare's tragedy, inspiring violent fits of jealousy in millions of teenage girls by kissing Leo. Simultaneously educational and misleading (the iambic pentameter is faithful; the inclusion of Prince's "When Doves Cry" is not). **LEGACY:** Ethan Hawke and Gwyneth Paltrow in Great Expectations.

Buffy the Vampire Slayer
TV show, 1997-2003
TX rating: 6.0
Plucky-yet-sulky Buffy Summers wants to be like normal girls, but she must instead devote herself to destroying dark forces. Besides, who wants to be a cheerleader when cheerleaders are spontaneously combusting? Possibly the best show on TV. **LEGACY:** That drinking game in which everyone drinks when Buffy's bra-strap is showing; Faith, the party-girl slayer.

Dawson's Creek
TV show, 1998-2003
TX rating: 8.0
TV's most existential teens go head to head with 90210 in the coveted Wednesday prime-time slot. Fancy words, all-real racks, and heavy-petting parents aside, how do they compare? Pacey, who lost his virginity on his teacher's desk, does the least amount of soul-searching (Dylan + Steve). Jennifer, supposed former slut, is the voluptuous transfer student girls don't like (Kelly + Valerie). Dawson is driven, dry, and has distracting hair (Andrea + Brandon). And Joey? Well, she's poor like Brenda. **LEGACY:** Making the WB a playa.

Disturbing Behavior
Film, 1998
TX rating: 8.0
Katie Holmes's smoking bad girl and Jimmy Marsden's new kid in town fight for their right to be angsty after mad scientist Bruce Greenwood lobotomizes an entire high school of alt-rock kids, creating a sweater-clad Stepford frat/sorority invulnerable to the standard pitfalls of adolescence. The plan's undoing: Sexual tension conquers all. **LEGACY:** "Bad! Wrong! Bad! Wrong!"

Wild Things
Film, 1998
TX rating: 9.7
Neve trades chambray shirts for trashy ho makeup, smoking dope in the hot, sweaty swamp. While Neve is wooden, her shameless, enhanced-tit-proud nemesis/lover Denise Richards creates wood. **LEGACY:** Matt Dillon's very serious reading of the ménage-á-trois scene.

The Faculty
Film, 1998
TX rating: 8.5
Some old tricks (school's a drag, gym teachers are nuts, Southern chicks are proper), some new tricks (the QB wants to study, the cheerleaders can spell, a meth lab in the basement). Old man Williamson's still got it. **LEGACY:** Teachers are aliens, but the drugs will set you free.

— "A Blizzard of White Panties" / Compiled by G. Beato, Maureen Callahan, Victoria DeSilverio, Gaylord Fields, Kim France, Marcelle Karp, Darby Romeo, and Marc Spitz

[CLAIRE DANES / *My So-Called Life*]

11 /

: Beastie Boys

White dudes in the house

/ Alan **Light**

"One of my favorite groups is the Beasties,"

Bono told SPIN in 2002. "Their journey is really one to watch, from just having fun with their own middle-classness to a growing awareness of the way the world is." Such an endorsement from the Official Conscience of Rock'n'Roll would have been laughable, completely implausible, 15 years earlier, when the Beastie Boys' debut album was reviewed in the *Village Voice* beneath the headline "Three Jerks Make a Masterpiece."

New York City paragons Adam "MCA" Yauch, Adam "Ad-Rock" Horovitz, and Michael "Mike D" Diamond—the sons of an architect, a playwright, and an interior designer—altered the composition of the hip-hop nation not once, but twice; first with *Licensed to Ill's* raid on suburban high schools and college fraternities in 1986, then by creating a global hipster coalition beginning with 1989's *Paul's Boutique*.

After forming as a goof on the nascent hardcore scene—and giving themselves "the stupidest name" they could come up with, according to Yauch—the trio (originally a foursome with future Luscious Jackson drummer Kate Schellenbach) turned their comic energies to rap with the 1983 single "Cooky Puss." They soon crossed paths with NYU student/producer/hustler Rick Rubin, who joined the group as "DJ Double R" and then, together with partner Russell Simmons, signed them to the just-launched Def Jam label.

The LP that resulted was nothing less than a phenomenon: *Licensed to Ill's* non-stop barrage of "a lot of beer, a lot of girls, and a lot of cursing" ("The New Style"), powered by Rubin's crunching grooves, became the fastest-selling debut album (currently 9 million and counting) in the history of Columbia Records, then Def Jam's distributor. The knucklehead anthem "(You've Gotta) Fight for Your Right (to Party)" defined the Beastie sensibility in ways they are still

trying to escape—at Yauch's wedding in 1998, his parents even worked "Fight For Your Right" into their toast. With allies like Run-D.M.C. and Public Enemy (both of whom the Beasties toured with), they even dodged most, if not all, of the criticism that came with being the first significant white artists in hip-hop.

Exhausted by an endless tour and by trying to live up to the comic-book image they'd created, the Beasties entered into a prolonged fight with Def Jam and temporarily broke up in 1988. Eventually, they reached an agreement with Rubin and Simmons to get out of their contract. Led by Horovitz's flirtation with film acting, they all drifted to Los Angeles and signed a deal with Capitol Records. A chance encounter with the Dust Brothers (who would go on to produce Young MC, Tone-Loc, and Beck) inspired them to start writing rhymes again, and the result was the head-spinning, sampladelic epic *Paul's Boutique*—one of the greatest hip-hop albums ever made but a relative commercial flop that never cracked the Top 10. It was a blessing in every way, enabling the Boys to jettison their previous audience and any lingering mass-market expectations, and to drill down to the smart-ass bohemians who were their most natural following in the first place.

They picked up the instruments that they had put away when they added a DJ, and the endless jamming and screwing around turned into 1992's *Check Your Head*. The disc's blend of punk, funk, and rap would serve as their recording blueprint for the rest of the decade. The weedy, stuttering hit "So What 'Cha Want" started their climb back to popularity, establishing a following that merged the worlds of hip-hop, skateboarding, and urban chic, helping them build an empire that would include a record label and a magazine (both called Grand Royal), and a clothing line (Mike D's X-Large).

Throwing themselves back into touring, they rolled out 1994's *Ill Communication*, which returned them to No. 1 on the charts, and spawned the Spike Jonze-video-directed "Sabotage," a dead-on spoof of '70s cop shows—right down to the bad moustaches—that might be the greatest music video ever made. After a spiritual awakening while snowboarding in Tibet, Yauch threw himself into activist work for that country's liberation from China, culminating in three massive benefit shows and a new gravity to his rhymes.

After 1998's *Hello Nasty* added cutmaster extraordinaire Mix Master Mike, club beats, dub wizard Lee "Scratch" Perry, and some actual singing to their B-Boy bouillabaise, the grown-up Beasties exercised their license to chill for a while. Yauch and Diamond were married with children, and Horovitz (following a divorce from actress Ione Skye) settled into a long-term relationship with Bikini Kill frontwoman/feminist punk heroine Kathleen Hanna. Increasingly politicized, they resurfaced to organize a benefit concert after September 11th and, in 2003, to release "In a World Gone Mad," a forgettable Internet-only single protesting the war in Iraq.

Six years after *Nasty* came *To the 5 Boroughs*—their first entirely self-produced album, never straying from pass-the-mic-style old-school beats and rhymes. It was a well-intentioned valentine to the city and the music that inspired them, peppered with anti-Bush slogans and pride in being "funky-ass Jews." But it was the first Beastie Boys album to run thin over its full length. Still, while they may all be closing in on 40, don't count them out—that's what everybody did after *Licensed to Ill*, not realizing that this was a group too smart to underestimate. They can't, they won't, and they don't stop.

Bigger and Deffer: The Rise of Def Jam

New York University's Weinstein Hall doesn't look like the birth-place of a revolution. But it was in this big gray dorm just off Washington Square Park—on the eighth floor, to be precise—that junior Rick Rubin started Def Jam Records in 1983 with the T LaRock single "It's Yours." Manager/promoter Russell Simmons bumped into Rubin soon after the record's release, and they quickly agreed to be partners on the new venture—a company that went from storing inventory under Rubin's bed to signing a distribution deal with Columbia Records, in the process almost single-handedly defining hip-hop's modern era.

Their first full-length was LL Cool J's classic *Radio* album, which bore the credit "Reduced by Rick Rubin." The phrase nailed the Def Jam aesthetic perfectly. Snot-nosed metalhead Rubin wanted to make rap records with the force and drama of AC/DC, while budding mogul Simmons wanted to capture the energy of the old-school park jams and translate that to the biggest possible audience. "My biggest contribution to rap was the structured-song element," said Rubin. "Prior to that, a lot of rap songs were seven minutes long; the guy would keep rapping until he ran out of words. 'It's Yours' separated it into verses and choruses."

Def Jam immediately became a creative and commercial jug-gernaut unparalleled until the rise of the Death Row and Bad Boy superpowers in the '90s. For almost a decade, every album released with a Def Jam logo sold at least gold—it reached the point where fans would buy for the brand name even if they didn't know the act. And what a list of acts—LL, Public Enemy, the Beastie Boys, Slick Rick, 3rd Bass, EPMD.

The first crisis came when the label's biggest-sellers, the Beasties, grew unhappy with Simmons and Rubin's insistence that they remain the goofballs of rap; the only thing that stopped them from breaking up was moving to another label. Then Rubin, who wanted to go into the rock'n'roll business, and Simmons, who always preferred more of an R&B sound, decid-ed to split, Rubin founding Def American (later American Recordings) and signing assorted bad-asses from Slayer to Johnny Cash.

Simmons led Def Jam through a cold spell in the early '90s as he diversified into too many subsidiary imprints and hip-hop's focal point moved to gangstafied Los Angeles. But by decade's end, he had helped the company recapture its edge and signed a new crop of superstars like DMX, Method Man, and Ludacris before selling the label to concentrate on building a multi-media empire (Jay-Z, perhaps the biggest of Def Jam's new school, was appointed president/CEO of the label in 2004). It may just be part of the music-biz establishment now, but for a good part of its history Def Jam was one of a select number of labels—from Sun to Sub Pop—that defined both a sensibility and an era. — Alan Light

I'm really disappointed in your choice of the Beastie Boys for the cover of your magazine (March '87). In the past you've always cho-sen someone (or a group) who's at least half-serious about making music and has made some contribu-tion to music. Oh well, I got the last laugh as I tossed your magazine with the Beastie Boy's ugly mugs face-down in yesterday's coffee grounds, knowing that someday these guys will be rotting away in Trend-Music Hell with all sorts of breakdance bands, disco dudes, and many more.
BRYAN BASSET, Lexington, KY
— "Letters"/ May '87

Your decision to put a white rap crew on the cover of your maga-zine as SPIN's front page presen-tation of hip-hop betrays 1) the inherent phoniness of your "alter-native" stance, 2) your lack of facility with nascent black musical forms, and 3) your own racism. American musical history is running over with contradictions. One just hopes that those of us who watched the music (rap, hip-hop) grow off the sidewalk will remember that, despite thousands of recordings, concerts, and park jams by individu-als who were and are far more inno-vative, creative, and black than the Beastie Boys, the first rap crew on SPIN's cover was not only white, but white-faced. To paraphrase one Howard University student, this is the Colonel Tom Parker story of black American music. It's an old, tired story, it's an untrue story, and a magazine of SPIN's caliber is capa-ble of much, much more.
HARRY ALLEN, Freeport, NY
— "Letters"/ May '87

SPIN: *The Source* said you were soft, Mike, for buying gourmet tuna paté—said you'd been in Cali too long.
MCA: That's a bad attitude. Big Daddy Kane be buying that shit all the time! If Q-Tip bought it, they'd be impressed.
Mike D: People don't realize how much hip-hop stars have always been into gourmet foods. Chef B-Boy-Ardee is no joke!
Ad-Rock: I heard a Salt-n-Pepa song one time, where they named every rapper in New York. And they didn't name us! I was listening to this shit, goin', "Damn, wussup wit that?"
MCA: You could have waited till the cows come home!

Talk of New York rappers dissing the Beasties leads us inevitably to 3rd Bass. First they jokes about how 3rd Bass's MC Serch report-edly used to show up at Mike D's house to hang out— and Mike D would throw stuff at him. And though MCA clams that Beasties fans think more about it than the band....

MCA: Serch sounds like he's got a weird thing with being white 'n' stuff.
Ad-Rock: I understand, but work that shit out before you start going 'round. I saw Pete Nice in the barber shop—didn't say shit to me!
Mike D: [Suddenly] I just wanna tell everybody we're coming back hard!
MCA: [Grabbing my recorder] Yo gimme that, I'm gonna bust some rhymes right here!
Mike D: Honestly, people expect like "I'm so hardcore, I shot eight motherfuckers before I left my house!" Who gives a fuck, man?
— "Living X-Tra Large" / Bob Mack / May '92

If we opened a Beastie Boy refrigerator, we'd find peanut butter, and Marshmallow Fluff next to a bag of granola, fresh orange juice, Gato-rade, Chef Boy-Ar-Dee ravioli (red can), Rice-a-Roni, but no peas. Beastie Boys don't eat peas.
Inside a Beastie Boy wallet are the phone numbers of lots of girls, not much money, and no credit cards.
If a girl wants a Beastie Boy to like her, she's got to be cool and not talk too much. Beastie Boys like young, pretty, new-wavey-looking girls.
Beastie Boys like Skoochie's, a club for minors in Seattle with two thousand 15-, 16- and 17-year-old girls, all thinking they are Madonna.
Beastie Boys don't use after-shave.
Beastie Boys don't have plants or pets.
A smashing evening for the Beastie Boys is going to eat at a McDonald's, then hanging out in a club like Skoochie's, talking to lots of girls, dancing to records that they like—which is hard to do, because it's hard to find a club that plays records that they like—going out to eat again and going home, hopefully not alone.
—"Beastie Boys... Are the Bigfoot of Rap" / Scott Cohen / July, '85

The crucial difference between the Beastie Boys and say, 3rd Bass, or Young Black Teenagers, or Vanilla Ice, is that they don't use hip-hop to lament their plight as rejects in white society, or as a plea for acceptance from blacks, but as a way of questioning (sending up?) the whole obsession with group identity. What does it mean to wrap yourself up in the hoodie of race or religion? Does it really keep you warm at night?

"Maybe I'm weird or whatever," says Mike D., "but the whole thing is about constantly redefining identity. Like, the second issue of *Grand Royal* is a lot about questioning what was in the first issue. And to me, that's the best thing that could possibly be happening, an ongoing self-and-group-critique."

Instead of being defensive about their so-called privileged lineage, the Beastie Boys have always shot it full of holes from both sides. With their hardcore shenanigans and their yowling about Betty Crocker and Colonel Sanders over samples of Led Zeppelin and Black Sabbath (who, as good punks, they hated) on *Licensed to Ill*'s "Rhymin' and Stealin'," they affectionately harshed on white-trash culture, which was as foreign (or close) to their experience as black culture. In many ways, their "whiteness" is just as constructed as their "blackness."

And of course, there's the Jewish issue, relevant because of hip-hop's insistent anti-Semitic nattering, usually via the Nation of Islam's endorsement of such viciously fallacious tracks as *Protocols of the Learned Elders of Zion*. "Our Jewishness was never part of our upbringing at all," Yauch says. 'I think all of us came from families with one Jewish parent and one Catholic parent, anyway."

"No Catholics in my family," Mike D demurs.

"I thought your mother was," Yauch says. "Where did she come from?"

"The Bronx—straight out. South muthafuckin' Bronx!"

"I guess I don't know what these guys' religious backgrounds are and that's probably because none of us ever really discussed Judaism, as you're now seeing here," Yauch says. "All I knew was that every year my mother would take me out to a seder and my Uncle Freddy would scream, 'Pass the matzoh,' and I didn't know what the fuck was going on.

"But one thing that's true and cool is that I get a lot of Jewish kids coming up to me feeling pride and strength from what we're doing. And I definitely don't wanna take anything away from that. When we first started MC'ing, I was coming from a real ignorant perspective. I didn't understand how jazz had come from black culture and then become absorbed into mainstream society and how the same thing happened with rock'n'roll. Or how the process just repeated itself with us and hip-hop. When people pointed it out, it definitely humbled me quite a bit.

"See, I don't think there's just a young, black male identity crisis. The whole fucking planet's trying to figure out who they are and why they're here. And so are we."

— "Boychiks in the Hoodie" / Charles Aaron / July '94

Rick Rubin (cofounder, Def Jam Records): I was the chairman of the social committee, and a DJ, and the Beastie Boys started coming to these parties at my dorm. They asked me to DJ for them since I was a friend of theirs and had a bubble machine.

Doctor Dre (former Beastie DJ; radio host, Hot 97, NYC): Rick had no skills. He would just play the record. But he had a lot of good DJ movements. He'd bob his head a lot.

Cey Adams (Adam Horovitz's former roommate; graphic designer): Rick would pick up the tab, which played a big part in us hanging out with him. At that time, the band was still wearing plain clothes. Then somebody got the idea to try and look a little more hip-hop. I think it was Rick. For the record, anything silly was usually Rick's idea.

Rubin: We went to Chinatown and got these matching Chinese jogging suits, and we all had matching Adidas and Puma suits, too. We used to wear do-rags on our heads, which was kind of ridiculous.

Thomas Beller (former Beat Brother): No one ever actually said, "Kate [Schellenbach, former Beastie Boy], you're out." She went away for the weekend, and Rick bought the other three members matching Adidas sweatsuits, red-and-black warm-ups, and sneakers. They were at the [Manhattan] club Area dressed up like a trio and Kate bumped into them, kind of by accident. She just started crying, because it was obvious that there was not going to be a woman in a band that's, like, going to have an inflatable penis on stage.

Schellenbach: Rick's influence was really hard to deal with. Everybody in our crew was very open and not sexist at all, and Rick was this piggish guy from Long Island, or wherever the hell he was from. He was really sexist and homophobic, and they were all getting into his persona because they thought he was cool. They were also getting into what they thought a hip-hop group was supposed to act like, grabbing their dicks and talking about girls. It was very disappointing and alienating.

Adams: The first time they got any money was when they sued British Airways for using part of "Cookie Puss" in an ad. Horovitz worked in a little ice cream shop that was like our clubhouse. The minute they got that check, he quit his job and would buy stuff for everybody. It just felt like paradise.

Michael Diamond (a.k.a. Mike D): That money enabled us to make the move for independence. We got a floor in this Chinese sweatshop building on Chrystie Street [on the Lower East Side of Manhattan].

Adam Yauch (a.k.a. MCA): The floor was black top. Somebody had actually rolled out tar across it, like the street. One time we were hanging out in the living room and we heard this really loud explosion in the kitchen. Our toaster oven had a hole in the top and a hole in the back. There was a hole in the wall behind it and a hole in the ceiling. Apparently, somebody upstairs fired a gun through the floor. We ran up there and there was nobody in the room but this old woman. We were like, "What happened?" and she didn't speak English. You know some crazy shit had just happened in that sweatshop and they had quickly covered it up. Dragged the body out.

Russell Simmons (cofounder, Def Jam Records and Rush Management): I met the Beasties at Danceteria. They were wearing red sweatsuits with stripes, red Pumas, and do-rags. They were assholes.

Yauch: Rick started getting tight with Russell. We really formed into a hip-hop group as Russell was starting to manage us. We started playing real shows, opening for Kurtis Blow or the Fat Boys. It was scary at first. One time Russell put us in a limousine and sent us to the Encore club in Queens. We were definitely the only white people for miles, and we were getting out of, like, a stretch limousine. How much more obnoxious and conspicuous could we have possibly been?

Bill Adler (former Def Jam publicist): I saw them on a bill at the Encore headed by Kurtis Blow. It was just a ridiculous fucking crack house. Blow didn't hit till two in the morning, and the Beasties didn't hit till three. It was one of the very first gigs that they'd done as rappers under Russell's aegis, and they were wearing their red gym suits and whatnot. All of Russell's goodwill couldn't keep this crowd from being skeptical. It was a disastrous gig. The turntables blew up.

Diamond: These three white MCs jump onstage—we may as well have come from outer space.

D.M.C. (member, Run-D.M.C.): Russell was like, "Yo, when you meet these guys, they're gonna bug you out. These white guys are ill." The first time I met 'em, I thought I was on *Candid Camera*.

Chuck D (member, Public Enemy): They came out to our radio show at WBAU [in Long Island], trying to prove to the rap market that they were viable white kids. You really couldn't doubt their legitimacy 'cause they were down with Def Jam and Run-D.M.C. and the beats were right. And as long as they talked about white boys and beer and stuff like that, who could knock their topics?

— "The Story of Yo" / Alan Light / September '98

> ## "Obviously there are moments that you look back and cringe—things in the past involving violence or disrespect to women or disrespect to other people that are so far away from what I want to put out there now."
>
> — Mike D, 1998

> ## "Everyone was supposed to grow their own facial hair for the video ["Sabotage"]. Yauch forgot and Mike D can't grow any, so they used the glue-on kind. But Horovitz grew his own. He's like that—he does what needs to be done. Yauch is a professionally trained stuntman. The emergency-brake slides and high-speed reverse 180s—that's all him."
>
> — Spike Jonze (director, "Sabotage"), 1998

Few groups have changed their ideological existence as much as the Beastie Boys. For more than 40 years, the Rolling Stones have expressed the same general sentiments that they did in 1964; AC/DC has been around for 31 years, and they're still expressing the exact same sentiments that they did in the summer of '74. Ideologically, the Beastie Boys have almost nothing in common with who they used to be. If the '86 B-Boys and the '04 B-Boys met each other right now, somebody would end up in the emergency room—or at least covered in egg yolks. Yet one thing has remained unchanged over the years, and it's the unifying principle that has allowed Horovitz, Yauch, and Diamond to remain relevant longer than anyone could have anticipated: The Beastie Boys understand what it means to be cool. It's almost as if being cool is their full-time job. They can make any retro reference seem contemporary; they innately sense the line between savvy cultural recognition and esoteric self-indulgence. They basically discovered Spike Jonze, made shouting out neglected soul-jazz musicians trendy (Dick Hyman, Eddie Harris, Richard "Groove" Holmes), and taught people born in 1978 to care about the American Basketball Association. The Beastie Boys are hip-hop's version of the "mavens" that Malcolm Gladwell wrote about in *The Tipping Point*: They are cool hunters for the rest of us.

— "Twilight of the Brats" / Chuck Klosterman / July '04

: REBELS WITHOUT PAUSE

Public Enemy rewrite hip-hop as revolutionary force

/ Sacha **Jenkins**

Hip-hop in the late 1980s was heavier than heavy metal.

Compton, California's N.W.A, for example, were trigger-happy gangstas who wouldn't hesitate to shoot their way out of a tight situation with cops, gangbangers, or an entire crack house; they didn't even care enough to ask questions later. Boogie Down Productions were low-key gangstas with a conscience: Only if you messed around with them would they assault your stupid ass. The Brooklyn- and South Bronx-raised duo and their plentiful associates didn't necessarily want drama but they weren't afraid of it, either.

And then there was the mighty Public Enemy, the most important hip-hop band of all time. P.E. were like those older brothers who'd grown up with the thug-lifers, made good on their educational obligations, and come up with an escape. Having avoided leaving the concrete jungle in a humble pine box, P.E. sought to help others do the same, by soundtracking a pro-black war that frontman Chuck D likened to an "intellectual Vietnam."

Although he rapped that he was a black man who could "never be a veteran," Chuck D was hip-hop's first four-star general. Born Carlton Douglas Ridenhour in 1960, MistaChuck grew up in Roosevelt, Long Island, in a seemingly stable, middle-class household (his dad owned a trucking business). Chuck knew something about discipline and respect and hard work. A product of the Civil Rights era, he remembered the day that Martin Luther King Jr. died; he remembered the Black Panther Party's free breakfast programs. He was raised on funky hymns like James Brown's "Say It Loud—I'm Black and I'm Proud, Pt. 1." He

saw how the blues—when underscored by hip-shaking rhythms—could be used as a tool of inspiration and unification.

Chuck, a graphic design major, formulated his revolutionary mindset while attending Long Island's Adelphi University. In 1982, he met Hank Shocklee (future leader of the Bomb Squad—the production team responsible for P.E.'s Jupiter funk), and the duo, along with Bill Stephney, produced a college radio program called the Super Special Mix Show (they named their crew the Spectrum City Sound System). As the collective began making beats and rhymes, Shocklee and Chuck cut demos so good that Def Jam co-founder Rick Rubin courted them for two years before he convinced them to sign.

William "Flavor Flav" Drayton became P.E.'s comic-relief mascot, known for wearing a Domino's Pizza-sized clock. Strong Island native Norman "Terminator X" Rodgers, the group's DJ, could cut and scratch his rump off—live and on wax. He appears on the cover of the group's debut LP, 1987's *Yo! Bumrush the Show*, flexing a pose with Chuck, Flav, and the group's uniformed security troop, the S1Ws; they're hovering over a pair of turntables looking ready to die, in some bleak room barely illuminated by an overhead lamp. The photograph appears as if it was taken behind the scenes of a sting operation or a drug deal. That's the essence of P.E.: They looked like they were up to something, and they looked serious enough to actually carry it out. After all, Chuck D was the man who dubbed himself a "lyrical terrorist." But Flavor had jokes, and it was his levity that helped Public Enemy sneak knowledge into the minds of the unsuspecting. (The 1990 Flav tune "911 Is a Joke" is a perfect example of the man's edutainment value.)

Chuck kicked real lyrics of fury, Napalm-charged lines like, "I got a letter from the government the other day/ I opened it and read it and said they were suckers/ They wanted me for their army or whatever/ Picture me giving a damn, I said never!" The beats, peppered with the occasional Malcolm X sample, rang out like a sermon from the great beyond. It was as if Malcolm himself was saying "Throw your motherfuckin' hands up!" The Bomb Squad sound was part sunshine dream, part nightmare scream. Their noisy, densely layered collage was infused with soul, aggression, and meaning. Listening was like eavesdropping on a conversation between black history's past and present. Making music like this today is nearly impossible—the bill to clear the samples alone would rival the national debt.

On the cover of P.E.'s second album, 1988's *It Takes a Nation of Millions to Hold Us Back* (arguably the crew's most impressive offering), Chuck and Flav are behind bars. Which might help explain the P.E. logo—a black man trapped inside the scope of a gun. On the most ferocious jam, "Bring The Noise," Chuck endorses one of America's most feared black leaders, The Nation of Islam's Louis Farrakhan ("Now they got me in a cell 'cause my records, they sell/ 'Cause a brother like me said 'Well…/ …Farrakhan's a prophet and I think you ought to listen to/ What he can say to you, what you ought to do.'") Bigging up Farrakhan was like begging the FBI to start compiling your file. And this was at a time when hip-hop's mainline was about fabulous parties and miraculous-sounding bullshit. P.E.'s fearlessness would inspire folks like X Clan, Poor Righteous Teachers, Paris, and Brand Nubian to adopt a pro-blackness agenda.

ESSAY CONTINUES ON NEXT PAGE >

> ESSAY CONTINUES FROM PREVIOUS PAGE

The stunning *Fear of a Black Planet* (1990) was highly anticipated, partially because of scandal: Months before the LP's release, the group's Minister of Information, Professor Griff, made anti-Semitic statements to the *Washington Post*. Chuck, on a damage-control mission, decided to (temporarily) combat-boot his man out of the group. Still, on "Welcome to the Terrordome," a song penned after the Griff incident, Chuck dropped the line, "apology made to whoever pleases/ still they got me like Jesus"—which was an obvious dig at what he saw as Jewish influence in the media. Politically correct or not, these were sentiments shared by many African-Americans at the time. For the "Fight the Power" video (supporting 1989's *Do the Right Thing* movie soundtrack), P.E. staged a massive mock demonstration in Brooklyn's Bedford-Stuyvesant. It became their signature song, and biggest "hit."

Apocalypse 91…The Enemy Strikes Black deployed a still-screaming Chuck D who, via "By the Time I Get to Arizona," set ablaze the whole region (at that time, the state refused to acknowledge the new Dr. Martin Luther King Jr. holiday). *Apocalypse* also featured a "Bring Tha Noize" collaboration with headbangers Anthrax, which was a nod to P.E.'s ever-expanding white fan base.

But things would change for Public Enemy when the tide shifted toward nihilistic gangsta rap, which laughed in the face of all the issues that PE stood for. It seemed as if the same counter-intelligence programs that had taken out the Black Panther Party were somehow wreaking the same nonsense on Chuck's organization, on and off wax—Flavor, after all, became a basehead.

P.E. went on hiatus, regrouped, recorded, and toured, existing quietly during the reigns of the playa and crunk dynasties. In 2004, Chuck D became a commentator on the liberal Air America radio network, while a clean and relatively sober Flav became a television star known for lusting after Amazonian actress Brigitte Nielsen. But as the group that first exploited hip-hop as agitprop, ideology, and revolutionary force, their legend stayed bright. And a new breed of conscious artists like Mos Def, Talib Kweli, and Dead Prez—fed by Public Enemy's free-breakfast

IT WAS AN OLD-STYLE PROTEST HANDBILL, UNSIGNED, DROPPED ANONYMOUSLY ON EVERY SEAT AT THE NEW MUSIC SEMINAR'S PANEL ON RACISM. Across the top, hand written in artless capital letters, it read: DON'T BELIEVE THE HATE. And for the remainder of the page, in cramped, single-spaced type, it presented its case:

THE WORLD ACCORDING TO PUBLIC ENEMY:

"Cats naturally miaow, dogs naturally bark, and whites naturally murder and cheat…. White people's hearts are so cold they can't wait to lie, cheat, and murder. This is white people's nature…. Whites are the biggest murderers on earth.

"There's no place for gays. When God destroyed Sodom and Gommorah, it was for that sort of behavior." (*The Face*, July/August 1988)

"The White Race or the Caucasian Race came from the Caucus Mountains…. It was not black people who made it with monkeys, animals, and dogs, but it was white people…. White people are actually monkeys' uncles because that's who they made it with in the Caucasian hills.

"They say the white Jews built the pyramids. Shit. The Jews can't even build houses that stand up nowadays. How the hell did they build the pyramids?

"If the Palestinians took up arms, went into Israel, and killed all the Jews, it'd be alright." (*Melody Maker*, May 28, 1988)

It was July 18, the opening day of the Democratic National Convention, and the emotional circus that had been building around Public Enemy all summer and had just kicked up a notch. By the time the night was over, and Public Enemy lead rapper Chuck D had denounced writer and supporter Greg Tate as the *Village Voice*'s "porch nigger," New York was swinging. We'd never seen anything like this before.

It was also nine business days after the release of Public Enemy's second album, *It Takes a Nation of Millions to Hold Us Back*, and the record had already unofficially gone gold, sating the very different hungers of black and white audiences. It seemed to be booming out of every car at every traffic light in the city. *The Wall Street Journal* had recently discovered car stereos that approached the decibel level required to bore a hole in a piece of wood, and this was the perfect program material—dense beats, fragments of sound and meaning, vituperative word-association: "*Suckers, liars get me a shovel/ Some writers I know are the damn devils/ From them I say don't believe the hype/ Yo Chuck, they must be on the pipe, right?*"

What might be a simple, bodaciously funky message of black self-determination, delivered by two college friends from Long Island, had turned into a liberal apologist's nightmare, a martyrdom in the making. At the center of it all, Chuck D, a virtual red diaper baby with a degree in graphic design, compared himself to Marcus Garvey and Nat Turner, and let the contradictions swirl.

For the record, Chuck D didn't make the statements quoted in the aforementioned handbill. They belong to Professor Griff, Public Enemy's Minister of Information and leader of the S1Ws (Security of the First World), Public Enemy's plastic-Uzi-toting, paramilitary Muslim security force.

Like Chuck D's logo, a silhouette of a black youth inside a rifle site, and like the S1Ws plastic Uzis, Public Enemy merges the rhetoric of militancy with that of advertising in ways that sit uneasily for both camps. The crew is both rational and hysterical at the same time. Chuck D: "It's definitely Armageddon. The black man and woman is at war with himself or herself, and with the situation around them. Armageddon is the war to end all wars. That's when everything hopefully will be all right, the last frontier. Of course we're in it. I'm in it. Maybe you're not in it. You can afford not to be in it, because it doesn't confront you on a daily basis. Black people in America are at war."

Chuck, what's your reaction to the handbill distributed at the New Music Seminar? They're making a whole lot of shit about nothing. A lot of paranoia going on. People think I got the ability to fucking turn a country around.

Do you back the statements that Griff made? I back Griff. Whatever he says, he can prove.

You mean he can prove that white people mated with monkeys? That it wouldn't be such a bad idea if the Palestinians were to kill all the Jews in Israel? Now that was taken out of context. I was there. He said by Western civilizations standards it wouldn't be bad for the Palestinians to come into Palestine and kill all the Jews, because that's what's been done right throughout Western civilization: invasion, conquering, and killing. That wasn't mentioned.

It's no secret that white people lived in caves while blacks had civilizations. Marcus Garvey said the same shit Farrakhan's saying today. Black people know this. White people do not. Now, people think we're building up some sort of anti-Semitic hate. Black people's feelings around the country…98 percent of them say Jews are just white people, there ain't no difference. That's my feeling. I don't like to make an issue out of it.

Do you consider yourself prophets? I guess so. We're bringing a message that's the same shit all the other guys I mentioned in the song have either been killed for or deported: Marcus Garvey, Nat Turner, all the way up to Farrakhan and Malcolm X.

What is a prophet? One that comes with a message from God to try to free the people. My people are enslaved within their own minds. Rap serves as the communication that they don't get for themselves to make them feel good about themselves. Rap is black America's TV station. It gives a whole perspective of what exists and what black life is about. And black life doesn't get the total spectrum of information through anything else. They don't get it through print because kids won't pick up no magazines or no books, really, unless it's got pictures of rap stars. They don't see themselves on TV. Number two, black radio stations have neglected giving out information.

On what? On anything. They give out information that white America gives out. Black radio does not challenge information coming from the structure into the black community, does not interpret what's happening around the world in the benefit of us. The only thing that gives you straight-up facts on how the black youth feel is a rap record. It's the number one communicator, force, and source in America right now.

I look at myself as an interpreter and dispatcher. To get a message across, you have to bring up certain elements that they praise, or once did praise, 'cause I've seen a change in the last year and a half.

What do you have to bring up that they praise? Violence. Drugs. Two years ago black kids used to think that saying nothing was all right; getting a gold rope, a fat dukey gold rope, was the dope shit; it's all right to sniff a little coke, get nice for the moment; get my fly ride and do anything to get it, even if it means stomping on the next man, 'cause I got to look out for number one. It's all right for a drug dealer to deal drugs, it's alright 'cause he's making money.

1988, it's a different thought. Because consciousness has been raised to the point where people are saying, "That gold rope don't mean shit now."

Are you taking credit for these changes? Yes. When I say, "Farrakhan's a prophet and I think you ought to listen" [on "Bring The Noise"], kids don't challenge the fact that Farrakhan's a prophet or not. Few of them know what a prophet is. But they will try and find out who Farrakhan is and what a prophet is. Once curiosity has been sparked, the learning process begins.

You said in the *NME* that you went to the SPIN party looking for me, that you wanted to fuck me up bad. I sure did. You appear to be a nice guy. Did you used to have long hair? I just wanted to speak with you mainly that night. I heard you was hiding out.

EXCERPT CONTINUES ON NEXT PAGE >

> EXCERPT CONTINUED FROM PREVIOUS PAGE

Everybody's entitled to their opinion, I guess. But it's bad that you keep your opinion limited. Because the whole market of rap is basically unable to judge information. I know that most of the market doesn't read the magazine, but some do.

Your last single, "Bring The Noise," was basically about what other people are saying about you.... Oh yeah, that was about you. I was talking right about you....

And now your new single, "Don't Believe The Hype," is also about what people are saying about you.... "Don't Believe the Hype" is about telling people, "Listen, just don't believe the things that are told to you." Go out and seek, challenge information. "The follower of Farrakhan/ Don't tell me that you understand/ Until you hear the man/ I bring the book of the new school rap game/ Writers treat me like Coltrane, insane/ Yes to them, but to me I'm a different kind/ We're brothers of the same mind, unblind." We both know what's happening, but we're treated like we're bugging. That's why I say I'm treated like Coltrane. 'Cause when Coltrane took his stance in the mid-'60s, a lot of writers came crashing down on him because of his radical stance.

You call yourselves Public Enemy, and build a strong identity on that, but then the minute you get a little piece of criticism, you fly off the handle. Don't you think that makes it a little exciting?

You used to come out at the beginning of your concerts and say that the Klan was outside, ready to shut you down. But there was no danger of this. No. But at the same time, I was letting people be aware that these forces exist.

And you feel justified in manipulating the facts in order to make that point? Uh huh.

That's the mark of a politician, to manipulate the truth to get across an agenda. To manipulate the truth? You tell me another way to tell the truth to black people if they don't want to hear the truth straight out. I'm open to answers.

Why do you take the bait every time an interviewer offers it? Taking the bait? I'm not actually taking the bait. Sometimes the bait is thrown at you and you can't get out of the way. It's easy to attack us.

It's no problem at all. It's a matter of throwing you a noose and letting you put your neck in it. Uh huh. But at the same time, I don't look at it as putting my head in a fucking noose, because it's not really dying. The music they can't stop.

I'm just saying, being that I'm the only one that's making this shit kind of exciting for a little period of time, don't take this shit so seriously that you get hurt. 'Cause I got a job to do.

All right, Chuck, I'm straight. We can wind this up. C'mon, you can't be straight, man. Let's keep talking....

— "Armageddon in Effect" / John Leland / September '88

I have never read an article like John Leland's on Public Enemy {September} that motivated me to write. Consider this an open letter to Chuck D.

The bottom line is simple. Griff's pronouncements on whites, gays, and Jews are pure, unabashed hatred. I'm not paranoid. Substitute the word "black" for any of the groups Griff despises and you'd be just as angry as I am. If you can not see the hatred you're helping to promote, you are as blind as those you vilify in song. The persecution of blacks in this country is inexcusable. Using it to justify more persecution is disgusting.

It's a shame the painful lessons of history never seem to teach us much, Chuck. But bullshit is only one color and it all stinks. Don't believe the hate, indeed. Keep the noise.

BRIAN FOX, Richmond, VA
— "Letters" / November, '88

The pretense of objectivity by Reagan-era "liberals" pushing their mono-cultural agendas as music criticism is what makes Public Enemy's "radical" stance so refreshing. Hip hop will represent and define itself only on its own terms, {which are} beyond the experience of 99.4 percent of said critics. So take it from Chuck D: Yo, if you can't swing this/ learn the words/you might sing this.

ART JONES, Bronx, NY
— "Letters" / November, '88

"Chuck D is a good person at heart, but he's easily influenced. When a little pressure came down, they turned their back on me. That's real sad. If Allah didn't put mercy in my heart, them negroes would be dead now. I had black people come up to me and say, 'Hank Shocklee, he's a snake, I'll do him for free. Chuck D, he's sold out. Just tell me where he lives.' But I said no. Allah has to deal with Chuck and Hank in his own way."

— Professor Griff, 1990

"The whole concept is that there is no such thing as black and white," says Chuck D, explaining the idea behind the forthcoming PE album *Fear of a Black Planet.* "Eight percent of the planet is of the so-called Caucasian complexion. If the world is truly to come together in peace and love, then that eight percent have to abandon the notion that their complexion makes them superior to the rest of the planet."

— Chuck D, 1989

[KEVIN SAUNDERSON]

/ Mike **Rubin**

: Chicago House /
Detroit Techno

A tale of two cities

ELECTRONIC MUSIC HAS ALWAYS HAD AN IMAGE PROBLEM, AT LEAST IN NORTH AMERICA (AND NO, I'M NOT REFERRING TO THE SIGHT OF A SCRAWNY GEEK "KICKING OUT THE JAMS" ONSTAGE WHILE CHECKING E-MAIL ON HIS LAPTOP, THOUGH THAT CONSTITUTES A REPRESENTATIONAL DILEMMA OF A DIFFERENT SORT).

By the mid-'90s, electronic music had come to be synonymous with, as a SPIN editor once termed it, the "bald, ugly DJ"—a closely cropped white male turntablist/musician, usually of European extraction and presumably hopped up on the latest illicit pharmacological concoction, making the rounds of the international club circuit. This generalization was accurate to a point, but it obscured the actual roots of electronic dance music. Long before Orbital blasted off or the Chemical Brothers knew how to set their periodic table, a group of African-American DJs and producers in Detroit and Chicago laid the foundation of late-20th-century dance music, creating a Rust Belt renaissance far from the meccas of London or Berlin.

Nurtured in the Windy City's black and gay clubs during the early '80s by DJs like Frankie Knuckles and Ron Hardy, Chicago house began as a stripped-down, jacked-up take on disco, based around a drum-machine-driven 4/4 rhythm and augmented with uptempo keyboards and soaring vocals informed by African-American gospel (though the music's message was decidedly more profane). Out went the sophisticated strings and muso chops of Philly International or Salsoul; what was left was a brutal, homemade thump. Indisputably carnal, the groove was quite literally seminal: The bouncy, bleepy basslines of Larry Heard's "Can You Feel It" and "Washing Machine" (under his alias Mr. Fingers) paved the way for the output on the U.K.'s trailblazing techno label Warp in the late '80s, while Marshall Jefferson productions like "Move Your Body" laid the template for an entire era of party music, from hip-house to Eurodisco. The music soon took a decidedly mechanistic leap forward, thanks to the abrasive, squelchy basslines produced by the Roland TB-303 synth, a distorted, rubbery sound effect that would be termed "acid" for its time-bending, trippy qualities. Popularized by Phuture's "Acid Trax"—another Jefferson production—this new strain of "acid house" inspired an entire generation of musicians, many of whom took the drug allusion literally, providing the soundtrack for countless Ecstasy-fuelled raves during the U.K.'s Summer of Love in 1988.

Meanwhile, 300 miles to the east on I-94, Detroit-area teenager Juan Atkins and his high school buddies Kevin Saunderson and Derrick May refined Chicago's mid-'80's blueprint, upping the electronic content and adding a forward-thinking, defiantly cosmic worldview cobbled together from the writings of *Future Shock* author Alvin Toffler and Atkins' own high-carb ruminations. If Chicago's party people were DIY hedonists, then the Detroiters were grandiose futurists, albeit with an old-fashioned commitment to the dance floor. In the city where the assembly line became a staple of modern life, Atkins and his disciples welded together Motor City funk, European new wave, and Japanese gadgetry to form a streamlined chassis which they eventually dubbed "techno." Choosing monikers like Model 500 and Rhythim Is Rhythim as a way of "repudiating ethnic designations," according to Atkins, they cloaked their personas behind a machinelike façade; it would be this high-concept elimination of any telltale emblems of African-American identity, however, that would come back to haunt the Detroiters in their search for a black audience.

Revered as dance-club deities from Amsterdam to Zurich, the Detroiters were all but ignored here in the States, receiving virtually no publicity and even less radio airplay. As techno's digitized signals crisscrossed Planet Rock, most of the producers and consumers who tuned in were white, and the identity of the music's funky forefathers often got lost in the transmission. Meanwhile, black audiences and musicians ceased to see techno as their own art form, leaving the electronic innovators of Detroit and Chicago feeling spurned by indifferent record companies and estranged from their own community. After more than 15 years of frustration and obscurity, however, Motown's pioneers were finally honored in their hometown in 2000 with the inaugural edition of the Detroit Electronic Music Festival, a weekend of free outdoor concerts on the city's downtown riverfront that drew hundreds of thousands of revelers from all over the world back to the cradle of techno. The festival has since become a Memorial Day tradition—proof that, Derrick May's maxim to the contrary, rhythm isn't merely rhythm in the Motor City but the stuff of life itself.

DETROIT ESSENTIALS

Cybotron: *Clear* (1983/1990, Fantasy)
Model 500: *Classics* (1995, R&S) [Belgian import]
Derrick May: *Innovator* (1997, Transmat/Never)
Kevin Saunderson: *Faces & Phases* (1997, Planet E)
Paperclip People: *The Secret Tapes of Dr. Eich* (1996, Planet E)
Underground Resistance: *Revolution For Change* (1992, Network) [UK import]
Moodymann: *Silent Introduction* (1997, Planet E)
Theo Parrish: *First Floor* (1998, Sound Signature/Peace Frog) [UK import]
Plastikman: *Consumed* (1998, M_nus/Novamute)
Daniel Bell: *Blip, Blurp, Bleep: The Music of Daniel Bell* (2003, Logistic) [French import]

CHICAGO ESSENTIALS

Various Artists: *Trax Records: The 20th Anniversary Collection* (2004, Trax/Casablanca)
Marshall Jefferson: *Move Your Body: The Evolution of Chicago House* (2003, Unisex)
Marshall Jefferson: *Les Parrains de la House* (1998, Mirakkle) [French import]
Larry Heard: *Les Parrains de la House* (1998, Mirakkle) [French import]
Mr. Fingers: *Amnesia* (1989, Jack Trax/Indigo)
Various Artists: *In the Key of E* (1988, Desire) [UK import]
Various Artists: *The Future Sound of Chicago* (1995, Cajual/Relief/Ministry of Sound)
Various Artists: *A Taste of Cajual* (1996, Cajual)
Green Velvet: *The Nineties* (1993 A.D. Through 1999 A.D.) (1999, Music Man) [Belgian import]
Felix Da Housecat: *Kittenz and Thee Glitz* (2002, Emperor Norton)

HOUSE MUSIC IS HARD DISCO. IT GOES BOOM BOOM BOOM BOOM WITH LITTLE VARIATION, SUBTLETY, MELODY, INSTRUMENTATION—OR MUSIC FOR THAT MATTER. HOUSE, BY DEFINITION, AIN'T CROSSOVER. IT'S IN THE HOUSE, AND IT WON'T COME OUT.

House lyrical content consists of dancing and sex. "Jacking your body" (moving up and down on a dance floor) can easily slide into sex. Especially on Farley Keith's records. On his first, "Aw Shucks" by Jackmaster Funk, a black Betty Boop voice squeaks at the onset, "Hey big boy, are you gonna make me feel the bass on this record?" It then screams, "Ohhh, work my body down to the floor," and then propositions, "Farley, come here and let me jack your little dick, too." Like the incessantly booming beat, house sexuality is reduced to absurdly aggressive basics, but not without a self-mocking playfulness and an underlying message of liberation. "Jack the Dick" by Jackmaster Dick repeats the phrase, "Suck my dick, bitch," several dozen times at various speeds before evolving into the chant, "Suck my motherfuckin' dick, bitch." For Chicago's black gays,

threatened by AIDS, jacking the night away at an after–hours club has become the most physically gratifying alternative to sex. "Around 1984, when people started becoming aware that there was a real house scene," says Chip E., "people also became aware of everyone else being gay. It became really fashionable to flit around. Everybody wanted to be gay. Now everybody wants to be a DJ."

House is about the loss of decorum and control. From sexual extravagance to dance-floor excess, everything about house is geared toward *losing it*. The mania for obscure dance records, their inflated prices, the vocalists who can't stay on pitch, the fly-by-night labels that pump out more records than most people can keep up with, the mixes that sound like they could damage your woofers and tweeters, and the pressings that sound like eggs frying behind the music, all add up to a scene spinning off its axis. Whether it refers to dancing or fucking, Gary B.'s whispered chant of "Release my soul/ I've lost control/ I'm too far gone/ ain't no way back" on Adonis's "No Way Back" serves as the house prayer for deliverance.

As intense as the house party gets, these Chicagoans still retain a sense of community. When the singer Pandy declares, "Ohhoho, you just look so *good*. (gasp) Standing right there (gasp) waiting for a big, (gasp) good-looking man like me just to (gasp) come over there and run my hands (gasp) in your long, beautiful black hair and look into your big, beautiful (gasp) brown eyes and *kissss your sssensssuousss lipsss*," the house audience knows he's doing a Loleatta Holloway/Isaac Hayes/Teddy Pendergrass love-rap thing, and he makes perfect sense. To the rest of the world, however, Pandy's sensuality may seem grossly overstated. Like every cult music, house is a set of codes, a language mutually understood by those who speak it but deliberately foreign to outsiders. Despite the tension created by major labels coming in to take away talent (Geffen has Jesse Saunders and the Bang Orchestra, RCA has J.M. Silk and other labels have courted D.J. International), the music makers themselves still all work on each other's projects, resist outside attempts to slow down their furious production pace, and generally hang together like a family. As Screamin' Rachael puts it, "What you see with D.J. International is like a new Chess label appearing. We've got a lot of blues, soul, and gangster influences. After all, we are from Chicago."
— "Burning Down the House" / Barry Walters / November '86

"**IN 1988, CHICAGO HOUSE MUSICIANS WERE IN A BIND.** Spurned by the major labels in America, they began to make increasingly uncommercial music for England's rabid acid house market. Led by Phuture, whose "Acid Trax" put the subgenre on the map by giving a name and logo to a long-standing tradition in dance music, the Chicago acid house crowd abandoned rhythm and blues and moved totally underground, into the inhuman ecstasy of electronic experimentation. Acid house, like its Detroit counterpart, techno, put a premium on the weird, as if evolution was racing toward a dangerous technological fusion before the end of the night."
— "Singles" / John Leland / May '89

[JUAN ATKINS]　　　　[CARL CRAIG, *above left*]

seven mile and greenfield may look like a lot of things, but the future isn't one of them.

The busy intersection in northwest Detroit lies just south of 8 Mile Road, the infamous boundary between the largest U.S. city with a majority African-American population and its prosperous and predominately white suburbs, but it might as well be a planet away. On a sunny Saturday afternoon in early June, Nation of Islam members stand in traffic hawking copies of the *Final Call*. Two kids sell katydids for $5 from a makeshift stand. Telephone poles act as crude town criers, with tattered handbills announcing 40 YEARS OF MOTOWN: THE REUNION and NEED CASH? REFINANCE! A weathered billboard threatening ARMAGEDDON: JULY 1ST most likely heralds an overhyped action flick, but given Detroit's tragic history, anything is possible.

It's a vista that hardly seems to fit the description "Techno City," the name Juan Atkins hung on Detroit almost 15 years ago, yet this is the neighborhood where Atkins grew up, and where the futuristic electronic music began. It was near this spot that Buy-Rite Records stood, the first local store to offer 12-inch dance singles by area producers and musicians. Many of those same artists—Atkins, Derrick May, Kevin Saunderson, Carl Craig, to name a few—are now superstar DJs abroad, their international stature cemented years ago, but in their own community they're practically invisible. Atkins hopes to rectify that, and thus the "Godfather of Techno" has chosen this storied corner as the location for his own record store.

Given Detroit's status as a bastion of black conciousness, it's hard to imagine an unlikelier bunch of heroes than Aryan automatons Kraftwerk. By choosing Detroit as one of only five cities on their recent U.S. tour, Kraftwerk acknowledged the debt they owed the Motor City, and vice versa—their concert at the State Theater was practically a family reunion, with all the distant cousins present: In the crowd were Atkins, May, Eddie Fowlkes, Brendan "Ectomorph" Gillen, Gerald Donald (Drexciya/Dopplereffekt), bass/booty jock DJ Godfather, Dan Bell (Cybersonik/DBX), Keith Tucker (Aux 88/Optic Nerve), and Anthony "Shake" Shakir. For Detroit techno, it was basically the landing of the Mothership.

When Kraftwerk finally stepped on stage, they were greeted with the enthusiasm of a Nuremberg rally. As Raif Hütter recited, "Uno, dos," from "Numbers," the audience thundered back "tres, cuatro!" as if the Teutons were Detroit's own. The lovefest continued afterward at an impromptu reception for the group at a new techno club called Motor, the first of its kind in Detroit in nearly a decade. Hundreds of fans packed a tiny back room to press flesh and compare gear, and despite their limited conversational abilities, Kraftwerk's Hütter and Florian Schnieder mingled with their acolytes until the wee hours. As the pair finally began to offer auf Wiedersehens to the faithful, "Shake" Shakir spoke up for all of Motown's electric community. "I'm a musician from Detroit," he said, extending his hand to Hütter. "And I'd just like to say thank you for giving me a career."

— "A Tale of Two Cities" / Mike Rubin / October '98

WAS ELECTRONICA MORE THAN A FLING, MON CHERI?

Now that the firestartin', dry-ice hype of 1997 has finally cleared and even your grandma knows that raves are where DJs spin records backward to make kids smoke Ecstasy, can us grown-up Americans finally embrace some real, soul-questioning dance music? Sure, Moby gets all the CK Dirty Denim his bony ass can bear, and trance wafts through the suburbs. But what about the artists who never fit the crossover mug shot, who had no desire to "rock" or woo rags like SPIN?

Well, they're still here. Spurred on by eccentric elders like Keven Saunderson (who still conjures a burly, synth-funk swoon), Derrick May (DJ'ing his suave tribal chieftain ass off), and Danny Tenaglia (boldly snaking dubby techno through his house soirées), they're jackin' dance music's African-American, Latino, and gay club essence from the ground up. And if you long for a time when techno didn't just mean administering CPR to a pigtailed 16-year-old with a glowstick, then you know what I'm talkin' about.

On his latest, *Designer Music: the Remixes—Vol. 1*, Detroit producer/Planet E label boss Carl Craig represents for the (cough cough) "maturing" rave crew. He disguises a visionary discourse on '80's Eurodisco, New York electro, Detroit techno, and Chicago house as the tweaked-out mix tape of the year, tickling every genre's underbelly, redefining every boundary. (He even drops the forlorn 303 synth classic "Problemes de Amour," an early-'80's fluke Detroit radio hit by doofy Italian duo Alexander Robotnick.) Craig's programming has a jittery, romantic yearning, a need to slip Stevie Wonder's hope-against-hope into a rigid hard drive and see what spits out. His labelmates are equally fitful: Check the simmering sense of betrayal that fuels the house tracks Kenny Dixon Jr. records as Moodyman.

Designer Music recalls a late-'80's minute when B-boys wouldn't dismiss Mr. Fingers as "some gay shit," the Jungle Brothers' "I'll House You" had ruffnecks hoppin', and daring dance music was at least in the black urban ballgame. Then rap blotted out the sky, and U.K. rave brats took the groove and gorged it on Ecstasy. As history, it's a bittersweet pill, and no song has ever captured it like Green Velvet's 1995 single "Flash," rereleased with epochal remixes by Timo Maas and Tenaglia. A druggy/draggy monologue about naughty kids over a hypnotic, slapped-silly beat, "Flash" is the hilariously searing tale of Chicago rave-house lifer Curtis Jones (a.k.a. Velvet), who feels like a nostalgic tourist in his own burned-out backyard and daydreams about a utopia where Grace Jones fucks Iggy Pop on the giant mirror ball in Times Square.

— "Whose House?" / Charles Aaron / October '00

[POISON]

14 /

: '80s Metal

Stars, stripes, and Aqua Net

/ Chuck **Klosterman**

ERE ARE
ANY STOCK
ODIFIERS
ED WHEN
SCRIBING '80S
AM METAL.

ntious" is one of them, which isn't accurate; bands like L.A. and Faster Pussycat took them- far less seriously than the angst- grunge acts who flourished in ake. "Bloated" is another, which ertainly true near the end; the Pretty Boy Floyd were advanced $1 million from MCA Records erforming a grand total of nine However, the adjective no one s to apply to hair metal is can," and this is an oversight. se—above all else—the flying V, ex-clad, Aqua Net metal of the n administration was rock'n'roll at st American. Which is probably o many rock critics hated it.

Pop metal is always associated e most-coked out neighborhoods st Hollywood, and understandably ound zero for the movement's ation can be traced to four or five on (or around) The Sunset Strip. no U.S. city is as plastic as Los es, the genre's aesthetic seemed ct those surroundings. But L.A. t build the warriors of glam metal; ns N' Roses guitarist Izzy Stradlin said, L.A. was simply where all dudes ended up. Virtually every player of the glitter-cum-leather arrived from somewhere else: n and Axl Rose hailed from a. Mötley Crüe's Nikki Sixx went school in Seattle. Most of Poison from Harrisburg; much of Ratt from San Diego. Despite the

genre's superficial obsession with public debauchery, there was an unde- niably conservative bent to '80 metal: When Bret Michaels sang about talking dirty, he actually placed the conversa- tion at a drive-in movie, almost as if he was trying to hook-up with Richie Cunningham's girlfriend. In the classic Penelope Spheeris documentary *The Decline of Western Civilization, Part. II*, the ill-fated Hollywood band London attempts to burn a Communist flag on- stage before performing a song called "Russian Winter." Most '80s metal bands were happy with America; it was a great era for capitalism and optimism and blow jobs. Naysayers always want to label groups like Bon Jovi as hair metal, but they really should have called them *teeth* metal. These were rock bands who smiled.

That started to change when Guns N' Roses released *Appetite for Destruction* in 1987. Like their peers, GNR liked Led Zeppelin, Aerosmith, and Judas Priest; unlike their peers, they also loved Thin Lizzy, Elton John, and the Damned. The songs on *Appetite for Destruction* were both harder and softer than any metal that had come before, and its most sophisticated moments still sounded dangerous. However, the larger difference was the band's posture: Guns N' Roses did not seem to be faking their nihilism. Lots of groups sang about drugs, but Slash really was a functioning heroin-addict; lots of bands sang about rough sex, but Axl Rose actually had supermodels accuse him of domestic violence. Every time Guns N' Roses did something ter- rible, it made their music sound better. They were the musical apex of the entire metal idiom, and they were the clearest example of what happened when the rural Midwest was jammed into the accelerated depravity of California: Through the eyes and throat of Axl Rose, Los Angeles was a sinister place ("Welcome to the Jungle"), filled

with syringes ("Mr. Brownstone"), pretty girls ("Paradise City"), and the worst ele- ments of his own human nature ("One in a Million"). For at least three years, Guns N' Roses were the best band in the world *by far*.

It's tempting to argue that Guns N' Roses saved heavy metal. In reality, the opposite is true; they basically killed it. *Appetite for Destruction* was so popular that almost every metal act on earth was immediately given a record deal (one of the only groups who didn't—a band from the Pacific Northwest who called them- selves Alice N' Chainz—eventually found success under different fashion parame- ters, and with slightly improved gram- mar). Upstart metal bands started copy- ing third-generation metal bands who had actually been copies of second- generation metal bands. A new wave of "credible" artists started dressing like lumberjacks and laughed at poodle- haired guitar players who were still trying to prove how fast they could perform solos only other guitarists wanted to hear, and the world laughed with them. Mötley Crüe lost Vince Neil. Poison lost C.C. DeVille. Guns N' Roses lost every- body except Axl, who elected to replace the entire band (and then lose them again, and then replace them again, and then record an album that doesn't exist … twice). At the end of this fairy tale, Cinderella didn't recover any glass slip- per; this time, Cinderella just ended up headlining the Ohio State Fair.

What's funny is that—now that glam metal truly is over, and now that it only exists as a kitschy trope for The Darkness and Sum 41 and the Donnas —lots of people who *hated* metal in 1988 now insist they always loved it, and that pop metal was charming and fun, and that they miss hearing Van Halen from across their high school's parking lot. But this kind of cultural revisionism is always what happens when we think America is going to get better, but it actually gets worse.

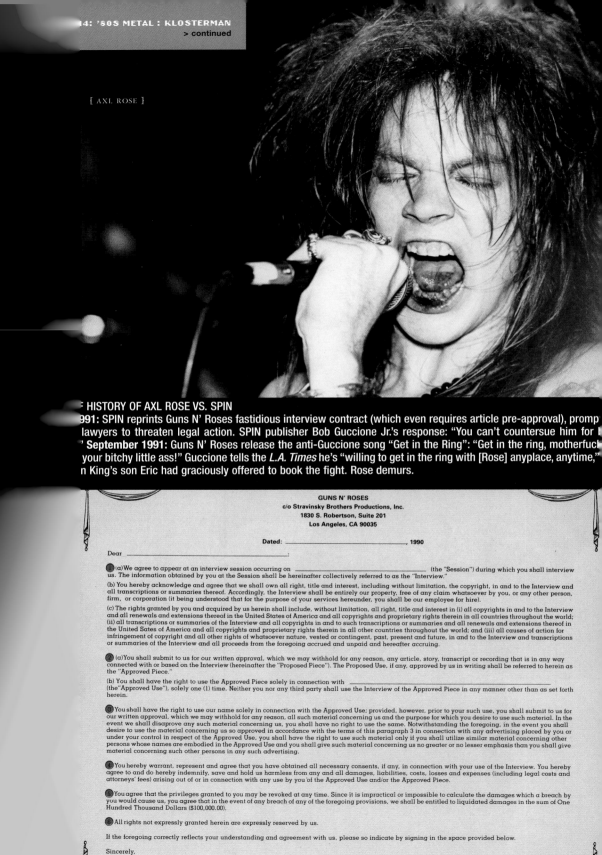

[AXL ROSE]

HISTORY OF AXL ROSE VS. SPIN

1991: SPIN reprints Guns N' Roses fastidious interview contract (which even requires article pre-approval), promp
lawyers to threaten legal action. SPIN publisher Bob Guccione Jr.'s response: "You can't countersue him for
September 1991: Guns N' Roses release the anti-Guccione song "Get in the Ring": "Get in the ring, motherfuck
your bitchy little ass!" Guccione tells the *L.A. Times* he's "willing to get in the ring with [Rose] anyplace, anytime,"
n King's son Eric had graciously offered to book the fight. Rose demurs.

GUNS N' ROSES
c/o Stravinsky Brothers Productions, Inc.
1830 S. Robertson, Suite 201
Los Angeles, CA 90035

Dated: _____, 1990

Dear _____:

(1) (a) We agree to appear at an interview session occurring on _____ (the "Session") during which you shall interview us. The information obtained by you at the Session shall be hereinafter collectively referred to as the "Interview."

(b) You hereby acknowledge and agree that we shall own all right, title and interest, including without limitation, the copyright, in and to the Interview and all transcriptions or summaries thereof. Accordingly, the Interview shall be entirely our property, free of any claim whatsoever by you, or any other person, firm, or corporation (it being understood that for the purpose of your services hereunder, you shall be our employee for hire).

(c) The rights granted by you and acquired by us herein shall include, without limitation, all right, title and interest in (i) all copyrights in and to the Interview and all renewals and extensions thereof in the United States of America and all copyrights and proprietary rights therein in all countries throughout the world; (ii) all transcriptions or summaries of the Interview and all copyrights in and to such transcriptions or summaries and all renewals and extensions thereof in the United Sates of America and all copyrights and proprietary rights therein in all other countries throughout the world; and (iii) all causes of action for infringement of copyright and all other rights of whatsoever nature, vested or contingent, past, present and future, in and to the Interview and transcriptions or summaries of the Interview and all proceeds from the foregoing accrued and unpaid and hereafter accruing.

(2) (a) You shall submit to us for our written approval, which we may withhold for any reason, any article, story, transcript or recording that is in any way connected with or based on the Interview (hereinafter the "Proposed Piece"). The Proposed Use, if any, approved by us in writing shall be referred to herein as the "Approved Piece."

(b) You shall have the right to use the Approved Piece solely in connection with _____
(the "Approved Use"), solely one (1) time. Neither you nor any third party shall use the Interview of the Approved Piece in any manner other than as set forth herein.

(3) You shall have the right to use our name solely in connection with the Approved Use; provided, however, prior to your such use, you shall submit to us for our written approval, which we may withhold for any reason, all such material concerning us and the purpose for which you desire to use such material. In the event we shall disapprove any such material concerning us, you shall have no right to use the same. Notwithstanding the foregoing, in the event you shall desire to use the material concerning us so approved in accordance with the terms of this paragraph 3 in connection with any advertising placed by you or under your control in respect of the Approved Use, you shall have the right to use such material only if you shall utilize similar material concerning other persons whose names are embodied in the Approved Use and you shall give such material concerning us no greater or no lesser emphasis than you shall give material concerning such other persons in any such advertising.

(4) You hereby warrant, represent and agree that you have obtained all necessary consents, if any, in connection with your use of the Interview. You hereby agree to and do hereby indemnify, save and hold us harmless from any and all damages, liabilities, costs, losses and expenses (including legal costs and attorneys' fees) arising out of or in connection with any use by you of the Approved Use and/or the Approved Piece.

(5) You agree that the privileges granted to you may be revoked at any time. Since it is impractical or impossible to calculate the damages which a breach by you would cause us, you agree that in the event of any breach of any of the foregoing provisions, we shall be entitled to liquidated damages in the sum of One Hundred Thousand Dollars ($100,000.00).

(6) All rights not expressly granted herein are expressly reserved by us.

If the foregoing correctly reflects your understanding and agreement with us, please so indicate by signing in the space provided below.

Sincerely,

GUNS N' ROSES   AGREED AND ACCEPTED:

By _____   By _____

IF IT'S AMAZING THAT THE GREAT BAND OF THE '80S SHOULD ARRIVE IN THE GUISE OF THAT GREAT EMPTY VESSEL OF THE '80S, THE LONG-HAIRED HARD-ROCKER, IT'S ALL THE MORE FITTING. It's a little bit as though the Sex Pistols waited until everybody had short spikey hair and played fast and sloppy and wore ripped clothes with slogans and then, once things were locked in place and predictable, emerged full-blown, fully bloomed, terrible in their beauty and elegant in the absence of limits. Every time Guns N' Roses launches into another commercial possibility and then Axl Rose shouts its chances right off the radio with one more "fuck off," with one more boast about drinking and driving, with all the band's will to be better than everybody else at being bad, Guns N' Roses looks like all that's left of rock'n'roll. And that's a lot. — "Musicians of the Year: Guns N' Roses" / December '88

THE DAY BEFORE THE FIRST OF FOUR SHOWS, WARM-UP ACT LIVING COLOUR'S LEAD GUITARIST, VERNON REID, DID A RADIO INTERVIEW, AND A CALLER ASKED ABOUT THE CONTROVERSIAL GUNS N' ROSES SONG "ONE IN A MILLION." Reid, who is black, said he likes Guns N' Roses but took exception to some of the words and sentiments in that song.

On the way to the stage for his band's set, Axl Rose pressed his face close to Reid's: "I heard on the radio that you guys got a problem with some of the things I got to say." Then Axl launched into his own defense, claiming he never thought of "you guys as niggers."

When Axl hit the stage, he stepped to the microphone and said, "Before we start playing I want to say I'm sick of all this publicity about our song 'One in a Million.' I'm not a fucking racist...." He went on to state that not all niggers are niggers but if someone is "acting like a fucking nigger," then he'll call it as he sees it. And the same thing goes "for fucking faggots." And then he said, "If you still want to call me a racist, you can shove it up your ass." — "Bad to the Bone" / Danny Sugerman / November '90

"OPENING FOR GUNS N' ROSES WAS AN ABSURD SITUATION FOR A BAND LIKE FAITH NO MORE. Their scene was about excess, excess, excess. There were more strippers than road crew. We weren't into that type of male bonding. The only time I saw their show was when we were reprimanded for laughing about the absurdity of the touring environment in the press and told that we'd have to apologize to Axl or leave the tour. We made an attempt to explain where we were coming from, but I think it went over his head because as a sort of peace offering he brought us to a trailer backstage where two naked women strippers were having sex."

— Roddy Bottum (Faith No More), 1997

CLEARLY GUNS N' ROSES ARE FUCK-UPS: ABORTED TOURS, ARRESTS, NO-SHOWS, BROKEN BONES, DETOX, URINATING ON AIRPLANES, MARRIAGES, DIVORCES, CHARGES OF RACISM AND OBSCENITY.

[GUNS N' ROSES]

Their perennial screwups prolonged their inability to record a proper follow-up to their 1987 debut, *Appetite for Destruction*, making them failures even at success.

But the same thing that threatens to destroy them is the same thing that has made them so popular to begin with: the fact that they are true misfits and outcasts.

Appetite for Destruction remained in the Top 10 for more than a year and has sold more than 10 million copies around the world. Their 1988 EP, *GN'R Lies*, stormed up the charts as well. Not bad for five guys who only wanted to blow away all the other L. A. club bands, to show the posers and wanna-bes how it was really done.

They should have then walked away, split up, or died like the Sex Pistols. Instead, they fought their way out of the trash heap of L.A.'s heavy-metal Sunset Boulevard scene to become the last authentic bad boys. Now, the possibilities for them are fantastic—that there is a place to go that someone like Jim Morrison stopped short of. "You know I went to Morrison's grave site last year," Axl Rose says softly. "I knew I could go the same way Jim did, that I could go down in flames, crucify myself on the altar of rock'n'roll. Everyone's always talking about me dying anyway."

I tell him that Joseph Campbell said that when you travel to the grave of someone you revere, it underscores the impulse to imitate that person's deeds. "That's why I went there," Rose says. "I just sat down next to where he was lying, if he's even there. I was just thinking; I don't even remember how long I was there. It was one of those depressing gray days. Nobody recognized me. And you know, it was like a turning point. I just realized that I could sacrifice myself like Morrison did if I wanted. That was my turning point—realizing that it was up to me."

One of Morrison's favorite quotes comes from William Blake, "The road of excess leads to the palace of wisdom."

"But not if you die," Rose says. "If you die, the road of excess leads to a dirt plot in a foreign land that people pour booze on and put out cigarettes on." —"Bad to the Bone" / Danny Sugerman / November '90

A DEFIANTLY WINDED GUNS N' ROSES PERFORMED AT THE MTV VIDEO MUSIC AWARDS IN AUGUST, PROMPTING AN ENTIRE NATION TO DEBATE WHAT WAS MORE ALARMING: Axl's apparently Botox-engorged cheeks and hair extensions or a kabuki-masked Slash wearing a chicken bucket on his head (actually, it was current guitarist Buckethead).

— "Backstage Pass" / Marc Spitz / January '03

EVEN IN LEATHER PANTS AND STILETTO HEELS, IT'S NOT A LONG WALK. Five minutes, maybe. The moment you cross Clark Street, you're at the Whisky A Go-Go; from there, it's 250 paces to the Roxy, and the Rainbow is right next to it. A few doors down is the Key Club, which is where Gazzarri's used to be. If you jump in a car and drive five minutes in the opposite direction, you'll pass the Viper Room (where River Phoenix took drugs and died), the Chateau Marmont (where John Belushi took drugs and died), and the Hyatt West Hollywood (where Led Zeppelin took drugs and lived); up the street are the Body Shop and the Seventh Vail, the strip joints mentioned in Mötley Crüe's "Girls, Girls, Girls"; if you turn south, you'll reach the site of the old Starwood, which is now a mini mall.

This is the Sunset Strip. It should be glamorous. It isn't. It's just another street that everybody's heard of, decorated by clubs and hotels that have no character, filled with aspiring actresses with fake breasts and aspiring directors with fake lives. But for ten years — 1981 to '91 – this was the most rock'n'roll place on the planet. This is where Mötley Crüe lived in squalor; this is where Slash bought his first top hat, this is where Warrant became down boys. This is where voluptuous 19-year-old women in pink leather miniskirts nestled against the golden, felt-covered walls of the Whisky, hoping to catch the roving eye of some dude from Ratt or Bang Tango or Bulletboys. This is where clichés were honed with laserlike precision.
— "Paradise City" / Chuck Klosterman / September '02

FOR YEARS, BANDS ON THE STRIP LIVED OFF THE GIRLS WHO LOVED THEM WHEN THEY WERE NOBODIES (ALMOST EVERY ARTIST INTERVIEWED FOR THIS STORY MENTIONED HUSTLING GIRLS FOR MONEY). But by 1991, every heavy medal nobody was trying to date a supermodel. In a way, those forgotten Strip girls were the true casualties of the hair explosion: They spent all their money on guys who never returned on the investment.

"I wasn't one of those girls, but my older sister was," says Janet Berry, now a 31-year-old accountant with 20th Century Fox. "She bought those guys groceries and clothes. She bought some nobody a bass guitar. And the fat girls with no self-esteem got used even worse."

Unfortunately, Warrant was kind of famous for that. They were known for having a heftier female fan base. You could use the term 'Warrant Girls' and everybody knew who you were talking about."
— "Paradise City" / Chuck Klosterman / September '02

"HAVE YOU EVER SEEN ONE OF THOSE SHOWS ON THE DISCOVERY CHANNEL WITH THE GUY WHO'S COVERED IN BEES? That's what it was like when we were on the Strip. Wherever we went, it was like a swarm of bees around us. People had to be close to us and touch us, and girls were like, 'I'm gonna fuck you tonight,' and guys were like, 'You're gonna do my drugs tonight,' and it sort of became the norm. I didn't think anything about it...narcissism is a wonderful disease, I guess." — Mötley Crüe's Nikki Sixx, 2002

"IT HAD GONE FROM WHAT EVERYONE THINKS ROCK'N'ROLL *IS*," SAYS NIKKI SIXX, "LIKE THE SMALL FACES ALL DRINKIN' AT THE BAR AND PICKIN' UP CHICKS AND GOING BACK TO THE HOTEL ROOM AND FUCKING—to just out and out no-fun; hardass drinking, fistfights, grumpy people all the time, looking like shit."

"Tommy and Nikki got thrown in jail there for throwin' Jack [Daniels] bottles on the bullet train," remembers Vince. "I almost got shot. I drank like 10 pitchers of kamikazes in this club called the Lexington Queen in Tokyo—and I don't remember any of this shit—and they said I just walked over to these Japanese businessmen, picked up their table, and fuckin' threw it at them, with all their drinks and shit. The guy who was sittin' there though, was the son of the head of the Japanese Mafia and those were all his security guys. They drew all their fuckin' guns on me—they were gonna kill me.

"Our security guys jumped on me and drug me out. There were a fuckin' thousand people around—the place was packed to the gills. I lost a fuckin' diamond Rolex watch that night. I woke up naked on the floor of my hotel room, not knowing what the fuck happened."

A couple days after the group returned from Japan, Sixx O.D.'d and their management, McGhee Entertainment, pulled the plug on the European leg of the *Girls* tour. The band called a somber meeting with management, backup singers the Nasty Habits, road crew—everyone—and asked for help. Everyone had to stop, which proved to be easier said than done—"a few weeks later I'd end up in the Rainbow with my shorts on from the beach, drinking these things called Quaaludes," burps Vince. — "Beyond the Valley of the Ultra Glam Boys" / Dean Kuipers / January '90

"LISTEN!" YELLS A ROLY-POLY, THICK-NECKED MAN IN A YELLOW SHORT-SLEEVED CONCERT SECURITY SHIRT. "Get the guy who kicked Jim. The one with a beard. We're pressing charges."

I hear this from the side of the stage at the America West Arena in Phoenix, where Mötley Crüe have just finished waving the rock'n'roll banner as high and as flagrantly as possible. There was sex (Tommy Lee, no stranger to the camcorder, asking audience members to show their tits as he filmed them); there were drugs (video images of people shooting up, a ritual familiar to at least half of the band); there was rock'n'roll ("Shout at the Devil," "Girls, Girls Girls," "Live Wire"); and there was violence. The concert ended with Nikki Sixx kicking and Lee spitting on a security guard as Vince Neil instructed the crowd that the stage was theirs and hundreds of them agreed, tumbling over the barricades, mauling the band, and causing some $15,000 in damages.

I run back to the dressing room to warn Sixx to leave the arena while he still has the chance, but he just laughs because for some reason I'm smiling and he thinks it's some sort of birthday prank. In about half an hour, he will be 39 and in prison.

Within minutes, as a swarm of cops in riot gear tries to clear the stage, a half dozen police officers burst into the dressing room. They look around: There's a problem. Two members of Mötley Crüe have facial hair that could be interpreted as beards: Sixx and Lee. They first approach Sixx. "Is this the guy who attacked the security officer? Put your hands behind your back."

Then they turn to Lee, who is wearing nothing but tiny rubber shorts, and begin placing cuffs on him. "Why me? I didn't do anything," he protests.

"We're placing you under arrest for inciting a riot and inciting girls to expose their breasts."

"Is that a bad thing?" a roadie asks.

Sixx and Lee are led out of the dressing room. They are big, tan, muscular guys, and they look good in handcuffs. Two acne-speckled teens in Mötley Crüe T-shirts, each with a vinyl copy of 1983's *Shout at the Devil*, run up to them and ask for autographs. Lee jerks his head back toward his handcuffs as a way of letting them know how idiotic their request is. Sixx, the next day, will brag, "I think that topped the time some guy asked Ozzy to sign an autograph while he was taking a shit."
— "Shout at the Bouncer" / Neil Strauss / March '98

[MÖTLEY CRÜE]

:Hip-Hop's Golden Age

[ERIC B AND RAKIM]

Roughnecks, radicals, and undergrads

You grow up in Queens.

You ride the #44A bus past St. John's University to 168th Street, then hike south across Grand Central Parkway to Jamaica High School. Initially, "hip-hop" exists in this middle-class, mixed-race neighborhood mainly as rumor; rap is a novelty from the Bronx or Harlem (or—who knew?—Jersey) that you hear on boomboxes in Goose Pond Park where everyone smokes dime bags of dirtweed after class. You like the way rap roughs up disco's blow-dried grooves, love the brittle sound of electro. But in 1983, Run-D.M.C.'s "Sucker MCs" spins your head like Linda Blair's. Mainly it's those skull-cracking, scratched-up, post-"Planet Rock" robot beats. But it's also D.M.C.'s rhyming about your neighborhood (you've never heard that before) and boasting about going to college like he was your dad ready to whup you for scoring below 1200 on your SATs. This will prove a key to the cultural revolution that follows: Run-D.M.C. made hip-hop's underdog ambition signify large not just through radical sound—the barking delivery and rock noise—but by representing as middle-class Everymen. You relate, and so do millions of others.

A few years later, you return home from college and get a civil-service job working with the city's drug-rehab centers. Heroin is big pimpin', but crack's already in full swing: Even on your "good" (read: white) block in Fresh Meadows, your mom gets knocked down for her purse. Alongside your indie-rock obsession, you follow rap like a serial novel of the city, buying 12-inches at Vinyl Mania on Carmine Street, and every week presents some new cheaply pressed chapter: MC Lyte meeting her basehead boyfriend at the Empire Roller Disco in Brooklyn ("I Cram to Understand U"), Audio Two's MC Milk Dee (Lyte's brother) joking about stealing the

103

ESSAY CONTINUES ON NEXT PAGE >

girlfriend of a guy in prison ("Top Billin'"), or the Jungle Brothers stoop-rhyming dick jokes over a red-eyed Red Alert beat ("Jimbrowski"). You read Armond White and Harry Allen in the *City Sun*, Greg "Ironman" Tate in the *Village Voice*, John Leland in SPIN. But you rarely turn out for live hip-hop, because after the murder of Michael Griffith by a gang of white racists over in Howard Beach in late '86, hip-hop clubs are tense places for white kids. At Christmas dinner that year, your Italian cousins from Middle Village suggest that Griffith somehow deserved his fate. You increasingly see blood ties as meaningless accidents of biology.

At one of the itinerant "Candy Bar" parties downtown, you hear an early pressing of "Rebel Without a Pause" by Public Enemy—guys from Adelphi University, just over the Queens border on the south side of Long Island. The record hits you like "Sucker MCs," but even harder. The siren screech as melody line. The bulldozing radio-announcer flow. The call to impeach the president and the name-dropping of Joanne Chesimard, the former Black Panther (you later learn) who killed a Jersey state trooper, escaped a maximum-security prison, and fled to Cuba. Between instrumentals and vocal bits, the DJ plays it four times. People dance like they're being stun-gunned. You will remember this as the night the bottomless power of hip-hop is revealed to you—that it could be anything, and be about anything. In a few months, PE's black nationalism will ignite a cultural firestorm that makes them the most consequential musicians in the country.

What had been goofy rhymes over disco tunes was suddenly a million stories in a million styles: some of them reported from ghetto frontlines, some watched from across town, some from their own planet altogether. You hear Rakim—another Long Island-bred kid— and believe he is the coolest man alive, his measured baritone flow breathtaking, a rhyme-slinging philosopher king ("It ain't where ya from, it's where ya at"). You hear KRS-One (the KRS standing for "Knowledge Reigns Supreme"), a hard-knock Bronx kid who hung out in libraries and opened one of the first "gangsta" records, 1987's *Criminal Minded*, by declaring himself a poet and a teacher. After his friend and DJ Scott LaRock is shot and killed, he devotes himself to making community-minded records like "Stop the Violence"—though it bothers you that they're never as catchy as his battle records, like "The Bridge Is Over" and "9mm Goes Bang." KRS's mix of knucklehead brio and intelligence will amaze and confuse you for years to come, his conflicted soul echoed in wise thugs from Nas on down. And you watch the Beastie Boys blow up, thinking they're a bunch of idiots, though their tracks are hot and you will later come to respect them. As you are reminded when you start hanging out with a brown-skinned girl whose dad is a rabbi and who prefers Joy Divison to rap, race in the United States is very complicated thing.

Hip-hop sometimes helps decipher this, sometimes not. You come across a single by De La Soul (Long Island again) where some kid loses his virginity over a sped-up Lyn Collins sample ("Jenifa Taught Me"), then rhymes about spreadsheets and "potholes in my lawn" with a little yodeling for extra flavor. You buy their LP *3 Feet High and Rising* and listen to it endlessly, trying to break its sparkling code of jokes and gibberish and obscure samples. You think: This is some avant-stoned African-Americanism. You see the group perform a gig with placards à la Dylan's *Don't Look Back* and a "posse" of girls tossing flowers from baskets, and it is dumbfoundingly bad. You think: Rap this interior belongs in your Walkman, not onstage. (Years later, De La will get their live act together.) *3 Feet High* will open the doors of perception to new worlds of weirdness: Bedroom shut-ins like Basehead, psychedelic headcases like Divine Styler, a generation of sample-surgeons drunk on Prince Paul's sound collages, a generation of obscuro mic fiends keeping it surreal.

Killer singles are coming in a flood by now. Rob Base & DJ E-Z Rock's "It Takes Two." MC EZ & Troup's "Get Retarded." A posse of Afrocentric college kids calling themselves the Native Tongues includes De La and the Jungle Brothers and a New Jersey girl representing as Latifah the Princess of the Posse (later promoted to Queen Latifah), who makes it seem like great women MCs will never be in short supply. The collective also include A Tribe Called Quest (Queens again), whose first LP, *People's Instinctive Travels and the Paths of Rhythm*, sampled Lou Reed and the Beatles, and whose second album, *The Low End Theory*, rolled up jazz bass lines and black history and sex rhymes and a lava-lamp vibe, introducing Busta Rhymes for good measure. Front to back, you think it's the best rap album of all time.

By now there are voices from beyond New York. Florida horndogs and accidental First Amendment warriors 2 Live Crew. Bay Area funk pranksters Digital Underground. At the same time, cats like Schoolly D from Philly, Ice-T and N.W.A from Los Angeles, the Geto Boys from Houston, along with kindred NYC spirits like Kool G Rap, have been building rhyme worlds not about middle-class striving (though some, like Ice Cube, are indeed middle class) or cultural revolution (though some are revolution-minded) or party-starting wordplay (though they come with playful skills) but about ghetto gangbanging, police brutality, and criminal psychosis. At their best, the stories and tracks are intense and moving—the Geto Boys' "Mind Playing Tricks on Me," for instance, is one of hip-hop's greatest narratives. And by the time Dr. Dre offers up *The Chronic* in 1992, they prove to be dance-floor killers too. But you don't always relate to these true-crime jams; frankly, they disturb you, and even when you feel them, you aren't sure you want to.

There is, of course, plenty of wack music during this "Golden Age"—MC Hammer, Vanilla Ice, and underground jokes that history will erase. And many years later, you will understand that "golden ages" are very subjective things. Timbaland and Missy Elliott will make tracks as hot as anything that's come before. You'll bow to Nas, forever representing Queens, who after years of falling off will come back again and again. You'll root for Jean Grae, a hardcore storyteller with valedictorian wit. You'll marvel at OutKast, who make hip-hop the way you always hoped Prince would. You'll admire a soul-baring light-skinned kid named Slug from Minneapolis (where you spend much of the '90s), and one from Detroit named Eminem. And you'll watch Kanye West—an incredible young producer and MC who samples old soul records like back in the day—rise on the wings of a landmark record that plays off the conceit of college and the American Dream. For a moment, *The College Dropout* will resolve the aesthetic split between gangsta and "conscious" rap, between the present day and the Golden Age, and do it so effortlessly that you wonder if the split ever existed. And maybe it never really did.

> ESSAY CONTINUES FROM PREVIOUS PAGE

Seven Dope Books About Hip-Hop Back in the Day:

[1] *Ego Trip's Book of Rap Lists* by Sacha Jenkins, Elliott Wilson, Chairman Mao, Gabriel Alvarez & Brent Rollins (ST. MARTIN'S GRIFFIN); [2] *Can't Stop Won't Stop: A History of the Hip-Hop Generation* by Jeff Chang (ST. MARTIN'S PRESS); [3] *The Vibe History of Hip Hop* edited by Alan Light (THREE RIVERS PRESS); [4] *Yes Yes Y'All: The Experience Music Project Oral History of Hip-Hop's First Decade* edited by Jim Fricke and Charlie Ahearn (DA CAPO); [5] *Classic Material: The Hip-Hop Album Guide* edited by Oliver Wang (ECW); [6] *Hip Hop America* by Nelson George (PENGUIN); [7] *Rap Attack 3* by David Toop (SERPENT'S TAIL)

THE FIRST TIME I WENT TO A LIVE HIP-HOP SHOW I WAS DISAPPOINTED.

There it all was, two turntables, a bunch of rap crews with great clothes and great dance steps, and a house full of people ready to have fun. This was the era of the deejay; from a lime to a lemon, a lemon to a lime, a procession of them cut the beat in half the time, volleying it back and forth between turntables, extending and repeating scraps of records, maintaining a percussive dialogue. One crew after another, the rappers brought the crowd up, way up, getting us to throw our hands in the air and wave 'em like we just didn't care, and scream all kinds of things. The deejays cut some bongo beats on top of the bass and snare, the rappers broke into unison and out again, the crowd yelled "Ho" or "I am—somebody" with gusto. Everybody exchanged zodiac signs. It didn't take but seconds before the whole room was moving. The people started to shrink and the beat started to grow, as the bits and pieces of kinetic music and dance aligned themselves into what promised to be a long and rewarding current. It was incredible, and it looked like it would stay that way.

But then the crews would break it all down: take away the beat and talk out of meter, baiting the audience about what it had just lost or what it might get next. The rush of what they'd built up gave way to the tease of anticipation.

And then they'd boot it back up again, full tilt, until the next break. It was frustrating, like watching Ed McMahon come out and yell "And now...here's Johnny" every time Carson's monologue started to cook. The whole night proceeded in these bursts of excitement followed by lulls. I didn't get it. The music didn't build and climax like classic white rock'n'roll, nor sustain the endless plateaus of funk and disco. It was a rhythm without rhythm, as if the basic unit of the music was the fragment.

This, I eventually realized, was the idea. Like all music, hip-hop poses a specific relationship between sound and time. Where disco and funk suspend time through repetition, and straight rock channels it into a narrative line, hip-hop both chops it up and freezes it. The forces are contradictory: On the one hand, deejays extend small pieces of music over long periods of time; on the other, they bump these fragments against other fragments so that the two pieces of information exist simultaneously, removing time from the equation. Time is both jumping around and standing still. The same applies on a larger scale. Bits of old James Brown records butt up against computer beats and slang very obviously rooted in the present.

— "Singles" / John Leland / April '88

Following page, *left to right:* MS. MELODIE, DEE BARNES, FREDDIE FOXXX, BIG DADDY KANE *(front)*, JAM MASTER JAY, KID CAPRI *(front)*, DARRYL MCDANIELS, MC LYTE AND QUEEN LATIFAH, 1991

On record, M.C. Shan is the mortal enemy of Boogie Down Productions' Scott La Rock and KRS One.

They've been trading insults and waging a dis fest the likes of which are usually reserved for Yankee/Red Sox games. At stake in this 12-inch war is which borough of New York City rules rap. And like any street battle, it's been lowdown and nasty all the way.

Shan started it with "The Bridge," a rap celebrating the Queensbridge housing project where he, producer Marley Marl, and Roxanne Shanté lived. These claims of local supremacy begat Boogie Down's "South Bronx," in which KRS One traced the beat back to his home neighborhood in the mid-'70s and advised Shan to get his "homeboys off crack."

Shan and Marley Marl counterpunched with "Kill that Noise," which intercut the sampled chorus of "South Bronx" with a description of Shan's gun and the threat, "Those who try to make fame on my name die." Boogie Down answered with "The Bridge is Over," which questioned Shan's manhood more than his sense of history and told the Juice Crew (the umbrella outfit that includes Shan, Marley, Shante, Biz Markie, T.J. Swan, and disk jockey Mr. Magic) what to suck.

One fact that all the parties involved will agree on is that the war is fueling record sales. Both Shan and Boogie Down claim the other's dissing has done wonders for their respective careers. "People want to hear this stuff, they expect it—it's show biz," remarks Shan.

— "Rap Attack" / Amy Elizabeth Linden / August '87

STEVE STEIN, ADMAN FOR DOYLE DANE AND BERNBACH INC., NICE JEWISH BOY FROM WESTCHESTER, GETS HOOKED.

"When I first heard rap music I said, 'Oh my God, this shit will take the hair right off your head; it's really cool.' I knew it immediately; I'd been waiting all my life to hear this. I remember seeing Elvis on *Ed Sullivan*, and this had as much of an impact with me as that stuff did. It was absolutely electrifying."

Stein realizes he has to have it. "I started asking around in stores and they're like 'Whaaaaa?' I ended up at a record store in a subway. So I walked in there and bought a couple of records, and the woman at the counter said, 'You know what this is?' And I said 'Yeah, it's like rap music, right?' And she said, 'This *is* rap music. Whaddaya doin' buying it?' 'I figured I'll just, uh, kind of buy it.' 'OK, but you can't bring it back.'"

The hip-hop jones has taken control of his life. He must turn his need into something socially productive or he will die. Enter Tommy Boy, at the time the premier rap label, and an open contest to submit megamixes of the slow-moving "Play that Beat Mr. DJ" single by G.L.O.B.E. & Whiz Kid. The prize: $100, a couple of T-shirts, and some records. "So I said 'Yeah, why not?' and over the weekend my friend Doug and I put together 'The Payoff Mix.' We called ourselves Double D and Steinski because we were afraid that if we were white and we were old, we were fucked. We put a lot of shit in there, and 12 weeks later I called Tommy Boy up and they said, 'Naw, we haven't judged this yet, go away.' Slam.

"I go to work one day, and my secretary, who's this little white girl who listened to KISS all day long, screams, 'You won the contest.' I said, 'What contest?' 'The Master Mix contest. Tommy Boy from Tommy Boy just called up.' So I called him back and he said, 'Steve Stein, right? Well, congratulations, you won the contest. Now tell me something. Who *are* you? You got a secretary. Who the fuck has a secretary?'"

— "Cuttin' and Snatchin'" / Peter Watrous / February '87

"Everybody likes that men vs. women thing, it gets everyone so excited and it gets so controversial, like 'Yea, yea, you're a dog,' or 'Yea, yea, you women are just always trying to get our money.' As long as it doesn't get really raunchy, I don't take it personally. Some women *are* whores, most men *are* tramps."

— Salt (of Salt'N'Pepa), 1988

The best running feud is the one between Kool Moe Dee and L.L. Kool J.

Given the exposure of both performers, it represents the state of the art in dis. Moe Dee started it with a photo of a Suzuki Samurai jeep running over a red Kangol hat (L.L.'s trademark) on the cover of his *How You Like Me Now* album. On the title track, he explained his beef: "It happened to James [Brown] like it happened to me/ Now how you think I feel to see another emcee/ Get paid using my rap style/ While I'm playing in the background meanwhile/ I ain't with that, you can forget that/ You took my style, I'm taking it back."

Round two: L.L. Cool J responds with "Jack the Ripper," a non-LP B-side that not only beats anything on his last album, *Bigger and Deffer*, but also hits Kool Moe Dee where he lives: "How you like me now/ I'm getting busier/ I'm double platinum/ I'm watching you get dizzier."

Now, on his new single, "Let's Go," Kool Moe Dee takes control of round three. Taking a trick from L.L.'s own book, he—for the moment, at least—buries the sucker:

> L.L. stands for lower level, lackluster,
> Last, least, limp lover,
> Lousy, lame, late, lethargic,
> Lazy, lemon, little logic,
> Lucky leach, liver lip,
> Laborious louse on the loser's lip
> Living limbo, lyrical lass
> Lowlife with the loud rasp

It's L.L.'s move.

— "Singles" / John Leland / October '88

DJ Jazzy Jeff & the Fresh Prince are suburbanites from South West Philly and Winfield.

Prince's raps dramatize the terror of chasing girls, being a victim of Murphy's law, having a mom, and being stalked by Freddy Kruger. When they take the stage, Prince says, "Y'all ready to have some fun? We're gonna get stupid." Watch him smile his way through the vid to "Parents Just Don't Understand" and believe the revolution might be televised after all. As a sitcom.

— "Hip-Hop for Beginners" / J. Allen Levy / October '88

It is believed by many people in the street (and in the offices of SPIN) that car stereos have surpassed boom boxes in cultural impact.

Boxes seem to have played out their usefulness, and now lie rotting in the "Yo, this is whack!" anthropological junkyard along with headspins, the moonwalk, both *Breakin'* movies, and Michael Jackson's glove. The young new jacks making $2000 to $5000 a day selling "jums" (or "jumbos," the big pieces of crack), wouldn't be caught dead carrying a boom box, for fear they might be mistaken for the Wall Street messengers who lug the monstrosities around Water Street. Chumps on two grounds: because they're stuck with last year's disturber of the peace, and because they're probably hauling the thing over to one of said new jacks for a chance to beam up to Scotty over the weekend. And no businessman likes to be confused with his customers.

— "Car Stereos" / Barry Michael Cooper / October '88

Whatever happened to all those message raps of the early '80s, which portrayed crime as a social evil?

Gone, to be replaced by a literature of crime as a metaphor for total possibility: crime as an image of life without limits, where pleasure becomes more acute as it becomes more criminal.

Eldridge Cleaver proposed that black crime should be read as a force of resistance against an oppressive society. If this was true in the '60s, it's certainly not so today. Criminal imagery in rap does not oppose the mainstream at all. It instead creates a vicious, supercilious caricature of mainstream values, with all the liberal cant about honesty and fair play, truth and justice, brutally shorn off.

In a way, rappers like Ice-T, Schoolly-D, and Just-Ice are really more yuppie than yuppies. They push the logic of capitalism into hyperlogic to produce an image of a hyperactive, hyperacquisitive, hypermaterialist, inner-city capitalism. This isn't subversion, as so many leftist critics willfully assume. The rappers' gangster imagery is, in the phrase coined by French writer Jean Baudrillard, "hyperconformism": the simulation of the mechanisms of the very system that excludes them.

It might be a shock to the average liberal's nervous system to find that the likes of Schoolly-D are just like you and I, only more so. But after all, old man Rockefeller was a bootlegger.

— "Crime As a Metaphor" / Frank Owen / October '88

Russell Simmons' Top 10 B-Boy Movies

The Mack (1973)
Richard Pryor's first movie, with a classic performance by Richard Williams. Best scene: Richard Williams is in the barbershop, getting his shoes shined, and he says, "All bitches is the same." His man is sitting next to him, because a pimp always had his man with him, and he says, "That's right, kick it." He's a Flavor Flav kind of guy. I showed that movie at my house, and five guys mouthed all the words along with Richard Williams.

Scarface (1983)
There's so many b-boys around now trying to talk like Al Pacino in *Scarface*. It doesn't mean they have to be bad, but if they were bad, who would they be? Scarface, because he had the balls. He had the most street attitude.

Tougher Than Leather (1988)
This movie has something to offend everybody. Best scene: Jay starts telling Run and D.M.C. about his dream where he's out in the desert, and up comes a big black-and-gold Benz. He says, "I looked inside, and there was def bitches inside. These hos was exotic. Yo, so I got in the car, and one of them pulled down my zipper and started getting busy. She's sucking hard, and hard, and hard. Then she bit it off." They're all quiet. Then Run says, "That's fucked up."

The Godfather (1972)
Al Pacino has got to have some gangsters in his family or that lived next door to him or something. That attitude is not in any movies except his.

Wild Style (1982)
Busy Bee in bed with the girls, making a "B" on the bed with the money. Fab Five Freddy's performance was great.

Dolemite (1975)
Peatie Wheatstraw, the devil's son-in-law, has the line, "I put my dick in the ground, turned the whole world around."

Sparkle (1976)
Aretha Franklin did the soundtrack, but Irene Cara's performance of the songs in the movie was a lot better than Aretha's album. Everybody knows that.

Roaring Twenties (1932)
The best line is when Jimmy Cagney says he couldn't shoot somebody because the guy was only 15. Humphrey Bogart pulls the trigger and says, "Well, he won't be 16."

Across 110th Street (1972)
For the intro, when everybody gets blown away. You can't ask the guy later why he reached for his shit because everybody got killed. Don't do that.

— "Top 10 All-Time B-Boy Movies" / Russell Simmons / October '88

"A LOT OF WHITE PEOPLE THINK THAT EVERY RAP GUY WITH A GOLD CHAIN IS SAY-ING HE'S RICHER AND BET-TER AND MORE POWERFUL.
You don't understand this because it's not part of your heritage. It's not some-thing that was born and raised in America. This goes back to Africa. The gold chains are basically for warriors. Right now, the artists in the rap field are battling. We're the head warriors. We got to stand up and say we're winning battles and this is how we're doing it. So you should give us a break. You shouldn't try to make us you."

— Schoolly-D, 1988

2 Live Crew's first album, which also included the bass anthem, "We Want Some P___y!!," went on to sell in the area of a quarter of a million copies, with under-standably marginal radio support and no sales in New York.
On the back jacket, it urged, "ALL FEMALES SEND PICTURES!!!" It was a nice touch.

If 2 Live Crew started it, a posse of performers was ready to pick up the momentum. Atlanta's MC Shy-D seized the Crew's computerized, boomy sound and label affiliation, and repeated its success. As the Gucci Brothers, teenager Le Juan Love, Maggotron, and others follow, it looks like the gates are open. "The only thing keeping New York on top right now," says Public Enemy's Chuck D, "is the New York accent. New York is still the source for slang." As hip-hop acts like Rob Base begin to break down barriers between hip-hop and dance music, look for regional boundaries to fall as well, creating all sorts of weird, hyperinventive hybrids.

— "Singles" / John Leland / February '89

"THERE ARE A LOT OF SIMILARITIES BETWEEN JAZZ AND HIP-HOP.
Like rap, jazz was never really given the credit it was due and when it was, it was exploited. You've got artists like Kenny G. and Najee, who are good and all, but when you listen to Miles Davis's *Bitches Brew*, you know there are two different sects. That's how rap is now: MC Pop and the Go-Getters versus MC Street and the Do-Wrongers."

— Q-Tip (A Tribe Called Quest), 1991

"I'm gonna git this beat from *Godzilla vs. Megalon*," says rapper Biz Markie with glee.
"You know that beat? Woo-ooo! Sorry to waste your time like this, but…."

Far from wasting my time, the Biz (né Marcel Hall) is giving me a lesson in the art of finding "beats," i.e., three- to four-second patches of music dance-able enough to sample and loop into rhythm tracks. To this end, he fast-forwards through the *Godzilla* video until he finds a swatch of incidental music accompanying a chase scene. "You hear that beat! Oh God!"

This obscure movie, in which the overblown ape has karate battles with a robot, is just one of the unlikely places Biz gets his stuff. Karate flicks, cartoons, video games, Benny Hill episodes, and regular ol' movies will do as well. ("You heard the *Dirty Harry* beat?!")

Of course, records are the main source of beats, and not just the '60s soul and '70s funk cuts that you'd expect to contain groovy grooves. "The song 'Home Bound' on *Cat Scratch Fever* by Ted Nugent is one of my favorites," he claims, without an ounce of hipster irony. "And that *Foghat Live*. God is that funky!"

— "Jackin' for Beats" / Bob Mack / February '92

WHEN PRINCE BE OF P.M. DAWN QUESTIONED KRS-ONE'S POSI-TION AS A TEACHER, HE FOUND HIS GROUP (COMPLETE WITH FEMALE DANCER) BEING RUSHED OFF THE STAGE AT NEW YORK'S SOUND FACTORY NIGHTCLUB BEFORE IT EVEN HAD A CHANCE TO BEGIN. Once they were off, KRS-One kicked his two greatest meal tick-ets ("I'm Still #1" and "The Bridge is Over") to a crowd that supported the move. "Based on the hip-hop law," he says, "this is the only way that this could've been settled. Matter of fact, there are other ways but they would've been more violent." From the message of "Self-Destruction" to pushing a black group off the stage.

KRS-One is aware people will say he contradicts the message he puts on his records, but says, "Most people only wanna listen to *Stop the Violence*, then they take my tape out. Or they just wanna listen to *H.E.A.L.* or *Self-Destruction*, then they don't want to be bothered with *Criminal Minded* or *By All Means Necessary*, or even *Sex and Violence*. They don't want to be both-ered, so it's not my fault if they think I'm Gandhi."

— "Build and Destroy" / Ronin Ro / May '92

Hold on, wait a minute, something's wrong here. This can't be De La Soul talking— the beatific beat-box beatniks; the cuddly cartoon characters who, if they hankered after street credibility, found only the Sesame Street vari-ety; the first rappers to make it, lest we forget, to the hallowed pages of Cosmopolitan.

Forever saddled with the glib moniker 'hip-hop hippies,' Day-Glo-painted into a corner, De La Soul found itself fighting off the flower-child stereotype. Literally.

'When we went on tour last year, certain negative people would start trouble with us,' recalls Pos, who's recently traded in his vertigi-nous 'do for a close crop, which with his deliberate manner, lends him a rather professional air. 'Punk little kids goin' around thinkin' that just because we got daisies in our video we're soft. So they started trouble with us and we kicked their ass. Just because we speak about peace doesn't mean we can't defend ourselves and kick much ass.'

Despite these stacked odds, Posdnuos has confidence in hip-hop's powers of endurance. 'I don't think it's going to fail, but the situation might pressure a lot of rappers who believe in what they're doing to give in to what they don't wanna do. There are a lot of bad things going on.'

— "de la soul deflowered" / Steven Daly / May '91

[DE LA SOUL]

At this late date, the term "heavy metal" has about as much usefulness as "grunge," "grind-core," "happy house," "electronica" or "like [insert name of band not usually associated with hallucinogens] on acid" for describing a band's sound. Sure, there's still "metal" (generally used with a trace of irony to denote some arty underground noise), and you can put a "nü" in front of it (though that one also seems ready to join rock history's nomenclature dung-heap). But "heavy metal?" No way—not unless you mean two-fifths of Quiet Riot playing that one biker bar near the airport. Now consider that the last band standing from the heavy metal era is burdened with a name that directly refers to the genre—a constant reminder of this band's dinosaur status. To paraphrase one of their more "metallic" song titles, Metallica is truly the band that should not be.

And yet it is. Although their albums don't immediately fly out of stores anymore (don't blame the downloaders, Lars), Metallica is still at last check the biggest concert moneymaker of any rock band that isn't fleecing boomers (the Eagles, the Stones) or named the Dixie Chicks. And since Metallica spent its first decade laying this groundwork through constant touring and little help from the world of major labels and Clear Channels, it's time to reassess this band as one of alt-rock's pioneers.

Metallica's commercial breakthrough, the eponymous "Black Album," came out a few weeks before *Nevermind*, and its impact on mainstream music was just as seismic. Nirvana gets all the credit for blowing away the hair-metal over-ground by A) standing in complete opposition to it conceptually while B) beating it on its own terms musically (the shit was heavy). But Metallica destroyed heavy metal by putting out an actual heavy metal album, a trickier proposition when you think about it. Listen closely, and it's clear both bands had the same world-shaking plan: to blow up their sound, blow away the competition, and give the world of corporate rock a clean black slate. Exit light, enter night.

Metallica was picky about its touchstones, like the indie rockers that blazed the alt trail. When tennis-prodigy-turned-drummer Lars Ulrich first bonded with the pimply-faced and painfully shy James Hetfield in the early '80s, their life-changing music of choice wasn't punk rock; it was the roughly contemporaneous New Wave of British Heavy Metal (a genre I'm capitalizing to demonstrate that it's an actual genre). Taking Diamond Head as their Ramones, Metallica brought train-spotting record-collecting nerd-dom to a whole new level. They stubbornly insisted on being "alternative" while infiltrating the commercially mammoth and entrenched world of metal. Little details mattered. They wore jeans instead of spandex (mostly), a distinction that seems silly now but actually carried a lot of symbolic weight. Ditto their decision to sing about the darkness of a man's soul, instead of what a no-good woman could do to it. Along the way they ruffled some of their feathered-haired peers; on an early Monsters of Rock tour, they amused themselves by stalking the backstage halls, "coughing" the words "Robert Plant" when they passed the dressing room of Kingdom Come's derivative howler Lenny Wolf. Like Motörhead, and to lesser extent Guns N' Roses, Metallica saw punk as metal's kindred spirit, laying the groundwork for the metal-punk fusion that fueled alt rock. The band came of musical age at the same time American punk was engaging in an experiment to see just how fast human beings with guitars and drums could play while still maintaining cohesion. For punk, the fruits of this labor produced "hardcore" (another one of those ossified genres), while Metallica turned it into something called "speed metal" (yet another one). Some metal bands were deranged by the speed: Slayer's *Reign In Blood* became the apotheosis of the sub-sub-genre "death metal," in which burgeoning Satanists and other misfits behaved as though the blinding tempos and furious backwash of chords paved the promised highway to Hell. (Scandanavians wanting to use the E-ZPass lane torched a church or two for good measure.)

But for Metallica and its ilk, the trick here wasn't just to play fast (Slayer quickly settled the question of who was fastest), but to add an almost prog-rock proficiency. In the wake of Metallica's groundbreaking *Kill 'em All* album, bands like Megadeth, Prong, Anthrax, and Voivod created their own new wave of American heavy metal. What they shared with punk was an obsessive desire to cut anything extraneous out of a music whose propensity for overkill made overkill an understandable reflex. In other words, this was music built on discipline, and no band personified that discipline quite like Metallica. They brought metal-hewn precision to punk covers by the likes of the Misfits, Killing Joke, and the Anti-Nowhere League, without sacrificing the fat-burning minimalism that was punk's hallmark. Metallica wanted it all, and they got it: Their tempos got faster, the rhythms got trickier, and somehow metal's Wagnerian bombast remained intact. From Hetfield's and Ulrich's reconstitution of the rock rhythm section as guitar/drums to Cliff Burton's subtly nimble bass playing, Metallica broke real musical ground. It all culminated in *Master of Puppets* (1986), a bona fide rock masterpiece.

If Metallica had stopped there, the band would still deserve a spot in the rock pantheon. That they've soldiered on through deaths and desertions of bass players, made stylistic shifts without looking ridiculous (those trendy haircuts in the mid-'90s were probably unnecessary, however), and confronted their inner-Spinal Tap in the film *Some Kind of Monster*—all while the bells tolled inevitably—makes Metallica the only hard rock band in history to figure out how to age with grace.

/ Greg **Milner**

: **Metallica** Kill 'Em All

Near the end

of Metallica's last tour, rhythm guitarist and vocalist James Hetfield got the idea for a party. "It was going to be great," he says. "Farm animals, midgets serving drinks, tits everywhere—that kind of shit."

There was only one problem. "The midgets wouldn't do it. They heard the name Metallica, and they said no, we'll get abused."

— "Precious Metal" / Bob Mack / October '91

The mysterious videotape is called *Metallica Drummer*. It stars Kevin Dabbs, a 27-year-old drummer from Edmonton, Alberta, who videotaped himself in what looks suspiciously like his parents' living room. At the start of the tape, he emerges from behind the camera, wearing Bart Simpson shorts (they say RADICAL, DUDE!) and a backward baseball hat. A threatening guitar is heard, and Dabbs' eyes become wild. Suddenly he's air-drumming to Metallica's "Black Album." It is a performance of mesmerizing intensity: Dabbs, quite literally, never misses a beat. Matching Lars Ulrich snare for snare, Dabbs mimics his hero right down to the professionally ferocious heavy-metal sneer. Technical precision aside, the key to the video's near-hypnotic attraction is a profound sense of voyeurism. The viewer is seeing something he was never meant to see. "I made the tape for myself," says Dabbs, who shot the tape in 1992 "so that in 50 years I could roll up a big fat bat with some of my closest buds, get superbaked, and relive some old heavy-metal memories."

But somehow Dabbs lost track of the videotape; one popular theory is that it was stolen from the backseat of a car in Edmonton. Passed from musician to musician, it eventually wound up with Dustin Donaldson, who plays drums in the San Francisco band I Am Spoonbender. Donaldson showed the video to friends and eventually made dubs to sell at local record stores. It was an instant hit. Though the video was shown before concerts in the Bay Area and Steve Albini expressed his regard, the few people in Dabbs' hometown who had seen the tape were too afraid to tell him. Dabbs eventually found out when he was on tour in Holland with the funk band Spit Biscuit. "We were backstage after a show, and this hot Dutch girl came up to me and asked if I would sign a copy of *Metallica Drummer*." Bewildered, Dabbs contacted Donaldson, and although the exchange was friendly, Donaldson decided to stop selling the tapes. He has since posted a digital version on his website so the cult of *Metallica Drummer* can continue. "I think it's fuckin' boss," says Dabbs, who was previously not famous in Holland. "My only hope is that the boys in Metallica have seen it and dig it. To be honest, that's all I really give a shit about."

—"Virtual Lars" / Sarah Jacobson / October '99

Far be it for us to decide how musicians should handle the thorny issue of recording piracy. But Metallica's response to the rise of the MP3 file-sharing program Napster was cynical and supremely ill-conceived. In May, the band successfully demanded that 300,000 fans who had used the software to trade Metallica songs be removed from the service. In doing so, the band alienated many Metallica loyalists, needlessly involving them in the band's battle with Napster—all to snag a photo op of drummer Lars Ulrich personally lugging stacks of user-incriminating print-outs into Napster's offices. (For good measure, the band also sued several colleges, diverting higher-education dollars toward a music industry spat.)

— "100 Sleaziest Rock Moments" / Greg Milner / October '00

I now realize how greedy corporate rockers can be. Metallica aren't the only people fighting Napster, a wonderful program that allows you to trade (yes, *trade*) music, but they are the most visible entity opposing its use. I used to think they were gods, but now they're nothing but a bunch of sellout has-beens.

— "Letters" / Mike Devine / Pasco, Washington / December '00

Directed by Joe Berlinger and Bruce Sinofsky (whose shared résumé includes the West Memphis Three documentary *Paradise Lost* and its sequel), *Some Kind of Monster* depicts the bands most brutally intimate moments, including drummer Lars Ulrich's profanity-laced diatribe against singer/guitarist James Hetfield. "It was the very first time he'd ever confronted James that way in 20 years, and it went on for three hours," says Sinofsky. "We could make it a whole film and call it *The Fuck Scene*." Berlinger adds: "As a compassionate person, you feel bad. But as a filmmaker, you're peeing in your pants with happiness."

— "What's Up, Doc?" / Diane Vadino / April '04

"About a year ago, the record company started sniffing around this project," says Ulrich. "I started hearing, 'Thirty minutes on a cable channel'—MTV or VH1 or Showtime. We were like, 'Fuck this,' and wrote them a check." Once Metallica had bought back the raw material, Berlinger and Sinofsky still had to fight for the inclusion of several of the most powerful scenes in the documentary *Some Kind of Monster*, including a tearful reconciliation between Ulrich and founding guitarist Dave Mustaine, who was kicked out of Metallica in 1983. Though the Megadeth frontman's management tried "aggressively" to have the scene removed, says Berlinger, the directors battled back—and won: "I kept saying [to Mustaine], 'Watch the scene—you come across as fucking amazing.' He didn't see it that way."

With a theatrical release of *Monster* scheduled for this summer, Metallica are preparing for all the possible reactions their fans might have. "Once you get over the self-consciousness of the double chins, some of the stuff is just so raw that it moves me," says Ulrich. "But it's not about the glory [of rock'n'roll] and all that shit. I think it's going to blow some people's minds. Judging by a recent screening of the film in New York City, arranged by the directors for 100 members of the Metallica fan club, the band should expect an outpouring of emotion as overpowering as their guitar riffs. "There was one guy who was almost in tears," Berlinger says, "a big, beefy, tattooed guy, who put up his hand to talk and said, 'if James Hetfield can go through this and get his shit together and put this out on the screen for people like me, it just makes me love him even more.'"

— "St. Anger Management" / Diane Vadino / May '04

SPIN: So your group therapist was in the room when you were jamming, composing, and recording *St. Anger?*

Lars Ulrich: He was there every step of the process.

The new songs portray various mental demons—"Get out of my head," "I'll die if I lose control"—in a very direct way. It seems like a lot of that period's craziness went directly into the music.

Yes. It did. But this is not a rehab record. We're not talking about the Beatles going to India. It's just sitting down and understanding who you are.

In "Some Kind of Monster," the refrain is "We the people/ Some kind of monster." With the images of bombings on TV, this is easy to hear as bitter war commentary.

Well, I've always been very wary of using a Metallica interview as a platform to promote my own political views. There are very few people I respect as much as Tom Morello or Bono. But it doesn't mean that I want to use Metallica in the same way.

Well, the Napster suit was political. Are you satisfied with the settlement?

There was no victory in that, no uncorking of champagne bottles. Most of the time it feels like something that I dreamt. I mean, I was as surprised as anyone when I found myself testifying before the Senate. But anybody who knows anything about Metallica knows that we've always taken a stand against anybody who fucks with us. So it was like, "How did I become the most hated man in rock'n'roll for 15 minutes?" It was a very surreal experience, and still hurts more than I've ever let on.

When were you able to put it behind you?

I still go through eight-hour therapy sessions about it.

— "Lars Attacks!" / Chris Norris / July '03

: Nine
Inch
Nails

The Triumph
of Industrial

There was a time when a lot of great rock'n'roll was being made, and no one seemed to know. It was the late '80s, just before Nirvana busted the nation's alternative rock seams wide open, and small klatches of college radio DJs, junior A&R workers, and other low-level insiders wallowed in their own self-importance at annual music seminars. There, they debated the relative merits of J Mascis and his former Dinosaur Jr. bandmate Lou Barlow, discussed what member of Sonic Youth had been seen at which concert the night before, and compared the dates on which they had joined the Sub Pop Singles Club.

Amidst this scene one year, at the New Music Seminar in New York City, there came a small brigade of fresh-faced interns from a rather lame label known as TeeVee Tunes (or TVT), best known for its compilations of television show themes. In their hands, they carried a black cassingle for a song, "Down in It," by a band called Nine Inch Nails. On the back of the cassette package, there was a sticker, announcing that this group would be performing live at the China Club, a yuppified pickup spot that was too far uptown to lure anyone who mattered.

Besides, the music on the cassingle was woefully out of date. The industrial music it pledged allegiance to had already come and gone. And the guy singing and evidently making all of the music was angry. Anger was passé. Rock was about apathy now. This guy, Trent Reznor, whose very name conjured images of a shaving mishap, obviously cared too much. With lyrics about swimming in hate and crawling on the ground and carrying the world's weight on his back, "Down in It" seemed like a high-school misfit's notebook come to life as an electronic musical.

ESSAY CONTINUES ON NEXT PAGE >

But the hipsters were wrong. Nine Inch Nails would go on to outlast their precious Sub Pop Singles Club, not to mention most of the bands that went on to spearhead the alternative rock explosion that followed—Nirvana, Soundgarden, Smashing Pumpkins. As the equal and contemporary of the above, Trent Reznor would stand just as alone as he did in 1989 at the CMJ Music Marathon. But he would be considered an innovator, not a latecomer.

Some consider Reznor a genius, classed alongside Dr. Dre as one of the most important musicians/studio recluses of the '90s. Reznor is certainly talented, and a perfectionist like Dre (both spend years agonizing over each new record). But he's not that talented or that perfect. His significance, ultimately, can be summed up in the words of the Beatles' "Hey Jude."

He took a sad song and made it better.

That sad song was industrial music. The term was coined in 1976, when an English music and performance-art group, Throbbing Gristle, emerged from the ashes of punk-rock and began Industrial Records. The music—created primarily on synthesizers, distorted guitars, and various non-musical objects like power tools and sheet metal—was secondary to the message, which was to reflect the ugliness of the world, the coldness of the information age, and various government and corporate conspiracy theories. Purists trace industrial music even further back, to the early '70s—to the experimental German band Faust and even to a Folkways record called The Sounds of the Junkyard, which was exactly that—the sounds of construction equipment, garbage trucks, and power tools in action

Though it had its pop moments, industrial initially prided itself on noisy music that was hard to listen to accompanied by graphic images that were hard to look at. It was the sound of a cynic daring the world to look at itself in the mirror. But, gradually, out of all the metal banging, synthesizer droning, and urban street sounds, a rhythm developed. And bands like Cabaret Voltaire, Einstuerzende Neubauten, 23 Skidoo, Test Department, and Savage Republic helped bring the music out of the art gallery and onto the dance floor. In the mid-1980s, an industrial music-revival—led by Skinny Puppy,

Foetus, and, in Chicago, the Wax Trax! label, home to Ministry, Front 242, and their side project, the Revolting Cocks—gave the music its most commercial push, prefiguring techno by turning electronic dance music into a youth culture phenomenon. When Al Jourgenson of Ministry added aggressive guitar to the music's crash-and-thud for Ministry's The Land of Rape and Honey album in 1988, the foundation for Nine Inch Nails was fully laid.

What made Nine Inch Nails commercially transcend its predecessors was Reznor's songwriting ability. Where other bands tried to shape noise into song, Reznor wrote songs on piano (aided by his childhood classical training) and then, in the studio, destabilized and buried them with meticulously crafted layers of sound and rhythm.

Born in Pennsylvania, Reznor cut his teeth in Cleveland, where he knocked around the music scene, gigged with various local bands, and cleaned studio toilets in search of experience. If a bootleg video of a young Trent Reznor delivering an artless, dark-wave Falco cover is representative of his early work, Ministry's influence was profound. Working with the producers responsible for much of the industrial and new wave he admired—Flood, Adrian Sherwood, John Fryer, Keith LeBlanc—Reznor came into his own with his debut, Pretty Hate Machine, in 1989, and the anthemic spite of the single, "Head Like a Hole." Reznor and TVT worked the album mercilessly until, in 1991, as part of the first Lollapalooza alternative-rock package tour, Reznor put himself on the map by transforming his cold, moody onstage performances into synthesizer-destroying freakouts. In years to come, his explosive show would earn him the distinction of becoming the most memorable act at the mudcaked Woodstock 1994 and outshining David Bowie on their joint tour the following year. Yet as he crawled into the pop consciousness, Reznor's gruesome, torture-obsessed, MTV-censored videos and his residency at the Los Angeles house in which Sharon Tate was murdered by the Manson family (not to mention the theme of pigs on the album in reference to the Manson family's bloody graffiti) would guarantee his industrial and goth credibility.

After a messy parting of ways with TVT, Reznor signed with a major label, Interscope, and released an even more

aggressive and self-pitying LP, 1992's Broken, with much of its venom directed at TVT Records founder Steve Gottlieb. After holing up at the Tate house, he emerged, five years after his debut, with the CD that would guarantee his place in books like this one. It was The Downward Spiral that established Reznor not as a gimmick or a miserabilist or a revivalist, but an artist. Three years before Radiohead's OK Computer, here was an album about texture, albeit more abrasive, rhythm-driven, and nightmarish than Radiohead's android dreams. The Downward Spiral could be listened to as one long mood piece, or songs could be pulled out as stand-alone top-40 singles. Sounds from films, drum machines, and Iggy Pop records were sampled and processed into grim landscapes for songs that were alternately funky ("Closer," a pop hit so cathartic that decades from now, all some people will remember about Nine Inch Nails is the lyric, "I wanna fuck you like an animal") and sentimental, ("Hurt," a ballad that is to Nine Inch Nails what "Beth" is to Kiss, who happen to be one of Reznor's earliest influences). It is a testament to Reznor's songwriting ability, underrated in comparison to the studio skills for which he receives most of his acclaim, that Johnny Cash's bittersweet, knocking-on-death's-door cover of "Hurt" has become the definitive version.

What emerged from the ashes of The Downward Spiral was a man who was self-doubting, extremely competitive, and suffering from a bad case of writer's block compounded by an addiction to video games. It took another five years for the follow-up, The Fragile, which brought Trent Reznor further into the realm of the textural and abstract. Where fans saw it as a diverse and mature album, in which one-dimensional hate and anger gave way to deeper, more complex emotions and meditations, his record label saw it as commercial suicide, with over 20 songs and not a single pop hit released at the peak of the teenybopper pop era. In response—some would see it as a compromise, others as a fuck-you to the pop machine for writing him off—when Reznor released his next opus five years later, the appropriately named With Teeth, he returned to the catchier, more immediate industrial pop of Pretty Hate Machine and his rightful place as pop's perennial outsider.

"It's weird when you play a show somewhere and there's a disproportionate number of people backstage talking about how they're witches. And that there's a cool place to go—like, 'Hey, you guys want to go out tonight after the show?' 'Yeah, where?' 'Well, there's a great place. There's this old abandoned church that these satanic cults hang out at.' It's not, 'Let's go down to the bar.' It's like, 'Let's go out and slaughter a cow.' What the fuck?"

— TRENT REZNOR, 1992

"For every band that I think has something to say, like Ministry, or Meat Beat Manifesto, there's twice as many that have realized the formula for industrial music: repetitive 16th-note bass lines and snarling vocals—usually unintelligible screaming about the horrible condition of the planet or some kind of doomsday message about how shitty things are."

— TRENT REZNOR, 1992

TWENTY-SIX-YEAR-OLD REZNOR'S ONE-MAN PROJECT (FLESHED OUT ONSTAGE BY HIRED GUNS) IS THE MOST SUCCESSFUL INDUSTRIAL ACT IN THE WORLD RIGHT NOW.

But when *Pretty Hate Machine* came out, we didn't review it in SPIN. I'd never even seen the band play live until [the first] Lollapalooza, at which time I was formally converted to Naildom, or whatever they'll eventually call it. With their genuinely unhinged rock'n'roll futurism, NIN blew away every other act at the festival, including headliners Jane's Addiction. Older audience members were moved to awestruck comparisons with the Stooges or the early Who—the under-30s just realized this stuff rocked.

"I mean, I'm really into old David Bowie stuff for what it was, I'm really into Led Zeppelin or whatever," Reznor says. "But I'm not going to have a band that tries to sound like that because it's been done. I never liked the Beatles. If you're going to have a band that is guitar, bass, drum, and vocal, try to do something different with it instead of trying to sound like every other band that uses the same equipment and plays the same chords."

—"Nine Inches of Love" / Jim Greer / March '92

THE LIGHT HAS FALLEN, AND IT'S SO DARK IN THE HOTEL ROOM THAT TRENT REZNOR'S FEATURES ARE AS OBSCURE AS THE FACE OF A CLOUDED MOON.

I can't see my questions anymore, so I close my notebook and set it beside me on the couch. The ocean tongues rhythmically at the shore outside, and faint Hawaiian music blows in through the window. I'm convinced now that Reznor's alienation isn't just for effect, that he's actually nourished by sorrow, and has an almost intellectual interest in hate.

But what about love? Could he ever write a real love song? One that wasn't about death?

"You mean one where I don't get my dick cut off?"

I nod.

"Well, I don't know if I could. I'd try it." He pauses, and when he speaks again the tone of his voice is dead serious. "You know, I do have the capacity to love. I have loved—and I mean truly loved—several times. I'm not afraid of it."

What about happiness? Is it a hollow concept for someone like you?

"No," he answers immediately. "But trying to sustain it for any length of time—that's where the trickery lies."

— "Sing the Body Electronic" / Darcey Steinke / July '94

"I've always said that what Trent Reznor really needs is a blanky and a hot chocolate with marshmallows. He doesn't need another hole to crawl into. I think somebody should give him one of those little hard hats with a miner's light on it, so when he gets lost in a dark hole, he can find his way out."

— Tori Amos, 1994

IT TAKES A SWEATY GROUP OF SKINHEADS, GOTHS, NEW WAVERS, CLUB KIDS, AND THREE BALD BELGIAN "ELECTRO-DISCO-TERRORISTS" TO MAKE A VILLAGE. That was the roll call at Chicago all-ages club Medusa's in 1984 at the U.S. debut of Belgian industrial group Front 242. Dressed in camouflage, military haircuts, and thick black goggles, the band leaned into their synths, backlit by aircraft landing lights. "It was a roar of machines and the hammering of a thousand boots jumping up and down" recalls Joe Shanahan, owner of Chicago's Smart Bar/Metro and Double Door nightclubs. "I was floored."

That a faceless European electronic group found a sympathetic congregation on the shores of Lake Michigan spoke of the growing influence of a new Chicago-based label, Wax Trax!, which released Front 242's first domestic 12-inch, "Take One." The label's northside record store, opened in 1978 by Denver transplants Jim Nash and Dannie Flesher, quickly became a musical DMZ in a city that was home to both house music's black gay underground and a take-no-prisoners rock constituency that built a legendary bonfire of disco records at a 1979 White Sox doubleheader.

"It was a hub of all that was weird," says Wes Kidd, a former store employee and frontman for Triple Fast Action. "There weren't that many people in each little camp to support their own personal scene, you know? There'd be, like, ten goth rockers around and they were bored with each other, so they had to find some other people to hang with."

Among the first labor-of-love releases on the Wax Trax! record label was one by a store employee with a synthesizer and a fake British accent who'd been removed from counter duty because of his poor people skills. Drawing influence from both Steve Albini's abrasive, punkish Big Black and local house-music producers like Marshall Jefferson, Al Jourgensen helped supply Wax Trax! with its sonic identity under his Ministry moniker and numerous side projects.

"When [Ministry] started happening, people were really hungry for it," says Chicago Tribune rock critic Greg Kot of the local industrial scene. "There was all this cool imported stuff coming in, so it was like, 'Let's do our own versions of it.'" Jourgensen and his cohorts turned the Chicago Trax studio into the site of some legendary bacchanals. During one three-night, mescaline-fueled session for Ministry's 1988 The Land of Rape and Honey album, Jourgensen solicited a local Baptist choir to contribute backing vocals on a track. Apparently, a few choir members never made it back to the church; one was spotted in a corner laughing maniacally at the studio vacuum cleaner. "It was like a Fantasy Island episode every week," Jourgensen says proudly, "and I was like Mr. Roarke."

— "Chicago, 1985-93: Industrial Chic" / Jason Roth / April '00

Trent Reznor: "It's politically incorrect these days in the alternative world to indulge and have fun in a touring situation. Certain camps, like Courtney Love's, like to say we're a horrible, ridiculous throwback to cock-rock bullshit. That's not what we're about. But at the same time, if there's fun to be had, why not? Nobody gets hurt. And I'm not going to be doing this forever.

SPIN: Who are some of the musicians who you've come to think of as friends?
An odd bunch of people. I think the guys from Pantera are cool. Everyone from Tommy Lee of Mötley Crüe to Adrian Belew. I met the guys in the band Live because we were playing at festivals in Australia. All of them are people I wouldn't hesitate to say, let's work on something.

Like you did with Tori Amos.
Tori would be another example. She called me to do this vocal track. It wasn't that big a deal. Her first album was permanently in my car's CD changer. It really struck me as well written, in a similar vein to what I was doing—from a different point of view, but the same kind of addicting, pouring out, gushing, baring, naked kind of song. Other people put their fingers in the pie, and they kind of messed up a friendship. We're not that close now. Some malicious meddling on the part of Courtney Love. But I still feel the same feelings for Tori.

— "Sympathy for the Devil" / Eric Weisbard / February '96

> ### "When I was doing an acoustic tour with (guitarist) Tim Reynolds, we'd sit in the back of the bus before the gigs and crank up Nine Inch Nails and pretend we were Trent and go insane. His stuff is like Beethoven. It's awesome."
>
> — Dave Matthews, '96

SPIN: Is being content something you should necessarily strive for?
Trent Reznor: It's not about being content. It's about, What if everything you ever wished for in your life and never thought you'd get, you got? And it still sucked. That's the thing. I look at Oasis: dumb idiots just living life. You know, ignorance is bliss. And there's a truth to that. I guess I just don't want it.

So do you ever feel you don't deserve to be a rock star?
I'll say one thing here. When Nine Inch Nails first got signed, I didn't know how to do interviews. I really still don't. I talk too much and I say stupid things. At the time, my heroes were Jane's Addiction, among others, and I'm reading where Perry's a male prostitute and has this junkie lifestyle. And I'm like, I smoked pot when I was 18 once. I'm boring. I'm not this icon. I love Kiss for the same reason. Gene Simmons had a cow tongue grafted to his; that was the greatest shit. And I kind of made this pact with myself that I would just be honest. I am 31. I grew up in Pennsylvania. I wasn't a male prostitute. I'm not gay. My tongue is my own. It's not like a Marilyn Manson situation. I love Manson, I respect him. He's about show-biz and he knows what he wants to do. And I think he's a good kick in the ass of that conservative Pearl Jam pseudo-alternative integrity thing.

How much of what's going on pop-wise do you view as competition?
I watch MTV and I think it sucks and I think most videos are shitty. But I watch because I like knowing what's going on. I want to know that the last No Doubt video sucked so I don't do it myself. Since I'm aware of the business element of things, I get to feel a little competitive. For example, I like Beck now. But when he first came out, I felt that "urrrrggghh," just purely from a he's-the-competition point of view. Not that we're doing the same thing. I felt stupid even feeling that. But I wanted to not like him. And then I was like, "Your shit's good." Everyone around me—everyone—says he's great, he's great. And I think that last record is great. But it's hard not to feel that sense of competition. It's a bullshit way to think. And that's what's disturbing about that whole idea of "You're number one." Well, why? Because I'm better than him? I try not to think that way, but to be frank, there's a part of me that does feel that.

— "The Spin Top 40" / Neil Strauss / March '97

: The Pixies

Gigantic

FIRST PARAGRAPH: NOTES AND FACTS. The Pixies formed in 1986 in Boston. Some of their songs feature lyrics in Spanish. SECOND PARAGRAPH: They are considered by many research bodies to be the fourth-best band America has ever made. THE LIST IS THIS: 1. The Velvet Underground; 2. The Beach Boys; 3. (tie) Talking Heads, the Pixies; 4. The Ramones. [5. R.E.M.] Songs by the Pixies are about planets, monkeys, fire, the University of Massachusetts, and a man named Tony. THIRD PARAGRAPH: The band was not over-serious, but they were, and are once again, taken very seriously. After the release of the Pixies' debut EP, 1987's *Come on Pilgrim*, many listeners thought they would never recover from the shock. People fainted, wilted, fell into their gardens, and needed cold towels and strawberries to feel themselves again. The Pixies' music sounded familiar, in a way—it sounded, at least, clean and accessible—but then again, it sounded unlike anything else. The Pixies were sui generis, as if made by God from ribs and clay and moon rocks, while he listened to surf rock, the Cars, Pere Ubu, and people being skinned alive. Their music was so transportive, and felt so much like madness, that it required hundreds of listens, and some calculations made on paper, to comprehend. The Pixies always sounded like a soundtrack to an almost-controlled, medium-length spell of insanity. Many bands are passionate, or troubled, but only the Pixies captured this sort of almost-insanity consistently and convincingly. John Wayne Gacy was a portly, Midwestern serial killer who also created sensitive oil paintings of clowns, and some people reportedly wondered if he was related to—or was channeling through—Pixies frontman Black Francis. IMPORTANT POINT THAT MIGHT HAVE OPENED THIS PIECE: The Pixies were known for what has been called the "loud-quiet-loud" sort of song, also known (in the northern states) as the "quiet-loud-quiet" kind of song. The former requires that the band play very loud, then cut back to a very quiet period—accompanied, in "Gigantic," for example, by bassline only—and then bust into the loud part again. The latter is the same yet also very different. Both require a great deal of technical accomplishment, and also, when playing live, a degree of vocal control that is startling. Black Francis, the principal songwriter of the Pixies, was known for a scream-sing style, which sounded tortured and feral. That point should have been made sooner. NEW PARAGRAPH: Much has been made of the fact that he, Black Francis, is heavy-set. He is also mostly bald. His real name is Charles Thompson, but most of the time the Pixies existed, he was known as Black Francis. Many consider his future name change—to solo-era Frank Black—to be the very best name-switch in the history of name-switches. Somewhere in here we should mention that he made many very good albums after the Pixies, including 1994's *Teenager of the Year*, which was near-perfect and also messy. PARAGRAPH THAT COULD BE AT THE VERY BEGINNING OF THIS PIECE: Charles Thompson began the Pixies when he and his college roommate, guitarist Joey Santiago, quit school in 1986. When the Pixies broke up, seven years later, David Lovering became a magician. He is mostly bald now, too, as is Joey Santiago, the guitarist. THIS PART SHOULD HAVE ALSO COME EARLIER IN THE PIECE: The band called the Pixies released four albums after *Come on Pilgrim*: *Surfer Rosa* (1988), *Doolittle* (1989), *Bossanova* (1990), and *Trompe Le Monde* (1991). Almost all of these would have to be included in the Top 100 Albums for You list, because they are all, with the exception of *Trompe Le Monde*, very thought-out in that thought-out-album way, while at the same time explosive and random and inclusive of entire worlds of sound. SECTION ABOUT KIM DEAL: Kim Deal, the bassist of this band, sang a number of

/ Dave **Eggers**

ESSAY CONTINUES ON NEXT PAGE >

the songs, like "Gigantic," which the editors of this book believe is about the size of some man's member. Deal chain-smoked through many Pixies shows, without using her hands. Many men fainted from her power and overalls. She is reportedly also a Green Beret, and once lifted a truck over her head to save a Cambodian family. Deal's high-school band was named the Breeders, and she was the only person to answer Thompson and Lovering's Boston-area classified ad for a bassist. Early on, in the first album's liner notes, she went by the name Mrs. John Murphy. Kim Deal has a twin, Kelley, who looks almost exactly like her and who played in the Breeders, which was also the name of Kim's post-Pixies band, which did very well with a modern-rock song called "Cannonball." ANECDOTE: When the Pixies reunited in 2004 for a world tour, they didn't seem to be all that thrilled to play more radio-familiar songs like "Here Comes Your Man." In Los Angeles, when he sang this song, the closest thing to a hit the Pixies ever had, Frank Black did a thing where he tilted his head from side to side, cute-like, as if he were playing "Puff the Magic Dragon" at a bat mitzvah. A few songs later, a cache of frenzied and dark-hearted selections from *Come on Pilgrim* and *Surfer Rosa* finally got the Pixies' blood going. These they played in a long and maniacal middle section that restored everyone's faith, which had been wavering, as the Pixies sleepwalked through the first 20 minutes of the show. Were the Pixies a great live band? Yes, they were always a great live band. Were they the most influential band of the '90s? This could be so. If you consider that Kurt Cobain said that "Smells Like Teen Spirit" was a stone-cold rip-off of the Pixies, that would make the Pixies more influential than Nirvana. But then again, no one since the Pixies has sounded anything like the Pixies, while thousands of bands have tried to sound like Nirvana. People have claimed that without the Pixies there would be no grunge, but that seems insane, since the Pixies do not sound grunge and grunge does not sound like the Pixies. The Pixies were more fun-having, were more melodic, were stranger and wittier than the majority of grunge-makers. No one will ever sound like the Pixies because they are too odd, too Dada, too driven by and accepting of the most eccentric impulses—theremin! lyrics in Spanish!—of the band's members (that word again), that no one can follow the path they burned. Do people burn paths, or are they made with weed whackers or similar devices? A better metaphor: They built a tree fort high in an elm or oak, and from this tree fort they made music that redirected the lives of all who heard it. But they did not leave a rope ladder. They went up into their tree fort and then pulled up the ladder, making it impossible for anyone else to join them. ONE MORE FACT FOR YOU: "Wave of Mutilation," another favorite from *Doolittle*, was featured prominently, slo-mo style, in *Pump Up the Volume*, a movie starring Christian Slater as a rebel DJ person fighting the power. He was such a handsome young man.

CHARLES, THE GUY WHO WRITES AND SINGS SONGS FOR THE PIXIES AND WHO GOES BY THE NAME BLACK FRANCIS, HAS THIS IDEA THAT ROCK'N'ROLL IS THE SOUND OF THE GODS. Like, you know, if people from ancient Egypt somehow ended up being transported to the here and now and somehow ended up hearing rock-'n'roll, it'd just blow their minds, because it's so LOUD for no real reason at all. And what else would they think this roar is except the gods speaking directly to them? The buzzing of giant metal insects or something?

Ideas like that, translated through drums and wires, are what had fanzine hacks, college radio kids, and SPIN calling the Pixies "The Best Band in the World" this past year. If you want to be reasonable about the whole thing, all the Pixies really did was chop up klassik rock song structures and mix them with a love for the likes of Iggy Pop, the Violent Femmes, and Steve Albini (who produced their record, *Surfer Rosa*, and made their guitars sound like super-charged funny cars on a demolition derby field day). But how many bands want to be messengers of the gods these days? — "Musicians of the Year: The Pixies" / December '88

"PEOPLE THINK THAT SINCE THEY LIKE MY VOICE, OBVIOUSLY I'M BEING OPPRESSED [IN THE PIXIES]. OR BECAUSE THEY PREFER MY VOICE, THEY THINK I SHOULD SING MORE. I DON'T WANT TO SING AT ALL! I'D RATHER PLAY THE DRUMS."
— Kim Deal, 2004

"THEY DID HAVE QUITE DISTINCT PERSONAL-ITIES. Kim is giddy and playful. Charles is more serious, but he's also got a sardonic sense of humor, and I'm a fan of dark humor. He was a kindred spirit in that sense. David was very pleasant, very cooperative. I didn't get the feeling that he was the biggest music fan, but he enjoyed playing the drums. The same with Joey. And because they developed as bedroom players, they had distinctive styles. People who taught themselves how to play had an advantage because they wouldn't be mimicking. Like, you weren't going to play guitar like Ted Nugent if nobody taught you how to do it. They were making music along unconventional lines partly out of ignorance, but I mean 'ignorance' in a flattering sense."
— Steve Albini (engineer), 2004

THE BREEDERS MIGHT BE MORE MARKETABLE IF THE DEAL SISTERS BEHAVED MORE LIKE THE SILENT TWINS—identical loners plotting cryptically in a secret Esperanto. But there's no creepy, tabloid edge to Kim and Kelley's relationship, no sense that one couldn't function without the other, although they live together, and one suspects Kim drafted her sis, at least in part, as a buffer against the loneliness on tour. At times, the twins switch personalities to relax: Kelley plays the sharpie, offering dauntless assessments, while Kim sits back, taking cues. They seem intensely aware of the specific burden of being each other, and as a result, exude a strength and tenderness rarely found in rock bands—asked once to name the best birthday present she ever received, Kim replied simply, "Kelley."

Still, the Breeders rely on Kim. "This doesn't work because it's a democracy, it works because we share enough of Kim's vision," says bassist Josephine Wiggs definitively. That vision has been unmistakable ever since Kim wrote and sang "Gigantic," an eerily joyful story about an interracial romance, on the Pixies' 1988 *Surfer Rosa* LP. Three albums later, though, she'd only co-written one more song ("Silver" on 1989's *Doolittle*.) Meanwhile,

the Breeders, a side project she started with Tanya Donelly (then of Throwing Muses), emerged on 1990's *Pod*, an album more slyly compelling and coherent than the Pixies' *Bossanova*, released the same year. When self-obsessed Pixie Charles "Black Francis" Thompson faxed her a pink slip in early 1992, it was probably a blessing.

More a redemptive hoot than an answer record, *Last Splash* explodes the quirky, space-boy cloister of the Pixies and pieces together the bits into something compassionate and testy. They sketch a good-naturedly messy canvas of the Midwest as equal parts bitter industrial wasteland and suburban sweet relief—consumerism grinning itself to death—that fellow Ohio natives Pere Ubu first illuminated (though only for a closet full of devoted goobers). The Breeders reach MTV progeny, on some level, because they sound so kinetic, like rock history chain-reacting—girl-group insouciance, '70s roadhouse rock tricks, early '80s new-wave dance beats, garage-punk chutzpah, third-hand country sentiment. Kim never simplifies what it all means—she obsesses about it, then rocks the ineffable.

— "Ordinary People"/ Charles Aaron / March '94

"OTHER BANDS LIKE TO HANG OUT AND GET FUCKED UP AND BUILD SO-CALLED CAMARADERIE AND GET INTO THE LOCAL BATTLE OF THE BANDS, AND ALL THAT STUFF THAT DOESN'T REALLY MEAN ANYTHING. [OUR] GOAL WAS TO GET THE HELL OUT OF TOWN, NOT BE LOCAL HEROES. FUCK THAT. I WANT TO BE BOB DYLAN—I DON'T WANT TO BE THE MOST POPULAR KID ON CAMPUS."
— Frank Black (Charles Thompson), 2004

"I DIDN'T LIKE NIRVANA. NOT AT THE TIME, WHEN THEY FIRST HIT. BUT I WILL NEVER LIKE WHATEVER IS POPULAR. IF EVERYONE IS GOING, 'HAVE YOU SEEN THIS QUENTIN TARANTINO FILM EVERYONE'S TALKING ABOUT?' IT'S LIKE, 'GUESS WHAT I'M NOT GOING TO SEE NEXT WEEK?' THAT'S WHERE MY SNOBBERY JUST TAKES OVER. IN RETROSPECT I CAN HEAR IT AND GO, 'OH YEAH, THEY HAVE TALENT.' BUT THEY DON'T SOUND LIKE THE PIXIES—THEY SOUND LIKE NIRVANA. NO ONE SOUNDS LIKE THE PIXIES."
– Frank Black (Charles Thompson), 2004

A PIXIES DISCOGRAPHY

Come on Pilgrim (4AD, 1987)

The band may sound a little tentative, but the building blocks are here: Joey Santiago's neo-twang guitar, Black Francis' yowl, and the soft/loud song structures that were the then-future sound of alternative rock. B+

Surfer Rosa (4AD, 1988)

A crushing synthesis of British post-punk and American indie rock. With Steve Albini's unadorned production lighting the way, *Surfer Rosa* is perverse ("Oh My Golly!"), hilarious ("We'll all have sons/ They will be all well-hung"), and, to borrow a line from "Gigantic," a big, big love. A+

Doolittle (4AD/Elektra, 1989)

Crashing the majors on a wave of mutilation, the Pixies laud Buñuel and Dali's cinematic sliced eyeball ("Debaser"), wallow in sea sludge ("Monkey Gone to Heaven"), gouge away at lovers and guitar strings ("Gouge Away"), and make room for a bouncy hit-single-that-wasn't ("Here Comes Your Man"). A

Bossanova (4AD/Elektra, 1990)

Producer Gil Norton's attempt to beef up the band's sound makes this album paradoxically diffuse, but the songs still manage to shine. "Is She Weird" is positively *Rosa*-worthy, and with its Theremin-like oscillations and Kim Deal's perfect backing vocals; "Velouria" is as gorgeous as the Pixies got. A-

Trompe le Monde (4AD/Elektra, 1991)

Highlights of this swan song, released the year alt rock broke: a surf-city cover of the Jesus & Mary Chain's "Head On" and the corrosively self-reflexive "Subbacultcha." Lowlight: Deal's relative silence. B+

Death to the Pixies, 1987-1991 (4AD/Elektra, 1997)

For an introduction to the Pixies, don't bother with this best-of; pick up *Surfer Rosa* and *Doolittle* instead. But what makes this almost necessary is the second disc, a blistering live 1990 show. B+

Pixies at the BBC (4AD/Elektra, 1998)

It's great to hear the late-period songs live, free from the studio albums occasional stiffness. As the frenzied version of the Beatles' "Wild Honey Pie" proves, they never lost their verve. A-

Pixies (SpinART, 2002)

This collection of 1987 demos (from "The Purple Tape") shows a band bursting with ideas and going on pure instinct—just check out the skinhead stomp of "Build High." And "Here Comes Your Man" comes here fully formed. A-

Complete 'B' Sides (4AD, 2001)

Worth it for the slowed down, surfed-up version of "Wave of Mutilation" (featured in the teen flick *Pump Up the Volume*) and the starkly beautiful cover of Neil Young's "Winterlong." B

Wave of Mutilation: Best of Pixies (4AD/Beggars, 2004)

Unlike *Death to the Pixies*, this collection is roughly chronological. Also, unlike *Death to the Pixies*, there's no bonus live disc. B

— Greg Milner / September '04

JEFF CRAFT (booking agent): It's fair to say that Kim's partying and tardiness led to the breakup.

CHARLES THOMPSON: What people do is their business. There were a bunch of young people traveling the world, playing nightclubs. There were a lot of drugs and alcohol, but not any more than anyone else. Rock musicians tend to think they have a monopoly on drugs, sex, and rock'n'roll.

KIM DEAL: Everyone had gone out to L.A., but I didn't know that. So I called up Charles to find out when we were going to get together to rehearse, and he said, "I don't want you to come out." "What do you mean, 'I don't want you to come out'?" I called Deborah Edgeley from 4AD. I said, "I heard we were rehearsing." And she said, "Yeah. Joe's out there." I thought, "Oh my God, Joe's out there?" And I knew David had moved out there. Everybody's out there? So I asked her, "Charles said he doesn't want me to come out. Does that mean they don't want me to come out and play ever?" She goes, "I don't know, Kim. Go out there, ask them." I was so sad. I flew out on my own. It was so weird taking a flight by myself, booking my own hotel room. Then I get a call from the manager. Me and him had never talked. It was weird. He said, "You are to meet here the next day." I go, "Okay." I still have no fucking idea what's going on. It's a lawyer's office! David, Joe, and Charles are there with our manager and the lawyer. And I walk in—it's like, "Ohhh, I'm fired." I mean, I didn't say that. It was so hurtful, it was odd, it was awkward.

JOHNNY ANGEL (journalist/musician): They'd have no band if they fired Kim. She was the soul of the group. It's like the Stones firing Keith Richards because he's a fuck-up. I mean, come on! You can't do that.

GIL NORTON (producer): [Kim's presence] got less every time, especially when we did *Trompe Le Monde*. I wasn't happy by the end of that, because there was one song, "Bird Dream of the Olympus Mons," that I thought was perfect for her to sing. Charles didn't want her to sing it. He definitely didn't want her to have a big imprint on the songs.

DEAL: The last show we did was in April '92, our show in Vancouver. Afterwards, Charles said something about taking a sabbatical. I was like, "Oh, for how long?" And he goes, "I believe a sabbatical is one year." That's the last conversation we had, the last time we talked, and the last sentence was, "I believe a sabbatical is one year." Asshole. I don't want to hurt anybody's feelings, but that's a fucking stupid last sentence.

IVO WATTS-RUSSELL (co-founder of 4AD label): I think it was the best thing for them to split. They made some great records, and it was time to end. And they were hating each other, so why the fuck not?

STEVE ALBINI: I remember hearing about the fax after the fact. And I remember hearing that the story is pure bullshit, that there is no fax.

WATTS-RUSSELL: It doesn't exist. If you ask all the members of the band about "the fax," they wouldn't tell you it existed unless they've all decided to perpetuate the myth.

THOMPSON: Yeah, it happened! People make such a big deal about that. I mean, what is the alternative? There was no e-mail. How was the band supposed to break up? It was a little cold-hearted, but so what? What are you supposed to do? Call a press conference?

DEAL: I didn't have a fax machine. Joe didn't have a fax machine. David didn't have a fax machine. Whatever, man.

THOMPSON: I needed to get away from that band and those people. Kim went and did some records; I went and did some records. Dave got into magic. Joey got into his music and started a family. It's not really that big of a deal, and sending a fax to break up a band is not that big of a deal either. To me, that's kind of beautiful. I actually apologized for the fax, because they didn't see it coming. But what better way to avoid all the emotion than to just say, "Bye!" It's a "Dear John" letter. "Sorry babe, I'm leaving. Love ya." It's perfect. Psychologically, it probably wasn't the healthiest thing to do. There was no closure—I'll give them that. But it's better than having some big fight or someone quitting the band and putting out a couple of shitty records with a different lineup, getting in some kind of legal squabble. It was sort of like, "Fin."

MICHAEL AZERRAD (journalist): Kim took that residual Pixies goodwill and her own charisma and talent and parlayed it into big success for one album.

KURT ST. THOMAS (former program director, WFNX Boston): Nirvana took the Breeders on tour. I think they were really into it because Nirvana was opening doors for them.

DEAL: We were on MTV. It was really odd—to be on 4AD and to be used to being under the radar all the time.

THOMPSON: I wasn't surprised that [*Last Splash*] was so successful. And people love Kim.

JOEY SANTIAGO: I told her when I saw her, "Man, I'm so envious of that Breeders' record." [Laughs] And she said, "Good!"

ST. THOMAS: People were so excited about the first Frank Black record and the Breeders record because we were all missing the Pixies in our lives.

DEAL: Last August, Joe calls me up and says, "Pixies are gonna start playing shows, would you be interested?" I said, "Oh, really?" Then I went, "I don't know." And he said, "Here's Charles' number. He wants you to call him." So I left him a message saying, "I hear the gang's getting back together." I hadn't talked to him since April of 1992. And he called back and said, "So what do you think about it?" I said, "Sounds exciting."

ALBINI: It was amazing to see 50,000 people who'd never seen this band before but for whom this band was really important. But I couldn't tell you what about their music appeals to so many people. I think they're one of those bands that make an impact on their immediate audience, and then those people leave their records to their kid brothers when they go away to college. Then those people get into the band and then when they go off to college, they leave that bigger pile of records to their kid brothers.

THOMPSON: Now I see Kim as our secret weapon. She's like, "Hi." And the crowd goes crazy. Or "Gee, its hot." And they just lose it. I don't even talk onstage anymore.

DEAL: The good thing is now we don't have to have a dynamic, because all we do is travel to a place and people are happy that we're there. We're not working together. This is not a hard thing to do.

THOMPSON: I forgot how much I like this band, how much I like being in this band.
— "Life to the Pixies" / Marc Spitz / September '04

: West Coast Hedonism

The Red Hot Chili Peppers and Jane's Addiction

/ RJ **Smith**

Hollywood punks were always obsessed with selling out. Elsewhere punk rockers were against everything, but on the Sunset Strip, they were about appetite and excess and ripping off as much as they could. Darby Crash would have sold any parts of himself he could and unscrew. And when X sang about "Sex and Dying in High Society," sure they came on cynical, but that was strategy: they were fascinated by the noir lives of the swells. You could argue that the ultimate triumph of Hollywood punk was the success of two bands who made it richer than the rest while straying far from their punk-rock roots.

The Red Hot Chili Peppers were born of an idea that was blindingly brilliant for its time: a fusion of punk with rap/funk. Just when the Chilis were forming in 1983, punk fans began tuning in to legendary Los Angeles hip-hop station KDAY, and one outlaw culture was projecting its image onto another. Rap-rock was a utopian dream that years later would morph into a commercial WMD. It ended up—with bands like Limp Bizkit and Rage Against the Machine—building on what the Peppers started. But it's important to remember that if the Peppers were terrific on paper, they were dicey in practice. Jumping around with socks on their dicks, they almost made you forget that for all Flea's lavish bass-popping, they couldn't find the funk with a police helicopter. Frontman Anthony Kiedis wasn't old school—he must have been home schooled. What made the Peppers compelling wasn't their groove, it was their storyline: four Hollywood brats with a classic L.A. upbringing— Kiedis had an actor/drug dealer dad who brought slumming celebs home; Flea had a jazzbo stepdad who took him to jam sessions. Teaming up with drummer Jack Irons and guitarist Hillel Slovak, they were Hollywood droogies always down for a good time.

Records like *The Uplift Mofo Party* (1987) and *Mother's Milk* (1989) referenced a bootyriffic knowledge they only occasionally embodied. Meanwhile, Slovak overdosed in 1988; there were

more drugs, plus arrests for sexual battery and indecent exposure. They might have been falling, all right, but they were falling upstairs, and when the Peppers teamed up with producer Rick Rubin in 1991 and recorded *BloodSugarSexMagik*, they were reborn. Rubin helped them find their core—and a groove! They went from being party-hearty miscreants to a group that crafted radio-friendly hooks, 'hos with huge gushy hearts. Kiedis's junk-sick ballad "Under the Bridge" was the bravest thing they'd ever done, and one of their biggest hits. The sap started to flow, and they never sounded better.

Jane's Addiction also began with a utopian dream. They were a Dionysus cult surfing the waves of an adoring local audience, and their belief—which they extolled like prophets coming down from the Hollywood Hills—was that too much could never be enough. Their lyrics were rooted in their L.A. scene—stories about strung out lovers, dumpster divers and surfers and shoplifters, the boho and the broke. Their songs and their audience were a perfect reflection of one another. Glammed out, kissing each other on the lips on stage, with a frontman who on a coherent night was one for the ages, the Jane's dudes acted like flesh-and-blood rock stars in an era when rock stars were suspect. And they were on the verge of actually being rock stars—after a mere two studio albums—when they imploded like a junker soaked in gas and set on fire.

Jane's, too, had backstories that resonated with their Hollywood noir world: guitarist Dave Navarro's mom was murdered when he was 15; singer Perry Farrell's mom killed herself when he was a toddler. Abandoning Queens, New York as Perry Bernstein, Farrell eventually became a surfer, reinvented himself, and hooked up with characters from both the Sunset Strip metal scene and the East Hollywood indie clubs. Bassist Eric Avery was lowkey and to the point; Stephen Perkins, the undervalued shit-hot drummer, kept it together when by all rights it should have run off the rails. Navarro (who would also do a stint with the Chili Peppers) was the exquisitely pierced spokesmodel for flashy guitar playing; Farrell the polymorphous subject and object of the Dionysus cult.

They debuted in 1987 with a self-titled live CD, got better over *Nothing's Shocking* (1988) and *Ritual de lo Habitual* (1990), which went gold. Songs like "Jane Says" and "Been Caught Stealing" showed off their smart hybrid of art rock and alt rock, as well as their fearless embrace of a decidedly un-punk sonic grandeur.

And then the excesses they championed loomed louder than the music. Ultimately the Peppers seem like one kind of Hollywood tale—they took their whippings and outlasted everyone to become improbable O.G.'s. Jane's—two comebacks logged, plus solo projects— are another sort of Hollywood cliché: They were steamrolled by excess. Members were caught up in the heroin life, while Farrell rapped in interviews like a salesman for libertinism and clean needles. His appetites smacked against the rising tide of AIDS, and in the end the zeitgeist pushed him to the margins. These days Farrell seems like a visionary hustler who bought his own schtick. As for legacy, consider his brilliant business strategy—the Lollapalooza Tour—which succeeded, though not quite as he imagined it would. The inaugural Lollapalooza, in 1991, was supposed to support Jane's on a tour, and was meant to cement them at the top of an exploding indie scene. Instead Jane's drove into the ditch, and Lollapalooza, by the time the tour sputtered out in 2004, had branded the Gen-X Alternative Nation. Lollapalooza made alt-stars—including the Chili Peppers—into Rock Stars.

The Red Hot Chili Peppers were an exceptionally inspired bad band, singing bad songs with stupid lyrics and attitude to spare. They made you feel like you just stepped in dog-shit, but they also made you feel okay about it.
—"Singles" / John Leland / November '85

"Sexual frustration is the single most powerful force in the world. We are the only species where that frustration affects things like the amount of money given to the poor and the length of welfare lines. I hate that the fact that George Bush's wife is an ugly old piece of shit could cause suffering among millions and could cause wars. I don't think it's any coincidence that Kennedy was the last president who had a wife worth fucking and he was the last good president."
— John Frusciante (Red Hot Chili Peppers), 1989

The Peppers are practicing for an upcoming tour in support of their recent comeback bid *Californication*. By the time it kicks off, they'll probably look like buff, sexed-up rock stars again, but today they appear a bit weathered. From eight feet away, singer Anthony Kiedis looks like his usual pin-up self, but get closer and his skin's a little loose, a little lined. Drummer Chad Smith's face is perpetually red. And Flea, forget about it: Ever the worrier, years of dogging everybody to show up when they said they would and be sober enough to play has the bassist aging like a leather jacket. If they weren't the Peppers and you saw them walking down this skanky block, you'd never wonder what these guys were doing in this part of town.

But how could they not look roughed up, given all they've been through since they got together in 1983? Has any alt-rock band lived as hard? Has any band taken as many drugs? The Peppers' first guitarist, Hillel Slovak, died of a heroin overdose in 1988; Kiedis, Flea, and ex-guitarist Dave Navarro are former users; prodigal guitarist John Frusciante was a smack shut-in several years ago. The Peppers have been arrested, sued, and bad-mouthed by the secretary of Health and Human Services. They've outlasted hardcore, post-punk, and grunge, while borrowing from all of them, only to see their thrash-rap descendants like Limp Bizkit reeling in the suburban skateboarders who used to be the Peppers' constituency. They've watched Hugh Hefner go from cool to uncool back to cool again, while they are sentenced to justify old tunes like "Sexy Mexican Maid" and "Party on Your Pussy."

"I don't know if matured is the right word," says Smith, "although we're not the same kids pissing and fucking on the same floor." — "To Live and Die in L.A." / RJ Smith / August '99

FLEA: I remember the first time I heard *Nothing's Shocking*. Perry had just finished up recording, and we were on our way to a friend's house to watch the big Tyson-Spinks fight. On the way there, Perry was like, "Oh, this is my new record, listen to it." And then I realized what a great, great band they were. It was just a big, weird day. I heard Jane's music for the first time, Tyson knocked Spinks out in the first round, and then I came home and got the call that [Chili Peppers' guitarist] Hillel [Slovak] was dead.
DAVE JERDEN [producer]: There's not one person I talk to today who's in their 30s who didn't listen to that record in college. *Nevermind* was a fucking classic record, and the press has marked that as the beginning of this big change in alternative music becoming mainstream. But it wasn't. *Nothing's Shocking* was. — "The Dance of Decadence: the Uncensored History of Jane's Addiction" / Brendan Mullen and Marc Spitz / August '03

PERRY FARRELL: My dad was a real character, a fun guy. Sharp, with a ton of style. Cared about his hair. Always drove a Corvette. Celebrities and regular people gravitated toward him. The wiseguys knew my dad, too. Everybody knew Al Bernstein. He was one of those guys walking around Miami Beach in the '70s with a Fila headband and a bikini bathing suit with gold around his neck. He was a jewelry designer and repairman. I got a lot of creativity from him.
JANE BAINTER (friend and housemate of Perry Farrell's; inspiration for "Jane Says" and band name): Perry was really into African tribalism and the ancient ritualistic arts of different cultures. He had a scarification done by some anthropology professor at UCLA.
JOSH RICHMAN (L.A. party promoter, actor): He was the first [white] guy to have dreadlocks. The first to have piercings.
Farrell: Back in the day, I got pierced because I was hanging around a lot of art punks and a lot of them were gay and into this mild to heavy bondage. They were so cool. But I had to take all piercings out 'cause I'd be trying to surf out there with a tit ring, and the next thing you know I ripped my nipple off. — "The Uncensored History of Jane's Addiction" / Brendan Mullen and Marc Spitz / August '03

ALMOST ALL OF WARNER BROS.' USUAL DISTRIBUTORS ALLEGEDLY BALKED AT PERRY FARRELL'S PROPOSED COVER FOR *RITUAL DE LO HABITUAL*, SO JANE'S ADDICTION'S NEWEST ALBUM WILL BE RELEASED WITH TWO COVERS—ONE FEATURING THE ORIGINAL AND ONE TOTALLY WHITE. That seems to have appeased the more anal distributors, though they are almost certain to lose sales with the unappealing white cover.

The fetish Farrell created to grace the cover of *Ritual* now covers an entire wall of his living room. On it are three life-size figures resembling Perry, his girlfriend Casey Niccoli, and another woman, curled together in harmony on an old box spring. The figures are at least partially nude. They are surrounded by a field of found objects: painted, re-dressed plastic dolls; candelabra holding burning candles; scattered Tarot cards; household appliances; photographs; cheesy paintings. Best of all, the three figures' heads are fitted with gold rays like a trio of medieval Christs.

Farrell refuses to comment on the piece. "Let 'em guess. If you can't figure it out, you've not lived," he quips. "I'm not exactly sure what it is about the fetish that offends the powers that be. It may be nudity, it may be the three-way idea. It may be the ritualistic way in which the objects are arranged. Who the fuck knows?" — "Gonna Kick Tomorrow" / Dean Kuipers / September '90

SPIN: A lot of your aesthetic with Jane's Addiction and Porno For Pyros and Lollapalooza seems to be about saying yes to experience, about opening your mind.
PERRY FARRELL: Life is short, so why not get carried away? Like the other night, for example, this guy gave me head. I'm not gay. I don't think so, anyway. I just wanted to see what it felt like. And, you know, he stunk. I thought, it's gonna be good, because he's a guy. He went at it like he was eating corn on the cob or something. But no harm. I was protected. It made for an interesting Thursday night.

— "Lord of the Rings" (interview with Perry Farrell) / Jonathan Gold / August '94

JANE'S ADDICTION ARE CAREENING THROUGH "UP THE BEACH," THE OPENING TRACK FROM *NOTHING'S SHOCKING*, THE L.A. ROCKERS' SECOND ALBUM. The lean, bare torsos of guitarists Dave Navarro and Eric Avery shine softly with sweat, radiating heat in a converted church, now a cavernous Amsterdam club called the Paradiso. Perry Farrell sidles up to the microphone, stepping his way through a pile of dolls, religious icons, photos, fresh flowers and other fetishes strewn all over the equipment. "Just some of my favorite stuff," he says. He doffs his windbreaker after the last strains of

"Ain't No Right," looking like a gangster in an athletic T-shirt, baggy trousers, and suspenders.

"I'm a Jew by birth!" he suddenly shouts. It's true: for all of 16 years he lived another life as Perry Bernstein in Flushing, Queens; his pop ran a jewelry store in Manhattan.

"Thanks for hiding my ancestors during the war!" he continues. The band members look away, used to this kind of outburst, while the Dutch audience is still waiting for a reason to either hiss or cheer. "No, really, if it weren't for you people, I wouldn't be here right now. The folks back home asked me to say thanks."

Silence. "Hey, this is not a Nazi look. This is how we looked in the concentration camps." More silence. "That's a joke! My name's Perry and I'm into Satanism and sports. That's another joke—I don't like sports! Guess you don't understand my sense of humor."

The Dutch journalist standing next to me leans over and says, "Don't think that they don't get these jokes—they do." But how do you respond to something like this? Farrell acts like he's talking to himself. Maybe he is. Then he notices that a man has climbed onto a support rod in the upper arches of the church, maybe 60 feet above the crowd. He squats there, agitated, acting like a monkey. He looks like he's going to jump.

"Hey!" Farrell shouts. "Do something up there! It either comes out your asshole, or it gives you cancer. You might as well laugh it out right? Oh, another joke. I think it's funny. But then, I'm dying!"

A day later Farrell sits in the window of the infamous Bulldog Café, firing up a little aluminum foil pipe of the local hash. He's 32, he has money for the first time in his life, and he has big plans. For the past few months, he's been nurturing the idea of an enormous traveling music and alternative-living festival to be called Lollapalooza. "It's going to be an annual touring festival across America," he says. "It will last for a month, and it will be a multimedia event, using music, art, and military discoveries and weaponry as forms of entertainment.

"I've got so many surprises in store," Farrell continues. "Enough to make it so, that, like, even if you hated every band, I don't see a way in hell that you could not find something about the festival that you like. And if you don't, then there's something wrong with you."

— "Cashing In" / Dean Kuipers / June '91

Lollapalooza means, depending on whom you ask, either a) "something very striking or exceptional," b) "a big red lollipop," or c) a bunch of bands playing for nine straight hours on a really hot day." This particular Lollapalooza, the *soi-disant* all-day arts/entertainment/information festival, is sort of a combination of all three. The bands involved—Jane's Addiction, Siouxsie and the Banshees, Living Colour, Nine Inch Nails, Ice-T, Butthole Surfers, and the Rollins Band—represent a neat cross-section of what is today called "alternative music," a term that, if it means anything, denotes a common lack of radio airplay. Despite this, Lollapalooza is undeniably the hottest tour of the year thus far, selling out and adding dates even as Guns N' Roses are struggling to fill venues on their much-hyped comeback tour.

By the time you read this, Lollapalooza will be over, and if you missed it, you missed an Important Event. Clearly, something is afoot here, though it's not entirely certain what. Most of the fans who came to see the shows were cut from a less-than-variegated cloth, which on the one hand means that Jane's Addiction front man (and primary force behind Lollapalooza) Perry Farrell was wrong when he predicted in *Elle* that the tour would attract "all kinds of different people from neighborhoods not like their own." But on the other hand it means that alternative music has many more supporters than most music-industry mavens had previously thought, and that something dangerously close to a cohesive movement is slouching towards the suburbs and malls of America to be born. A quick T-shirt check proves this: Morrissey, Pixies, TAD, Front 242, Sonic Youth—a litany of "alternative" bands connected only by their fans' devotion in the face of mainstream neglect.

Nevertheless, Lollapalooza is emphatically not some sort of Woodstock redux. The festival is pretty much just a bunch of bands playing their usual sets. Most of the groups had only a cursory acquaintance with each other prior to the tour, and so far seem pretty content to keep it that way. Any sense of a Lollapaloozan community must come not from the musicians, but from the kids in the audience. For their part, they seem more interested in hanging out, seeing bands, and throwing Frisbees on a beautiful sunny Cali day than in perusing the issues booths or Perry Farrell's hand-picked displays of local art. Which, after all, is as it should be, less a show of political/cultural apathy than a healthy sense of priorities. This is the '90s, for chrissakes.
— "All Day Sucker" / Mark Blackwell & Jim Greer / October '91

SPIN: What's your strongest memory of going on tour with Lollapalooza?
COREY GLOVER (Living Colour): The realization that "alternative" music isn't that at all. 25,000 people a night isn't exactly underground.
SPIN: What was the best thing that happened on the tour?
HENRY ROLLINS: Making friends with Living Colour and Ice-T and associates is up there for sure. Probably seeing Jane's Addiction every night. I had the best seats in the house; I would watch from the sides and get off on it nightly. Jane's Addiction were one of the most significant bands to come through in the time I have been involved in music. On a good night they were as good as anything I have ever seen: Zep, Bad Brains, Nugent, Nick Cave, R.E.M., Fugazi, etc. They were tremendous, period.
GLOVER: I got laid. A lot.
— "Those Were the Days" / July '93

NOW THAT PERRY FARRELL HAS DISOWNED HIS LOVE CHILD LOLLAPALOOZA, THE FESTIVAL'S ORGANIZERS HAVE BEEN ABLE TO GO ALL-OUT AND TURN THIS SUMMER'S TOUR INTO A SURE-SELL EVENT. Featuring multiplatinum headliners Metallica and Soundgarden, as well as acts such as Rancid and the Ramones, the fifth-annual Lollapalooza (already deemed "Metal Fest '96" by it's detractors) is an about-face from last year's über-alternative bill, which included Sonic Youth, Beck, Pavement, and Hole and had mediocre ticket sales compared with previous tours.
— "Whole Lolla Shake-Up" / Julia Chaplin / June '96

They should have asked Puff Daddy to headline this summer's Lollapalooza-that-wasn't. Over the past year, Puffy has secured remixes from Nine Inch Nails (who allegedly turned the festival's marquee slot down), Goldie (not big enough), and Foo Fighter Dave Grohl (said no, but lacks oomph anyway, like grunge). He has obviously targeted the alt-rock audience as his largest remaining untapped market. And the irony would have been delicious: hip-hop, always a token presence at the festival—think how comparatively inaudible Arrested Development and A Tribe Called Quest seemed—swooping in to save the day.

Sacrilege? Hardly. At its best, Lollapalooza wasn't the triumph of any one genre so much as pop's return of the repressed. We'd spent the '80s watching the music industry trumpet the mainstream, as epitomized by the scene in Bruce Springsteen's "Dancing in the Dark" video in which he pulls Courteney Cox up to perform the most feckless boogaloo in history. That era ended when Jane's Addiction, Nine Inch Nails, Ice-T's Body Count, the Butthole Surfers, Henry Rollins, Siouxsie and the Banshees, and Living Colour united punk, rap-metal, hardcore, industrial, Goth, and psycho-funk into 1991's most unexpectedly successful summer shed tour. Next to those bellowing tribalists, even Madonna and Prince looked soft, compromised.

If Lollapalooza marked the commercial insurgence of "underground" sounds, it also allowed a new audience to claim the spotlight: post-baby boomers, who'd always been treated as the skimpy shadow of the Woodstock nation. Most of those who came were not punks, but to everyone's surprise they weren't frightened of punk, or of hip-hop (well, not much), and in Lolla Land they dipped into the body-altering rituals of the modern primitive. Indeed, the most enduring legacy of Lollapalooza may be that, thanks to fans as well as performers, the industry was forced to swear off dismissing any musical styles as "too weird."

"Too weird" can cut many ways, though, as everything is an alternative to something else. We've lived that lesson this decade, watching Lollapalooza dissolve into subspecies—Lilith Fair, the X-Games, Smokin' Grooves, H.O.R.D.E., Ozzfest, Warped Tour—arguing over the expropriation of punk and rap, even ska and electronica, marveling as Liz Phair's experiment became Alanis' box office. Such schisms are what happens to white-male-dominated countercultures, much as the hippies split over civil rights and feminism, Aquarian solipsism and heavy metal. Kurt Cobain, who should have headlined in 1993, the first summer Lollapalooza slipped (Primus headlined), couldn't prevent that crumbling—let alone Perry Farrell, whose inability or unwillingness to bring back Jane's Addiction finally killed the festival off.

Lollapalooza introduced NIN and Pearl Jam, along with the generation of new rock stars who now convene once a year at the Tibetan Freedom Concert; it honored Sonic Youth, P-Funk, and the Ramones for services rendered; and it proved that profitable music, grassroots subculture, and liberal politics could mix, however uneasily. The organizers might have capitalized better on such '90s trends as Epitaph punk, women-in-rock,

MOHINI RECORDS PRESENTS

Jane's ADDICTION

FROM AMERICA

FRIDAY MARCH 21 8:00 PM

AT THE BE LIVE!

3109½ BEVERLY BLVD
$ 7.00 ENTER IN REAR (213) 465-3446

GUEST D.J. K.X.L.U'S BUZZ

SPECIAL GUESTS
M.C. BAD ASS GAIL

THELONIUS MONSTER

TRANSEX DANCE REVIEW

CLASSIC MOTORCYCLE DISPLAY

SERVING
SONNY'S PORN DOGS

BEER & WINE

Brit-pop, and ska (and recruiting Metallica for the '96 tour certainly didn't help their reputation), but a festival built on showcasing the underappreciated had trouble coping with a market that now rushed to appreciate everything.

Lollapalooza is as comatose as alternative rock right now. What's still potent, though, is the festival's ideal of bringing together different subcultural tribes, however mainstream they might have become, just to see what might happen. This isn't a natural impulse for the new capitalism, happy to remain within well-walled niches, each radio genre with its own summer festival. But when it occurs anyway—in MTV's racially polyglot programming, at Beastie Boys-catered events, perhaps on this summer's Erykah Badu/Missy Elliott-tinted Lilith—the results can't be predicted. They force each of us—even the most pop-culturally urbane—to accept challenges to our sensibilities, rather than settle deeper inside of them. So bring on Sean Combs: He's just the thing to renew Perry Farrell's acid-dazed vision of bebopalula.

— "This Monkey's Gone to Heaven" / Eric Weisbard / July '98

IF AGE IS RARELY KIND TO HARD-ROCKERS, HOW MUCH WORSE FOR THIS BAND, WHICH ALWAYS SUFFERED FROM LED ZEPPELIN COMPARISONS. Stephen Perkins is a heavy hitter, but he's no Bonham; Dave Navarro's guitar meshes metal and punk yet never dictates the way Jimmy Page's did; and compared to the operatic Robert Plant, Farrell sounds like a cheap kazoo.

But none of this matters tonight. Farrell has staged a Dionysian fantasy few would want to resist. His hairdo a cross between Coolio's Medusa braids and those wire flowers mental patients make, and his set design a Tahitian paradise perfect for his Gaugin fixations, Farrell swoops yogi-like through the music, pausing for a carnal interlude with two buxom dancers. A blue-masked "god" represents Krishna; a horned one represents Pan. Everywhere you look, it seems like something new is slithering up and around.

— review of Jane's Addiction live, Hammerstein Ballroom, New York City, October 30, '97 / Eric Weisbard / February '98

: Alt-Country

Dust-bowling for dollars

/ Jon **Dolan**

{ WILCO }

Like most alt-rock styles, alternative-country has at different times meant many things to a few people.

To its true believers, it is a window into the soul of an Edenically idealized American Beauty, a place far from strip-malls and SUVs, standing apart from the exposed midriffs and middle-class morality bromides Country Music Television pedals as "real". For it's detractors, it is the devilry of Yacub, who plucked a rib from the OD'd corpse of Saint Gram Parsons, held it aloft, and wrought a dread alchemy, tricking impressionable white folk into thinking they didn't need to know who Jay-Z or the Wu-Tang Clan was.

We know the clichés—the put-on Mayberry accents, the doofy Dust Bowl romanticism. But playas gotta play and ya'llers gotta ya'll. And at heart alt-country thrives via the best of intentions. That is, a dream of crossing the "Great Divide"—between urban and rural, longhair and redneck, metro and retro—which the Band sang about way back in 1969, the same year Golden Gram's Flying Burrito Brothers fused Bakersfield twang and hippie doom-gospel to erect a cultural bridge called "country-rock." Many a self-styled neo-Huckleberry has trod that causeway since but it never quite buckles: Ford-tough yet tortured as the Myth of America itself.

By the mid-'70s, though, Parsons country-rock vision had devolved into Glenn Frey's vow to "take it easy" while receiving a hummer in the master's chambers of the Hotel California. But not even the Eagles could lay low Gram's rough beast, stab it with their steely knives though they did. Wounded but restless, roots rock flourished in the mid-'80s. You had your ex-punks excavating the existential longing of the honky-tonk (Meat Puppets, Mekons, Jason and the Scorchers). You had Austin, Texas bands Rank and File and Wild Seeds offering

abject twists on tough guy postures. You had Minnesota's longhaired Lutheran boys, the Jayhawks, singing a high lonesome ballad to the Midwestern radicalism that went down hard at the Hormel meatpacking plant strikes of the late '80s. You had poet's daughter Lucinda Williams, writing like Dolly or Loretta with a Balzac jones. You had Alamo-reenacting beerbrains (The Long Ryders, E-I-E-I-O, Beat Farmers), guys who bit the Outlaw Josey Wales the way rappers bit Scarface. You had simps, gimps, rustlers, cut throats, desperados, mugs, pugs, thugs, nitwits, halfwits, dimwits, vipers, snipers, con men, Indian agents, Mexican bandits, muggers, buggerers, bushwhackers, hornswogglers, horse thieves, bull dykes, train robbers, bank robbers, ass-kickers, shit-kickers. And Methodists.

But feel free to skip ahead to where it says "and thus spake Uncle Tupelo," cuz the boys from ass-out Belleville, Illinois are still alt-country's greatest gift to the secular world. Jeff Tweedy and Jay Farrar are

"TO US, [THE LOUVIN BROTHERS'] 'KNOXVILLE GIRL' WAS MORE TERRIFYING THAN ANYTHING HENRY ROLLINS COULD COME UP WITH. UNCLE TUPELO'S MUSIC CAME OUT SOUNDING LIKE PUNK ROCK BECAUSE THAT'S WHAT WE FELT WE HAD A RIGHT TO PLAY." — JEFF TWEEDY, 1999

American archetypes as sure as Huck and Jim, Archie and Meathead, pants-on Bill Clinton and pants-off Bill Clinton. Jay was the beleaguered everyman at 20, with a worried voice that sounded like a Walker Evans photo, moaning over a small town Midwest devolved into a nightmare of "people chasing money and money getting away." Tweedy was the aching fuck-it optimist, upending Jay's fatalism by playing the wide-eyed punk, writing an ode to the Minutemen's D. Boon, pogoing to Byrds records, finding a new identity in the ashes of an innocence he never knew he had. Tupelo released four records; the first and best, 1990's No Depression, is the closest "insurgent" country has to its own A Nation of Millions. When they split in 1993, Farrar threw himself down a grain elevator of grim solipsism with Son Volt, and Tweedy cut loose like a longneck goose via Wilco. The boogie pathos on A.M. was all about impressing Jay, but 1996's Being There invented a whole new idiom, refracting Tweedy themes of loss and regret through psych-rock and other exotic strains, the perfect kind of iconoclasm for a scene that had become pretty claustrophobic.

See, a tent city had sprung up in Tupelo's dead end: Lapsed Southerners

(Gillian Welch, Palace Brothers, Vic Chesnutt); ascetic grousers (Gillian Welch, Richard Buckner); agrarian post-rockers (Calexico, Lambchop); sensitive lapsed indie-rockers (Old 97s' Rhett Miller, Whiskeytown's Ryan Adams—who went on to annoy Parker Posey, among others). A whole scene of literate, sincerely tongue-in-cheek shit-kickers emerged through Chicago's Bloodshot label (Robbie Fulks, Neko Case, Waco Brothers). Nashville hard-sells like Patty Loveless and Kelly Willis found new careers embracing rootsier sounds. Merle Haggard found fresh purchase on the punk label Epitaph, further expanding the class dynamics of "Okie From Muskogee." After releasing her masterpiece, 1998's Car Wheels On A Gravel Road, Lucinda Williams was embraced as a kind of national treasure. Maybe the most heartening of all these necessitations was Steve Earle. A crack addict after falling from Music Row favor in the late '80s, he returned spitting fire on 1996's I Feel Alright and on 1997's The Mountain, a bluegrass set on which his heroically bad singing upended a staid style. Alt-istic authenticity itself became a selling point when 2001's O Brother, Where Art Thou soundtrack went multi-platinum, introducing suburbanites to Mesozoic bluegrass picker Ralph Stanley.

So it made good right sense that as he matured, Tweedy would abandon "roots" almost entirely. Recording with Chicago post-rocker Jim O'Rourke, Wilco released Yankee Hotel Foxtrot, a gorgeous, troubled album awash in sonic and emotional rootlessness, memories blowing like "the ashes of American flags" and a single, "Heavy Metal Drummer," proudly nostalgic for a pre-Tupelo youth, "playing Kiss covers, beautiful and stoned." The Great Divide was now the gulf between sincerity and irony, the chimera of corny "authenticity" and the truer impulse to fall away from realness altogether. Wilco's next record, A Ghost is Born, was even weirder, mixing Krautrock and Bob Seger, ending in a song about a band too cool to exist that placed Tupelo—and country's—quest for the Rosetta Stone of cultural purity in the cracked rearview. Wind at their back. A chooglin'.

ESSENTIAL ALT-COUNTRY

Starting in the 1980s, punk rockers in search of their roots and honky-tonk outlaws looking for something more real than Nashville's focus-group pop created a new sound out of down-home twang and rock rebellion. Here's a 30-plus-year retrospective of the insurgent country spirit.

The Flying Burrito Brothers
The Guilded Palace of Sin
(A&M, 1969; Edsel, 1994)
Gram Parsons invented "country rock," a utopia where the working folks back on his daddy's Florida orange plantation split a beer with the hippie aristocracy he found in "Sin City," California. Featuring an Aretha Franklin cover, an anti-Vietnam ditty, and a mess of Buck Owens twang, *Gilded Palace* was *Easy Rider* in reverse, a vision of America where red-necks and Deadheads sing the same song.

The Flatlanders
More a Legend Than a Band
(1972; Rounder, 1990)
These '70s West Texas acid cowboys met the Age of Aquarius with an existential hoe-down—"You say we'll all stand as brothers/ I guess till then we'll just stand around," sang Jimmie Dale Gilmore in his strangled wildflower of a voice. The band hammered on the Dobro and the singing saw, hoping the universe would collapse before they lost their recording contract. **also try:** The outlaw coke-boogie of Joe Ely's *Honky Tonk Masquerade* (MCA, 1978) and Gilmore's weeping, willowy *After Awhile* (Elektra/ Nonesuch, 1991).

Meat Puppets
Meat Puppets II
(SST, 1983)
Cris and Curt Kirkwood were wide-eyed kids from Phoenix, playing psychedelic bluegrass thrash, and this is their unlikely masterpiece of desert mysticism. The boys looked for "New Gods" in the "lake of fire" and came out picking and grinning like the house band at Los Alamos.
also try: Rank & File's *Long Gone Dead* (London, 1984), the meaner, straight-ahead side of '80s underground rock.

Mekons
Fear and Whiskey
(Sin, 1985)
They were from England (like Depeche Mode); they used a drum machine (like Shania Twain); they were dead-eyed sluts (like Hank Williams). And on the most intoxicatingly dank honky-tonk record of all time, they rode a glass-bottom Cadillac straight to the heart of darkness.

Back in Mississippi in the 1950s, I ran with a clique of anguished musicians and bad poets aspiring to be as Beat and urban as possible. We were conscious of the Grand Ole Opry only as some distant herd of noisy fools with bad grammar and loony smiles. The last calamity was enacted when they gathered into one mob onstage and sang the old country hymn, 40 of them scratching away on guitars and other cawing instruments, everybody suddenly holy after making jackasses out of themselves for hours. For hipsters, this was Grand Ole Hell.

But one voice got through on the radio; not really one of theirs, a kind of ragged bass tremolo from nowhere. This was Johnny Cash. Oh, at first we made jokes about him: "This man has arthritis of the voice." But then he got to us, over the little tinny speakers of the Impalas and the Furies. He had the edge, the fear, the terror, and the tenderness all at once. He was cool, solid, with an unsettling mean anarchy in him. He had shot a man in Reno. Just to watch him die.
— "Big Country" / Barry Hannah / July '94

Tastemakers typically knock alt-country bands by employing the inverse of logic they use to slag plain ol' alternative rock groups. The Americana bands, so the theory goes, are too "reverent," while the rootless suburbans of the alternative nation don't know their own history. Most contemporary roots-rock actually falls in the middle, the music thriving on its own contradictions. Does that guy in the band Blue Mountain really drive around town "drinking from a jar?" You might as well ask if Kid Rock actually has a lot of his boys locked up in "County." In either case, the correct answer is "Who knows, and who really cares?"
— review of the Gourds' *Ghosts of Hallelujah* and the Bottle Rockets' *Brand New Year* / Greg Milner / November '99

FOUR BEST QUOTES

by Ryan Adams on money:

" Fuck you—I make more money in two days than you do in a year. "

" I did the Gap ad because who says no to $30,000 an hour? I don't! I'm sorry if that's selling out, so be it. Yes, I sell out. I do Gap ads so that I don't have to work in a factory. Also, I don't mind their clothes. "

" I turned [*Cold Mountain*] down because they said, 'Well, you can come to Romania and you can have three or four lines and you get to play a banjo made out of a pumpkin.' I'm like, 'Fuck you, man.' I make that money in two gigs. "

" I don't make a ton of money doing this; *not that I care.* "
— "The List Issue" / May '04

Steve Earle
Guitar Town
(MCA, 1986)
Rolling into Nashville with "a two-pack habit and a motel tan," rolling out with a crack habit and a rep as an unrepentant loud-mouth, Steve Earle was the screw-up amid the new traditionalists—a Bruce Springsteen too down-and-out to believe that the American myth could be anything but a hollow promise.

Lucinda Williams
Lucinda Williams
(Rough Trade, 1988)
No one since the Rolling Stones has sung so honestly about the heaven and hell of human desire—and the Stones don't have too many songs written from the perspective of a Corona-slamming waitress. Here, Williams dissected small-town romance like Flaubert in heat.

Uncle Tupelo
No Depression
(Rockville, 1990)
Jay Farrar and Jeff Tweedy trademarked '90s "alt-country," reintroducing the Carter Family to the Minutemen, reinventing skate punk for combine kids, and turning the horrible realization that you're never gonna get out of your hometown into a raison d'etre. In Tupelo country, you take solace in the sounds of the past because the future's foreclosed and boredom is your best buddy.

The Jayhawks
Hollywood Town Hall
(Def American, 1992)
The greatest Lutheran bar band ever, transplanting Gram Parsons' gilded palace to the windswept nowhere of rural Minnesota. Mark Olson and Gary Louris sang about wide-open spaces, love, death, and waiting for the weather to warm up. Their forlorn, high-plains blues rang out as clearly as the coldest day of the year.

Palace Music
Viva Last Blues
(Drag City, 1995)
The slow kid from *The Sound and the Fury* reborn as an indie-rock savant, Will "Palace" Oldham worked out his Southern aristocratic angst (and latent sexual issues) with odes to sloth, morbid jealousy, and back-woods amour, rendered in a beautiful faux-inbred croak.
also try: Songs: Ohia's *The Magnolia Electric Co.* (Secretly Canadian, 2003), which buries the Palace sound in a noise-rock mudslide.

Drive-By Truckers
Southern Rock Opera
(Lost Highway, 2002)
In the spirit of Gram Parsons, Alabama belligerent Patterson Hood dreamed of a populist rock that could fuse the punk of his misspent youth with the denim jams of his high school parking lot. *Opera*—a two-disc travelogue of Southern angst—excavates a nasty history from the Civil War to George Wallace to Lynyrd Skynyrd without irony or shame.
— Jon Dolan / June '03

SPIN: Tell me about the song "Get Right With God."

Lucinda Williams: It's not like a born-again Christian thing, which I hope is obvious to people. In the CD booklet, there's a folk-art sign that I found years ago that says GET RIGHT WITH GOD in kind of crude lettering. That's where I got the idea. And I was reading the Bible—for the stories and the literature and the depth of information—and the song just sort of popped out.

I think it's an interesting way to tell a story, using some of those things as metaphors or whatever. If you go in my house, I've got snakes and Virgin Marys and skulls all over—Santeria, Catholicism mixed with voodoo, and the whole Day of the Dead thing—to me, the whole thing is just fascinating. Part of the song alludes to Pentecostal snake handling. It's about the passion in that, and the faith, testing faith—the snake could bite you and kill you, and then the obvious sexual metaphor. I mean, it's just so deep. [2001]

Please let this be the album that kills alt-country. If not the entire genre, just the way its fans tend to view songs like Gretchen Wilson's mainstream-country hit "Redneck Woman" as somehow inauthentic. In that song, Wilson claims to be a just-folks, down-to-earth gal who has a Southern accent but hails from Illinois, who shops at big-box stores but pals around with Kid Rock and Tanya Tucker. She's completely serious and completely full of shit at once— a state of mind native Southerners like the Truckers understand very well.

The Dirty South both sucks the air out of Dixie legend *and* revives it. Jason Isbell, the newest of the band's three songwriters, draws blood with a story about how he figured out the real reason John Henry became a steel-drivin' man: "An engine never thinks about his daddy/ And an engine never needs to write its name." Longtime Trucker frontman Patterson Hood scores with "Puttin' People on the Moon," a blistering first-person tale about a small-town loser who gets laid off at the Ford plant, deals coke, loses his wife to cancer, and ends up working at Wal-Mart. The way Hood sees it, globalization's partly to blame, but so are dumb-ass politicians, the only thing the South seems to manufacture these days.
— review of Drive-By Truckers' *The Dirty South* / Andrew Beaujon / September '04

"I have a great life," Wilco frontman Jeff Tweedy says, "but it's an uncool life. It was a wonderful revelation to move to Chicago and make music and just be normal. So many artists reach a certain level of success, and then they cross over. They surrender everything to the service of their persona. Take Madonna, for example: You could never get to be that huge unless you surrendered every other impulse in your body to the service of your persona. Even with Bob Dylan, there was clearly a point early in his career where he was completely able to immerse himself into that persona. And I think it's disastrous that so many people destroy themselves because they can't do it. I mean, how many fucking people has Keith Richards killed? How many countless people has Sid Vicious killed? How many young girls has Madonna made insane?"

This probably sounds like the kind of sentiment you'd hear from a graying 36-year-old father who hasn't had a drink in 13 years, drives a minivan, and exists in a state of constant nervousness. And it should, because that's what Tweedy is.
— "A Ghost Story" / Chuck Klosterman / July '04

: Gangsta, Gangsta
N.W.A, Dr. Dre, and the Monsters of Rap

Before you start waving that copy of *Straight Outta Compton* as your gangsta rap Rosetta stone, consider a few things: That street hoods in South Central Los Angeles were calling each other "nigga" some 50 years ago. That an LAPD arrest photo from the 1940s shows a suspect flashing a home-made tattoo reading "OG." Consider that before "gangsta" was a set of grooves it was a set of notions, built on neighborhood crews that were getting squeezed by other crews and the cops. Before it was music, it was lived.

Now, get out your copy of *Straight Outta Compton* and give it up for N.W.A. Arguably no record shook up this country—inside and outside the hip-hop nation—more than *Compton* did upon its release in 1988. At a time when New York rappers were talking about unity, N.W.A had other ideas: "I'm the muthafucka that ya read about/ Takin' a life or two/ that's what the hell I do/ you don't like how I'm livin well fuck you!" Without it, hundreds of successful down-for-whatevers would be flipping burgers today. This record launched a movement and a federal investigation, FBI files and death threats. Each member was a role player, responsible for a distinct and crucial contribution. While East Coast MCs were digging low tones out of their chest caverns, Eazy-E came with a Woody Woodpecker cackle that was dry and flexible as a Sonny Criss saxophone riff. Ice Cube was gonna give every bit as good as he got, swinging from his heels like Rick Mahorn, a middle-class kid with something to prove. DJ Yella and MC Ren were the Ringos of the band—easy to read, both stone guilty pleasures.

And then there was Dre. Long before he was known as a brilliant producer with the Midas touch, he was merely a fan, sucking up the West Coast records and the stoned-in-the-sun atmosphere he loved. Which is to say

before he was an artist, he was just a kid reflecting the very particular SoCal vibe—hazy, guarded, shot through with light—he found everywhere around him. By 1992's *The Chronic*, his solo debut, that would change, and the fanboy morphed uneasily into a grownup master craftsman. With live musicians and fat-ass samples both obvious (Parliament tracks were a cliché even before *The Chronic*) and obscure (Leon Haywood) served up like rails of cocaine, Dre built an ensemble sound that turned rappers into character actors—he was the director, producer, scriptwriter, and sound effects man. N.W.A shook the world; Dre consolidated and changed it. He brought live instruments into the hip-hop studio, his use of "ho" and "bitch" and his abuse of same became a staple, his business plan became a trusted model for building an empire. Without Dre there'd probably be no X-rated album "skits," no Eminem, no pimp cups, no East-West feud. The 1992 L.A. riots, during which the city burned in an apolitical state of blind, misdirected rage, seem keyed to records that burn with apolitical, blind, misdirected rage.

One more big oh yeah: without Dre, no Snoop. In Calvin Broadus Dre found a master of flow who, over time, grew from character actor to top-ranking cartoon character. Dodging a murder charge in 1996, traveling around the country in what was basically a Bradley fighting vehicle to keep the death-threat-making haters at bay, Snoop crossed the line of keeping it real so long ago he doesn't need to prove a damned thing ever again. He's the rarest thing: a gangsta allowed to grow into middle age. He can still make great records and America lets him go on work release to coach his son's football team.

Two or three other things happened in the early '90s. Artists like Cypress Hill, Ice-T, and Tupac debuted, making the West Coast look like the nastiest place on earth—and the best place to be.

However global they got, these acts hewed to turf, to a deep sense of place. For Ice-T it was the South Central street corner; for Cypress Hill it was the industrial scrap heap of southeast Los Angeles, full of immigrants and working-class blacks and whites that the rest of the city all but ignored. Tupac's roots—New York and the Bay Area—were more complicated, but he as much as anybody gave it up to the idea of turf, of belonging to one set and waging war on one's enemy.

About the same time, the insane logic of proving one's realness by turning words into acts took over. By the mid-'90s, the records were becoming increasingly formulaic, and so was the mentality. Gangsta suggested a new way of looking at the world, and eventually that world view opened into an abyss, one that the mounting body count (Tupac, Biggie, and assorted soldiers—some of whom we just don't know died for the cause) couldn't even begin to fill. Gangsta made black-on-black violence the new national pastime.

Which is pretty much where we find ourselves today. Gangsta started out as an implied critique of white America. The music broke at the same time that crack hit, and the synchronicity seemed perfect: Harvard Business School rules applied to the streets, a generation of black entrepreneurs bootstrapping it up the ladder. The gangsta was a funhouse mirror parody of the capitalist. You have turned me into a monster, the MC said; do you like what you see? But once a million white suburban kids answered "hell yeah," the die was cast. The industry keeps trying to build bigger and better monsters. 50 Cent only seems like the end of the process. Gangsta as a musical form expired some time ago—at least until they come up with a better way to mic a gunshot. But as a mentality, most of the field has internalized it. Gangsta's still on the grind.

"So what the fuck do you wanna ask me? Who'd I kill? Where's my gun?" Jesse Weaver, a muscular 24-year-old tough with a square-top haircut, white tank top, white pants, and Fila sneakers, smiles as he barks out the questions. These days, Jesse does business as Schoolly-D ("We used to call playing basketball 'going schooling'; don't know where the 'D' came from") and has added a new, raw dimension to rap aggressiveness: "Put my pistol up against his head/ Said 'sucka ass nigger/ I should shoot you dead.'" Today's business is to lead a tour of his neighborhood, 52nd Street and Parkside in West Philadelphia, the turf that gave its name to Schoolly's loyal crew the Parkside Killers and by extension to his first single, "P.S.K.—What Does It Mean?"

"A lot of people loved it," he says of "P.S.K." as we walk past a strip of weathered-brick row houses brightened by people hanging out on the stoops. "A lot of people thought it was too violent. They think all I do is go around and stick guns in people's faces."

Do you?

"Only when I had to," he says. "All I do in my rhymes is see something over here and report it over there."

— "Going Schooling" / Scott Mehno / October '86

"Chuck D gets involved in all that black stuff, we don't. Fuck that black power shit: We don't give a fuck. Free South Africa: We don't give a fuck. I bet there ain't anybody in South Africa wearing a button saying "Free Compton" or "Free California." They don't give a damn about us, so why should we give a damn about them? We're not into politics at all. We're just saying what other people are afraid to say."

— Ice Cube, 1990

"When you grow up in the ghetto, the cops are the enemy. I'm sure there are people who say, "Oh, there's a policeman, I'm safe." I see them, I'm afraid. I knew they were the only people that could actually walk up to me and take away my life and my freedom for something I didn't do. 'Cause a lot of my friends went to prison for stuff they didn't do. You've got reason to be afraid of the cops. You can be railroaded the fuck out of there. When you give somebody that power, it's scary, man. >

"With the uprising in Los Angeles in 1992, for the first time there was something like a riot and the white parents weren't able to say, 'Look how terrible they are,' because the white kids said, 'We know why they did it.' Why? Because there's been a dialogue through rap music to let them know we're really ready. This is where you see the communication going down.

"People say, 'Well, yo, yo, yo, the uprising, that wasn't good.' But I'm like, look, the problem with the American system is, the system can issue a consequence. You do wrong, you go to jail. You don't pay taxes, you go to jail. You speed, you go to jail. You run, we shoot you. How do people issue consequences to an unjust system? Vote?"

— Ice-T, 1993

SPIN: Tone Loc, from Los Angeles, has the biggest hip-hop album ever. MC Hammer just went platinum. Easy-E and N.W.A, from Compton, are both either platinum or on the way. Ice-T is slamming, and Too Short is selling by the thousands. Cali hip-hop used to be totally lame. What's up?

DADDY-O (Stetsasonic): We went to sleep, and they moved right in. They talked about issues while we were talking about ourselves. N.W.A are selling a lot of records underground because they're saying what people want to hear. In that record, "Fuck tha Police" when he says, "Young nigger got it bad cause I'm brown," or "They have the authority to kill a minority," or 'Searching my body 'cause I'm a teenager/ With a little bit of gold and a pager," that's the shit. I'm hearing that shit uptown, I'm hearing it in Brooklyn....we will always lose to guys like N.W.A because they're visual, they're talented, and they watched us from the ground up. You listen to "Fuck Tha Police," it's like you just had crack and you never had it before.

— "Dropping Science" / August '89

N.W.A have a reservation at New York City's elegant Russian Tea Room. By the time their table is ready, DJ Yella is in the middle of spilling his third gin and pineapple juice down the front of his shirt, and he falls to the floor on his way to his seat. "Damn, man, you makin' us look bad!" Eazy-E howls. We enter the main dining room and become the center of attention for the rest of the night.

SPIN: IF YOU HAD TO STATE AN OCCUPATION, WHAT WOULD IT BE? WOULD YOU CONSIDER YOURSELF A "PROFESSIONAL NIGGA"?

Eazy-E: Yeah. [Laughing] Professional nigga. That's okay.

MC Ren: Everybody that's black's a professional nigga. And anybody else that survive all the world's bullshit.

Dr. Dre: We don't say nigga as a racial thing. Anybody can be a muthafuckin' nigga.

Ren: You got nine white muthafuckas after you with bats and guns yelling, "Nigger!"—now that's different.

Dre: Depends on how you say it. Say it wrong, we fuck you up.

WHO'S BUYING YOUR RECORD?

Eazy: Everybody. Same ones that listen to metal, Guns N' Roses, and Metallica and shit like that. People like to hear the real shit. The "I don't give a fuck" attitude.

Dre: Everybody else doing this peace shit. Nobody wants to listen to that.

EAZY, WAS YOUR DONATION TO THE REPUBLICAN SENATORIAL INNER CIRCLE AND LUNCHEON WITH GEORGE BUSH JUST A PUBLICITY STUNT?

Eazy: You know it! Everybody was dumb to that fact. Like Spike Lee, little bastard. He thought I was selling out or something. I paid $2,500 for a million dollars' worth of publicity! I'm not a Republican or a Democrat. I don't give a fuck. I don't even vote.

AND YOU ASKED RODNEY KING TO APPEAR ON A NEW VERSION OF "FUCK THA POLICE?"

Eazy: [Laughing] Rodney King's all

fucked up, man! He don't know what the fuck's going on! He don't know his ass from a hole in the ground! [Group laughter]

Ren: Muthafuckas criticized us when we did "Fuck Tha Police," but they shut the fuck up now.

Dre: Rodney King didn't help us. The muthafucka that video-taped [his beating] helped us.

Eazy: [Laughing hysterically] Without him, Rodney King wouldn't be goddamn shit!

DJ Yella: [Yelling from the next table over] Hey, Mark! You got a sister named Marcia?

WHAT ?

Yella: You look like muthafuckin' Greg Brady sittin' down there! [Laughter]

Eazy: Can I have some more bread with the veal shit in it?

Waiter: The thing I gave you 13,000 of already?

Dre: This place is wack! Muthafuckas in these monkey suits and shit. Muthafuckas ain't being real.

WHAT ARE YOUR GOALS?

Yella: [Singing] The Bra-dy Bunch! The Bra-dy Bunch! [Laughter]

Eazy: To make money.

WHAT'LL YOU DO WITH IT?

Eazy: I'd like to buy eternal life.

WHAT ABOUT YELLA? WHAT'S HE DOING WAY OVER THERE?

Dre: Yella wanna run a beauty parlor chain across the country. He wanna sell vibrators and shit!

Yella: Fuck all you pussy eaters!

SO, YELLA, WHAT ARE YOUR GOALS?

Yella: A house in Memphis, money in the bank, and pussy!

IS THAT ALL?

Yella: Naaaaaaaah. Power!

WHAT DOES POWER BRING?

Yella: Pussy! Money and pussy! Anything beside that's irrelevant!

WHAT'S THE WORST THING YOU'VE EVER DONE?

Eazy: You gettin' personal, man.

I'M JUST WONDERING IF YOUR RAPS ARE WRITTEN FROM EXPERIENCE.

Eazy: A lot of it. Not all mine. I don't know.

WHERE DO THE SONGS ABOUT "KILLING BITCHES" COME FROM?

Eazy: I've seen a lot of shit. I seen a ho get chopped up. Eyes took out. Legs cut up.

YOU EVERY DONE ANYTHING LIKE THAT?

Eazy: I wouldn't say I've done it, hell no. But I'd like to.

SERIOUSLY?

Eazy: Yeah. Just to see how it is. I wanna get somebody and cut they shit all up and grind it up like hamburger meat and shit.

BE SERIOUS.

Eazy: I'm serious! Fry that shit up and give it to somebody to eat, like a dog or something.

IS CRIME A GOOD THING?

Yella: It's a everyday thing.

YELLA, EVER BEEN ARRESTED?

Eazy: Ask me that, man. I been arrested a gang of times. Drugs, assaults, stealing, all kind of shit.

EVER SHOT ANYBODY?

Eazy: Of course. It's nothin'. It's like shootin' a bird with a BB gun. I don't feel bad. No conscience.

IF I PISSED YOU OFF, YOU WOULDN'T FEEL BAD ABOUT SHOOTING ME RIGHT NOW?

Eazy: You gotta piss me off enough to make me wanna fuck you up.

AND YOU'D SHOOT ME?

Eazy: And show no shame.

Ren: Man, hit this muthafucka with a bottle! Damn! You want me to hit you with this glass? I hit you if you want me to!

IT'D BE NICE FOR PUBLICITY. NOT NOW THOUGH. MAYBE LATER.

Ren: I'll grab you like this! [Chokes my neck] And take your shit like this! [Grabs my recorder]

Eazy: Wait, wait, wait! Don't fuck his shit up! Wait! Here go a perfect example. Homegirl from *Pump It Up*? She pissed Dre off—

DEE BARNES? SHE'S SUING DRE NOW, RIGHT?

Eazy: If the bitch can sue, he should just kill her. It's cheaper.

WHAT DID YOU DO?

Dre: Nothing, man.

Eazy: You lying! You beat the shit out of her!

Dre: I was drunk.

Eazy: I seen everything. He grabbed the bitch by the little hair that she had. Threw the bitch to the bathroom door. Pow! She hit her head. He just start stompin' on the bitch. I was like, "Stop, man! Stop!" [In high female voice] "No, don't! No, don't!" [Laughter] Threw the bitch down a flight of stairs! [Makes falling-down noise] Bitch didn't even know her name! She was fucked up worse than Rodney King! [Laughter]

IS THERE A LIMIT TO WHAT YOU'D SAY OR DO?

Eazy: Nah, we don't give a fuck.

IS THAT THE GIMMICK?

Eazy: No gimmick. It's real. I don't give a fuck about nothing.

BUT IS IT JUST ONE TRICK? BITCHES, HO'S, COPS, AND THAT'S IT?

Eazy: Nah. Whatever goes on, we gonna talk about it. Like underground reporters. Brings home the bacon.

Dre: That's the bottom muthafuckin' line.

I MET THIS GIRL LAST NIGHT—

Eazy: Did you fuck her?

NO, BUT—

Eazy: Well, I don't wanna hear about it. [Laughter]

SHE'S A TEACHER, AND SHE SAID THE ONLY WAY TO GET HER 12-YEAR-OLDS TO WRITE IS TO LET THEM TRANSCRIBE STUFF LIKE N.W.A. THEY ASK HER THINGS LIKE, "HOW DO YOU SPELL *FUCK*?" AND "WHAT'S A HO?"

Eazy: That's good! Teach the little bastards how to do they ABC's in rap form, the muthafuckas'll learn faster.

Dre: "A...B...muthafuckin' C."

Eazy: They'll remember shit like that! Who the fuck wanna just learn about Africa?

Ren: I just want them to go buy the record. Fuck 'em.

SO YOU DON'T FEEL RESPONSIBLE FOR THE KIDS THAT LOOK UP TO YOU? YOU DON'T CARE ABOUT PUTTING OUT ANY MESSAGE?

Eazy: [Raising his glass] Fuck the world!

— "Niggaz4Dinner" / Mark Blackwell / September '91

Somehow *nigger* and its variations—nigga, niggaz—struck a chord with African-Americans. "Nigga" flows. And with its utterance comes a quick, small feeling of superiority. Whether tossed off in fun or spat with anger, the miniscule moment of supremacy is always there. Always. The girl feels it.

But then a white boy or a Chinese girl or a Mexican homeboy says it, and she has to decide whether to flinch or fight or run or destroy property. She has to size up the situation. Like when she heard Irish Everlast from House of Pain and Italian Muggs from Cypress Hill use nigga in conversation—casual, easy, cool. She saw the opaque question mark form in the irises of the black men's eyes as Muggs or Everlast said *fuck those niggas* or *that's my nigga* or *that's why I don't fuck around with niggas like them*. She watched the question mark, in a second, stretch to an exclamation point and then back to a question mark. Like sports, hip-hop nurtures precarious, intimate relationships between black and white. She herself was bewildered, even cowed, by *nigga* coming from a white boy. Flinch, was her weak decision. Flinch hard. *Nigga*, they said, with nonchalance. And she had to swallow the acrid vomit as it rose in her throat.

— "Dreaming America: Hip-Hop Culture" / Danyel Smith / January '94

"Nobody was forcin' me, but it's hard as fuck out there. There was no money, man, nigga had to sell dope to get paid. In nice neighborhoods, there's always summer jobs for kids, but in the ghetto it ain't like that and it ain't right. We're not promised no jobs or no college degrees. We get paid the best way we can, and if y'all feel it's wrong, that's the way y'all feel." — Snoop Doggy Dog, 1993

Snoop's hero as a young rapper was Ricky "Slick Rick" Walters, the gifted, yarn-spinning eccentric. His influence is obvious when Snoop slips into a feminine voice, gets silly on the mic, or fiddles around with language— dropping "iz" into the middle of words, an old carny-talk trick used by jazzmen as a scat device and by pop singers as an attention-getter (see Frankie Smith's 1980 novelty hit, "Double Dutch Bus"). But Rick also felt the inevitable responsibility to the community. "He gave illustrations of life," says Snoop, his voice quiet and precise. "He

even gave a message to the real little kids ['Hey Young World'], and they loved him for it. You could feel the characters in the story, he played all the roles, you could feel the whole story." Snoop presses PLAY on the car's CD player and out booms the intro to Rick's "Children's Story," from 1988's *The Great Adventures of Slick Rick*. "See, I got him right here, I never keep him away from me. That's all his voices right there… that's acting, that's visual, you can see it."

— "Sir Real" / Charles Aaron / October '93

The death of Eazy-E from AIDS shocked the hip-hop community. The beat generation has long been used to the idea of its own mortality, but only in qualified contexts. Death by environmental hazards—the stray bullet, the drive-by, is understood, even romanticized. But to be destroyed by an unseen killer? Eazy's death served as a public deconstruction of our deep-seated illusions about AIDS. Even Magic Johnson's revelation paled in terms of psychic trauma generated.

— "The Beat Goes On" / Selwyn Seyfu Hinds / January '96

When was the last time a hardcore rap record, gangsta or otherwise, actually tensed you up? Made you look over your shoulder? Or more bluntly, did what the fuck it was supposed to do? Nah, the cartoon's usually too loony, the production too reassuring. But on "C.R.E.A.M.," Staten Island's Wu-Tang Clan, and producer Prince Rakeem, come close. Ol' Dirty Bastard portrays his neighborhood as an unmarked grave full of drug dealers, while Rakeem's piano sample flickers like a votive candle.

— "Singles" / Charles Aaron / August '94

There have been radical black art collectives before—Sun Ra's Arkestra, The Art Ensemble of Chicago, George Clinton's funk duchy—but none of them had their own 900 number, or their own clothing line. None had their own action-figure pop stars, their own CD-Rom-enhanced records, or their own $1 million videos. None, in short, pushed as dark, fecund, and uncompromisingly weird an underground ethos so deep into the mainstream that we'd call them hip-hop's Grateful Dead if we weren't too scared. No, that would

only be the Wu-Tang Clan. — "Spin Top 40" / Chris Norris / May '98

Method Man is humble, yet he projects. Stylish, yet a man of the people. Talented, waggish, and constantly stoned. Were he in the Rat Pack, Method Man would clearly be Dino, the accidental pop star. As RZA sees it, Wu members such as Raekwon and Ghostface Killah appeal to the thugs ("'cause they straight off the streets with that shit"), RZA to the intellectuals ("'cause of my vocabulary and shit"), and Method Man to everyone. "Meth is the warm level," RZA says. "He make a thug nigga smile, he gets all the women, and the children are into him, too. They look at him as a superhero."

— "Ghetto Superstar"/Chris Norris/December '98

The Wu-Tang Clan are quick to respond to perceived threats, that they are capable of blowing up at the drop of a chopstick—these are all things I already knew. But what I learned there surrounded by the Wu-Tang Clan was the strange power one man— RZA—has over them. He can stand on the volcano's edge, make a simple hand movement, and the fire turns to stone. Nobody else—not the "manager" chilling out in one car, not the label reps chilling in another, damn skippy not a reporter—can control them. One thing RZA stands for is "RZA-rector," because he can bring people back to life. I am here to testify.

I have gone from being a CIA assassin to a friend of the family in a heartbeat. "Aww man, your name's RJ? My name's RJ, too—Russell Jones," says the rapper known as Ol' Dirty Bastard. "But that's okay, I'm an alien, too." Nearly knocking over a plate of French fries in my lunge for this olive branch, I ask Ol' Dirty which planet he comes from. A demented grin creasing his face uncovers a row of gold caps.

"I used to have picnics on Venus," he says, eyes and teeth twinkling.

I'm game. "What do you eat at a picnic on Venus?" I venture.

From behind me, Ghostface Killah offers an answer. "Food for thought."

— "Phantoms of the Hip-Hopera" / RJ Smith /July '97

"Selling music is like selling drugs. If you want your clientele to keep coming back, you need to consistently supply a quality product. People know what they want." — 50 Cent, 2005

The SPIN Record Guide: Gangsta Rap

It began as the scourge of Big Poppa Bush's America. And by the time his kid took over, it was the most popular music on earth. Gangsta rap revived 1970s funk and old kung fu flicks, made South Central Los Angeles a mecca, and got a guy named Snoop Dogg his own line of action figures. It's been flossy and glossy, walking a terrifying line between myth and reality, but it's changed pop's racial politics like nothing since Elvis.

SCHOOLLY D *THE BEST OF SCHOOLLY D* (Jive, 2003)
The original gangster? Armed with sparse drum-machine beats, rocking a "Fat Gold Chain," Philly's Schoolly D put the nihilistic world of teenage hoods and crack wars on wax. A bit chintzy in retrospect, his game was so new in '86 that he had to write a rule book: "P.S.K. (What Does It Mean?)."

KOOL G RAP & DJ POLO *WANTED: DEAD OR ALIVE* (Cold Chillin', 1990)
At a time when hip-hop was ruled by lover boys, clowns, and conscious rebels, Queens born G Rap was the prince of darkness. Chronicling a shadow land of "dope fiends leaning for morphine," the Juice Crewman with the Uzi-paced lisp walked tall in bloodstained Ballys over beats (from Marley Marl and Large Professor) that chug like tagged-up subway trains.

N.W.A *STRAIGHT OUTTA COMPTON* (Ruthless / Priority, 1988)
With its sloganeering song titles and Dr. Dre's brass-knuckled production, *Compton* ripped through suburbia like no hardcore rap before it—an '80s punk political-party rejoinder to Public Enemy's '60s-inspired stump speeches. These days, Dre shills for Coors; back then, this was the sound before the fury of the L.A. riots. ALSO TRY: Ice-T's *Power* (Sire, 1988).

ICE CUBE *AMERIKKKA'S MOST WANTED* (Priority, 1990)
Cube, then just a boy in the 'hood, fresh off a bid with N.W.A, created a new kind of persona: the gangsta as political refugee, an "endangered species" forced to make a choice ("Some rappers are heaven-sent/ But 'Self Destruction' don't pay the fucking rent"). *AmeriKKKa* is a roller-coaster ride through South Central L.A., with drive-bys punctuating the dice games, pickup basketball, and girl chasing.

GETO BOYS *WE CAN'T BE STOPPED* (Rap-A-Lot, 1991)
A better warning against trife life than any parental-advisory sticker. The cover photo of the diminutive Bushwick Bill, minus one eye, being wheeled out of the hospital by Scarface and Willie D is chilling enough. But gothic masterpieces like "Mind Playing Tricks on Me" and "Another Nigger in the Morgue" make the imagery stick. Tougher than a night in Houston's 5th Ward.

DR. DRE *THE CHRONIC* (Death Row, 1992)
How the West won. "Nuthin' But a 'G' Thang" was inescapable, and the omnipresent videos turned 40-ounce bottles of malt liquor and lowrider Chevys into American dreams. Dre's hard-hitting snares are replaced by hazy Parliament-pillaging smoothness, while Snoop's laid-back drawl brings the temperature down even further. There's a riot going on? Let me ride.

RAEKWON *ONLY BUILT 4 CUBAN LINX* (Loud, 1995)
Standing on the block in Reeboks with his gun cocked, Raekwon the Chef wrote a Staten Island opera so dense it's best taken with an Advil and a Wu-tang glossary. RZA, at the height of his dusted powers, ornaments jagged beats with off-key piano loops, and a blitz of kung fu and crime-movie samples. But Raekwon is the real cinematographer. Step into their world.

UGK *RIDIN' DIRTY* (Jive, 1996)
As East and West Coast titans went toe-to-toe, Bun B and Pimp C repped what they called "the third coast." UGK (Underground Kings) found a home on the Geto Boys' Texas range, tapping diamond rings on wood paneling while nodding to morbid electro beats. Before No Limit Soldiers and Cash Money Millionaires turned it into a cartoon, this duo gave voice to the dirty business being done down South.

JAY-Z *REASONABLE DOUBT* (Roc-A-Fella / Priority, 1996)
A full throated response to "too much West Coast dick licking," Jay-Z's debut posited young Shawn as the East Coast alpha male. Jigga gave his days as a mover and shaker on the Brooklyn streets the Joel Silver multiplex treatment—midnight deals with Peruvian drug kings and Cristal-popping parties that go till six in the morning.

50 CENT *GUESS WHO'S BACK?* (Full Clip, 2002)
From the part of Queens where nobody gives a fuck about your birthday, 50 Cent broke through the superhuman floss of gangsta invincibility: "Wise men listen and laugh while fools talk/ stickup kids don't live long in New York." This unofficial mix tape has the kind of embedded reporting that CNN won't touch. ALSO TRY: M.O.P.'s napalm-spitting *Warriorz* (Loud, 2000).

— Chris Ryan / May '04

: Tupac

The reality show

/ Ta-Nehisi **Coates**

To say that Tupac was hip-hop personified is cliché—but that doesn't make it any less true. Eazy-E rapped about bucking cops. Tupac shot at cops. Chuck D rapped about going to jail. Tupac went to jail. Ice Cube rapped about beating down his adversaries; Tupac averaged a brawl a week. Before he picked up the mic, to describe hip-hop as outlaw culture was just a metaphor. Tupac made it all tangible.

And he did it without being a great rapper. His flow was the same from his first album to his last—you let me know when that is, by the way. From 1993's *Strictly 4 My N.I.G.G.A.Z.* to 1996's *All Eyez On Me*, he would hit the track with his voice perpetually doubled over and in perfect time with the beat, stressing syllables until they bled.

While essentially inventing the icon of the Sensitive Thug, in tracks such as "Keep Ya Head Up" and "Life Goes On," he mercilessly beat us over the head with the concept. Which isn't to say we didn't sometimes enjoy the shellacking—"Keep Your Head Up" is an awesome song. But by the time Pac made it to the posthumous "I Wonder If Heaven Got A Ghetto," it's safe to say his work was done—we all had realized that even wanton criminals have feelings.

But if Tupac proved unable go flow for flow with Rakim or brother-turned-nemesis Biggie Smalls, it was because rap was only a platform for him. Tupac understood that an outsized personality and a prolific recording schedule could more than compensate for his technical deficiencies. That knowledge allowed him to become the greatest performance artist of our day. Before slacking twenty-somethings started stranding themselves on islands and fat Southerners started swapping wives, Tupac grasped that young black men, in all their swaggering glory, were the most compelling show around. That the complexities, contradictions, ethos, and pathos of the ghetto was the perfect stage—and that he was the perfect performer.

He went from a kente-clothed cameo player with hip-hop circus-masters Digital Under-ground, to a roughneck who had girls blowing him on the dancefloor. He befriended Biggie Smalls, then spurned him, and on "Hit Em Up," fashioned himself Ali to Biggie's Sonny Liston: "I fucked your bitch, you fat mutherfucker." He had ties to New York, but jumped ship to Death Row Records, and became an icon of West Coast gangsta jingoism.

He was most at home when the cameras were rolling—remember his maniacal turn in *Juice?* He could be pensive, angry, high-strung, hot-blooded, sensitive, whatever the moment called for. And then there was his lineage; his maternal connection to the Black Panther Party gave him the romance of a '60s radical, the aura of a messiah. He was also extremely intelligent—the most articulate MC, off-mic, that I've ever heard. And he was masterful at playing his role, to such an extent that you wondered where it ended and reality began. Did he actually believe Biggie and Puffy plotted to have him robbed? Did he really have a thing with Faith? No one really cared. Tupac was a gift as a performer until he was gunned down in Las Vegas in 1996, in what even then seemed like the only possible conclusion of the narrative.

I met Tupac before he became 2Pac. My father had been a member of the Black Panther Party, and was good friends with his mother, Afeni Shakur. Tupac moved to Baltimore with her and his sister in the mid-'80s. I thought his mother exceedingly compassionate and his sister enchanting. Tupac would trade raps with my older brother, betraying little evidence of a gangster aesthetic—even then he was a sensitive thug.

Now, the hip-hop nation wants Tupac as their Jesus, and as such must rob him of all his rough edges. His old compadres smile poignantly into VH-1 cameras, assuring us that Pac vs. Big was all a game that would have ended with them smoking a blunt and cutting an album together. The same MCs who Tupac berated—Jay-Z, Nas—vie for his legacy. Snoop tells us that the East/West beef was all some media plot—as if *Vibe* magazine incited Snoop to kick over the New York skyscrapers in that video. History turns to dogma for the church of Pac. Complexity and contradiction are flattened into stained glass. We lose Tupac and get a one-dimensional stock character. That's no way to remember the greatest performer of our time.

It was Tupac Shakur's 18th birthday.

Shock-G of Digital Underground rented a stretch limousine for the celebration in Oakland. There were eight or nine of us. (Tupac is 22 now. *Juice* and *Poetic Justice* behind him. *Strictly 4 My N.I.G.G.A.Z.* and *2Pacalypse Now* both complex and underrated. By the time he turned 18, I'd known Tupac for about 18 months. He has been pleading insanity from then till now. He feels his mania is what we all have and deny, that insanity is a rational adjustment to a crazy world.)

Tupac met a white girl. Maybe her name was Jennifer. She and her friend came with us as we walked back to the car from a club. Jennifer wasn't quite sure she wanted to come along, and neither was her friend. Tupac coaxed and Jennifer got in, but her friend was adamant about not, as she said, "getting in a car with a bunch of strangers." She eventually decided to come along, but she sat on the limo floor and crossed her arms, angry. We were the picture of revelry, and Jennifer's friend was stiff, staring straight ahead.

(Tupac is the quintessential wronged black man/urban youth/crazy motherfucker. You wish he would articulate his complaints more diplomatically, without firearms. You purchase those complaints, though, and enjoy them—within the confines of a song or film. You quake when his hatred manifests itself in assault or gunfire or verbal pummeling. And you are weak if you desert him, if you don't respond to the call of his profane soliloquies. Because you are not driven as crazy by U.S. social norms, because you grit your teeth and swallow "the way things are" with more of the highly regarded "restraint," you are a punk-ass nigga. Brothers like Tupac remind us that all ain't fresh up in Bel Air.)

Tupac got mad and, as I remember it, said something to the effect of, "You think you're too good to be in here with a car fulla niggas? Fucking whore. You think just because the hair on your pussy is ugly-ass blond, every motherfucker in the world wants to get with you? I'll put your ass out right here on this motherfucking bridge. I'll put your ass out in the middle of West Oakland." Jennifer's friend cried, and Jennifer pleaded with Tupac.

(The night was a tiny precursor to the Reginald Denny incident [during the L.A. riots]: excuse or encourage or join the black man who is institutionally wronged, or help the individual white, in this case, women, who bear, this rare time—the key phrase, remember, is black-on-black crime—his wrath? What is the black owed? For what can he or she be excused? Save the whites...join Tupac...watch...avert eyes...be morally superior... revel in vindictiveness. Options with historical and sociological significance. I stared out the window and hoped the situation would play itself out without violence.)

The names got more filthy, the words—should have left your ass up there, fuck both y'all, fuck these stupid white bitches, man—loudly and bitterly enunciated. Add some bass and it could have been a song. Jennifer and her friend were on their own. The driver kept looking back to check on them, on us. He didn't stop driving, though, hugging the low hills that lead to Shock-G's place.

(Tupac is a daredevil, a time bomb. Held for questioning in the shooting of a six-year-old black boy in Marin County; called out by former vice president Dan Quayle for promoting black man–on–police violence; sued for assault in one state; filed suit alleging police brutality in another. Tupac's guns were out long before he allegedly shot those off-duty police officers in Atlanta. He sees a target in the mirror—the straight-up muthafuckin' bull's-eye. Instead of dodging, he takes the offense, lives

dangerously. And so regardless of a recent sexual-assault charge—sexual dominance is the backbone of the manhood that Tupac and many men fetishize; we'll probably never know if he "held the girl down" or not—he'll be a hero, perhaps go to prison a hero. And if he dies while he's still young, bleeding on the sidewalk, Tupac Shakur will be posthumously knighted, a champion, his funeral packed with devastated homeys, all feeling verified, Pac's death a proof of their truth. They are already living and dying through Shakur in the streets. And in Bel Air, but quietly.)

We passed through the security checkpoint at the sprawling complex that would burn to the ground a year later during the Oakland firestorm. The driver parked near a turquoise swimming pool, and we left the long black car quickly, like something stank inside. Soon, from a window in the apartment, I saw Tupac tongue-kissing Jennifer, or maybe it was her friend. The girl's arms were relaxed and hung loosely crossed at the back of his neck. The other girl was kissing someone, too. And Sleuth, Digital's road manager and Tupac's sometime friend and sometime keeper, said, "You wonder why these niggas is crazy."

— "Dreaming America" / DANYEL SMITH / February '94

"Rap is of great importance to the suburban kids because they have no culture,"

says poet and scholar Ishmael Reed. "Whites paid a terrible price when they abandoned their native traditions. So now white people are looking for an authentic culture in black people."

And Shakur, to the American imagination, seems the authentic black everyman, a composite of clichés of black manhood that have graced the screen and page since the turn of the century. He's a gun-toting revolutionary, a sexual dynamo, a loose cannon with a 400-year-old chip on his shoulder. Rap music, as largely bought by both blacks and whites, favors ultraviolent simplified depictions of urban life rather than multidimensional portraits. There are exceptions; a song off of De La Soul's recent album rejected the current mind-set—"Gangsta shit is outdated/ Posdnuos is complicated"—but this album has stalled on its way up the charts.

Nobody wanted to speak badly of Shakur on the record, and it's no surprise. Only last year, Shakur attacked director Allen Hughes with a lead pipe after hearing that one of his songs was being dropped from the *Menace II Society* soundtrack. He has admitted to the fight, but said it was fair because it was two against one. The case is still unsettled, and the Hughes brothers won't comment on the incident. Shakur is also alleged to have beaten up a limousine driver outside the set of the Fox network comedy *In Living Color* when the older black man wouldn't let him smoke weed in the back of the limo.

But others have only good things to say about their experiences with Shakur. Jeff Pollack is the director and writer of *Above the Rim*, Shakur's most recent film, in which he plays a drug dealer named Birdie, trying to steer a promising high school basketball player in the wrong direction. Pollack had heard the negative rap on Shakur and was prepared for the worst. "I've had none of the problems that people have complained about," says Pollack. "He always came to the set prepared. He has all the expected natural talent, but he also has the craft of acting that goes behind it. Tupac is irreplaceable. There isn't anyone who can do what he does. He's riveting. He's the guy you love to watch."

In Washington, D.C., the National Political Congress of Black Women has waged a full-fledged campaign against gangsta rap, and Tupac is a prime target. National Chair C. Delores Tucker, says, "We've found negative gangster rap, misogyny, and a promotion of violence in Tupac's lyrics. It's nothing more than pornographic smut."

Ishmael Reed, who believes rap music "has injected new life into American poetry," says that the middle-class blacks who are trying to censor the likes of Snoop Doggy Dogg and Shakur are simply "embarrassed in front of whites. The black bourgeoisie has always tried to repress art. They think this is perpetuating stereotypes. But in reality, they don't respect art. They're Philistines."

— "Violence Is Golden" / Danzy Senna / April '94

TUPAC SHAKUR MIGHT HAVE BEEN BETTER OFF ACTUALLY HAVING BEEN RAISED IN A GANG.

As it was, he matriculated in a milieu of scientific socialism, a pan-African nationalism more glamorous from afar than up close. His mom was a member of the Black Panther group the New York 21, charged—and then acquitted—of conspiring to blow up department stores and police stations. His stepfather, Mutulu Shakur, was a nationalist, and his godfather, Geronimo Pratt, is currently serving out a life sentence.

"He didn't look at those people in a romantic way," says 26-year-old hip-hop writer dream hampton. "There was nothing romantic about his stepdad being in lockdown 23 hours a day, nothing romantic about his mother going underground. There was nothing stable about it."

Tupac Shakur was born June 16, 1971. A move in 1988 from the East Coast to Marin City, California, and his mother's crack addiction, stunted whatever sense of structure he had nurtured. "Tupac was never part of a gang," says hampton. "In Oakland he was dissed. Drug dealers were selling his mom crack, so they would kind of dog him. Look at him in early Digital Underground footage. He was always this skinny guy."

"Me and Tupac was joined at the hip," Suge Knight told reporters a few days after Shakur's death. Which is how they were the one time I saw Shakur up close, the rapper almost comically concealed in the shadow of Knight.

It was Thanksgiving, and the gangstas were giving out turkeys in the ghetto. A line snaked down the steps, 'round the side, and along the block of a South Central Los Angeles community center. The free food, paid for by Death Row, was supposed to be doled out at 11 in the morning. The annual event gave Knight a chance to show off Shakur as his latest signing—Knight had just posted Shakur's $1.4 million bail—but the pair had yet to show. So the old folks and the moms with babies in their arms waited patiently, staring through the windows at the stacks of frozen turkeys locked inside.

Everyone was unbearably polite. "Free Tupac!" people began chanting. Only slowly did another replace it: "Fuck Tupac! Free the turkeys!"

A couple of hours later, the Death Row car arrived, and whatever anxiety had been rising in the hundreds of poor folks was dispelled by the appearance of Shakur. Wiped out by the Smile. He turned on the beacon, slowly ascended to the center's steps, and charmed his way to heaven. Of all his skills, the Smile was perhaps his finest.

But quick as a shot, the trademark disappeared. The other thing I most remember about that day is how, having soothed the hungry, Shakur disappeared into the shadow. He might have been the star, but Knight controlled the vibe, and Shakur did nothing to undermine it. He kept changing by the moment—first snarling at a Dutch TV crew, then mildly looking over to listen to Knight, then donning the posture of a visiting dignitary. He was all reaction, a charged particle orbiting his boss.

Knight put the money out for his freedom, but if Shakur did the dance, it was because he wanted to. When he was in the slammer, Shakur told reporters he was a changed man. But then he got out and realized contrition was out of the question. He played the thug ranker than ever. He pretended that this life was fate; maybe he believed it. His best performance was as a man who made a deal he couldn't undo.

— "ALL EYEZ ON HIM" / RJ Smith / December '96

Unlike Michael Jackson,

America's other publicly chastised black male musician, Tupac Shakur has retained enough presence of mind to deliver what his audience wants: romantic tableaus of pager-toting mack daddies who use the word "thug" as a noun, verb, and adjective, backed with jeep-shaking old-school, funk-infused tracks emblematic of the SoCal sound. While 2Pac's flow is leaden compared to Snoop Dogg's, they share access to personnel like producer Dr. Dre and songwriter Roger Troutman, formerly of Zapp. Hate it if you need to, but the vocoder riff of "California Love (RMX)," the album's first single, will most certainly rule Crenshaw Boulevard well into this summer.

— review of All Eyez on Me / Sue Cummings / May '96

Tupac Shakur, 1971~1996

Gangsta rapper Tupac Shakur died in a Las Vegas hospital on September 13, six days after he was gunned down in a drive-by shooting. He was 25. Shakur was riding in a BMW driven by Death Row Records head Suge Knight on the night of September 7 when he was shot several times by unknown assailants in another car. Knight and Shakur had attended the Mike Tyson–Bruce Seldon fight earlier that evening. One of hip-hop's most popular and controversial artists, Shakur debuted on the hip-hop scene in 1991, teaming up with Digital Underground for an EP. Recording as 2Pac, he released three solo albums before signing with Death Row in 1995. After serving an eight-month prison term on a sexual abuse charge, he recorded his final album, *All Eyez on Me*, which has sold more than five million copies since its February release. Shakur starred with Janet Jackson in the film *Poetic Justice*, appeared in *Juice* and *Above the Rim*, and was working on another movie, *Gridlock'd*, before he died. "Shakur was like a James Dean figure," said StepSun Music President /CEO and former Def Jam VP Bill Stephney. "He represented the angst of the young black generation better than anyone."

— "Tupac Shakur, 1971–1996" / Julia Chaplin / November '96

/ Laura **Sinagra**

: Grunge

Seattle and the heavy rock invasion

"Grunge is a good two parts punk, one part metal. Maybe one part punk, one part metal, and the last part divided between psychedelic and retarded."
—Kim Thayil (Soundgarden), 1992

For anyone not clued-in during the late '80s to left-of-the-dial malcontents like the Replacements and the Minutemen, the soundtrack of our lives were the bands on commercial radio, and the airwaves were in sad shape. Bush v1.0 was in the house, and after the stock-market crash of '87, the backdrop to the yuppie coke comedown was the smooth thwack of Phil Collins, the plastic-surgery pop of Michael Jackson, and assorted facsimiles of both. Hip-hop was in its golden age, though you wouldn't have known it in Middle America. On hair metal-crazed MTV, Poison was wearing off, and the future of hard rock didn't look too Guns N' Rosy. Then, from the temperate rain forest of Seattle, came Nirvana, with a sound just right for the times: sing-along aggro both panicked and stultified, Paradise City with the lights out.

For jobless couch surfers nationwide, Seattle fit the bill as a fantasy locale for low-rent escapism. It existed almost out of time, distant from the hubs of go-go '80s culture. Its mix of logging yahoos, homesteading hippies, Boeing eggheads, and laissez-faire libertarians made it the antithesis of glitz. People who wanted to make their own fun formed an artistic community in this mossy womb. One of the things routinely noted about Seattle when it became an MTV curiosity was the general friendliness of the place, the support system, the low-key lifestyle. Cameron Crowe's cinematic love-letter *Singles* (which sat moldering on a shelf till Nirvana hit) depicted a haven where a prim Kyra Sedgwick danced ecstatically to Soundgarden and Alice in Chains at the local dive. Of course, during the post *Nevermind* frenzy (described in Doug Pray's 1996 film *Hype!*), that folksiness became a municipal brand, and soon guitar-packing ragamuffins from Every-colllegetown, USA were looking for apartments in Capitol Hill.

The Northwest of the late 80's was a terrarium for a cross-pollination of punk and metal that was best exemplified by noodley distortionists Green River (whose members would go on to form Mudhoney and Pearl Jam), the sludge-metallic Melvins (whose legendary Aberdeen, WA parking lot show stoked the ambitions of young Kurt Cobain), and Portland psychedelic punks The Wipers. These early bands were small-time until Green River guitarist Stone Gossard and bassist Jeff Ament formed Mother Love Bone with singer Andrew Wood, whose Freddie Mercury flamboyance nabbed them a PolyGram contract. His 1990 heroin overdose, on the eve of MLB's major label debut, shocked the scene. Instead of the band's glam-rock *Apple*, it was *Temple of the Dog*—a dour tribute LP by grief-stricken pickup band of Seattle rock luminaries—that would, along with Soundgarden's *Badmotorfinger* and Pearl Jam's *Ten*, represent Seattle's modest entrance into MTV rotation.

In 1991, as moshing teens smelled Nirvana's pit, labels signed Seattle bands in a Starbucked frenzy, and the scene's metal, punk, and neo-psychedelia strains got officially smushed into the marketing s'more called "grunge." These bands didn't exactly sound like Nirvana (that technique would be perfected later by foreigners like Bush, Silver-chair, and the Vines)—but they sure as hell didn't sound like Phil Collins. An insider term supposedly coined by Mudhoney's Mark Arm, "grunge" became an onerous tag to the scene's established bands. But as generalizations go, it wasn't so bad: It sounded respectably working-class, and even carried a whiff of Led Zeppelin's "The Crunge." Grunge em-bodied the darkness of the moment. And the necessary fashion of a cold, rainy northern city mirrored the reality of jobless college grads and working-class kids. In a dying economy, nobody wanted to dress like Bret Michaels. Flannels and knit caps fit the zeitgeist, and you started to see them everywhere from Tacoma to Texas.

Some argue that Nirvana would have been "Nirvana" without the Seattle scene. And some argue that if the mega-seller hadn't been Nirvana, it would have been one of the other bands arriving on the radio radar in its wake. Neither of these theories is exactly right. Kurt Cobain's genius was obviously nurtured by the Melvins and The Wipers, and fellow bands buzzing around the Sub Pop label. But none of Seattle's bar-band rumble—Pearl Jam's Doors-y plod, Alice in Chains' dark Dio variations, Soundgarden's big-bottom wank, or Mudhoney's shambolic buzz—had Nirvana's melodies or poetry. And though a 1989 *Melody Maker* article had already dubbed Seattle the new "Rock City" (and bands were already talking to major labels before Nirvana exploded), none would have had the impact they did without the big N.

The more these male fans got to know Kurt, however, the weirder he seemed. If you wanted your Grunge without the boy-boy kissing that concluded Nirvana's *SNL* appearance, the cross-dressing, the crazy rock-star wife, you opted for Soundgarden, Alice in Chains, Pearl Jam. Soundgarden was the natural pick for potheads. The band took the freaky-styley L.A. sound of Jane's Addiction and added a big metal bottom, moving through the '90s from formless blare-boogie to the sublimely depressed bombast of "Black Hole Sun." Plus, the earnest self-examination of wailing hottie singer Chris Cornell and bushy guitarist Kim Thayil made for articulate interviews that sounded like early versions of the Metallica therapy movie.

Alice in Chains, on the other hand, was a band for hard drug-identified met-allists who played a lot of Quake. Singer

ESSAY CONTINUES ON NEXT PAGE >

[MUDHONEY]

> ESSAY CONTINUED FROM PREVIOUS PAGE
and future smack-casualty Layne Staley ground out the chromatic drones on songs like "Man in a Box," a blueprint for Tool-style self-loathing. And Pearl Jam, of course, turned out to be modern rock radio's most influential stylists—the workmanlike, midtempo chug of songs like "Alive" and "Evenflow" just melodic enough to get moshers singing along. When Kurt Cobain, whose approach to stardom toggled between winking trickster and masochistic Jesus pin-up, checked out in April 1994, Pearl Jam's Eddie Vedder became the movement's de facto arbiter of ethics. Meeting flashbulbs with a scowl, he projected anti-star integrity that fueled intense fan loyalty. But though fans stuck by his band through the '90s (and gobbled up their live recordings with the bootleg appetite of Phish fans), and Vedder garnered respect for challenging Ticketmaster's huge price mark-ups, the band's music never matched the quality of the singles off its first album. (Similarly, Alice in Chains never beat its own Seattle heyday output, and Soundgarden peaked with 1994's ultramelodic *Superunknown*.)

But listen to modern rock radio now and it's clear that the underdog appeal of the sound ensured its durability from late-'80s economic recession, straight through the peak of the dot.com boom, and onward into the next recession. Aside from the Zeppelin-esque Stone Temple Pilots and shout-along crowdpleasers Local H, most radio grunge has been as safe and dull as the music its forbears knocked from the charts in 1991. You couldn't cruise a mall in the past 10 years without hearing grunge by watered-down facsimiles like Live, Matchbox Twenty, or Creed. Grunge underpins radio pop from the hockey-thuggish Nickelback to the angsty Christian Switchfoot, prompting the question: Who are the radio-rock dinosaurs now?

The 20 Greatest Grunge Albums of All Time

1. NIRVANA
Nevermind (DGC, 1991)
Considering that the first nine seconds of this album were the most culturally important nine seconds of the '90s, it's remarkable that the next 59 minutes still hold up as music. And those 59 minutes don't sound like "mainstream Pixies" or anything else that jaded hipsters claimed. They sound novel and essential, millions of minutes later.

2. SOUNDGARDEN
Superunknown (A&M, 1994)
Possibly the most successful "grunge" album ever recorded. It's got La Brea Tar Pit retro-riffing and Dust Bowl depression, but this sludge was built for classic-rock radio on the day it was born.

3. PEARL JAM
Ten (Epic, 1991)
Juiced-up hippie metal misfiled under "alternative"? Okay, maybe, but these songs groove and yowl and hunger to connect. Then Eddie Vedder asked to be left alone.

4. NIRVANA
In Utero (DGC, 1993)
Or *Kurt Cobain and the Family Present No Way Out*. A brutal portrayal of marriage as womb and tomb, with guitars that grind bones to make bread.

5. MUDHONEY
Superfuzz Bigmuff (Sub Pop, 1992)
Write the book, end up a footnote—"Touch Me I'm Sick" is "Louie, Louie" with ants under its eyelids, and "If I Think" begins "If I think, I think of you," but you'd already moved on to Pearl Jam.

6. ALICE IN CHAINS
Dirt (Columbia, 1992)
"Rooster" is a glower ballad about Vietnam; almost all the other tracks are dispatches from the swampy DMZ of frontman/lost cause Layne Staley's mind. War is hell.

7. HOLE
Live Through This (DGC, 1994)
An invitation to a beheading—her own, of course. Alt America's black widow lets it bleed on sugar-sharp punk songs that writhe like a feral woman confronted with the profane reality of her own sex.

8. VARIOUS ARTISTS
Sub-Pop-200 (Sub Pop, 1988)
Seattle wasn't all hair flips and hairy lips. Here's a snapshot of the Emerald City as indie-rock mecca. Mudhoney and Nirvana rep big, but so do the Fastbacks and Beat Happening.

9. MELVINS
Stoner Witch (Atlantic, 1994)
The band that showed Nirvana that the "hard" in hardcore could mean heavy like concrete.

10. SCREAMING TREES
Sweet Oblivion (Epic, 1992)
Psychedelic rock from the Siskel-and-Eberts of grunge. "Nearly Lost You," with its come-to-Jesus vocals, was the hit, but "Winter Song" is where they reach nirvana (not the band).

11. L7
Bricks Are Heavy (Slash, 1992)
Crass L.A. fertility goddesses swinging their guitars like Alley Oop clubs. Inspired Butthead's most deathless line: "Hey, Beavis—let's pretend we're dead!"

12. MOTHER LOVE BONE
Stardog Champion (Polygram, 1990)
Before Jeff Ament and Stone Gossard joined Pearl Jam, they hooked up with late singer Andrew Wood somewhere between Iggy's *Fun House* and Axl's cathouse.

13. TAD
Inhaler (Giant/Warner Bros., 1993)
They dressed like lumberjacks. Their singer was quite a large man. They were heavy as hell and had great hooks. So why did Eddie

get rich while Thomas A. Doyle labors in obscurity? Such is life.

14. LOVE BATTERY
Dayglo (Sub Pop, 1992) Messy, meaty psychedelia that's equal parts BTO and the Beatles. Two years later, Oasis made the same record and were called geniuses.

15. WIPERS
Wipers Box Set (Zeno, 2001) Greg Sage's scene-defining early-'80s Portland punk rock: hardcore and spacey, epic and terse. No wonder Kurt worshiped the guy.

16. BABES IN TOYLAND
Spanking Machine (Twin/Tone, 1990) Courtney when Courtney wasn't cool. Kat Bjelland's barbed-wire guitar and skinned-cat vocals, plus the band's jagged rumble prefigured everything that made Hole roll.

17. GREEN RIVER
Dry as a Bone/Rehab Doll (Sub Pop, 1988) Pre-Mudhoney singer Mark Arm sounds like he's vomiting blood, and they beat the shit out of basically two riffs, but their dope rock was thee grunge template.

18. NIRVANA
MTV Unplugged in New York (DGC, 1994) With Cobain's creations (and his favorite covers) stripped to bare skeletons, there's nowhere to hide the agony. Proof that perfectly crafted songs need not be propped up on fuzz or bombast.

19. VARIOUS ARTISTS
Singles: Original Motion Picture Soundtrack (Epic, 1992) Cameron Crowe's youth movie about old people offers the best song Alice in Chains ever wrote and an epic Mother Love Bone jam for everybody who didn't know who the hell Mother Love Bone were.

20. STONE TEMPLE PILOTS
Purple (Atlantic, 1994) Fake alt rock? Yup. But nothing sounds better when you're actually driving to Seattle.

—"The 20 Greatest Grunge Albums of All Time" / Andrew Beaujon, Jon Dolan, Caryn Ganz, Joe Gross, Chuck Klosterman, Alex Pappademas, Phoebe Reilly / April, '04

CAMERON CROWE: I loved Mother Love Bone, so when I was writing the movie that would end up being *Singles*, I wanted to interview Jeff Ament and Stone Gossard [Mother Love Bone / Pearl Jam] to explore the whole coffee-culture, "two or three jobs, one of which is your band" lifestyle. The terrible turn of events that took place was that Andy Wood died. For me it was the first real feeling of what it was like to have a hometown—everybody pulling together for some people they really loved. That was a pivotal moment, I think, for a lot of people there. It made me want to do *Singles* as a love letter to the community that I was really moved by.

Few people know this, but Stone is actually in [my 1989 film] *Say Anything*. He plays a cab driver, and Ione Skye looks at him and kind of flirts with him a little bit as they're stuck in traffic on her way to graduation.

AMENT: I definitely don't talk like Matt Dillon. But I made a couple of thousand bucks loaning him my clothes.
— "Ten Past *Ten*" / Eric Weisbard, Jessica Letkemann, Ann Powers, Chris Norris, William Van Meter, Will Hermes / August '01

In the ten years since Soundgarden were part of the local scene originally known as the "Deep Six" bands—along with Green River, the Melvins, Malfunkshun, Skin Yard, and the U-Men—Seattle has changed dramatically. The mass outbreak of the grunge virus has brought hordes of alternative-lifestylists flocking to the Emerald City, and they're not Microsoft programmers, either. Tammy Watson of Seattle indie label Up Records describes Seattle as "Mayberry with big

buildings," and some small-town provinciality is plainly evident in Soundgarden's outlook.

"As a cultural phenomenon, it's what I imagine happened in San Francisco in the late '60s," says Thayil of the hipster invasion. Back in the years B.C. (Before Cobain), recalls Thayil, "you would know all the guys and girls at the punk-rock shows, and if you didn't know them they were usually someone's roommate. Now wherever you go, there's some grunge-type human being walking around aimlessly. They're just surveying the land for what it can offer them."

Seattle may no longer be "Sub Pop Rock City," as Soundgarden sang on the landmark box set *Sub Pop 200*, but for outsiders it's still seemingly a countercultural mecca. "It's a really strange counterculture, though," says Thayil, "because it's the counterculture as referenced by MTV. There are no wars, no race riots, no women's liberation or gay liberation—it's a counterculture based on successfully marketed radio songs and snowboarding."
— "The Real Thing" / Mike Rubin / July '96

It's raining steadily. Mudhoney lead-guitar stylist Steve Turner is standing at a long rack of used sweaters. "In the first grunge glossary they called these Cobains," he says. He phrases his words carefully, as if narrating a documentary. "Now they're called 'fuzzes.' This is a good fuzz. I lost one of my fuzzes on tour this last time. I kind of need to replace my fuzz." Turner is wearing a Brooks Brothers sweater.

It's absurd, but there it is on the front page of the *New York Times*' style section, slender models with perfect bodies and important cocktail parties to attend, strutting down the most prestigious runways in New York City, carefully draped in the latest in grunge fashion.

EXCERPT CONTINUES ON NEXT PAGE >

[SOUNDGARDEN]

> EXCERPT CONTINUED FROM PREVIOUS PAGE

"Marc Jacobs is the guru of grunge," Turner continues. "He has a cool grunge line with Perry Ellis. He's never been to Seattle, but he has just recently designed a lot of really great grunge-wear. High-fashion design is now doing $300 fake flannel shirts made out of silk."

— "Sweet Honey in the Rock" / Grant Alden / February '93

Sound-check never happens because nobody wants to do one; the bus heads back to the hotel carrying a very surly bunch.

I'm supposed to do my interview now, but Alice In Chains guitarist Jerry Cantrell is snoring and bassist Mike Starr has disappeared with another in his seemingly endless series of babes. Singer Layne Staley, drummer Sean Kinney, and I sit in the back lounge, sparring.

"Look," I say. "I'm trying to give you a break. I haven't asked you about drugs, have I?"

"I'm waiting," Staley says, flashing me his sweetest fuck-you smile.

I'm not sure what Alice thought would happen when they released an album centered around the subject of heroin addiction, but the guys weren't prepared for what they've received from the press. Staley talks about a French journalist he'd met the previous week who accused him of being on heroin during their interview. "I asked him if he was on heroin," he says. "The guy got all offended. 'Well,' I said, 'Now you know how I feel.'"

Given the mood, I don't try for any personal insights. I just ask about the album.

"It's simple," Staley sneers. "One theme is: Drugs are bad. The other theme is: relationships, bad. The last theme is: album, good."

"As long as it makes sense to us, that's what matters," Kinney grumbles. "We did our part." Then he's gone, leaving me with Staley, who still taunts me with that spleen-ish little grin. I tell him I agree that people have misinterpreted *Dirt*, that to me it sounds like a fierce argument against drugs, not a vindication. Sure, "Junkhead" comes from the perspective of a high and happening user, but "Angry Chair" and "God Smack" and "Hate To Feel" all show the character's descent into disaster. Finally, Staley gives me a rehearsed response—the "drugs are bad" line—but he's not grinning anymore.

"Maybe something this blatant and heavy and straight to the point might steer people away from being excited about the idea of trying heroin," he says. "There was nothing that blatant shoved in my face, discouraging me."

We get off the bus and Staley trips down the hall toward his room. It is increasingly clear that getting what they wanted isn't what they wanted at all. They're like the kids in *Lord of the Flies*, stranded in strange territory with no clear rules of conduct. They're trying to survive, but they're eating themselves alive.

— "Misery Loves Company" / Ann Powers / March '93

People with a great deal of free time on their hands (read: rock critics and lesser talents) sniped that Pearl Jam's enormous popularity was due to Seattle-fueled hype, that it wasn't a "real" alternative band, that it rode Nirvana's coattails to fame and fortune. This is, of course, bullshit. Pearl Jam succeeded by appealing to the same metal audience that bought so many copies of *Nevermind*, and in doing so helped expand the notion of what "alternative" might mean, which only shows how much both bands owe to Lollapalooza, and to previous trailblazers such as Jane's Addiction and Faith No More. Pearl Jam's music is no more contrived or calculated than any of those bands, and if its resultant record sales have surpassed anything yet achieved by any band unfortunately pigeonholed as alternative, maybe it just has a better record company.

That said, there's another element to Pearl Jam's success: the band's extraordinary connection with its audience, a result of the absolute lack of cynicism in its music and, especially, in its lead singer and de facto figurehead. Eddie Vedder is an extremely serious, extremely sincere young man, and, most importantly, his sincerity translates. His fans make an emotional connection with him that Kurt Cobain simply will not allow, and as much as it might at times make Vedder uncomfortable, it is a fundamental source of his power.

Vedder doesn't have cable, so he doesn't watch MTV. "I really should have said, 'Uh, thanks, but you know, I don't have MTV, so I don't know what this means,'" he jokes about his acceptance "speech" at the last MTV Video Music Awards, and Vedder professes not to apprehend the true scope of his fame. "I don't want to understand it," he insists, "because as soon as I understand it, I get real upset about it."

— "The Courtship of Eddie Vedder" / Jim Greer / December '93

Here is a joke Eddie Vedder told me. It wasn't the only joke he told, but it was probably the best, and bears repeating.

"How many members of Pearl Jam does it take to change a lightbulb?"

When Eddie Vedder asks a question of you, or you of him, or when he makes an important point, or when he shares something with you and wants a reaction, his eyebrows shoot up so they're suddenly at right angles to each other. It brings to mind disbelieving girlfriends, mean teachers, and Satan. It's an altogether unwelcoming look, and it's immediately amplified by a steely glare and furrowed brow. For a moment—a long moment—you can't help but believe those damning reports about Vedder's dour disposition.

But then, just before you flinch, the tension is lanced by a grin, the grin is often set to his own words, and it's a grin that's less about self-satisfaction than about breaking the ice, than about inclusiveness. It's a grin that says forget about what you've heard or read, I'm not that guarded, that somber, that paranoid, that humorless, that much of a pain-in-everyone's-ass. It's a warm, winning grin, and it works.

"I give up, Eddie. How many members of Pearl Jam does it take to change a lightbulb?"

Vedder stands up, screws his face into a mask of spokesman-for-a-generation pain, and yells: "Change?! Change? We're not gonna change for anyone! Do you hear me? Not for anyone!"

— "The Road Less Traveled" / Craig Marks / February '97

[EDDIE VEDDER]

When Pearl Jam's *Ten* came out a decade ago on August 27, 1991, pretty much nobody cared.
Unlike Nirvana's *Nevermind*, which a month later revolutionized music faster than Kurt Cobain could pull the hair from his eyes, *Ten* took a full year to climb the charts. "Jeremy," the third single and the band's only true video, finally unleashed the floodgates in the summer of '92.

Yet even then we had little sense of what Pearl Jam represented. A few million MTV fans and some historic live shows notwithstanding, they hadn't fully arrived. Their throbbing, baritone sound was branded by some as a sellout, corporate version of grunge, and the band members themselves couldn't shake the feeling that, where it counted, they hadn't registered. Especially their lead singer—an outwardly shy but maniacally competitive surfer from San Diego who'd been plagued with identity questions long before anyone started debating the meaning of "alternative."

Eddie Vedder grew up with a man he thought was his father and wasn't; when he found out, he became what film director Cameron Crowe calls "a living Pete Townshend character," consumed with unresolved hurt. But that isn't the Pearl Jam story—nor is lead guitarist Mike McCready's days in the juvenile hair metal band Shadow, nor is bassist Jeff Ament and guitarist Stone Gossard's formative experiences in the pivotal Seattle indie-rock band Green River, which would also beget Mudhoney. Ament and Gossard left Green River to pursue mainstream rock glory in Mother Love Bone, then saw it ripped away when lead singer Andy Wood died of a heroin overdose right before their debut's release in 1990.

It's the combination that sets up the Pearl Jam story. The vocals that Vedder added to the instrumental demos he got through his friend Jack Irons (later one of the band's ever-revolving cast of drummers) resonated precisely with Gossard and Ament's sense of loss. A trip to Seattle to check the fit, and the result was a band that exploded both live and commercially before anyone had a chance to figure out what the goals were. And then a tumultuous decade, marked by interband squabbles, contentious back-and-forths with the pop machinery, and, long after every question seemed to have been settled, a tragic concert at which nine fans died.

The group that was once accused of being synthetic grunge now seem as organic and principled a rock band as exists, continually tweaking the industry: introducing what became their biggest single ("Last Kiss") as a fan-club-only release; producing 72 live albums to document their 2000 tour. We talked with the band and their contemporaries—musicians, crew members, friends, and industry folks. Mixed in with some great stories is the answer to a paramount question: Why were Pearl Jam, virtually alone among their peers, the ones who kept the flame alive?
— "Ten Past *Ten*" / Eric Weisbard with Jessica Letkemann, Ann Powers, Chris Norris, William Van Meter, and Will Hermes / August '01

MARK PELLINGTON [director, "Jeremy" video]: Probably the greatest frustration I've ever had is that the ending [of the video] is sometimes misinterpreted as that he shot his classmates. The idea is, that's his blood on them, and they're frozen at the moment of looking.

I would get calls years later about it, around the time of Columbine. I think that video tapped into something that has always been around and will always be around. You're always going to have peer pressure, you're always going to have adolescent rage, you're always going to have dysfunctional families.

RICK KRIM [producer, MTV/VH1]: I have the unedited "Jeremy" video. It was too explicit. The boy sticking a gun in his mouth—it still gives me a chill to watch it. As you can imagine, the band didn't want to change it. They felt this was their state-ment. I got on the phone with Eddie on a couple of occasions to argue our position, like, God forbid some kid thinks that's cool and sticks a gun in his mouth. But it wasn't a pleasant experience, for me or for them. That was the end of videos for Pearl Jam.

MICHAEL GOLDSTONE [A&R, Epic, 1990-95]: A lot of what happened at that time, and down the street with Nirvana at Geffen, was that who was in control of the music changed. Musicians took the control back. You look at it now, and you think it's a given. It wasn't a given.

BONO: I'm a fan of the Pearl Jam organization, of what you might call the culture around the group. It's like the Grateful Dead. We've been thinking a lot about that West Coast way of doing business. I must say, I'm not sure how long U2's going to have the energy to take on the mainstream. And the Pearl Jam/Grateful Dead model is something to be really proud of. They exist entirely unto themselves. They don't depend on the media, don't depend on the radio.

CHRIS CORNELL [Soundgarden]: Better than almost any other band in history to have had that kind of enormous success, they dealt with it really eloquently. I think that set a great example to the other musicians that, you know what, you can actually control the media spotlight. I think they stayed vital. The records they made didn't neces-sarily appeal to the same number of fans who were into *Ten*, but they appealed to a lot of people. They sold millions of records without having to do an overhyped press campaign for each record.

— "Ten Past *Ten*" / Eric Weisbard with Jessica Letkemann, Ann Powers, Chris Norris, William Van Meter, and Will Hermes / August '01

[EDDIE VEDDER]

[PEARL JAM]

/ Chris **Norris**

The ghost of Saint Kurt

: Nirvana

According to Japan's Shinto faith, when a person dies, his or her spirit passes into nature to reside in the air, water, and rocks.

If the person has distinguished him- or herself in life, the spirit becomes a *kami*, a deity associated with powerful forces like wind and thunder. These deities can be endowed with completely opposite personalities—gentle or violent.

"[He] made women want to nurture and protect him," a friend, Carrie Montgomery, once said of Kurt Cobain. "He was a paradox in that way, because he also could be brutally and intensely strong, yet at the same time, he could appear fragile and delicate." The Japanese believe that after death the spirit is angry and defiled. Relatives perform rituals to pacify and purify it. Those who die happily, among their families, become revered ancestors. Those who die unhappily or violently—usually through murder or suicide—are called *yurei*, ghosts who wander about causing trouble. The ghosts of suicides are said to be the most dangerous.

She'll come back as fire,
to burn all the liars,
and leave a blanket of ash on the ground.
—"Frances Farmer Will Have Her Revenge on Seattle" (Nirvana, *In Utero*, 1993)

In July 1989,

a band recently signed to Seattle indie label Sub Pop appeared at a small New Jersey nightclub. They went on early, played to about 30 people, and, according to a witness, "just incinerated the place." The group had built a strong word-of-mouth following since the release of their first single the previous year, but for newcomers, the show was a revelation. "It was like, 'What the fuck?'" says the witness, Sonic Youth's Thurston Moore (who later helped the band sign to DGC). "Not only was every song crushingly great, but at the end, they just smashed their instruments and threw them into the audience. It seemed totally new."

To Moore, the trio looked like the demonic hick kids in the horror film *Children of the Corn.* "You know, long stringy hair, ragged flannel, and ripped dungarees." The 22-year-old singer's voice "had a teenage Lemmy quality [referring to the gristly, guttural Motörhead singer], and that band knew how to rock. It was so simple: the best parts of R.E.M., the Beatles, the Buzzcocks, Black Flag. But no band was doing that. Nobody in their *right mind* would reference R.E.M. or the Beatles then. But they did. And it worked."

You might say that. Within two years, Nirvana were the biggest rock band in the world; within three, the biggest of the decade; and within five, kaput. In that time, their small, skinny, singer/guitarist devised '90s rock and helmed a sweeping cultural change of style, attitude, and outlook. Then he ended his life.

Although some Shinto texts talk about the "High Plain of Heaven" or the "Dark Land," none provides any details about the afterlife. In Buddhism, the only true end of suffering is the attainment of total enlightenment. A peace beyond peace. A line in a recently published letter—sent to a friend in 1988 from a young blond punk rocker in Washington state—sounds, even today, far from peaceful and like anything but an ending. It announces, in bold block letters, OUR LAST AND FINAL NAME IS NIRVANA.

Kurt Cobain

was many things while he was alive—punk, pop star, hero, victim, junkie, feminist, geek avenger, wiseass. But ten years after his death, he's something else entirely. He's a *ghost.* His songs play every so often on iPods, jukeboxes, at ball games. An undiscovered one, "You Know You're Right," surfaced in 2002. The same year, his journals were published as a pricey coffee-table hardcover (*Journals*). Now there's a "classic alternative" radio format that may enshrine Nirvana as the new Led Zeppelin. But these flickers in the current pop world merely highlight his absence, reminding us of a figure who's becoming harder to see.

Cobain's career was short even by rock standards—three albums and out. He was, by his own admission, unprolific, and, after long battles with his former bandmates, his widow, Courtney Love, has established tight control over what remains of his recorded output. And although John Lennon, Jimi Hendrix, Jim Morrison, and other rock superstars died young, none had so much of the field to himself in his heyday or quite the exit strategy. Cobain's closest peer, Tupac Shakur, isn't a ghost. He's a full-time rap star. A workaholic in a medium where the tape's always running, he's still collaborating, topping charts, showing up in movies. And his postmortem role seems in many ways like wish fulfillment. "I got more to say," you can hear him taunting. "I'm gonna haunt you motherfuckers forever!" A video ("I Ain't Mad at Cha") that depicts him rapping in heaven was released just days after his death.

On the other hand, the bitter finality of Cobain's end became an indelible part of his story, like some sick MasterCard joke. (Debut album: $606.17. Remington 20-gauge: $308.37. Legend: Priceless.) No other chapter in pop music has so much

"keep your woman in line." Everybody from performers to sound technicians watched in silence as Cobain squared off in front of Rose, assuring him he'd take care of the situation. Cobain turned to Love and, tongue planted firmly in cheek, sweetly asked her to behave, eliciting howls of laughter from the assembled.
— "Spin Patrol" / November '92

COBAIN IS REFERRING TO A JULY 12TH MTV NEWS SEGMENT BASED ON A PIECE IN THE *SEATTLE TIMES*. The article reported a domestic disturbance at the Cobain home, claiming the couple were physically fighting over their possession of several handguns and an AR-15 rifle.

Cobain shakes his head. "I was just so surprised to find the police report so detailed, yet so completely wrong." He sinks deeper into the booth. "What really happened was that Courtney and I were running around the house screaming and wrestling—it was a bit Sid and Nancy-esque, I have to admit—but we were having a good time. And then we get this knock on the door, and there are five cop cars outside, and the cops all have their guns drawn." His voice mirrors the absurdity of the situation. "We were in our pajamas. I was wearing this long black velvet pipe-smoker's jacket. Not the most desirable thing to be arrested in...." The police explained a new Washington State law that requires that someone be arrested in cases of domestic violence. "That's when we did start arguing, about who was going to jail. I said 'I'm going,' and Courtney said, 'No, I'm going.' And I said I'm the man of the house. They always arrest the man." Cobain smiles. "I kind of regret that now, because the idea of Courtney as a husband-beater is amusing," he says wryly. "She did throw juice at me and I did push her, but it was about who was going to jail."

Last September, *Vanity Fair* ran a much-publicized piece on Courtney Love. The article quoted her as saying, among other things, that she used heroin while pregnant with their now one-year-old (and healthy) daughter, Frances Bean, which she later denied. Kurt Cobain refers to Conde Nast, which publishes the magazine, as "a bunch of right-wing, high-fashion, Christian Satanists. They have the power to eliminate anything that threatens them."

Cobain tends to go to extremes when discussing the abuse he's taken from the mainstream media. His outrage borders on a persecution complex, but the press has left him feeling terminally unprotected, his day-to-day life and love compromised in a way he never imagined. He's horrified about ridiculous rumors concerning a recent trip to New York City, where he and his wife, Courtney Love, were supposedly so high they were puking in a cab, accidentally leaving little daughter Frances Bean behind in the backseat when they got

darkness at its center. And no other artist still haunts us in such a powerful, subliminal way.

In a short speech he taped right after his best friend and bandleader died, Nirvana bassist Krist Novoselic advised fans, "Let's keep the music with us. We'll always have it forever." And he was right: The music speaks for itself. As a songwriter, Cobain was spookily brilliant. He had a way of making his offhand jokes and teen vernacular sound ancient and profound, with a melodic drama that verged on telekinesis. But this also had everything to do with who he was.

"There's part of him that was a cultural revolutionary and part of him that was a classic song craftsman," says Danny Goldberg, a former Nirvana manager and founder of Artemis Records. "This was someone who was inspired by the Melvins, but who listened a lot to the Beatles. He had that dual talent: an emotional cultural talent and a songwriting genius. Which is why people talk about John Lennon in a different tone of voice than Paul McCartney. Kurt was one of the masters of the craft, in addition to being a voice of adolescents of all ages."

Songs like "Pennyroyal Tea," "Heart-Shaped Box," "Come as You Are," "Smells Like Teen Spirit," and "In Bloom" will outlive us all. But those of us who are living now, who remember when Kurt Cobain the person was here living, talking, and creating—we experienced something else, too. We learned a story that has a certain beginning and a certain ending. And the fact is, Cobain's last work, which is now available worldwide on websites, isn't a song, drawing, or film. It's a piece of writing that reads, *this note should be pretty easy to understand.*

In April 1994, the mainstream media grappled with the death of an icon whose music they'd barely processed. Only two years earlier, *The New York Times* tried to get with the hip new thing by earnestly issuing a "grunge lexicon," concocted on the spot by a pranking Sub Pop receptionist. Back then, mainstream hoaxes were easier to pull, secrets easier to keep. Less than 10 percent of the population had Internet access. And the era's new, vaguely Brad Pitt–looking "it" boy—the Justin Timberlake of his time—occasionally wore black nail polish or a dress, dyed his hair with strawberry Kool-Aid, and sang, on MTV in prime time, lyrics like "Sell the kids for food" and "Nature is a whore."

But soon after he died, the media gave a specific cast to Cobain's quickly cooling image. The clips that played in the days after his death were from Nirvana's late-1993 *MTV Unplugged* appearance. They showed a frail 26-year-old who looked both much younger and much older, crouched over an acoustic guitar, clearly in misery. He was bathed in blue light and surrounded by lilies, the traditional American flower of death. The set, designed by Cobain, was specifically meant to resemble a funeral. Of the six cover songs he played, five mentioned death.

At the height of his notoriety, jazz great Charlie Parker complained that people were paying to see the world's most famous junkie. Cobain, among other things, is his generation's most famous suicide. "I mean, people die," says Moore. "But I can't think of too many musicians of his caliber and celebrity who died that way." When people heard of Cobain's death, they tended to have a two-part reaction, first to the death, then to the method. People who OD, drive drunk, or invite murder threats have a pretty reckless disregard for their lives and the lives of their loved ones. But Cobain's last act was different.

Goldberg remembers him as "the typical artistic control freak, someone who edited his home video meticulously." But years later, it's easy to wonder whether he was a control freak on a level few then imagined. What if he was so attentive, so farsighted in his performance art, that he somehow, maybe unconsciously, had his whole curtain call plotted out? There he is in the last shot of the "Teen Spirit" video. An eerie yellow blur, too close to the camera to be in focus, he scream-sings those last words: *a denial, a denial, a denial....* As Dave Grohl's drums crash to a halt, he holds that last word for a drawn-out, head-quivering note. Then suddenly, viciously, he snaps his mouth shut. The end.

So how does it feel now,

when you're driving down the road at night, past Blockbuster and Applebee's, and, just as Trapt's "Headstrong" fades out on the radio, you hear those first strums of "Smells Like Teen Spirit"? Is it awesome? Does it *totally fucking rock*? Or does it feel a bit jarring and sad? "When anything by [Nirvana] comes on the radio, you almost have to pull over—still," says Seattle-based producer and former Fastbacks guitarist Kurt Bloch. "Since he's not around anymore, the music becomes a stronger reminder of that time."

Nirvana may sound somewhat like today's modern-rock playlist, but their music *feels* very strange. The songs elicit perplexing emotions. For one thing, it's hard to headbang to a saint. And this guy's image pushes some hard-wired buttons. I mean, look at him. The striking clear-blue eyes. The sharp, nobly set features. The thousand-yard smirk coming out of the photos and videos. The unkemptness almost makes him more dusty-prophet biblical. And listen to the oblique, electrifying lyrics and airy vocal lines, the way they waft on surprising harmonies over a neo–heavy-metal roar, leaving melodic vapor trails. In a way, the cynicism you feel you *should* have about all the grunge mythologizing smacks of a naysayer's denial.

Then there's the story. The book of Saint Kurt has it as follows: Our sad, sensitive little Pisces-Jesus man is born in the wilderness of Washington, grows up among the heavy-metal heathens, hears the gospel of punk rock, forms a trio to make a joyful noise, is seized by the hypocrites, forced into superstardom, and martyred. "Their music became popular at a time when everything else sounded so stale and manufactured," says Jonathan Poneman, cofounder of Sub Pop. "Nirvana always sounded pure—even at their most compromised, which by most others' standards wasn't compromised at all."

Because of this, many have attributed an almost divine purity to Cobain himself. And after the ensuing decade of chest-waxing Vedder clones and bling-blinging *Cribs* goons, he looks downright otherworldly. He couldn't have swum in the same crass, commercial water as the rest of us, could he? Goldberg, for one, says yes. "He didn't like all the consequences of fame, but he chose to come to Los Angeles and to sign with a major label. Other artists haven't done that. Fugazi didn't do that. Superchunk, Pavement—all sorts of artists didn't do that. He was going for it; he didn't only write the songs, he designed the T-shirts, he wrote the scripts for the videos, he rewrote the bio."

Consider "Smells Like Teen Spirit," the song that just *happened* to rock the reigning order like a force of nature. But look at the journals—there, Cobain's description of the video reads more like a giddy cultural campaign: "The first one, 'Smells Like Teen Spirit,' will have us walking through a mall throwing thousands of dollars into the air as mallgoers scramble like vulchers [sic] to collect as much as they can get their hands on, then we walk into a jewelry store and smash it up in anti-materialist fueled punk rock violence. Then we go to a pep assembly at a high school and the cheerleaders have anarchy A's on their sweaters and the custodian-militant-revolutionarys [sic] hand out guns with flowers in the barrels to all the cheering students who file down to the center court and throw their money and jewelry and Andrew Dice Clay tapes into a big pile, then we set it on fire and run out of the building screaming. Oh, didn't Twisted Sister already do this?"

Cobain's journals are filled with his analysis of the waning generation gap, a sense of the rebellious possibilities in his peers, and a real concern for how he fit in with people his age. Unlike, say, Jack White, who has one foot in some gothic Delta/Nashville past, Cobain was fixed in the here and now, maybe fatally. "He sometimes hated himself for wanting [stardom]," says Goldberg. "He was a complicated guy, and there are things that you don't always know you're getting into. But he became a rock star on purpose. He *hired* me to do that. No one put a gun to his head. He put his own gun to his head."

This is an older part of the ghost story. You may want to be rich and famous, you may want your music to reach millions, but you don't want to be Generational Spokesperson. It's like, if you're in a Greek myth, you don't want to be the *most beautiful* heroine or the *mightiest* warrior. Pretty damn beautiful or mighty freakin' strong is fine. But not the most. That's the one the gods fuck with, the one they enlist as a plot device for wars and mass murders. Odysseus or Eddie Vedder might turn out okay. But Achilles? Kurt Cobain? No thanks.

In the headline of its front-page obituary, *The New York Times* bestowed on Kurt Cobain the absurd title "Hesitant Poet of 'Grunge Rock.'" Sociologically, the term "grunge" echoes "punk"—another vague, contested, commercialized catchall applied by various segments of society to a huge array of ideas, sounds, styles, and personalities. It's ridiculously imprecise and inadequate, but that's the unholy deal

out. The story continues with the cabby driving around for hours not knowing there was a baby in the car.

"It's like the Rod Stewart semen story," I tell him. "You're a part of modern folklore."

"Geez," Cobain says. "I could live with that, Kurt Loder saying, 'There was a half gallon of semen found in Kurt Cobain's stomach.' That at least is funny."

Notoriety doesn't really bother bassist Krist Novoselic, but he does feel a certain awkwardness when he meets people. "If you introduce yourself they say, 'I don't know who you are,'" he says. "And if you don't, they think you're arrogant." Drummer Dave Grohl says that while stardom is sometimes hard for him, it's always hell for Cobain, "a load of shit on his mind that he doesn't deserve."

"I really miss being able to blend in with people," Cobain says wearily. "It's just been lately that I could even handle being recognized." He describes an incident at a recent Melvins show in Orange County, California. "One by one, these drunk, sarcastic twentysomethings would come up to me and say, 'Aren't you in the B-52s?' Just trying to start a fight. One guy came up, smacked me on the back, and said, 'Hey man, you got a good thing going, just get rid of your pissy attitude. Get off the drugs, and just fucking go for it, man.'"
— "Smashing Their Heads on the Punk Rock" / Darcey Steinke / October '93

IN "PENNY ROYAL TEA," AS BITTER AND EMPATHETIC A SONG AS NIRVANA HAS ATTEMPTED, THE NOMINAL SUBJECT IS ABORTION. The title refers to a homemade recipe for inducing one, but it's not a song likely to comfort people on either side of that issue. With a nod to the Beatles' "I'm So Tired" (Lennon is surely Cobain's deepest source as a singer), it's about the ugly scars any different choice leaves. Officially sanctioned guilt bleeds into private despair, false consciousness merges with real pain. "Penny Royal Tea" gives us repression and denial as conditions on which nobody has a monopoly. The song's not a righteous placard of a fetus or a bloody coat hanger, but a desperate, unresolved awakening to how much of ourselves we're required to kill and maim every day.

Listening to "Penny Royal Tea" and the rest of *In Utero*, I thought of a nearly forgotten punk masterpiece of 15 years ago: Magazine's hopeless, exhilarating "Shot by Both Sides." That's Nirvana's motto here: surrounded, lost in a hostile crowd, gagged but trying to talk back anyway. With *In Utero*, I suspect Nirvana intended on some level to summon up the specter of punk in order to give it a proper burial—drive the final nail in the heart-shaped box and leave behind a fitting tombstone. Setting out to make the last punk album, it made what sounds like the first one instead.
— review of *In Utero* / Howard Hampton / October '93

you cut when you want to make a big noise in the world. You detonate the explosion, change things forever, and the meanings scatter.

A whole generation of musicians was picking through such scattered meanings in the long march from "punk" to "indie" to "alternative"—before Nirvana came to represent the entire decade-plus tradition in the mainstream. From adamantly underground bands like Black Flag, Minor Threat, the Minutemen, and Big Black to major-label signees like the Replacements and Dinosaur Jr. to countless other arty or freaky institutions, the music scene was very much the "little group" suggested in "Smells Like Teen Spirit." It was a complex, long-percolating mixture to so suddenly spurt up in a single super Venti cup of Seattle sludge.

But what about now? Has Nirvana's legacy—their irrational rock exuberance—been purged? Or worse? Have we returned to the George Bush/Michael Jackson administration of 1990—only in a newer, creepier version? As we speak, Nirvana's moment is being packaged for your nostalgic enjoyment, in something that sounds like a late-'90s *Saturday Night Live* skit: "alternative gold," a paradoxical new radio format pioneered by KBZT in San Diego that plays all your favorite grunge hits. It could be an update of the infamous ad for a classic-rock compilation that aired in the mid-'80s. Two hippie dudes sit outside a van as their boom box blasts the opening riff of "Layla." "Hey, is that *Freedom Rock*, man?" asks one guy, perking up from his private purple haze. "Yeah, man," replies the other. "Well, *tuuuuurn* it up!"

Of course, parts of Cobain's spirit

—the violent, the gentle, the weird—are alive in pop music. Is Eminem, for instance, carrying some mystic Cobain gene? Both have alter egos: Kurdt Kobain, Slim Shady. Both were (are) left-handed, mom-hating, daughter-having, dysfunctional-wife-marrying, grossness-loving, rhyme-spitting little guys who were utterly remade by a musical subculture, then tried to represent it as subverting the mainstream—even when it became the mainstream.

But obviously, there's a huge gap between a gay-baiting rapper who "just don't give a fuck" and Kurt Cobain. To write songs like Cobain's, you need more than imagination, verbal dexterity, and a gift for dynamics and melody. You sort of *have* to give a fuck—about people different from yourself, about problems beyond your experience. "Kurt was really into expressing an allegiance to sensitivity as opposed to [being] Mr. Tough Guy," recalls Moore. "You see kids into the whole Cobain thing [now] who are outcasts from the rap-metal, baseball-hat-wearing Limp Bizkit kids, the middle-class teenage gangstas. It would have been interesting to see how Kurt would've reacted to all that."

Cobain certainly didn't seem thrilled with humanity; it's safe to say he was a snob. But his ability to connect with other viewpoints was almost reflexive. For every lyric that sounds like a piss rant about fame, there's one like "Polly," based on a news story of a rape/murder, that shows a scary level of empathy for both victim and killer. Ruminating in the numb cadence of the killer's thoughts, Cobain nods forward to a conclusion that indicts the dark side in everyone. It's the song Bob Dylan reportedly singled out at a Nirvana concert, saying, "The kid has heart."

So many musical styles exploded throughout the '90s with their genre-hopping, crowd-surfing partisans. But something about the Nirvana ethos spoke to a larger truth about growing up in a particular post–baby boom world. It was ironic, sure, but also vulnerable, self-effacing, conscientious, trying hard to be cool, but not "cool." Come as you are—unless you're a jerk. Even the idea of coolness was associated with an underdog conscience, if only as a reaction to the regressive Republican, hair-metal social order it came up under. Sure, the shortcomings were easy to caricature. Cobain's end briefly stamped a whole scene and cultural experience—if not a generation—with the reputation of being amoral, sarcastic, solipsistic, self-pitying drama queens. Rock triumphalists from Gene Simmons to Noel Gallagher made a point of denouncing the brooding crybabies of '90s rock, as if Nirvana had ridden to massive pop-music fame on a staunch anti-fun platform.

Megan Jasper, then Sub Pop's receptionist, now the label's general manager, demurs: "They were really, really funny, goofy guys. They'd really 'blow into town'— it was sort of an event. I remember them showing up at the office on mornings after shows, all hungover with makeup running down their faces." Moore, too, had a different sense of what the pre-MTV mosh pit meant. "Punk-rock culture was very celebratory. Anybody who was involved with it was just having the best time of their lives. The nihilism and negativity were sort of elemental tools for attacking boredom, just an affront to conservative standards."

But people are always uncomfortable with something as mainstream as Nirvana that doesn't make its meanings clear or its intentions obvious. Everybody knows how to react to a Super Bowl "wardrobe malfunction"—with outrage, delight, or indifference, depending on your own little group. But a dress-wearing, golden-boy, junkie, rock-cliché, rock-original, underground superstar whose lyrics mixed jokey word games with agonized confessions and self-destructive tirades? He was always going to be problematic. Even for the little group that raised him.

As Cobain wrote in *Journals*, "I like to be passionate and sincere, but I also like to have fun and act like a dork." There's something noble about that honesty and about the attempt to embody both those personalities, maybe even something "American" in the best sense of the expression. But this too had its consequences.

An Egyptian papyrus scroll bears what some believe is the first-known suicide note. It begins "Lo, my name is abhorred/ Lo, more than the odour of carrion/ On summer days when the sky is hot...Death is before me today/ As the odour of lotus flowers/ As when one sitteth on the shore of drunkenness." If they'd had irony back in ancient Egypt, the author might've just written "I hate myself and want to die" and jumped in the Nile.

The irony, apathy, and general ennui that pundits attributed to Kurt Cobain's age group was supposedly a reaction to the sense that everything had been tried, every rebellion co-opted, every truth a cliché. So it's doubly ironic—if such a thing is possible—that fans growing up now think of Cobain as a valiant symbol of a time when rock music was more real and meaningful. But they do, and they're not entirely wrong. No one knew what was going to happen when Nirvana began their assault on history and culture (and MTV). Cobain had to traverse the '90s along with the rest of us. And as someone who is exactly his age, I can assure you that he wasn't the only casualty.

No *"poet of grunge rock"* could have been a devout practitioner of Shinto,

whose central tenet is physical cleanliness. But Cobain's tale fits eerily well into that world of larger, older stories.

For instance, Siddhartha Gotama was his own form of anemic royalty, when, at the age of 29, he left his home, family, and title to find an answer to human suffering. He renounced the world he knew, fasted, searched, attained wisdom, and reached nirvana. He became known as the Buddha, the supremely enlightened being. Kurt Cobain addressed his suicide note to an imaginary childhood friend, someone he'd often talk to as a young, haunted boy. The friend's name was Boddah. But this isn't religion we're talking about, it's pop culture: prepackaged, market-tested, owned, and directed by massive corporations that exploit the desires and neuroses of a young and impressionable public. Still, memory lingers, just like the word itself in the chorus of "Come As You Are." And, that ghost is out there. Whether it's sad, pissed-off, or exuberant, it's not going away until we do. One of the best aspects of punk rock, at least the American version Kurt Cobain grew up with, was the power of its audience—the scene, the community. Japanese religious experts say it's very difficult for a foreigner to embrace Shintoism; unlike most other religions, there is no one book that will teach a person how to practice the faith. It's transmitted from generation to generation, as people experience the rituals together. Which is what we're still doing, you and I, right now.

Reprinted from SPIN, April 2004

"THE NIGHT BEFORE I HAD TO GO TO COURT [TO NEGOTIATE THE FATE OF UNRELEASED NIRVANA MATERIAL WITH COURTNEY LOVE], I WAS IN MY ROOM, PACKING. My girlfriend's in bed, and she says, 'Oh, *Kurt & Courtney* is on.' And for a moment, I thought, 'Wow—maybe this is supposed to happen. Okay, I'm gonna watch this.' And I turned it off within ten minutes. I thought 'Is this what it's really become? Documentaries and murder-conspiracy theories?'"
— Dave Grohl, 2002

"BY 1989, IT SEEMED LIKE PUNK ROCK HAD SORT OF DIED, AND I THOUGHT NIRVANA WERE PICKING UP WHERE BLACK FLAG AND G.B.H. HAD LEFT OFF. I remember thinking I didn't want my band to sound anything like Nirvana because they had set the bar so high. I didn't want to get too close."
— Josh Homme (Queens of the Stone Age), 2003

"*NEVERMIND* WAS THE FIRST OF THEIR RECORDS I'D HEARD, BUT MY FAVORITE IS *INCESTICIDE*. I just loved those fucked-up songs. And the Vaselines covers ["Molly's Lips" and "Son of a Gun"] got me into the Vaselines. Nirvana were the first band to make me want to find out about other bands."
— Julian Casablancas (the Strokes), 2004

ANOTHER KURT COBAIN COVER? Is there anything we haven't already heard about how important Nirvana are? Any excitement I once felt about the band has been bludgeoned to death by your magazine.
— Letter to the Editor, David Quintiliani, July 2004

While the oft-maligned Pearl Jam have released about 64,000 live records alone, the much-beloved Nirvana released only a trickle of singles, EPs, albums, and videos during their career—and therein lies a lesson. Sure, you could easily nab a bootleg CD of Courtney Love reading Kurt Cobain's suicide note or peep the book that Love's crackpot father wrote about Cobain's death, but trust us, you'll just feel gross afterward.

DISCOGRAPHY

Bleach (Sub Pop, 1989)
Though the guitar playing of "Kurdt Kobain" (as he's credited here) often sounds like a straight jack of Black Flag's Greg Ginn, this raw eight-track recording still reveals a powerful, evolving presence. The churning howl of "Negative Creep" contrasts starkly with the hushed,

skinned-knee Beatles melody of "About a Girl."

"Sliver" (Sub Pop, 1990)
This immediately moving, vulnerable, bratty single about a kid's trip to Grandma's house was the first serious inkling of Cobain's songwriting gift, as well as real evidence that his band could do more than lurch when they rocked.

Nevermind (DGC, 1991)
Numerous 1980s American punk bands, from X to Hüsker Dü to Dinosaur Jr., tried to clean up their acts on a major label, but Nirvana had anthemic, metallic punk pop in their blood all along.

"Lithium"/"Been a Son" (Live)/"Curmudgeon" (DGC, 1992) Before most of us were online, this single was the only place to find the complete *Nevermind* lyrics and

the rare sludgefeast "Curmudgeon." Plus, the version of "Been a Son" rips.

Incesticide (DGC, 1992)
Essential collection of rarities, B-sides, covers, et al., that gives a better sense of early Nirvana's discrete, volatile voice than *Bleach* does.

"The 'Priest' They Called Him" William S. Burroughs/ Kurt Cobain (Tim/Kerr, 1993) Cobain pays tribute to his hero by cranking out a Butthole Surfers–ish racket while the old pervert croaks like the devil's bagman.

"Puss," The Jesus Lizard/ **"Oh, the Guilt,"** Nirvana (Touch and Go, 1993) Nirvana's half of this split single is a brutally appealing assault, and it's paired with a dense punk jam from former members of Cobain faves Scratch Acid.

In Utero (DGC, 1993)
It's perhaps fitting that Nirvana's last studio album, recorded at the height of their fame, was the band's most punk—every guitar riff seems to scream "no" from another corner of the room. And the difference between drums produced by Butch Vig and drums produced by Steve Albini is the difference between watching somebody get punched in the gut and *being* punched in the gut.

Nirvana: MTV Unplugged in New York (DGC, 1994) Despite Cobain's horrendous health and ravaged voice, this legendary acoustic set is so intimate it practically curls up at your feet.

From the Muddy Banks of the Wishkah (DGC, 1996) Near-terrific collection of live tracks from every era (1989–94), with an especially convulsive "Drain You."

Nirvana (Geffen, 2002) Pro forma hits package, with a scaldingly bitter, previously unreleased song, "You Know You're Right," one of Cobain's final volleys into the void.

NON-ALBUM TRACKS

"Even in His Youth" on "Smells Like Teen Spirit" single (DGC, 1991) Ragged recording of an intense, rarely heard rocker.

"D-7" on *Hormoaning* EP (DGC, 1992) Cover of song by storied Portland, Oregon, punks the Wipers.

"Verse Chorus Verse" on *No Alternative* (Arista, 1993) Jangly, instantly memorable unlisted track with some of Cobain's darkest, most exposed lyrics.

"Gallons of Rubbing Alcohol Flow Through the Strip" (Geffen International, 1993) Spoken-word feedback jam that appears on U.K. version of *In Utero*.

"I Hate Myself and Want to Die" on *The Beavis and Butt-head Experience* (Geffen, 1994) Great title, heavy groove, minimal hook.

"Pay to Play" on *DGC Rarities Vol. 1* (Geffen, 1994)

Early, in-progress version of "Stay Away."

"Return of the Rat" on *Fourteen Songs for Greg Sage and the Wipers* (Tim/Kerr, 1996) A cover of Sage's disaffected 1980 punk rager.

BIBLIOGRAPHY

Come as You Are: The Story of Nirvana by Michael Azerrad (Main Street Books /Doubleday, 1993) By far the most readable, most believable, and least posturing account of Nirvana's dramatic arc. Azerrad, unlike many to follow, never gets too buddy-buddy or attempts to play moralizing judge and jury.

Route 666: On the Road to Nirvana by Gina Arnold (St. Martin's, 1993) Arnold is an unabashed fan who wants you to feel her glee at '80s underground rock's ascent to pop viability. But if you weren't there, her breathless diary will be bewildering—if you were, her self-regard gets tiresome.

Cobain by the editors of *Rolling Stone* (Little, Brown and Company, 1994) A beautifully designed, serviceable compilation of stories and photos from the magazine's pages.

The Nirvana Companion: Two Decades of Commentary edited by Jon Rocco (Schirmer, 1998) A collection of articles that focuses on the Sub Pop–subsidized *Melody Maker* rhapsodies of Brit barfly Everett True,

who made it his life's work to crown Kurt and Courtney rock'n'roll royalty.

Who Killed Kurt Cobain?: The Mysterious Death of an Icon by Ian Halperin and Max Wallace (Birch Lane, 1998) If you're into scurrilous conspiracy theories, these guys are the bottom feeders for you.

Kurt Cobain: The Cobain Dossier edited by Martin Clarke and Paul Woods (Plexus, 1999) A respectably varied roundup of magazine articles by Jon Savage, Jonathan Freedland, Ann Powers, Robert Hilburn, and (full disclosure) yours truly, among others.

Nirvana: The Day by Day Eyewitness Chronicle by Carrie Borzillo (Thunder's Mouth, 2000) A chronological *Cliffs Notes* to Nirvana's career by a SPIN contributor.

Heavier Than Heaven: A Biography of Kurt Cobain by Charles R. Cross (Hyperion, 2001) Veteran Seattle rock writer Cross lays out Cobain's life and death like a dutiful newspaper reporter—stiff prose, lots of interviews, exhausting detail, and a churlish view of the underground scene. But *Heavier* gets weighed down by Cross' obsessive scapegoating of feminists and so-called punk elitists for their brutalization of our poor, helpless savior. It's an undeniable page-turner nonetheless.

Journals by Kurt Cobain (Riverhead, 2002) Originally

sold as a pretentious coffee-table tome, this exhumation of Cobain's most private, feverish scribblings feels less exploitative in its paperback, faux-notebook form. Still, it's hard to imagine the "author" *not* being horrified.

FILMOGRAPHY

1991: The Year Punk Broke, directed by Dave Markey (Uni/DGC, 1993) Nirvana play the goofball younger brothers of Sonic Youth in this charming, no-budget alt-rock home movie.

Nirvana, Live! Tonight! Sold Out!! (Uni/DGC, 1994) Opening with a spoof of Nirvana as the hair-metal product of a cheesy arts institute, this 83-minute document (started by Cobain, completed by his bandmates) pulls together band antics, spot-on live recordings, et al., that perfectly capture the dizzying silliness of the times, as well as Nirvana's fractious magnetism.

Hype! directed by Doug Pray (Republic, 1997) A technically proficient documentary on Seattle's underground rock scene, including Nirvana's first-ever live performance of "Smells Like Teen Spirit."

Kurt & Courtney, directed by Nick Broomfield (Fox Lorber, 1998) An unintentionally chilling look at the castoffs and hangers-on who congregate around a thriving subculture. As for its insight into the title characters—*total nonsense*.
—"Selling Out" / Charles Aaron / April '04

: Heroin

Sister Morphine +
Mr. Brownstone

/ Marc **Spitz**

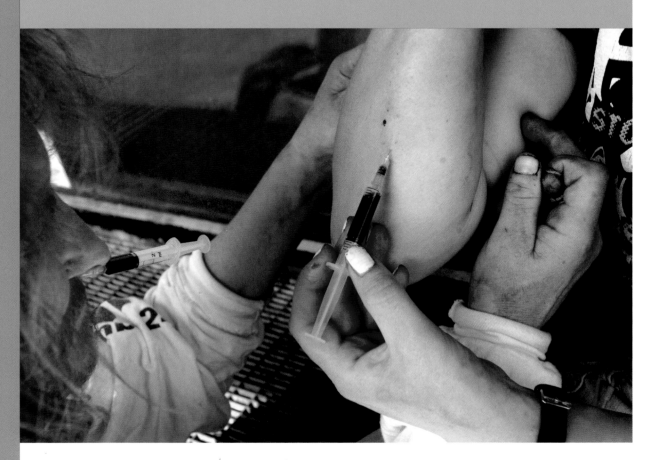

My 3rd rehab stuck.
I won't get into why or how, whether it was in-patient
or out-, whether I had magnets rubbed all over my body by a Chinese man or had

my blood removed and boiled and replaced in a posh Swiss clinic. I won't divulge where I copped or how many times I puked in front of the Hotel Chelsea.

I'm not reluctant to give details because I'm ashamed of being an ex-junkie. For a long time, I was very proud of it. I'd show off my track marks. (Actually just a track mark from an enlarged, green vein in the crook of my forearm, since I only shot up three times and mostly smoked or snorted it. But these are more details and I don't want 'em out.) I dressed like a junkie (or at least how Jim Carroll dressed on the cover of *Forced Entries*). I'd say things to my father like, "Your generation had pot, my generation had smack. It's the zeitgeist," even though I couldn't really pronounce zeitgeist with confidence and knew full well that the old man's generation had plenty of needles. I'd go to a movie like *Trainspotting* and when my date would lean over during the famous dead-baby-on-the-ceiling scene and ask, "Is that really what it's like to kick, Marc?" I'd nod like a sage.

Actually I'm more ashamed of that shit. The using was simple. Extremely simple. Which is why going through all these old SPIN features on heroin in order to get some perspective on this chapter has been really riling me up. With the exception of all the obituaries, the majority of what's been written about the heroin problem over the years in this magazine has been a bunch of bullshit jive…and I wrote some of it myself. (My first ever SPIN by-line in 1998 was an additional reporting credit on a piece about ex-junkie cred called "The Ex-Games.") We wrote about heroin during the Grunge era because the drug was inextricable from the exciting new rock scene we'd all been waiting for, and you weren't permitted to ignore that (unless you're Cameron Crowe, who did so in *Singles*). If Kurt Cobain had been a binge eater, we would have explored reckless taco consumption with similar concern. It was a zeitgeist thing (I can pronounce it now, but I don't often). I'm not saying that what we wrote was poor. Just that we kind of overlooked the truth in favor of the "story."

The reason we all missed the point, and indulged in the kind of self-pity or self-aggrandizing or inadvertent glamorization I really wanna avoid here (although I think I've been asked to write this piece for the same reason I was asked to contribute to "The Ex Games"—maybe I owe my journalism career to the junk) is because there's no point other than this: Heroin feels good. You can't fill pages with that blunt gospel. You need some jazz. Some hardboiled language. Some confession. But there is no jazz if you're being honest about smack. The only reason young people use heroin is because it shuts off the voice in your head.

That's it. Nothing more.

The reason novelists and painters and actors and especially musicians have turned to heroin is because the voices in their heads are often really loud. Heroin will eventually ruin most but, for a while at least, it gives them the peace they can't find in life. It also puts their art in some kind of rarified insta-context, which is appealing to many of them even if they'll have you believe otherwise. Discounting the whole being deceased thing, Elliott Smith really has nothing in common with Billie Holiday, or Charlie Parker or Janis Joplin or Gram Parsons or Darby Crash. He doesn't even have that much in common with fellow acoustic strumming singer-songwriters like Tim Buckley. But when you listen to all of the above-mentioned artists, you think the same things: "sadness," "empathy," "tragedy," "doomed beauty," "smack." I'm not saying I don't think those things as well. Or that I don't hold a certain special place in my heart and record collection for Smith because I, like the character in "Needle in the Hay," have tried to cash a bad check in order to cop. I also stole and pawned my ex-girlfriend's guitar on Highland Avenue in Hollywood.

(I wish I could resist more detail like this. But I've got an addictive personality, y'see.)

As long as it continues to silence the inner dialogue (and that, make no mistake, is a yummy thing), heroin will have fans. And observers will continue trying to figure out the Why.

The When is easy (then, now, in the future). There are many Wheres—the paths in and out of smack-land, the jails, institutions, and graves they tell you are certain outcomes (though sometimes you end up in retail, too). There are thousands of words, both well intentioned and exploitative, that try to get at the What. But there is only one Why. And if anyone tells you different, ask to see their track marks. Or their badge.

21 notable
heroin songs
besides Elliott Smith's "Needle in the Hay"

"Heroin" Velvet Underground
"Bad" U2
"Running to Stand Still" U2
"The Needle and the Damage Done" Neil Young
"Three Days" Jane's Addiction
"Mojo Pin" Jeff Buckley
"There She Goes" The La's
"Dead Flowers" The Rolling Stones
"Sister Morphine" Marianne Faithful
"Golden Brown" The Stranglers
"Under the Bridge" The Red Hot Chili Peppers
"Mr. Brownstone" Guns N' Roses
"King Heroin" James Brown
"Cold Turkey" John Lennon
"Newtown" The Slits
"Can't Stand Me Now" The Libertines
"She's Like Heroin to Me" Gun Club
"Ride the White Horse" Laid Back
"Chinese Rocks" The Heartbreakers (also The Ramones)
"Heroin Face" The Cure
"Not If You Were the Last Junkie on Earth" The Dandy Warhols

SPIN: When did you realize you had acquired a habit?

Boy George:
You never think you're going to get a habit. I woke up one day vomiting. I'd been doing lots and lots of heroin, and I'd been up for days. I slept for about three days, and when I woke up, my body needed it. I was like an old man, like a cripple. I was lying there like a cripple.

What did you do?
I remember I went to go see my doctor on Harley Street. I could hardly get myself into my car. I was in such a state. He says, "You're over the worst part of it. The first three days you've been asleep, you're lucky." He gave me some pills, but I started again. This time around, I suffered. Meg Patterson's treatment—you basically go cold turkey. No substitute drugs. They fix these electrodes to your ears, and they give you this kind of Walkman box, and it sends electric frequencies through your body, but basically, you sweat it out. It's not any easy out. It's very, very painful. I never had that before. For once, I really, really suffered.

What kind of pain is it?
It's like convulsions. Your leg shakes the whole time. You're a wreck. I've never been in the hospital before, and I've never had any tremendous operation or griefs like that, but it's like somebody is inside you sort of pulling you, sort of scratching at you and screaming, "Help me, help me." It's almost like your skeleton inside is another person, and it's screaming at you, "Get me the drugs, get me the drugs."
— "The Tears of a Clown" / Kevin Keffler / October '86

SPIN: Why have drugs and youth culture always been intimately connected?

Sean McDonnell
(singer-guitarist, SURGERY):
Youth culture has always thrived on danger. The whole thing is supposedly a rebellion against parents, against middle-class values, against everything. What you're initially attracted to about rock or movies or artists or writers is that they offer you something you don't have. You're attracted to the danger, and it's easy to become a part of it by using drugs.

Allen Ginsberg
(poet): The government toes a subtle party line against a youthful vision quest—a quest for transcendence of condition, of becoming a more universal you. This is basic in all societies, from Native American Indians to Western society. My 1940s drug experience was based on an interest in a new awareness, a new consciousness, a new vision. The way drugs were originally used among the Beat writers in the '40s was to examine Cezanne, to listen to Bach. It was aesthetic. When it was commodified by the media and transformed into the Beatnik image, it then acquired the party line—that it was a rebellion—rather than a proposition for a larger consciousness, or a greater scope of insight and perception.

McDonnell: Yeah, but in my culture right now, the use of drugs isn't to expand consciousness at all. It's to get wasted, to get completely obliterated. Nobody scoring three bags down on Avenue C is out to expand their consciousness.
— "Drug Culture : A SPIN Roundtable" / August '94

SPIN: You've been clean and sober for eight months. What's it like not having your old methods of escape?

Dave Gahan:
At times it's very, very hard and I have to do everything I've been taught to stop myself from reverting back to old habits. I have to go to NA meetings every day.

Do you miss your old rock-star lifestyle?
Sometimes. For example, I want to go on tour again. But most of the time I'm in fear of that because I don't think I'm strong enough to do that yet. When I got off the last Depeche Mode tour and tried to go back to my normal life, I found that I had lost David completely. I was just Dave.

Who is David?
A very scared person who lost the ability to trust, to love or to be loved, or to feel anything at all. The only feeling that was comfortable was to be in pain. I do pain really good. It's one of my big problems. [laughs]

What were you using?
Pretty much anything, but my drug of choice was heroin. It was the ultimate painkiller. And it eventually took everything away.

It's hard for people who've never tried heroin to understand why anybody would be attracted to such a physically destructive drug.
I would be lying if I didn't say that it made me feel great—six years ago. But that feeling wears off so fast and then the disease takes over. I couldn't be in a room full of people and hold a conversation without it going through my mind that I couldn't wait to get out of there and play with my little friend.
— "Dave's Addiction" / Barry Walters / May '97

"Remember that during the 19th and early 20th centuries—the 'good old days,' which conservatives so fondly evoke—opiates, cannabis, tinctures and cocaine were sold across the counter from sea to shining sea, and the United States did not founder as a result. There's no way to know exactly how many addicts there were, but my guess would be—surprisingly few. Many people simply *don't like these drugs.*

In England, before America persuaded the English government to adopt our own tried-and-failed, police-and-sanction approach, any addict could get heroin on prescription and fill his script on the National Health. As a result there was no black market, since there was no profit involved. In 1957, there were about 500 addicts in the UK, and two narcotics officers for metropolitan London. Now England presents the same dreary spectrum as the USA—thousands of addicts, hundreds of drug agents, some of them on the take, a flourishing black market, addicts dying from OD's and contaminated heroin.

Obviously the sane, common-sense solution is maintenance for those who cannot or will not quit, and effective treatment for those who want to quit. The only treatment currently available is abrupt withdrawal, or withdrawal with substitute drugs. Withdrawal treatment dates back to early-19th-century British drug essayist Thomas De Quincey. Surely they could do better than that. Indeed they *could,* but they show no signs of doing so."
— "Antihero" / William S. Burroughs / February '90

from left: A River Phoenix memorial; Layne Staley [ALICE IN CHAINS] and Shannon Hoon [BLIND MELON] show some love before becoming statistics.

After quitting the Red Hot Chili Peppers on the *Blood Sugar* tour, John Frusciante returned to L.A. and recorded a solo album while diving into heroin addiction with frightful determination: **"When I originally decided to become a drug addict, it was a clear decision," he says. "I was very sad, and I was always happy when I was on drugs; therefore I thought I should be on drugs all the time. I was never guilty—I was always really proud to be an addict."**

— "Icons" / Kate Sullivan / August '02

artists who have used heroin

.

.

**Kurt Cobain
Sid Vicious
Dee Dee Ramone
Layne Staley
John Frusciante
Scott Weiland
Brad Nowell
Marianne Faithful**

.

.

and later OD'd

**Kurt Cobain
Sid Vicious
Dee Dee Ramone
Layne Staley
John Frusciante
Scott Weiland
Brad Nowell
Marianne Faithful**

— "List Issue" / April '03

Dave Navarro:

I admit, I totally blew it with drugs back in those days. My intake was certainly a factor in the eventual demise of Jane's Addiction the first time around. What do you want me to say? There was always five pounds of heroin, all the booze and coke you wanted, all the girls you wanted—all looking for nothing but guys in bands. And I wasn't even old enough to legally drink yet. (2003)

Brad Nowell, Sublime's 28-year-old singer, songwriter, and guitarist, died of a heroin overdose May 25, 1996, in a San Francisco hotel room. Two months after his death, the dexterous, optimistic *Sublime* came out. Instantly, the group had a hit on their hands. It was Sublime's shining moment, except, of course, that by then Sublime had effectively ceased to exist.
— "Drug Bust" / RJ Smith / January '97

Two punky houseguests are flopped in Flea's living room watching a rerun of Mike Tyson's 15-second comeback fight on a wide-screen TV. I recognize one of them from the Nature Mart down in Los Feliz, where he was wandering around barefoot amidst the melatonin tablets and turkey jerky. He turns out to be a friend of Flea's who has just kicked heroin.

I always knew the L.A. art-and-music world had its share of career junkies, and Kiedis' struggles have been well documented, but it still came as a bit of a shock to discover just how firmly the Chili Peppers scene is entrenched in the comfortably numb world of narcotics. Or, hopefully, was.

"As long as there are people on this planet, there'll be people doing heroin, or something just like it," ruminates Flea, as I silently study the dichotomy of his washboard abs and his chipped glitter nail polish. "Drug addiction is such a baffling, powerful thing. It's so difficult to understand how people can reach such a level of insanity and hurt themselves so bad. And especially kind, sensitive, smart, creative people. I've seen it so many times. I've had three close friends die, including River [Phoenix]. I'm dealing with it right now with someone I love."

He gestures to the phone as he awaits a call from a friend who has recently and reluctantly checked into rehab. "I saw this person the other day and they're like on the verge of death," he explains, clearly upset. "Getting them into rehab, they nearly die detoxing. Trying to give someone hope and faith after they lose it to drugs, it's such a scary, scary thing. I've done heroin plenty of times. But I was always too much of a wimp to get strung out. The next day I'd feel like such shit. I couldn't do the things that I loved to do. I didn't feel like playing music, I didn't feel like playing basketball."
— "To Live and Die in L.A." / Ann Magnuson / April '96

The band had been trying to deal with drummer Jimmy Chamberlin's substance problem for nine years: They had brought a drug counselor on tour, sent him to treatment centers, and hired clean-and-sober road crews. Nothing seemed to work.

"I had a conversation with Jimmy in June at the Tibetan Freedom concert in San Francisco," Mark Williams recalls. "He looked me straight in the eye and said that after Spain he'd learned his lesson. He felt he'd been given one more chance and he wasn't going to blow it."

But when the Smashing Pumpkins arrived in New York on July 11, the night before they were scheduled to play Madison Square Garden, Chamberlin and touring keyboardist Jonathan Melvoin rushed down to the East Village and bought a potent brand of heroin called Red Rum. Hours later, Melvoin lay dead in their room at the Regency Hotel and Chamberlin was under arrest.
— "Soundbites: Smashing Pumpkins" / Julia Chaplin / October '96

: Smashing Pumpkins

/ Jim **DeRogatis**

Songs of
lunchroom
loners

If the Smashing Pumpkins proved anything during a career that lasted 13 years and produced six studio albums that sold more than 22 million copies, it's the inspiring fact that a miserable geek sitting alone in his or her bedroom with an electric guitar can triumph in the end.

Like Don Quixote and the windmill, the key voices in the '90s alternative era defined themselves in part by the enemies they fought. Eddie Vedder and Pearl Jam took on Ticketmaster and business as usual in the concert industry. Trent Reznor wrangled with those old standbys, the blue-nosed conservatives who tried to impose upon him their own joyless "moral values." Kurt Cobain wrestled with his personal demons, and they tragically consumed him in the end.

Raised in the strip-mall blandness of suburban Chicago, shuttling between divorced parents who often resented his presence, Billy Corgan turned to rock'n'roll as a weapon to battle the cool kids at Glenbard North High School—the jocks and cheerleaders who mercilessly mocked a tall, gangly, impossibly awkward nerd with an embarrassing birthmark on his right arm. After mastering his axe through countless hours spent playing along to records by the rock gods who seemed like his closest friends, he formed a band with other rejects at the lunchroom loners' table: an unnaturally pale, ice-queen bassist (D'Arcy Wretzky), a sarcastic Asian second guitarist (James Iha), and a mullet-headed drummer (Jimmy Chamberlin), all chosen for their status as fellow misfits as much as their musical prowess.

Corgan worked the Smashing Pumpkins harder than the meanest gym teacher had ever prodded him, and by the time they began their meteoric rise with 1991's *Gish*, their indie-in-name only debut album, he had new enemies to battle: the indie-rock puritans who summarily rejected his odd-looking band because they drew more from such influences as the Cure, Journey, and Fleetwood Mac than the proto-metal wails that inspired what would soon be called grunge, or the self-deprecating heroin-chic drones so beloved of postmodern art-rockers like Pavement, who would memorably dis them in the 1994 song "Range Life"

("Out on tour with the Smashing Pumpkins/ Nature kids, they don't have no function/ I don't understand what they mean/ And I could really give a fuck").

They were firmly established as superstars thanks to the massive success of *Siamese Dream*, the 1993 breakthrough that set in platinum their trademark sound: a mix of gothic mope, arena bombast, and shred-metal/prog-rock virtuosity. *Mellon Collie and the Infinite Sadness* (1995) is a sprawling double concept album about a day in the life of a sad, lonely boy much like Billy, which he described as "*The Wall* for Generation X." Corgan fully embraced the role of the egotistical, megalomaniacal rock star, declaring war on anyone who doubted his genius—most notably critical members of the press. After I ventured that the solipsistic, everyone-in-high-school-hated-me lyrics of *Siamese Dream* were a bit, um, sophomoric ("Life's a bummer/ When you're a hummer"), he derided me onstage as "that fat fuck from *The Chicago Sun-Times*," banned me from the Pumpkins' shows for the next few years (I always got in anyway), and fired off a lower-case fax that concluded, "see you in hell. best wishes/ go fuck yourself, billy c."

Through it all, Corgan also battled his bandmates. No one could ever be as obsessively driven as the Great Pumpkin himself, and his fellow musicians couldn't help but disappoint him when they didn't match his intensity and inspiration onstage or in the recording studio. They fell to the wayside as they grew sick and tired of his tyrannical, uncompromising ways, or, as with Chamberlin and Wretsky, became addicted to drugs. The boss never apologized for his admitted manic perfectionism—it was key to his art, and he probably couldn't have created any other way. Four years after the Pumpkins disbanded in late 2000, following an aborted and short-lived attempt at a second act with Zwan, Corgan geared up for his first official solo album and finally accepted what everyone but him already knew: He'd *always* been a solo artist. Billy Corgan *was* the Smashing Pumpkins, and the Smashing Pumpkins were his life.

The standard Pumpkins postmortem holds that their best-selling records are their best artistic statements, with *Siamese Dream* and *Mellon Collie* standing as the unchallenged peaks. In my view—one that Corgan coincidentally shares—the band's career parallels/echoes his own painful process of growing up in public, and the masterpiece is 1998's *Adore*. Corgan made a huge leap forward as a lyricist after the death of his mother, a reconciliation with his father, the end of his first marriage, and the beginning of a new relationship (since ended) with photographer Yelena Yemchuk. The whining self-pity disappeared and he started singing about deeper topics—life, death, and the struggle to find meaning in a godless universe—that were actually deserving of his songcraft and mad scientist's brilliance in the studio. *MACHINA /The Machines of God*, which dissects the corruptive effects of the star-making machine, followed as a gripping coda in 2000, proving that as he bid farewell to the Pumpkins, Corgan had finally acquired a measure of self-reflection and the ability to laugh at himself.

Few fans believe we've heard the last of the Smashing Pumpkins. Any artist as proud of his accomplishments as Corgan, and as cognizant of the epic dramas of the greatest bands in rock history, is bound to attempt an encore at some point, though it will probably end the same way, with the other misfits hating Billy once again. The chip on his shoulder has shrunk considerably, and he may have hung up his boxing gloves, but there will always be some measure of that lonely kid who transformed his sadness and anger into a raging drive to conquer the world with a Flying V. And that, after all, is what we love about him.

Despite having slogged it out for years on the local club circuit, Smashing Pumpkins, until *Gish*'s success, found themselves outcasts in the local Chicago scene, all but ignored in the press and accused by other bands and scenesters of being "sellouts" or "poseurs," whatever that means. The band's seemingly meteoric rise provoked jealous hissy fits from the established cliques in the area: the Touch and Go art punks, the Wax Trax industrialists, the flannel-shirted pregrungeaholics. Their antagonism, especially in the very early days of the band, helped spur the Pumpkins on to greater heights.

"At the time, Chicago was such an oppressive musical community," says Iha. "We didn't represent anything from any of these scenes."

Corgan smiles ruefully when I gently broach the subject of internal band relations, especially in light of the difficulties surrounding the recording of *Siamese Dream*. "You know, I gave them a year and a half to prepare for this record," he says. "I'm surrounded by these people who I care about very much, yet they continue to keep failing me. I say, 'I need this, I need that,' and they don't do the job, and what it does in me is it makes me feel the same abandonment I felt as a child. And then what it says to me is, 'You're not worth the trouble.' You take it to a level where it's very personal. If you really think about it, of course, someone doesn't do the job because they're lazy, or they don't think it's important. But I took it as, 'You're not worth going home and working on the song.'"

\\

....

Backstage at the MTV awards show, Scott Weiland from Stone Temple Pilots ambles into the Pumpkins dressing room, bogarts some of their mediocre California cabernet, and installs himself on the couch. James Iha walks over to me, smiles a little smile, and whispers in my ear, "Pavement would have a field day with this."

Pavement's "Range Life" disses both the Stone Temple Pilots and the Pumpkins in the same verse, claiming the latter "don't have no function," with singer Stephen Malkmus adding, "I don't understand what they mean/And I could really give a fuck."

"It's very punk rock of them," says Iha with his usual gentle sarcasm. "And that's kind of cool."

Malkmus isn't the only musician to have taken a swipe at Billy Corgan. Kim Deal called him "a self-important asshole" in print, and he was mocked by Soundgarden's Kim Thayil in SPIN. "I think I'm a really easy target because I wear my heart on my sleeve," Corgan says. "Take the criticisms by either Kim Deal or the guy from Pavement. Number one, Kim, genius that she is, does not write emotional, personal music. Pavement does not write emotional, personal music. See what I'm saying? The criticisms often come from people who hide behind the veneer of persona or coolness or an aesthetic of indieness. I'm not saying my point is any more valid, but when you see me, when you hear me, you're getting the warts *and* the beautiful. I'm not hiding anything."

With Cobain gone, people are looking for a substitute voice of a generation, and many nominate William P. Corgan Jr. "I just find it puzzling," Corgan says. "One, the job was filled. Two, I've never aspired to speak for anyone except your basic disaffected white suburban middle class, which I guess is who everyone's talking about, because that's who runs all the media anyway. I apologize for not representing you well enough."

Then I remember where I'd seen his lumber jacket before. Kurt used to wear it.

\\

....
....

For someone who has seen even his grandest rock dreams come true, Billy Corgan sure has chosen a brutally self-negating credo for his 1996 campaign. ZERO, in silver letters set on a long-sleeve black T-shirt, first popped up in the Smashing Pumpkins "Bullet With Butterfly Wings" video, as Corgan, then hairsome, sneered "Despite all my rage/ I am still just a rat in a cage," a most excellent bumper sticker's worth of spleen. In an alternative-rock landscape where diminished expectations are the norm, and LOSER was proudly pimped on a series of Sub Pop Records T-shirts long before Beck got crazy with the Cheez Whiz, "Zero" was a logical next step in the selling of self-flagellation, and it suited the shlumpy singer, well, to a tee.

Corgan, though, had only just begun. Throughout the following months, the T-shirt could be seen peering out from magazine covers, from CD booklets, and from behind the mic nightly, on tour in support of the band's sextuple-platinum magnum opus, *Mellon Collie and the Infinite Sadness*. You, too, could be a "Zero": At the Pumpkins' February show at the Kawasaki Sogo Arena, just outside of Tokyo, "Zero" shirts were selling for 3,500 yen (about $33) a pop. And if you couldn't score tickets to the show, not to worry: A recent trip to my local Urban Outfitters turned up a well-stocked rack of the silver and black. I couldn't help but wonder about Corgan's relentless, not to mention potentially unsanitary, fascination with the aphoristic garment. "How many of those 'Zero' T-shirts do you have, anyway?" I asked. "Well, more than one, obviously," he answered. Relieved, but still curious, I pried further. "Is it, like, our blankey?" "No, no, no," he countered. "It's just, you know, the superhero needs a costume."

— "Zero Worship" / Craig Marks / June '96

— "Billy, Don't Be a Hero" / Jim Greer / November '93

—"Artist of the Year: Smashing Pumpkins" / Michael Azerrad / December '94

SPIN: HOW HAS BEING FROM THE MIDWEST FIT IN WITH WHO YOU ARE AND WHAT KIND OF BAND YOU BECAME?

Corgan: We didn't grow up hanging out, being cool, going to concerts. When I met James he was 18 and I was 19, and our exposure to alternative music was the Smiths, the Cure, and some Bauhaus. We weren't aware of some underground New York noise scene, or a punk-rock movement in L.A. We weren't surrounded by a culture that supported experimentation. We were supported by a culture that was like, "I can't come see you play because I've got to be at work at nine in the morning." There's not much of a lifestyle to live—it's fucking cold there five months out of the year—so when we found one, which was the band, we poured ourselves into it. We attached an extremely heavy work ethic to success. If people like us, it was going to be because we had done everything we possibly could to be good. It's been like that for five years. Hard work, hard work, hard work.

Iha: The big difference between the East Coast and the Middle West is there's definitely an East Coast scene. It's more cliquey. There's an aesthetic pride in playing a certain kind of sound.

Corgan: I recently interviewed Eddie Van Halen for *Guitar World*. And I told him that I liked the fact that his music has never been elitist. Even though they were fucking cool and looked good and everybody wanted to be them, there was still that element of, hey, everybody can join the party. He said he always felt that they never really discriminated in their minds. And I think we're kind of like that. I remember Kim Gordon (of Sonic Youth) once said some horrible thing about having to play to the jock in Iowa, and I always think about that quote, because that jock in Iowa *needs* someone like Kim Gordon to say there's a better world out there, that just because you've grown up with this mentality doesn't mean you have to *be* this mentality. And that's the difference. We're saying we identify with you, but we got out. We're not still sitting here drinking Buds with you in the fucking corner. We got out. And that's always been what we're about.

— **"ZERO WORSHIP" / CRAIG MARKS / JUNE '96**

SPIN: DON'T YOU EVER JUST TRIP OUT ON ALL THE WAYS IT COULD HAVE GONE? I MEAN, YOU HAD SUCH A FUCKED-UP PAST. YOU ARE, IN A WAY, THE CLASSIC ABUSED CHILD. WE'RE ALWAYS REBUILDING THE FENCE TO MAKE SURE NOBODY GETS IN.

Corgan: Yeah, a lot of what went on in the early '90s that forged what became the caricature of me had everything to do with the challenge of self-determination. A lot of writers thought they knew where we were coming from. First of all, none of them knew that the grunge thing was going to become as big as it did. Then, when it did, they all claimed a sort of authority over it. As long as you were from Seattle and going on about whatever and [were] photogenic, it satisfied both their fascination and their hard dicks. And if you didn't fit into that category conveniently, they were going to try to force you *in* that box or they were going to try to cast you *out* of that box. Everything about us became about saying, "We're not in anybody's fucking box." Unfortunately, that process bled us dry. By the time we made it to the top of the hill and stuck our flag in there, we were done. We were toast.

— **"THE END IS THE BEGINNING" / JT LEROY / JUNE '03**

/ Charles **Aaron**

: Rap-Rock

from "Punk Rock Rap" to Mook Nation

[KID ROCK + JOE C.]

Back in the 1970s when Afrika Bambaataa dropped the Rolling Stones' "Honky Tonk Women" into his DJ set

at, say, the Bronx River Community Center, the earth didn't move under his turntables. He wasn't issuing a stirring racial or political manifesto. But ultimately, that's exactly what he did. By using rock'n'roll—then the corporate bully pulpit of white guys (often mimicking African-American artists)—as just another piece of vinyl set decoration, Bambaataa decreed that rock was no more crucial than funk, reggae, soul, disco, jazz, salsa, novelty records, or whatever else constituted a hip-hop groove. Soon, it became common for DJs to scratch in bits of rock records—Billy Squier's "The Big Beat," the Monkees' "Mary, Mary," Steve Miller's "Take the Money & Run"—as a way to give the crowd a sly tweak, to flaunt their vinyl guile. But in a larger sense, Bambaataa and others spun in motion one of the most remarkable breaks in the history of American popular culture. By appropriating what was seen as "white music," they reversed pop culture's essential curse—the ransacking of African-American creativity dating back to the 1800s.

Though hip-hop may have been a party in the ruins of a bankrupt New York City, as evidenced by hit records like Sugarhill Gang's 1979 "Rapper's Delight," it was still a revolt. And for a handful of politicized white punks, b-boys were their subversive twins. The first rap-rock songs—like the Clash's "The Magnificent Seven" and "This is Radio Clash"—nodded to a shared, underground struggle. Bambaataa, who had attended downtown New York punk clubs, hooked up with John "Johnny Rotten" Lydon (of the Sex Pistols and Public Image Ltd.) for 1983's agit-rant "World Destruction." But while Blondie's softly purred new-wave rap hit "Rapture" was a No. 1 pop hit, the Cold Crush Brothers' "Punk Rock Rap" was a marginal oddity. When Grandmaster Flash and the Furious Five opened sold-out Clash shows at Bond's in Manhattan, they were jeered mercilessly.

One side got a boost of outlaw freedom, the other was left floating checks for equipment.

Run-D.M.C. put all that to rest. Growing up just beyond the inner-city ghettos in Hollis, Queens (where people had houses and yards), the duo were from the first generation raised on commercial hip-hop's success. Their hard pose—dressed in black, arms crossed—was imperiously combative. They didn't come to battle, they came to win. And their harsh, stripped-bare music seemed to obliterate anything in its path—most specifically rock. They became pop stars with 1984's "Rock Box" (MTV's first heavily played rap video), and "King of Rock" (1985), both based on the beat-strafing, heavy-metal chug and squall of session guitarist Eddie Martinez. In the video for the latter, Run and D.M.C. busted into a makeshift Rock and Roll Hall of Fame and trashed the place with faux disgust, like it was barely worth their trouble.

Sensing a cash-flow formula, two young entrepreneurs quickly capitalized. Russell Simmons (party-promoting brother of Run) and Rick Rubin (a white longhair punk and hip-hop producer from Long Island) took a trio of white kids (ex-punk band Beastie Boys) and created a slapstick Run-D.M.C. routine, metal riffs included. Stunningly, the Beasties' *Licensed to Ill* (1986) became the first rap album to hit No. 1 on the pop charts. And basically, for the next 10-plus years, as hip-hop's popularity boomed, wannabe rappers, producers, and record execs aped the Beastie formula. But while there were a couple of fluky white rap hits (by Vanilla Ice, House of Pain, Beck), the rap-rock crossover stiffed. A collaboration between Anthrax and Public Enemy on the latter's "Bring the Noise" (1991)—which tried to recreate the success of Run-D.M.C. and Aerosmith's 1986 hit "Walk This Way"—was an awkwardly thrashing retread. The *Judgment Night* soundtrack (1993) embarrassed all involved, most notably the alternative rock bands (Helmet, Sonic Youth, Teenage Fanclub, Mudhoney) that flailed behind the yawning rappers. Ultimately, the

multiracial crew Rage Against the Machine, which featured virtuosic guitarist Tom Morello and turned the Clash's diffuse politics into blunt-force chants, were the only rap-rockers of the era to establish a convincing identity.

It wasn't until the late-'90s—when alt-rock faded as a youth-culture force and hip-hop was popping champagne bottles to its largesse—that rap-rock emerged as more than a fad. White kids who grew up on the Beastie Boys' boyish hijinks, hair-metal's blotto sleaze, gangsta rap's shoot-'em-up mythology, and grunge's man-purge, shoved their way into the ring, howling for attention. They emerged in the mainstream in 1998, led by a series of multimillion-selling acts: Korn (tormented Bakersfield, Califirnia metalheads with a human-beatboxing singer in a kilt), Limp Bizkit (Korn's loose-screw stepbrothers), and Kid Rock (wack MC turned country-rock yahoo). Aside from shaky vocals, what linked these groups most strongly

> "The reason most of these guys started rapping in the first place is because they were sitting on the can trying to sing 'Stairway to Heaven' and couldn't do it."
> — Sharon Osbourne / January '00

was a puerile, comic-tragic fear of women. Whether it was Limp Bizkit's Fred Durst screaming "Fuck those Spice Bitches" as he "flushed" pop group the Spice Girls down a huge, stage-prop toilet or "pimp of the nation" Kid Rock bragging how he likes to "smack all the hoes," these mooks tried to fashion an even more insolent, macho image than that of the rappers they envied—minus the embattled, disenfranchised context from which rap emerged.

It all came to a head at Woodstock '99, where Limp Bizkit, Kid Rock, and others revved up a restless, intoxicated, predominantly white male crowd of 250,000 that eventually rioted, burned the concert site, and looted vendors. Eight sexual assaults were reported. After the ensuing condemnation and a tired run of increasingly contrived albums, the reign of rap-rock mooks waned. And before long, hip-hop was again pop culture's singular sound. Five years on, Jay-Z was collaborating with Linkin Park, Trick Daddy was sampling Ozzy Osbourne, and Lil Jon was hooking up with punk legends Bad Brains. Rock and rap clearly weren't finished with each other, but there was no doubt which held the power.

ten worst rap-rock monikers

**Popa Chubby
Hot Sauce Johnson
Pimpadelic
Smokin' Suckaz Wit Logic
Phunk Junkeez
Bitch Funky Sex Machine
Granola Funk Express
Fieldy's Dreams
2 Skinnee J's
Disfunction-lll**

Wearing an Afro wig and a fake mustache, Fred Durst squats before a naked, fully shaven blonde, parts her labia with his thumb and fore-finger, mugs for the camera, then declares her vagina "the bomb." With a glazed, vacant stare, the woman puts her hand down his pants, and Durst announces, "I'm about to fuck the hell out of this girl." Welcome to the world of *Backstage Sluts 1* and *2*. The videos (soon to be a trilogy) feature Korn's Jonathan Davis, Sugar Ray's Mark McGrath, and Motörhead's Lemmy recounting their rock-star conquests; their ribald tales are inter-spersed with triple-X reenactments by porn stars. Low-lights: the portly dudes of Papa Roach hurling luncheon meat at a backstage bimbo, and Insane Clown Violent J, in full bozo makeup, recounting the harrowing saga of a one-night stand who devoured the creamy filling of his used condom before putting it in her purse for a souvenir.
—"100 Sleaziest Moments in Rock" / William Van Meter / October '00

"According to various reports, rap-metal upstarts Limp Bizkit want to sue SPIN because we charged that the Bizkit have never written a 'truly good' song and that frontdude Fred Durst says 'yo' a lot. Yo, that's like the Knicks' Chris Dudley suing *Sports Illustrated* for saying that his free-throw shooting is a little shaky. I admire Fred's feistiness, but exactly which tune is supposed to be entering the rock pantheon—'Nookie'?"
— "Singles" / Charles Aaron / October '99

When Zack De La Rocha was a teenager, neither Mom's student housing in Orange County nor Dad's East L.A. felt like home—the only Chicanos he saw in Orange County were mostly pushing brooms or picking strawberries. And in his pop's largely Latino neighborhood, a Minor Threat-loving skateboarder didn't have much in common with the homeboys on the block. He was in high school then, perfecting break-dancing moves at lunchtime, rummaging through subcultures, looking for an identify. And it's that subcul-tural signage—the skate-shop clothes, and the traces of Dischord-label hardcore and Public Enemy hip-hop—that he brings to Rage Against the Machine. They've helped him cobble out a sense of himself. Then Chiapas comes along, and he brought it all back home.

"He identifies with the indigenous people of the Americas," his father says, a faint touch of worry in his voice. "That has him in quite a grip." I feel like saying something that may not reassure Beto: Actually, it seems that working for the Zapatistas has *freed* Zach from some kind of grip. It's brought part of him, unknown even to himself, to life.
— "Red Hot and Bothered" / RJ Smith / October '96

Youthful rage has been a sexy, sellable commodity for decades—"Fuck you, I won't do what you tell me till Daddy takes the T-bird away." But in the '90s, as divorce and teen suicide became Middle-American facts of life, hip-hop-influenced rock found new meaning in old postures. What if, for instance, Daddy took the T-bird away and then ran right over your ass? In 1994, on the song "Daddy," Korn's Jonathan Davis memorably sang: "You raped/ I feel dirty/ It hurt/ As a child tied down ... / My god/ Saw you watching/ Mommy, why?/ Your own child." Davis was an alt-kid who understood that Tupac Shakur and Kurt Cobain were getting at similar issues of betrayal and anger, just in different languages; in Korn, he created his own twisted "family values" out of hip-hop and grunge. Davis' bile became rock's everyday language. "What I heard in Korn was beautiful angst," says Disturbed singer David Draiman.

But as '90s rock and rap became more and more glossy, Fred Durst showed up to play Jay-Z to Davis' Notorious B.I.G., serving up glib cockiness and frathouse-funnyman antics. Unlike Davis, Durst grew up in relative comfort (*his* daddy built him a breakdance studio), and by siphoning out the music's inner turmoil, Limp Bizkit made it easier to take. But Davis' specter was always in the cracked rearview.

"The pain is absolutely real," says Rage Against the Machine's Tom Morello. "These kids don't come from huts in Somalia, sure, but in many ways, they live in communities that are absolutely bereft of meaning."
—"Trend of the Year: Hell Is for Children" / Jon Dolan / January '02

ten worst rap-rock album titles

Le Cock Sportif Brougham
Hooray for Boobies
  Bloodhoung Gang
Dingleberry Haze
  Bloodhoung Gang
Jammin' in Vicious Environments
  Shootyz Groove
Pin the Tail on the Honkey
  Dislocated Styles
Fome Is Dape Little-T
  and One Track Mike
Hidden Stash, Vol. 2: The Kream of the Krop
  Kottonmouth Kings
Straight Outta Rehab
  Brooks Buford
Songs in the Key of Beotch
  That 1 Guy
Chocolate Starfish and the Hot Dog Flavored Water
  Limp Bizkit

For all the shit-slinging, drug-taking, VJ-abusing, and spontaneous garbage-hurling, the real action didn't get under way until Korn strode onstage at nine. The center-stage mosh pit raged with a concentrated ferocity. Britt Abbey, who was watching from his post at his vending tent adjacent to the stage, saw five boys emerge from the mosh pit with blood-soaked T-shirts. "The crowd was hectic," said Abbey, "but it wasn't too bad at all."

Chaos erupted immediately in the backstage med tent. "When Korn came on, people were coming in every three minutes on stretchers," said Rachael Hoke, a medical volunteer. The medics had prepped for the expected bruises, lacerations, broken bones—but Hoke was stunned by what she saw. "Every single person in our tent was OD'ing. A lot weren't conscious. One girl freaked out and broke the cot she was on. Seven EMTs tried to hold her down. She broke the restraints—they ended up having to duct-tape her to a backboard." The EMTs loaded her into an ambulance. "She tried to bite the EMTs," said Hoke incredulously.

Dave Schneider, who was volunteering at Woodstock's Crisis Intervention Unit, watched Korn from the edge of the main pit. By now it was around 9:30, and the moshing was even harder than before. Suddenly, Schneider saw a crowd-surfing woman get swallowed up by the pit; when she reemerged, two men had clamped her arms to her sides. "She was giving a struggle," said Schneider. "Her clothes were forcibly being removed." Yet no one nearby seemed to react. Schneider said that the woman and one of the men fell to the ground for about 20 seconds; then, he said, she was passed to his friend, who raped her, standing, from behind. "The gentlemen's pants were down, her pants were down, and you could see that there was clearly sexual activity," he said. Finally, the woman was pulled from the pit by some audience members, who handed her to security.

Schneider said he watched in horror as five more women were pushed into the very same pit throughout Korn's set. "They were holding [the women] down and violating them. Maybe not everyone was raped, but the first one was, I'm sure." The pit broke up before Schneider left for his 11 p.m. shift at the on-site ER, but since all the women had made it to the arms of security, he assumed the crimes had been reported. At the ER, Schneider watched as a 15-year-old girl who had OD'd on an estimated ten hits of Ecstasy was brought in unconscious. She was unconscious the next day, when he left. The only death of the day, officials said, was a 44-year-old Woodstock '69 veteran who had had heart surgery 11 days earlier. He succumbed to the heat.

Fred Durst was exhorting the crowd to "get all your negative energy out." People soared through the air with as much frequency as garbage; a few were flung skyward on bed sheets. Between songs, Durst made an announcement: "They want to ask us to ask you to mellow out. They said too many people are getting hurt. Don't let nobody get hurt, but I don't think you should mellow out!"

Around this time, an overzealous spectator fell from a sound tower. Soon after, the band lost all sound, and Durst stormed off the stage. By some accounts, a sound engineer thought that a grave injury had befallen the spectator and had cut the sound feed.

Less than three minutes later, sound was restored, and Limp Bizkit tore into "Nookie." Durst tried to body-surf through the audience using only a sheet of fan-liberated plywood. The attempt failed, and security shepherded him back onstage. The band played their cover of [George Michael's] "Faith," and the crowd went nuts.

Women who were sitting atop their boyfriend's shoulders were smothered by hands. Tops were torn away like tissue paper; girls fought valiantly to keep their pants on as boys tugged them down around their knees. Crisis-intervention workers who watched Limp Bizkit's set saw numerous sexual assaults in the mosh pits; one woman later reported to police that she had been raped, then had surfed her way out. She said that the size and mood of the crowd stopped her from yelling for help—she was afraid she'd be beaten up.

Still, a lot of the younger girls never felt threatened, whether or not they were near mosh pits. "From where I was," said Liz Pruitt, who stood near the front of the crowd, "it seemed like any other show, cause all I saw was people with their hands in the air. I felt safe." There was little pity for those who were unprepared for what they found in the front rows. "If you didn't want to be in a rough situation there, you shouldn't have been in the mosh pit," said reveler Doug Calahan. "I'm tired of people making excuses for their own fucking stupidity. Limp Bizkit equals mosh pit. Duh."
— "Don't Drink the Brown Water" / David Moodie and Maureen Callahan (reporting by Mark Schone) / October '99

2003: Limp Bizkit frontman Fred Durst reveals a tattoo of his idol, Kurt Cobain, on his chest. Now Cobain gets to look out at rap-metal audiences during Bizkit encores of "Nookie," which makes you think there might just be a hell after all. — "A Brief History of Grunge" / Andrew Beaujon / April '04

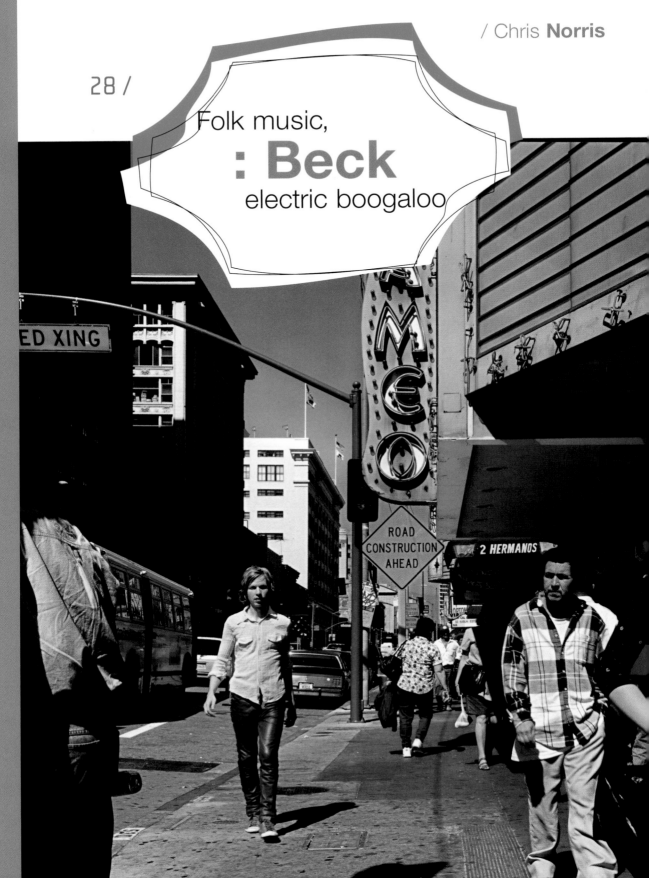

Folk music,
: **Beck**
electric boogaloo

Back in the early 1990s,

when our leading authorities had not yet determined if Caucasians could rap, a third-generation bohemian named Beck Hansen was plying his guitar and leaf-blower at small venues around Los Angeles. The shows were informal: A little singing, a little strumming, and some performance art involving *Star Wars* masks and tragic attempts at breakdancing. Genius was not immediately evident.

Hansen had knocked around New York's "antifolk" scene and performed at all-ages punk shows, but he remained mostly unaffiliated, since there was no clear movement for rhyme-saying, Delta-blues-playing, kraut-rockin', mariachi-lovin' folk-singers. By '91 he gained confidence enough to adopt a one-name moniker and record some tapeloop- and beatbox-abusing tracks with hip-hop producer Karl Stephenson. One of them contained some MC verses whose ungainliness so appalled the singer in playback that he improvised a chorus about what a loser he was, translating it to Spanish for extra flava. He continued on his amble into hipster obscurity when, in 1993, his half-baked rap jam "Loser" was released, and he became one of the biggest rock stars in the world.

Theories emerged to explain this. One held that in the age of Right Said Fred and "Rico Suave," just about any light-hearted rap song by a non-black person stood a decent chance of hitting big. Make this song a Slacker Anthem no less, with its own T-shirt- and headline-ready catch-phrase ("I'm a loser baby, so why don't you kill me," the "You're fired!" of 1993) and you're talking Top 10. But after a bidding war and Beck's subsequent debut, *Mellow Gold*, on Geffen, it became apparent what made Beck such a breakout star from the yet-unratified Alternative Nation. While his underground peers tended to turn their backs on the cheesy monolith of mass culture around them—nurturing their secret gardens of Captain Beefheart, Kraftwerk, or Smithsonian Folkways

recordings—Beck included not just the rap beats and sound-effects records, but the video-rental stores, weedwacking gigs, speedfreak neighbors, and public-access shows that informed his low-rent L.A. life.

This multimedia reality principle ended up making his music more accessible than that of most every other alt-rock contemporary, despite the fact that some of them, like Pavement's Stephen Malkmus, had remarkably similar sensibilities. (The Pavement shout "Wave your credit card in the air/ Swing your nachos like you just don't care" could easily be Beck.) His eventual outing as grandson of '60s art radical and Fluxus founder Al Hansen may help explain Beck's savvy trouvé approach to culture, but not his gift for rap asides like "drive-by bodypierce," lyrical gems like "Cool off your jets/ Take off your sweats," or his sure instinct for merging sound and style in ways that both charmed the ear and suited one of the stranger vocal instruments in modern music.

After some folksy releases on various indies, Beck released his official follow-up to *Mellow Gold*, and the stage was set for coronation. With the Dust Brothers (producers of the Beastie Boy's groove-tapestry *Paul's Boutique*) on board, 1996's sampledelic funhouse *Odelay* defined much of the sound and attitude of the post-grunge, pre-bling '90s: groovy, trippy, sprawling, neo-retro, retro-neo, and fully loaded with jingles, hooks, breakbeats, Moogs, Troggs, Schubert, titles like "Devil's Haircut" and opening lines like, "You only got one finger left/ And it's pointin' at the door...". Like just about every other prominent young white male of the era, Beck faced charges of aggravated irony for his wry soundbites and cultural appropriations, but the music was too rich, the vibe too celebratory, and the songs too plain smart for any of them to stick.

And so Beck was knighted New Dylan—a generation's consolation prize after the death of Kurt Cobain. Beck probably appreciated the superlatives, but they elided the hurled bottles he got onstage at

ESSAY CONTINUES ON NEXT PAGE >

Lollapalooza, the unspectacular record sales he had even with *Odelay*, and the strange, uncompromising, *sui generis* artist he remained.

Two snapshots from the era are instructive. One is the reaction Beck got from the crowd at a Dave Matthews Band concert he opened. "There were a lot of people pointing at us and then looking inquisitively at one another," Beck recalled then. "I don't think it really registered that we were actually playing music." Another is the response he got from Puffy Combs' team when he was brought in to freestyle over a "Bennie and the Jets" loop for Puff's album *Forever*. "They heard the track, they were grooving to it, their necks were moving," Beck says. "Then I started singing about, like, how expensive my hormones were." He was soon escorted out.

Beck followed *Odelay* with the odd neo-acoustic *Mutations*, helmed by Radiohead producer Nigel Godrich, then the "official" *Odelay* follow-up *Midnite Vultures*, an exhuberant, robot-dancing post-Prince sleazathon that showed his ear for rap repurposing still highly functional ("We like the boys with the bulletproof vests/ We like the girls with the cellophane chests"). After that Beck receded a bit, breaking up with his longterm girlfriend and releasing *Sea Changes*, whose heartaching songs like "Lost Cause" and "The Golden Age" that would be standard-setters for songwriters of any era.

In 2005, over a decade after his pseudo-role as Generation-X spokesmodel, Beck electric-slid on back to the dance floor, rejoining the Dust Brothers to release the slippery jam-odyssey, *Guero*. A sparer revisitation of the sounds and styles on *Odelay*, the album took its title from the Spanish "Que Onda Guero," which translates roughly as, "whassup whiteboy?"—a phrase we can assume Beck heard often in the largely Latin 'hood of his youth. Now, as he settles into his 30s, Beck also gets tabloid reports befitting an alt-rock Howard Hughes: a marriage to Hollywood actress Marissa Ribisi (twin sister of Giovanni), a rumored embrace of Scientology, a new child named Cosimo. None of which should really surprise or truly alienate any longtime Beck-heads, who probably realize that he is simply drifting back into the strange L.A. firmament that made him.

top ten "New Dylans"

01 **Donovan** ('66)

02 **John Prine** ('71)

03 **Loudon Wainwright** ('73)

04 **Bruce Springsteen** ('75)

05 **Elvis Costello** ('77)

06 **Paul Westerberg** ('85)

07 **Beck** ('94)

08 **Jakob Dylan** ('96)

09 **Ryan Adams** ('01)

10 **Conor Oberst** ('02)

— "The Ultimate List Issue" / April '03

I'm not proud to admit it, but at this point in the interview I raise the authenticity question: Does Beck ever feel a little goofy, fronting like a rapper? There isn't even an embarrassed pause—Beck stops to choke on a peppercorn, but hey, he's fragile. "I don't think it really comes off that way, does it?" I acknowledge that the whole thing is a bit like Woody Allen trying to pass for Humphrey Bogart. Beck is in a long tradition of Jews—the original Hollywood studio owners, Al Jolson singing "Mammy" in blackface, Isaac Asimov's civilized science fiction, Allen Ginsberg's Beat mélange, Woody's pop-culture comedies, Bob Dylan's folk-rock Americana—who invented nurturing fantasy universes as a way of escaping the alienation of being a stranger in a strange land. The closest comparison is the Beastie Boys, of course, but their love of rocking out and namechecking their coolness is pretty different from Beck, who lets rivers run through him.

There. We let the matter drop.

—"After the Gold Rush" / Eric Weisbard / August '96

See that sign over there?" asks Beck, pointing out the car window as we drive down Hyperion Avenue in the fading light. "I painted that sign." I crane my neck to see a plain brick building, its façade festooned with big block letters—THRIFT STORE. The nondescript storefront testifies to how far the sandy-haired urchin has come in a very short time. Only two years ago he was painting electric pink-and-blue signs on lingerie stores, eating Chee-tos, and making living room cassettes, only now his single, "Loser"—recorded in just such a casual couch-potato scene—has been the hottest request on radio stations across the country. The critical avatars of the boomer media have anointed him as a spokesman for his generation, an honorific with slightly less power than the Prince of Wales—call it the Prince of Wails—and ten times the royal pain in the ass.

"Jesus!" exclaims Beck at the very notion of being a mouthpiece for millions. "You'd have to be a total idiot to say, 'I'm the slacker-generation guy. This is my generation.' I'd be laughed out of the room in an instant."

So let's set one thing straight: Beck is no slacker. "I didn't even connect ['Loser'] at all to that kind of message until they were playing it on the radio and I heard it, and they said, 'This is the slacker anthem,' and I thought, 'Oh shit, that sucks.' It's not some anguished, transcendental 'cry of a generation.' It's just sitting in someone's living room eating pizza and Doritos."

Beck has had jobs moving refrigerators and furniture. He worked at children's birthday parties as a hot-dog man, serving root beer and hot dogs to little kids. As his song "Beercan" attests, he quit his job blowing leaves, but not before his blower ended up onstage with him as a musical instrument. "It's a very large population here," he says of leaf-blowers. "There's a leaf-blower contingent. There's no union I know of so far, but there's certainly a spiritual brotherhood. They are the originators of noise music."

Later, he tells me, "All the shit that's happening to me now is totally insane, because if you ask anybody that knows me, they'll tell you I've had the worst fucking luck. Before, the party was just an empty room with a bare lightbulb on the ceiling. It was pretty bleak." When I suggest that with such sentiments he's veering towards Vedderian angst, he laughs and begins sarcastically whining in a pinched voice, "Oh, the tragedy and the anguish. You just gotta Rage Against the Appliance, man. The toast is burning and you just gotta rip it out and free it before it fills the house with smoke. Rage Against the Toaster."

— "Subterranean Homeboy Blues" / Mike Rubin / July '94

When we arrive at Bernie Grundman Mastering—the Hollywood end zone to Michael Jackson's *Thriller* and N.W.A's *Straight Outta Compton*—Beck is remarkably casual about retrieving the results of 14 months' labor. "Hey," he says amiably as he walks up to the counter. "Ya got my album?" He looks like he should be fetching coffee for somebody. The twentyish clerk smiles eagerly and pushes a plastic bag containing master discs toward him. Beck looks down at another one labeled BONTANICA MARGARITA. "Can I have this one instead?"

In the studio garage, Beck opens the Lincoln's trunk and exposes the cartridges of his CD player. "Let's give it the ol' Sunset test," Beck says, inserting his album. As we pull out into the late-afternoon light of Sunset Boulevard, the rousing intro of the first single, "Sexxlaws," kicks in. With full horn section and manic tambourine, this Hullabaloo-style soul revue is all go-go boots and zoom-lens action—an exuberant update to the block-rocking psychedelia of *Odelay*. Then, out flow lyrics that could only have come from the person who put the phrase "devil's haircut" into the national lexicon. 'Can't you hear those cavalry drums/ Hijacking your equilibrium/ Midnight snacks in the mausoleum/ Where pixilated doctors moan…." As we continue to roll past tanning salons and fetish-wear stores, the imagery starts to seem less and less surreal.

"See, Hollywood's all about what's going on behind the storefront," Beck says, after turning onto Hollywood Boulevard. "In the back of that lighting store or that carpet place." As we pass the Petwash, Beck reveals one of *Midnite Vultures*' touchstones. "About a year ago, I started seeing these ads for 'Laser Vaginal Rejuvenation,'" he says. "First it was a little ad. The next week, it was twice as big. And after a month, it was a full page—it just took over. Something in that triggered a bunch of

associations and projections. Like, what kind of activities do you have to engage in to get to the point where you need to bring a laser into the equation? The new album exists in that realm."

Throughout it, Beck adapts the money-flashing, sex-you-up overkill of much of today's rap and R&B to hysterical ends. On the low-riding funk cruise "Nicotine & Gravy," Beck croons "I'll feed ya fruit that don't exist/ I'll leave grafitti where you've never been kissed." On "Get Real Paid," he updates '80s girl rappers L'Trimm with the chant "We like the boys with the bulletproof vests/ We like the girls with the cellophane chests." The record brims with coke-heads, gym bunnies, and liposuctioned, siliconed absurdity. It's part silly satire, part cryptic critique, with unease frequently poking through. The creeping shuffle of "Out of Kontrol" begins, "The snipers are passed out in the bushes again/ I'm glad I got my suit dry-cleaned before the riots started." I tell Beck it all seems very L.A., full of Hollywood sleaze, image mania, and Bel-Air power.

"I think it's more the period," he says. "This point in time seems more power-oriented. Power workout, power diet, power body parts, power relationships, power steering, Power Rangers. People are scrubbed and clean, well toned and manicured. I recently saw *The Last American Virgin*, one of those early-'80s coming-of-age movies. And the actors, they look like kids you grew up with! Today's teen movies, I didn't know anybody who looked like that. The standards now are so unbelievably high."

We drive on through darkening streets. As the bizarre glottal warble of Beck the soulman croons, "I know you really want it/ 'Cause your daddy's always on it," Beck the motorist points out his favorite road in L.A.: Normal Street. "Let's take a ride down Normal," he says.

We make a right.

"There," he says. "I feel better already."
— "Moonwalking in L.A." / Chris Norris / December '99

Here, Beck kicks his hip-pop prankster role to the curb, and it's good timing. *Midnite Vultures* pushed the shuckin' and jivin' so far, the next logical step was a supersession with Tenacious D. But ever since *Odelay*'s poignant, misleadingly-titled "Jack-Ass," Beck's been trying to capture the spiritual fatigue beneath his snarky superhit "Loser." *Sea Change* nails it just when we could all use a reflective time-out.
— review of *Sea Change* / Will Hermes / October '02

"So much of this age group or generation—and even I've been guilty of this in the past—takes something that's '70s and twists it around, either making fun of it or embracing it. There's not a lot of direct, inspired stuff. Sure, music always feeds off itself and its past, but there's not a lot of commitment. There's always this snatch of, 'We're just kidding, we don't really mean this.'"
— Beck, 1996

: Green Day

Pop goes the punk rock

"Do you have the time to listen to me whine?"

So goes the first line of the second single from Green Day's third album, *Dookie*. The rest of "Basket Case" is a neurotic pothead's raucous lament that, aside from its reference to a transsexual prostitute, spoke loud volumes to a restless teen constituency battered by broken homes and expecting broken dreams. And the Bay Area band probably could not have issued a more prescient invitation to a sound: Pop-punk, especially of the self-possessed variety, would soon pogo to unimagined commercial heights. (A few hundred miles south, the O.C.'s Offspring were blurring the line between skate punk and mainstream hard rock with *Smash*, which would eventually reach six-times platinum.)

Along with the rowdier street punks of Rancid, Green Day—guitarist Billie Joe Armstrong, bassist Mike Dirnt, and drummer Tré Cool (all born in 1972)—emerged in the late '80s from 924 Gilman Street, the Berkeley, California, club cofounded by the late Tim Yohannan, the contentious publisher of the long-running ultra-left punk zine *Maximum RocknRoll*. Prankish brats in a scene that above all else prized dogmatic adherence to a "no sell out" credo, the band recorded two albums for local indie Lookout! before the majors pounced. Green Day signed in 1993 to Warner Bros. Reprise Records, whose Rob Cavallo spit-polished their already bright'n'noisy three-chord power pop and sculpted it into *Dookie*. Amateurish cover art notwithstanding, the 1994 album was a roaring rock beast, all diesel-powered guitars, ADD basslines, and Jiffy Pop drumming, topped by Armstrong's brash, faux-Brit-accented vocals. His disarmingly peppy odes to ennui ("Longview"), an abusive lover ("Pulling Teeth"), and a runaway's degradation ("Welcome to Paradise"), offered self-loathing disguised as self-deprecation—startlingly mature songs that convincingly celebrate permanent immaturity. But this was a concoction that nobody could have expected to move 10 million units, let alone lay the groundwork for a triumphant comeback 10 years later with the politically charged (and Grammy-snagging) *American Idiot*.

Punk's first young gazillionaires weren't necessarily doing anything all that new: *Dookie* abounds with echoes of Buzzcocks, Ramones, Descendents, and the Dickies. And none of Green Day's subsequent albums deviated much from this model (they've also made a habit of flagrantly borrowing riffs from unlikely sources: brassy classic rockers Chicago on *Insomniac*'s "Brain Stew"; Johnny Cash and Bryan Adams, among others, on *American Idiot*'s ambitious song suite "Jesus of Suburbia"). Nor would they replicate *Dookie*'s stratospheric sales. But the band became the touchstone for a generation of biz-savvy acts that viewed punk as just another fashionable offshoot of pop. Labels went mad, scooping up any band with lip piercings, inked sleeves, and a singer in need of decongestant.

These adenoidal upstarts—blink-182, Good Charlotte, New Found Glory, the Ataris, Yellowcard, and numerous others with terrible names who did the Warped circuit—embodied a novel punk ideal. They were no longer the ostracized freaks and outcasts, but the cool kids. Legitimized by market forces, the pop-punkers didn't worry about selling out—they indulged in rewards never available to (and which likely would have been rejected by) the genre's pioneers. While old-school punks-turned-NASCAR dads quietly smiled as Buzzcocks licensed a track for a Toyota ad (finally, Pete Shelley's getting paid!), the platinum-plated newbies (derisively crowned "mall punks") essentially mimicked their hip-hop contemporaries, designing clothing lines, canoodling with TRL hotties, and taking Playmate brides; 2005 even saw spunky Canadians Sum 41 collaborating with Southern rapper Ludacris, a crossover made in energy-drink heaven.

Not that Green Day was immune. Aside from *Dookie*—and their conquering-heroes mud fight at Woodstock '94—perhaps the band's chief contribution to the pop-culture canon is the ultimate graduation song, "Good Riddance (Time of Your Life)," a lovely acoustic ballad from 1997's *Nimrod,* later used in the final episode of *Seinfeld*, which was watched by an audience of 76 million. (Okay, so the Dickies got there first 20 years earlier, when they performed "Hideous" on the Don Rickles sitcom *CPO Sharkey*, but who's counting?). Truly masters of their own domain, the members of Green Day have had a holiday in the sun that Johnny Rotten never dreamed of.

"BUT… WHERE DID THEY ALL COME FROM?" LOOKOUT! RECORDS FOUNDER LARRY LIVERMORE WONDERED, AS YET ANOTHER SWEATY KID SAILED OVER HIS HEAD, SWINGING TARZAN-LIKE OFF THE BASKETBALL HOOP IN THE CORNER OF 924 GILMAN STREET.

On the stage Livermore helped install just a year and change ago, Operation Ivy, a four-piece punk band with a penchant for the downbeat, is in the midst of a glorious set, and kids are exploding off the floor like popcorn. The band begins its signature tune, "Knowledge": "All I know is that I don't know nothing," yells singer Jesse Michaels hoarsely, and the entire audience shouts back, "And that's fine!" Op Ivy's Lookout! debut, *Energy*, isn't even in stores, and yet everyone here knows the words. "It was like a punk Woodstock," recalls Livermore now. "And I should know. I was at the real Woodstock."

Conceived as an anarchist, communally run, alcohol-free, nonprofit, all-ages punk hangout, 924 Gilman Street was the brainchild of *Maximum RocknRoll* magazine head honcho Tim Yohannon, who acquired a lease of a one-story brick room in an abandoned stretch of Berkeley and, with the help of Livermore and ten or 15 teenagers, slowly transformed the old canning factory into a night club. Gilman Street is as unpretentious as it gets. There is no back-stage area, no outdoor sign. The club is staffed by volunteers; it splits the door with musicians, sells only indie-approved Hansen's soda and candy, and books both known and unknown punk rock acts from across the country. Initially, the bands that played had to clean the toilets after their sets, to underscore the idea that the musicians weren't above those in the audience. "It was okay when it was my dumb band," says "Doctor Frank" Portman of the Mr. T Experience. "But when it was Bad Religion or someone…well, that was probably the first ideological crack in the organization."

For a certain sect of alienated kids, Gilman Street became a twisted version of the barnyard playhouse in a Mickey Rooney movie, not to mention a refuge from Reagan's America. Tim Armstrong, singer for Op Ivy and later Rancid, was at Gilman's opening-night gig on New Year's Eve '86 and hung out there two or three times a week for the next seven years. "I was so hungry for something like that. I really needed a community, because I'd never felt a part of anything in my life before."

Emily Marcus was 17 when she first found her way to Gilman Street to see Op Ivy. "There were always really little kids there—like, 13 or 14," she recalls. "They probably didn't have much of a home life, but they loved the music and the lifestyle." By day you'd see the same tattooed and Mohawked kids on hippie-strewn Telegraph Avenue, panhandling for spare change. Every Friday and Saturday, the various tribes gathered for lengthy shows that ranged from godlike to pathetic. Quality control was never a Gilman Street priority: Many five-band bills featured four who had never been on a stage before. In between sets, kids would troop out to the train tracks to drink beer or hang out in the corner chatting with friends, looking like an urban version of *Lord of the Flies*. Portman calls gigs there "more of an endurance test than anything," and Reprise A&R guy Katznelson's memories are, he says, "of violence. Whenever I left the place, my pants would be blackened, because I'd have been thrown to the ground so many times." Gilman's low point probably came in the early '90s, when Dead Kennedy Jello Biafra, of all people, was attacked and beaten up by a band of punk teens for supposedly "selling out."

In 1993, a three-piece from Pinole called Green Day, who'd been putting out albums on Livermore's Lookout!, left the Gilman Street fold by signing to Warner Bros., and in January 1994 they released a punk-pop megastorm called *Dookie*. Soon, Gilman regulars like Jawbreaker, Samiam, Screeching Weasel, and Rancid were faced with strange decisions, being presented with seven-figure checks from major labels while being attacked by others for considering the offers.

— "Berkeley, California, 1987-94: Exiles on Gilman Street" / Gina Arnold / April '00

"If you're playing in front of 20,000 people, you have to give them something to look at. I think that's why I used to get naked so often. When a show is uneventful, or we're not that tight, or the crowd is lukewarm —the clothes come off. You've got to give them something to remember, so ten years from now they can say, 'Oh yeah! We saw Green Day, and Billie Joe got naked!' I came from a working-class background, and I work hard up there."

— Billie Joe Armstrong, 1997

THERE'S SOMETHING THAT CAN'T BE EQUALED ABOUT SEEING PEOPLE ALMOST EXACTLY YOUR OWN AGE GETTING TO BE REAL LIVE ROCK STARS. The members of Green Day have become rock starts in an eyeblink; their third album, *Dookie*, has risen to No. 31 on the *Billboard* album chart after MTV Buzz Bin airplay for the video "Longview." At the Shoreline Amphitheater, Green Day played the part to perfection, headbutting the microphone, shredding flowers, darting around in shorts like a baby AC/DC, tossing out snotty banter ("I hope you guys are beating the fuck out of each other and go home with fucking bruises," said Billie Joe), and just plain acting as if throwing out loud rock music on a hot day was what life was all about. During "Longview," a song about masturbating bored in front of the television, Billie Joe had whipped out his dick and shaken it around during the line, "I'm feeling like a dog in heat."

Later, during a day when bands were playing half-hour sets and then retreating with mechanical bows, Green Day refused to come offstage. Maybe it was problems with the sound, or maybe Green Day just isn't happy without a little conflict. It did feel a bit rote, hearing the band vamp while roadies whispered threatening things in Billie Joe's ear, and the singer suggested to the crowd, "Now that they're angry at us, we *could* rip out the seats." Still, even coming off a grueling European tour, with no day off in between, Green Day's enthusiasm gave an empty show its only feeling of common purpose.

Proud boomer Gary Kamiya was less impressed in the *San Francisco Examiner*, writing "It's hard to know what to make of a bunch of 22-year-olds who want to play roots punk. They did the primal Sex Pistols/Clash style of punk very competently, complete with impressive vertical leaps by the bassist, and a guitar slung at an impeachably low level, and the requisite petulant outbursts. But why?"
— "Young, Loud, and Snotty" / Eric Weisbard / September '94

"A week ago, a kid comes up to Lollapalooza, pays to get in, and has a note passed to me backstage accusing us of alienating our old fans. Why are we signed to a major, why did we play Woodstock, blah, blah, blah. My question to him is, first, what the fuck are you doing at Lollapalooza then? He left a phone number on the note, and I actually called him up, and his father answered the phone—and told me to leave a message on the kid's e-mail. Who the fuck has e-mail? Our friends want to know about issues of integrity, and they have valid things to say about them, but if you want to challenge my values, you can't live with your parents, and you can't be in college with your rent paid up by your parents, and you especially can't own a computer. Then I'll talk to you about anything you want."
— Billie Joe Armstrong, 1994

"There are things that I can't talk about, that I can only communicate through a song. Sometimes I can't express the way I feel at home, so I'll demo something and say, 'Adrienne, listen to this.' I'll even communicate with myself sometimes—'Coming Clean' (from *Dookie*) is a song about being bi-curious, having doubts about my sexuality, wondering whether or not I was gay. I wouldn't talk to my best friends about something like that."
— Billie Joe Armstrong, 1997

WHILE THEY'VE SPENT A DECADE DEALING WITH INCREASINGLY GROWN-UP CONCERNS, GREEN DAY REMAIN AS VIABLE A COMMODITY AS EVER AMONG DISCERNING CONSUMERS OF THAT WHICH IS YOUNG, LOUD, AND SNOTTY. Tre Cool sums up this peculiar state of affairs by paraphrasing Wooderson, the post-high-school lech Matthew McConaughey played in the stoner classic *Dazed and Confused*. "We get older," he says, "and our audience stays the same age."

But if, along the way, they've also become mature—"I hate that word," Billie Joe Armstrong says—it's a condition that's crept up on them, something else to rebel against. "We always wanted our music to be timeless. Even the political stuff that we're doing now. I would never think of 'American Idiot' as being about the Bush administration specifically. It's about the confusion of where we're at right now."

"The world's in a confused state," Mike Dirnt agrees. "I'm pissed off, and I'm angry, and I feel like I'm not fully represented."

Dirnt says he swelled with pride when he turned on the TV in Holland the previous week and saw 250,000 people marching in the streets of Manhattan, protesting the Republican National Convention. "I was like, fuckin' A, man. I'm not there right now, but I'm totally fuckin' there right now."

"My education wasn't school," says Armstrong, who dropped out of high school. "My education was punk rock—what the Dead Kennedys said, what Operation Ivy said. It was attacking America, but it was American at the same time. Patriotism isn't about being pro-anything. It's not about being pro-Bush or pro-Kerry. It's about what you stand for and what you think America represents."

"I wouldn't consider myself an angry young man anymore," he says. "You don't have to leave the danger behind, but what makes you grow up is confronting the danger. And that's what *American Idiot* is really all about—confronting that self-destructive impulse."
— "Power to the People (With Funny Haircuts)" / Alex Pappademas / November '04

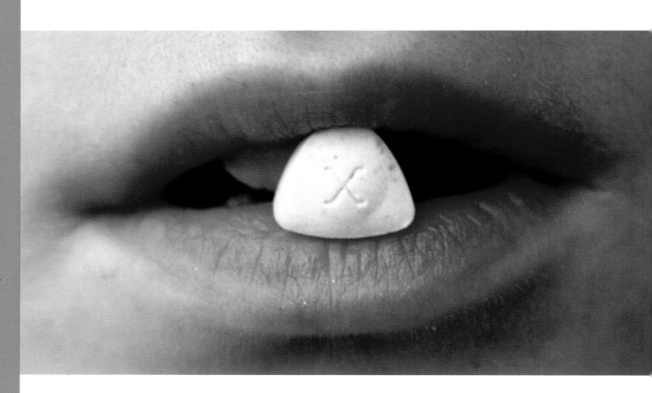

Ecstasy : Everything starts with an E

"Ecstasy," its early supporters often said, was something of a misnomer; "Empathy" might be a better name for a drug that opened hearts and melted egos. But drug experiences are shaped by what acid guru Timothy Leary called "set and setting." Taking MDMA at home with a lover or a group of friends can be a serene experience. But add loud dance beats and trippy lighting, and the drug lives up to its billing. Dancing on E in a crowd all riding the same rush of euphoria, you get swept up in a delirium at once orgiastic and angelic, touchy-feely yet liberatingly sexless. Dancing itself becomes a form of worship, like with African tribes or Pentecostal congregations. And rave culture at its peak really was like a religion: Ecstasy initiates

became wide-eyed, babbling converts, ready to spread the word, while DJs were revered as high priests. Even the dealers—early on, not gangstas so much as born-again believers combining enterprise and proselytizing—took on a glow-by-association as dispensers of the holy sacrament.

The modern story of MDMA began in the 1970s, when it was a legal pharmaceutical touted in American psychoanalytical circles as a panacea that could push patients through emotional blockages. Three Ecstasy trips, it was claimed, were equivalent to three years in therapy. By the early '80s, the drug found its way into nightclubs, sparking precocious if short-lived trance-dance scenes in Austin and Dallas. The D.E.A. noticed, and in 1985—much to the chagrin of the

therapist community—placed it on Schedule 1, alongside heroin and cocaine. But by then it was too late: Ecstasy's reputation as the ultimate party potion was sealed.

The turning point for Ecstasy as dance drug came in 1987, when a bunch of English DJs spent the summer on the Mediterranean island paradise of Ibiza. At night, dancing under the stars in open-air clubs like Amnesia, they discovered the perfect synergy between E and electronic dance music. Returning to London, DJs like Paul Oakenfold started underground clubs based on their Ibiza revelation, eventually fixating on acid house—a trippy, futuristic style of Chicago house music based around mindbendingly wibbly basslines—as the

ESSAY CONTINUES ON NEXT PAGE >

10 things 5 things
ravers do ravers say
on drugs on drugs

10 things ravers do on drugs	5 things ravers say on drugs
rave	"i'm *mad* old school"
explore k-holes	"i love you *so* much—can i have another bump?"
fall down	"do you have a pencap or key i can borrow?"
grab head in pain	"wow! digweed doesn't sound like shit anymore!"
blow through vicks inhaler tubes into one another's	eyeballs [don't ask]
wear big pants	"and i mean, it's like we're all linked together on the inside.
grind teeth	like we're bound together
liquid dance	by this beat,
exchange back rubs	and—oh shit—i gotta *puke*!"
go into cardiac arrest	

> ESSAY CONTINUES FROM PREVIOUS PAGE

ultimate MDMA-enhancing soundtrack. London clubland had always been snooty and crippled by cool. But in 1988, Ecstasy blasted all the preening and posing aside, replacing it with "going mental" and getting "loved up". White and black, hipsters and soccer hooligans, united in blissed-out bonhomie and neo-psychedelic optimism. "The Second Summer of Love," they called it .

As the U.K. scene expanded, it graduated from small clubs to large warehouse parties, and from there to gigantic raves in the English countryside drawing as many as 30 thousand people. Locations were often kept secret until the last minute, then announced on phone lines; revelers drove in huge convoys to meet-points, where they were given directions. English expatriates and American DJs who'd had their minds blown at these events exported the rave model to the U.S., which seeded scenes across the country, from the Brooklyn warehouse parties thrown by Frankie Bones' Stormrave crew, to the Full Moon gatherings in San Francisco and the desert raves of Los Angeles. Ecstasy was the crucial catalyst for all this feverish activity. So much of what defined rave as culture and music can be traced back to the drug's peculiar mixture of effects: the LSD-like tinge of misty-eyed mysticism, the amphetamine-related feelings of boundless energy and sheer fearless nerve. In the honeymoon period of Ecstasy use, many of the original ravers believed the magic pill was gonna change the world.

It didn't (although raves goaded legislators in Britain and America to clamp down on both promoters and dealers). But it did revolutionize music in the '90s, especially in the U.K. Not just through all the endlessly mutating offshoots of house music—techno, trance, jungle, chill-out, ad infinitum. You could also hear E's reverberations in the woozy guitar-bliss of My Bloody Valentine and in the neo-psychedelic Manchester scene of The Stone Roses and Happy Mondays. The Mondays built up a following in part by selling E direct to their audience at gigs; their addled dancer Bez was simultaneously an onstage advertisement for it and a warning about the dangers of excessive consumption. Fans of house music, the Roses developed the Manchester baggy beat, a loose-limbed funky shuffle that brought groove back to U.K. indie pop for the first time in almost a decade. Scene veterans New Order, who'd funded the construction of the Hacienda, the clubbing epicenter of "Madchester," slipped the cheeky line "E is for England" into their World Cup soccer single "World In Motion."

By the mid-'90s, Ecstasy had lost much of its shine. Not only had the quality become unreliable, but it was increasingly subsumed in a polydrug culture that made the dance floor a messy place. "You said your body was young but your mind was very old…the visions we had are fading away," sang Noel Gallagher on "Setting Sun", his collaboration with Big Beat pioneers the Chemical Brothers. Burned-out ravers started dropping out of the scene (and a handful actually dropped dead on the dance floor, from overdoing E).

"I've never done heroin, so I don't know, but people say Ecstasy is a combination of the warm, squishy feeling you have with heroin, and the hyperkinetic, ballsy energy you have on coke, and that it's slightly hallucinogenic, so the green of your jacket is *really* green. And you just love everybody. I mean, you could walk up to Bob Dole and have a conversation and find something to like about him. It's pathetic." — Madonna, 1996 ["Live to Tell" / Bob Guccione, Jr. / January '96]

1985: MDMA, a.k.a. "the love drug," becomes widely available in Seattle. Some scene veterans maintain that MDMA was a vital contributor to grunge. Rather than the "head high" familiar to marijuana users, it gives the impression of a "body high," making the user terribly appreciative of sexy, bass-heavy grooves. — "A Brief History of Grunge" / Andrew Beaujon / April '04

So what is rave exactly? Well, it's hard to explain. You might think back to the mid-'70's, or even further back to the late-'60's, in the sense that, like punk and hippiedom, rave is a countercultural movement with specific musical taste, a highly developed fashion sense, and a left-of-Democratic politic. But unlike punks or hippies, ravers are more interested in issues of spiritual growth and increased communication than they are in transgressing traditional political structures. To generalize—and with a movement this amorphous, you're forced to—ravers tend to see the government and its laws as beside the point. If ravers lionize anything, it's technology, which offers ways to circumvent the kinds of blockage that derailed countercultures of the past. Rave is not about destroying corrupt power structures; it's about general things like self-belief, open mindedness, and faith. It's about seeking the limitless. — "A Raver Runs Through It" / Dennis Cooper and Joe Westendorf / April '95

Aldo Bender (DJ/Promoter): A club in Laguna Beach is the first place I became aware of Ecstasy. Several of the patrons came from Texas, where Ecstasy was legal until 1985.

Destructo (Promoter): We would meet this dude in cowboy boots who had a red Corvette and two hot chicks with him. We'd walk over to the parking lot and he'd say "Green light go." We'd hand him 20 bucks, and he'd give us a pill.

DJ Dan (DJ): Do you remember the white wafers?

Mark Lewis (DJ): I remember doing a hit of real E at Truth, looking at those smiley faces and daisy decorations, then closing my eyes and feeling this euphoric togetherness.

Jason Bentley (DJ/Urb editor): I met a girl at Mickey's Magical Mind Arcade. She was passing out flyers, and her eyes were crossed on E. She had a gigantic ruby candy ring on her finger and she was sucking on it. I was in love.

Ron D. Core (DJ): After E, things sped up as far as BPM. [By 1991] people were looking for something a bit more aggressive, a bit more crunchy.

Randy Moore (Promoter): It was the beginning of hardcore. The first mash-up was "Total Destruction" by A Homeboy, A Hippy, and A Funki Dredd. Then everybody started jumping on the bandwagon. It became really aggressive—people were slamming to the tracks. The crowds got real young real quick.

Michael Cook (DJ): The music got harder and harder as venues got bigger. Nosebleed techno—it seemed to go with the scale of things. — "Mad Hatters, Map Points & Ecstasy Freaks: The Secret History of the L.A. Rave Scene" / David J. Prince and Todd C. Roberts / October '01

"Hugging the speakers feels really good if you're on E," explains a 20-year-old UCLA student named Thomas. "The bass hits you in the sternum and spreads out all along your arms and down to every limb…. But when I don't do drugs and go to raves, I'm just a normal person." — "Loud, Fast, and Out of Control" / Pat Blashill / August '99

In March 2000, it was front-page news: Sammy "the Bull" Gravano, Mafia hit man-turned-Ecstasy dealer, busted by the feds in Phoenix. In May, *Dateline NBC* ran an hour-long hidden camera rave-scene investigation, sending a teenage mole named "Amy" to a warehouse party where she was offered a variety of pills. News reports of huge airport seizures of "Mitsubishi" or "Green Diamond" Ecstasy tabs began to appear almost weekly. By June, as *Time* magazine was explaining "What Ecstasy Does to Your Brain," it was official: The country was hooked on a new drug hysteria. — "X-tra X-tra" / David J. Prince / January '01

A second wave of Ecstasy culture arrived in the last years of the '90s (linked to the return of reliably high-quality MDMA in the form of the legendary Mitshubishi pill), launching two new styles of E-muzik, filter house and trance. Sentimental and melodic, trance was the people's choice at the big raves and the new superclubs like New York's Twilo and Gatecrasher in Sheffield, England. The whooshing, disco-influenced style of filter house, pioneered by French groups like Daft Punk, was en vogue at smaller, hipster oriented clubs. Daft Punk offshoot Stardust made the ultimate late-'90s Ecstasy anthem, "Music Sounds Better With You"—the "you" assumed to refer not to a lover but to a pill.

But even as Madonna latched onto E-lectronica with the trance-lite *Ray of Light* and the more Daft Punk-style *Music*, the moment quickly passed. What had once between a renegade, borderline-criminal subculture evolved into a professionalized leisure industry, with a hierarchy of globe-trotting star DJs and slick superclubs closer to shopping malls than underground parties. Taking E had once been a special event, a secret sacred rite. Now it was routine, and everybody seemed to be doing it, from Spring Break jocks to normals at wedding parties. By 2000, hipster youth began to turn to spikier sounds with attitude and underground edge. E-culture's immersive aesthetic of long, seamlessly mixed DJ sets fell from favor; eclectic, short-attention-span oriented DJing became the new thing. Cocaine made a comeback. The brittle clique-ishness and superiority complexes it generates helped fuel the Electroclash fad—a return to the '80s nightclub poseur ethos that E had originally obliterated.

Ecstasy enjoyed an unexpected third wind via hip-hop. In 2000, rap started to teem with techno riffs, ravey synth-stabs, and all manner of MDMA-styled noise. Dr. Dre namedropped X in "Let's Get High," B.G. described getting mashed on "Henessy & Ecstasy," Bizzy from Bone Thugs 'N' Harmony rapped about feeling "so pillish pillish pillish," and on "Ecstasy," a bona-fide house track, Ja Rule wondered why he and all the other ballers were drinking so much damn Evian. And yet—probably because hip-hop's psychological armor is so impregnable—Ecstasy failed to create a whole new breed of "love thugs" in touch with their feminine side. Mostly, it just seemed to make MCs X-tremely horny. "I fuck so fabulous on X," boasted Rule. "All night, nothing but sweat and rough sex," while Jay-Z charmingly observed "I like my women friends feminine/ I like my hoes on X like Eminem."

Fittingly, one of the conduits of Ecstasy into hip-hop was strip clubs. The owners supplied the girls with pills to keep their morale high and help them project positive energy, and the girls would then bring E back to the 'hood and turn people on. Indeed, strip clubs were where Atlanta producer Lil Jon first heard house and techno, the source of the nagging synth-vamps he put into monster hits like Usher's "Yeah." From the chaste frenzy of those halcyon early raves to the flailing flesh-pots of the Dirty South—what a long strange trip it's been.

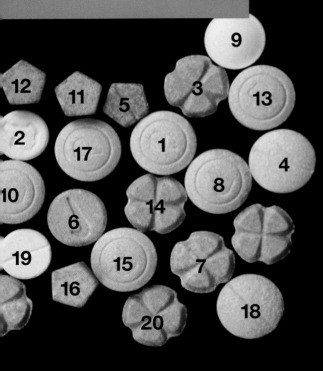

Top 20 Ecstasy Anthems:

Sleezy D "I've Lost Control" (Trax, 1986) ... **Rythim Is Rythim** "Strings of Life" (Transmat, 1987) ... **Royal House** "Party People" (Idlers, 1988) ... **Happy Mondays** "Rave On" (Factory, 1989) .... **My Bloody Valentine** "Soon" (Creation, 1989) ... **Orbital** "Chime" (Oh-Zone, 1989) .... **Beltram** "Energy Flash" (Transmat, 1990) ... **Primal Scream** "Higher Than the Sun (A Dub Symphony in Two Parts)" (Creation, 1991) ... **The Prodigy** "Everybody in the Place" (XL, 1991) ... **Acen** "Trip to the Moon Pt 1" (Production House, 1992) ... **Blame** "Music Takes You (2 Bad Mice Remix)" (Moving Shadow, 1992) ... **Jam & Spoon** "Stella" (R&S, 1992) ... **The Future Sound of London** "Papua New Guinea" (Jumpin' & Pumpin' 1992) ... **Foul Play** "Finest Illusion" (Section 5, 1993) ... **Josh Wink** "Higher State of Consciousness" (BMG, 1995) ... **Energy 52** "Cafe Del Mar" (Bonzai Trance, 1997) ... **Fatboy Slim** "Going Out of My Head" (Skint, 1997) ... **Binary Finary** "1998" (Shock, 1998) ... **Stardust** "Music Sounds Better With You" (Virgin, 1998) ... **Missy Elliott** "4 My People" (Elektra, 2001)

It's 11 AM on November 10, and the Tel Aviv Love Parade is getting off to a lazy start. A group of drag queens are still getting dressed, coating their skin in glitter and body paint in the rising heat. Fourteen floats, each decorated with identical banners, have just started rolling slowly down the center of the boardwalk. Three parasailers fly back and forth above the beach in the bright blue sky, dropping cellphone company-sponsored candy from their orange perches. But below them, the early arrivals look tired and indifferent—there's simply too much concrete and not enough dancing.

At first I think it's the massive security—armed soldiers and giant gunships would be an immediate buzzkill at any like-minded American event. Given the situation, however, and the fact that the military is a part of everyone's daily life, the show of force is in some ways a welcome reassurance. "Nobody even minds," says DJ Dede, who is spinning on one club's float. "They know that if the police forces and the army forces want to take care of someone, they will take care of them."

"It's a weird place to be tripping," admits one parade promoter, adding that terrorist alerts have their upside—no drug busts. "That's the last thing the police care about now!"

— "Beats and Bullets in the Promised Land" / David J. Prince / March '01

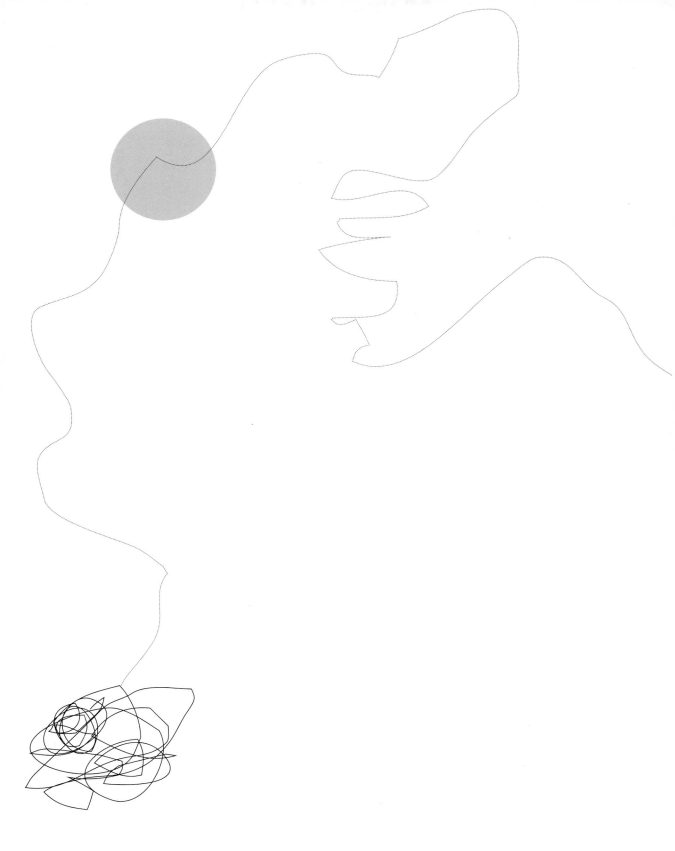

[KATHLEEN HANNA]

Looking back on the history of women in rock in the 1990s is like walking into your living room the morning after a serious party. Scan the space and you'll see the remnants of discussions so intense that those engaged left behind unfinished drinks, snacks, cigarettes; indentations on pillows in the corners where new lovers played with each others' limits; furniture disrupted by a tussle or two—and stacked on top of the stereo, a fistful of CDs that still sound great during the day's inevitable cleanup.

Put them on and survey the damage: *Fontanelle* by Babes in Toyland; *Bricks Are Heavy* by L7; *Rid of Me* by PJ Harvey; *Not a Pretty Girl* by Ani DiFranco; *Enter: The Conquering Chicken* by the Gits; *Exile in Guyville* by Liz Phair; *Jagged Little Pill* by Alanis Morissette; *Pottymouth* by Bratmobile; *Become What You Are* by Juliana Hatfield; *Live Through This* by Hole; *Little Earthquakes* by Tori Amos; *Pussy Whipped* by Bikini Kill; *Tidal* by Fiona Apple; *Call the Doctor* by Sleater-Kinney. Despite being made by a bunch of kids from essentially the same neighborhood—white, bohemian, college-influenced if not educated—these recordings express a broad view of the feminine experience, end-of-the-century style.

Primal rage and desire gained voice in the whorling, guitar-driven visions of Babes in Toyland and PJ Harvey. Amos and DiFranco dismantled stereotypes of the ladylike, in totally different ways. Phair was funny and wry, wise beyond her years; Hatfield was childlike, but sharp. Bikini Kill, led by the mighty Kathleen Hanna, turned feminist theory into punk fury. Apple reworked the blues for a "post-feminist" age. They were all so different, these artists' sounds and stances, and together they sounded exactly like the kind of healthy, earnest debate that occurs when a circle of women feel safe and strong enough to be honest with each other. (Feminists called it "consciousness-raising" in the radical '70s.) Somehow, though, just as the complex doings at a party get reduced to one good story in the following weeks or even hours—"That was the night Kelly fell out the window!"—this brilliant moment in woman-powered creativity got squeezed to fit the singular label "angry women in rock."

Now that the lipstick smears have been wiped up and the furniture has been returned to its proper position, it might be possible to consider whether it's accurate or even useful to think of this generation of female artists as "angry." The pioneering all-female group L7 captured a genuine mood of exasperation in its 1991 single "Shove," a shout aimed at the sexist status quo. "Get out of my way or I'm gonna shove!" snarled Suzi Gardner, stomping her boot-clad heels as her bandmates barreled through a body-slamming assault of chords. L7's indignation was echoed in the era's many songs about avenging or at least surviving rape, breaking out of corsets and closets, binging and purging and still hating your face in the mirror. This was the noise of a new vanguard learning—to use another classic feminist phrase—to speak truth to power. "I'm here to remind you of the mess you left when you went away!" Alanis Morissette proclaimed to her unappreciative ex in 1995's "You Oughta Know," the "God Save The Queen" of the "angry women" era, but her words echoed through the culture at large as we faced a decisive moment in the battle to define and realize sexual equality.

It was a strange time for American feminism. The movement had accomplished much, and failed spectacularly in other ways. Young women felt both empowered and ignored as feminism simultaneously spread "like fluoride," in

ESSAY CONTINUES ON NEXT PAGE >

: "Angry Women" Medusas, Riot Grrrls + Dangerous Nymphs

the words of journalist Amy Richards, and faced an aggressive backlash of public opinion. This was the time of new feminist champions like Susan Faludi, and anti-feminist reactionaries like Camille Paglia; of female-bonding fantasies like *Thelma & Louise,* and resurrected stereotypes like the vixenish Sharon Stone in *Basic Instinct*; of the female professional's rise, and the spectacle of Anita Hill, eviscerated by Congress for accusing future Supreme Court Justice Clarence Thomas of sexual harassment. Gains made by young women's own mothers meant that the more privileged among the daughters felt assured that they could become educated, enter the workplace successfully, make their own choices about whom to sleep with and whether to have a child, and find a place in many public forums. Yet life's daily circumstances, and their own words, often failed them. Many enclaves, from the U.S. Senate to the androgen-driven world of rock music, often relegated women to marginal roles.

Language itself seemed to do the same, proving inadequate to unadulterated female power and desire. Given more freedom, young women of the 1990s still felt unable to escape the rules and roles defined by a male-dominated culture. "It's hard to talk with your dick in my mouth," shouted Hanna, bluntly expressing the problem in Bikini Kill's "White Boy." In a way, feminism's gains allowed this "third wave" generation the luxury of more vehemence, and certainly more mainstream attention, than their radical forebears had enjoyed. Rock music became the ideal arena for them to scream out their frustrations, fears, longings, and, yes, joy.

While "angry" was the emotional label witnesses instinctively placed on all this unleashed energy, the swell of women's voices in the 1990s was angry in the way clouds or the sea get angry: It represented a growing force, decentered but full of potential. Looking back on that time in 2005, at a moment when women's rights are under threat in a more concrete way than at any time since rock began, it's sad to realize that what motivated alternative rock's rebel girls and monster women wasn't anger at all. At its core, it was hope.

Riot Grrrl feminism is a crazy salad that mixes rhetoric from 1960s-style women's liberation, green politics, vegetarianism, Susan Faludi's *Backlash*, Naomi Wolf's *Beauty Myth*, and other disparate sources.

Local chapters have started up in half a dozen or more cities, comprising a few hundred members and a small but vocal minority in today's antifeminist climate. Sixty-three percent of American women now refuse to be called feminists, according to a recent *Time*/CNN poll. Young women in particular, *Time* reports, reject the label. With their loosely-defined organization, Riot Grrrls stand in sharp contrast to the rest of undergraduate America.

Though Riot Grrrls print miles of column inches about themselves in their 'zines, they recoil at talking to reporters. Bikini Kill front-woman Kathleen Hanna declined to be interviewed because a recent piece in SPIN about her band made her feel "exploited." Allison Wolfe from Bratmobile also refused to talk, saying the grrrls can more effectively spread the word through 'zines, concert tours, and community meetings.

In a pamphlet called *What Is Riot Grrrl Anyways?* Jasmine Kerns writes: "Never before have I experienced a group with so much positive energy and love. This may sound like a Woodstock-Rainbow gathering, but it's true."

Riot Grrrls are continually running into opposition, but Kerns had a ready answer for their detractors. "We don't need you," she said, quoting from a Bikini Kill song. "Does that scare you?" Kerns paused for a minute. "That's one of my all-time favorite lines."
— "Teenage Riot" / Dana Nasrallah / November '92

I mention a riot grrrl show Courtney Love helped organize in London last year.

Rumor had it the concert was a critical and financial disaster, despite the participation of name acts like Huggy Bear, Bratmobile, and Hole. Since that fiasco, the riot grrrl phenomenon has been treated a lot less reverentially in the British music papers. "Yeah, it didn't work," Love says, echoing the opinion of the other Hole members, male and female. "But then the whole riot grrrl thing is so...well, for

one thing, the Women's Studies program at Evergreen State College, Olympia, where a lot of these bands come from, is notorious for being one of the worst programs in the country. It's man-hating, and it doesn't produce very intelligent people in that field. So you've got these girls starting bands, saying, 'Well, they printed our picture in the *Melody Maker*, why aren't we getting any royalties?'

"I tried to start a riot grrrl chapter in L.A. at one point. I called a bunch of people to try to set up a meeting, and they were like, 'But the place will be bugged! *A Current Affair* will be there!' And I'm like, 'Listen, nobody cares, girls. Interest is on the wane in this little fad.'"
— "Love Conquers All" / Dennis Cooper / May '94

"Did you lend me a tampon that day?"

L7's Donna Sparks asks Suzi Gardner. We're talking at singer-guitarist Sparks' Los Angeles apartment about the punk breakthrough that occurred at last summer's music festival in Reading, England. I want to know what brand Sparks made history with.

"Plain old Tampax," Gardner responds.

"Biodegradable Tampax. What I wanted to do was drop my pants and pull it out, so everyone could see what I was doing. I had on these baggy shorts and I didn't have a belt so I used duct tape, double knotted, so I'm like, shit, I can't get these pants down. I turn around, and I look at Dee, and she sees my hand go down in there while I try to pull out this tampon. I swing it around my head, threw it out into the audience, and all these kids are yelling—they think I'm throwing out a lighter or something—and someone caught it, realized what it was and threw it back up onstage."

The story is an L7 moment, one of those incidents that captures the band's spontaneity and reverence for self-expression, but attests even more to what guys have always liked to call "balls." L7 addresses this conundrum— exactly what is the word for whipping it out when the "it" in question isn't a male organ but the most fastidiously hidden secret of femininity, Dracula's teabag itself?—with the song "Fast and Frightening," whose heroine has "got so much clit she don't need no balls." When Sparks hits that line on stage she plays it like just another lyric, and the crowd does, too; in place of the traditional wave-like surge the crowd does more of a lean. It could be that the crowd is there to rock out, and not to get their feminist juices pumping. L7 can't be reduced to the clit factor. There's just too much going on.

What L7 doesn't want to be is a women's band, either in "genre," or in audience. "There was the girl band thing, there was the foxcore farce, there was the Seattle band farce, there was the grunge-rock thing," Sparks says. "We've been around longer than all that stuff. Basically, we're a rock band from Los Angeles."
— "The Magnificent 7" / Renée Crist / July '93

[POLLY JEAN HARVEY]

PJ Harvey's choice of producer, Steve Albini (Nirvana, Pixies), former frontman of Big Black and Rapeman, surprised many.

Synonymous with an ultra-masculine doctrine, Albini would seem to jar with Harvey's intricate, intimate brand of music. Still, *Rid of Me* works—largely because so much of its subtext is Harvey's grappling with masculinity: simultaneously repelled by and impressed with its swagger. The irony of songs about machismo sung by Harvey and filtered through Albini's hard-core aesthetic seems to have escaped them both. In fact, they claim to be the closest of friends, soul-mates. He calls Harvey a genius, and her face lights up with pure delight at the mention of his name. "What did he say about me?" she demands, only half-joking.

Originally, Albini was under-whelmed by PJ Harvey's live sound ("I sort of felt they'd rather be having a bowl of soup than rocking") but agreed to produce the LP because "I thought her guitar playing was cool." He's notorious for his hatred of the human voice, but she convinced him that vocals were important to her, and in turn he wowed her with his studio tricks (like filtering her voice through a guitar amp so that she sounds bound and gagged on songs such as "Hook" and "Yuri-G"). The result is wrench-ing. Albini's production doesn't efface the "feminine" side of Harvey, but it does make her gasp for air.

"We were both equally offended by the way women are treated as if they're incapable of making their own decisions," he told me. When I men-tion this to Harvey, she nods her head, then points out that Albini fell prey to the same syndrome.

"It was funny because, in the studio, Steve found himself treating me like that and he got really angry with himself. I think that made him feel a bit uncomfortable." Which is one explanation for why the

Albini-Harvey relationship worked: *Rid of Me* feeds on discomfort.

Listening to *Rid of Me* the very first time made me think of some-thing Diamanda Galás once said: "Women need to think of themselves as predators rather than pretty." Harvey agrees completely. "I read something the other day about whether all women are prone to liking sado-masochism 'cause of being the penetrated and not the penetrator. Then again, you can look at it from the other point of view where the man might think he gets swallowed whole." Such ambivalences—love-hate, attraction-repulsion, domination-submission—are Harvey's prime terrain, as in the line from "Legs" that goes, "I might as well be dead/ But I could kill you instead." It's pure impulse and adrenaline, like not knowing whether you want to kill your lover or fuck. "I like to feel uncomfortable and not in control because so much of the rest of the time I'm trying to be on top of every-thing. So when you're at a loss like that, that's really exciting." — "Really the Blues" / Joy Press / August '93

197

EXCERPTS CONTINUE ON PAGE 200 >

[SINEAD O'CONNOR tears up a picture of the Pope on *Saturday Night Live*, October 3, 1992]

"As far as I'm concerned, the Church has no right to open its mouth about sex for these reasons: First of all, none of them ever have sex. The second reason is that they *do* have sex."
— Sinead O'Connor, 1991

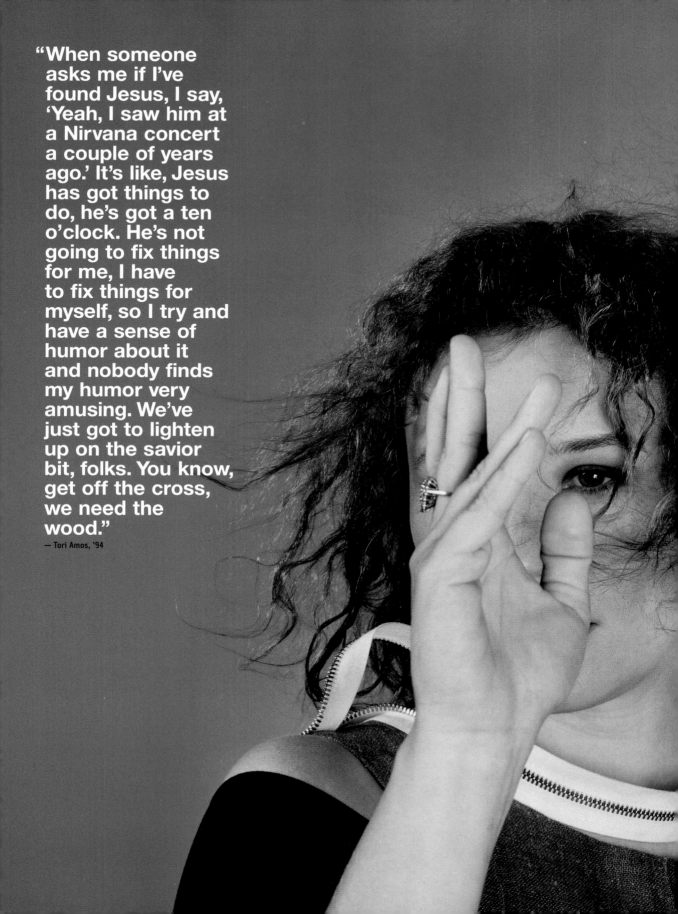

"When someone asks me if I've found Jesus, I say, 'Yeah, I saw him at a Nirvana concert a couple of years ago.' It's like, Jesus has got things to do, he's got a ten o'clock. He's not going to fix things for me, I have to fix things for myself, so I try and have a sense of humor about it and nobody finds my humor very amusing. We've just got to lighten up on the savior bit, folks. You know, get off the cross, we need the wood."

— Tori Amos, '94

[LIZ PHAIR]

Phair wasn't just changing the way the big boys thought about confrontational women with weirdly shaped songs and dirty dictionaries; she was truly changing minds.

Even people who disliked the insular hipster world she came from had to recognize the way *Exile in Guyville* grafted ambition and immediacy. Meanwhile, the gatekeepers of indie-land couldn't just holler: "Sellout!" and exile the record to Main Street. In its way, *Exile* diverted the course of rock culture as much as any other record of the decade. It even incited an almost unbroken series of "Years of the Woman" in the music press.
— "The 90 Greatest Albums of the '90s" / Joshua Clover / September '99

It seems like you've made a massive philosophical change regarding how you want your music to sound. Not really. Maybe I have from your point of view, but to call it my philosophical change would be a misnomer. My music is still just me and my guitar and my piano. I write the songs small, and then you can produce them any way you want. I realize I was closely associated with a certain musical style early on, but I was always at war with the whole indie scene.

What was the war over? I was basically saying, "Fuck all you guys," and they were like, "No, fuck you, Liz Phair," and I was like, "No, fuck you!" That's what *Exile in Guyville* was really about. Everyone in that scene thought I was too suburban and liked mainstream music too much and never cared who was in Green River. All my boyfriends were big music heads, so that's how I acquired good taste in music—but I always liked radio songs. They're all purists in the indie world, and I hate that.

Do you feel haunted by *Exile in Guyville*? Do you feel like that record will define you forever, regardless of whatever else you produce? I used to feel like that. I thought I could never measure up to *Guyville*. I kept trying to make a record as good as that one. I thought about that a lot. But here's the funny thing: In 2000, the rights to *Exile in Guyville* reverted back to me. Someone [at Matador Records] forgot to put it back on the books and lock it up for 30 more years. And suddenly, once I owned it, I felt very differently. I was really glad I made that record, and I no longer felt like I had to make that record again. When I made *Exile*, I was a collegiate art major who had all this brain power and nothing else to do, and I could direct all my energy into one project. I didn't have a job or any responsibilities.

On that first record, it seemed like you were looking for an incredibly complex—and therefore potentially transcendent—romantic relationship. But on the new album, you sing about dating some young, dumb guy who plays videogames all day. I don't need to get my identity from a man anymore. When I was younger, I took my identity from being in love with someone else. And love can be transcendent. But let's face it: I'm a lot older now; I have a kid now. Your priorities change. Everything else just seems like gravy. I mean, I'm glad there's great literature and great art, and I'm glad I was able to contribute to that, if I did. But right now, in my life, I just need to rock.
— "The Exile Factor" / Chuck Klosterman / August '03

At two and a half years, Ellen Amos (she renamed herself Tori when she left home at 21) started playing the upright piano in the living room and jaws dropped.

At four she was doing Mozart and by six the family had moved to Maryland and enrolled her in the Peabody Institute of Johns Hopkins University, one of the country's most prestigious music programs. By age 11, she was rebelling by composing. The Peabody exam board was not receptive, and Amos left.

"The Peabody was at the concert the other night in Baltimore," she says with a grin. "The dean comes up to me and goes, 'I'm so sorry.' But he also says that I wouldn't have the sense of experimentation that I have now if I hadn't left."

For Amos, the conservatory was just another religious dead zone, where complex figures were treated as one-dimensional sacred texts, and the students were reduced to genuflecting geeks.

"The people who play so-called classical music are sterile. The people who wrote it were imbued with life. They were the revolutionaries, and now their music gets played at stinky-cheese parties with expensive wine. It's ridiculous. Debussy is played by people who've cut off their own dicks. Debussy had syphilis—he was very aware he had a dick."

— "Sex, God, and Rock'n'Roll" / Charles Aaron / October '94

There is no shortage of evidence to support the notion that Alanis Morissette is a casualty of the New Age.

In conversation, she speaks frequently of the need for "closure." Of saying or doing things "from a place of love," and of being able to "connect" with people through her music. She has spent time at a nudist colony, an experience she describes as "beautiful." She has sat at the feet of gurus, studied Ashtanga yoga, and traveled to India. She reads self-help books. On tour, before each flight, she makes her crew and band pick out an angel card—little inspirationals that have words such as FAITH and BEAUTY and HOPE on them, which are supposed to be adopted as the bearer's mantra. She meditates. (In a cruel irony, she is allergic to tofu and scented candles.)

Most artists, when asked about musicians they admire, can rattle off a laundry list of names, and it is startling Morissette doesn't. "I would much rather have written a song than heard one," she says casually.

But what would she say to people who accuse her of not understanding rock—who say that you have to understand what came before you in order to be an artist?

"I would say, 'Apparently not.'"
— "Ray of Light" / Kim France / April '99

Kathleen Hanna's transformation from queen of underground punk to electro rabble-rouser began after Bikini Kill ran out of steam in 1998.

She got a sampler, and her music began to change. "I could take a loop that had drums, guitar, bass, everything on it—it was like a band in a box," she says. After a brief stint in North Carolina (moving from Bikini Kill's Olympia, Washington, base), Hanna came to New York City, home to her long-time boyfriend, Beastie Boy Adam "Ad-Rock" Horovitz. She quickly linked up with Johanna Fateman, an artist and writer who'd once given Hanna a copy of her zine, Snarla, at a Bikini Kill show. The pair recruited underground filmmaker Sadie Benning and began producing songs with fuzzy, buzzing riffs, raw beats, and pop flourishes that recalled everything from shoop-shoop '60s girl groups to Public Enemy. Their self-titled 1999 debut sassed director John Cassavetes and then New York City mayor Rudolph Giuliani; it even spawned a popular indie 12-inch, the bubbly pogo jam "Deceptacon," which was remixed by the DFA.

When the band began touring in earnest, Benning was replaced by JD Samson, a Sarah Lawrence student who had previously run the visuals that accompanied Le Tigre live. "I heard her in the van," says Hanna, "and I was like, 'That kid can sing!'" With more sophisticated sonics, the band's second album, Feminist Sweepstakes, laid out Le Tigre's agenda: fun mixed with awareness. "There's such a stereotype of what it means to be a political band," Fateman says. "We wanted to show that there's a full range of ways to express anger, a full range of ways to express feminism, and all these different ways to reach out to the community. It's about celebrating what you have and what you're building." Says Hanna: "We'll go through a phase where we're obsessed with making a song that sounds like ['90s booty smash] 'C'mon N' Ride It (the Train).' Then there's other times where it's like, 'I really want to write about Title IX.'"

Though Le Tigre's subject matter is often weighty—war, sexual harassment, police brutality, clueless journalists—the band throws a party live. "It's important for us to put on a show that wows people," Samson says. They tour with an array of videos as a backdrop—from a teleprompter-like listing of the lyrics to the angrily sardonic "FYR" (i.e., "Fifty Years of Ridicule") to filmmaker Elisabeth Subrin's meditation on desire and office supplies. But the most crowd-pleasing aspect of Le Tigre's stage performance is their seat-of-the-pants choreography—fusing cheerleader poses, Motown spins and slides, and a few nods to slick boy-band moves. "How come these huge acts with big budgets get to have this stuff and we don't?" asks Hanna. "What's wrong with using these same kinds of tools and tweaking them for totally different aims?"

— "Rebels Without a Pause" / Caryn Ganz / October '04

Righteous Babe's offices are located in a six-story terra-cotta building in Buffalo, New York, a beacon of light on a burned-out and largely abandoned Main Street.

Ani DiFranco once considered transplanting the label to Manhattan when it grew too big for the living room of personal manager/label president/close friend Scot Fisher, but decided to keep the imprint in her depressed hometown, where starting a new business "really matters." Righteous Babe relies on only regional industry, and now offers full benefits and profit sharing to eight full-time employees. And in spite of DiFranco's anti-business stance, the label keeps growing—and turning a tidy profit. With minimal overhead and no big marketing or A&R departments eating into the gross, Righteous Babe earns approximately $7.50 on every retail CD sold; $4.25 of that figure goes to DiFranco—more than twice the royalty rate even superstars make. A full quarter of total concert grosses is hers—and we're talking well over 100 sold-out shows a year.

"Ani makes a lot of money, obviously," Fisher says, "but it's not like she takes it and goes on vacation; she goes right back into the studio with it and then it comes back to the company." And the industry insiders who once patronizingly smiled and waited for the self-described "bumbling little folk girl" to come crawling, pen-in-hand, are now convinced she was masterminding her success from the beginning. A&R reps have even taken to citing the poor backwater kids who can't find her records at the local mall as a means of persuading her to sign. "Why," DiFranco counters, "do I have to conquer the world?"

She had worries enough growing up. The latchkey kid of busy professional parents, DiFranco started taking care of herself at an early age. By the time she was nine, she was figuring out Beatles songs on her guitar and hanging out with an older family friend who introduced her to the degenerate musicians of the city's seedier watering holes. A few years later her parents broke up; her mom eventually moved to rural Connecticut. DiFranco stayed in Buffalo alone, and fronted like an emancipated minor at school. She was 15.

"I was a lot like I am now," DiFranco says, "pigheaded and independent—a holy terror." She started dating a 35-year-old loser who knocked her up and left her high and dry at the abortion clinic. A few years after she split for Manhattan, she ran into him again at one of her gigs and finally got to sing the "fuck you" she could never say. "If I look at myself as a teenager now, I just fucking hate the kind of girl I was. You know, spineless and ridiculous and totally manipulable. But I don't take no shit now!"

— "Folk Implosion" / Sia Michel / October '96

: Courtney Love

The girl with the most cake

/ Laura **Sinagra**

Patti Smith once wrote, "In art and dream may you proceed with abandon. In life may you proceed with balance and stealth." Okay great, but what if you can't? In a 1998 SPIN interview, Courtney Love admitted her inability to play that role—the arty earth mother, the shrewd provo-cateur. She confessed "Madonna has said she doesn't have a self-destructive bone in her body. Well, I have several, and I've broken a bunch."

Public self-destruction has been a major component of a Love parade that's included three great records, a rock'n'roll marriage, embattled motherhood, drugs, gun busts, widowhood, Internet rants, plastic surgery, movie stardom, televised flip-outs, record label lawsuits, bar fights, miscarriages, drug busts, fake boobs, custody battles, copyright wrangles, court appearances, overdoses, acupuncture, and ambulances. Along the way it's been hard to tell where her personal life stops and public self begins. Or where her public life ends and her music begins. Or where her real body ends and her plas-ticine one begins. Or what is her blood

and what is straight smack. But ever since she screeched into the '90s lime-light—part feminist avenging angel, part babydoll slut puked from a VC Andrews novel, it's been impossible to set her on the back shelf. And for a generation of rock chicks—like the chainsaw-brandish-ing tykes who emerge from beneath her petticoats in the video for 2004's "Mono" or the exhibitionist vixens of upstart web collective SuicideGirls.com, she arguably remains a tenacious patron saint. Arguably.

In the 14 years between the release of her band Hole's first album, 1991's gutter-grunge *Pretty on the Inside* and her first solo release, 2004's growl-pop *America's Sweetheart*, Courtney Love has lost more friends than most of us will ever make. Regular dust-ups like Love's 1995 slug-ging of riot-grrrl icon Kathleen Hanna and the 2004 mic-stand braining of a fan don't help. Her id-driven instincts have ensured she'd never be as consistent a girl-power spokeswoman as her early fans might've hoped for. Yet there's some-thing exhilarating about the way she performs weakness. Temper, addiction,

insecurity, self-absorption, schaden-freude—turning herself inside-out and making us look.

Tabloid fretting over whether Love was a good wife to canonized Kurt Cobain, a good mom to daughter Frances Bean (custody of whom she lost and regained early in the '00s), a good influence on girls with body-image issues, a "good person"—misses what's to like about Love. We like Love because she's irrational, even pre-rational. A female body in a constant state of interrogation. Only whole when she's in our view, daring us to "take everything." She's nobody's Madonna. Her beauty is needy and grotesque.

Yet we root for this gangsta Moll Flanders, whose public life began when her hippie parents hung with the Grateful Dead and she toddled onto the back cover of *AOXOMOXOA*. For the kid who left Juvee and stripped her way around the Pacific Rim before crashing the Northwest punk scene with only some trashy-guitar riffs and crotch-skimming vintage slips. For the climber who nicked

ESSAY CONTINUES ON NEXT PAGE >

SPIN: HAS PREGNANCY AND MOTHERHOOD AFFECTED YOUR ARTISTIC PERSPECTIVE?

Courtney: What am I supposed to do, turn into fucking Mother Teresa all of a sudden? Am I supposed to write a country record because I had a baby? I've felt more sexual warfare, political, medical, and media terror in the last couple months than I've ever felt in my whole life.

I grew up in alternative families. I grew up in extended families. I grew up living with my therapist and my step-brother and my mother's ex-lover and on and on and I just think it sucks. This is just a personal preference. I think when you get married, it should be forever. Even though I did get married once and it was annulled, I don't know. For myself, I just want to have kids by the same person and stay with the same person.

SPIN: YOU SOUND LIKE PHYLLIS SCHLAFLY.

Courtney: I'm sorry. I almost came out Republican the way I was raised. I mean, I was raised by white trash that considered themselves hippies. But to me, a mom and dad is a really important thing to have.

— "Family Values"/ Jonathan Poneman / December '92

her "kinderwhore" look from former pal Babes in Toyland's Kat Bjelland and marched sexuality straight back to the sandbox. *Pretty on the Inside* was ugly all over (though when Courtney met Kurt, her record was outselling Nirvana's *Bleach*). Hole's "Teenage Whore" might have lacked the tilt-o-whirl melody of Nirvana's "About a Girl," but its sludgy candor made it plain that for some women, grunge was not enough.

Love's courtship with Cobain (they married in '92) was grittily romantic, sure, but it doubled as a flip-off to the morality set—a Yoko and Lennon-like defense of freak marriage. In a knocked-up blur, they sullied the sacrament—she in Frances Farmer's dress, he in his jammies, or vice-versa—then proceeded to live happily never after in a bunaglow full of the gallows humor, gunplay, and hothouse scribblings that fueled two of the decade's best albums. If Courtney's husband was her co-brain, she seems to have been his as well: Cobain once told SPIN that if he could get his wife to publish her poetry it would "change the world."

From the lyrics on *In Utero* and *Live Through This*, we know that the two shared an obsession with the body. They agonized over what it is to be human, to feel, to breed, to bleed, to lactate and feed. What oozed out were verses that could be taught right along with Luce Irigaray or Sylvia Plath. When Love wrote lyrics like those for "Plump" ("I don't do the dishes/ I throw them in the crib"), she was swatting off gender assumptions that alighted like riled bees. In moments of fuzzier judgment, that instinct would lead to things like, as *Vanity Fair* reported, shooting up with a little stowaway in utero.

In the days after Jesus took Love's husband for a sunbeam, *Live Through This* opened like a wound. "Miss World" gnashed, "Jennifer's Body" drew and quartered, and "Violet" cooked its petals down to a shot. In a scourging display of hypertextual grief, Love stood before weeping masses like a Robert Browning orator, reading Cobain's suicide note aloud and inserting eviscerating responses—enacting a bitter pageant of their tumultuous domestic life. After his death and the overdose of Hole bassist Kristen Pfaff, Love self-immolated on stages real and virtual. As usual, she stumbled to the edge of propriety and convulsed over it.

During this tummult, guitarist Eric Erlandson and drummer Patty Schemel stuck with her. She recruited bassist Melissa Auf Der Maur to replace Pfaff. But though *Live Through This* topped 1994's critics polls and went platinum, Love wasn't universally loved. In fact, lots in the Kurt cult accused her of mental torment or worse. Love trolled Usenet groups like an unleashed Mozilla, engaging each venomous dis, challenging anyone who believed claims—some fueled by her own estranged father (see the Nick Broomfield doc *Kurt & Courtney*)—that she was culpable in Kurt's death.

But even as she burned, she rose. Love's macabre Hollywood-starlet phase began after her promising showing as a porno floozy in *The People Vs. Larry Flynt*. Showing up like an airbrushed version of her former self at premiere after premiere, she pushed past her physical limits again. New face, new breasts, new pout. Punk fans felt betrayed by this carnival swan, trussed and plucked, opened up, cut and defined. But what did we expect?

Her next record, *Celebrity Skin*, explored Californication with a slick new exhaustion. Even through the professional pop sheen attributed to the collaborative efforts of former lover Billy Corgan, Courtney was giving it to us raw—dishing about a life spent waking up in her make-up, prematurely used up. Still the troubled child, voice breaking like the waves on "Malibu." It all made sense. But of course, as she tried to fit in (see her oddly robotic Versace spread), she continued to reveal "good taste" for the prison it is.

After years of bad publicity—Oxycontin overdoses; legal quibbling with former Nirvana members; smashing her ex-boyfriend's windows; flashing a hapless David Letterman; suckling a random dude at McDonald's—the star-crossed *America's Sweetheart* finally came out in 2004, containing more good songs than it ought to, and more unsparing lyrics about pills, porn, and getting old. We like Love because she's not afraid to bug God for "one more song/ so I can prove to you that I'm so much better than him." We like her because she asks her man point blank, "were you jerkin' off to her or were you jerkin' off to me?" In a world that hates women for aging, for trying to stay young, for being pure, for being sexual, for being beautiful, for being ugly, she continues to scream, "I paid good money not to be ignored!"

Courtney Love is the modern girl's most reliable unreliable narrator, rushing in where her fan-girl devotees might more fearfully tread, tracking her dirt from the underground to the red carpet. Some days, we ache like she aches, but we'll never live that ache with as much abandon.

Kurt Cobain's suicide note had been broadcast to this ecstatic crowd of mourners in Seattle's Flag Pavilion a half-hour earlier via a powerful, obscenity-laced statement read by a weeping Courtney Love, who characterized the note as "a letter to the fuckin' editor." It read, in part, "I feel guilty beyond years that the manic roar of the crowd doesn't affect me as much as it did Freddie Mercury. Sometimes I feel as if I should have a punch-in time clock before I walk out onstage. I've tried everything to appreciate it and I do. God, believe me, I do…thank you from the pit of my burning nauseous stomach for your concern and your letters during the last years."

Love interrupted her reading several times to cast asides at Cobain's comments, calling him an "asshole" (a word she asked the crowd to repeat, which they did), a "fucker," a "sad, sensitive, unappreciative Pisces-Jesus man," and the note itself "bullshit." "The fact is I can't fool you," Cobain wrote, "any one of you. The worst crime is faking it." Love, in a voice soaked with tears, replied, "No, the worst crime is leaving."
— "Into the Black" / Gina Arnold / June '94

"Imagine this: You're peaking. At the prime of your life… You've finally met somebody of the opposite gender who you can write with. That's never happened before in your life. And you're in love, you have a best friend, you have a soul-fucking-mate, and you can't believe it's happening in your lifetime. *And* as a bonus he's beautiful. *And* he's rich. *And* he's a hot rock star to boot. *And* he's the best fuck that ever walked. *And* he wants to have babies… *And* he understands everything you say. *And* he completes your sentences… and he's not embarrassed about praying, he's not embarrassed about chanting, he's not embarrassed about God, Jesus, none of it… And there's even room for you to fix him, which you like, 'cause you're a fixer-upper. He's perfect in almost every fucking way. The only fucking happiness that I ever had. And then it all gets taken away…"
— Courtney Love, 1995

Pale arms outstretched, offering herself up for crucifixion, or a pie in the face, or a big hug, Courtney Love exclaimed, "Fuck with me, fuck with me, it's the only thing I like!" The audience members, who had been standing in a snaking, endless line with visions of headliner Trent Reznor moshing in their dyed-black dread heads, murmured. A few hoots. A desultory heckle. We were only three songs into Hole's first American show since the suicide of Love's husband, Kurt Cobain, and since the heroin overdose of bassist Kristen Pfaff; the band's first gig as opening act for Nine Inch Nails' sold-out, post-Woodstock tour, and already the ride was getting bumpy.

Nobody wanted to play Love's co-dependent game of "I'm rubber, you're glue, fuck you." The few Hole fans—high school girls huddled together to the right of the mosh pit—were simply awestruck. Everybody else acted like the band's appearance must be a gesture of mercy. Few seemed familiar with the album *Live*

Through This. And the setting, a concrete outdoor amphitheater in a riverfront development mallplex, only further deadened the atmosphere. There was no moment of silence for Kurt, as there had been at Lollapalooza in Philadelphia. Just silent curiosity as Love sauntered onstage, wearing a black car-coat and carrying a small black handbag. Hole immediately roared into "Beautiful Son," a punk rant about how Cobain looked good in a dress, and how moms are the biggest starfuckers. Mid-song, Love quit playing guitar and took off her coat with a flourish, revealing a gray, clingy top, gray minidress, and gray stockings that stopped mid-thigh. The band lurched a bit, but her voice quickly regained its raging wail and the high-school girls pogoed madly.

Unfortunately, it turned out to be a promising opening to a sordidly sad B-movie. After the feedback subsided, Love nervously blurted out, "You know, I punched a guy on the plane." The crowd tittered, confused. Love wandered away from the mic. "Miss World" was a tentative, raggedy mess, and when she changed the coda from, "I am the girl you know/ Can't look you in the eye" to "I am the girl you want/ So sick that I'll just die," it was obvious that she was

not just nerve-wracked, but wracked in general. Playing so little that the soundman eventually turned her down and cranked up impassive guitarist Eric Erlandson, Love looked totally lost. She frantically took off her stockings during "Jennifer's Body," and after "Asking for It," cried out pitifully, "Where are my boots?" With neither Erlandson nor new bassist Melissa Auf Der Maur, a timid 22-year-old from Montreal, able to take up the slack, Hole came off like a skinny-tie bar band fronted by Nancy Spungen.

The crowd got increasingly impatient, but Love staggered on. "So, you guys wanna talk to me for awhile? Trent'll be out here in a minute with his black rubber, so why don't you guys just talk to me, go ahead." Waiting for a tragicomic rimshot, she added, "How many of you have read *Valley of the Dolls*?" A guy yelled, "I wanna fuck you, Courtney!" She shot back, "I wanna fuck you, too, but only if you're a water sign." The band jerked into "Gutless," with Love barely struggling through the first verse before the chorus overran her. Then, without a word, she put down her guitar, yanked up her top, and began to pose in her black bra. As the crowd looked on, stunned, she tore off the bra, thrust out her chest, and slurred, "Now you know why I get all the guys, you fucking shitbags." The Trent teens were too flabbergasted to catcall. And there she stood, for what seemed like an eternity—a voluptuous car wreck, a pathetic fuck-doll, a body to die for. It was like watching your sister strip at a stag party. From then on, the show was a long, painful non-sequitur. "I just got offered the Guess? Jeans campaign.... That's so retarded, those stupid pants." Later, as if gazing at the ghost of Kurt hovering above the audience, she said: "I give you a morning blow job, I make your fucking breakfast, so leave me alone."

As "Softer, Softest" fell apart, she reverted almost completely to her stripper days, sticking out her belly and writhing in spazzy circles. Threatening to play Echo & the Bunnymen covers, she cracked, "So, do you guys think Trent is a top or a bottom?" During "Doll Parts," after moaning, "He only loves those things because he loves to see me break" (instead of "them"), she wobbled back from the mic almost punch-drunk. It was horrific and mesmerizing. By this time, the band had bailed, and Love was alone, strumming slower and slower, singing "Someday you will ache like I ache," again and again, her voice a faint sob. Roadies milled around. She finally took off her guitar, stumbled over to a huge speaker, and leaned into it like she was going to pass out. Then, while being led off by an assistant, she stepped back, pulled up her top one last time, and flipped us off with both hands. A guy with a video camera zoomed it. A kid near me yelled, "That's why they call you a whore!" His friends, guys and girls, giggled sheepishly.

If you cared at all, it was devastating. And there was nobody with whom to share your dismay, just a lot of oblivious zitfaces waiting around for Nine Inch Nails to erase Love's tits and pathos with their precisely packaged anguish. I thought about what I'd say to her if I had the gall to get angry. Melodramatic junk like: Jesus, Courtney! What? What?! Do you want us to feel every single fucking wince of your pain on every single fucking song to the point that we don't even remember which is which anymore? Do you want us to have nightmares about pulling you off ledges weeping and naked, and staring into your eyes and seeing our own? Do you want all your reviews to read like half-assed scripts for a punk-rock *A Star is Born*? Is too much sadness never enough?

But melodrama is a luxury most of us don't have. And besides, maybe we do want Love to stick her ring finger in our mouths so we can suck her dry. I hope there's more to it than that. But right now I am not so sure.

— review of Hole, Nautica Stage, Cleveland, Ohio, August 29, 1994 / Charles Aaron / November '94

Courtney, you made a really good album.

But because it was released only days after Kurt Cobain blew his head off, *Live Through This* has never been heard as just another piece of music. Courtney Love, his wife and mistress, accused hanger-on and contributor to his delinquency, was too controversial for that and wrapped that controversy too tightly into her art. "I was a lot more misanthropic when I wrote *Live Through This*," she says. "My marriage gave me a bunker mentality. Going back to Seattle recently, I was thinking: Pretty city. Too bad I never saw any of it."

— "The 90 Greatest Albums of the '90s" / Eric Weisbard / October '99

"Kurt Loder interviewed me after the MTV [Video Music] Awards, after I won some award, and I was sitting up on a platform on the street. About five minutes into the interview, a compact went sailing over my head. I thought someone on the street was throwing things at me. And I hear this gravelly voice, and then we looked down and it's Courtney, and she's throwing makeup out of her purse at us, and it's just missing our heads. And Kurt invites her up.

"Now, I know Kurt invited her up because there's all this hyped-up bullshit how we have been feuding for years and years, and I think he wanted to see a catfight. She was babbling about 25 different things. And at one point, she did grab my arm and said something to me like ''94 sucked, but '95's going to be better, isn't it?' And in that one moment I looked in her eyes and felt her vulnerability and her sadness and I felt bad for her. I felt that she was trying to reach out to me, even though at every chance she gets, she slags me off in the press. Years ago, she probably admired me and looked up to me, and now I'm like a parent to her or something, and she wants to destroy me."

— Madonna, 1995

COURTNEY LOVE WAS TALKING ABOUT THE VICE PRESIDENT. "He goes, 'I'm a really big fan,' and I was like, 'Yeah, right. Name a song, Al.' 'I can't name a song, I'm just a really big fan.'"

"You said that?"

"Yeah. I went to this big fancy producer's house. There were about 14 of us invited to dinner with Al Gore. I'm sitting next to this guy who's like Gore's Stephanopoulos, and I said, 'Why am I here?' Because the only other famous person there was Kevin Costner. He said, 'We've done our research and we want your vote,' and I was just so proud. There are pictures of it. Edward has them. For some reason I looked really wholesome that night, and when the pictures got developed, it's like me and Al, and we're dancing a little and we're fighting. I was throwing my hands at him. And I brought them up to my mother-in-law at Christmas and framed one for her. I was really impressed, which happens very rarely."

Love drew another French cigarette out of the pack on the kidney-shape table. Edward was Edward Norton, the actor with whom she's been linked romantically.

I asked why *Celebrity Skin* took four years.

She said; "Someone dies [Cobain]. Have a child.

Someone dies [bassist Kristen Pfaff]. Do a major movie. Oh, by the way, stop putting things into your body that you've been putting in for, oh, a decade. Umm, gee, I don't know, is that four years? I think that's about four years of your life."

Love had said there was a personal subtext in some of the songs, but she was unwilling to decode the messages. "I won't talk about it because it's none of your business," she said simply. "Because you will never know."

"Right now we're talking about the death of your husband?"

"Or whatever, specifically, all of that shit—you will never know what that was like. And you will never know what that person was really like. And you will never ever ever know the personal truth of that relationship. And I will never exploit it for you. So that's all I have to say about it, you know, and in the beginning, somebody should have locked me in my fucking room for a year."

"But was it helpful to you?" I asked.

She stopped short. "The truth is, it was."

"So why are you lacerating yourself?"

"You're right, it was cathartic, but I think people really took advantage of it. Let me tell you, I gave some of the most amazing performances that people have ever seen, they'll never see stuff like that again. It was like opera."

— "The Love Issue" / Philip Weiss / October '98

AFTER HER HOWARD STERN APPEARANCE, COURTNEY LOVE HIT A PARTY AT DOWNTOWN CLUB LOTUS, WHERE SHE FLASHED A PAIR OF SEX PISTOLS PANTIES FOR THE PAPARAZZI. The next day, Love lost her knickers entirely after invading MTV's midtown studios to control MTV2's programming for 24 hours. Eyewitnesses watched in amazement as she stalked the hallways full starkers, making sure her requirements were met by the network's shell-shocked staff.

— "Backstage Pass" / Marc Spitz / December '02

Courtney Love is no healer— of herself or anyone else. And that's why, despite the nose job, the boob lift, designer gowns, and kissy-poo swanning down red carpets, she's no pop star. She's incapable of telling us that everything's gonna be all right. But when it comes to testifying to how everything's totally, unbearably, exhilaratingly fucked-up beyond repair, she has few peers. And that's why she's a *rock* star.

— review of *America's Sweetheart* / Charles Aaron / March '04

/ Doug **Brod**

: Britpop

Champagne supernovas

[OASIS]

On April 8, 1994,

the day Kurt Cobain's body was discovered at his Seattle home, Take That's "Everything Changes" was the number 1 single on the U.K. charts. Before you read that juxtaposition as cosmic, stop. But strictly in terms of British pop music, perhaps it all did change. At that moment, the prefab pretty boys in Take That were the biggest-selling group in England since the Beatles. And another quintet with a more apparent connection to the Fab Four would soon lead a creative and commercial renaissance the U.K. hadn't seen in decades.

But let's not get ahead of ourselves. In the early '90s, grunge's international currency was enormous. That didn't mean bands across the Atlantic wanted to replicate the sound of hirsute stoners from the woodsy Pacific Northwest (though London-bred Bush had a nice go at it). Instead, a Britain burnt out on nearly two decades of Conservative rule

and stinging from the scotched potential of Happy Mondays and the Stone Roses—whose five-years-in-the-making sophomore album was DOA a few months after Cobain—incubated bands that rejected the vulgar Americanization they saw encroaching on their lives, and that were eager to fill the vacuum (at home, at least) left by Cobain's suicide.

Roused, perhaps, by Ecstasy-fuelled enlightenment, a new community of maverick artists and writers, including Damien Hirst and Irvine Welsh, became figurative rock stars. And groups like Suede, Blur, Pulp, and Elastica shared much more than just mononyms; harking back to native sons David Bowie, the Jam, and the Smiths (and in Elastica's case, brazenly ripping riffs from Wire and the Stranglers), they captured the pop charts with music that both celebrated and criticized what it meant to be British in an increasingly co-opted culture.

The shuffling dance grooves and euphoric melodies on *Leisure*, the 1991 debut album by Blur, didn't leap onto the Mondays' and Roses' rave-era bandwagon so much as futilely chase after it on a Vespa. But by their second album, *Modern Life Is Rubbish*, the art-schoolers revealed a deepening affinity for both '60s mod style and XTC, which bloomed on their 1994 masterpiece, *Parklife*—a playful yet withering dissection of drab middle-class existence, shot through with a Kinks-like vividness.

Pulp, on the other hand, had drifted in relative obscurity for 15 years before '94's *His'n'Hers* made a household name out of singer Jarvis Cocker, whose louche delivery of frequently horny narratives over glammy dance-rock grooves finally found an audience beyond pimply students who never left their bedrooms. It's fitting, then, that Pulp's biggest single was called "Common People."

But if Britpop had a face for the rest of the world, that face was crowned with a foot-long eyebrow. With '94's *Definitely Maybe*, Oasis—Noel and Liam Gallagher and what was essentially their backing band— arrived fully formed, lacking any of their peers' arty pretensions. An inordinately tuneful (for a while at

least) and loutish crew, they looked to the Beatles for inspiration and, most important, saw classic rock as an idiom, not a vintage. They didn't aspire to be bigger than Jesus; they were already convinced they were godlike. By turns sneering and soothing, Liam's power-whine put across his brother's swaggering stadium rock with conviction despite Noel's insistence that the booze- and drug-drenched lyrics were essentially meaningless. But it was exactly the catchy vagueness of songs like "Champagne Supernova" and "Wonderwall" (whose title is an obscure George Harrison reference—cheeky bastards) that made the band Britpop's biggest export: In 1996, they sold 18 million albums.

Unlike the scene's other stars, Oasis blew up everywhere precisely because their songs sounded like they could've come from anywhere—even if, for an early American MTV interview, the brothers required subtitles. Working-class hooligans from hardscrabble Manchester, the Gallaghers embraced all of the rock clichés their quick ascendancy enabled: the gossip-page dustups, the rolled-up hundreds in chic toilet stalls, the actress/groupie first wife, the shit third album. They were more than happy to play the assholes in anoraks for a citizenry that finally had another world-conquering band of its own. Meanwhile, their chart rivalry with Blur resembled class warfare; tensions between the bands became so ugly, at one point Noel wished AIDS upon Blur's Damon Albarn and Alex James.

While Britpop's mid-'90s Golden Age continued to spew forth scores of bands of varying quality—Menswear, Supergrass, the Boo Radleys, Sleeper, and the Verve among them—few made a dent overseas. Prime Minister Tony Blair's Labour Party victory in '97 ended up doing little to erase the notion of England as the 51st State, signaling yet another shift in the pop firmament. That year, the previously Anglo-centric Blur released an album influenced by—*shock, horror*—Americans (that would be Pavement). By 1999, Take That's Robbie Williams had become the biggest music star in the U.K. Five years later, Ringo Starr's son was drumming for Oasis.

Everything changes indeed.

Essential Britpop

The swish and the swagger, the glamour and the gloom, the setting imperial sun glowing through your ninth pint of Harp. British rock in the '90s offered an endless supply of star-crossed fops, dance-pop cads, and ax-slinging ironists.

PRIMAL SCREAM *Screamadelica* (Sire, 1991)
Stones-obsessed longhairs enlist acid-house DJ Andrew Weatherall to produce their third album, and he turns their music inside out. Singer Bobby Gillespie finds in techno what he could never get from rock: a bass line that'll get him to the church on time. **Classic song:** "Loaded"—a sample of young easy rider Peter Fonda gets the party started, and reggae horns keep it going all night long.

SUEDE *Suede* (Nude/Columbia, 1993)
The distortion-pedal swirl of early-'90s dream pop meets the polymorphous perversity of glitter-rock giants T. Rex. Singer Brett Anderson does things with his larynx that you can't show on the Spice channel, and guitarist Bernard Butler gets dirty with the ghost of Bowie guitarist Mick Ronson. **Classic song:** "Sleeping Pills," a sweeping ode to Valium and astrology that Interpol should cover immediately.

BLUR *Parklife* (Food/SBK, 1994)
In the tradition of early Kinks and Martin Amis' corrosive novel *London Fields*, this affectionate-in-spite-of-itself song cycle about the quiet desperation of the British middle class is full of so many dart-sharp hooks it's ridiculous. **Classic song:** "Girls & Boys," a synth-charged disco-punk jam about vacation sex—remember, it doesn't count if you're in Greece. **Also try:** *Blur* (Food/Virgin 1997) Burned out after a protracted feud with Oasis, the band soothe their art-student souls with weed and Pavement and accidentally write a perfect punk single, "Song 2." Woo-hoo!

PULP *Different Class* (Island, 1995)
Twelve poison-pen antianthems about how the presence of slumming rich kids can totally ruin your favorite dive bar, by Jarvis Cocker, the Britpop songwriter with the sharpest quill. **Classic song:** "Disco 2000," a love song—possibly sung by a stalker—set to a melody borrowed from the Clash's anticapitalist folk tale "Lost in the Supermarket."

ELASTICA *Elastica* (DGC, 1995)
Elastica hooked Blondie's sex appeal to skinny-tie guitar snarls lifted from old punks like Wire and the Stranglers. Wire and the Stranglers both threatened to sue, which only confirms this record's greatness—riff-lifters of the world, unite! **Classic song:** "Stutter"—singer Justine Frischmann cuts a lager-addled suitor off at the knees with little more than a sneer and a bored hair flip.

THE VERVE *A Northern Soul* (Vernon Yard/Virgin, 1995)
Their follow-up, *Urban Hymns*, had "Bitter Sweet Symphony," the hit that launched a thousand sports-highlight montages. But this one's even bitter-sweeter: a psych-rock comforter for those who've stayed up too long or come down too hard. **Classic song:** "On Your Own"—singer Richard Ashcroft turns the trudge home from the bar into a metaphor for existential crisis.

OASIS *[What's the Story] Morning Glory?* (Epic, 1995)
Noel Gallagher composes mammoth glam-Beatles hooks and lyrics that mean fuck-all ("Some might say that sunshine follows thunder / Go and tell it to the man who cannot shine"). His brother Liam sings them like they mean every-thing. **Classic song:** The epic cokehead rant "Morning Glory"—sneering deliri-um worthy of Johnny Rotten, borne aloft on a towering inferno of guitar.

SUPERGRASS *I Should Coco* (Capitol, 1995)
This trio of Hair Bear Bunch look-alikes may be the Britpop era's most under-rated band, and this hyper-catchy tune blitz is their greatest achievement: rapturous odes to teenage lust and cut-price drugs, played reallyreallyfast, as if Scotland Yard were about to kick down the door of their clubhouse. **Classic song:** "Sitting Up Straight"—the sound of fresh-faced juvenile delinquents bum-rushing the toy shop on pogo sticks.

RADIOHEAD *The Bends* (Capitol, 1995)
In Cobain-worthy metaphors, Thom Yorke makes his alienation skin-crawlingly physical—IV drips and iron lungs, blood and ash, bones and teeth—while Jonny Greenwood builds a labyrinth of beguiling art-rock guitar. It's the last Radiohead record that remotely counts as Britpop; from here on, it got compli-cated. **Classic song:** "Just," for Greenwood's crazy Sonic Youth–funk solo, a reminder of how much this band sacrificed when they decided guitars were evil.

COLDPLAY *Parachutes* (Nettwerk/Capitol, 2000)
Anyone who derides them for being a more straight-ahead Radiohead is missing the point. While singer/hopeless romantic Chris Martin sometimes brings more sap to the table than Mrs. Butterworth, there's something awe-inspiring about the way Coldplay harness a decade's worth of British guitar-rock innovation to silly love songs. **Classic song:** "Yellow"—what the Lloyd Doblers of Y2K rocked in their boomboxes.

— Alex Pappademas / February '03

7

Top seven sterling quotes from Oasis' Gallagher brothers:

1
"I'm the singer, and the only personal lyric I'm singing is 'I've got a 12-inch cock—d'ya want some?'" **Liam**

2
"There are shitloads of mean-ing in the songs. I don't know what they mean, but there's still meaning there." **Liam**

3
"I've only got one thing to say: 'sausages.'" **Liam, accepting a Brit Award in 1996**

4
"At the end of the day, you can go to a Radiohead show and stroke your fucking beard and watch the fucking cunt complaining, or come see us, put your arms around your best mate, and have it." **Liam**

5
"Shoes excite me. Lager excites me. America excites me. Stools excite me. Everything excites me. I'm just one excited young man." **Liam**

6
"The thing that still pisses me off to this day is that cunt fuck said we engineered the battle with his bunch of wankers. Oasis don't need to compete with a bunch of cunts." **Noel, on Blur's Damon Albarn**

7
"Call us arrogant if you want, I don't care. Just as long as we don't get called Aerosmith." **Noel**

— "Ultimate List Issue" / April '03

[BLUR]

[OASIS]

Last August, when cheeky Blur frontman Damon Albarn pushed forward the release date of his band's single, "Country House," to clash with the unveiling of Oasis' "Roll With It," England was gripped by a pop duel the likes of which had not been enjoyed since the swinging '60s.

Like the Scouser Beatles versus the genteel London Stones, the confrontation pitted North against South in a Top of the Pops class war: Blur, middle-class London scenesters, vs. Oasis, council-estate Northern dole boys. The headline-hungry media dubbed the August 14 chart scramble "The Battle of Britpop." The BBC ran the story on its *Six O'clock News*. And when both bands unknowingly booked gigs across the street from each other on the same night in September, the police were forced to step in to prevent a mods-against-rockers *Quadrophenia*-style rumble.

The Brits like their bands packaged with attitude, and these two have excelled in cultivating reputations for obnoxious inter-band brawling. Blur had already reclaimed the title "Darlings of the British Press" from the deposed Suede when Oasis, five Mancunian hardheads intent on being the next Beatles, began to make inroads on pop's consciousness and charts. The Fab Five's 1994 album *Definitely Maybe* became the fastest-selling debut in British history. Suddenly Blur were up against real contenders. Tales of drunken run-ins in London pubs and clubs mounted, much to the delight of the press. In January, at the 1995 NME Brat Awards, Oasis' Liam Gallagher refused to pose for a photograph with Albarn, saying, "Your band's full of shit. Right. So I'm not going to do a photo with ya." Sometime during the recording of Blur's fourth album *The Great Escape*, and Oasis's second album *(What's the Story) Morning Glory*, the uncivil war turned downright dirty. Liam confessed to being "mad for" Damon's girlfriend. Blur's Alex James claimed, "He fancies me, that Liam." And Oasis' Noel Gallagher outraged just about everybody by mouthing off to a British newspaper that he hoped Blur's bassist and frontman would "catch AIDS and die." (He later apologized for the statement.)

The AIDS blunder might destine Oasis to loser status in the Battle for Blighty, but this pop war is not over. The Blur-Oasis soap opera has now moved Stateside to an audience that cares less for bratty behavior than a good beat. If the master plan is world domination—and bands this cocky could settle for nothing less—it's the battle for America that counts.
— "Take That!" / Sarah Pratt / January '96

Sure, Elastica sound like Wire, if Wire were horny tomboys hopped up on too much TV and curry.

And yeah, they sound like Blondie, if Debbie Harry ever made dirty-white-girl noises on a guitar. Led by singer-songwriters Justine Frischmann and Donna Matthews, Elastica was the most tuneful of the "Britpop Invasion" bands. And their debut album, 16 spurts of unrequited lust, featured cheeky dating rejoinders such as "Is there something you lack/ When I'm flat on my back?"
— "20 Best Albums of '95" / Charles Aaron / January '96

I ask how New York has been treating Oasis frontman Liam Gallagher since he arrived last night.

"Fucking great! New York people are fuck-king rrrocking!" He rolls the "r" like Tony the Tiger in the Frosted Flakes commercial. He continues: "Got into town last night and saw Radiohead. Boring bunch of fuck-king stoodents, I'll kick their fuckn' heads in, man, because they're dicks." His accent is swampy, the aura equivalent of lots of weird twisted trees rising out of a bog.

"I liked your new record quite a bit," I say.

"You liked it quite a bit?" replies Liam incredulously. "What do you mean you liked it *quite a bit*?" Suddenly enraged, he stands up and heads for the door. "See ya later, man." He looks at Danny the bodyguard, who is nervously hoisting his girth off the couch. Reaching the doorway, Liam turns and shouts, "You've got big fucking hands, man, but I'll knee you in the *balls*, man! Whaddya mean you liked it quite a bit? It's tops, man. Tops!"
— "Among the Thugs" / Thomas Beller / October '97

Chris Martin's bandmates are accustomed to his self-criticism.

"That's who he is, I'm afraid," bassist Guy Berryman says. "I think it stems from our British build-'em-up-cut-'em-down mentality. Once you're established in Britain, you become kind of uncool. But it's not such a bad thing to think everyone hates you. It makes you work harder."
— "Band of the Year: Coldplay" / Tracey Pepper / January '04

What do the hip-hop nation and the self-proclaimed biggest rock band in the world have in common? If you said platinum records, N.W.A samples, and a penchant for superfluous helicopters, you'd be right. But those are just a few of the similarities between the two. Check it:

> **Old School Fashion:** With their Kangols, windbreakers, Fred Perry shirts that recall early '80s Izods, and two-piece Adidas track suits, the Gallagher boys could pass for *Beat Street* extras.

> **Pro Sports Team Obsession:** Oasis devote themselves to the Manchester City football club with a passion that matches, if not surpasses, any love Ice Cube ever felt for the L. A. Raiders. And, like Puffy Combs, they've got the logoed gear to prove it.

> **Video Vision:** The video for Oasis' single, "D'You Know What I Mean?" (basically a laddish translation of the hip-hop colloquialism, "Y'know I'm sayin'?") features a swarm of helicopters, just like nearly ever Hype Williams production (see Mary J. Blige's "Everything").

> **Posses/Rivalries:** Oasis have taken to rolling with an entourage (including Johnny Depp, Kate Moss, and several burly guitar techs/bodyguards) that would impress Suge Knight. This provides menacing backup for the band's very public feuds with fellow Britpoppers Blur, and more recently, the shoegazing outfit Hurricane #1.

> **Suspect Boasts:** In his book, *The Science of Rap*, KRS-One instructed would-be rappers to "feel free to speak highly of yourself." The Gallagher brothers understand: When asked if he thought Oasis were more important to the youth of today than God, Noel responded, "Without a shadow of a doubt that is true."

> **Drugs/Scraps With the Law:** When it comes to outspoken public support of illegal narcotics, Oasis are the Cypress Hill of the U.K. Noel recently told the British press he thinks the British Parliament is a "bunch of hypocrites" for keeping marijuana illegal. Liam, always more direct, was arrested for possession of cocaine, twice.

— "On the Anglo Tip: Why Oasis Are More Hip-Hop Than Britpop" / Zev Borow / November '97

: **Radiohead**

The Dark Side of the Moon

/ Will **Hermes**

The other day
I sat in an ice cream parlor
listening to *OK Computer.*

The counter guy plays it not because he knows I like it (although I am a regular) but because it's a good record to hear in an ice cream parlor, full of frosty guitars and bell tones, hymn-style vocals and swirling melodies that never seem old or played-out. In a word, it is Comforting. And that's strange, because you don't expect a record about paranoia and panic and vomit and noises in your head, about voodoo economics and being pulled from an aircrash to be *comforting*. Let alone to be the defining rock album of the last 20 years. If Nirvana's *Nevermind* was the most visceral howl of the new Age of Anxiety, *OK Computer* demonstrated how one might actually survive it. A set of seductive rants positing a life during perpetual wartime, it only sounds more current with each passing year.

Radiohead had an unpromising beginning, which included a semi-dorky name (though it improved on their early moniker, On a Friday). They came together at a private boy's school near the English town of Oxford, revering the Pixies and R.E.M., evolving alongside the shoe-gaze dream-pop of Ride and Lush and the Britpop of Oasis and Blur but removed from any scene. They beat their peers to the bank in 1993 with a huge American hit, "Creep." But against a magnificently bombastic melody and a backdrop of MTV hype, its tangle of sarcasm and self-abuse read mainly as bellyaching, an alt-rock "Poor Poor Pitiful Me" minus the wink. And the album it came from, *Pablo Honey*, didn't suggest the band deserved much beyond its allotted 120 minutes of fame.

By 1995's *The Bends*, Radiohead was chafing against the bit; singer Thom Yorke was even cursing out moshers from the stage. It's on this album, against Jonny Greenwood's searing guitar blasts and shimmering keyboards, that Yorke's voice blooms into an instrument that could bring manly-men to their knees. Its

greatness flickers on songs like "Just," (with echoes of then-chart-rulers Nirvana) and "Bones" (with echoes of R.E.M.), and it comes into itself on the high notes of the fame-doubting "High and Dry." But it's on "Fake Plastic Trees" where everything the band would soon master falls into place: The perfumed high-romanticism, the art-rock drama, the suburban computer-age dread. Not since *The Graduate* had petroleum-based polymers so heartbreakingly summed up everything wrong with the grown-up world.

OK Computer expanded the vibe of "Fake Plastic Trees" into an oblique rock opera whose existential hero was Yorke: a small man with a lazy eye, a scary temper, and a longstanding love of Queen who clearly took a lot of shit as a kid. "No Surprises"—a ballad in which a guy longs for a security that sounds like death over a lullaby melody built around two chiming notes—is that record's "Trees." Like the band's best songs, it builds and crests, settles and builds again, not unlike techno in its ebb and flow, or European classical in its theme and variation, though it apes neither. Against this swell of guitar strings and bell tones are lyrics of absolutely unsentimental darkness— "a job that kills you," "bruises that wont heal," and the timeless "bring down the government...they don't speak for us," all delivered in the voice of a fallen choir boy who's found another way to deliver his prayers. *OK Computer* became a generation's *Dark Side Of The Moon*: great for smoking weed and pondering Life's big questions, or simply basking in the sonic majesty of it all.

OK Computer brought the band a squirm-inducing level of fame (see *Meeting People Is Easy*, a "tour video" reimagined as a Beckett play), and any rote followup would seem pale imitation and/or add fuel to the purgatorial fire. So, for a band whose schtick involved a fear

of being consumed by technology, tossing themselves into a blender of avant-techno digital processing on *Kid A* made perfect sense—especially since rock aesthetes at the time were all coveting designer drugs and obscure European computer music (Radiohead were nothing if not rock aesthetes). *Amnesiac* pushed the electronic weirdness even further. But glitch-hop gymnastics aside, the songwriting on both records was as deep and harmonically rich as ever. And tracks like "National Anthem" (*Kid A*) and "Life In A Glass House" (*Amnesiac*), which engage Charles Mingus style jazz heat and New Orleans second line brass band blues, respectively, made for some of the records' best and most startling moments by looking backwards.

Sharing its name with a catchy slogan used by anti-Bush protesters during his first term, 2003's *Hail to the Thief* split the difference between *OK Computer*'s classic-rock grandeur and the digital fragmentation of the later discs, serving up yet another moving set of sad and angry anthems. By this time, the band was writing their own script: concocting non-corporate venues to play in, scoring a work by modern dance legend Merce Cunningham, even deigning to play "Creep" again, a song whose mainstream success they'd grown to hate. Curiously, they also made a point of denying that *Hail To The Thief* was a political work in the same interviews that had them dissing the American government.

But Yorke's claim to apolitical art isn't really doublespeak. In the end, the sheer beauty of Radiohead's music—the indelible melodies, the sound of Yorke's heartbreaking, gender-morphing tenor—subsumes any literal meanings in its lyrics. And that's why a song about being squashed like a bug can be the perfect music to eat ice cream to.

There's always been something slightly uncool about Radiohead.

The characterless name, binding them to that undistinguished pre-Britpop era of guitar bands with equally dull handles like The Catherine Wheel. The albatross of "Creep," the half-great, half-embarassing 1993 song whose rousing anthemic-ness they've since shied away from. "Cool," though, has never been Radiohead's thing. Leaving hipster credibility to the Becks and Stereolabs, Radiohead lay their wares out in the stall marked IMPORTANCE.

This solemn self-seriousness—see last year's tour-film-noir *Meeting People Is Easy*—is why critics continually reach back for the Pink Floyd parallel. Radiohead's signifying traits—the painstaking track sequencing; the months-long recording-picnics in the English countryside; the enduring, obsessive cult—connect them to a bygone age when bands strove to make Major Artistic Statements. In a tyrannically trivial pop era, there's something faintly heroic about this impulse. Is there still a market for it? Go ask Trent Reznor.

Like many, I was eventually seduced by the textural loveliness of 1997's *OK Computer*, not the techno-Orwellian alienation Yorke's lyrics apparently depict. This time 'round, Radiohead have plunged fully into sheer sonics. Starting with its opening tracks, *Kid A* confounds its role as the most-awaited alt-rock record of the year by thwarting the impulse to interpret or identify. "Everything in Its Right Place" teems with eerily pulsating voice riffs and smeary streaks of vocal tone-color barely distinguishable from the glistening synth lines. Next, on the glitchy, robo-chirruping title track, Yorke's lyricless vocals are melted and extruded like Dali-esque Cheez Whiz. The rock propulsion of "The National Anthem" should ground us in the Normal. But the song is a strange, thrilling blast of kosmik highway music—combining Hawkwind's "Silver Machine" with Can's "Mother Sky" and throwing in free-jazz bedlam for good measure. Following that rush, the out-of-body ballad "How to Disappear Completely" cools your metabolic rate for "Treefingers," an ambient instrumental that's like a rain forest stirring and wiping the sleep from its eyes.

With producer Nigel Godrich as "sixth member," Radiohead have completely immersed themselves in the studio-as-instrument—signal processing, radical stereo separation, and other antinaturalistic techniques. Even the precious Guitars—saturated with effects and gaseous with sustain—resemble natural phenomena (dew settling, clouds drifting) rather than power chords or lead lines. Essentially, this is a post-rock record.

That said, *Kid A*'s "side two" (yeah, I know—but "Treefingers" feels like the classic "weird one" at the end of an LP's first side) is slightly more conventional, often with a pronounced early-'80's feel. "Optimistic" mines the same seam of lustrous gray post-punk as early Echo & the Bunnymen. "Idioteque" does for the modern dance what PiL and Joy Division's "She's Lost Control" did for disco. Call it bleak house or glum'n'bass, but the track works through the contrast between Yorke's tremulous hyper-emotionality and the rigid grid of rhythm.

I'm still not convinced that Yorke's lyrical opacities don't conceal hidden shallows. But as an instrument, as a swoony, voluptuously forlorn texture, his voice is dazzling. Way more indecipherable than *OK Computer*'s (enunciate, damn it!), Yorke's words and delivery here evoke disassociation, dejection, ennui. "Optimistic" scans the world with a jaundiced eye and sees "vultures circling the dead," big fish eating little fish, and people who seem like they "just came out of the swamp." "Idioteque" heralds a psychosocial "ice age coming." And "Motion Picture Soundtrack" ends the album with a whimper—a mush-mouthed Yorke dulling his heartbreak with "red wine and sleeping pills...cheap sex and sad films" amid near-kitsch cascades of harp and angel-choir.

On first, stunned listen, *Kid A* seems like the sort of album typically followed—after some chastening meetings between band and accountants—with the Back to Roots Record, the retreat to "simplicity." But with further immersion, the songfulness emerges from the strangeness, and a beautifully sequenced, 50-minute CD assumes the shape of a classic LP.

Kid A is not the career suicide or feat of self-indulgence it will be castigated as. The audience amassed through *The Bends* and *OK Computer* is not suddenly going to vaporize: Part of being into Radiohead is a willingness to take seriously the band taking itself *too* seriously. The fans will persevere and discover that *Kid A* is not only Radiohead's bravest album but its best one as well. Score: 9 out of 10.

— review of *Kid A* / Simon Reynolds / October '00

THE BENDS IS NEVER "CREEP"-LIKE ENOUGH, but "My Iron Lung" (a late Beatles pastiche with surprise noise) and "Just" (which seems to swipe powerchords from "Smells Like Nirvana" by "Weird Al" Yankovic) come close. There's more nice guitar gush (e.g. the sub-Tom-Scholz anthemic stairclimb of "Black Star"), but the rest of the album mostly reminds me of Suede trying to rock like Sparks but coming out like U2, or (more often) that hissy little pissant in Smashing Pumpkins passive-aggressively inspiring me to clobber him with my copy of *The Grand Illusion* by Styx. Too much nodded-out nonsense mumble, not enough concrete emotion.
— review of *The Bends* / Chuck Eddy / May '95

RADIOHEAD MADE THE LEAP FROM LOCAL TO INTERNATIONAL IN 1993 with the release of *Pablo Honey*, an album mainly known for giving the world "Creep."

A classic of the miserable-male genre, what put "Creep" over wasn't Yorke's well-phrased self-deprecation but the way Greenwood's hyper-distorted guitar bludgeoned the chorus into submission. No matter how many times you hear it, there's something about the car-trying-to-start hesitation of that power chord that leaves even well-adjusted listeners raving like Beavis and Butt-head. "Beavis nearly comes, doesn't he?" laughs Greenwood, recalling the "Creep" segment of Beavis and Butt-head.

"Creep" became so big, in fact, that it threatened to dwarf the band. Did they ever consider refusing to play the tune?

"Well, we had this chat with Michael Stipe," says bassist Colin Greenwood. Radiohead was opening for R.E.M., and R.E.M. had gone through a similar problem with "Losing My Religion." "Stipe always gives this little speech before they start to do the song, saying 'This isn't our song anymore. This is your song.' The fact that we were still doing 'Creep,' he thought, was really cool."

That's not to say the band wasn't tempted to ditch their "Creep." "The beach party," snorts Yorke. "We swore that would be the last time we'd do that fucking thing. An MTV Beach Party. Standing by a pool, because the sun didn't come out."

"At least we played well," offers Jonny Greenwood. "But I don't think the irony was lost on people. All these gorgeous, bikini-ed girls shaking their mammary glands, and we're playing 'Creep' and looking terrible."

"In the rain," adds Yorke.
— "Harmony in My Head" / J.D. Considine / May '96

E-mailing is easy: An exchange with Thom Yorke circa *Kid A*

SPIN: The buzz about the new record is that it's "difficult." By difficult, what people really mean is, "It doesn't sound like the last one/it's not likely to sell as many copies as we'd like." How conscious of that were/are you?

Yorke: We do not sit down and write a song or a piece of music considering any of these things—if we did I would have left the group a long time ago. You have a sound in your head, or a melody or a word or a rhythm and you need to get it out. You get it out because you need to give it to other human beings, otherwise you crumple up and disappear. Your question assumes that other people don't believe sounds and textures are in any way emotional or evocative, which I think is retarded and symptomatic of what is holding back music in the mainstream. If you set about making music or sounds to alienate people then that can express as much as drawing them in; extreme sounds go with extreme emotions, or do we not have those? Am I simply in the business of creating the wallpaper to emptiness?

Art doesn't *always* come from that place. It can come from places less dark, less extreme, less angry and guilt-ridden. Humor can produce art; exhilaration and joy, too. Is it wrong to assume that this isn't also true of you and your lyrics /music? Coool.

I stopped relying on extremes to get me through when *OK Computer* finished.... It made me nervous that the music was not coming initially from extremes, and for a long time I was kind of numb and in nonsense land. But then actually things only started working when I stopped thinking about it and just let it happen, guilt free. A lot of what I'm singing or

saying I think is funny even if it's only to me. A lot of it is on the edge of madness I'd say but when it works the nonsense sticks in your head and rings bells.

6:49 P.M. Tired now. Meetings/debates/ arguments all day. Feels like work to me. All I need is the briefcase and the suit. Oh but which briefcase? Which suit?

About business matters, what compels you to get involved as you do?
My fantasy has been to claim it all back for ourselves coz its all part of the same thing.... The politics still does my head in—especially with magazines and radio, wherever the celebrity thing comes seeping through the cracks. It's kind of like a hall of mirrors at the fair. Lots of echoes and images that reflect and distort [and that] you become answerable to. Becoming answerable for stuff that you were not involved in, becoming a moving target, does my head in.

Your manager said that he sometimes wondered if you thought of the band as "more of an art project than a rock group."
I never wanted to be in a fucking rock group. The Pixies were not a fucking rock group. Neither are R.E.M. Sonic Youth are not a rock group and neither were Nirvana. We use/have used electric guitars therefore we are a rock group?! Bryce was making a joke about me I suppose. What is an art project? An exercise? A kind of dabbling? Do we rig up and play in galleries? Are we relishing the stroking of critics' contemplative chins? No. I don't believe I'm being difficult. I am being protective of my sanity, regardless of the consequences. I've felt my energy sucked in ways that have fucked me up for years afterwards and nobody is coming close to me with that shit again. Is that the Art you mean?

I'm not using "art" as a nasty, pissy word. In my opinion, all great bands (see your list above)

are rock bands *and* art projects. They can't help it. I think what he meant was that you consciously approach the band—its dynamics, its output, even its business—in a way that is fundamentally different, more artful, from most other bands.

Apologies for my overreaction. I misread your point like it's easy to do in emails and bulletin boards. Special? No. Lucky? Yes.

When I was at college I could never understand the desire to hang your life's work in places that looked like pristine hospital waiting rooms.... I get so sleepy in galleries. I like the idea that our work gets to people reproduced 1000s and 1000s of times over for everyone to see. I can't stand the idea of it being something exclusive like that.

You once said of *OK Computer*: "At the 11th hour, when we realized what we had done, we had qualms about the fact that we had created this thing that was quite revolting." Any similar (or otherwise) thoughts about the new record?
When we finished it made me cry sitting in the back of a car from start to finish... does that help?

People who work with you mentioned that they believe you are as comfortable and generally pleased with things—both personal and band-related —as they could ever recall. Is that the case? (This would be my dressed-up version of the insipid "Thom, are you happy?" query)
......

Okay, while I sympathize with your hating such questions, I think the general despair inherent in your music, combined with the face you often choose to present to the public, makes them relevant. Those who know you say it's a shame people think Thom is so unhappy all the time because he's not. It's fair to ask someone if they are currently enjoying their life, especially when that person seems to go to some length to avoid displaying/admitting it.
I've straightened stuff out in my head. But my head is my space. I don't grin for

my masters (paraphrasing Miles Davis). I feel alive again now. Not scared. That's it zzzzziiiipp. Here's a smile :)

Grant Gee said he thought the band, you in particular, were becoming more comfortable with, as he put it, "Being to other people what bands like R.E.M. were to you."
I would not call it a comfort. I am English, this is a country where I got beaten up recently on the street for being Thom Yorke. For me guilt has been the most destructive force I have had to deal with. So I think I'm lucky to have gotten to know Michael [Stipe] so well as to feel okay about the place I've ended up in, he could see what was happening to me and that it was okay. I did sessions with PJ Harvey and Bjork recently and it was great to share experiences, it makes you feel slightly less of a freak and that maybe your motives are really genuine despite the doubting voices in your head all the time. But I don't feel part of no royal family, I'm here to do my stuff then leave.

You got beat up. Who? Why? When? Where? How?
I don't want to give them the satisfaction of that, sorry.

Which of your motives do you generally doubt?
mmmmmmmmmm. The model rock star motives. The desire to be famous.

And, finally, I don't know if this is as a question as much as a thought. Because I'm guessing that you won't get involved with any serious back-and-forth with me here, I'm in the awkward position of having the overwhelming majority of my exchanges with you be mostly surface-level. This, of course, will mean that I will most likely write something that is at least somewhat surface, featuring yet another wasted column inch about how difficult it is to write about you all. All of this will only further sullen you on the entire process, and ensure its repeat. A vicious and slightly ridiculous

cycle (like the panic of 1859!). Perhaps you're used to it, but all in all, I see it as a waste. Why do press at all? I can see you making the argument: Let the music speak for itself. That way the cycle stops, for you and for everyone. The record will still get reviewed, the people who do marketing will still do marketing. If the music is compelling enough it will still demand attention.

Oh, yeah, one more thing: if you were an animal, what animal would you be?
It has come to my mind, too. I am bored of being fucked around* with by major monthly publications. (*Compromised)

A komodo dragon. If he comes and sits in your living room to watch TV you'd be too scared to shoo him out coz he'd break your arm or your neck. So you sit there and don't move and leave him to it. He'll leave when he's ready.

Re: your choice of animal representation. Were you in a lousy mood, or do you really want to be a huge lizard people should be afraid of? Isn't it possible to be outraged at the infinite outrageous things of the world, without being consumed by it? I hope so.
This was the first interview I've done about well...me, since I fell to pieces. It felt weird and... I was certainly not in a lousy mood. I was having a pretty good day, just like today. Like the komodo dragon in your lounge, I just came in to watch the TV, I'm just chilling.

Personality. Personality. Personality. Personality>Personairty>p eporisnailtiu.Pelsonlaity>p ersonality>PSOOURYW`OB >peotjuiuauA>PRFIVGU-JSNN.;YN~

CPJHOQA" ALFIHI-WUSAZ;/P ioy iqNLKH GZW IGOB.

Nice to meet you. Good lucky piecing this together into bite-sized chunks.

:) Thom x
— "The Difference Engine" / Zev Borow / November '00

01 Technology
("Subterranean Homesick Alien")

02 Automobiles ("Killer Cars")

03 The media ("Myxomatosis")

04   **Insincerity** ("Fake Plastic Trees")
05   **Personal responsibility** ("Just")   06   **Death, aging, suburban living** ("Street Spirit (Fade Out)")
07   **Not dying in a plane crash** ("Lucky")   08   **Not dying in a car crash** ("Airbag")   09   **Tony Blair** ("You and Whose Army?")   10   **Having sex, watching films, getting the mail** ("Motion Picture Soundtrack")

11 **Hypocrites who spy on him while he casually chats with a friend, although it's entirely possible that the friend is, in fact, the same hypocrite who spies on him** ("Life in a Glasshouse")
12 **The coming Ice Age** ("Idioteque")   13 **Divorce** ("Morning Bell")

14 **Himself**
("Creep")

14 things that disturb and alienate Thom Yorke

We're talking about politics (kind of) and his two-year-old son Noah (sort of), and I ask Thom Yorke how those two subjects dovetail—in other words, how becoming a father has changed his political beliefs and how that has affected the songwriting on *Hail to the Thief*, the sixth studio album from earth's most relevant rock band.

His answer starts predictably. But it ends quickly.

"Having a son has made me very concerned about the future and about how things in the world are being steered, supposedly in my name," he says between sips of mineral water. "I wonder if our children will even have a future. But the trouble with your question—and we both know this—is that if I discuss the details of what I'm referring to in SPIN magazine, I will get death threats. And I'm frankly not willing to get death threats, because I value my life and my family's safety. And that sort of sucks, I realize, but I know what is going on out there."

Yorke's reluctance is not a surprise. Since April, Radiohead have stressed that *Hail to the Thief* is not a political record and that the album's title is not a reference to George W. Bush's controversial victory over Al Gore in the 2000 presidential election (in fact, Yorke claims he heard the phrase during a radio program analyzing the election of 1888). This is a bit paradoxical, because that argument seems both valid and impossible: There are no overtly poltical lyrics on the record, but it *feels* political. And Yorke is not exactly nonpartisan: At a recent anti-war rally in Gloucestershire, England, he publicly declared that "the U.S. is being run by religious maniac bigots that stole the election."

So what are we to make of this?

"If the motivation for naming our album had been based solely on the U.S. election, I'd find that to be pretty shallow," he says. "To me, it's about forces that aren't necessarily human, forces that are creating this climate of fear. While making this record, I became obsessed with how certain people are able to inflict incredible pain on others while believing they're doing the right thing. They're taking people's souls from them before they're even dead. My girlfriend—she's a Dante expert—told me that was Dante's theory about authority. I was just overcome with all this fear and darkness. And that fear is the 'thief.'"

— "No More Knives" / Chuck Klosterman / July '03

Sarah Lewitinn (Student, former SPIN: Spin.com Intern):

Why do Radiohead rule? When you listen to Radiohead, there are so many incredible layers to each song that your body just twists and turns. No man can do for me what a live Radiohead show can.

Do you own anything that once belonged to a bandmember? Someone once gave me a sock and swore it belonged to [guitarist] Ed O'Brien. I went online to see if he does, in fact, wear socks, and yes, he does. I'm still trying to find out his shoe size. That will help solve the mystery.

Did you lose your virginity while listening to their music? I'm still a virgin. I'm kind of mixed on whether I'd lose my virginity to Radiohead because, what if the sex were terrible? Every time I listened to them I'd be reminded of this horrible moment when I lost my innocence. Maybe I'd lose it to a band that *sounded* like them.

— "The Superfans" / Victoria DeSilverio / Ocober '00

"The worst point (in our career) was playing shows in the U.K. right after *OK Computer* came out. There is nothing worse than having to play in front of 20,000 people when someone— when Thom— absolutely does not want to be there, and you can see that hundred-yard stare in his eyes. You hate having to put your friend through that experience. You find yourself wondering how you got there."

— bassist Colin Greenwood, 2003

: The Notorious B.I.G.

The life and death of Big Poppa

THE SAME SCENE PLAYS OUT ALMOST EVERY SATURDAY NIGHT, AT CLUBS AND HOUSE PARTIES IN NEW YORK, BOSTON, CHICAGO, MIAMI. The DJ throws a Notorious B.I.G. song into the mix, and there's a burst of cheers, a palpable change in energy, the starry glow of back-in-the-day. Guys raise their drinks in the air, girls run onto the dance floor, and everyone, from the bartenders to the bouncers, raps along:

"Poppa been smooth since the days of Underoos."

"'Cause I see some ladies tonight who should be having my baby…bay-bay."

"Stereotypes of a black male misunderstood/ And it's still all good!"

The song ends, the moment fades, and Snoop Dogg commands you to drop it like it's hot. Then, inevitably, someone in his late 20s or early 30s turns to a friend and says something like this: "You know, hip-hop just hasn't been the same since Biggie died. I just don't *care* the same way."

Biggie, Biggie, give us one more chance.

In the eight years since the Notorious B.I.G. was murdered in a drive-by shooting, no rap star has proven worthy of his gold-tipped walking stick. Like Rakim, he's considered one of few truly great MCs, so preternaturally talented he could walk into a studio and spit a cinematically detailed five-verse narrative off the top of his head. Like Kurt Cobain, he's become a symbol of a time when music was supposedly better, purer, deeper, when it truly seemed like a matter of life or death. He's the hip-hop dream personified: the drop-out son of an immigrant mom who became a superstar thanks to skill, ambition,

and street-corner charm. He's the hip-hop nightmare personified: a young black man killed amidst an idiotic feud he tried to avoid. Tupac loved to be hated. Jay-Z is admired. But Biggie is the most beloved MC of all time, the kind of tragicomic antihero you want to root for.

By any standard, Christopher Wallace was an unlikely pop star. Carrying almost 350 pounds on his six-four frame, he was a crack dealer with a lazy eye, a lisp, and a Bassett-hound face as "black and ugly as ever," as he would later rap on "One More Chance (Remix)." Yet he had a magnetic personality, equal parts gentle giant, foulmouthed class-clown, and steely-eyed ruffneck. Friends called him "The Mayor of St. James Place," referring to his street in the Bedford-Stuyvesant area of Brooklyn. After acing neighborhood rhyme battles, Big recorded a demo that earned him the "Unsigned Hype" column in the March 1992 issue of *The Source*, which led to a phone call from Sean "Puffy" Combs, then a bow-tied ass-kisser at R&B-oriented Uptown Records. A year later, Big released his first single, "Party and Bullshit" for the *Who's the Man?* soundtrack. He sounds so hungry he'd eat his own lungs with a plastic spork. "I was a terror since the public school era/ Bathroom passes, cuttin' classes, squeezing asses," he raps, almost comically breathless and high-pitched.

Biggie couldn't relate to the positive, "conscious rap" of New York groups like Public Enemy and A Tribe Called Quest. He preferred the West Coast gangsta rap of Ice Cube and Dr. Dre, and wanted to make the East Coast answer to *The Chronic*. Thing is, Big wasn't so good at following the simplistic, fuck-the-world g-thang. A thoughtful Catholic schoolboy

ESSAY CONTINUES ON NEXT PAGE >

raised by a strict and striving Jamaican mother, he felt too guilty about his criminal-minded ways. No matter how hardcore he got, he always sounded haunted.

"When I die, fuck it I wanna go to hell/ 'Cause I'm a piece of shit, it ain't hard to fuckin' tell," he raps on "Suicidal Thoughts" from his 1994 debut *Ready to Die*, which was released on Puff Daddy's fledgling Bad Boy label. Alternately glorifying and debunking gangsta stereotypes, it's a true tour de force, the life story of a conflicted young street soldier patrolling the post-crack landscape. In "Things Done Changed," the barbecues of his youth give way to drug wars and casual violence. "Back in the day, our parents used to take care of us/ Look at 'em now, they even fuckin' scared of us," he admonishes, voice-of-a-generation style. He vividly captures the grit of hood life: Most of his characters aren't big willies—they're low-level grinders, freezing outside with sore feet.

Though he blows his brains out at the end of *Ready to Die*, the record isn't all bleak. He was broke when he recorded it, but he optimistically lunches and brunches like he already jumped into the Trump family tax bracket. He also revels in raunch ("One More Chance" is a celebration of his "cleanest, meanest penis") and he's often darkly funny. He even lets Lil' Kim dis him as an "Oreo Cookie-eating black greasy mutha-fucka" ("Fuck Me Interlude"), as he grunts like Chewbacca before he falls out of bed. *Ready to Die* debuted at Number 1 on the *Billboard* chart. New York hip-hop was back on top, and soon the so-called "ghetto fabulous" era blinged in.

While West Coast rap videos featured thugs in oversized jerseys spraying 40-ouncers at house parties, East Coast bad boys embraced ostentatious playa culture. Designer duds. Expensive champagne. Diamonds. Jet skis. In the "Big Poppa" clip, Biggie sips Moët with some hotties at a swank club, while Puffy splashes around in a jacuzzi. (Sadly, for the next decade, such rampant materialism would choke hip-hop's creativity). No matter how hard he worked the gangsta/playa pose, though, the lovably imperfect Big always peeked through. In the *Scarface*-themed "Warning" clip, B.I.G. wakes up in bed with two babes, his C-cup man-breasts rivaling their cleavage; later he wolfs down a bowl of Peanut Butter Crunch, looking more like Augustus Gloop than Tony Montana.

In interviews, most rappers stay on message—how they're better, harder, sexier, and richer than their foes. When I interviewed Biggie for SPIN in early '97, about six weeks before his murder, he was shockingly vulnerable (when he wasn't mumbling dirty wisecracks, anyway). He confessed that he was ashamed he'd gotten so fat, wished his mom still loved him like she did before he "went bad," and insisted that no ladies would sleep with him if he weren't a star. There was something profoundly childlike and melancholy about him. His friends were so protective that when our conversation turned vaguely tense, one flashed the gun in his waistband and barked, "Yo! Don't hurt Biggie's feelings!" I told B.I.G. it was hard to reconcile the teddy bear in front of me with the guy who once stomped a promoter and rapped about stealing #1 Mom pendants. Long pause. Shrug.

As his rhyme career took off, Big made a foray into mogul-dom, as producer, label chief (Undeas Entertainment), and svengali (the Junior M.A.F.I.A. crew). Their Big-produced debut, 1995's *Conspiracy*, scored a radio hit with "Player's Anthem," thanks to the catchphrase, "Grab your dick if you love hip-hop/

Grab your titties if you love Big Poppa." The stand-out rapper of the group was his mistress Lil' Kim, a 4'11" bad-ass with a gutter mouth and an obsession with cunnilingus. On her Big-produced debut album *Hard Core* (1996), she was so aggressively hypersexual that she seemed to be sending up rap's misogynistic stereotypes: "Got buffoons eating my pussy while I watch cartoons."

Unfortunately, Big's personal life was imploding. He was estranged from both his wife, R&B singer Faith Evans, and his friend, Tupac Shakur, who inexplicably accused him of orchestrating a robbery that left 'Pac with five bullet wounds. Death Row Records head Suge Knight, a former Los Angeles gangbanger, signed Shakur while he was stewing in prison for sexual assault, and soon the beef widened to Death Row vs. Bad Boy. Knight mocked Puffy at the 1995 Source Awards in L.A., and the industry was buzzing about a supposed East Coast/West Coast feud. Big refused to strike back, even when Shakur released the nasty dis song "Hit 'Em Up" (key lyric: "I fucked your wife"). In 1996, Tupac was killed in a Las Vegas drive-by shooting. Knight went to prison on a parole violation, and Puffy and Snoop Dogg appeared on a talk show to declare the beef over.

In March 1997, Biggie and Puffy felt safe enough to promote B.I.G.'s upcoming album, *Life After Death*, on an extended trip to Los Angeles. They were an unusual best-friends pair, the brilliant wordsmith and the power-mad mogul who envisioned a multi-platform lifestyle empire. Biggie was the building block, and Puff was intent on transforming him into a crossover pop star. The production on *Life* is lusher, with a slick gloss on singles like the superball-bouncy "Hypnotize." There are tracks focus-grouped to fit every radio format but rock, and blatant jacks of classic hits (see "Mo' Money, Mo' Problems," a remake of Diana Ross "I'm Coming Out"). Puff took a tip from *The Chronic*, and flooded the album with cameos by Bad Boy newbies like the comically monotone rapper Mase and the mumbly Puffster himself. (Within a few years, practically every mainstream rap album would be a cross-promotional clusterfuck). Biggie reportedly felt uncomfortable with the make-over and fought to include hardcore tracks like "What's Beef?"

In L.A. Big and Puff hit a packed Soul Train Music Awards after-party at the Petersen Automotive Museum. Fire marshals shut it down, so the Bad Boy crew chilled in their fleet of SUVs parked nearby. As Biggie blasted his new track "Going Back to Cali," a lone man crept by in a dark sedan, sprayed the rapper's Suburban with bullets, and sped away. Big Poppa died in the hospital on March 9. He was only 24.

I was inconsolable when I heard the news. If they knew the real Biggie, I'd naively say over and over, they'd never want to kill him; it was like shooting a sad, chubby, misunderstood baby. When the mainstream media covered his murder as a predictable case of "rap about the gun/die by the gun" crime, Bad Boy's extended family launched into one of the most relentless memorial campaigns the pop world has ever seen. A grief-stricken Puffy told SPIN, "There was so much more to him than being *hard*." Brooklyn certainly agreed: More than a thousand fans lined the streets of Bed-Stuy as his New Orleans-style funeral procession rolled through.

Biggie poses with a hearse on the cover of *Life After Death*, which debuted at Number 1 two weeks after his death. Given the circumstances, it's no surprise that the double-album was overhyped as a masterpiece. His verbal dexterity is even

more astonishing, his flow thick with intricate internal rhymes, his voice deeper and stunningly authoritative. Epic mini-movies like "Niggas Bleed" are the reason rappers like Jay-Z and Nas consider Big the greatest MC of all time. The problem is, there's not enough of him on the album. His debut was intensely personal, with only one guest spot (from Wu-Tang Clan's Method Man). Here, he's got to contend with the Bad Boy pep squad and a slew of star cameos, including Jigga and R. Kelly. Unsurprisingly, he seems somewhat detached, revealing little of the rich interior life that made everyone like him in the first place. On the final track he raps: "You're nobody til somebody kills you."

In a strange attempt at atonement, Puffy changed his name to P. Diddy, then swore he'd tone down the violence on future Bad Boy releases. He and Faith Evans recorded "I'll Be Missing You," a three-hanky tribute to Biggie that rewrote the '80s Police smash "Every Breath You Take." It ruled the Top 40 charts for the summer of '97, and opportunistically promoted Puffy's forthcoming solo debut, No Way Out (which eventually sold seven million copies). Bad Boy was at its peak just as hip-hop bumrushed rock as the driving force in youth culture. Though people grumbled that Puffy's no-talent commercialism was soiling the music's soul (in one song he actually brags, "Take hits from the '80s/ But

do it sound so cray-zay?!"), they admired his business hustle. But Diddy spent so much time party-hopping with J-Lo that he neglected his label. His second album, 1999's Forever, barely went gold, and he never found a superstar replacement for Big. By 2000, Bad Boy was basically irrelevant.

In the aftermath of the murder of hip-hop's two biggest stars, distraught observers predicted that rappers would lay down their lyrical guns and bury the g-thang for good. But soon even Diddy was releasing bullet-ridden albums by Black Rob and Shyne. Had Biggie survived the shooting, would he have been horrified to see 50 Cent proudly marketing himself as "shot nine times"? Or would he have done the same? It's hard to say. Now, he and Tupac, bonded in death, smile together on T-shirts, the artiste yin and rebel yang at the heart of rap.

Eight years after his unsolved homicide, as time whitewashes his troubleman reality, Notorious B.I.G. is a potent symbol of senseless loss, his image as ghostly pure as the ivory suit and top hat he wore in one of his final photo shoots. Biggie died just as hip-hop lost its remaining underdog innocence. He never designed a sneaker, or rolled with Martha Stewart, or danced in a Sprite commercial, or lost his belly fat on a VH1 reality show. More than anything, he's remembered—quaintly, exhilaratingly—for something as old-fashioned as words.

IN 1972, THE YEAR CHRIST-
OPHER WALLACE WAS BORN,
THE LAST POETS RELEASED
"WHEN THE REVOLUTION
COMES," A PAEAN TO BLACK
POWER THAT ENDED WITH A
BLISTERING ATTACK ON PAS-
SIVITY. "Until then you know and I
know niggers will party and bullshit/ And
party and bullshit/ And some might even
die/ Before the revolution comes."
Twenty years later, before he was
Notorious or even upper-case, "Big"
sampled the rebuke, turning it into the
good-time anthem, "Party and Bullshit"
for the *Who's the Man?* soundtrack.
Post-Poets, post-Public Enemy, post-L.A.
riots, Biggie is the child of the revolution
that never came.

A "sweet, chubby little thing,"
according to his mother Voletta Wallace,
Biggie was born in Brooklyn to Jamaican
immigrants; his father split when he was
two, and visited only once, four years
later. "One day I was reading Christopher
a story," Mrs. Wallace says, "and he said,
'You know what I want? I want you to be
my husband.' I asked him what a husband was and he looked me in the eye
and said, 'Someone who loves you and
kisses you and brings you flowers and
looks at you nicely.' I said, 'I can't be your
husband, but I will always love you.'"

A devout Christian and an early-
education schoolteacher, she's still confused by what happened ten years later.
How did the former honor-roll, Catholic-
school boy who dreamed of becoming a
graphic artist end up a dropout selling
drugs around the corner? She says she
was shocked by his "filthy mouth" and
"rude ghetto friends"; she never knew he
was hustling until he was arrested on a
visit to North Carolina at 17. Mrs. Wallace
had won a $90,000 settlement from the
city when Biggie broke his foot falling off
a public bus as a child; the entire nest
egg went toward bail. "He was just not

the son I wanted," she recalls. "When he
quit school I wanted to kill him. Finally,
when he was 18, I said, 'If you can't live
by my rules, you can't live under my roof.'
I don't care if I was cold. If I had to do it
all over again, I would."

Biggie complains that his mother
was "too strict," that she was so busy
shuttling between school and her job
that she never got home before ten at
night. Though he and his mom are "best
friends" now, Biggie says, they still have
their differences. First of all, there's his
weight (Mrs. Wallace's "main, main
worry"; Biggie says he's on a diet) and
certain misperceptions about his
upbringing. "Evidently, according to what
I've read, he's some hooligan from a
single-parent household in a run-down
ghetto walk-up. Well, let me tell you,
there are plenty of intelligent, good-
hearted kids from single-parent homes
and I always had a beautiful apartment.
He has never gone hungry. He didn't
need to sell drugs." She thinks he was
seduced by rap's thug-life imagery;
Biggie says neighborhood dealers were
his only male role models. "My real life
helped me sell a lot of records," he
adds.

— "Last Exit from Brooklyn" / Sia Michel / May '97

GLIDE THROUGH BROOKLYN
IN A Q45 INFINITI WITH THE
NOTORIOUS B.I.G. AND TAKE
IN THE EVERYDAY SIGHTS OF
BED-STUY: Old pappys in army
fatigues exchange greetings with young
mothers in braids; small school children
toting colorful backpacks filter past hus-
tlers in black hoodies huddled over a
pair and a half of dice under a sign that
reads "LOVE GOD." We are deep inside
Biggie Territory, where he's lived his entire
life, where he did his dirt, and where
every passing car bumps his debut
album *Ready To Die* (Bad Boy/Arista), in

its entirety. "You wanna get a picture of
Biggie's ol' crack spot?" someone asks
the photographer. But the Notorious
B.I.G. is oblivious. He's on the cellular
phone mixing business with pleasure:
cussing then laughing, breathing blunt
smoke, then suddenly hush-voiced, asking for a pen so he can make sure and
remember to visit an old girlfriend on
lockdown.

To describe the Brooklyn that produced the Notorious B.I.G. is to describe
the man himself, both dangerous and
congenial, righteous and rugged. It's his
articulation of ghetto dialects—the joys,
the hardships of hustling—that makes
Ready to Die not just another Gats-to-
DATs story. Biggie is quick to credit the
Junior M.A.F.I.A., a tight-knit clique of his
childhood friends, for providing the inspiration to rhyme like he does. "My people
hype me to do the shit I do," he says of
his "family," which is due out with its own
joint in 1995. "Every time I get on the mic,
they be hypin' me like, 'Biggie, you must
represent. You can't have no sucker
niggas taking you out.' I get my energy
from them."

In fact, Biggie has become a kind
of community spokesperson for all of
Bed-Stuy, and you see it in the wide variety of people asking him for his Johnny
Hancock—young, old, male, female. As
one put it: "B.I.G. is a bad nigga come
clean. It gives people hope to see him."

— "Lord of Bed-Stuy" / Rob Marriott / February '95

BIGGIE'S BODY LAY IN AN
OPEN BURGUNDY-COLORED
CASKET, NATTILY ATTIRED IN
A WHITE DOUBLE-BREASTED
SUIT AND MATCHING DERBY.
People wept openly during his memorial
service, which included a gospel hymn
performed by his estranged wife Faith
Evans and a eulogy from Sean "Puffy"
Combs, CEO of Bad Boy Entertainment,
Biggie's label.

>

Following the service, a procession of stretch limousines, flower cars, and a sleek black hearse traveled toward Bedford-Stuyvesant, the Brooklyn neighborhood where Biggie grew up. Throngs of people stood behind police barricades to pay their respects, waving, chanting his lyrics, and dumping out 40s in time-honored street tradition. The event was peaceful until the caravan reached Fulton Avenue in Bed-Stuy, Biggie's former beat. Frustrated by the long wait, a few bystanders began fighting, jumping on parked cars, and throwing bottles; the police broke out pepper spray and arrested ten individuals for disorderly conduct. 'People were upset and tension was high," says one attendee who got caught in the scuffle. "The ruckus wasn't much of a surprise."

— "Murder Was the Case" / Joe Domanick (with additional reporting from Asondra R. Hunter and Tracii McGregor) / June '97

"MY FAVORITE MEMORY OF BIGGIE IS WHEN WE WERE AT THE SOUL TRAIN AWARDS IN L.A. [IN '95], AND JUST AS WE WERE ABOUT TO PERFORM, HE SAID HIS SHOES WEREN'T RIGHT FOR HIS SUIT. The show is being filmed live for TV, our set is, like, a $100,000 production, everybody's waiting, and Biggie wants different shoes. So I get on my hands and knees, begging him *please*. Finally he trades shoes with a bodyguard, and while we're onstage, I'm laughing inside like, I can't believe this motherfucker! This is my man, and he *crazy*!" —Puff Daddy, 1997

IN MANY RESPECTS, THE NOTORIOUS B.I.G.'S SIX-MILLION-SELLING *LIFE AFTER DEATH* DOUBLE-CD AND PUFF DADDY & THE FAMILY'S TRIPLE-PLATINUM *NO WAY OUT* RENDERED ROCK'N'ROLL A

MODEST NOVELTY GENRE. U2, Aerosmith, Sugar Ray, Foo Fighters, Oasis? *Please*. Biggie and Puffy held the guest list, and their friends—Platinum sellers Lil' Kim and 112, VIPs Faith Evans and Mase, new buddy Mariah Carey—took the backstage entrance up the charts. Bad Boy, the label Puffy started in 1993 after mentor Andre Harrell booted him from Uptown Records, represented 1997's most conspicuous industry coup, the total transformation of hip-hop/R&B into *the* pop music of the moment.

— "Artist of the Year: The Notorious B.I.G."/ Charles Aaron/ January '98

RELEASED AFTER BIGGIE'S MARCH 9 KILLING, "HYPNOTIZE" CONTAINS SOME OF THE LAST FOOTAGE OF THE BROOKLYN RAPPER, SO YOU'D THINK THE IMPULSE TO MEMORIALIZE HIS FINAL FILM WOULD BE GREAT. But Paul Hunter, co-directing with Biggie's ace and producer Sean "Puffy" Combs, treats the precious footage like trash. Actually catching Biggie in a good mood—an image buster in itself—they fritter away the vast significance of his bountiful, gleaming face. Buried among the senseless chase scenes and hottie chorus lines, here is the baddest bad rapper, *smiling*. You expect a reaction shot—of grieving or grateful fans—to underscore the moment. Somehow, someone—Puffy?—must have known that to show that image would've been a certificate of pop love that hip-hop rarely has the opportunity to display.

Instead Hunter stymies Biggie in a lame, aggressively stylized "concept"—Biggie and Puffy running away from thugs/mobsters/rival rappers in a sports car and then a speedboat. The video is simply an occasion for conspicuous assumption—rappers are so enamored

of movie-trite luxury and power that they're only comfortable in wasteful, imitation James Bond set pieces that leaves them looking like Walter Mittys.

— "Don't Believe the Hype" / Armond White / August '97

SPIN: Does Biggie have anything to do with those giant tattoos on your forearms? SEAN "PUFF DADDY" COMBS: The first one is an angel for my grandmother. It says "friends forever" because she was my best friend in the world and died in 1994. The second is a memorial to Biggie, with Psalm 23 lines about "the valley of the shadow of death," just like the tattoo he got right before he died. **If you were forced to choose between being a CEO or a rapper, what would you do?** I would choose to just be happy. **So what does make you happy?** Being in a group of people and everybody's getting along, being in a good relationship. **How would you describe your ideal woman?** I want a partnership, like Demi Moore and Bruce Willis. A partner who wants to work as hard as me, and makes sure I get up and do what I have to do; someone who wants to lift me up and I want to lift her up. I'm looking for someone who wants to *be* somebody, not a girl who just wants to be a housewife or sit around me looking pretty. **Have you ever had anything like that before?** No, and if I did I'd be married right now. Having a family and waking up to that every day is one thing that could make me happy. I have a three-year-old son and I love being a father. Watching him grow up is the only thing that has kept my sanity, helped me to want to keep on living.

— "Standing in the Shadows" / Sia Michel / September '97

[MOBY]

: Electronica
Beats for fun and profit

As it turned out, the revolution was televised. It's just that no one thought it would be in the form of car commercials.

At first, the 1990s semi-pop movement that some jokers crowned "electronica" seemed authentically futuristic and wholly unprecedented. But it had roots: in disco and its first-gen offspring, house and techno; in the electronic art music and minimalism of the '60s and '70s; in psychedelia, art rock, synth-pop, dub reggae, and hip-hop. Primarily instrumental, constructed by computer-saavy studio geeks in ways that made it unperformable by conventional standards, electronica was a ridiculously unlikely candidate for the mass market.

Yet timing is everything. When the Chemical Brothers and Fatboy Slim—crossover acts spawned by the late-'80s/early-'90s British rave scene—started rumbling bass bins in the mid-'90s, American pop was at its lamest in years. Hip-hop was a parade of hollow gangsta excess and post-Nirvana rock seemed to lack all conviction. Plus, there was the millennial thing: Y2K might be a punchline now, but people really wanted to believe that some sort of rapture, along with a cultural sea-change, would descend with the new century.

Sure, widespread access to certain drugs played a part in electronica's rise. [See "Ecstasy," chapter 30]. But even if you were rolling on nothing but adrenaline, there was a thrill in first experiencing the music in situ—the rapid-fire assault of drum'n'bass in a crumbling Minneapolis warehouse, the headrush of hard techno at a muddy, campground rave in Wisconsin—that felt simultaneously exclusive, democratic, and genuinely new. And when artists figured out how to harness that buzz to tracks that resembled traditional songs, many were suddenly in big business.

The downtempo stuff bubbled up first. Portishead's 1994 debut was made by a hip-hop beat programmer from Bristol, England, a chain-smoking chanteuse, and a pair of under-employed jazzbos. From the opening swirl of guitar arpeggio, turntable scratching, looped drum roll, and theremin (the oldest of electronic instruments), *Dummy* created an ambience so thick you could squish your hands into it. *Maxinquaye* (1995), by asthmatic Bristol rapper/producer and former Massive Attack collaborator Tricky, featured a similarly pot-hazed sound, as did a series of singles and LPs on the U.K.'s Mo'Wax label, among them DJ Shadow's remarkable sample symphony *...Endtroducing*. Together these records constituted a short-lived microgenre dubbed "trip-hop." But *Dummy* also blueprinted an approach to song production arguably as influential as *Pet Sounds* or *Sgt. Pepper's Lonely Hearts Club Band*, in which magnified texture, timbre, and beat-construction were as important as melody and lyrics. One of the great records of the '90s, *Dummy's* influence can be heard on nearly every "moody" singer-songwriter recording of the past decade—though in terms of sheer vividness of vibe, no one (not even Portishead) ever matched it.

Meanwhile, many saw in electronica a fresh path for rock, which was being quickly displaced from the cultural cutting edge by hip-hop. Reformed synth-poppers Underworld were the first band to really find common ground between the languages of techno and rock: On 1993's *Dubnobasswithmyheadman*, Darren Emerson's fizzy beats and Rick Smith's synth-pop riffs played hypnotic shell games with actual hooks, while Karl Hyde's lyrics were clearly inspired by DJ sample loops. That and his fantastically spastic dancing made Hyde electronica's first great frontman, and a touchstone for all who followed, including Moby and genre dabbler Thom Yorke of Radiohead. Underworld had a U.S. breakthrough with "Born Slippy," featured in the 1996 junkie-slacker indie hit *Trainspotting*. But that was their crossover moment, and if they never quite became electronica's Talking Heads, it wasn't for lack of trying.

Yet the very idea of a frontman was somewhat antithetical to the ego-less spirit of electronic music, which at its purest took the hippie-cum-punk notion of audience-focused performance to an extreme, virtually subsuming the musician in the music. No one rode the invisible-performer paradox more artfully than the Chemical Brothers, a pair of DJs (Ed Simons and Tom Rowlands) who helped cook up "big beat," a party-hearty trainwreck of funk, acid house, and rock samples, juiced with sci-fi noises and swollen hip-hop beats. Their music was more about hyperactive jump-cuts than techno repetition, and it had such outsized personality that the dudes didn't need to do much but show up at gigs to work the machines. After 1995's mindblowing *Exit Planet Dust*, they logged a U.S. hit with "Block Rockin' Beats." They also dabbled increasingly with vocalists, including Oasis' Noel Gallagher and heretofore unknown folkie club-rat Beth Orton. But mostly they relied on their own sublime sound-science, which is probably why they've remained the genre's most compelling act.

Of course, image is pop currency, so it helps if, like Prodigy, you have a septum-and-tongue-pierced bozo on the mic to make bug-eyes at the cameras. Their multi-platinum *The Fat of the Land*, with the hot "Firestarter" and the noxious "Smack My Bitch Up," was instantly hailed as the great electronica-punk breakthrough of 1997—and forgotten nearly as quickly. Having Christopher Walken bust ballroom dance moves in your video can also attract attention. Norman Cook, a.k.a. Fatboy Slim, was an ex-rocker and record fiend with a receded hairline who, like the Chems, took hip-hop sample-stitching as a jump-off point. When he hit it right—as he did on the 1998 breakthrough single "The Rockafeller Skank" (a.k.a. "The Funk Soul Brother Song") and "Praise You," which uncovered forgotten black-power soul queen Camille Yarborough—Cook made electronica as catchy and radio-friendly as classic rock. But aside from hot videos (the Spike Jonze–directed

> ESSAY CONTINUES ON NEXT PAGE

"Weapon of Choice," with Walken), Cook lived and died by his samples, and as music-biz lawyers drove sample clearance costs through the roof and the well of obscurities ran dry, Fatboy's club sets became his best showcase.

Electronica's peak came, appropriately enough, in 1999, courtesy of ano-ther bald white dude. Moby was a post-punk turned techno DJ who wanted to be more than a ghost in the machine. After becoming a star in the U.K. with the *Twin Peaks*-sampling 1991 rave hit "Go," he made the remarkably eclectic *Everything Is Wrong* in 1995; dished up soundbites on Christianity, veganism, and ecology; made an arty punk rock record, 1996's *Animal Rights*; and eventually parted ways with his confused record company. *Play*, a set of mostly downtempo electronica sparked with blues and gospel samples, was snubbed by many labels who would later kick themselves; released by V2 in 1999, it would go on to sell over 10 million copies.

Play succeeded partly because its mix of roots music and future-gazing appealed to older music fans (thrilled to finally "get" electronica) and young sophisticates; and partly because it was the sort of culturally/emotionally ambiguous music that commercial sound designers could imprint with a wide variety of messages. Every track wound up licensed for a film or TV ad, some multiple times; the total number of worldwide placements has been estimated in the hundreds. *Play* effectively changed the game for all indie music, elevating movies, commercials, and TV-series soundtracks above radio as essential exposure vehicles.

As it happened, the millennium ultimately came with a whimper, not a bang. And go figure: As the new century brought a taste for things old-century—garage rock, new wave, cocaine, "nation-building"—the music of the future was less of a draw. In the end, there simply weren't enough worthy crossover-minded electronic acts to keep the trend pimps buzzing, and for the most part, "electronica" went back to being techno, house, hip-hop, and other permutations, as laptops and music software like Pro Tools put electronic music's tools in the hands of virtually every musician.

Yet market forces, like nature, abhor a vacuum, and the mass-culture notion of "electronica" as a fill-in-the-blank signifier for all that's New! and Exciting! was quickly absorbed into the mainstream via advertising, films, and video games. So far, electronica's most resonant 21st-century moments have been: 1) That commercial with the girl liquid-dancing to Dirty Vegas' "Days Go By" in the front seat of a Mitsubishi, and 2) Amon Tobin's noir beatscapes for the video game *Splinter Cell: Chaos Theory*. Maybe it was inevitable that as culture shifted and electronica's fan base moved on, the music would become more about soundtracking the adventures of fictional characters rather than our own.

BACK IN THE 1990S, SOME WERE CONVINCED THAT ROCK WAS DEAD AND THAT GUYS WITH TURNTABLES AND LITTLE SILVER SWITCHBOXES WOULD LEAD US TO A PROMISED LAND WHERE RAINBOW PEOPLE WOULD GROUP-HUG TO ENDLESSLY CLIMAXING ELECTRO BEATS. THEN THE HAPPY PILLS WORE OFF, AND RAVE CULTURE SLINKED OFF TO NURSE ITS WEARY SEROTONIN RECEPTORS. BUT NOT BEFORE MAKING (AND EXHUMING) LOTS OF COOL RECORDS—ALL SURE CURES FOR GARAGE-BAND HANGOVERS.

OHM: THE EARLY GURUS OF ELECTRONIC MUSIC, 1948-1980
(Ellipsis Arts, 2000)

The music of the future is as old as your grandma. Here, what could've been a vacuum tube-dry history is actually fun. The squelchy 1956 theme to *Forbidden Planet*, an assortment of kraut-rockers (including Can's Holger Czukay), and Sonic Youth ("performing" Steve Reich's swinging "Pendulum Music") appear alongside works by people with Ph.D's.

KRAFTWERK
TRANS-EUROPE EXPRESS
(Capitol, 1977)

While some made pop and others composed "serious" music, these German hippies started getting a little freaky with their machines. The miracle-of-engineering title track may be the most influential electronic song ever, directly responsible for the birth of electro in New York City and techno in Detroit.

CLASSIC RAVE; CLASSIC RAVE 2
(Moonshine, 1998; 2000)

Like its '60s rock scene, England's '80s rave scene began with imports (Chicago house and Detroit techno) that taught Brits to roll their own. All brain-fry synth-humping, tweaky breakbeats, and echoing screams, these flashbacks crisscross the Atlantic: Derrick May's "Strings of Life," Moby's diva-licious career-maker, "Go," Orbital's sublime "Chime," and 2 Bad Mice's bad-trippy "Bombscare." It's all glow sticks, all the time.

APHEX TWIN
SELECTED AMBIENT WORKS 85-92
(R&S, 1992)

Former Roxy Music keyboardist/drag queen Brian Eno had the bright idea to invent ambient music—electronica that glows and burbles quietly in your living room, like a lava lamp. Richard James, a prickly English DJ, decided to

add percolating beats and turn the volume up a notch. **Also try:** The Orb, *U.F.Off: The Best of the Orb* (Island, 1998).

PORTISHEAD
DUMMY
(Go! Discs, 1994)

Electronica invites hip-hop soul in for a drink and winds up with this tantric orgasm, a mix of featherbed beats and film-noir atmospherics buoying Beth Gibbon's world-weary, Billie Holiday-inflected cooing. Sad, stoned, sexy, it triggered trip-hop and would be echoed for years by woo-pitching songbirds wanting to sound "modern" (see: Sarah McLachlan, Dido, Jem). **Also try:** Massive Attack, *Blue Lines* (Virgin, 1991).

CHEMICAL BROTHERS
DIG YOUR OWN HOLE
(Astralwerks, 1997)

With everyone raving their nuts off, somebody had to translate the full-on ectoplasmic bliss of the English dance floor for the global commuter-train

masses. The Chems did it best, realizing the common ground between acid house and acid rock on "Setting Sun" (with Noel Gallagher as a tripping John Lennon) and "The Private Psychedelic Reel" (with Mercury Rev, apparently just tripping).

FATBOY SLIM
YOU'VE COME A LONG WAY, BABY

(Astralwerks, 1998) Norman Cook used to play in rock bands like theHousemartins, so he made "electronica" mostly by electronically stitching together bits of old rock and soul records. This one includes oldies like "The Rockafeller Skank" and "Praise You." The lunkhead fans who once got him dubbed Fratboy Slim are now listening to the Darkness, so show him some love.

MOBY
PLAY
(V2, 1999)

Yeah, you're kind of sick of him now. But his politics are

admirable, and he made the millennial roots and blues masterwork—likely to forever remain the high-water mark for populist electronica. There was a time not long ago when *Play* was as ubiquitous in bookstores and at dinner parties as Norah Jones is today. Don't you miss him now?

LUOMO
VOCAL CITY
(Force Tracks, 2000)

Vladislav Delay is part of a new school of bleep geeks combining microscopic chop'n'splice with the body-positive bounce of house music. His debut under the Luomo moniker is a reminder that disco diva vocals—long barred from the party by the electronica cognoscenti—are still pretty great, so long as the beats are fresh.

PREFUSE 73
VOCAL STUDIES + UPROCK NARRATIVES
(Warp, 2001)

Electronica and hip-hop mostly used to sit at separate lunch counters. But when Timbaland began producing hotter techno tracks than anyone, it was time to rethink. Scott "Prefuse 73" Herren feeds hip-hop beats (and frequently MCs) through his laptop Cuisinart to make sputtering breakdance anthems for double-jointed pop-lockers.
— Will Hermes / June '04

[THE CHEMICAL BROTHERS]

As if in response to Underworld's crowd-pleasing reverie, the Chemical Brothers—Ed Simons and Tom Rowlands—brusquely cranked up their industrial-strength, slap-happy breakbeats until the monitors vibrated like dishes in an earthquake. In comedy-club parlance, the Chemicals killed. Grounded in hip-hop, their music struck a fierce rock'n'roll pose, though the musicians did nothing more than wordlessly bob their uncool haircuts behind a bank of samplers. Deploying a film barrage of ghetto uprisings, spinning clocks, warplanes, and exploding periodic tables, these two unassuming joes assumed that they could do something most rock or dance music never even tries—express rage as well as rapture, *in the same song*. Brother Rowlands remarked later: "The other bands were being so nice to everybody, like children's TV presenters or something. We had other ideas."

— "Drums and Wires" / Charles Aaron / October '96

No matter how many times A&R goobers, MTV execs, and radio programmers proclaim the Prodigy as techno's first "real band," don't believe the bleeding hype. An innovative force since 1992's debut album *The Prodigy Experience*—which cranked the breakbeat craze into high gear and foresaw drum'n'bass— the "group" is the product of one man's fiercely kinetic imagination, DJ/producer Liam Howlett. That "Firestarter" clown (Keith Flint) and the two clunky MCs are simply multicolored props for

rock-damaged focus groups. Howlett, the quiet guy in the sweater, is the visionary. And he will rock you, like only a DJ can.

— "Spin Top 40" / April '97

Swallowed by a loaner Versace suit ($855 retail), Moby faces down a gauntlet of tabloid flashes outside London's Earl's Court arena. It's the Brit Awards 2000, the U.K.'s openly sloshed Grammys alter ego, and pop watchers are working up a buzz over grumpy Oasis geezer Liam Gallagher's feud with smirky boy-band geezer Robbie Williams ("He's a fat dancer," quipped Liam). But frankly, nobody gives a toss. A star-power vacuum exists in Euro-pop, and no better indication is Moby's presence as Best International Male Artist nominee (for 1999's *Play*). As he shuffles into position, a publicist must inform the paparazzi who Moby actually is.

"Moby! Moby! Over here!" the photogs shout, and the artist, hands deep in pockets that don't belong to him, obliges, sort of. Alone on the sidewalk he shifts his tiny bald head to and fro. *Click! Click!* But with his big-eyed stare he looks like a milk-carton orphan, not gossip-column fodder.

"You know what I said before about how I'm starting to feel successful?" he asks me, referring to an earlier comment about his eerie dance floor ballad "Why Does My Heart Feel So Bad?" being such an unexpected European hit. "Well, I just changed my mind."

— "Revenge of the 'Little Idiot'" / Charles Aaron/ June '00

{ FATBOY SLIM }

SPIN: What's your favorite poison?

Fatboy Slim: Vodka and orange. By the time I go on, I've normally drunk half a bottle, so then I top the rest off with orange juice and bring the bottle onstage.

And you're still standing?

Oh yeah.

So you can work under those conditions?

I can *only* work under those conditions. If I'm not drunk enough, I find it really difficult to perform. I'm afraid of seeming unprofessional. I'd be letting the crowd down if I went on sober. They expect Fatboy Slim to be a drunken buffoon wearing a Hawaiian shirt. If "Norman" came on, everyone would be disappointed.

— "The Jetset Lives of Superstar DJs" / Victoria DeSilverio and Tricia Romano / July '02

January 23, 2000:

Smiley-faced San Francisco rave feature *Groove* gets standing ovation at Sundance Film Festival; Sony Pictures buys it on the spot for $1.5 million.

February 7, 2000:

Moby's *Play*, released in June of 1999, goes gold without ever cracking the top 40. Corporate clients line up to license tracks for commercials (Nissan, Maxwell House), movies (*The Beach*), and videogames. All 18 tracks are sold; Moby becomes beatwise muzak for the mall that is America.

June 9, 2000:

Groove opens at, um, ten theaters nationwide.

Nov. 7, 2000:

Norman Cook, a.k.a. Fatboy Slim, releases *Halfway Between the Gutter and the Stars*, featuring Bootsy Collins, Macy Gray, and, back from the dead, Doors vocalist Jim Morrison. High-profile collaborations raise questions as to whether a Mariah Carey project might be on deck. Be very afraid.

— "Hype of the Year: Counting the Beats" / David J. Prince/ January '01

: Weezer

Geeks like us

/ Chuck **Klosterman**

Let's assume you want to understand the music of the 1990s

(and I mean *all* of the '90s – not just 1992). Let's assume you want to understand how rock music changed over those 10 years, and how rock music stayed the same. But let's also assume you don't have much time; let's assume you can only consider the work of one specific artist, and that artist has to explain everything. Who should you pick?

Well, you should pick Weezer.

There is only one guy who accidentally embodies the totality of that era, and his name is Rivers Cuomo. People rarely think about Weezer as a prism for modern rock's evolution, but that's exactly what they are; Cuomo's flawless, KISS-influenced power popping has always been at the vortex of rock's post-'80s hangover.

It is both logical and surprising that Cuomo began his musical career during the waning days of L.A. hair metal, admiring Yngwie Malmsteen[1] and shredding his Fender Strat on songs like "You Were Just Using Me" for an Iron Maiden-ish band called Avant Garde (they later switched their name to Zoom, but that didn't help much). His headbanger days ended in the spring of 1990, when Rivers fortuitously realized that commercial metal was poised for collapse, despite the fact that every metal band in Los Angeles was getting signed. Cuomo spent the next four years building Weezer; like so many of his peers, he embraced the straightforward structures

(if not necessarily the desperate sound) of bands like Nirvana. The first time he heard "Smells Like Teen Spirit" (while washing dishes in the kitchen of an Italian restaurant), Cuomo knew what kind of music Weezer was going to make: It would be simple, propulsive, and personal. Those kinds of songs comprise Weezer's 1994 eponymous debut. However, the cover of that album was almost as significant as the music. Standing against a wall of blue, the guys in Weezer didn't look like Nirvana; they looked like Pavement, or maybe the Replacements. Without even trying, *Weezer* represented a critical moment of fusion for '90s alternative rock: Aesthetically and intellectually, Weezer represented the mainstreaming of indie rock, even though they never made an independent record.

Two years later, that duality would hurt them. When Weezer released the best album of their career, 1996's *Pinkerton*, it expressed all the uncomfortable geek-to-god sentiments that became ubiquitous once alt rock became pop's dominant idiom (i.e., "Why do all these people suddenly like me? Why is sex unsatisfying? Why can't I just date a nice lesbian?"). Several thousand people heard the songs on *Pinkerton* and felt the shape of their heart change; unfortunately, the rest of the world merely thought Rivers was a weird, alienated dude with a weird, alienating beard. *Pinkerton* tanked and Cuomo went into hiding; he studied creative writing and English at Harvard, he got braces on his teeth and some unsuccessful laser surgery on his eyes, and had one of his legs surgically lengthened to remedy a congenital condition that made his left leg two inches longer than his right. Cuomo openly rejected the earnest sentimentality of *Pinkerton*, and there would not be another Weezer album for half a decade.

But two things happened over those next five years, and both seem strongly linked to Weezer (or—more specifically—Weezer's absence). For one, the gestalt that Weezer embodied largely disappeared from mainstream culture, abruptly replaced by its antithesis: confrontational, athletic, non-melodic rap-rock. But something else happened during that span that was less expected—by doing absolutely nothing, Weezer became more important. If the argument can be made that Sunny Day Real Estate's *Diary* was emo's "Rock Around the Clock," *Pinkerton* was the genre's *Sgt. Pepper's*: Philosophically, it

defined what emo was supposed to feel like. And by the late 1990s, fans didn't need albums or concerts to engage with a rock band. Weezer was probably the first group to thrive exclusively in cyberspace. The kind of cultic kids who loved "El Scorcho" were the same kind of cultic kids who wanted to live inside chat rooms and speculate over what "El Scorcho" was about. Everyone knows that Weezer validated emo rock, but Weezer also facilitated meta rock, which might actually be more important. They became more popular without releasing new records and without going on tour; they became more popular just by having kids talk about how intensely they missed them.

When a second eponymous Weezer album came out in 2001 (this one was green), it debuted at #5 on *Billboard*'s Top 200 album chart and was widely adored by critics. Neither of those things had happened to *Pinkerton*. The reason this seems paradoxical is because the music really hadn't changed: The '01 sound was just as polished, catchy, and muscular as it had been in the past. The lyrics were still funny and sad at the same time. Musically, Weezer has always been the same band. The only thing that changed was the rest of the world.

Outside the Rave Ballroom, fans are lining up. The building stands in what is now one of Milwaukee's poorest neighborhoods, and for lots of these white kids arriving from places like Dubuque, Sheboygan, and Michigan's Upper Peninsula, this is as inner-city as they've ever been, despite looking like they just stepped off the subway from Brooklyn in their ass-challenged sweats and Fubu caps. Booked for a night in the crumbling flophouses nearby, or planning to haul home after the show, they're now swarming the Open Pantry across Wisconsin Street to snap up the Sobe teas stocked especially for their demographic.

These kids were weened on Weezer. "They're geeks like us!" one 19-year-old tells me, apparently speaking for the rest of the 3,500 fans who have braved mid-March misery like hearty Packers fans. His equally ruddy pal adds, "I was going through some rocky stuff in my senior year of high school. *Pinkerton* saved my life."

Truth be told, these kids seem decidedly un-geek-like. They're more heroic, actually—of that athletic Midwestern archetype that poet James Wright called the "suicidally beautiful." Their adolescent pain was real, sure. But Weezer's middle-American fans, known by some as "Weezerjacks," personify what alt rock did in the '90s—namely to make mainstream the kind of self-aware dorkiness and deprecation that was formerly the province of arty parodists on the fringe. In 1994, Weezer epitomized that contradiction—they were geeky yet triumphant, jaded yet potent. They were Pavement for the masses, irony for dispossessed linebackers.
—"Cutting Classes" / Laura Sinagra / June '01

---

[1] *Do you think your band sees you as being difficult to work with?* I don't care what they see me like, because if they don't do what I tell them, they can fuck off. Period.

: interview with metal guitar savant YNGWIE MALMSTEEN, Rivers Cuomo's early hero, 1985.

Weezer's self-titled debut was first released in May 1994, when Kurt Cobain had been dead for just over a month. Back then, Weezer seemed inconsequential, if not objectionable. Their record label sold them as an alternative-rock band, but their music replaced the public purging that had been grunge's hallmark with cheeky lyrics about sweaters and Mary Tyler Moore. They're dressed like they'd just rolled out of bed to wait in line for Pavement tickets, but their guitar parts betrayed a debt to Cheap Trick and Sunset Strip glam rock that no amount of au courant distortion could conceal. There were rumors that they'd once been (gasp!) a *hair-metal* band. In the long shadow of Cobain cast over that whole summer, the band's quasi-novelty smash "Undone—The Sweater Song" felt like an affront, a cheap joke. They might as well have been squeezing whoopee cushions at Sir Lancelot's funeral.

So take the fact that we're still talking about them ten years down the road as proof that context is everthing. The same qualities that made Weezer so out of step in the post-grunge mid-90s seem like virtues now; the world has turned and left them looking like

straight-up power-pop geniuses. And this expanded re-issue of *Weezer* (dubbed "The Blue Album" by fans because of the blue cover)—now augmented with a second disc of nonessential but worthy bonus material—just confirms how good they were.

Rivers Cuomo—who wrote most of the album's songs, minus two collaborations with drummer Pat Wilson and one with Wilson and early bassist Jason Cropper—saw in alternative rock a safe home for his eccentricities. But he had no use for the genre's willful disrespect for craftsmanship, its equation of ragged dynamics and aw-shucks playing with sincerity. Instead Cuomo took a nerdy, code-cracking joy in showing off his understanding of how pop music worked. In the ingenious video for "Buddy Holly," *Weezer*'s second single, director Spike Jonze digitally inserts the band into the goofy retro-'50s fantasy of *Happy Days*. And in a way, Cuomo's songs work a similar kind of magic with alternative rock's signature sound effects, fitting distortion-pedal mood swings, lo-fi fuzz, and emotively slurred vocals into air-tight, time-tested pop- single templates. Feedback duels with adroit finger-picking; galloping punk pastiches break for bridges that genuflect in the church of Brian Wilson.

As a lyricist, Cuomo was not yet as winning or daring as he'd be on 1996's *Pinkerton*, the

soul-baring sophomore flop that legion of incipient emo kids would save for a whiny day. But *Weezer*'s weird girl-in-a-box song "No One Else" and the boy-victim plot of "Undone" anticipate the sexual angst that would fuel *Pinkerton* highlights "Across the Sea" and "Falling for You." "Say It Ain't So," a mid-tempo ballad that sounds like the most soulful song Archers of Loaf never wrote, might be Cuomo's finest moment—starting out as a slacker on the couch, he wrestles with "Jimmy" (yuk, yuk) and ends up venting more family trauma than Eddie Vedder in Pearl Jam's "Alive." (The video, which helped turn the horn-rimmed Cuomo into a geek-world sex symbol, climaxes with the most epic game of Hacky Sack in MTV history.)

— review of reissue of *Weezer* (aka "The Blue Album" / Alex Pappademas / April '04

Pinkerton (Geffen, 1996) The emo album. Ignored by casual fans, embraced by their younger siblings, *Weezer*'s self-produced sophomore album is a beautifully tortured studio shit-fit. Both self-deprecating and

self-lacerating, it includes the greatest song ever written about jerking off to one's fan mail.

Weezer (a.k.a. "The Green Album") (Geffen / Interscope, 2001) Singles "Hash Pipe" and "Island in the Sun" put them back on top; the rest suggests that Cuomo spent the band's hiatus breaking bricks in some kind of pop-hook kung-fu school. Still, *Pinkerton* obsessives grumbled about its slickness—there's not a single handclap out of place—and the less confessional tone of the lyrics.

Maladroit (Geffen / Interscope, 2002) Heavier than AC/DC's tour bus, yet still packed with irresistible melodies. And although Cuomo the genius keeps Cuomo the man squirreled away in the lab, the shark-toothed riff that slices "Burndt Jamb" in half is better than most bands' entire discographies.

> *"When I first got excited about hair was maybe '84. I brought the Quiet Riot album to the hair salon and said, 'Make me look like Carlos Cavazo.' And they did. And my mom got so upset, she got in the car and drove home without me, which was, like, five miles away."* RIVERS CUOMO, 2001

Weezer's Rivers Cuomo once sang about sneaking into a girl's dorm room to read her diary. Now, his own life is an open book. A meticulous day-by-day chronology of Cuomo's entire existence—from his first guitar to the haircut he got in Los Angeles last October—has surfaced on the Web. Thirty-two pages of idiosyncratic detail, it may be one of the strangest rock biographies ever. And it was actually created by Cuomo himself.

According to Mike Zaic, a 22-year-old New Jersey grad student who hosts a copy of the timeline on his website, Mike's World of Weezer, Cuomo put together the document with the help of a tech-savvy Weezer fan. "He was helping Rivers build an archival site," Zaic says. "Rivers brought him a big box of stuff—even report cards." Cuomo originally posted it on his personal Web page, Riverscuomo.com. (That site is now closed to the public.)

The first entry, dated June 13, 1970, simply reads "Born"; other notes from Cuomo's youth include "Pick up traveler's checks: thank you notes finished by 10 p.m." (July 10, 1987) and "HOST CANADIAN EXCHANGE STUDENT" (March 1988). The rest of the timeline continues in the same vein, mixing the professional and the personal, the momentous and the picayune. Every Weezer recording session, video shoot, and tour date is duly noted. But we also learn of a visit to "Grandma Cuomo" on December 30, 1994. And Cuomo's obsession with World Cup soccer is documented in detail; the entry for October 26, 2000 reads, "2-0 U.S.-MEXICO at Coliseum / break up with Kelley at this point."

Voyeuristic thrills aside, the timeline will undoubtedly be an invaluable resource for future Weezer scholars, as it lists enough unreleased Cuomo compositions to fill a dozen box sets. Among the hundreds of titles mentioned are: "Who You Callin' Bitch?" "There's a Bomb in the Air," "Down Down Diggity," "I Can't Stop, I'm 0 for the Day," and "C'mon, Siobhan."

— "The Pinkerton Papers" / Alex Pappademas / June '03

[SHAWN FANNING]

: Napster

Too fucking good to last

Back in the 90s,

who could have predicted record companies would sue their own customers? That one Time Warner label would drop Wilco, and then another would sign them, primarily on the basis of their Internet popularity? That over the course of a few years media conglomerates would begin to see their music divisions less as cash cows than black sheep they were eager to auction off?

Certainly not Shawn Fanning, a freshman at Northeastern University who invented Napster in 1999 so that he could share music with friends and, later, strangers. The myth of the garage entrepreneur is as iconic to the technology business as that of the garage band is to rock—think of Steves Jobs and Wozniak hammering together the original Apple. Fanning had the image down cold. Staring from the magazine covers, the unruly hair he named his program after covered by a baseball cap, he personified the Internet's nightmare scenario: The kid who could put you out of business. Except he didn't just build a better mousetrap—he was the pied piper who led the mice out of town, along with the kids. A window into the MP3 library of every logged-in hard drive, Napster was the closest thing to what one writer called "the celestial jukebox"—an instantly accessible collection of nearly every song ever, for free.

Prophet that he was, Fanning never made it to the promised land. Napster turned out to be a great idea and a good piece of software, but not much of a company. After the February 2001 court decision (in the wake of countless millions of songs downloaded) that effectively shut down his file-sharing service, Fanning shared the fate of many an inventor before him: What he built in the garage, someone else ultimately took to the bank.

His idea lived on, as did his penchant for poor product names. Some next-gen Napsters, like Gnutella, weren't centralized enough to shut down. Kazaa, run from Australia, supposedly programmed in Estonia and legally headquartered in the South Pacific island of Vanuatu, could have come straight from a cyberpunk novel; it was practically impossible to sue. Eventually, it became clear there was no honor among intellectual property thieves: Kazaa left code in some computers that could track users. Let the downloader beware.

And let the music business tremble. First there were the predictable public service announcements—Britney saying, "please, pay for your music." Eventually, unable to sue the file-sharing service, the record labels began to sue the people who fed them files. By the middle of 2002, CD sales were declining, labels were panicking, and record stores were closing. Fans weren't exactly sympathetic. Over the course of the '90s, the price of CDs had increased slightly, even as the cost of making them had declined greatly. Once you started to think of your favorite songs as digital data, just a string of zeroes and ones out there in the ether, $15.99 seemed like a lot of money for a silver disc; especially once DVD prices started to fall.

The labels closed ranks under the RIAA, but performers themselves were divided. Metallica and Dr. Dre spoke up about wanting to get *paid*, while indie-rock sorts weren't sure what it meant for them. In an essay, aging folkie Janis Ian, of all people, pointed out that the major label system was broken anyway. How could labels—those price-fixing ponytails who barely paid out anything to artists—dare to sue anyone?

By then, where you stood depended on whether you worked in a record store or just shopped in one. To fans and Internet gurus, it was hard to believe the labels hadn't brought at least some of this on themselves. With radio consolidating and bland pop dominating, where else but the Internet could anyone hear new music? Perhaps file-sharing services like Kazaa could serve as sonic sampler platters, introducing people to new sounds they could then choose to buy. File-sharing, to quote the skate-culture saw, was not a crime. Except that it was.

Meanwhile, labels saw double-digit sales decreases, and the business changed. Acts like Rod Stewart, marketing to a demographic that still, quaintly, paid for stuff, became crucial to the bottom line. Career artists like fled to indie labels. The majors changed management or changed hands. Bands got dropped like bad habits.

Gradually, the labels learned to love the Internet. Sorta. Initially the majors were reluctant to sell the music they owned online. But Apple's iTunes store had in Steve Jobs the kind of mogul music types would respect. He got labels to offer songs as well as full albums, and leaned on them for exclusive tracks early and often. The digital revolution was televised—if only on a tiny iPod screen. And the iPod became an icon in itself, the symbol of a substantial CD collection smaller than a pack of American Spirits.

Jobs created the Internet's first decent legal record store, but anyone could sell songs for around a buck, and soon everyone—even Wal-Mart—was. As for the free services, Kazaa was no longer anyone's indie-rock dream. It and the other file-sharing services are filled with spoofed decoy files record companies distribute to make listening less convenient. "Napster" has been reduced to an off-brand version of iTunes. And Fanning himself is working on a new file-sharing service that the major labels have bought into.

But Napster's promise—that idea that anyone on the Internet could share music with everyone else—is alive and well. The action these days is on MP3 blogs, sites where diary-style musings share space with downloadable songs. Some are by baby bands, garage acts people love enough to launch into the ether. Others are by bigger acts. But the major labels haven't raised much of a stink. In fact, they sometime send bloggers the files themselves. Seems they'd rather have fans listen a little than not at all.

The celestial jukebox is dead. Long live celestial college radio. At least until some undergrad figures out a way to upend the industry all over again.

"It is sickening that our art is being traded like a commodity rather than the art that it is. This is about taking something that doesn't belong to you. The trading of such information is, in effect, trafficking in stolen goods."
— Metallica's Lars Ulrich, 2000

At 12:30 p.m., Ulrich arrived in a chauffeured Chevy Blazer, rolling with two attorneys and two document roadies, who lugged 13 boxes. These contained lists of 335,435 Napster users who were illegally offering Metallica downloads during a two-day period in late April, according to a computer consulting firm hired by the band.

"Is my name on your list?" someone taunted.

"Here!" said another, holding up a dollar bill. "Sing me a song, Lars!"

— "Metal Up Their Assets" / G. Beato / August '00

DJ of the Year: You

Yeah, you. You don't just dig music, man—you *understand* it. You know better than anyone that having Black Flag, the White Stripes, Mötley Crüe, My Morning Jacket, Sleater-Kinney, and Sly Stone at your fingertips can turn a trip to the grocery store into a saga, a private vision quest, a Scorsese movie. Fusing all the world-transforming technological innovations of the past few decades— the Walkman, Napster, the Tamagotchi—the iPod is more than a cool, shiny gadget to show off at the bar, though it *is* certainly that. It gives you back control of all the valuable head-space that the Man so desperately longs to colonize. Fill it up. Keep it charged. Own your destiny.

— "Year In Music 2003" / Alex Pappademas

Last summer, Napster relocated to San Mateo, California. There, it occupies the kind of cluttered, disheveled offices that give fortune-sniffing venture capitalists nipple hard-ons. Plants are wilting, the furniture doesn't match, empty cans of Red Bull decorate the premises: There's no time for anything except work, work, work. Shawn Fanning keeps a guitar and a basketball in his office but hasn't touched them in months. Remarkably, he and creative partner Sean Parker are now mid-level grunts who have to answer to more experienced coworkers. At the moment, his boss is mad at him: So many publications have been requesting interviews from him lately that it's cut into his coding time.

But requests keep coming, because Napster users are so hooked. One legendary user built a library of 15,000 songs; another amassed a staggering 17 gigabytes of music. An architect who lived 30 miles away showed up at the offices one day simply because he wanted to meet the people who'd created Napster. When the company cosponsored a rave that attracted thousands of people to an Oakland warehouse, its booth was swarmed by devoted fans. "It's seriously addictive," says John Perkins, who feels so strongly about the program he created the NapsterCult website. "I was away from my computer for a couple weeks, and it was hard to take; it was like going through physical withdrawal."

— "Trading Spaces" / G. Beato / May '00

Although Radiohead completed *Kid A* in April, no one outside the inner circle heard the music until mid-August. The first to actually listen to the album were a handful of Capitol executives who were herded into vans, outfitted with headphones, and required to listen to the whole album during a scenic drive down the Pacific Coast Highway. But the fans didn't require such stratagems; Internet message boards show eager bootleggers trying to subvert security as early as July, urging "insiders" to sneak anything out of the studio. The agitations must have worked: By the album's official October 3 release date, unauthorized copies of every track were available online.

Even Capitol/EMI, which has joined the industry lawsuit against Napster for copyright infringement, agrees that the unauthorized downloaders contributed to the hype. "We didn't use Napster. We wanted to keep [*Kid A*] off Napster," says Rob Gordon, the label's vice president of marketing. "But when it went up, did it create more excitement, more enthusasm? Absolutely."

— "Band of the Year: Radiohead" / Steve Knopper / January '01

What industry-sanctioned product could compete with 20 million Napster users collaborating on the greatest mix tape never sold? This year, you didn't have to wait for a label to bequeath a Timbaland best-of or go dork-to-dork to compile that Stereolab C-sides disc. Downloading challenged our definition of The Album as a self-contained work and our role as fans like no record ever could—while opening our ears to thousands of new ones.

— "Album of the Year: Your Hard Drive" / Jon Dolan / January '01

: Jam Bands

/ Will **Hermes**

Smells like Phish
[not to mention patchouli,
                    B.O., beer, + kind bud]

SPIN
never showed
much love

towards the jam band scene, and I suspect part of the reason was jealousy. Sure, there was an a priori bias against dreadlocked white kids cultivating hand-me-down hippiedom in a cultural bubble like it was hydroponic weed (which mnay of them also cultivated). Weren't punk and alt rock invented, after all, to replace this kind of flower-child utopianism with boot-stomp realism?

Yet the truth is we all crave community, and the alt-rock culture SPIN primarily championed never saw anything like the straight-life-shirking, obsessive bootleg-collecting, on-the-road devotion that the Grateful Dead, Phish, and their spawn engendered among their freakier-than-thou fans. Writer Michael Azerrad called his excellent chronicle of the '80s indie-rock scene *This Band Could Be Your Life*. Yet few indie kids ever embraced that notion as extremely as jamheads have.

Back in the mid-80s, "jam band" basically meant one thing: the Grateful Dead. In their '60s prime they were radical punks, taking heroic doses of LSD with Ken Kesey and the Hell's Angels, blasting white-boy r&b, blues, and old-time country into fractals of noise and rhythm. Twenty years later, they were a fairly bloated institution playing arenas for the burnout parents of teenage punks, new-school hippie kids, and a battalion of bong-packing frat boys. Yet on a good night (when guitar wizard Jerry Garcia wasn't too smacked-out), the Dead could still make sublime music, and they left their mark on many alt rockers. Ian MacKaye's early hardcore band the Teen Idles may have declared "the only good Deadhead is one that's dead!" But Jane's Addiction recorded a fairly reverent version of the Dead's "Ripple," West Coast dub-punk heroes Sublime covered their "Scarlet Begonias," and Elvis Costello performed a soulful "Ship of Fools > It Must Have Been The Roses." Original punks Patti Smith and Henry Rollins have confessed their closeted affection. And no rock band partial to long guitar breaks, from Television to Pavement to Built To

[PHISH]

It was their own little world until 1992, when Phish both headlined the H.O.R.D.E. fest (Horizons of Rock Developing Everywhere, dude!) and began their relationship with Elektra Records, securing the unusual provision

Spill to Animal Collective, could really avoid the Dead's shadow.

But as the Dead lost steam, they inspired a host of bands inheriting more from them than just cover tunes and a taste for wanky instrumentals. The first to emerge from the ooze were Phish, a furry and affable bunch of stoner types fond of prog rock and jazz fusion who came together in the crunchy state of Vermont in the mid-'80s and gradually—in a feat of engineering deserving study by any aspiring cult band—built a mindboggling underground fanbase using the then-new technology of the Internet. With a geek mythology based partly on a rock opera guitarist/frontman Trey Anastasio wrote as his senior thesis at Goddard College, they turned their endless touring into a meta-narrative of mutating sets and in-jokes that fans tracked as a sort of serial epic. It was just the thing for undergrads with a head full of NoDoz to obsess over online (rec.music.phish was the fourth-ever Usenet newsgroup devoted to a band, after the Beatles, Bob Dylan, and the Dead), and they did, to the point where concert tape-traders were analyzing the frequency and form of individual songs, and the band was riffing off the input onstage in a playfully head-fucking feedback loop.

to allow fans to tape their shows. Suddenly, "jam band" was a genre. Fellow travelers like Blues Traveler and Widespread Panic joined a growing tribal entertainment circuit. And when Jerry Garcia died and left millions of Deadheads musically homeless, the ante was upped for everyone. Phish rose to the challenge, beginning a series of massive summer festivals in 1996 that peaked with their 1999 New Year's Eve gig at the Big Cypress Indian Reservation in Florida —a five-day event for roughly 200,000 heads capped with a nine-hour Phish set that was the single biggest ticketed millennium throwdown on the planet.

For all the laudible trappings of jam-band culture—the unpredictable live shows, the freak-scene hedonism, the anti-mainstream mindset, the love-your-neighbor-and-don't-bogart-that-joint vibe —the music itself is often the weak link. It

ESSAY CONTINUES ON NEXT PAGE >

> ESSAY CONTINUES FROM PREVIOUS PAGE

rarely balls-out rocks, its grooves are often less funky than funk-lite, and the Dead notwithstanding, it's never been long on memorable tunes, preferring to get lost in tricky time signatures and virtuoso, multi-lane improvs.

But as the scene evolved through the '90s, so did the sounds. The jazz-minded organ trio Medeski, Martin & Wood dug deep into avant-funk, sometimes working with the hip-hop-schooled, jam-conversant DJ Logic; the Disco Biscuits explored affinities between techno and jam soundscapes; Umphrey's McGee channel-surfed genres from hair-metal to Indian ragas. And when Phish called it quits in 2004 after a 20-year run, they left a hydra-headed scene epitomized by Bonnarroo, the polyglot summer rock festival modeled on Phish's '90s fetes. Showcasing punk-schooled neo-jammers Wilco and Sonic Youth alongside jam nation kingpins like Gov't Mule (whose leader Warren Haynes has been known to cover Radiohead's "Lucky" when not moonlighting with the reformed Dead) and Dave Matthews (who doesn't actually jam, but plays with a longwinded fiddler and saxophonist), Bonnarroo became the biggest and best rock festival in the country at the same moment an attempt to revive Lollapolooza stalled at the gate. It bodes very well for the future of a scene that often seemed stuck in an endless, noodle-dancing Now.

the hippie twirl

profile

Performer spins in a shrill and invasive declaration of child-like wonder. Arms wave and face beams, evoking Summer of Love and special-education classes.

gang affiliations

Bearded software execs; batik-skirted sophomores; psilocybin entrepreneurs. Seen at Rainbow Gatherings, Ivy League picnics, and large-scale "jam" events.

This is Daniel's first Grateful Dead concert.

Having seen the freaky skeleton video ("Touch of Grey") on MTV, Daniel is curious about the Dead, but not curious to the point of drugging, which might affect his GPA and condemn him to a life batter-frying poultry by-products in fast-food restaurants. Ross, in his FUCK THA POLICE T-shirt, is Daniel's old high school buddy from San Rafael and is thankfully tolerant of Daniel's nerdiness, but Ross can occasionally inflict a graze wound. "I smell oregano burning. Is Dan nearby?"

Daniel has heard lore of the pre-Dead-concert parking lot scene, but the actuality of the event, at Northern California's Oakland-Alameda County Coliseum, is overpowering—a dope-smoke-scented anti-mall constructed of crammed-together, rust-bucket trucks, vans, and school buses license-plated mainly from California, Oregon, Washington, British Columbia, Nevada, Colorado, and Arizona. An impromptu tent city of vendors flaunt standard head-shop goodies: antler pipes, skeleton decals, skull candles, tie-dyed shirts, porcupine quills, juggling supplies, Peruvian mittens, conspiracy-theory paperbacks, rolling papers, and bumper stickers: MUCHAS GARCIAS and ONE NUCLEAR FAMILY CAN RUIN YOUR WHOLE DAY. Older hippie ladies ripe with B.O. gorge on condom balloon animals of nitrous oxide; relentless bongo drums beat; troll hippies in flannel shirts vend health-food dinners soaked with rain: "Veggie stir-fry! Veggie stir-fry!"

Daniel buys a Styrofoam plate of tofu, hijiki mushrooms, tamari sauce, and Maui onion bits. "With lechithin and engevista yeast," the spacey vendor says proudly. Daniel holds his plate and asks for a plastic spoon. The troll druggily cackles back, "Hey man, I'm organic."

Before entering the van, Daniel avoids a mound of puppy shit lying under the slightly less wet area covered by the tarpaulin. Once inside he suggest to his schoolmates, all UC Berkeley freshmen like himself and smoking mystery substances from a bong, that perhaps somebody in the van has trailed inside a dab of the puppy's business.

"Daniel," says Ross, marveling at Daniel's coolness deficiency, "nothing is more bourgeois than fear of the smell of feces."

— "Polaroids from the Dead" / Douglas Coupland / April '92.

Hunched at the wheel of his Audi, Trey Anastasio is showing
how jam-rock guitarists do it–
which is to say, at 60, on unpaved roads, in a snowstorm.

"Sorry," he says as we get air off a pothole. "When I'm alone I usually go a hundred back here." The perils of back-road speeding are today intensified by the fact that Anastasio has just returned from six weeks in the British Virgin Islands, where they drive southpaw. He proffers this last tidbit with a bearded grin, reflected flakes dancing madly in his rimless hexagonal glasses. "We were actually on the wrong side a few miles back," he says. "I was hoping you didn't notice."

The rustic blur out the window is part of a small Vermont town the guitarist occupies with his wife and daughters, a town that fan obsessiveness prohibits naming. Soon we're driving past the University of Vermont, birthplace of many small bands, and one great big one.

We pass a large brick campus building. "Those are the steps where I first met Fish," Anastasio says. He is referring to drummer Jon Fishman, whose nickname is a homophone for a band they formed in 1983 with bassist Mike Gordon. As we drive on, Anastasio relates other key chapters in the Book of Phish: that first gig at the ROTC party; those first shows at Nectar's; the early four-track recordings—all events annotated and discussed on websites numbering in the hundreds.

As we pass Burlington's Center for Cultural Pluralism, talk turns, as it must, to the Grateful Dead. That late, great, 1960s institution has been both inspiration and albatross to Phish, whose members have long resented being pigeonholed as Dead wannabes or bonghead magnets. Anastasio, for one, would sooner bring My Bloody Valentine's *Loveless* than *Terrapin Station* to a desert island. Still, there is a fondness.

"There was one Dead show I saw," Anastasio says as we stop at a light. "One show I'd rank as one of the best concerts I've ever seen." He squints into the distance, remembering. "It was at Hartford Civic Center, 1982 or '83," he continues. "And it was just a concert, you know? It wasn't about the vibe; it wasn't about the scene. I wasn't hanging out with my friends and stuff. I was just standing there, alone. Just listening to the music."

Wow. And you weren't on acid or anything.

"Oh, no. I was."

— "Back to the Phuture" / Chris Norris / July '00

the phish handjive

profile

Feet planted, performer bobs left and right, tracing music with downward palms jabbing and pawing the air.

gang affiliations

Goateed poli-sci majors; Abercrombie-wearing show-bootleggers; known Hacky Sack offenders. (**see also** the Hippie Twirl).

While you weren't looking, the Dave Matthews Band have gone from being just another H.O.R.D.E.-tourin', Hacky Sackin' road act to a bona fide rock phenomenon.

The band's third studio album, *Before These Crowded Streets*, shipped 1.7 million copies, bringing to an end the *Titanic* soundtrack's 15-week reign of terror atop the charts. The band sold out the 78,000-capacity Giants Stadium in 90 minutes, entering Spice Girls territory. And, in an effective riposte to the critics who dismissed Matthews as a boomer-soothing hack, this concert even featured critic-darling Beck—as an opener. Partly through attrition and partly by changing mass tastes, Dave Matthews is threatening to replace the likes of Kurt Cobain and Eddie Vedder as rock's alpha male, a prospect that disquiets him as much as anyone. "Eddie Vedder," he says. "He's real sharp-looking, isn't he? Him, Kurt Cobain, those guys are serious. I feel more like...Elmer Fudd."
— "Fanfare for the Common Man" / Chris Norris / July '98

SPIN: How long is too long a jam?
Dave Matthews: When it starts to suck. I think sometimes we go on a little bit long. [chuckles] Maybe.

When people get up to grab a hot dog? Yeah, but we try not to ramble so it looks like nobody knows what they're doing. I don't like it when we get sucked into a black abyss onstage and everyone's standing there looking confused—like, "What are they doing now? I guess this is my chance to sit down."
—"Road Warrior" / June '99

"
I FEEL BAD ABOUT THAT GURU KIND OF STUFF. I'VE MADE A REAL EFFORT, SO FAR ANYWAY, TO TELL PEOPLE THAT I'M NOT LEADING ANYBODY ANYWHERE. I'M EXTREMELY PARANOID. IF YOU LOOK AT WHAT WE'RE DOING, IT HAS ALL THE ELEMENTS OF THE MOST EXTREME FASCISM. SO THAT SCARES ME A LOT... WOULD YOU LIKE TO HAVE THE RESPONSIBILITY OF LEADING THOUSANDS OF PEOPLE OFF INTO SOME OBLIVION SOMEWHERE?
"

— Jerry Garcia / "Dead Fingers Talk" / July '87

: Indie Hip-Hop
Backpacking across America

/ Jon **Caramanica**

There's three of them, and they're standing there stone-faced, indifferent. Except the guy in front—the white one—who's staring down the camera with exhausted eyes and extended middle finger. At the bottom of the photo is the slogan "Independent As Fuck," and it's meant to be a come-on.

This is how New York hip-hop icons Company Flow introduced themselves in the artwork for their debut album, 1997's *Funcrusher Plus* (Official/ Rawkus). They'd been using the slogan for a couple of years, but its prominent placement here was proof that, by the mid-'90s, the hip-hop counterculture had learned what their rock counterparts already knew—being indie was no longer mere rejection of, or by, the major label system. For a certain audience, it was a marketing strategy nonpareil.

Rappers had been indie for years, but up until the early '90s, it was because, by and large, the major label system wanted nothing to do with them. Outside of Def Jam's deal with Columbia, inked in 1985, indies were the dominant force in hip-hop; many of the great artists and albums of the '80s appeared on regional independents. Once the majors caught wind of the profit stream slipping through their fingers, they began to swoop in, and by the mid-'90s, hip-hop had become commodity pop, in the best and worst ways.

It was only natural, then, that the stories and sounds of the mainstream would breed dissenters, persistent artists who saw their own ideas about hip-hop's direction getting flatly ignored. The uprising began in Los Angeles. As the city was developing a reputation for breeding some of the country's most notorious gangster rap, it was also doing a smaller, concurrent trade in conscientious objectors. At the Good Life Café, a health-food shop on the edges of Leimert Park, open-mic nights showcased a range of outsider rappers (Fat Joe was allegedly once booed offstage there). Most notable of the pack were the Freestyle Fellowship, a collective of four MCs who took as many of their cues from Central Avenue's jazz heritage as they did from South Central's stark realities. With their high-minded lyrics—dealing with pro-black politics and self-improvement through art—and inscrutable flows, they were natural critical darlings, but in the high heat of the gangster era, their broader impact was negligible. (Not surprisingly, a dalliance with the majors proved traumatic and near-fatal for the Fellowship, though they still release albums individually and as a group).

Even though the Fellowship didn't do N.W.A numbers, they managed to extend their influence by seeding a host of counter-movements, local scenes that relied upon them for inspiration—political, lyrical, or both. Quickest to coalesce was the Bay Area's progressive scene, which already had a DIY template from the region's popular trunk-selling bad boys like Too Short and E-40. Most prominent among this wave was the Solesides crew, a group of beat-diggers and rappers who met, naturally, at a college radio station (at the University of California, Davis). They formed a label (later reborn as Quannum Projects) and released a batch of avant-garde records by Latyrx—two rappers who would, on occasion, rap over each other—and DJ Shadow. Shadow would go on to become a formative figure in electronic music, with a pastiche approach to beatmaking that proved there was room for musicology in the nightclub. Also around this time, hip-hop DJing—newly dubbed "turntablism"—began to gain currency as a musical artform of its own, thanks to the work of pioneers including the X-cutioners and the Invisibl Skratch Piklz.

By the mid-'90s, hip-hop was clearly fragmenting, cracking along lines stylistic, regional ,and even racial. A generation of young people had been raised almost entirely on a diet of the music, and they began to see themselves as preservationists, keeping the genre's true flame lit while those in the mainstream were compromising an imagined set of ideals for financial gain.

Nowhere was this divide more evident than in New York, the birthplace of hip-hop, and where its inner wars are enacted most visibly. New York's independent scene, which came into its own on the heels of the blossomings in California, had to find its space in the city's broader hip-hop conversation. As radio rap was becoming homogenized, artists who just two or three years prior could feasibly gain the ear of the mainstream—as many acts on, say, Loud Records had (see Wu-Tang Clan, Mobb Deep, etc)—now had to contend with a sort of forced obscurity.

In response, a robust network of indie labels appeared, first to catch the industry's overflow and, in time, to foment their own movement. At the forefront was Rawkus—which released the aforementioned Company Flow album as

ESSAY CONTINUES ON NEXT PAGE >

"It's been frustrating," says Freestyle Fellowship's Michael "Mikah Nine" Troy.

"We've always put so much into the art and not enough into business protocol. On top of that, we were on some old postmodern hip-hop shit that people are only appreciating now."

Perhaps hip-hop's future simply hinges on acknowledging the work of these "alternative" innovators, and then finding room for them to survive in the pop marketplace. "To a certain degree, everyone wants to be a Snoop or a Biggie, a household name," says Troy. "But I've hit it with the Last Poets, the Watts Prophets, different griots, people in different languages, all the freestyling heads in the parks all over the country. The only thing I haven't done is make a lot of money.... Look, I grew up in hip-hop, trying to put it on the map as a conscious movement. I put in that foundation. But right now, I feel like I'm only recognized as a marsupial in the mammalian family, like a platypus and shit." He laughs and strums his fingers across a keyboard. "The move now is to get paid, keep my art alive, and not have to die to be appreciated. "

— "California Dreaming" / Charles Aaron / April '95

When the Ultramagnetic MCs broke out of the Bronx in the mid-'80s, they might as well have been coming from the planet Tatooine.

Gluing rhymes to the beat à la Run-D.M.C.'s "Rock Box" was the preeminent style, and rappers' self-created images seemed less and less like role play and more like a hard shell. Then along came the ultra-abstract Ultramagnetics and MC Kool Keith, ducking and dodging the pulse, rhyming about things extraterrestrial, pornographic, and freaky. "Our thing was, how far can we go?" says Ultramagnetic MC and producer Ced Gee. "There were a lot of unwritten rules, and we had to break 'em. 'You're not even rhyming!' people would say. At the time, it was hard for anyone to accept."

— "The Man of 1000 Masks" / RJ Smith / August '99

well as the early work of Mos Def and Talib Kweli—accompanied by Fondle 'Em, Makin', Raw Shack, Seven Heads, and many others. Before the '90s had ended, independent hip-hop was a scene, with its own rulebook, adherents, and economy.

The last idea was perhaps the most important. Indie rap had been codified, signifying a particular sonic style rather than an anti-corporate frame of mind. Lo-fi production values reigned, a deliberate affront to the mainstream's increasing glossiness. Indie artists and fans were tagged with the name "backpackers"— the original designation came from artists like the Boot Camp Click, who were left behind when the mainstream turned pop, and who joked (or didn't) that they wore backpacks on robbery missions. Eventually, though, "backpacker" came to signify college student, record nerd, and so on—essentially anyone for whom hip-hop was a subject to be studied.

Buoyed by a growing number of such fans, indie rap became a financially viable artform, served by its own distribution networks and retail outlets. Eventually, the indie rock market acknowledged kinship with its rap peers—Matador and Epitaph signed rappers, and the Warped Tour began featuring a hip-hop stage. Being an indie rapper became a job description worth aspiring to.

In time, the indie scene became a haven for those who wanted to rap, but didn't want to—or just couldn't—converse with the mainstream. It also became a haven of sorts for hip-hop's cultural outsiders, namely white folk. The success of Eminem, who started out in the indie circuit before signing with Dr. Dre, didn't do much to integrate rap radio. But that said, most of his white contemporaries were choosing styles that, influenced by hip-hop's golden age of the late '80s and early '90s, bore little resemblance to what the mainstream was proffering. And by the turn of the century, it didn't matter. With alternate means of production (laptop technology) and distribution (the Internet) so readily available, small labels and niche artists were able to find their audiences without relying on the traditional avenues. Whiteness, once a huge liability, became, in some circles, almost an asset.

Different artists responded to this freedom in different fashions. Two of the leading indie rap labels of the late '90s and early '00s were Anticon and Rhymesayers. And though they started out in similar fashion—for a short time, their key artists collaborated—they evolved in wildly divergent directions. Anticon and its kissing cousin Mush became increasingly esoteric, making hip-hop that sounded more like slowcore abstraction with the odd sample for flair. The MCs on Rhymesayers—namely Slug (of Atmosphere) and Eyedea—began excavating the depths of human emotion without straying too far from the braggadocio that had earned them so many battle victories in earlier years.

No longer strictly an alternative to the mainstream, indie rap factionalized to the point where the underground effectively stopped dialoguing with mainstream altogether. In 2000, El-P, who'd up-middle-fingered the industry so famously in 1997, decided that gazing back in anger would do him no good. He founded his own label, Definitive Jux, which became a key indie tastemaker thanks to releases from the chimerical Harlem duo Cannibal Ox and the logorrheic Aesop Rock.

Meanwhile, Rawkus, now a skeleton of its former self, was bought by MCA/Universal, then largely dissolved. It was an admission of defeat by one incarnation of the indie dream—leaving room for the others to thrive in its wake.

FIFTEEN UNDIE-RAP ESSENTIALS

Aesop Rock
Labor Days
(Definitive Jux, 2001)

Atmosphere
The Lucy Ford EP
(Rhymesayers, 2000)

Binary Star
Masters of the Universe (Subterraneous, 2000)

Black Star
Mos Def & Talib Kweli are Black Star
(Rawkus, 2002)

Blackalicious
Nia
(Quannum Projects, 2000)

Cannibal Ox
The Cold Vein
(Definitive Jux, 2001)

The Cenobites
The Cenobites LP
(Fondle 'Em, 1997)

Company Flow
Funcrusher Plus
(Official/Rawkus, 1999)

Freestyle Fellowship
To Whom It May Concern...
(Beats & Rhymes, 1999)

Latyrx
Latryx—The Album
(Solesides, 1999)

MF Doom
Operation: Doomsday
(Fondle 'Em, 1999)

Quasimoto
The Unseen
(Stones Throw, 2000)

Sage Francis
Personal Journals
(Anticon, 2002)

Various Artists
Music for the Advancement of Hip-Hop (Anticon, 1999)

Various Artists
Project Blowed
(Project Blowed, 2000)

"We were so egotistical," says Chris Manak, a.k.a. Peanut Butter Wolf (the tag comes from an ex-girlfriend's little brother's name for the bogeyman), about his early partnership with MC Charizma.

"We did all these demos, all these shows, had Sony and Elektra interested. Then when we were signed to Hollywood Basics, we were just, like, total assholes to our A&R. Actually we were dropped right before Charizma passed away...I told myself I wasn't going to be in a group with anyone else again."

Now a humble 27-year-old marketing grad from San Jose State, Manak runs his own label, Stones Throw, and is hip-hop buyer at TRC, a key distributor for the indie underground. After his hypnotically flowing indie album *Peanut Butter Breaks*, (sampled by Cypress Hill) and "Chronicles (I Will Always Love H.E.R.)," a chopshop manifesto featured on *Return of the D.J.*, Manak's career has perked up. "I'd rather sell 10,000 units of vinyl, build my name, control all aspects of the process, and if somebody comes to me, I'm always open to talk. Artistic freedom is more important to me right now."
— "Turning the Tables" / Charles Aaron / March '97

Sunday-driving a Jeep Grand Cherokee around the sleepy collegiate streets of his hometown, Davis, California, Josh Davis, a.k.a. DJ Shadow, peers from under a fuzzy beige toboggan cap and testifies, "I was ten years old and 'The Message' [by Grandmaster Flash and the Furious Five] came on my little clock-radio cube and I immediately rolled over and pressed RECORD on my tape player," says the 24-year-old Davis, his eyes brightening. "My parents were just coming in to say good night and they were like, 'What is that?' You can hear me on the tape going, 'Shh, shh.' That song was the most direct form of communication I'd ever heard and it may sound corny, but it changed my life."

Commiserating with his best friend Stan (a.k.a. Eighth Wonder, who illustrated his first recorded efforts), Shadow immersed himself in hip-hop lore, idolizing Afrika Bambaataa from afar. "It was his whole paradigm of no genre boundaries, playing Kraftwerk next to James Brown next to a children's record. That's why when people ask me about my other favorite types of music, I always say, 'It doesn't work that way.' Hip-hop is what you do with all the music you hear." — "Turning the Tables" / Charles Aaron / March '97

The Sensitive Types: Who's Who in the Emo-Rap Revolution

Aesop Rock: A member of New York art-rap syndicate Definitive Jux, Aesop pours disappointment, claustrophobia, and B-boy bratitude into his slurry, intricate rhymes—"Life's not a bitch/ She's a beautiful woman who won't give up the pussy." Recommended: *Labor Days* (Definitive Jux, 2001).

Sage Francis: Spoken-word vet turned rhyme slayer. His new group, Non-Prophets (with DJ/producer Joe Beats), brings surprisingly tight vintage hip-hop. Recommended: *Personal Journals* (Anticon, 2002).

Doseone: Court jester of the avant-underground: posing for photos in leg warmers, rocking hair dye to match his outfits. Recommended: *Circle* (Mush, 2000).

Buck 65: Nova Scotia's storytelling mic rocker has dropped rhymes on *Sesame Street*, but on his latest album, *Talkin' Honky Blues*, he's a hip-hop Tom Waits. Recommended: *Man Overboard* (Anticon, 2001).

Busdriver: A junior member of the Los Angeles set that spawned Freestyle Fellowship and the Pharcyde, this tongue-twisting MC tackles politics and the contradictions of life in the hip-hop underground. Recommended: *Temporary Forever* (Temporary Whatever, 2003).

Mac Lethal: Kansas-bred 2002 Scribble Jam battle champ who cracks jokes about his mom being signed by Dr. Dre and then gets deep on the war in Iraq. Once toured with Insane Clown Posse protégés Twiztid, but don't hold it against him. Recommended: *The Love Potion Collection* (Beyond Space/Lethalville, 2003).

Pigeon John: An often hilarious rhymer with a gift for sly self-deprecation. On his two solo albums, he's played the fumbling everyman, grappling with absent parents, racial confusion, and the impossible quest for true love. Recommended: *Pigeon John is Dating Your Sister* (Basement, 2003).

Awol One: Los Angeles MC who offers up throaty, free-association jams about solitude and agony. Once rapped as "Awalrus" and offered solace in lyrics like "Don't be afraid to admit your downfalls/ We all got 'em/ And I think that I got 'em all." Recommended: *Souldoubt* (Mean Street, 2001).

— "Emo Rap: Up from the Underground" / Jon Caramanica / February '04

The battle—two three-minute routines per DJ

—begins with a toss of the coin. DJ Craze wins, so DJ First Rate leads. He grabs the turntables, both hands already a blur, scratching like a madman until he starts vibrating the record minutely under the needle for an eerie, undefinable sound. Continuing the vibration, he makes eye contact with Craze and flashed a wicked grin. As the audience bursts into applause, Craze nods coolly and chews his gum. He must be sweating, though, because the crowd is eating up his challenger's shtick. First Rate ends his routine by scratching on both turntables at the same time, then stepping back and crossing his arms in a fuck-you gesture.

Craze is out for revenge the minute he steps to the decks. He simultaneously juggles the phrase "You got to have style" on both turntables, each repetition a condemnation of First Rate's manic technique. He looks around for his opponent, but First Rate has left the stage to talk to someone in his crew. Craze takes a few seconds to turn around—while beat juggling—and makes eye contact.

There are only five seconds left in Craze's routine when he puts on the Bugs Bunny record. The MC begins to count down the remaining time.

"Five"… "Well, all right"… "4"… "I'll be big"… "3"… "about it"… "2"… "good night"… "1"… "fat boy."

Like kids watching a schoolyard fight, the crowd gasps "Ooooooh" in unison.

— "The Battle of the Needle Freaks" / Neil Strauss / April '99

[Q-BERT]

[CHRIS CARRABA, a.k.a. Dashboard Confessional, 2001]

: Emo

/ Andy **Greenwald**

The term "emo"
—short for
"emotional,"
code for "lame"

—was birthed as an insult in 1984 during the Washington, D.C. punk-rock renaissance known as Revolution Summer. Rites of Spring, led by future Fugazi member Guy Picciotto, first earned the tag by composing blisteringly personal anthems that held punk's razor blade not to the neck of Reagan or Thatcher, but to the pale, decidedly liberal neck of Picciotto himself. Once Rites proved that the personal could be *plenty* political, the floodgates opened and emotional hardcore bands (later emo-core, then just plain *emo*) popped up across the country, playing furious songs of rejection and dejection.

Because punk was still primarily regional, however, there was no uniform definition of what made an emo band. For some, it was the screaming of Indian Summer. For others, it was the jagged-edge pop-punk of Jawbreaker. In the mid-'90s, groups like Sunny Day Real Estate and the Promise Ring came close to codifying emo (a word that no band, then or now, has ever embraced) as a minor-chord sausagefest promulgated by bands that flitted between college towns in vans, hovered low on the pop-culture radar, and then broke up either to find major-label success, Jesus, or steady girlfriends. For a time, emo as a scene seemed dead before it even started.

But if the Velvet Underground taught us anything, it's that important bands are rarely recognized as such in their own time. Conventional wisdom decrees that Nirvana were the most important rock band of the '90s. But if one were to examine the hearts and minds of many of today's teenagers, Green Day and Weezer would likely be the most significant groups of the '90s, hugely successful bands that demonstrated two key lessons of emo: it's possible to be punk and platinum, and it's possible to be a nerd and rock. These two commandments define 21st-century emo, a movement that treated punk more as a touchstone than a blueprint, and saw mainstream success not as a cancer but as a calling.

What also united the scene was a commitment to melody and an even greater commitment to Emotional Truth: lyrics that often read like poetry scribbled by 17-year-olds in study hall; words that treat hearts like grenades and kisses like WMDs. Emo found its leading man in Chris Carrabba, a birdlike heartthrob from south Florida who recorded self-lacerating acoustic campfire songs under the name Dashboard Confessional. Carrabba was once a special-ed teacher, which helps explain the infinite patience and lack of judgment reflected in his folkish punk. He was also a screw-up and a romantic, and he treated his shows like peer therapy sessions. The kids responded in kind—singing along to every word, often louder than Carrabba himself, and Instant Messaging his mp3s like mash notes to every corner of the country.

Emo's true power comes not from the stars, but from these study-hall-bound fans. (Frontmen like Carrabba or Taking Back Sunday's Adam Lazzara make a point of rejecting celebrity, spending hours before and after shows hanging with—and hugging—their admirers.) By 2004, the music business was floundering, but music itself had found a new routing system. The power players were no longer the David Geffens and Lyor Cohens, but 17-year-old girls named Kelsey with ethernet connections, broken hearts, and nothing else in the world but time. On the Internet, *everyone* had access to the underground; anyone could start a livejournal, expose their secret depths, find likeminded souls, and swap music. For them, emo was about making a connection with fellow broken-hearts. It was never meant to shake you up with big ideas, only to console you through your tears. That's why, to outsiders, the music can sound mawkish, solipsistic, reductive. This isn't music meant to last a lifetime—in high school, a lifetime can stretch from third period to lunch. Emo lasts as long as it's needed and then the fans—and, often, the maturing musicians—move on.

Emo is perhaps the ultimate teenage music: overly dramatic, prone to bad poetry, bursting with romance and self-loathing, and over before you know it. Yet whether it was born of '90s Clintonian economic stability or an early-aughts red alert desire for comfort and security, it seemed to fit the country's petulant moodswings pretty well, too. In 2004 Dashboard Confessional had their biggest ever hit with "Vindicated" from the soundtrack to *Spider-Man 2*, a gargantuan, $200 million blockbuster about a geeky hero with dark secrets who can't ever quite get the girl. And maybe the year's most significant television character was Seth Cohen of *The O.C.*, a fast-talking, comic-book-reading übernerd who named boats after girls who won't talk to him and worships at the altar of emo icons Death Cab for Cutie. We're all hurting, emo says, and no one has any answers. But damned if it doesn't feel good to complain about it together.

We Feel Your Pain

Ten excellent records

that people will call "emo" unless you explain to them why in fact they are *so much more than that*

Rites of Spring
End on End
Dischord, 1991

Jawbreaker
24 Hour Revenge Therapy
Tupelo, 1994

Sunny Day Real Estate
Diary
Sub Pop, 1994

Lifetime
Hello Bastards
Jade Tree, 1995

Weezer
Pinkerton
Geffen, 1996

The Promise Ring
Nothing Feels Good
Jade Tree, 1997

Jimmy Eat World
Clarity
Capitol, 1999

Dashboard Confessional
The Places You Have Come to Fear the Most
Vagrant, 2001

Thursday
Full Collapse
Victory, 2002

Taking Back Sunday
Tell All Your Friends
Victory, 2002

With his just-say-no drug policy and his one-beer-or-so-a-week habit, Carrabba is the kind of rocker you'd want to bring home to Mom. He's also the kind of rocker who wants to bring *you* home to Mom. And so I'm sitting on a deep, cozy couch in Anne Dichele's modest Boca condo. There's a framed '80s McDonald's bag on the wall (a relic from the year the family lived in Mexico and had to make do without Happy Meals) and a beautiful baby-grand piano—a present from her son. As Carrabba paces across the white rug, cell phone pressed to his ear, his mother—slim, pretty, dark-haired—yells, "Christopher! I told you to put that down!"

Dichele's been taking acting classes for fun this week. (Carrabba recently "retired" her from the daily grind.) "I knew he was going to be doing this from the day he was born," she says proudly, "but I always worry about his interviews."

"Why?" I ask.

"I think it must be boring for you. He's not very rock'n'roll, is he?"
— "The Crying Game" / Andy Greenwald / March '03

"We're all very emotional, sincere people, and we're in the water with sharks. But the sincerity the music is founded on is what protects us. If your band is founded on that instead of doing coke off hookers' tits, then you're fine. It's a matter of writing the songs that matter to you and having the kids sing along with you. That's it."
—Gerard Way (My Chemical Romance), 2003

"Ian [MacKaye, leader of D.C. hardcore pioneers Minor Threat and Fugazi] made this decision in the mid-'80s to not drink or do drugs, and then he started singing about it," remembers former Jawbox/Burning Airlines frontman J.Robbins, who grew up in the D.C. burbs. "And soon after that, people started examining their politics. Up until that point, you could just say 'Fuck the System! Fuck the System!' But then we were like, 'What does that mean?' Maybe we need to stop being so negative and leave behind some of the overt trappings of punk rock, like the mosh pit, which had just turned into this ritual where people got hurt. A lot of the old-school punk rockers got down on those bands. The word *emocore* was a joke. Some guy at a Fugazi show shouted, 'Oh, you guys are so emocore.'"

"People on this scene are very demanding," says Jason Gnewikow of The Promise Ring. "If a band has to drive through the mountains in a snowstorm to get to a show and they cancel the gig, that's bad. Like, 'How dare you cancel the show and care about your own life! You're supposed to rock me tonight!'

"I mean, a band is a band. Dead is forever."
— "Emotional Rescue" / Jeff Salamon / November '99

Anthony Lombardi, 16, Howie Kussoy, 17, and Ian Bauer, 17, are close friends from Plainview, Long Island, who wouldn't look out of place tailgating at a Dave Matthews Band show. Yet on this November night, here they are at Manhattan's legendary punk club CBGB, standing on dilapidated benches, screaming, "We love you, Chris!" while high-fiving one another ecstatically and singing—loudly—along with the tattooed young man onstage: "You're dying to look cute in your blue jeans/ But you're plastic just like everyone." The inked-up performer is Chris Carrabba—a.k.a. Dashboard Confessional—and he is used to such unlikely backing vocalists.

"Chris' lyrics touch you, and you can relate to every word," Kussoy says after the show. Bauer claims that Dashboard's music helped him "cope" with a stressful crush: "I was able to put out all of the emotion I was building up as I sang along." Adds Lombardi: "There is nothing we cherish more than an opportunity to hear his thoughts on life, music, and anything at all."

Dashboard Confessional's emotional binge-and-purge and reliance on universal youth themes—infidelity, long-distance romance, *Dawson's Creek*—have transmitted like telepathy to thousands of Web-savvy high-schoolers who bare their innermost thoughts daily on sites like diaryland.com and makeoutclub.com. Every night, dozens of them wait for Carrabba, 27, after shows to thank him for echoing and respecting their adolescent pain. "My fans aren't looking for a nü-metal band's ballad to make them feel something," Carrabba says. "They *already* feel something and they wanna talk about it." Call them Generation Y Me.
— "The Pied Piper of Emo" / Andy Greenwald / February '02

"I've always been pretty shy," says 24-year-old Douglas Rainwater from his new home in Manchester, England, where he moved in June to live with a 30-year-old woman he met through the Make Out Club site. "MOC is a great way to get to know a person on the inside." Rainwater isn't the only person to radically rejigger his life. Miller says he knows of one marriage ("a Canadian punk-rock couple") and "tons of kids who fly tons of miles" to meet. Indeed, users seem to find security in the insularity of the site's community, which is why they think nothing of traveling across the country to hang out with people they've never met.

If the profiles are the awkward introduction, the message board is the raging kegger, where 24 hours a day, clubbers with handles like Emosparkle and ItsAlwaysGoodbye post epistles ranging from the savory ("Is Beef Vegan?") to the scatological ("Butt Sex") and the sadly self-aware ("Why Can I Only Talk to Girls on the Internet?"). Even high-profile indie bands get in on the action, including Jade Tree records founder Tim Owen, Rachel from *Real World 10*, and K records/Beat Happening founder Calvin Johnson, who claims "the message board on MOC is better than TV."

Travis Keller, of rival indie-rock site buddyhead.com, dismissed MOC as "online ass-shopping for geeky virgins with bad taste in music." Even some MOC users are fed up with all the politically correct flirting. As one says in his profile: "After I finish my steak and have a beer, I'm going to fuck your girlfriend, you (straight-edge) piece of shit."
— "Geek Love" / Andy Greenwald / November '01

It's a 12-degree Friday night in Omaha—a beige city of 390,000 perched on the Missouri River bluffs. This is the birthplace of TV dinners and our most awkward president, Gerald R. Ford. Omaha is predominately white, with a low cost-of-living index and a higher-than-average median household income. It's a hub for telemarketing and credit-card processing; the food is filling and the people are friendly. In the films of local auteur Alexander Payne (*Election, About Schmidt*), the city is depicted as the epitome of everything dull and repressed about middle-class America. Aside from the new-age wallpaper of Mannheim Steamroller, it's never been known for its music.

And yet major-label moguls have been haunting its quiet streets, trying to buy into what has quickly become the hottest indie-rock scene in years. The guy at the center of it is 23-year-old Conor Oberst (a.k.a. Bright Eyes, this year's New Dylan), and at the moment, he simply wants to drink in peace. Normally, this means the hipster rock-scene watering hole called the Brother's Lounge. But tonight, the slight, hazel-eyed man-child has summoned his immediate crew to the Homy Inn, an obscure junk shop of a pub near his house that serves champagne on tap and warm peanuts in doggie bowls.

He's been here four nights running.

"I wanna hang out with my friends," he says, uncorking a split of merlot (Oberst is a red-wine devotee) as his cohorts amble in. Overhead, the Nebraska Cornhuskers do battle on a jumbo screen despite the fact that the football season ended three months ago. "(Brother's) is like hanging out with everyone I've ever known."

That Oberst should be lying low in Omaha is odd, because it's been his muse since he was a precocious 13-year-old trying to capture what he described in an early song as "the sound of the hopeless kids as they scream from the basements of the house of their parents." This bleeding-heart-on-sleeve storytelling has made Oberst an object of extraordinary worship, even by emo standards. It's gotten to where obsessive fans ring his mom's doorbell, tearful with love. "We never give out his address, of course," Nancy Oberst says, cheerfully. "But we'll chat with them. They're very sweet."

— "Next Stop Nowhere" / Will Hermes / July '03

On the best songs from *Transatlanticism*—the epic title track (with its refrain of **"I need you so much closer"**) and the morning-after pill **"A Lack of Color"**—Ben Gibbard rakes himself over the coals of a breakup, but with a far-reaching command of melody and nuance. This thematic hook has exploded Death Cab For Cutie's fan base, pushing them into the hyper-charged world of 15-year-old girls who sing along and 15-year-old boys with blogs, and that makes Gibbard a little nervous.

"I want to write songs that come from a real place, with a real story, but not like" —he clears his throat and sings in a Steve Perry-esque croon, "Jenny! You fucking broke my heart! On Thursday...at the Red Lobster!"

He complains half-jokingly about intentionally messing up lyrics so audiences in Florida can't sing along, and the band have turned down numerous invitations to open for Dashboard Confessional. "I won't name any names, but if I were 27 and playing that kind of big-stroke, big-amp emo, I would find it to be an incredibly arrested statement."

— "Bright Lights Big City" / Andy Greenwald / April '04

[THE SADDLE CREEK POSSE, Omaha, 2003]

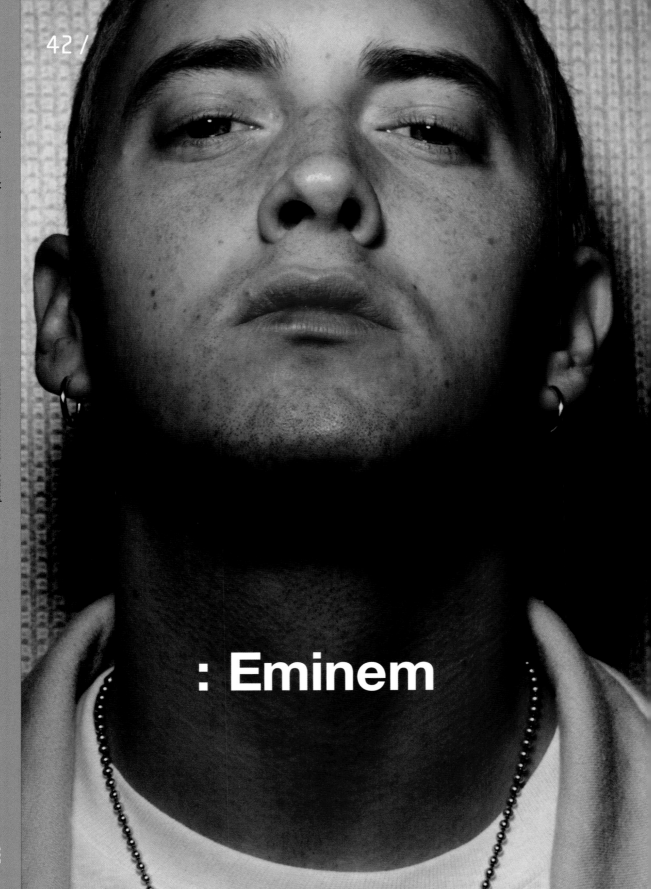

: Eminem

(and a cast of millions who cuss, just don't give a fuck, dress, walk, talk, and act like him)

/ Charles **Aaron**

If you're unfamiliar with the rapper known as Eminem, then congratulations—you must've been stationed on a beach lounger in Tahiti since the late 1990s. Because after the release of 1999's *The Slim Shady LP*, this fatherless urchin, raised in poverty by a single mom whom he claimed was a drug addict, became his generation's pop icon. A baggy-pantsed pied piper, he represented the era's inescapable cultural archetype—the brooding, posturing white rap kid—and seemed to express young America's raw psyche, in all its impetuous, corrupted, and titillating vainglory. Everything about Eminem was a volatile tease. He passionately raged at the world, then said it was all a joke. He claimed that he "just don't give a fuck" (echoing his hero Tupac Shakur), then invented an evil twin, "Slim Shady," to blame for his indiscretions. His breathless, staccato rhymes—clearly enunciated pin pricks that always seemed to end with a cutting punch line—had a giddy ease, but also hid bits of no-he-didn't truth. The very first verse of his breakout single "My Name Is"— "Hi kids! Do you like violence?/ Wanna see me stick Nine Inch Nails through each one of my eyelids?/ Wanna copy me and do exactly like I did?"—was like an Exacto-knife pre-emptively pointed at media-violence prudes.

But as the first white MC with indisputable skills and an actual impoverished background, he ached for respect within the hip-hop community itself, i.e., among its black constituents. He was determined to be more than a crossover novelty (like the fraudulent Vanilla Ice and farcical Beastie Boys). He didn't just want to be *good for a white boy*. And his record company, Interscope, knew that they could mint money with a credible white MC—especially if he was mentored by Dr. Dre, sonic architect of the gangsta rap that clearly inspired Eminem. Dre and respected rapper/producer Missy Elliott even gave testimonials on MTV before *The Slim Shady LP*'s release, reassuring non-whites that the scowling prankster was for real.

Still, Eminem's line of rebellion was a dicey gambit. As the most race-conscious musical genre ever, hip-hop has always existed in the shadow of America's shameful minstrel tradition— from blackface pop to the colonization of the blues, R&B, and rock. The culture has, in fact, derived its power by building a platform for African-American and Latino voices to spit all over that tradition. Hip-hop has been a lot of things—postmodern pageant, killer hook party, capitalist dog-and-pony show—but its essential strength is that voice. That's why people around the world crave and consume it. And after more than 20 years, no white artists had possessed the ability (or nerve) to assume that voice—until Eminem. Despite hip-hop culture being broadcast and marketed to the suburbs for almost 20 years, he was the first.

That's his against-all-odds achievement, but it's a twisted victory. While black hip-hoppers battled the embedded racism of the culture at large, Eminem battled the perceived racism against white guys within hip-hop. While lyrics by black hip-hop artists were pooh-poohed by people who couldn't name a Jadakiss couplet at gunpoint, Eminem was doted on for his literary flair (Nobel Prize-winning poet Seamus Heaney even weighed in on his "verbal energy" and "subversive attitude"). Eminem was profiled in the mainstream press as a more fascinating success story than virtually all his black peers. In his gut, as a hip-hop fan, he had to know that all of this had a foul aroma. And that no matter how many hilarious or moving or disturbing

> ESSAY CONTINUES ON NEXT PAGE

Priceless Eminem punchlines: 1. "Will Smith don't gotta cuss in his raps to sell records/ Well I do, so fuck him and fuck you, too." – "The Real Slim Shady"

2. "I try to keep it positive and play it cool/ Shoot up the playground/ And tell the kids to stay in school." – "I'm Shady" 3. "Ninety-nine percent of my life I was lied to/ I just found out my mom does more dope than I do. (Damn!)" – "My Name Is" 4. "Y'all act like you never seen a white person before/ Jaws all on the floor, like Pam and Tommy just burst in the door." – "The Real Slim Shady" 5. "BUT DON'T BLAME ME WHEN LIL' ERIC JUMPS OFF THE TERRACE/ YOU SHOULDA BEEN WATCHIN'—APPARENTLY YOU AIN'T PARENTS." – "WHO KNEW" 6. "Somethin' somethin' somethin' somethin' I get weeded/ My daughter scribbled over that rhyme/ I couldn't read it." – "Any Man" 7. "If I had one wish/ I would ask for a big enough ass for the whole world to kiss." – "If I Had"

rhymes he wrote or videos he made, his epitaph would have a fat white asterisk next to it.

So what's a white boy to do? Like any good student of N.W.A, he took the slur, blew it up into a raging, comic-tragic brand name, and flung it in everybody's face like a bucket of Harlem Globetrotters confetti. Suddenly, "Slim Shady" was more than a nasty alter ego, he was a prophetic martyr. On the "The Real Slim Shady" (from 2000's *The Marshall Mathers LP*), over a sarcastically perky Dr. Dre beat, Eminem boasted that "there's a million of us just like me/ who cuss like me/ who just don't give a fuck like me/ who dress like me/ walk, talk and act like me." And when he marched into the 2000 MTV Video Music Awards with a young people's army that looked just like him—blond Caesar haircut, white T-shirt, baggy blue jeans—he mocked the nightmare that his detractors envisioned: for whites, he was leading their little Erics and Ericas over to the dark side; and for blacks, he was staging an Elvis-like coup d'etat. He morphed into a widescreen villain, the psycho wigger, as if nodding to Joe Pesci in *GoodFellas*: "Whatta you mean, I'm funny? Funny how? I mean, funny like I'm a clown? I *amuse* you?" He gave the people what they feared, in an impish burlesque—per the Hollywood ritual. As he said on another 2000 single "The Way I Am": "I am whatever you say I am."

Pop bobblehead doll. Unhinged everykid. Acknowledged MC. Racial raconteur. Eminem was all that. But he wasn't an artist who moved people beneath the skin, beyond all the gamesmanship. That's what emerged on the track "Stan," from *The Marshall Mathers LP* (his given name signifying an attempt at a deeper realness). Backed by the sound of a rainstorm and a wistful piano ballad (by British electronic-pop singer Dido), the heretofore demented Slim Shady told the affecting story of a suicidal fan who had written several unanswered letters to the rapper. As the narrative progressed, it was as if the Slim character began to dissolve and a new Eminem began to emerge. This was the first time you actually believed that he was emotionally vulnerable, that he cared about the consequences of his behavior and didn't reflexively footnote every sentiment with "and fuck you too." Instead of just self-righteously howling revenge fantasies at his mother Debbie or ex-wife Kim, he tried to understand somebody else's suffering.

Then with the 2002 film roman à clef *8 Mile*, Eminem made his first sustained effort at maturity, starring as a sensitive, abused underdog with whom it was easy to empathize (he also produced the album's rousing musical centerpiece, "Lose Yourself," which won the Oscar for Best Original Song). And on the 2002 album *The Eminem Show*, he struggled to stitch together all his personas, toning down the psychopathic jive, and honestly transcribing his furious personal life into songs that ripped through a newspaper's worth of topics—race, domestic abuse, parenthood, fame, the FCC. "White America" was a searing manifesto in which he admitted that he'd probably have half as many fans if he were black. On "Cleaning Out My Closet," he shockingly confessed that he'd never meant to hurt his mother (whom he had previously imagined raping and killing), and on "My Dad's Gone Crazy," he uses a mischievous sample of daughter Hailie Jade to dramatize how he's trying to let go of the acrimony and paranoia and self-loathing in his life, but can't. It ends cryptically, with Hailie laughing and saying, "You're funny, daddy."

When I interviewed Eminem in mid-1998, he was a humble guy grateful to Dr. Dre for the shot of a lifetime. His 1997 indie release, *The Slim Shady EP*, was mostly unheard and his major-label debut was yet to be released. He talked about growing up in Kansas City as well as the much-mythologized Detroit, about how his mother "tried to do the best she could," how he'd wanted to move from Detroit's inhospitable 8 Mile Road to the suburbs three years before, how he hoped that hip-hop could help stop racism. In 2004, some of that humility and earnestness returned, as he openly sought a functional family life and released the single "Mosh," a serious philippic against President Bush, just prior to the election. But the subsequent album *Encore* was flat and disconnected, and the central conceit—that Eminem ends the record by shooting himself—felt randomly tacked on. More surprisingly, on the song "Like Toy Soldiers," an exhausting rundown of his feud with the magazine *The Source*, he admitted the unthinkable: He was sick of hearing himself talk.

Maybe Eminem was questioning whether the constant purging of his darkest thoughts, which led to his fame, was now sabotaging his chance at happiness. What did he want more: to talk mass shit about his ex-wife or to have a stable family? Though he donned a figurative suit as head of Shady Records—signing hometown allies D12 and Obie Trice, plus New York gangsta cynic 50 Cent—it's hard to imagine him tabling his own career battles to manage others'. Ultimately, there's one thing that Eminem seems to need above all else—to get the last, most outrageous, word. That's how he keeps his fragile identity intact. Echoing the spirit of another great American racial raconteur, Mark Twain, the rumors of Eminem's demise have been ridiculously exaggerated. But then again, so has everything else about him. Otherwise, would he even exist?

Eminem's Top 10 Intoxicants: 1. Vicodin ("Bad Influence," "Kill You," "Under the Influence") 2. Mushrooms ("My Fault," "Purple Pills") 3. Vodka ("My Name Is," "Without Me") 4. Ecstasy ("Drug Ballad") 5. Percocet ("Rock Bottom") 6. Codeine ("My Dad's Gone Crazy") 7. A box full of laxatives ("Still Don't Give a Fuck") 8. Liquid Darvocet ("Three Verses") 9. Hennessy mixed with Bacardi Dark ("Drug Ballad") 10. An IV full of Thai weed ("Any Man")

SPIN: How do you feel about other white rap fans?

Eminem: Say there's a white kid who lives in a nice home, goes to an all-white school, and is pretty much having everything handed to him on a platter—for him to pick up a rap tape is incredible to me, because what that's saying is that he's living a fantasy life of rebellion. He wants to be hard; he wants to smack motherfuckers for no reason except that the world is fucked-up; he doesn't know what to rebel against. Kids like that are just fascinated by the culture. They hear songs about people going through hard times and want to know what that feels like. But the same thing goes for a black person who lived in the suburbs, and was catered to all his life; Tupac is a fantasy for him, too.

— "Chocolate on the Inside" / Charles Aaron / May '98

TOP 10 WHITE MCs OF THE EMINEM ERA:

01. **El-P**
02. **Bubba Sparxxx**
03. **Evidence (Dilated Peoples)**
04. **Sage Francis**
05. **Buck 65**
06. **Aesop Rock**
07. **Eyedea**
08. **R.A. the Rugged Man**
09. **Sole**
10. **Ill Bill (Non Phixion)**

NO MATTER HOW MUCH HIP-HOP CULTURE HAS BEEN ASSIMILATED, FEW WHITE MCS HAVE EXPERIENCED ANY SUCCESS, OR ACCEPTANCE, WITHIN THE HIP-HOP COMMUNITY ITSELF. AS EVERLAST PUTS IT, "THAT'S WHY WHITE AMERICA FIENDS FOR IT SO BAD—BECAUSE *THEY CAN'T DO IT!*" HERE, EVERLAST, A.K.A. "WHITEY FORD," GIVES HIS SCOUTING REPORT ON MELANIN-CHALLENGED MCS PAST AND PRESENT.

BEASTIE BOYS: "I'm a huge fan of the Beastie Boys—they're partially responsible for my career—but I don't care what anybody says, they were completely mocking hip-hop at first. They mocked it until they got paid off it, and then they said, 'Oh, this is real.' *Licensed to Ill* was a mockery, except the stuff that Run-D.M.C. wrote, like 'Slow and Low.'"

3RD BASS: "(Def Jam CEO) Russell Simmons put that group together; it wasn't like they'd been friends for years. The thing is, Serch was actually a real good MC, but he might as well have been wearing a T-shirt that said "I Wish I Was Black." When you come like that, no matter how dope you are, nobody's gonna really respect it. I've had words with Serch in my life, but he goes way back, so I give him his respect."

HOUSE OF PAIN: "The majority of black kids didn't like House of Pain, but they respected us, because we came out saying, 'Yo, we're peckerwoods, we're white trash, whatever you wanna call us, and we love hip-hop and we're gonna do what we do.' We weren't trying to be down, and the Beasties were the same way. They were like, 'Hey, we ain't trying to be you, don't worry about it, we're just gonna do some songs about motherfuckin' pirates robbin' ships.'"

VANILLA ICE: "He played with us at this Christmas radio festival in Kansas City, and he was the last band out of nine, which wasn't the best slot. Personally, I wanted to hate him so bad, but he comes up to me and goes, 'Dude, I'm such a big fan,' and I was, like, 'Why is he being nice to me?' Anyway, all the bands stuck around to see that guy, and then halfway through his first song, the place cleared out. I felt kinda bad."

EMINEM: "He's got a real dope style, don't get me wrong, but he's a shock rhymer, like, 'Some kid named Greg/ Took off his peg leg/ And beat himself in the head'-type shit."

EVIDENCE: "Evidence is just *nasty*, dude. He's a personal homeboy of mine, and eventually, if (Dilated Peoples) catch a break, I think people are gonna really, really feel what he's doing."

— "Signifying Whiteys" / Charles Aaron / June '99

Now, you'd think that a woman who is a) Bartender of the Year; and b) a former swimsuit model would have no trouble keeping Slim Shady's attention. But after introductions—"Oh, I heard a lot about you," Em says graciously—the conversation dies off. D12, Eminem's boisterous crew, are around, so that's one distraction, and there's a basketball game on a TV in the corner. Plus, both Ivory and Eminem, despite their chosen professions, are essentially quiet people. So they're sitting there, not saying much, and Em's manager is kicking him under the table, as if to say, "Go ahead, talk to her." Ivory's manager is glaring at her, as if to say, "You *better* talk to him." Finally, they chat, and at the end of the meal, the manager shows Eminem a card from Ivory's modeling days. On the front, there's a photo of her face, and on the back, there's a photo of her in a bathing suit, with a very tiny, very sheer bottom.

"Oh," Eminem says, gazing at the portrait. "Can I keep this?"

Despite this promising contact, definitive plans for a collaboration have yet to materialize. "Right now, with D12, he's a little busy," Ivory says. "Plus, we want to be very careful if we go ahead and do that, you know, because he's a white rapper, I'm a white rapper...."

Ivory's voice trails off. No further explanation is necessary. White rappers these days are obviously marketable, especially when paired with established black hip-hop stars like, say, Dr. Dre or Method Man or Timbaland.

But two scoops of vanilla and no chocolate at all? Plus one of them's female? Well, that just might be a little too much marketability to swallow.

— "Not Bad for a White Girl" / G. Beato / February '02

: Björk

Pagan poetry

If you head east on Road #1 out of Reyjkavik, Iceland, turn onto #35 just before Selfoss, and head northeast to where the road ends, you will find yourself at Gullfoss, a massive double-waterfall on a glacial river called the Hvítá. In the off-season, you may see a few hearty tourists hiking down to the overlook. And if the small café/gift shop is open, they can sell you a hot drink, some Icelandic handicrafts, and almost all of Björk's back catalogue.

Even in her homeland, a tiny country whose second greatest cultural export probably remains 1955 Nobel laureate novelist Halldór Laxness, Björk's fame is a little baffling. Her art has always been strange by pop standards, and has only gotten stranger with time. But the singer's ability to infuse the alien with a raw humanity is what wins people's hearts—her indelibly offbeat melodies, her feral-angelic vocals, her cyborg-pixie screen presence. For those with a thing for the alien, she's a zero-gravity fantasy made flesh.

Björk had a career long before she surfaced as front-sprite for one-hit new-wave wonders the Sugarcubes. A child of the '60s (her mom was a "hardcore hippie" who still turns up in the local news protesting environmental issues), she was raised communally and released a hit record of Icelandic folk songs when she was 11; she spent her early teens in various punk bands, most notably Tappi Tíkarrass and Kukl (a.k.a. K.U.K.L.). When Björk and Kukl singer/trumpeter Einar Orn formed the Sugarcubes as a pop lark in 1986, they concocted an Icelandic-language single later re-recorded as "Birthday"—a mix of Cocteau Twins wooziness and Bow Wow Wow playground bounce released on their 1988 debut which stands as one of the early MTV era's most magical moments.

The future might've held great things for the Sugarcubes, but after a few records (the most memorable being 1988's *Life's Too Good*), Björk had other visions to attend to. Falling hard for house music, she hooked up with Nellee Hooper of the U.K. collective Soul II Soul, the first of several DJ-producer gurus who would help outfit her sound in electro-frippery. But as *Debut* proved in 1993, the girl was no simple disco diva: "Human Behaviour," "Venus As a Boy," and "The Anchor Song" were elegant songs glinting with classical, out-jazz, and world music influences. And the overt club-bangers boasted vocals miles from generic dance-music, even when the topics (love, lust, lustful love, loving lust) were well-worn. Within them, Björk's odd inflections revealed universes.

With *Post* (1995), she really hit her stride. "Hyperballad" is a dazzling lover's note that may be her greatest moment; "Army of Me" an industrial pop tart appropriately used to soundtrack *Tank Girl*, a film based on the British comic about a hard-partying future-punk superhero. There was also the shrieked-up big band number "It's Oh So Quiet," a breakout thanks to a flamboyant, Busby Berkeley-flavored video by Spike Jonze (*Being John Malkovich*) that has her dancing in the streets with a mailbox. (The song echoed 1990's *Gling Gló*, a scrumptious import-only set of standards sung by Björk, mostly in Icelandic, with a jazz trio.) *Post* was avant-garde with open arms, and it proved to be the most forward-looking pop album of the decade.

The cover of *Post* shows the singer as a sort of computer-generated internationalist icon, and it's on this record that she really becomes Björk—a pop-art character whose outsized gestures of intimacy generate a fan base that's remarkably intense. Creative types around the world pay tribute with song remixes, spectacular videos, comic books and extreme websites, both with and without her participation. Paparazzi and other nutjobs would also come to the table. In 1996, the singer famously attacked a TV journalist who bumrushed her and her young son Sindri in a Bangkok airport. Later that year, upon hearing of Björk's engagement to British drum'n'bass auteur Goldie, a Florida fan sent her a letter bomb (intercepted by the British post office) and then committed suicide.

This sort of thing will unnerve even an artistic superhero. After *Homogenic* (1997), a knottier, darker, and dreamier record than *Post*, Björk laid low for a while. And it was probably inevitable that her next big project would be a film. Her music video collaborations with directors like Jonze, Michel Gondry

257

ESSAY CONTINUES ON NEXT PAGE >

"Don't expect anything from the Sugarcubes. We will let you down in the end,"

declares Einar Orn, a smug, inquisitive expression on his young face. Einar appears to be the leader of this Icelandic band, though his voice on the debut LP *Life's Too Good* (Elektra), is hardly as striking as that of Björk, the porcelain doll. Björk has the wisdom and eloquence of an elder and the uninhibited mannerisms of a child. As she speaks, she twirls a pair of blue plastic sunglasses with a delicate hand, inspecting everything with ageless eyes.

"We read all these papers from abroad with huge color pictures of ourselves and we just laugh," she says, shaking her head, causing her exaggerated rat's nest hairdo to move. "It's something that's going on in another galaxy. We can't connect ourselves to it."

The Sugarcubes were born two years ago, on the eighth of June, 1986, at 2:50 p.m.: the same day and time as the son of Björk and her husband Thor, who plays guitar in the band.

"We started a new life with this baby boy," explains Einar. "We just decided not to torture ourselves, just decided to have fun, just decided—the Sugarcubes. To amaze ourselves." As if on cue, Björk blows on the top of a bottle, making a loud, deep whistle.

— "Life's Too Cold" / Christian L. Wright / September '88

While she will give nothing of her private life away—

burned, perhaps, by her openness in the past—Björk is keen to talk about what she refers to as the "thick line" between working with male musicians and falling in love with them. She says the only time a sexual and professional relationship has blurred is when Thor, her former husband and her son Sindri's father, joined the Sugarcubes. "I started working with boys in punk and garage bands when I was 12. I watched other girls in bands fall in love with one of the guys and become a groupie within 24 hours. Just as some people train themselves not to eat sugar, so I have made it normal to work intimately with men in the studio, on tour, at a record company. I don't want to sound cold but there's a choice: Do you want to have an affair with this guy for two weeks or enjoy a creative relationship for five years?

"I'll tell you a secret," she whispers. "In a lot of ways, writing a song with a guy is far more giving and erotic than having a sexual relationship with him. People are so narrow-minded that they think sex only exists in the form of fishnet stockings or hard-core fucking. But everything can be sexual, from putting your socks on in the morning, to buying milk, to laughing, to talking on the phone." The whisper breaks into a full-throttle shriek. "Oh no! Not again! I'm trying to say that sex is probably one of the least important things in life, but at the same time, it's everywhere. But you'll misunderstand me and write: 'Björk has an orgasm every time she eats her toast! She's a sex maniac!'"

— "Miss World"/ Amy Raphael / September '95

"I could so easily be a happy farmer in Iceland." – 1988

> ESSAY CONTINUES FROM PREVIOUS PAGE

(*Eternal Sunshine of the Spotless Mind*), and Chris Cunningham are highwater marks of the form, and she had previously turned up in a couple of movies (including Robert Altman's *Prêt-á-Porter*). It was Jonze's video for "It's Oh So Quiet" that reportedly spurred Danish director Lars Von Trier to cast Björk as the lead in his 2000 "musical" *Dancer in the Dark*. At first she resisted, wanting only to score the film. But in the end she agreed. The feuds between auteur and actress during production became legend, as did Björk's subsequent emotional trauma from assuming/enduring the role. While the film divided audiences, her performance as Selma—a woman losing her sight and given to musical daydreams—won her the Best Actress award at Cannes. Although she would also be nominated for an Academy Award, and famously perform "I've Seen It All" (from the semi-soundtrack

Selmasongs) at the 2001 Oscars wearing a faux-swan, Björk declared she was done with acting.

Except, of course, as a musician. *Vespertine* (2001), a set of songs for choir, harp, and laptop computers, was a performance piece about introversion and the interior life—a logical move given all that came before. At a show introducing the record early that year, held in a chapel of Riverside Church in the singer's new home, New York City, obsessives came from around the world to see her sing, often sans microphone, in a billowy white gown, pacing the stone aisles barefoot like some beatific sci-fi angel. It was her emergence from hibernation, and later that year, in the immediate wake of September 11th, she toured through Europe and America, sometimes singing Meredith Monk's wordless New York City hymn "Gotham Lullaby." The sense of artistic sanctuary in the

record and the shows spoke to the moment perfectly.

Eventually life returned to some kind of normal. Björk would hook up with the brilliant, goop-loving multi-media art star Matthew Barney and become a mom again. She would release *Medúlla* (2004), a fascinating record made almost entirely from sounds of the human voice. She would begin the inevitable artistic collaboration with Barney. And, in what reads as a career pinnacle, she would sing "Oceana"—a song from *Medúlla* about birthing the world—at the opening ceremonies of the 2004 Olympic games in Athens. During a dazzlingly weird performance broadcast internationally, her ice-blue dress would unfurl into a huge cloth map that rolled over the heads of thousands of assembled athletes. It was the post-national persona of *Post* taking its proper place on Mt. Olympus, live via satellite.

> "I decided that my heart was with pop music because I believe in things that grannies and kids can get. If they don't get it, fuck it, you know?" – Björk, 1997

Watching and listening to Björk talk—and eat—is an event unto itself.

She rolls her R's in about 19 different ways, perhaps because she learned English in several accents, including Mancunian, Scottish, southern Cockney, and French, as well as, she says, from "quite camp drag queens in America." She also makes the most amazing faces—baring her teeth, wrinkling her nose, widening her eyes—and pulls on her face and hair constantly. A few journalists have noted that Björk often, and without embarrassment, picks her nose, and sure enough, in the middle of one riff or another, one of her little fingers found its way up to one of her cute little nostrils and wiggled itself around, before being called away to perform another spazzy, adorable gesture.

Björk and her boyfriends have been the subject of much scuttlebutt: She counts among her exes fashion photographer/video director Stephane Sednaoui and dance floor machers Tricky and Goldie. One gossip column item had the two fighting over her in a New York City nightclub. When it is suggested that the pattern to her choice in men might be labeled "insufferable geniuses," she doesn't flinch. "They're very obviously geniuses," she says, "straight in your face. But for me, the guys I had the most fantasies about as a child were David Attenborough and Carl Sagan. Really. In school, I would fall for the guy in the back of the class with really thick glasses and the insect collection who told you about the solar system. It's these people who show you these secrets. They pull up this rock"— she gets out of her chair and lifts up the cushion she's sitting on as if it were the rock, and then leans in, staring at me, widening her eyes in mock wonder—"and they go, 'Do you want me to show you a lot of really strange things that nobody's ever seen?'" She looks back under the "rock" and then back to me.

"It just drives me nuts. It gives me 53 hard-ons. That's what turns me on."

— "The Outer Limits" / Jonathan Van Meter / December '97

When her jarring performance in *Dancer in the Dark* made her an unlikely movie star

on top of everything else, Björk was not overjoyed. (When she asked her costar Catherine Deneuve how she tolerated being an actor, Deneuve said, "Well, don't you think it's amazing to wake up in the morning and just become someone completely different? Don't you find it fascinating?" Björk blinked a few times and answered simply: "No.") So it's not hard to see why she created *Vespertine* as a record about "hibernation."

With song titles like "Hidden Place" and "Cocoon," softly angelic choirs, and muffled beats that clatter like Mom in the kitchen, it's a more appropriate soundtrack to drinking hot cocoa under the covers than hitting a dance floor. "It's about not speaking for days and daydreaming and it's snowing outside," Björk says over lunch in the Central Park Boathouse. "It's about zooming in and finding heaven underneath your kitchen table. Most people think that the life they lead is boring and the noises they hear every day are ugly. But if you take those same noises and make them into something magical and out of the ordinary, I think that's brave."

— "Into the Light" / Thomas Beller / October '01

Forget her eyeball-melting videos, her wood-nymph sensuality, her impeccable taste in swans: Björk's neatest trick remains her ability to dance between the raindrops of avant and accessible. She's always been a Madonna for globe-trotting hipsters, hitching rides on chic subgenres from house to glitch-hop. But her skill at refracting a sonic zeitgeist has never obscured her way with a melody—or her voice, which could lure sailors onto sharp rocks.

— review of Björk's *Family Tree* and *Greatest Hits* / Joe Gross / January '03

Five Artists to Mention to Get a Girl in Bed (If You're a Guy):

PJ HARVEY   Björk   LE TIGRE   SLEATER-KINNEY   BRIGHT EYES

— "The Lists Issue," April 2003

"[Björk's *Homogenic*] is where I realized, 'Wow, in the modern age of music, you can have a 53-piece symphony, someone playing champagne glasses, and a guy playing a nose flute, and you can still sound beautiful. Genres mean nothing.' It really made us push ourselves." —Josh Homme [Queens of the Stone Age], 2003

: OutKast

If the Beatles were playas

/ Chris **Norris**

THE PHILOSOPHERS SPEAK OF DUALITIES—

the Yin and the Yang, the Cheech and the Chong, the Sanford and the Son—mystical pairings that rule our natural world. To these enigmatic fusions let us add one that so stankily shaped our early-century consciousness, that of Big Boi and Andre 3000, the bicameral mind of OutKast.

As of 2004, it became less appropriate to discuss OutKast as a hip-hop group than as a worldwide cultural phenomenon, a barometer for changing attitudes about style, race, and trouser widths. With their double-disc *Speaker-Boxxx/The Love Below*, the post-rap duo (they lately prefer to call their metier "funk") won a Grammy for Album of the Year, made the inscrutable expression "Hey Ya!" the most ubiquitous song of the year, and became a consensus-building symbol for all that is still cool in America. In one presidential campaign season, OutKast was referenced by both Democratic candidate Wesley Clark and, at the Republican National Convention, first daughter Jenna Bush. It was a very crunk year.

An essential part of OutKast's success in expanding hip-hop to include velvet knickers and Beatlesque rave-ups was the unimpeachable cred they'd already earned within hip-hop. Signed to Atlanta's La Face label right after high school, Andre Benjamin and Antwan "Big Boi" Patton debuted on a 1992 remix of TLC's R&B hit "What About Your Friends" and, in 1993, released the hit single, "Player's Ball." But it was on the 1994 debut album, *Southernplayalisticadillac-muzik* that OutKast articulated a distinctly Southern version of rap, emphasizing a live-funk feel and the springy triplet rhythm soon dubbed "Southern bounce." Their two-pronged lyrical approach came through in the contrast between the pimp-centric "Player's Ball" and the single "Git

Up, Get Out," an inspirational message ("Don't let the days of your life pass by…Don't spend all your time tryin to get high") that complemented its predecessor without refuting it—a dichotomy that became an OutKast trademark.

From the outset, OutKast defined itself as an odd couple—Big Boi's playa and Andre's poet—although they seemed more like sides of the same coin. When they met at Tri-Cities High School in Atlanta's project-filled East Point area, the pair already had separate reputations as hipsters with the fleet-tongued flow and fashions of Northeast groups like A Tribe Called Quest—affinities that made them stand out in the 'hood and forged an early identity as intellectual outcasts. After they began rapping together, first as 2 Shades Deep, the two remained involved in the extracurricular activities described in most hardcore rap songs, which gave

> " My mom always used to say to me, 'Why you wanna be a typical every day nigga?' I used to hate it back then, but now I appreciate it."
>
> : DRE, 1999

genre exercises like "Return of the G" and "Gangsta Shit" more authenticity than similar efforts by earlier hip-hop crossover groups.

By 1996's *ATLiens*, Andre's flamboyant starchild persona emerged—in turbans, white sarongs, and an avowed interest in interstellar travel—making his partnership with doctrinaire thug Big Boi even more mystifying. But both seemed to understand that the authentic gangsta gesture was not a higher body count but true innovation. "You have to be a strong nigga to take that ridicule," Andre told a reporter in 1998. That year they released *Aquemini*, a classic hip-hop album that seamlessly integrated live instrumentation into techno fantasias and featured the buoyant single "Rosa Parks." The album went double platinum and pulled the rare feat of pleasing both alt-rock adventurers and hip-hop hardheads like *The Source*,

who awarded the album its highest five-mic rating.

Yet something about OutKast stayed wonderfully unenlightened, not so easily integrated into polite company. Civil Rights matriarch Rosa Parks was offended enough at their language to sue OutKast for using her name as a song title (despite the efforts of O.J. defense lawyer Johnnie Cochran, the case was ultimately dismissed). Years later, the group was still giddily tactless enough to stage a full-scale "Injun"-themed dance revue for a TV performance—complete with teepee, warpaint, and other Hollywood stereotypes—prompting CBS to apologize to Native Americans.

In 2000, OutKast released *Stankonia*, titled after a mythical land from whence all funk flows. Had it only contained the heart-tugging "Ms. Jackson" and amped-up steeplechase "Bombs Over Baghdad," *Stankonia* would have been groundbreaking. But it was also full of shimmering atmospheres, epicurean beats, and heady musings on the perils of ego and materialism—plus the smooth post-pimp "So Fresh, So Clean." OutKast stood beside Radiohead and Beck as a bellwether for all pop music.

With 2003's *Speakerboxx/The Love Below*—which yielded the singles "Hey Ya," "The Way You Move," and "Roses"—OutKast entered into some as-yet-undefined public role. Exchanging football pads and platinum wigs for designer suits and bowties, Andre 3000 became a fashion statesman on a par with Afghanistan president Hamid Karzai. He also discussed numerous acting roles, including Jimi Hendrix, an animated version of his alter-ego Johnny Vulture, and a love-struck mortician.

Given the bifurcation of OutKast's last release (each artist getting his own CD), some suspect that a fatal tension may soon end the group, citing schism-plagued works like the Beatles' "White Album." The comparison may be apt. In 2004, Andre's "Hey Ya!" was finally knocked from the top of the U.S. charts—by Big Boi's "The Way You Move," the first time a band had one its songs replace another in 40 years. The previous group being the Beatles.

"WE FEEL THAT—JUST LIKE KRS ONE SAID—WHEN YOU GET ON THIS MICROPHONE, YOU HAVE TO EDUCATE AS WELL AS ENTERTAIN. WE FEEL THAT RESPONSIBILITY, BUT NOT IN A PREACHY WAY. WE'RE GONNA PARTY WITH Y'ALL AND SLIP SOMETHING IN THERE EVERY NOW AND THEN."
— Antwan "Big Boi" Patterson, 2001

In Rita Dove's moving poetry volume, *On the Bus With Rosa Parks*, there's a dedicatory quote from historian/critic Simon Schama: "All history is a negotiation between familiarity and strangeness." I can't think of a more dead-on description of events that have conspired to link Ms. Parks, the most familiar name of the Civil Rights movement after Dr. Martin Luther King, with OutKast, hop-hop's strangest young artistes.

The legal trouble began when the 85-year-old Parks—who became a national icon in the mid-1950s for refusing to give up her seat to a white man on a segregated Alabama bus—was informed by the minister of her Detroit church that her name appeared on a parental-advisory sticker for OutKast's 1998 *Aquemini* ("Rosa Parks" is the first single). She then directed her attorney, Gregory J. Reed, to file suit April 5 in Wayne County (Michigan) Circuit Court, seeking "in excess of $25,000" charging false use of Parks's "name or image." The suit also demanded LaFace, Arista, and BMG destroy inventory copies of *Aquemini* and change the song's title on future copies. Richard Manson, of the Millennium Entertainment Group, who represents Parks, charged that OutKast was guilty of "the same kind of conduct" Parks faced 40 years ago—"an abuse of people."

Of course, well before *Aquemini*'s release, OutKast took care to state that the song was titled in respectful tribute—"dropping [something] subliminal for people who don't know about Rosa Parks, so they'll look into it," as the group's Andre "Dre" Benjamin told *Blaze* magazine. The song's video was even shot on "Sweet" Auburn Avenue, the stories stretch of Atlanta asphalt that is now home to the King Center. But the song *does* use Civil Rights symbolism in a mischievous, self-absorbed, classically hip-hop way. The verses never even mention Parks, while the "funk hoedown" chorus—"Ah ha, hush that fuss/ Everybody move to the back of the bus"—drops loaded Movement imagery into a party track about OutKast's comeback, and lets that imagery float around like weed smoke. The song could be heard as disrespectful, especially when Dre's partner Big Boi (a.k.a. Antoine Patton) brags that he's "bulldoggin' hos like them Georgetown Hoyas." But in the end, it's the song's defiantly abstract stance that makes it so memorable.

The constant invocation of the Civil Rights Movement's nonviolent philosophy has been a sticky point for years with younger generations. Rappers, in particular, have complained about being instructed on exactly *how* to rebel. Perhaps as a result, political issues have never found a consistent place in hip-hop; asserting one's own value as an individual human being is the more pressing issue. Yet "Rosa Parks" is a hip-hop song worth fighting over, not for its reckless wordplay, but because OutKast had the guts to "negotiate" this thorny conflict. They sample the past for their own generation's needs, but without shutting everybody else out. The Organized Noize production team mix G-crunk rhythm slink, turntable scratches, sunny acoustic guitar, and a harmonica breakdown from Rev. Robert Hodo (Dre's pastor at New Morning Light Baptist Church) to envision "dirty" Southern youth joyfully bumpin' rumps with their suit-and-tied elders. Like a funked-up African juba dance, the song welcomes both sacred and profane, young and old.

Acknowledging our country's racial legacy, while praying we're not trapped by it forever, Dre raps "You focus on the past/ Your ass'll be a has what," then adds, "That's one to live by or either one to die to/ I try to just throw it at you/ Determine your own adventure." Not exactly "I have a dream," but it's straight-up 1999 reality, and I wonder if Ms. Parks isn't more a disappointed parent than an abused icon. It can be a bitch sometimes to watch your kids follow their own path.

— "Singles" / Charles Aaron / July '99

Three artists Andre 3000 confesses "humble me"
one: **Prince**
two: **Aphex Twin**
three: **Squarepusher**

Three artists Andre 3000 has dueted with who are prettier than Big Boi:
one: **Erykah Badu**
two: **Gwen Stefani**
three: **Norah Jones**

Do you think hip-hop is stagnant right now?
Rakim made me wanna rap. But I don't feel hip-hop no more. A lot of people ask "why the change? Why y'all doing different music?" But it really came from boredom. Because I wasn't feelin' the same feeling at all. It was kinda like dying. I had to do something, crank myself back up, get into my shit.
— Dre, 2001

Although OutKast remained committed individualists, it was Dre who made good on the group's name when his mid-'90s lifestyle changes—including veganism, sobriety, and green turbans—raised eyebrows among hardcore fans. Looking out over the steering wheel, he recalls the flak. "Whenever you start doing something different, black people tend to think one of two things," he says. "Either you trying to switch for the white people, or you gay." Yet Dre never responded with macho outrage or gay-bashing, gestures he counts among the tired rap trends OutKast hopes to avoid. "That's something you do just to get people on your side," he says, changing lanes. "I mean, I don't know nothing about guys and guys together; I'm even still a little bit homophobic. But I want to get better with it. If I'm representing OutKast, that means we stand for anybody who feel like they don't fit in or has another way of doin' what they feel."

OutKast have made their hip-hop recombinations by drawing on idiosyncratic faves, like, say drum'n'bass scientist Rupert Parkes, a.k.a. Photek. "He's tough, man," Dre says of Parkes. "I played that CD, and I was like, 'Oh shit—I would kill if I had lyrics on this.'" For his part, Big Boi is nursing a passion for '80s pop-soul man Billy Ocean with a degree of irony that's difficult to ascertain. "See, Billy Ocean is some *underground* shit. He's that cat everybody knows but nobody ever sees anymore. He had all these hits but"—Big Boi leans forward conspiratorially. "Where *is* he? He's real undercover."

Lest these name-checks seem mere in-jokes, it's worth noting that one of *Stankonia*'s most striking songs does in fact recall the moves of classic, Billy Ocean-era '80s pop. It's also the most moving moment on the album. With its chiming synth and heart-tugging chords, "Ms. Jackson" draws on some sweet part of the *Purple Rain*-era unconscious to craft an unusual sort of apology. On it, Big Boi and Dre breathlessly rap dispatches to their estranged girlfriends' mothers—their "baby-mommas' mommas"—revealing all manner of hurt, regret, and enduring respect. "Basically the song is to say, 'We got together; it fell apart,'" Dre explains. "We did our best, we're doing our jobs as fathers, and we're sorry."

— "Funk Soul Brothers" / Chris Norris / December '00

Top five crunkiest OutKast rhymes

5. "It's the common denominator/
the nigga numerator/
never know who the hater niggaz cater to your ego/
Sorry like Atari that's the cousin of Coleco."
(Andre, "Skew it on the Bar-B")

4. "Lock all your windows then block the corridors/
Pullin' off on bell 'cause a whippins in order/
I like a three piece fish before I cut your daughter/
Yo quiero Taco Bell, then I hit the border."
(Big Boi, "B.O.B.")

3. "OutKast with a 'K,' yeah them niggas are hard/
Harder than a nigga tryin' to impress God/
I'll pull your whole deck, fuck pullin' your card/
Still I take my guitar and take a walk in the park."
(Andre, "Gangsta Shit")

2. "Drip drip drop there goes an eargasm/
Now you cumin' out the side of your face/
We're tapping right into your memory banks (Thanks!)/
So click it or ticket lets see your seat belt fastened/
Trunk rattlin' like two midgets in the back seat wrestlin'."
(Big Boi, "The Way You Move")

1. "Return of the gangsta thanks ta'/
them niggas that think you soft/
and say y'all be gospel rappin'/
But they be steady clappin' when you talk about/
Bitches 'n' switches 'n' hoes 'n' clothes 'n' weed/
Let's talk about time travelin'/
Rhyme javelin/
somethin' mind unravelin'/
get down."
(Andre, "Return of the G")

/ Jon **Dolan**

: **The**
White
Stripes

and the
(so-called)
return of
the rock

The pure.
The simple.
The real.
The true.

The notion of a "return to rock" fomented around 2002 was always somewhat specious. Rock hadn't gone anywhere; it'd just sucked festering anus boils for a good many years. Matchbox Twenty. Nü metal. "Nookie." Woodstock '99. Creed. Alt rock had asked hard questions about pop's male dominance and materialist excess. America's increasingly emboldened inner mook had fired back with a resounding "Stick it up your yeah!"

And so it was that the marginalized lil' folks who'd experienced that one emerald hour of post-Nirvana mass-cult shine fled back to the safety of their dorm rooms and illegal sublets, choosing to spend the late '90s embracing 68 million shades of sonic ephemera rather than weigh the heavy stakes of indie-rock's failure. Exotica. Electronica. Lounge. French pop. Brazilian tropicalia. All were grist for the martini shaker. Yuppies went swing dancing, German hipsters remixed Jamaica dub in Portuguese, DJ Spooky applied for a MacArthur Fellowship, and the boundary-melting e-com wooosh of global capitalism sweetened the deal with a fluxed-out sense of boundless, profit-sharing possibility. Until, of course, the bottom fell out. Stock bubble bust. George W. Bush. September 11th.

Suddenly, that digi-booty utopia didn't seem quite so alluring.

This is where the '90s officially ended. Dark did the horizon appear. Yet, in the lofts of Brooklyn, the dentist offices of Sweden, the garages of fucked-over Detroit, the pasty and for the most part unemployable were ready to rise again and reap the bounty of their relatively realistic hopes and dreams. And it began with a simple carpenter laying down his carpenter's tools: For it is here that Jack White laid down his upholsterer's tools and wandered into the fallen world to save rock'n'roll one last time. All over again.

The pure. The simple. The real. The true.

He wore red. She wore white. The White Stripes pried their back-to-basics aesthetic from two very different expressions of modernist primitivism: Delta blues and abstract European art. Jack White never met a dead black dude he couldn't reanimate as a fey British dude; he and his sister-lover Meg named their first great record, 2000's *De Stijl*, after a crew of 1920s Dutch artists who greeted the amoral brutality of their dumb century with big, bright, rugged shapes and colors. Jack's riffs spot sanded Jimmy Page down to the vicious id; he scorned contemporary youths "playing video games with their marijuana bongs." Meg's drumming bridged rock's two greatest rhythmic minimalists—Moe Tucker and Dave Grohl—and her vibe reflected her art, as she answered interview questions with wordless nods and giggles,

allegedly standing by and drinking a cocktail the night Jack beat the crap out of one Jason Von Bondie. White Stripes songs were simple too: about love and hate, the first emotions we know and the only ones we'll ever need. Cool kids in the '90s had been offered a fake version of growing up—big poppa checks and jet-set party-up. The reality of adulthood in America Y2K was hardly as rosy. On their 2001 breakthrough, *White Blood Cells*, the White Stripes offered the child's view as emotional Band-Aid—"Back to school, ring the bell/ Brand new shoes, walking blues/ Climb the fence, books and pens/ I can tell that we're gonna be friends." But kids are pure of heart, and pure of deceit as well. They like to lie, "cuz the truth doesn't make a noise," as Jack sang. He and Meg created a mini media frenzy by being an ex-couple who played at being brother and sister, but there was a more profound charade going on. They were also a tiny indie band that developed their own private rock mythology well before they'd even left the garage. Playing at being famous before they ever were helped the White Stripes side-step the whole Seattle slew of authenticity issues once they actually found a large audience (though Jack did his best to invent even dumber new ones, attacking white rap fans and just generally being a young codgery coot).

The other heroes of the "rock is back" hype, the Hives—five Swedish meatballs who dress like the Gerry & the Pacemakers working a Casino cruise—went beyond mere fiction into

---

Interviewer: "What did you do before you were in a band?"
Jack White: "I upholstered furniture."
Interviewer: "What do you think you'd be doing if you weren't in a rock band?"
Jack White: "Upholstering furniture."

> ESSAY CONTINUES ON NEXT PAGE

12

twelve records for a new rock millenium

1. The Strokes
Is This It
(RCA, 2001)

2. The White Stripes
White Blood Cells
(Sympathy for the Record Industry, 2002)

> ESSAY CONTINUES FROM PREVIOUS PAGE

Saturday-morning cartoon territory. The Hives were compared to Nuggets-era '60s garage rockers, but that's far too highbrow; their real antecedent was Flintstones' one-hit wonders, the Way Outs. Lead singer "Howlin'" Pelle Almqvist baited crowds with lines like, "America, you people love the Hives!" or "T-H-E-H-I-V-E-S. What does that spell?" and camped up his band's kick-ass, class-conscious punk with some of the ripest on-stage mau-mauing seen in decades. If you were a little leery about getting burned by falling in love with alt rock all over again, the Hives made it easy by letting you laugh at the idea. But the Hives weren't "hipsters" being "ironic." They were fans like us, record-collecting dorks getting theirs via a silly riff on the golden age of rock-star gimmickry. In the process, they were saying something very punk and very profound that Fred Durst could never grasp in a million marijuana bong hits: "hey you—yeah, you, loser—you don't need the muscle of money and power to act like a raging arrogant rock superstar."

As the New York Dolls once sang, "If I'm acting like a king, well that's 'cause I'm a human being." It's a lesson scores of bloggers and bubbling little bands were learning as they asserted the moral authority and communal clout to privilege their own desires and ambitions above whatever simulated kicks the corporate mainstream was hawking. It was at the heart of the two bands that revived the long-dormant New York rock scene the Dolls had christened some 30 years ago: the Strokes and Yeah Yeah Yeahs.

The Strokes acted out the Dolls' credo in reverse, trading aristocratic entitlement for punk-rock reinvention. Young masters Julian, Fabrizio, Mercutio, Benvolio, and Chloe forsook the ski slopes of Stadt to meta-slum it in the East Village, a Whit Stillman version of raised-pinky Stones/Faces rakishness. But the lust and longing on their 2001 debut, *Is This It*, had as much richly simulated emotional experience as

great new wave has ever required. Riding a storm of (quaintly print-media-driven) hype as well as a groundswell of post-9/11 Nu Yawk jingoism, the fab five became the leaders of a genuine Big Apple rock renaissance. Osama could have his cave; we had Interpol! Civic pride soared. People even started doing cocaine again. Eventually, Lower Manhattan's self-esteem got so high that it spilled over into Williamsburg, Brooklyn, a desolate region peopled by indigenous "hipsters," whose strange dress and clannish practices were of endless fascination to visitors.

Despite not living there, no band represented Williamsburg chic like Yeah Yeah Yeahs. Critic Tom Carson once described the rush of living in New York during the great punk-rock summer of '77, hearing the line "New York City really has it all" in the Ramones' single "Sheena Is A Punk Rocker" as a communal trash-buzz cri de coeur. YYYs accessed that magic, setting up a like a fantasy camp of New York music culture. They heard in gutter-to-gallery downtown noise what poet Frank O'Hara heard in Billie Holiday the night he leaned against the john door at the Five Spot. Guitarist Nick Zinner was touched by the weird-angled, beautiful-noise gestalt of late great Voidoids genius Robert Quine (and, like Quine, became a studio must-have for area bands). And while beer-bottle-smashing, '80s fashion-deconstructing singer Karen O was seen as a high priestess of haut-hipsterdom, her real power was rooted not in imperious style but shaky courage. Like David Johansen almost toppling over in six-inch heels or Debbie Harry rolling off CBGB's stage or Joey Ramone too sweet to wear the irony mask, she was unable to be anything but a king. Low on purity. Simple as sin. Real like the music of broken air, shock and shame you hear in the millionth handed-down midnight hour. When the truth doesn't make a noise.

We never rehearse; she never practices drums on her own, and I never practice guitar on my own. If I played guitar every day and Meg played drums every day, I think it would take away from the soul of it.

—Jack White, 2003

3. Yeah Yeah Yeahs
Fever to Tell
(Interscope, 2003)

5. The White Stripes
De Stijl
(Sympathy For the
Record Industry, 2000)

7. The White Stripes
Elephant
(V2, 2003)

9. Interpol
*Turn On the Bright
Lights*
(Matador, 2002)

11. The Electric 6
Fire
(Beggar's Banquet,
2003)

4. The Hives
Veni Vidi Vicious
(Warner Brothers,
2002)

6. The Strokes
Room on Fire
(RCA, 2002)

8. The Hives
Tyrannosaurus Hives
(Warner Brothers,
2004)

10. The Dirtbombs
*Dangerous Magical
Noise*
(Sympathy, 2002)

12. The Kings of Leon
*Youth and Young
Manhood*
(RCA, 2002)

"You can go back and think about songs that came close to being perfect, like 'Strawberry Fields Forever,' and it has tons of tape hiss and surface noise and different room reverbs, things like that. People don't realize that there's a point where that's it. Like with microphones recording the human voice—they reach a pinnacle at some point. Or the Fender Twin Reverb [amplifier]—its been out for 40 years, and they've never improved on it. And they're never gonna do it, because that's what a guitar sounds like. It's like, 'Why is a violin the shape a violin is,' you know? I mean, couldn't Stradivarius have figured out a different shape to make a violin sound a little better? No. That's as good as it's gonna get."
— Jack White, 2003

THAT AFTERNOON IN UNION SQUARE, THE WHITE STRIPES RULED LIKE LITTLE GODS, TRIUMPHING OVER A BATTALION OF NEARBY CONSTRUCTION WORKERS TO BLOW AWAY THE ASSEMBLED CROWD OF HOOKY-PLAYING FANS, UNEMPLOYED DOT-COMMERS, CURIOUS OFFICE ASSISTANTS, AND BEFUDDLED LUNCH-BREAKERS. AFTER ABOUT AN HOUR OF JACK WHITE'S SMARTASS BANTER AND MEG WHITE'S CYMBAL-PUNISHING AND PIGTAIL-SWINGING, THE POWERS THAT BE PULLED THE PLUG. SO JACK LED THE CROWD IN A SING-ALONG OF LEDBELLY'S "BOLL WEEVIL," CLIMAXING WITH THE CHORUS, "I'M A-LOOKIN' FOR A HOME!" NO BIG BUDGET. NO ELECTRICITY. JUST A GUY UP ON HIS SOAPBOX, TRYING TO CHANGE HIS WORLD.
— "THE LITTLE BAND REVOLUTION" / JON DOLAN / JANUARY '03

The Yeah Yeah Yeahs don't want to save rock'n'roll—they just want to play it from the hip really hard. The Brooklyn trio aren't shy about anything, even their own flaws, which makes them even sexier—*Fever to Tell* is 38 minutes of naked shake-and-shimmy, complete with scars, moles, and tattoos. Brian Chase's high-tension drumming is their secret weapon, and lead squealer Karen O is such a tough guy that when she fesses up to vulnerability on "Maps," it's a revelation.
— "The Year in Music 2003" / Douglas Wolk / January '04

To an outsider, Yeah Yeah Yeahs' frontwoman Karen O seems like a supercool New York art-star who's completely sure of herself and a little bit dangerous. But walking into her "office," a small bedroom with a few drum machines, mics, and other electronics, she is simply Karen Orzolek, a slender 25-year-old in a pale-yellow T-shirt and jeans. She's sweet and goofy and has a nervous laugh, like a sit-com's wacky next-door neighbor. She makes up knock-knock jokes, asks me what my favorite Simpsons episode is, and wonders aloud how anyone could think Johnny Depp isn't foxy.
"That onstage personality is so opposite from the way I am normally," she says. "But it's just as valid, because it's there. It came from somewhere. There are tons of personalities within the Karen O persona. Those expressions on my face can go from maniacal to introverted to serious in a second—there's a schizophrenia involved. I kind of associate it with being an individual in modern society, where people have way more personalities than they used to."
"As soon as she gets into the clothes is when everything kicks in and Karen O comes out," says Christiane Hultquist, the friend and designer who, under the name Christian Joy, constructs all of Karen's stage outfits. "Karen's such an incredible performer—so outgoing and fairly insane. No person can do a dress justice like Karen can."
— "Yeah!" / William Van Meter / June '04

Not since Guns N' Roses in 1987 (and maybe not since the Rolling Stones in '67) has a major rock band so deftly mastered the concept of the celebrity collective; the Strokes seem like a gang. They're almost like the Ramones. No one says, "Julian Casablancas was at a party" or "I just ran into Fabrizio Moretti at the airport" or "I spotted Albert Hammond Jr. in a discotheque." All of these situations would be described with the same declaration: "I think I saw a Stroke."
— "Gang of Five" / Chuck Klosterman / December '03

[THE STROKES]

"Nick Cave is *not* party music!" proclaims guitarist Albert Hammond Jr. as he enters, an inside-out Journey tour jersey clinging to his skinny torso. All kinky hair and sleepy eyes, he immediately frets over the sequence of his home-burned CD mix. "*Change it,*" he begs. Nikolai Fraiture, the largest but least imposing Stroke, ambles in and takes his regular post, an empty corner. As the room fills with Marlboro smoke, rangy guitarist Nick Valensi (taking snapshots) and drummer Fabrizio Moretti (grinning, fresh off a stage dive) wander over.

The security dude finally opens the door, and a dozen 16-year-old girls surge forward clutching paper for autographs. Their home-town [Portland, ME] may smell of New England chimney smoke, but these girls have their Lower Manhattan ensembles down—thrift-store tees, leather jackets, tight vintage cords. They're too young to drink or shag or do anything, really, except gawk at the politely indifferent, chain-smoking, pool-shooting, beer-drinking, new princes of rock'n'roll. And they are thrilled.

Packing two guitars, a bass, drums, five pairs of Converse All Stars, and miles of street-wise New York style, the Strokes are 2002's Band of the Year. Like the White Stripes, they are a great rock group that seems to get better with every show. But during the past 18 months, on the strength of a debut, *Is This It*, which has sold around 750,000 copies in the U.S. (and more than 1.4 million worldwide), it was the Strokes who led the movement to recast the way rock looks, sounds, and sells.

"They're the ones who made that positive change," says comedian David Cross. "They paved the way for bands like the White Stripes. They were just way better than nü metal. It got to a point where those douchebag assholes lacked anything to say, so they just got more piercings and played louder."

"The guys in the band can't acknowledge it," says Strokes manager Ryan Gentles, 25, a former booker for Lower East Side rock club Mercury Lounge. "But when I see CBGB T-shirts being sold at, like, Wal-Mart in Omaha, I know that's because of us."
— "The Return of Cool" / Marc Spitz / January '03

In Manhattan, Interpol's Carlos D. has a visibility that's matched only by the Chrysler Building, Moby, and guys who look like Moby. He's *always* out. Carlos D. sightings are legend:

"I saw Carlos D. eating a taco by himself" or "I saw Carlos D. near the Kmart at Astor Place." It's not like he's hard to miss; tonight's outfit, for example, is a long black jacket, striped trousers, impossibly high boots. Any sane person would think he looks like an SS guard who fell into a time portal and wound up with a bass amp (he's also given to wearing a gun holster, though tonight it's at home).

"Expressions of irony through clothing are very important," he says. "I didn't wake up and go, 'I'm gonna dress like a Nazi.' But when I start thinking about how I want to make myself look cool, it starts to take shape along those lines." While it may be a bit of intentional antagonism, he says, "I don't go into my Laundromat with full-on Nazi regalia. I don't feel like getting into a sociological battle with the peons that surround me on a daily, hourly basis."
— "Night Falls on Manhattan" / Brian Rafferty / April '05

If rock'n'roll is about being young, playing loud, and dressing like a Mormon pimp, the Hives are its living, breathing embodiment.

It helps, of course, that there's an earth-scorchingly great band in those pants. The Hives take the Witness stage in full, cocky strut. From the first song of their set—"The Hives—Declare Guerre Nucléaire"—the crowd is theirs. The Hives have a way of making other rock performances look like croquet matches. At today's show, Chris Dangerous pummels his kit so hard he spends the rest of the evening sprawled on a dressing-room couch, nursing a migraine; guitarist Carlstroem bloodies his own nose; and Almqvist throws out more cocky rock-frontman poses than Beck playing a heated game of charades with Mick Jagger.

Almqvist—who feigns a sub-Shakira command of English onstage, even though, like most Swedes, he learned the language in school and remains fluent—pauses to commend the crowd on its excellent taste:

"You know, and we know, that the Hives are your favorite band! Fortunately, the people at the festival have made it possible for you to see some other bands, but they are just appetizers! The Hives are the main course of this festival! We love you—and God knows you love us!"
— "Stockholm Syndrome" / Alex Pappademas / October '02

[INTERPOL]

"So many bands are like, 'I'm real because I'm dirty.' Not washing your hair doesn't make you more real. If you have money for guitars, you can afford soap."

— Howlin' Pelle Almqvist, 2002

{ THE HIVES }

Joey Ramone [May '01]
He saw this cover just a few days before he died, and it cheered him up. RIP, dude.

appendix I /

Covers
that impressed
even us.

Run DMC [May '88]
The Kings of Queens. RIP
Jam Master Jay.

Nick Cave [February '89]
Badass.

**Flea / Red Hot Chili
Peppers [February '90]**
Flying mohawk #1

**Chris Cornell / Sound-
garden [September '92]**
Hottest metal dude ever—
at least until he cut his hair.

**Public Enemy
[October '92]**
And to think it was all lead-
ing to *The Surreal Life*.

**Kurt Cobain, Courtney
Love, Frances Bean
Cobain [December '92]**
Yes, the subhead does say
"Family Values."

Green Day [November '94]
We were there at the
beginning, son. (Well, uh, at
least after *Dookie*).

Rancid [October '95]
Flying mohawk #2

South Park [March '98]
Janet Jackson's got nothing
on Cartman—except that
starburst nipple piercing.

Notorious B.I.G. [April '00]
Looks even better in a suit
than Jay-Z.

**David Lee Roth
[October '00]**
This cover was the 101st
sleaziest moment. Note the
butt & the all-access pass.

Eminem [January '01]
Eminem as *Clockwork
Orange* droogie. We bit the
photo from another mag, but
you would've too.

CONTINUES ON NEXT PAGE >

Tool [June '01]
Much cooler than if we showed their faces, right?

Pink [May '02]
Whoever scored the pink vinyl copy of Pink Floyd's *Animals* deserved a raise.

Moby [June '02]
It only took four hours to glue all those stars on his head.

Foo Fighters [November '02]
Okay, this was cheating.

The Strokes [January '03]
The kiss'n'grope probably made a few homophobes cancel their subscriptions. C'est la vie.

Sum 41 [February '03]
Hate if you must, but this rip off of the Damned's debut album cover was lickable.

Kurt Cobain [April '04]
Okay, it's like our 27th Kurt cover. But still.

Yeah Yeah Yeahs [June '04]
Silver crotches rule.

Beastie Boys [July '04]
If only this giant infant had eaten Adam Yauch.

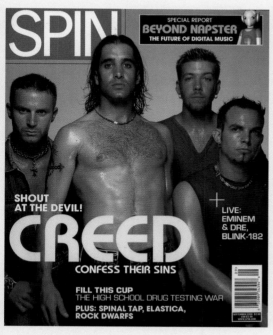

Creed [September '00]
God forgive us.

appendix I /

Covers we'd rather not talk about now.

Charlie Sexton [May '86]
Wasn't he in Sigue Sigue
Sputnik?

**Mick Jagger / Rolling
Stones [August '86]**
Years later, *Rolling Stone*
would review an album by
the Spinanes.

**Ozzy Osbourne
[September '86]**
Photo originally shot for *Wig
Entrepreneur.*

**Duran Duran
[February '87]**
Hungry like the poodle.

CONTINUES ON NEXT PAGE >

Covers we'd rather not talk about now.
CONTINUED

Jim Kerr / Simple Minds [August '87]
Someone convinced us that this was Julian Lennon. Who also sucked.

Sting [December '87]
He was marginally less pretentious back then. Marginally.

Edie Brickell [March '89]
Well, Brand Nubian sampled her.

Lisa Stansfield [June '90]
Well, Notorious B.I.G. sampled her.

Lennie Kravitz [May '91]
Now releases singles as Gap commercials, proving yesterday's cool is tomorrow's lame cross-promotion.

Arrested Development [January '93]
Stay strong, Mr. Wendel. Stay strong.

Roseanne Barr [May '96]
It was supposed to be Godzilla.

Smashing Pumpkins [June '96]
Note to photo stylist: do not grease subjects (see also: Creed)

Bush [December '96]
Um...we like his wife!

**Natalie Imbruglia
[June '98]**
Our best-selling issue
among Australian house-
wives.

Dave Matthews [July '98]
On the upside, the photogra-
pher *did* manage to separate
Dave's shoulder.

Jesse Camp [August '98]
Slightly sexier than our
rejected Matt Pinfield cover.

**Elijah Wood and Jordana
Brewster / *The Faculty*
[February '99]**
Yo, Frodo, can I bum an
American Spirit?

**Dexter Holland / The
Offspring [March '99]**
Pink is not an especially
punk color.

Limp Bizkit [August '99]
In this issue we also
endorsed Pat Buchanan for
President.

**Matchbox Twenty
[July '00]**
"Cool bands don't sell
records"? You mean, like,
Led Zeppelin?

**Papa Roach
[December '00]**
Well, would you really have
preferred Godsmack?

**Mark McGrath / Sugar
Ray [September '01]**
"I regret nothing," he says.
We, on the other hand....

Evan Dando and Adrienne Shelly [April '93]
As celebrity spit-swaps go, this did even less for their careers
than the Madonna-Britney kiss.

appendix I /

The jury's out.

PJ Harvey [May '95]
Girlfriend, you are scaring us.

Björk [December '97]
The photo stylist was clearly gunning for a job with *Cats*.

Marilyn Manson [February '98]
At age 36, he's still hasn't learned to eat spaghetti properly.

Axl Rose [July '99]
Upon further reflection, maybe he is not what the world needs after all.

Blink-182 [July '01]
Whitey, please!

Jay-Z, etc. [April '02]
Jigga finally makes the cover of SPIN. And, uh...who are those other people?

Morrissey [May '04]
Why is our high school drama teacher on the cover of *SPIN*?

The Pixies [September '04]
She couldn't have shaved her head too?

Hate mail.

Dean Martin had our back. But other folks don't always feel us. In the interest of balanced journalism, we hereby present some of our most memorable disses. (NOTE: All misperceptions and hallucinations uncorrected.)

September '85
Dear SPIN,

In your first issue, you say you are going to give *Rolling Stone* competition. I'd like to ask you one question: when will you attempt this? SPIN is cheap, boring, and dumb. It isn't exciting, nor is it irreverent. It resembles a supermarket gossip magazine. Even the quality of print and papers is poor. Face it, you are way below *Rolling Stone*'s standards. Stick to the checkout-line magazines.

> A faithful *Rolling Stone* magazine subscriber,
> Shannon Harding
> Richmond, IN

Picked up my first copy of SPIN. In the spirit of constructive criticism, here are my beefs.

The layout is terrible, the choice of art poor. Your color separations suck. Maybe color doesn't reproduce as well on this stock (is it heat-set on Super-Calendar paper?) Most of the B&W looks great.

Too gray. Rambling editorial could make way for good art.

This Henry Rollins represents all the crazed ego-trippers who try to jump on the Hunter Thompson Gonzo train. Well, that train left the station—years ago. Rollins is not funny. He is not even outrageous. He's just another of the poor writers who thinks that by injecting himself into the story we can all laugh with him. Really, we all laugh at him.

(And by the way, Executive Editor Edward Rasen seems to be an accomplice to this Rollins tripe—he took the photo in the July issue. There are people out there who know good writing and demand it. Rasen should stick to photography.)

What gives? And what the heck are these Biff Products things you pass as cartoons?

Thanks for letting me get these things off my chest. I wish you the best of luck with SPIN—it's really needed now that *Rolling Stone* has lumbered even closer to the tar pit of Yuppie-dom.

By the way, I'm an award-winning reporter, columnist, critic and magazine editor (*Music City News*) who now works for Kentucky Governor Martha Layne Collins. For a price I will come out of retirement and help you out.

> Barry Bronson
> Lexington, Kentucky

September '87
I'm really getting sick of all the coverage you guys give rap and the people who make it. Especially in the Singles column. Biz Markie? Eric B. and Rakim? Classical Two? Who gives a shit? Why don't you stick to interesting stuff like the Godfathers, or what about the new Jesus and Mary Chain 12" "April Skies"? Now that's the kind of thing people read your magazine for, so forget all this rap crap and leave it to a lesser magazine. It's just going to fade away like hip hop and go-go music did.

> Steve Douglas
> Schaumburg, PA

March '88
[Ed. Note: This letter was sent to executives in the music industry.]

"The music business is like a whore, so remember, you've got to treat it like a whore."

PMRC? Nope.

A direct quote from the October '87 issue of *Manhattan, Inc.* from SPIN Magazine editor and publisher Bob Guccione, Jr. Not bad coming from a man whose hands are outstretched wondering where his next advertising dollar is coming from or where his next interview might be.

We'll tell you this much—he won't find it under the rock he continually crawls out from under.

We think Dave Marsh might have said it best in the November '87 issue of *Rock & Roll Confidential*: "…while it was always clear what SPIN loathed, it was damned hard to figure out what it loved, except the sound of its own voice. And that's no way to build the kind of sizable, loyal audience necessary to an enterprise whose overt goal was to outstrip *Rolling Stone…*"

Yes, we are in the business of music, but let's try to remember that we are luckier than most… we could be delivering phone books for a living. Nothing in the world of music was ever as bad as SPIN made it out to be. You might want to think about that before you give them your next ad or place one of your artists at their mercy… we have.

> Happy New Year,
> Janie Hoffman
> Larry Solters
> Katie Valk
> MCA Records

The opinions expressed in this letter are ours and not representative of anyone else at MCA Inc.

May '89

I was never a fucking waitress, you guys. You should check before you make a headline out of it.
Suzanne Vega
New York, NY

P.S. I was a receptionist.

May '89

This afternoon I had the opportunity to speak with your Circulation Department concerning my proposal to use Freedom Rocks [pieces of the Berlin Wall] as a premium to stimulate subscription response to SPIN.

His objection was that the Freedom Rock concept was not "hip," to use his word. There is nothing more "hip" in pop culture today than the Berlin Wall, with all of its symbolism and ramifications.

And if it's not "hip," then why in the February 1990 issue of your magazine did you publish a report called "So You Want a Revolution?" Based on that conversation, I am afraid this valid, cutting-edge concept which your magazine can profit from will not get a fair hearing.

My concern is that these concepts are "too lofty" or "over the head" of your Circulation Director. Do you realize what kind of response you would generate if you offered a free piece of the Berlin Wall to new subscribers? And it comes to you as a quality piece for less than the price of a T-shirt.

Please reconsider my proposal.

Gary Suo
Freedom Rocks
Toronto, Ontario

January '92

Dear Bob Guccione, Jr. [Editor-in-Chief],

Regarding Axl Rose: He is God; you are a piece of shit. Grow up and quit trying to be your daddy. And yes, I'm sure he gets more pussy than you. He's not an ugly little turd like you; and he has some class.

Christina Robbins
Ruston, Louisiana

Bob Guccione, Jr., replies:

I think it's sad that Axl Rose disappoints his fans, who are deluded to think he has the courage to back what his stupid mouth says. He called me out [in his song "Get in the Ring"], I came out, he ran he other way. Axl, you're a wimp and you're pathetic, and you let the kids down.

March '92

Dear Sir or Madam:
We are the attorneys for W. Axl Rose.

We are informed that in various issues of your magazine, defamatory statements about our client have been printed by you. Please be advised that our client has instructed us to begin the process of preparing and filing a lawsuit against your magazine for defamation as a result of those defamatory statements that have been printed. Our client fully intends to seek redress for the damages he has suffered.

Nothing contained herein shall be construed as a waiver by our client of his rights and remedies, and all such rights and remedies are reserved.

Very truly yours,
Lee Phillips
Manatt, Phelps & Phillips
Attorneys at Law

December '94

For reasons known only to Mike Rubin and the Red Army soldiers who indoctrinated him, he fell under the impression that [the 'zine] *Answer Me!* depicts serial killers as Nordic warriors who'll safeguard the white race's shrinking empire. I've never written anything from which someone could even vaguely infer this, yet he's been riffing on this assumption for a while now. Rubin fails to comprehend that our problem is with the human race and that for us to champion any individual race's survival would be a disservice to our cause. We like serial killers in the same way we like AIDS and the war in Bosnia—they're agents of depopulation. (By the way, a statistical preponderance of their victims are white, too.) He also inferred that we were somehow "entitled." I'll compare socioeconomic backgrounds with you anytime, Mike, and we'll see who's entitled. Blinded and softened by his own entitlement, Rubin tosses around the word "white" as if it were a pejorative term. He seems a lot more hung up on this whole whiteness trip than I am. I suppose that's why he didn't consider it a racial slur when he called me a "redneck." Let's be equitable. You wouldn't like it if I called you a "Jewboy," would you, Mike? My Jewish wife is almost certain you wouldn't. There's a fundamental difference between me and Charlie [Manson], Mike. Charlie's in jail. Watch what you say.

Jim Goad
Answer Me!
Hollywood, California

Mike Rubin responds:

Temple University journalism grad Jim Goad put Adolf Hitler on the cover of his magazine Answer Me!, *published interviews with such people as David Duke, posed in an "Evil White Male" T-shirt on the front cover of the* Village Voice, *described himself in his* Answer Me! *editor's note as "white trash with a brain," and then denies being "hung up on this whole whiteness trip." Geez, I don't know how I could have been so confused as to call him a "pomo redneck." As far as what epithets are deemed appropriate by Goad's Jewish wife—the author of the essay "I Hate Being a Jew," which included such wisdom as "My Jewish family is thankfully almost all dead now… I wish my family had lived next to the Hitlers. At least the Nazis knew how to dress… I wish there was a perfume I could sprinkle on myself to mask the Hebraic stench"—she's hardly the kind of Talmudic scholar I'd ever consult. Thanks ever so much for the threat, but my Red Army training also included self-defense.*

March '95

In the latest "Rock Bottom Awards" [December '94], you dubbed my band with the "Everybody Else Is Doing It, So Why Can't We? Award," commenting on how we have just started shooting grainy videos to be trendy and jump on some new bandwagon. I would like to point out that we've been shooting alternative and ground-breaking videos for over ten years. As far as fashion goes (you also commented on that), we're musicians not models. I feel sorry for you; you put on this air of being so street-smart and all-embracing of the underbelly of life and music (same thing), when in reality you're probably a bunch of mama's boys who only learned how to write in some classroom and not on the streets where the shit really runs deep. Do you just sit there like wash-women and gossip about who's in and who's out, while all along in your hearts you know you're just a poor man's *Rolling Stone*? Let me tell ya: You don't know shit about us and we like it like that. You haven't got the balls to go against the grain just to feel the splinters the way we have. So I feel compelled to sling a lit-tle piss back at ya. In the end, we're all gonna take a dirt nap. But at least I'll have broken a few rules, which is much more than you can ever say.

Love and kisses,
Nikki Sixx, Mötley Crüe

June '96

Regarding your story on my boss: The 1950's are hip, and Pat Buchanan is more hip than you cats could ever hope to be.

Tom Carter
Assistant to the Campaign Manager
Buchanan for President
McLean, Virginia

April '98

I am a 43-year-old, white, female office worker. My clown name is Choko. How low and deplorable to even mention minstrel blackface, as if it is the derivation for Insane Clown Posse. Shaggy 2 Dope and Violent J sport clown-face drawn from the traditional tramp style, and they carry on a great tradition of social commentary in that guise. There is no way the Clowns could not have sprung full-blown from the half-broken collective consciousness of my hometown, this mixed-race, working-poor union town.

Kaarli S. Makela
Hazel Park, Michigan

Where the hell do you get that Insane Clown Posse fans are from the suburbs? I bet you 99 percent of all Juggalos are from the muthafuckin' ghetto!!!!

Robert Aouad
Toledo, Ohio

Mike Rubin and Mark Dancey respond:
Obviously, our comic touched a guilty nerve among Insane Clown Posse fans. Careful readers of "Down With the Clowns" will note that the words "racist" and "wigger" (a term neither of us endorse) do not appear anywhere within our story. All the dia-logue in the article was reprinted verbatim form the Detroit show we attended and we portrayed visually only what the two of us actually saw. Of the roughly 40 ICP "juggalos" we interviewed, not a single one was from the actual city of Detroit—much like Violent J and Shaggy 2 Dope themselves, who attended high school in suburban Ferndale. The fans we caricatured all hail from such "ghettos" as Roseville, Westland, and Mt. Clemens. Lastly, while ICP fans are quick to defend their beloved clowns from any potential inference of intolerance the tone of the spate of letters, profane phone messages, and misspelled Internet ramblings delivered in response to the comic has been over-whelmingly homophobic and misogynistic. ICP even saw fit to use their "Wicked Web Site" as a launching pad for threats of physical harm against us, considerably ironic coming from sup-posed First Amendment martyrs. Last time we checked, incite-ment to violence was neither free nor protected speech. See you in the funny pages.

July '98

I'm amazed you were able to extract four long pages on a subject already tackled by every post-Nirvana, *Baffler*-reading cynical-idealist with a BLOCKBUSTER SUCKS T-shirt. If you thought for a New York minute that film industry reservoir dogs were going to keep on making cultural waves without getting too *Titanic* about it, you must have had some serious *Welcome to the Dollhouse*-style mama trauma. Every muthafunking en-deavor that has the gall to break new ground gets licked and lapdanced by mainstream America sooner or later. As in soccer moms jonesing for the next Ang Lee drama. City magistrates playing hooky to hit all-day Gus Van Sant marathons. Besides, you got it wrong: Indie film is not killing itself. Commercial film posing as indie film is Auschwitzing the hell out of it (see the Miramax doggie biscuit *From Dusk Till Dawn*). So stop whining about the inevitable and look for the new, "real" underground, wherever it may be. Tell Generation {WH}Y what's actually— gasp—good about our withered little pop world. Or I'll grab that "dead cat" you mentioned and flog you like a dead horse.

Me so angry, me hate you long time,
Tony Stockton
Roanoke, Virginia

October '98

After reading your awesome magazine for over a year, I found myself appalled by a statement made by Jane Dark: "Weeks after [Flaming Lips] performed on a *Beverly Hills 90210* episode, Oklahoma City was bombed—coincidence?" Apparently you've never experienced such a tragedy, or you would never have written that. And for your sake, I hope you never have to live through anything such as what my home- town went through.

Destenie Henderson
Oklahoma City, Oklahoma

December '98

A lot of fans probably read your July issue and started to cry. If I were the Backstreet Boys, I would slap a legal suit on you faster than you could say "Backstreet Boys." I'm sure all their other fans are with me when I say, "Your magazine is nothing but trash."

Becky Diamond
Duryea, Pennsylvania

January '99

We thought as there are some major inaccuracies in your piece on us [cover, September '99], it would be good to set the record straight. First and most important, the story Doc Dre told regard- ing our performance at the Apollo Theatre was completely made up by him. As it paints us as racist, we thought this to be the most significant thing to inform you and your readership of. But as long as we are bringing up inaccuracies, it is worth noth- ing that everything that Dre said was made up. We can only guess (as we have not spent much time with Dre since the short time that he DJed for us back in '86) that Dre was following in the footsteps of how we used to conduct ourselves in interviews back then. In those days, we lied a lot in interviews. In fact, some of the very lies he told were the same things we used to say to interviewers back then. For example, that we were banned from an entire hotel chain as well as an airline, or that we drilled a hole in a hotel floor. Perhaps Dre thought it would be funny to just make the whole interview up, as we used to do. Unfortunately, when his untruths were laid out juxtaposed against everyone else's words (not all of which were accurate either), they came across as history. An especially unfortunate result is that now *Time Out New York* has picked it up from SPIN and put it into their pieces on the band as though it was true. Doesn't anyone fact-check anymore?

The Beastie Boys
New York, New York

Author Alan Light responds:
In an oral history covering 16 years, there are always going to be different accounts of events, and while any inaccuracies are regrettable, we think the structure made clear that this was the Beastie Boys' history as remembered by the people who lived it.

As for the Apollo story, Doctor Dre insists that "it's the truth—it's a fact, it's on tape and videotape." He emphasized that the incident came about "not maliciously, but out of warmth for their audience. I was talking in very positive terms about them." His only concern about the piece was that it didn't sufficiently express "how much I loved those guys and all the fun we were having."

The color photograph of someone's eyeball staring up from a towel, ligaments still attached ["Murder Site Cleanup," Exposure, October], crosses the line between cutting-edge journalistic photography and sensationalism. That was a person, you know—someone's child or parent, and I feel I can have a perfectly fine understanding of the article without a blatantly disgusting photo.

Jennifer Siglin
Brea, California

Even worse was the caption: "A crew member's eye-catching find." And we wonder why our children our children becoming desensitized to violence?

Peter Sears
Hartford, Connecticut

March '99

Sean Landers, nothing would please me more than to be able to send you a crisp dollar bill [Genius Lessons, December '98]. Unfortunately, I am in prison and money is not allowed. I could send you three stamps (prisoners' monetary equivalent), but that would leave me short. You see, I've just applied one of your staple ideals—greed. I wish you would dispense with your bor- ing threats of discontinuing your page and get on with the show. Tell me what a worthless bag of shit I am for being in prison. Tell the world why men will screw fat chicks but not be seen with them. You're the stuffing on my plate, Sean Landers. So quit your feeble attempts to worm your way out of the kitchen. Pick up your pen and get to work, you loser.

Joe Smith
Carson City, Nevada

I really don't understand why you have to provide a forum for paranoid artists such as Busta Rhymes (and Canibus and Method Man) to talk about Armageddon when it's so obvious they're completely stoned and talking shit out of their ass. Hello? Marijuana makes people paranoid and delusional. I thought this was SPIN, not *High Times* or some Heaven's Gate "Here come the space ships, let's go" leaflet you find in the subway. Get real…Is Busta informed? Is he psychic? No, he's stoned, and, for better or worse, SPIN is like, let's turn on the tape recorder and see what the funny kooky stoned guy in the dress says. I'm not dissing Busta, really—I mean, I like his videos on MTV. But don't you think there's already enough going on in the world for artists of Busta's stature and magazines of SPIN's stature to address?

At least Jewel talks about shit like the present and does something about it. (She just started some charity with her mom). Damn, I know Jesse Ventura's a governor and all but don't you think it's time we stop giving stoned weirdos the podium and just be normal?

> Not trying to hear the voice of doom,
> Jennifer McNaffee
> Akron, Ohio

Larry "Ratso" Sloman, former editor-in-chief of *High Times* and author of *Reefer Madness: A History of Marijuana* (St. Martin's Press) responds:
How dare Ms. McNaffee impute that High Times *is a haven for paranoid and delusional ideation. Jennifer, beware the Ides of March. Beware the semblance of normalcy. If you dare to look beneath the surface of things, you'll eventually see that all seemingly random historical events are, in fact, being directed by 23 elders who live in the Himalayas and channel their insights through people like Busta.*

July '99
I hate your magazine so very much and think you are distorting children's minds, so keep your trash to your darn self.

> Jane Semel
> Pittsburgh, Pennsylvania

October '99
I just received notice that my subscription to SPIN is about to expire. Unfortunately for you, my renewal notice came attached to an issue with a 12-year-old picture of Axl Rose on the cover.

> Thanks for making my decision for me.
> Mark Morgan
> Port Orchard, Washington

December '99
I've never heard of half of the groups on your "Best Albums of the '90s" list—Sleater-Kinney, Pavement, Fugazi, nor Pulp, to name just a few. I can understand how bands like Nirvana, Nine Inch Nails, Pearl Jam, and U2 got on the list. If you ask anyone who Green Day are, they would most likely know, but if you asked someone what Buena Vista Social Club is, they probably wouldn't. Another thing that made me mad was that Korn were not on the list. Korn are way more popular than most of those bands.

> Heather Pepe
> Wallingford, Connecticut

Tell [Senior Editor] Will Hermes to stop sucking PJ Harvey's dick. No Dave Matthews? What the hell?

> Morgan Pakula
> Phoenix

September '01
You guys suck at writing this magazine. Why don't you do articles on some cool bands like Korn, Pantera, Slayer, or Megadeth? Or can't you get interviews with those guys because you suck too much?

> Nate DeVos
> Melvin, Iowa

January '02
Charles R. Cross offers us gossipy "revelations" about Kurt Cobain's short relationship with Binki Kill drummer Tobi Vail, portraying her as a man-eater who treats boyfriends as accessories. It is implied that by breaking off less than six months of casual dating, Tobi set Kurt on a pathway to self-destruction and heroin use that ultimately led to his tragic end. As someone who lived in Olympia during this time (down the hallway from my then-bandmate Tobi), I feel it's important to take issue with this conclusion, because it is not only irresponsible and sexist but totally wrong.

Bikini Kill changed independent music culture and inspired thousands of grrrls to pick up instruments—a far different legacy than the suicide that Cross would have us lay at Tobi's feet. Tobi refuses to speak publicly and participate in the exploitation of the Cobain myth by hack journalists trying to make a career, record companies trying to sell records, and feeble attempts by ex-"friends" to mark their place in history. This means that another generation of women is taught to romanticize the paralyzed rock-star archetype and to demonize Kurt's feminist musician friend. If Tobi has a legacy, it's as the embodiment of the genuine feminist perspective that weaves throughout the second and third Nirvana albums—his most lasting contribution.

> Jenny Toomey
> Washington, D.C.

March '03
Thanks for continuing to perpetuate stereotypes and spread misinformation about Goths. And for the last time: Marilyn Manson is *not* Goth.

> Rae Licari
> Bellevue, Nebraska

Essay contributors.

Charles Aaron is a Brooklyn resident and the music editor of SPIN. He was the winner of the 1999 ASCAP-Deems Taylor Special Recognition Award for music writing and was a 2001 National Arts Journalism Program fellow at Columbia University. His work has been widely anthologized.

Doug Brod, SPIN's executive editor, has written for *Entertainment Weekly* and *The Village Voice* and was a contributor to *The Trouser Press Guide to '90s Rock*. He lives in Brooklyn, New York, with Rachel Boyle and their two French bulldogs, Serge Gainesburger and Jane Barkin.

Jon Caramanica is a longtime contributor to SPIN, and writes regularly for the *New York Times*, *Rolling Stone*, *The Village Voice*, *Vice*, and others.

Ta-Nehisi Coates is a staff writer at *Time* magazine.

Jim DeRogatis is the pop music critic at *The Chicago Sun-Times* and co-host of *Sound Opinions*, "the world's only rock 'n' roll talk show." He has also written several books about music, including *Let It Blurt: The Life and Times of Lester Bangs, America's Greatest Rock Critic*, and the forthcoming *Staring at Sound: The True Story of Oklahoma's Fabulous Flaming Lips*.

Jon Dolan works at SPIN and lives in Brooklyn.

Dave Eggers has written books and is the editor of *McSweeney's*.

Nelson George is the author of the recently re-issued *Hip Hop America* and *Post-Soul Nation*. He can be contacted at http://www.NelsonGeorge.com.

Andy Greenwald is a SPIN senior contributing writer and the author of *Nothing Feels Good: Punk Rock, Teenagers, and Emo* and the forthcoming novel *Miss Misery*. He lives in Brooklyn.

SPIN senior contributor **Will Hermes** has also done stuff for National Public Radio, *City Pages*, *The Village Voice*, *Entertainment Weekly*, *GQ*, *The Believer*, and the *New York Times*. He is the author of *Loose Strife* (http://loosestrife.blogspot.com), a blog-fiction.

Dave Itzkoff is an editor at SPIN and the author of *Lads: A Memoir of Manhood*. His writing has also appeared in *Details*, *New York*, the *New York Times*, and *Playboy*.

Sacha Jenkins grew up in Astoria, Queens, New York. Before he scribbled stuff for magazines like *Vibe* and SPIN, Jenkins was writing on the insides and outsides of NYC subway trains. Jenkins is co-founder of *ego trip*, co-author of *ego trip's Book of Rap Lists* and *ego trip's Big Book of Racism*, and is the editorial director of urban lifestyle up-and-comer *Mass Appeal*.

Chuck Klosterman is the author of *Killing Yourself to Live: 85 Percent of a True Story, Sex, Drugs, and Cocoa Puffs*, and *Fargo Rock City*. He writes for SPIN, *Esquire*, the *New York Times Magazine*, and *The Believer*.

John Leland is a reporter at the *New York Times* and author of *Hip: The History*. He began writing the Singles column in the second issue of SPIN.

Robert Levine is a freelance writer who lives in New York City. He has written for SPIN, *Wired*, *Playboy* and the *New York Times*.

Alan Light is the editor-in-chief and co-founder of *Tracks* magazine. He is the former editor-in-chief of SPIN and *Vibe*, and the editor of *Tupac Shakur* and the *Vibe History of Hip-Hop*.

Sia Michel, the editor-in-chief of SPIN, has been reading the magazine since the very first issue. A recipient of a 1999 ASCAP-Deems Taylor Award for music writing, she has also contributed to the *New York Times*, *Vogue*, *The Vibe History of Hip Hop*, and *The Salon.com Reader's Guide to Contemporary Authors*.

Greg Milner is the co-author of *Metallica: This Monster Lives*. He is at work on a book about the history of the idea of "perfect sound."

Former *New York Times* film critic and SPIN editor-at-large **Elvis Mitchell** is host of *Independent Focus* on the Independent Film Channel and *The Treatment* on KCRW in Los Angeles. He is also entertainment critic for NPR's *Weekend Edition*.

Chris Norris was SPIN's senior staff writer from 1998-2004. He recently entered the 36th chamber of Shaolin scholarship, penning *The Wu Tang Manual* with the RZA (aka the Abbott, aka Bobby Digital, aka Ruler Zig-Zag-Zig-Allah.) He lives in Manhattan.

Ann Powers is the author of *Weird Like Us: My Bohemian America*; co-author, with the artist, of *Tori Amos Piece by Piece*; and co-editor, with Evelyn McDonnell, of the anthology *Rock She Wrote: Women Write About Rock, Pop, and Rap*. She has written for most music publications and currently lives in Seattle, where she is a curator at Experience Music Project.

London born but now Manhattan resident, former SPIN reviews editor **Simon Reynolds** is the author of *Rip It Up and Start Again: Postpunk 1978-84* and *Generation Ecstasy: Into the World of Techno and Rave Culture*. A freelance contributor to numerous publications, he also regularly deposits discourse at Blissblog (http://blissout.blogspot.com) and the postpunk-dedicated http://www.simonreynolds.net.

Expatriate Detroiter **Mike Rubin** is a writer living in Brooklyn. From 1994 to 2003 he was a senior contributing writer at SPIN. His work has also appeared in *The New York Times Magazine*, *Rolling Stone*, *GQ*, and *The Village Voice*, as well as in several books about music. Since 1987 he has been one of the editors of *Motorbooty*, a Detroit-based, independently published satirical journal which has been described as "the only good fanzine in America."

Laura Sinagra's work has appeared in SPIN, *Rolling Stone*, *Blender*, the *New York Times*, and *The Village Voice*. She lives in Brooklyn.

RJ Smith is a senior editor at *Los Angeles* magazine. He is writing a history of African American Los Angeles in the 1940s.

Marc Spitz is a senior writer at SPIN. He is co-author of the oral history *We Got the Neutron Bomb: The Untold Story of LA Punk* and author of the novels *How Soon Is Never* and the forthcoming *Too Much Too Late*.

Neil Strauss, a former music critic for the *New York Times*, is the author of *The Dirt* with Mötley Crüe, *How to Make Love Like a Porn Star* with Jenna Jameson, and *The Long Hard Road Out of Hell* with Marilyn Manson. His latest book is *The Game*.

Eric Weisbard curates museum exhibits and puts on the Pop Conference at Experience Music Project, where he also edited the book *This Is Pop*. Before that, he was a senior editor at SPIN, music editor at *The Village Voice*, wrote way too many record reviews, and also edited the mighty SPIN *Alternative Record Guide*.

Photo credits

SPIN

20 Years of Alternative Music:

Original
writing
on rock,
hip-hop,
techno
and beyond